CRISIS AND CONFLICT IN NIGERIA

VOLUME I

JANUARY 1966–JULY 1967

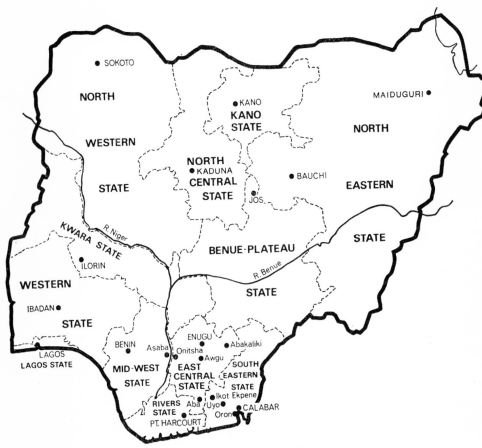

Nigeria: The Twelve States

CRISIS AND CONFLICT
IN NIGERIA

A Documentary Sourcebook 1966-1969

VOLUME I
JANUARY 1966–JULY 1967

A. H. M. KIRK-GREENE
Senior Research Fellow in African Studies
St. Antony's College, Oxford

LONDON
OXFORD UNIVERSITY PRESS
NEW YORK   IBADAN
1971

Oxford University Press, Ely House, London W.1

GLASGOW NEW YORK TORONTO MELBOURNE WELLINGTON
CAPE TOWN SALISBURY IBADAN NAIROBI DAR ES SALAAM LUSAKA ADDIS ABABA
BOMBAY CALCUTTA MADRAS KARACHI LAHORE DACCA
KUALA LUMPUR SINGAPORE HONG KONG TOKYO

SBN 19 215641 1

This edition
© Oxford University Press 1971

Printed in Great Britain
by R. & R. Clark Ltd., Edinburgh

To
NMF/18151283 and NMF/18151286

brother-officers in peace
and opponents in war;
and all those others
who lost their lives in violence
between 15 January 1966
and 15 January 1970
for the causes they believed in
Allah ya ji k'ansu

PREFACE

THE case study of political Nigeria in 1966–1970 can be expressed in terms of proven disenchantment. More importantly, it can be presented in terms of established accomplishment and of potential success. The narrative of Nigeria's momentary disrepute and postulated disintegration, and of her supreme achievement in overcoming the threats—predominantly internal yet on occasion unmistakably external—to her sovereignty is one that seems destined to be retold many times in our lifetime. How the one time showpiece of decolonizing Africa, its Government repeatedly hailed as the continent's exemplar of democratic institutions and its Prime Minister the paragon of unstampeded statesmanship, could manage to plummet from such an apogee of grace within less than six years of its independence and come so perilously close to collapse; how it could plunge first into brutal assassination, then into constitutional chaos, and finally into the bloodiest civil war of the twentieth century so that even African leaders themselves denounced the carnage as 'a shame on Africa'; how it succeeded in crushing rebellion and now accepts the challenge presented by the years of reconstruction; how it all happened, why, and who was to blame; all these are issues that will arouse many sorts of minds to continuing analysis and argument. The time-span is unlikely to be less than that covered by the shadows of suffering and suspicion inseparable from the aftermath of any civil war. It may, given the precedent of the American Civil War, last for longer: the rights and wrongs of that tragedy have their ardent advocates a hundred years and more after Gettysburg. The wounds of history do not heal quickly; some indeed leave their mark on the nation's soul for ever. Mercifully, history also suggests that, despite the unforgiving passions of the present, bruised memories can with the passage of years become less bitter and more forgetting even if they do not entirely erase the past. At the same time, the accuracy of such memories is apt to become blurred, so that in gladly forgetting what one no longer wishes to remember one may falter in the faithful recollection of what one wants to recall. Nigeria and the one time Republic of Biafra are no more likely than post-Hitlerian Europe or South Africa and the United States in their respective eras of reconstruction to be able to ignore Santayana's warning that those who do not remember the past are condemned to relive it.

In general terms, history claims to remain impartial in its chronicling even if it may depend on passion for its immediate inspiration. At its best, this impartiality, enhanced by a bipartisan approach, inclines towards neither side yet consciously presents the viewpoint of all parties before judgement is delivered, whether by itself or by other assessors.

To fulfil this inclusive role, the historical perspective derives strength from a consideration of the actuality of events as they were registered or believed at the time. The record thus stands available for subsequent review, for reinterpretation and rejection if need be, but for unchallengeable accuracy of reference in the first, unargued place.

Nowhere is this responsibility of the historian for objective and conscientious recording more important than during the inflamed and psychologically emotive period of war. Throughout the campaign it is far more important for those involved as well as those peripheral to the actual conflict to *believe* than to *know* the truth. In the pre-war crescendo months as much as during the fighting, what gains currency as accepted fact is often far more persuasive and influential than the facts themselves. The central theme of history, G. M. Young once said, is not exclusively the chronicling of what happened but also what people felt about it while it was happening. Here is a major challenge to the contemporary historian. In the post-bellum period, the sifting of truth from propaganda, of half-rumour from half-fact, and the balancing of claims against counter-allegations becomes another primary responsibility as the historian scrutinizes the records that gradually become available. This is the complementary essential task of the third-party historian. But just because he is a third, uninvolved party, his objective research may have many years to wait until reason is restored in men's minds and the total archives of both sides are freely and fairly open to public examination. Such a stage of unimpeded research has been nowhere reached at the time this preface is being written [March 1970]. For this reason the reports of a 'Nigerian' history of the war commissioned from a team of Federal scholars or as a public relations venture, or the dozen *parti pris* presentations of the Biafran side that have appeared in 1969 do not inspire much confidence that we shall be better off in learning early the full and detached story of 1966–70. Not till we can compare the parallel narratives of both sides, the Cabinet and War Council minutes of the several Governments, the Special Branch Reports on the civilian disturbances, the High Commands' directives on strategy, and the tactical orders from the field, and then set this picture against the established *obiter dicta* of the respective leaders, is any historian likely to feel himself in a strong enough position to claim to be prepared to write *the* history of the Nigerian Civil War.

To set the record of Nigeria's critical years 1966-70 straight is thus a task that awaits the historian uncommitted in his ideology and unhampered in his researches. But, at the risk of being held premature, we have been guided by what we look on as an even more urgent task. To us it seems to have priority in time and content. This is the preservation of the verbatim statements made by the leading *dramatis personae* of the Nigerian tragedy of 1966–70 as they were uttered and before they disappear or are dangerously half-remembered. With so much decreed by radio and not appearing in print till much later—the handling of the vital Decree No. 1 is an extreme case in point—the need for attention to this elusive material becomes great, especially for 1966.

Such is the mainspring of this documentary record. Evaluation, summary, and interpretation can wait; the systematic retrieval of the raw data on which alone these must be based cannot. In a situation that seems destined to provoke *engagé* attitudes for at least a generation, the final understanding must be insured against distortion of the record through either the inevitable erosion of time or else the more subtle and pernicious processes of second-hand repetition, revisionism, selective omission, and historical hindsight. Meticulous recording today can forestall the myths of tomorrow for those who do not wish to be mesmerized by them. The historical record must be established before the folk lore assumes its aura of authenticity. If there is to be hagiography, it must be a natural and not a self-induced process. Sympathy with Colonel Adebayo's wish 'we are all aware that we are writing history now and we want good history to be written about us' is balanced by the maxim *et semel emissum volat irrevocabile verbum*, reminding us of the irrevocability of the word once spoken. It is in this simplistic approach to one of the prime responsibilities of contemporaneous historiography—in this instance enhanced by some personal knowledge of the peoples who have had to endure the crises and the conflict here recorded—that this documentary sourcebook of public records has been conceived.

This is emphatically not a history of Nigeria's civil war. So far, no such book has been written. For its Wagnerian overture we have John Mackintosh's important symposium and Walter Schwarz's intimate account, both indispensable to an understanding of the mounting tension in Nigeria before the flashpoint of July 1967. Again, as I write, presentations of the Biafran case by Ojukwu, Uwechue, Nwankwo and Ifejika, as well as many by 'passionate whites', are appearing. Dr. Azikiwe's account has been delayed. Regrettably no book has yet appeared by a Nigerian giving the Federal side of the coin. A few perceptive articles on the decline and fall of the First Republic, notably Father James O'Connell's essay in Arthur Hazlewood's collected case studies *African Integration and Disintegration*, and many more on the four years of consequent turmoil are to be found in a number of scholarly journals (see the Bibliograpy included in Volume II). These two volumes here, if at all they have to be fitted into some kind of taxonomic straitjacket, are no more than a history towards the history of Nigeria's months of crisis and conflict between January 1966 and January 1970. The terminal date of 15 January has more than an attractive symmetry. Like the Ides of March, 15 January seems likely to retain a certain talismanic property in any future calendar of Nigerian history. By their very definition, any claim to inclusiveness or confidentiality of material in these volumes is discounted. As an item of hopefully widely-studied recension of existing sources (not all of them easily available or on occasion readily known) they principally seek to provide the answers to 'what' and often 'when'. They may in turn help later interpreters, with the public statements at their fingertips, authoritatively to discuss the many 'whys' and intelligently to suggest the many 'hows' to the queries that have time and time again naggingly occurred to us as we logged the record. The several books already published or in the press are likely to be contributions of one sort or another towards a further understanding of the problems and process of Nigeria 1966–70; some of those that are bound to appear in the years ahead may perhaps derive benefit from the documentary record that follows here. Thus historians may soon have enough basic data to write a provisional account of the war and chart the graph of the public declarations of political intent by its leadership which will satisfy the highest standards of objective scholarship until such time as the Nigerian and the former Biafran secret archives up to the very Cabinet level itself are made available to the generality of researchers. Selected access apart, there is no historical or political reason to expect such a bonus for some time to come.

In the meanwhile, no account worth its place in the literature will agree on every detail. Yet all seem likely to be based on one common premise: that the 'heroes' of the story of Nigeria 1966–70 will feature Gowon, Ojukwu, and Ironsi. 'We cannot escape history,' Abraham Lincoln once said to Congress, 'We will be remembered in spite of ourselves.' Lesser roles, yet by no means walking-on parts, will be allocated to such spokesmen-players as Hassan Katsina, Ejoor, Adebayo, and of course Nzeogwu in the first act, and subsequently to such speech makers as Enahoro, Awolowo, Arikpo, and Asika in the second half of the drama. As such, their verbatim statements assume an advanced quality of authority and historical significance.

The provenance of the documentation (see the Bibliography in Volume II) that makes up this sourcebook is wide but lays no claim to being exhaustive. Its pre-emptive cataloguing at this stage aims at no more than helping to provide a contribution towards eventual, total, and definitive examination of the mass of press copy, propaganda pamphlets, and radio emissions that has given the prematurely dubbed 'forgotten war' in Nigeria the greatest footage of newspaper comment—albeit the least campaign reporting, marked by a unique absence of dispatches from 'our war correspondent'—of any war in the history of Black Africa.

In the selection of actual *texts*, as opposed to the indication of the location of reports or complementary *comment*, one criterion has been inviolate. The limit we have set ourselves eschews in ninety-nine cases out of a hundred even first-hand speculation and political commentary however well informed, and allows only the actual declarations of the contending parties and their propaganda machinery, recorded in their own words and whenever possible at the very time. Deliberately, there is very little second-hand or third-party data, only the received statements of the major protagonists and their mass media. Very exceptionally and with due deliberation and warning, the local evaluation of a situation or event has been included. There has advisedly been no attempt to consult or quote from the confidential material that has been circulated to interested parties since 1966. I am planning to deposit some of such private and ephemeral materials in the Royal Commonwealth Society in response to its Librarian's call. Apart from those footnoted against citations in the text, a bibliographical note on some of the printed sources is appended to Volume II. Its rationale is to guide research supplementary to the limits imposed by the purpose of these two volumes.

I would like to pay tribute to the extensive and invaluable reportage available to the researcher in *West Africa* and *Africa Research Bulletin*. If I have preferred not to quote matter verbatim from their useful encapsulating pages but rather to reproduce the original sources themselves, I would nevertheless wish to draw attention here to the continuing excellence of these two guides to Africa day-by-day. Recourse to the archives of the B.B.C. Monitoring Service has formed a notable strengthening of my quest for verbatim texts and a separate acknowledgement is in order here. As I point out in the bibliographical note, few texts have been taken from the non-English language press since nearly all the documents are speeches of the protagonists or the work of their information media and these have, apart from Hausa, been almost entirely in English. This is in no way to imply that for commentary and *post-hoc* interpretation of events the non-English language world press, notably that of France, Germany, and Scandinavia, has not since 1968 carried a lot of reportage of high importance in another, nonverbatim, context. Consultation of Nigerian newspapers has been extensive. Given their sadly restricted availability in British universities and indeed their total absence for the vital eighteen months from January 1966, special attention has been paid to this source in Volume I. The decision which one to use for quoting the verbatim statements by Government spokesmen has perforce been selective. In favouring the *New Nigerian* I have been influenced by the readiness of its editorial co-operation, by its role as a leading newspaper of Nigeria, and by its importance in representing the novelty of an informed Northern public opinion so crucial over this period. In preferring for the British press *The Times* in Volume II, covering the period for which Nigerian newspapers are more easily available in the U.K., I have been guided solely by its status as a standard research tool for scholars.

This collection of documents will have justified itself if it achieves three ends. If it plays an enabling part in an eventually uncommitted understanding of what the leadership actually said during these months of crisis and conflict. If, too, it succeeds in having recorded, without interpolant emotion betraying us into alteration of the truth, the bulk of the major policy statements of the leading *dramatis personae* and the essence of their publicity, be this declaratory, explanatory, or accusatory, exactly as it was publicly received in Nigeria or former Biafra as well as by the outside world at the time. Above all, if it lays the foundation for, in the years ahead when passions cool and memories grow softer, a calm and scholarly assessment of the rights and wrongs of the conflict and of the degree of success or otherwise of those who, assuming responsibility for the well-being of Africa's greatest nation in the years of her direst peril, were seemingly frustrated in their efforts peaceably to reconcile, on the one hand, a tenaciously felt desire for the extension of the right to self-determination beyond its colonial context with on the other a no less fervently held and a legitimately founded belief in the indivisibility and integrity of 'one Nigeria'. Few would quarrel with the relevance of Abraham Lincoln's prayer during his own country's civil war: 'We here highly resolved that these dead shall not have died in vain and that this nation, under God, shall have a new birth of freedom.'

In a retrieval and recording operation of this nature, individual debts of thanks are too numerous to list exhaustively. Such an unavoidable omission should not be taken as indicative of ingratitude, and I would ask the many persons and institutions who so generously co-operated in my search for documents in Nigeria, Biafra, the United Kingdom, and the United States of America to accept this acknowledgement of help they have given even if they do not find the materials they kindly supplied reproduced here. Among those whose assistance in making available materials and information, often of a personal nature, I should like to acknowledge by a special word of thanks, are:

David Williams, Kaye Whiteman, and the editorial staff of *West Africa*, London;

Charles Sharp, Adamu Ciroma, and the editorial staff of the *New Nigerian*, Kaduna;

John Drysdale and the editorial staff of *Africa Research Bulletin*;

John Sheringham, Head of Output, B.B.C. Monitoring Service, Reading;

Kenneth Fairfax, Editor, External Services News, B.B.C. London;

Malam El-Nafaty of the Nigerian Broadcasting Corporation, Kaduna;

The Controller, the Broadcasting Corporation of Northern Nigeria;

William Norris of *The Times*;

Walter Schwarz of the *Guardian*;

Bridget Bloom of the *Financial Times*;

Colin Legum and John de St. Jorre of the *Observer*;

the Federal, Northern, Eastern, Western, and Mid-Western Ministries of Information, Nigeria;

the Senior Information Officer in the Nigerian High Commission, London;

the Information Attachés to the Federal Nigerian Embassy in Washington, D.C., and to the Nigerian Mission to the United Nations, New York;

the Biafran Representative's Office in London, Washington, and New York;

David Russell of Galitzine Chant Russell, London;

Galitzine Chant Russell for permission to reproduce the map;

The *Observer* Foreign News Service for permission to reproduce the Biafran poster 'Gowon Hates You';

H. Wm. Bernhardt Inc., Geneva;

George Knapp, External Development Services, London;

Press Section, Commonwealth Secretariat, London;

Overseas Press Section, Central Office of Information, London;

C. H. G. Nida Press Service, London;

West African Department, Foreign and Commonwealth Office, London;

United Nations Information Centres, New York and London;

the Conseillers de Presse, the French and Ivory Coast Embassies, London;

the Information Officers, Tanzanian and Zambian High Commissions, London;

the Information Division of the International Red Cross Committee, Geneva;

the Information Service of Joint Church Aid, Geneva;

the Information Service of Caritas, Rome;

the Secretary, Britain–Biafra Association, London;

the Secretary of the Committee for Peace in Nigeria, London;

the Secretary for the Co-ordinating Committee for Action on Nigeria/ Biafra;

the Press Cuttings Library of the Royal Institute for International Affairs, London;

the Librarians of Rhodes House and the Institute of Commonwealth Studies, Oxford; Royal Commonwealth Society; British Museum, Colindale; and the University of California, Los Angeles;

and to

Dame Margery Perham, for allowing me to consult her private collection of Biafran and Nigerian papers;

T. G. Brierly Esq., for making available his personal file of famine
  relief operations;

M. J. Dent Esq., for reading this MS. and giving it the benefit of his own
  research on the military and political events of 1966;

numerous, purposely unnamed, Nigerian, 'Biafran', and expatriate
  friends at home and abroad, for supplying local documentation and
  providing so much illuminating information in their discussions and
  correspondence;

the two Helens and Netta, for their tireless searching of the British daily
  press, scissors at the alert;

a kindly editor at Oxford University Press, for patiently accepting a
  somewhat curiously presented MS.;

and the Warden and Fellows of St. Antony's College, Oxford, for their
  generous hospitality and encouragement.

A. H. M. KIRK-GREENE
March 1970

St. Antony's College
Oxford

CONTENTS

B

JANUARY 1966

THE POLITICAL PROLOGUE

REDUCED to fundamentals, the post-independence years brought about the crystallization of two views of the Nigerian situation. Either there was no workable basis for the concept of one Nigeria, in which case the federal structure that had been deliberately sought by Nigeria's leaders during the successive constitutional conferences of the 1950s was at the best a compromise and at the worst a thing of patches concealing the fragility of would-be unity; or else the emergence of a national entity called Nigeria was genuinely believed to be possible and practicable, in which case no step towards its creation should be overlooked nor any justifiable risk in its promotion be shirked. Momentarily turning from the past to the future, those who have seen the outbreak of civil war as tantamount to the deathblow for any hope of Nigerian unity might do well to recall that America emerged stronger from her similar tragedy and France did not disintegrate after her similar 'night of the long knives' on that infamous St. Bartholomew's Eve four hundred years ago.

For all the undeniably unifying effect of the colonial overrule, these dichotomous attitudes have been sharpened in the *ex-post hoc* ratiocination of the 1966 peril as expounded in the propaganda war and in the soul-searching ultimate question of whether Nigeria and 'Biafra' are together, individually, or in no circumstances a real nation. On the one hand is found the extremist Northern rejection of the whole ethos of unity in the 1950s. This can be summed up in such criticism of Lugard's constitutional coming-togetherness expressed by its own parliamentary leaders, as, for example, Alhaji Sir Ahmadu Bello's cryptic comment that 'The mistake of 1914 has come to light';[1] or again, during the aftermath of the 1966 massacres, in the preamble to the memorandum submitted by the Northern delegation to the constitutional conference summoned in Lagos, where the injured feeling of the North's dislocation from its cultural legacy was put in these words: 'We have pretended for too long that there are no differences between the peoples of this country. The hard fact which we must honestly accept as of paramount importance in the Nigerian experiment, especially for the future, is that we *are* different peoples brought together by recent accidents of history. To pretend otherwise will be folly.'[2] There is less change here over the years than that sought by the doubtful honesty of those who quote Alhaji Sir Abubakar Tafawa Balewa's version of 'Since the amalgamation of the Southern and Northern Provinces in 1914, Nigeria has existed as one country only on paper.'[3] Those words were spoken in 1947, at a time when Northern members were still being

[1] Quoted from *House of Representatives (Lagos): Debates, 1953*, in his autobiography *My Life* (Cambridge, 1962), p. 133.
[2] *Memoranda submitted by the Delegations to the Ad Hoc Conference on Constitutional Proposals for Nigeria* (Lagos, 1967), p. 5. Two editions of this were published, one in Lagos and one in Enugu. See Bibliographical Note in Volume II.
[3] *Legislative Council Debates (Lagos); 20 March–2 April 1947*, p. 208.

initiated into the Lagos political process. If one wishes to cite Sir Abubakar in this context of Nigerian unity, his centripetal statements as Prime Minister are many and more valid.

For the contrary view, there has been the Eastern Region's emphasis of the 1914 amalgamation as the ultimate sanction of Nigeria's legal existence. This has been expressed in intellectuals' statements corresponding to Professor Ezera's dictum that 'it is only from *then* [1914] that any reference to what is today called Nigeria could, strictly speaking, begin',[1] or again, for all its advocacy of drawing apart in order to come together again, in the reluctance to concede any argument that reaches back beyond 1914, the year when:

the boldest constitutional experiment in this country was undertaken. . . . The Easterners were the first to embrace this idea [of a unified country] wholeheartedly [and] came to acquire a stake in the country as a whole and to identify themselves with the survival and progress of the political entity called Nigeria.[2]

Hence, too, the insistence that 'Biafra did *not* secede: Biafra was pushed out',[3] contrasts starkly with the Northern stand of 'Let them go, but first divide our assets',[4] and, at a grass-roots level, of 'We do not want Nigeria to be partitioned, but if in a unified Nigeria we see falsehood, harm, enslavement and oppression [by Ibos], then let us [Northerners] insist upon separation'.[5] Not for nothing was the cautious, separatist mood of the North in the early constitutional give-and-take of the 1950s deliberately echoed in the slogan shouted in the anti-unitary government riots of May 1966—*a raba, a ware*, let us part.[6] Indeed, each of the three major Regions had at one time or another, publicly or privately, done more than dream of secession. Each had come to the conclusion that, if pushed, it could and would go it alone, but on balance there was more to be gained from keeping the Federation than from quitting it. When actual war comes the polarization reaches its extreme, with Biafra's implacable rejection of national integration on the principle of the twelve states set in opposition to the grim Federal determination that 'to keep Nigeria one is a task that must be done'. Now the supreme task of the Federal Military Government be-

[1] Kalu Ezera, *Constitutional Developments in Nigeria* (Cambridge, 1960), p. 21.

[2] *The Problem of Nigerian Unity* (Aba, 1966), pp. 5–9.

[3] *Biafra Newsletter* (Enugu, January 1968), vol. i, no. 6, p. 8.

[4] Statement by the Sardauna of Sokoto, 29 December 1964 (Ministry of Information, Kaduna, Release No. 2266, 1964).

[5] Translated excerpt from a letter to the Editor, *Gaskiya ta fi Kwabo* (Zaria), 11 February 1960.

[6] The claim made by the Eastern Military Government that 'The D-Day [29 July] was given the code-name *Araba* (Hausa for "Secession") *Day*', as a sort of parallel to the code-name 'Exercise Damis[s]a' for the operations in Kaduna on 15 January 1966, has not been substantiated (*January 15: Before and After* (Enugu, 1967), p. 41. In further references this work is referred to as *January 15.*).

comes that of saving Nigeria from disintegration.[1] In General Gowon's own words:

> The struggle ahead is for the well-being of the present and future genera-tions of Nigerians. If it were possible for us to avoid chaos and civil war merely by drifting apart as some people claim that easy choice may have been taken. But we know that to take such a course will quickly lead to the disintegration of the existing regions in condition of chaos and to disastrous foreign interference. We now have to adopt the courageous course of facing the fundamental problem [of political imbalance brought about by too few states] that has plagued this country since the early fifties.[2]

Yet whether there did exist the basis for one Nigeria or not is perhaps now academic. Once one concedes the existence of an alternative, arguments to support it quickly accumulate: *in ka ji 'na k'iya' samun dama ne*, 'if you hear "I won't", that means there is an option', as the proverb has it. Thus, in the crisis and counter-crisis that derived directly from the assassinations of 15 January 1966, the issue of a unitary or federal system of government began to matter less than that of whether there was to be a government at all. In the final analysis, the Nigerian tragedy has been bedevilled by a set of oppositions—generalized, stereo-type, not necessarily of the same order and maybe imaginary, yet each widening the wound and reducing the hope of healing it: North *v* South, Islam *v* Christianity, alleged feudalism *v* assumed socialism, federal *v* unitary preferences, traditional authority *v* achieved elitism, haves *v* have-nots, each with sinister undertones of tension, irreconcilability and threatened withdrawal. None was entirely accurate. Nevertheless each opposing set had sufficient seed of truth within it to permit, and even fertilize, the growth of feared fact from the semi-fiction of its existence.

It is against such a background of *believed* oppositions, of dissent and distrust, that one must direct one's search for the roots of the disaster of 1966 and all that has ensued therefrom towards the events of the political past. It may be significant that it should be the very thesis of a Nigerian commission—and the first to show public awareness of the Regional sensitivities over an Africanization programme for the civil service—that at once comes to mind as we consider the real meaning of Nigeria 1966: 'A purely contemporary view of any problem is neces-sarily a limited and even distorted view. Every situation has its roots in the past . . . the past survives into the present; the present is indeed the past undergoing modification.'[3] These roots reach deep into Nigeria's history. Nor are they simply separable, for so intertwined has been their growth that it is equally legitimate to read into many of the pre-1966

---

[1] *The Struggle for One Nigeria* (Lagos, 1967), Preface.

[2] Radio broadcast, 27 May 1967.

[3] S. Phillipson and S. O. Adebo, *The Nigerianization of the Civil Service* (Lagos, 1954), p. 49.

Northern attitudes or into those of the East thereafter the words of
Isaac to Rebecca: 'Two nations are in thy womb, and two manner of
people shall be separated from thy bowels.'[1] If one were to plot the path
of Nigerian unity rather than that of her discord, the routes would,
historically, scarcely deviate one from the other, both being delineated
by the same landmarks since 1900.

But in Nigeria's descent into threatened national disintegration in
1966 and the humiliation of her signal inability to avert a civil war, the
factors of early fission were at least as prominent as those which existed
for some degree of fusion. This is not to deny the indications of a growing sense of one Nigeria. These were sharpened by the formulation of
the Six Year National Development Plan in 1962 and by the expanding output of Northern graduates meeting and competing with their
Southern counterparts on equal terms and with increasing mutual respect. It was among the secured new intelligentsia that the pointers to
something like a real national identity were at their most prominent.
From many students the answer 'I am a Nigerian' in reply to the
foreigner's ever-ready question of 'what's your tribe?' became a matter
of positively creative rather than negatively xenophobic pride. Many of
the radical intellectuals were honest as well as fashionable in their
adoption of a national posture; certain echelons of the upper-middle
civil service genuinely believed in a one-Nigerian approach; and, despite
the subsequent savage paradox of 1966, intimacy with the officer corps
gave one the most satisfying of all assurances that a 'Nigerian' could
emerge from that 'precarious lumping together of peoples whose
separate identity is at least as real a matter as their acceptance of
national unity.'[2] Such persons, the Colts rather than the Old Guard,
were not only able but were often also willing to look beyond the
horizons of ethnicity and work towards a Nigerian national identity.

Nevertheless, it is possible to look back in anger from the bloodbath
of 1966–70 and weigh every political event since 1950, or even earlier,
in terms of its impetus towards the final collapse of the First Republic.
For, in harsh summary, the continuing if occasionally latent animosity
between the North and the South never needed much pressure to erupt
angrily to the surface. Nor does such retrospect involve many *post-hoc*
judgements. 'History haunts us like a bitter shadow,' Chinua Achebe
once wrote. It seems valid, without subscribing to an inflexibly deter-
minist approach to Nigeria's experience, to interpret her past politics
as being the stuff from which her present history has been shaped. It is
in the belief that it was shadows from the past, and not a sudden darken-
ing of the moment, which broke upon Nigeria on 15 January 1966 that

---

[1] Genesis 25: 23.

[2] R. Emerson, 'Nationalism and Political Development', *Journal of Politics* (1960),
p. 3. Chief Awolowo's dictum that 'Nigeria is not a nation, it is a mere geographical expression' has nowadays acquired the status of a cliché—*Path To Nigerian Freedom*
(London, 1947), p. 47.

the introduction to this chronological presentation of policy documents has purposely assumed the approach of seeking historical precedents and patterns for the period up to 1966.

As far back as 1899 the Selborne Committee had, while recognizing the ultimate objective of one colonial administration for the three territories then under the separate direction of the Royal Niger Company, the Foreign and the Colonial Offices, preferred the reality of coexistence to the ideal of a single government. In proof of this, they advocated a demarcation, in terms that were to be echoed again and again until they reached their climax in 1967, between 'the Soudan regions governed by Mahommedans and the Pagan regions of the Niger Delta'.[1] So it was that the colony of Nigeria, conceived in the tripartite government of 1898, was born in the dual administration of 1914, proclaiming rather than playing down the Kiplingesque polarity of North being North and South being South. The incorporation of Lagos into the Southern Protectorate in 1906 was another opportunity, rejected rather than missed, for closer union. A third, and one of the clearly identifiable political cross-roads, was Lugard's commission in 1912 to amalgamate—not, let it be noted, to unify—the two Protectorates. But Lugard's commitment to what Lagos looked on as the nefarious 'Nigerian System'[2] ,with all it meant to him emotionally, albeit sincerely, and his brusque contempt of the South as he sensed it in the undignified atmosphere of Lagos politicking, meant that in his own mind there was little prospect that he would ever impose a unitary system of government and bring his favoured stable North into contaminatory contact with the fickle South.[3] So, realist of the present rather than dreamer of the future, he chose—if the word is not too strong in its hint of a seriously considered alternative—to perpetuate the classic cleavage between North and South. Had Lugard, without sacrificing his belief in the oil-and-water incompatibility of the two, gone further by refining Morel's scheme for dividing the country into four geographical groups of provinces,[4] or had he looked sympathetically on his Lieutenant-Governor Temple's proposal for splitting Nigeria into seven provinces,[5] or had the Willink Commission[6] of 1958 recommended the immediate

[1] C.O. 446/3, *Report of the Niger Committee* (4 August 1899).

[2] For a scathing attack on this version of indirect rule, see the editorial in *Lagos Weekly Record*, 1 February 1919.

[3] Cf. I. Nicolson's evaluation of Lugard's Governor-Generalship in his chapter 'The Machinery of the Federal and Regional Government', in J. Mackintosh (ed.), *Nigerian Government and Politics* (London, 1966), and his *The Administration of Nigeria 1900–1960* (London, 1969), *passim*.

[4] E. D. Morel, *Nigeria: its Peoples and its Problems* (London, 1911), especially the last three chapters.

[5] The official minute is reproduced in full in A. H. M. Kirk-Greene, *Lugard and the Amalgamation of Nigeria* (London, 1968), pp. 214–23.

[6] *Report of the Commission appointed to enquire into the fears of the Minorities*, Cmd. 505, 1958.

creation of more states and damn the consequences of delayed independence, it is open to question whether the bloody events that have determined the need for this book would ever have come to pass. This is not to say that some other form of crisis might not have broken upon those mini-states, such as that of insolvency in the lean period of the early 1930s, or of non-viability in the closer political association era of the late 1950s when the British Government seemed to believe as a moral and prudential imperative that there should be no decolonization without viability.[1] And so, from 1922 onwards, Nigeria was governed under a constitution that, if not satisfactory, had never excited any particular interest in its unitary shortcomings.[2] Though the North was purposely excluded from the deliberations of the Legislative Council in so far as ordinances affecting it could be enacted by the Governor alone there was no sustained protest at such an arrangement either by nationalist elements in the South or by the emirate representatives of the North. The mood was primarily one of indifference.

Nigeria's first experiment with a unitary constitution did not come until 1947. Although observers have decried the Richards constitution as enshrining its architect's unfavourable capacity to deal effectively with colonial nationalism and his 'special knack for antagonizing the educated elements—in Nigeria, at least, his name is at the bottom of the popularity list',[3] and politicians have vilified it, particularly in retrospect,[4] as the beginning of the end of any true pan-Nigerian concept, it did endorse an essentially central form of government and achieved a real political breakthrough by integrating the North with the South at the legislative level. In seeking to reconcile the principle of promoting Nigeria's unity with that of suitable provision for the wishes of the country's diverse elements it inevitably made use of the device of regionalism. But at heart its bias was unitary. However, when this constitution came up for revision in 1950, well ahead of schedule, and the people were widely consulted for the first time, the result was an unquestionably Nigerian (all but three of the fifty-three delegates to the conference were Nigerians) resolution demanding a substantial degree of full-scale regionalization. There were at that General Conference on the Constitution held at Ibadan several straws in the wind. In the light of the repeated references to the political arrangements of 1914, the threat by the Emirs of Katsina and Zaria to seek 'separation from the rest of Nigeria on the arrangements existing before 1914'[5] unless the North was given fifty per cent of the seats in the proposed House of

[1] The phrase is Professor W. J. M. Mackenzie's, used in his review of R. L. Watts, *New Federations*, in *Journal of Administration Overseas*, vol. vii, no. 1, 1968, p. 338.

[2] Cf. Alhaji Sir Ahmadu Bello, *My Life* (Cambridge, 1962), p. 60.

[3] James S. Coleman, *Nigeria: Background to Nationalism* (California, 1958), p. 275.

[4] e.g. Ezera, op. cit., pp. 76–7 and 81.

[5] *Proceedings of the General Conference on Review of the Constitution held at Ibadan, January 1950* (Lagos, 1950), p. 218.

Representatives in accordance with its preponderant population, takes
on special significance. The eventual decision, on the recommendation
of the Legislative Council when the conference failed to arrive at a conclusion, to allow the North's claim for her representation at the centre to
equal that of the West and East together, was one that was to dominate
the shaping of Nigeria's political culture until the First Republic ex-
ploded sixteen years later.

Yet even the measure of mutual non-interference guaranteed by the
increased regional autonomy and stronger regional legislatures derived
from the Macpherson constitution of 1951 was inadequate to hold the
ring. The Cabinet split of 1953 and the ugly public clash in April of the
same year over accepting a target date for securing self-government
marked a further parting of the ways. The North was fully aware of
what it was doing. The South may have seen, in the North's refusal to be
stampeded into premature self-government, their worst fears of Northern
feet-dragging and 'H.M.V. Stoogery' confirmed. Both the Action Group
and the National Council of Nigerian Citizens spokesmen denounced the
North in stinging terms.[1] In the North, it is doubtful whether the leaders
ever forgot the vulgar obscenities to which they were subjected by the
Lagos mob. To the Hausa *cin mutunci*, personal humiliation through
public abuse, is one of the most grievous social offences, outweighing in
its gravity physical assault. Close observation indicates that their treatment on this occasion was to colour the views of many Northerners on
the politics of the South right to the end of the First Republic—views
that, if they needed a booster, received it eleven years later when their
Ministers were belittled by the *Nigerian Outlook* as 'cattle-rearing legisla-
tors'.[2] The Sardauna's own bitter narrative[3] and his statement issued to
the press at the time[4] are vividly reinforced by this passage from the
composite account based on statements from Northern People's Congress Ministers and floor members made shortly after their return from
Lagos:

Trouble did not start until the day the House was adjourned excepting for
Mr. Awolowo's unhappy and deeply resented reference to Shehu Dan Fodio,
a reference which was to a high proportion of Northern members little short
of blasphemy in view of Shehu Dan Fodio's saintly status. After the House
was adjourned, however, when the members emerged they saw a crowd of
young Yorubas and Ibos milling round where their cars were parked. This
crowd of hooligans, which had been organised, was with some difficulty
driven back by the Police in order that the cars could have freedom of movement. There were loud shouts of 'thieves', 'Kolanut men', 'Kolanut Chief',
'no minds of their own', etc., also sarcastic repetitions of the customary

[1] Ezera, op. cit., p. 166.
[2] See the résumé of the articles of abuse printed in *Morning Post*, 25 July 1964.
[3] Bello, op. cit., pp. 133–5.
[4] *Daily Times*, 6 April 1953.

Northern salutation to a superior, also contemptuous reference to every member as a 'Minister'. The servants of members were later subjected to the same treatment. Groups of Ibos and Yorubas surrounded them and called them 'thieves' and 'slaves of the white man', 'stupid Hausas', 'the men who have no minds of their own'.[1]

From this incident the returning Northern delegation drew its determination to explore secession rather than ever again expose themselves to such abominable treatment. They were not likely to forgive or forget the terrible insult hurled at them in Chief Bode Thomas's gibe of 'gutless Africans'. The mood was evident in the Northern Legislature's acceptance within a matter of weeks[2] of the loosening Eight Point Programme and the setting up of the Northern Nigeria Self-Development Fund (significantly revived in 1967[3]). The East, too, has looked back to these events of 1953 as a point of no return. Much of Biafra's subsequent presentation of its case for international recognition, with its reiterated recall of 'ruthless massacres of Easterners by Northerners' and its identification of 'the most terrible being those of 1945 [Jos] and 1953 [Kano]',[4] underlined the injury done to the Ibos in those riots (by then Jos had been largely forgotten by the Northern man-in-the-street) and ascribed to May 1953 the beginning of an alleged but quite unproven genocidal policy towards their people. None the less, the bitterness of mutual contempt sensed in the parliamentary clash at Lagos was translated into such brutal physical terms in Kano, necessitating the deployment of troops on a scale unprecedented in the North since the pacification era of fifty years earlier—and unknown again until the smouldering sense of discontent in Tiv country burst into open revolt in 1964—that there is a plausible case for arguing 1953 as a watershed in the relationships of the new-found political parties. From then on their feelings towards one another were never again to be the same.

The constitutional conference of 1954 acknowledged the deep realities of the confrontation. 'It was clear that Nigeria', the Colonial Secretary recorded in his diary, 'if it was to be a nation, must be a federation, with as few subjects reserved for the Central Government as would preserve national unity.'[5] In exchange for a limited Exclusive List of powers exercised by the Federal Government and a substantial Concurrent List of areas where the Regional Governments could legislate, the North dropped the confederal Eight Point Programme for which it had elicited an urgent mandate from its electorate after the Lagos inci-

---

[1] *Report on the Kano Disturbances* (Kaduna, 1953), p. 4.

[2] The point was subsequently emphasized by the Eastern Government preparatory to its own secession in 1967. Cf. *The North and Constitutional Developments in Nigeria* (Enugu, 1966), *passim.*

[3] Address by the Military Governor of the North, 15 January 1967.

[4] *The Recognition of the Republic of Biafra* (Enugu, 1967), p. 1.

[5] Lord Chandos, *Memoirs*, quoted in Mackintosh, op. cit., p. 27.

dent of the previous April. The sense of legislative decentralization agreed on in 1964 is apparent in the common sobriquet of the 'Regionalization Constitution'. Its provision of separate Governors, separate Premiers and Cabinets and legislatures, separate judiciaries, separate public service commissions, civil services, marketing boards, and development plans, continued without effective protest through independence. Indeed, the few modifications negotiated at subsequent constitutional conferences simply served to emphasize the separateness of the three Regional Governments. Thus, by 1963, a fourth Region had been created with its full legislative and bureaucratic complement: three of the five national universities were unmistakably regionally oriented in all but their charters while the other two were conspicuous by the uneven composition of their undergraduate intake; the safeguards of independence entrenched in the establishment of a Judicial Service Commission had been swept away; the Federal police force had taken on a far more Regional aspect than the organization which the Willink Commission, appointed to inquire into the fears of the minorities, had in 1958 assumed to exist and had accepted as the best means of allaying such fears. Outside the Federal Civil Service and Foreign Service, only the army appeared to be a genuinely national institution. Yet in the first two, the North could justifiably complain that its people held less than 5% of the senior appointments. In the third, the strictly enforced Regional quotas for the officer cadres (and the unconcealed adjustment of entry standards that went therewith) as part of the North's belated attempt to match Ibo predominance in the commissioned ranks, aggravated by the reverse gap in the Regional provenance of the other ranks inherited from a classical colonial preference for *soi-disant* martial races, threatened to make as great a mockery of the supposedly federal nature of the armed forces as had tribalistic nepotism of the national statutory corporations.

This decentralization through a creeping extension of the power of the Regional Executives nevertheless stopped short at the crucial point in administrative devolution: the creation of more states. The North's adamant refusal to consider this move was, up to 1966, the target of continuous criticism from the Southern and Middle Belt politicians. Interestingly, the failure of the Willink Commission to recommend the creation of more states in 1958 has, since 1966, been the main moment to which many of the new Nigerian intellectuals have unhesitatingly pointed as the day when the country took the wrong turn and as the ultimate cause of the civil war—without perhaps remembering the Commission's precise terms of reference or always minding the probability of violent reaction from the political leaders, the people, and world anti-colonial opinion had any British-inspired move been made to postpone independence in order to set up more states and correct the built-in imbalances of the evolving federal structure. The Federal

Military Government has itself since made an important acknowledgement, although it too seems to have expected more from the Minorities
Commission than was within its competence:

In [our] common desire to win independence, many vital problems were
left unsolved. One of these outstanding problems was the creation of more
states which would have provided a more lasting foundation for stability of
the Federation of Nigeria. The British Government pointed out at the time
that if new states were to be created, the new states must be given at least
two years to settle down before independence could be granted. On reflection,
Nigerian leaders have admitted that the British were right and they were
wrong on this vital issue in hurrying to independence without solving the
problem of stability of the Federation.[1]

The self-examination has gone even deeper in its search for blame, and
has reiterated the cold douche reality of retrospect that 'time has proved
the British right'.[2] If it has, it has shown only that the remedy of more
states was an accurate diagnosis and not, as Nigeria has successfully
illustrated even in the middle of a war, that they needed as long as two
years before they began to function effectively. It is sad that, when the
North was in 1967 at last split into a number of states as the politicians
of the East had long been advocating, the dispersal of power came too
late to assuage their fears. Ironically the East's political goal of the
1950s, once achieved, was to become the very signal for their own
secession. The judgement of history is likely to set 1967 and 1958 along
with 1914, and maybe 1946 and 1954, as Nigeria's constitutional turning
points.

And so in 1960 Nigeria's leaders (with, be it noted, the enthusiastic
mandate of an exemplarily administered general election behind them[3])
moved into sovereignty, a federation rather than a nation, with as yet
little substance to the somewhat self-conscious label of 'Nigerian' and
with future hope rather than present truth in the sentiment of its
national anthem, first sung at the magic midnight hour of 30 September
1960, that 'Though tribe and tongue may differ, In brotherhood we stand.'

For all this, and despite the strains and stresses of divided and at
times mutually antagonistic authority, the first years seemed likely to
prove that the British and the Nigerians had been right to ignore the
Jeremiahs of unity and the advocates of balkanization and to accept
the admitted risk in pinning their hopes on a single nation within a loose
federal framework. World acclaim for the stability of Nigeria, its

[1] *The Struggle for One Nigeria* (Lagos, 1967), p. 3.
[2] *Nigeria: 12-State Structure the Only Way Out* (Lagos, 1968), p. 3.
[3] The assessment is that of K. W. Post, *The Nigerian Federal Election of 1959* (London,
1963). James O'Connell, in his brilliant study of political integration in Nigeria (A.
Hazlewood, *African Integration and Disintegration* (London, 1965), Chapter 5), makes a
related point about the Nigerian-ness of the Independence constitution which destroys
the stereotype of imposed colonial constitutions contributing to subsequent political
breakdown.

democratic institutions, its economic strength, and the statesmanlike maturity of its Prime Minister—especially when contrasted with the seeming brashness of unconventional Ghana—was generous; and even the impatient youth-movement activists who enviously felt that Dr Nkrumah had beaten Nigeria in the race to political leadership of the African continent that should by right have been theirs could be mollified by the sincerity of the respect accorded to Sir Abubakar Tafawa Balewa on the world scene. What discord there was was generally internalized. Despite the obvious tensions at home, Nigeria managed abroad (apart from the special case of the North's refusal to accept aid from Israel) to give the impression of generally presenting a unified front, though this is by no means to be taken that foreign policy decisions were arrived at in a spirit of national consensus.[1] With relief, observers began to discern signs of a gently growing feeling of 'we are Nigerians', along with an encouraging readiness on the part of the Regions more and more to accept tactful Federal guidance, notably exercised in attempts by Lagos to accommodate the interlocking and overlapping projects within the first National Development Plan. Nigeria, it seemed, had arrived.

In any evaluation of the causes of the Nigerian débacle—and particularly in answer to the question of what prompted the mounting of the military coup finally launched, or half-launched,[2] in January 1966— the inquirer is confronted by a seemingly endless chain of antecedents and reactions to actions. If, as some argue, the secession of May 1967 was urged by the hawkishness of Ibo intellectuals fearful of economic extinction and furious at Gowon's pre-emptive 'coup' of dividing the East into three states,[3] was this not precipitated by the massacres of October 1966, in turn the culmination of the bloody counter-coup of July, which was the Northern riposte to the moves of May and the murders of January, itself the East's protest at its failure constitutionally to secure its share of the national cake, which in turn . . .? The permutations of result and causality threaten to stretch back to before the name 'Nigeria' was ever coined, let alone appears on a map or assumes any reality as a polity. Nigerian politics impress by having a self-perpetuating house-that-Jack-built element. Event A leads to B, which induces C and so D ensues; the net result is E, the prelude to F

[1] The internal disagreement over foreign policy is well analysed by Claude S. Phillips *Nigerian Foreign Policy* (Evanston, 1964), and A. Akinyemi, 'Towards a Pax Nigeriana', unpublished D. Phil. thesis (Oxford, 1969).

[2] The phrase is used not so much to describe the relative failure of the mutiny of 15 January outside Kaduna but rather to allow for the theories of either a coup within a coup or of several coexistent plots, held by certain political commentators.

[3] Walter Schwarz has identified General Gowon's breaking of the four Regions into twelve States as the third coup of 1966–7, 'The coup of the minorities', *Nigeria* (London, 1968), p. 230. Radio Biafra called it 'a one-man coup d'état'.

and the *fons et origo* of. . . . This chain-reaction has too often been compounded of mutual misunderstanding born from dislike and distrust and turning into contempt, jealousy, and fear of domination. For all the sincerity of some pre-1966 leaders in seeking to bring about 'one Nigeria', proverbs in several local languages warn that incompatibles are placed together only with disastrous results. This message of fear and frightened reaction to it runs through the explanations by both Nigeria and Biafra of why the events of 15 January took place. The Western Region summarized the causes of 1966 as 'fears of domination of the Federation by one or other of its constituent units, suspicions as to the intentions of the various ethnic groups, and grievances as to the equitable distribution of amenities throughout the country'.[1] Other Governments were more specific in their allegations. Thus the North's belief that 'These manipulations [actions of the Ironsi régime] generated genuine fears in the minds of other Nigerians that they would be dominated by the Ibos'[2] and the Federal claim that 'ethnic groups tend to be chauvinistic but the Ibos were the most militantly chauvinistic and this naturally created apprehension in the minds of others'[3] are balanced by the Ibos' assertion that 'the world is being given to understand that there can be no peace and unity in Nigeria unless the country is ruled and dominated by the North.'[4] Similarly, the Federation's attribution of the riots of 1966 to the fact that 'a feeling of resentment and fear was created in the minds of the ordinary people'[5] is countered by the East's brutal explanation that 'a number of student-survivors from institutions of learning in Northern Nigeria [had] all the fingers of their right hands chopped off—that would help in curtailing, they were told, the educational lead of Eastern Nigeria over the North'.[6] Perhaps the totality of the sickening atmosphere of mutual distrust is best captured in the remarks of the Northern delegation to the constitutional conference of September 1966:

We all have our fears of one another. Some fear that opportunities in their own areas are limited and they would therefore wish to expound and venture unhampered in other parts. Some fear the sheer weight of numbers of other parts which they feel could be used to the detriment of their own interests. Some fear the sheer weight of skills and the aggressive drive of other groups which they feel has to be regulated if they are not to be left as the economic, social, and possibly political, under-dogs in their own areas of origin in the very near future. These fears may be real or imagined; they may be reasonable or petty. Whether they are genuine or not, they have to be taken

[1] Memorandum submitted by the Western Nigeria and Lagos Delegations, *The Ad Hoc Conference on the Nigerian Constitution* (Enugu, 1966), p. 97.

[2] *The Nigerian Situation: Facts and Background* (Zaria, 1966), p. 7.

[3] *The Collapse of Ojukwu's Rebellion and Prospects for Lasting Peace in Nigeria* (Lagos, 1968), p. 5.

[4] *The Problem of Nigerian Unity* (Aba, 1966), p. 26.

[5] *Government Statement on the Current Nigerian Situation* (Lagos, October 1966), p. 3.

[6] *Pogrom* (Enugu, 1966), p. 7.

account of because they influence to a considerable degree the actions of the groups towards one another and, more important perhaps, the daily actions of the individual in each group towards individuals from other groups.[1]

It was more than intellectual clever-cleverness that inspired a reviewer of a recent book on contemporary Nigeria to use the punnish title 'The Politics of Apart-hate'.[2] Such a frank isolation of the intensity and influence of the ethnic undercurrents in Nigeria's political mainstream is as sadly valid for the 1950s as it was for the 1960s. For the tragedy of 1967 is that many of its seeds were not, as is often claimed, sown in October or even July 1966 but in the 1950s or, as some see it, in 1914 or maybe in 1900 itself.

All sides have given general recognition to the fact that the fuse which eventually ignited when certain army officers put the match to it in January 1966 was laid in October 1965, at the time of the Western Region election and its aftermath of bloody violence. Whether there was also a powder-trail, as some would have it, deliberately laid back in the New Year constitutional crisis of 1965 has so far remained a matter of uncertainty.[3] The Federal Military Government's admission that the election was 'believed by many honest Nigerians to have been rigged on a very large scale'[4] and 'resulted in widespread rioting, arson and lawlessness,[5] for once coincides with the Biafran assessment that 'many Nigerians regarded [it] as the final test before despairing of constitutional, political and economic reform. . . . It sealed the fall of democracy under the last civilian régime [and] was indeed a national calamity'.[6] In brief, the Nigerian National Democratic Party, with the militant support of the N.P.C., foisted on the bitterly divided West the unpopular and improperly appointed Akintola. Here was a new political phenomenon. For the first time the N.P.C. showed itself prepared to risk its reputation (although it refused to alter its name to the 'Nigerian' Peoples' Congress) in the rough-house of an electoral campaign outside its home base. A scrutiny of the Nigerian press over the last months of 1965 affords some indication of the resentment engendered by what was to prove a suicidally insensitive incursion of the N.P.C. into the Southern political arena and by the Federal Government's preference for merely sending in minimum security forces rather than fulfilling the Prime Minister's threat to 'flood the West with troops' if there was any trouble and so declare a state of emergency on the justifiable precedent of 1962.[7]

[1] Memorandum submitted by the Northern Region. *Ad Hoc Conference* . . . p. 5 (Lagos), and p. 1 (Enugu).

[2] Review of W. Schwarz, *Nigeria*, in the *Guardian*, 21 June 1968.

[3] The Federal Military Government ascribes the first moves for a military take-over to December 1964, *Nigeria 1966* (Lagos, 1967), p. 5.

[4] *Current Nigerian Situation*, p. 2.

[5] *Struggle for One Nigeria*, p. 7.   [6] *January 15*, p. 8.

[7] The discrepancy was commented on abroad as well as in Nigeria. See *The Times*, 7 January 1966.

C

But if it is accepted that October 1965 was the flash-point, what made up the sombre clouds of the gathering storm? The political tensions of the 1950s had been disguised rather than relaxed in the euphoria engendered by 1960's independence. They were soon to re-emerge, as the potential for imbalance of the federal constitution began to be exploited. It would be possible to examine this fatal imbalance at a number of levels. For the sake of brevity, they could be reduced to two: those of political power (elections and the sweets of office) and of higher manpower (Nigerianization, élites, and education), the two converging in the passionate and ruthless race to secure and consolidate personal, party, and ethnic economic opportunities. This cut-throat antagonism was symbolized in the haves and have-nots struggle: the Dantesque nightmare of an economy expanding too slowly to absorb the unemployed school-leavers and surplus (so far only Southern) graduates, of trade union unrest, of nepotism, and of tribal discrimination in the allocation of jobs. Horace Walpole's classic exposition of the limited alternative, 'Downing Street or the Tower', had, in its application to the Nigerian scene, a far wider validity than to the political process alone.

An analysis of these areas of conflict, with their strong potential for a dénouement fit to justify the darkest fears of a lugubrious Dumont-Barnes[1] interpretation of modern Africa's chances, is beyond the scope of this introduction, but their total influence on shaping the events of January 1966 and beyond might, in other circumstances, fairly be assessed in a detailed study of the real implications of that single crisis where all three levels of tension converged, namely the census controversey of 1962–4. From here, to revert to our explosives metaphor, the gunpowder trail was laid, awaiting only the lighting of the fuse in October 1965 to result in the final conflagration on 15 January 1966. Indeed, comparative historians may be tempted to see the fate of Nigeria mirrored in the opening words of a recent study of France's collapse: 'The defeat of France in 1940 [Nigeria: 1966] began twenty years earlier, in the years immediately following the First [Nigeria: Second] World War'.[2]

A number of signposts to disaster may be identified in the post-Independence decline of Nigeria's political health. Each of them constituted, potentially and then progressively, a step towards the awful climax of constitutional overthrow and the assassination of her Prime Minister and two of her four Premiers. In phrasing the tragedy in these serial terms, the aim is not to conjure up the image of Nigeria advancing towards destruction with the inexorable and foredoomed helplessness of a Greek drama. What it does suggest is that, to alter the metaphor, the

---

[1] The reference is to the tenor of the survey of the African political continent given by Réne Dumont, *L'Afrique est mal partie* (Paris, 1961), and Leonard Barnes, *African Renaissance* (London, 1969).

[2] Guy Chapman, *Why France Collapsed* (London, 1969), p. 1.

threads of dénouement were being woven year by year from 1961 onwards, and that to the clear-sighted some kind of pattern of compromise
or confrontation cumulatively became distinguishable. By 1965 many
found the design so daunting that they concluded it was no longer a
question of *what* shape the finished product would take but simply a
matter of *when* the end would be. The most optimistic of the pessimists
clung to the belief—or was it merely a prayer?—that the inevitable
climax might be bloodless. Such is the human capacity for self-deception
in the cause of survival that few among them imagined anything quite
so traumatic as the appalling events set in train by the cataclysm of
15 January. 'If the evil men who started the events of January 1966,'
Colonel Hassan Katsina told a passing-out parade at the Nigerian
Defence Academy in 1967, 'had known the terrible consequences that
would follow, they would have hesitated: their act should now be a
lesson to all.'[1]

In our inquiry, we may leave aside speculation on how the cards
would have fallen had the A.G. and the N.C.N.C. felt able to sink their
differences in the Mid-West, the new 'cockpit of Nigerian politics',[2]
and thus seize the opportunity of driving the N.P.C. into a salutary
period of opposition through a Southern alliance after the results of the
1959 Federal election. In the event, it was to be the N.C.N.C. that came
(or, as some believe, was allowed to come) in from the cold and make up
the indispensable coalition with the N.P.C.

Six months of glorious self-confidence and justified self-congratula-
tion followed the Independence celebrations of October 1960. Then,
within the year, Nigeria encountered its first possible warning. This was
the sweeping victory of the N.P.C. in the Northern Regional election of
May 1961. Its tally of 94% of the seats eliminated Northern Elements
Progressive Union as an opposition and left only the A.G.-voting Tiv
in stubborn disagreement. Unexceptionable by accepted Nigerian
standards of political patronage and power bases, the result confirmed
the South's fear that, under the independence constitution, there was
now little to prevent the North winning a working majority at the next
Federal election.[3] Some heard the door slam, as early as 1961, on any
non-violent solution to the perpetuated situation of political imbalance
in the absence of a change of heart by the N.P.C.

Next came the breakdown of constitutional government in the
Western Region. Exactly a year after the entrenchment of the Northern
establishment at the polls, in May 1962 pressure groups from the ruling
parties at the centre persuaded the Prime Minister that an unseemly
rough-house in the Parliament building at Ibadan and the self-proclama-

[1] Colonel Hassan Usman Katsina's address to the cadets of the Nigerian Military
Academy, Kaduna, 12 August 1967.

[2] The phrase is Professor J. Mackintosh's.

[3] See James O'Connell, 'The Northern 1961 Election', *Nigerian Journal of Economic
and Social Studies*, Ibadan, July 1962.

tion of two rival Premiers was sufficient to declare a state of emergency in the West. The constitution was suspended and a sole Administrator appointed to run the disgraced Region on behalf of the Federal Government. The chaos had arisen from a violent public split in the A.G. leadership during the party's annual congress held at Jos in February when Awolowo had sought to dismiss Akintola from the Premiership on grounds of 'maladministration, anti-party activities, and gross indiscipline'[1] and Akintola, developing his earlier sneer at Awolowo followers as 'revolutionary babes who have not the astuteness to gain the party a single vote',[2] showed his preference for finding a role for the West in some sort of national government in Lagos rather than being permanently cold-shouldered by the N.P.C. and N.C.N.C. Worse was to follow, for Awolowo found himself arraigned and sentenced to a long prison sentence on a charge of treason and his A.G. had its name dragged through the mud in the public inquiries of the Coker judicial commission: no wonder that Awolowo felt moved to comment that for him and his party 'the twilight of democracy and the rule of law in Nigeria is changing into darkness'.[3]

One clear political lesson emerged from the Federal Government's declaration of an emergency. There had been a manifest violation of the tacit acceptance of the principle of what Professor Sklar has formulated as 'regional security' whereby each party was quietly left to control its own Region without interference.[4] The inference was clear. The apparently impregnable walls of regional power bastions could after all be breached by the heavy artillery of the centre. For all their dogged resistance to change or challenge from within their own sphere of one-party authority the Regions were not proof against coercion, constitutional though it was, from the Federal Government. The ease of this operation augured an ominous precedent in the hands of whichever party controlled the Federation. Furthermore, the North could draw another moral from the West's discomfort. The same disaster might overtake them if the N.P.C. leadership should be split by the Middle Belt politicians or a radical wing within the Hausa-Fulani-Kanuri ranks: the concept of 'one North, one people' was more imperative than ever.

The N.P.C.'s immature and unsuccessful involvement in the Mid-Western election of 1963 was another portent of just how high the price might be for the carving out of more states. The message now seemed clear that unless new states were to be created simultaneously, a piece-

---

[1] Quoted in Schwarz, op. cit., p. 134 (with incorrect reference to *West Africa*, 17 February 1962).

[2] *West Africa* (1962), p. 647. Akintola also accused Awolowo of being 'politically evil and dictatorial in approach', *West Africa* (1962), p. 579.

[3] Quoted by Schwarz, op. cit., p. 146.

[4] This very useful concept was devised by Richard L. Sklar. See his 'For National Reconciliation and a United National Front', *Nigerian Opinion*, Ibadan, vol. ii, no. 1, 1965, p. 5.

meal solution might prove to be bloodier and more embittering than no such fragmentation at all. With the North dedicated to the inviolability of its regional shape and sovereignty as an attitude of political faith, and the earlier campaign for Kabba-Ilorin separatism or a non-Fulani Middle Belt State adroitly overcome, or at least muted, by N.P.C. tactics, there seemed to be no likelihood of anyone at the Federal level advocating, to use General Gowon's subsequent words, the 'courageous course of facing the fundamental problem that has plagued this country since the early fifties'.[1] Yet there is irony again in the finale. When the time did come in May 1967 to create the states so long called for by so many as the only chance for Nigeria's political survival, the East's reaction was as abrupt in its rejection of such a decentralization by the Northern leaders as the North's had been bloody at the centralization imposed on it by an Eastern leader exactly twelve months previous. Gowon's 'divide and rule' was as much a do-or-die measure for national survival as Ironsi believed his 'unify and rule' to have been; yet both came too late to avert disaster.

Prominent in our story of *Sturm und Drang* stand the census figures. Too long to be recounted here,[2] the census story is important because, with electoral representation based on a population count, the South's only hope of wresting political dominance from the North constitutionally lay in proving that the combined population of the East, West, Mid-West, and Lagos exceeded that of the North. This hope, and belief in the East, was shattered by the Prime Minister's eventual acceptance, after many months of discreditable wrangling in public, of the revised census figures, which gave the North a count of 29·8 million (54%) against the East's 12·4 m., the West's 10·3 m. and the Mid-West's 2·5 m. out of the country's total of 55,653,821, thus confirming the majority (56%) established in the 1952 census.

The next two crises are on a lesser scale but their message was none the less significant and, in the long run, substantial. With Awolowo behind bars, Azikiwe constitutionally advanced above politics, and Okpara held in check by the Prime Minister's official approval of the census result, the North could survey the dispersal and dismay of its opponents with satisfaction. Better still, even the South could not agree among itself. The early months of 1964 saw a minor but equally virulent extension of the tribal overtones of the census disagreement. In rapid succession, pamphlets were published, with official connivance and at times sponsorship, to discredit one political party or another by alleging blatantly ethnic criteria for the composition and promotion prospects of the senior posts in such ostensibly Federal institutions as the Railway Corporation, the Ports Authority, the Airways, and the University of

[1] See p. 5.
[2] The most useful account to date is that given by J. Mackintosh, op. cit., pp. 547–60. The pamphlet literature on the census was considerable; no holds were barred.

Ibadan.[1] There was a further ugly recrudescence of this ethnic jealousy over high office when, a year later, accusations of tribalism over the appointment of a new Vice-Chancellor for the University of Lagos were injuriously bandied about and came to a head in physical violence and murderous intent. Though the acrimonious bickerings of teachers, staff, and students had become a regrettable and ridiculous feature of campus life at more than one Nigerian institution of higher education, it was not till after the fall of the civilian government that academics and the military alike publicly came out in robust condemnation of certain intellectuals as 'the worst pedlars of tribalism'[2] in the country's ethnic rat-race. When one adds to this unsightly quarrel the North *v* East rivalry over the siting of the multi-million iron and steel complex, whose eventual compromise solution threatened to make a laughing-stock of the principles of unified national economic planning to which such lip-service was paid by the politicians, a case could fairly be made out for seeing in the census controversy the microcosm of all the North-South suspicion, mistrust, fear, and animosity that marked this political decade of Nigeria's history.

The general strike of June 1964 is an event whose organization and long-term effects would reward a much closer analysis than they have so far experienced in any large-scale attempt to pinpoint the strength of the underlying feeling of discontent by the lower-paid wage-earners. Additionally, there was the growing gap between the literate electorate and most of the seemingly indifferent political class whom they had expectantly helped to vote into power. And what, after all, was left to a people with politics in their blood to argue about after independence had been achieved? Walter Schwarz once gave the answer: 'Politics was now about the allocation of jobs, scholarship, patronage and amenities'.[3] The remarkable success of the general strike has perhaps been underrated for its role as another nail in the coffin of the First Republic. While it was certainly of less immediate political importance, the eventual coming together of Nigeria's quarrelling trade unions into an effective Joint Action Committee and their rewarding promotion of the strike showed up the jelly-kneed element in the Federal Government. Ministers in Lagos asked for armed escorts and the slackening off in the conspicuous vulgarity of several well-known parliamentary figures did not escape the amused notice of the Lagos man-in-the-street. The strike underlined a lesson in labour affairs that may not have been properly learned by the Establishment in Lagos. The lesson was not, however, lost by the Lagos bureaucracy, who now were heard to speak quite

---

[1] Again, the pamphlet literature was extensive in its statistical allegations and counter-allegations. It reached its climax in publications over the Vice-Chancellorship of Lagos.

[2] Dr K. O. Dike, Vice-Chancellor's Address to Convocation, Ibadan, 1966, quoted in *West Africa* (1966), p. 783.

[3] Walter Schwarz, 'A Troubled People', *Help*, no. 10, 1969, p. 21.

openly of their responsibility for saving Nigeria from the mess made by the politicians.

The most perilous display of brinkmanship in the history of the First Republic stemmed directly from the census row. As the parties shuffled their alliances under the new umbrella symbols of Nigerian National Alliance and United Progressive Grand Alliance and the Sardauna confessed that 'the Ibos have never been true friends of the North and never will be',[1] the President allowed himself seemingly to become involved in the political scene. On dissolving Parliament at the beginning of December, Dr Azikiwe treated the nation to 'A Dawn Address'. He cited instances of corruption and intimidation in the electoral process on a horrifying Eatanswill scale of rottenness, and closed his message from Government House with this dramatic appeal:

I have one advice to give to our politicians. If they have decided to destroy our national unity, then they should summon a round-table conference to decide how our national assets should be divided before they seal their doom by satisfying their lust for office. I make this suggestion because it is better for us and for our many admirers abroad that we should disintegrate in peace and not in pieces. Should the politicians fail to heed this warning, then I will venture the prediction that the experience of the Democratic Republic of the Congo will be child's play if ever it comes to our turn to play such a tragic role.[2]

The deduction could be made that U.P.G.A. no longer fancied their chances of winning the forthcoming election. As the crisis deepened and an U.P.G.A. delegation called on the President to postpone the election because of the scandalous conduct of the campaign, Dr Azikiwe suggested inviting the U.N. to supervise a new Federal election.[3] The Prime Minister demurred at this affront to the country's competence and declined to cancel the election. U.P.G.A. called on the people to 'rally round so that we might save this nation from the forces of tyranny, despotism and feudalism, and from those who now seek to come to power at all costs'.[4] Uneasily, the nation went to the polls on 30 December.

The critical confrontation of the Prime Minister with Azikiwe, and the latter's suspected toying with the idea of assuming Presidential control after the East's gauche miscalculation of boycotting the election, brought the country to the very edge of disaster in the opening days of 1965. Nigeria had never been more ripe for military intervention and junior officers were not loath to mention the dreaded word coup in the Mess and among friends. Indeed it is to this election period that the

[1] Quoted, without source, by Schwarz, *Nigeria*, p. 164.
[2] *West African Pilot*, 11 December 1964.
[3] *Sixteen Days of Political Crisis (State House Diary)* (Lagos, 1965). Entry for 28 December 1964. See also Okoi Arikpo, *The Development of Modern Nigeria* (London, 1967), Chapter viii.
[4] Statement issued by U.P.G.A. through the N.C.N.C., 27 December 1964.

Federal Military Government was later to ascribe the first plot for a *coup d'état*, naming some of the very officers involved in the army mutiny almost exactly a year later.[1] The President's conclusion that he 'would rather resign than exercise the power to call on a person to form a government' was reversed by his sudden decision to cancel this broadcast message, but not before it had already been released to the Eastern press.[2] His eventual announcement that he had, after all, decided to reappoint Alhaji Sir Abubakar as Prime Minister and his acceptance of the five points for constitutional patch-work put forward by the Chief Justice were greeted with relief. These included determining the legality of the recent elections in constituencies where the number of voters were so small as to 'make a mockery of democracy', a constitutional review commission, and the immediate formation of a 'broad-based national government'.[3] Any literal preference by Sir Abubakar for such a 'broad-based national' government was obliged to give way to his party's determined refusal to treat with U.P.G.A. Thus the able A.G. men were still to be excluded from power. Those who censure the Prime Minister for his weakness, enforced rather than willed, in failing to order his Federal Cabinet in accord with the high and patriotic standards which he set himself should not overlook the razor-edged delicacy of his position within the N.P.C. as nothing more than the deputy leader of the party, and the uncomfortable knowledge, publicly pronounced, that the Prime Ministership had been entrusted by the Sardauna to one he had arrogantly stigmatized as 'my lieutenant'.

As the tension of early January began to relax, many were left wondering whether even Nigeria, with its genius for eleventh-hour compromise to wrench itself off a collision course, could survive another crisis like this one. Disenchanted, despondent, and likely doomed, the East had one last constitutional chance to save itself from the otherwise certain condemnation to a long-term politico-economic sentence as a second-class citizenry. If U.P.G.A. could secure the Western Region in the election due before the end of 1965—and the unpopularity of the usurper (*ole*, 'thief', was a common cry in Yorubaland by now) Akintola's client-government seemed to point towards a comfortable A.G. + N.C.N.C. victory given the precondition of a free and fair poll— then it would control three of the four Regional governments. Here was an opportunity to regain the advantage forfeited by Azikiwe and Awolowo in their mutually mistrusting refusal to come together in 1959 and redress the political imbalance by isolating the North and restricting the N.P.C.'s influence to Kaduna alone.

But the N.P.C. had no intention of committing political *felo de se*. Akintola had at all costs to be saved from the fate his government

[1] *Nigeria 1966*, p. 5.
[2] e.g., *West African Pilot*, 4 January 1965.
[3] *State House Diary*, entry for 3 January 1965.

deserved. The outcome was the crooked Western election of October 1965 and ultimate debasement of the democratic process in the reimposition of an unpopular government through chicanery and thuggery. The near-anarchy that prevailed in parts of the Region during the dying months of the year made Okpara's stricture on the recent Federal election, 'a colossal farce, a daylight fraud',[1] pale in comparison to the naked corruption and terrorism of the West. The indictment of electoral infamy made public by Esua, the Chairman of the Federal Electoral Commission, in a letter to the Governor of the West—'a valuable document in the psephology of a developing country'[2]—is by no means a complete catalogue of all the methods used to ensure a fraudulent result. As the deeper significance of the scandal of the Western Region results sank in, it became apparent that under the rules of the 1963 constitution by which the political game was then being played, the days of Nigeria as the world had learned to know it over the past decade were clearly numbered.

In this cumulative progression towards the internal collapse of 1966, particularly the key quarrel over the inflated census figures and the consequent crisis over the conduct and outcome of the ensuing general election which may well have constituted the ultimate point of no return, there merge the three eroding forces identified earlier: the disappointment of all but one of the political parties seeking power by constitutional means and with it the open sesame to 'life more abundant' for their expectant electorates; the disenchantment with the deteriorating quality of Nigeria's political culture by many of the intelligentsia at all levels; and the disillusion of the semi-educated underpaid and unemployed. These were the clouds of the threatening storm that was now to break.

'Five years after independence,' the Federal Military Government has since remarked in a disarmingly frank judgement, 'all these factors had combined to produce an explosive situation little short of a breakdown of law and order. It became increasingly clear that sooner or later there would be a fundamental, and probably violent, change.'[3]

That change came, in its most brutally violent form, in the early hours of Saturday, 15 January 1966.[4] There were, it seemed, some who

---

[1] A subsequent U.P.G.A. pamphlet on the 1964 Federal Election was entitled *The Big Fraud* (Yaba, 1965).

[2] Schwarz. op. cit., p. 185.

[3] *Struggle for One Nigeria*, p. 7.

[4] While this political prologue to the tragedy of 'Nigeria 1966' is in some measure derived from personal observation and documentation (the writer was fortunate in having been a nominal *d'an Kaduna*, 'one close to Kaduna' [in a socio-political as well as physical sense] between 1954 and 1965), its assumptions acquire a certain confirmation from other sources. The Nigerian literature up to 1963 is rich and its ample bibliographies render any discussion of it superfluous here. However, from the census, general strike, and Federal election of 1964 onwards, the political story has yet to be fully recounted and analysed. The ephemeral literature for the period 1966–70 is discussed in the note on sources appearing in Volume II. For obvious reasons the events of 1966 and their after-

were prepared to overlook the risk inherent in the motto attributed to
Mao that politics come out of the barrel of a gun. Thereafter, for the rest
of that fateful year in Nigeria's history, the nation and the world were
left to ponder on the possible completion of the W. B. Yeats stanza,
the opening words of which Chinua Achebe had made so famous in the
calmer climate of African literature:

> Things fall apart;
> The centre cannot hold;
> Mere anarchy is loosed upon the world.

---

math cannot yet be told in full; a completely satisfactory presentation must await the
opening of the archives of both sides. Meanwhile, in addition to the authoritative background studies of James S. Coleman, Richard L. Sklar, Ken W. Post, C. Syl Whitaker,
and Billy J. Dudley, each of which discusses the fortunes of the several Nigerian political
parties, the preliminary critiques of the vital years of 1964 and 1965 by John Mackintosh,
James O'Connell, Walter Schwarz, and Okoi Arikpo, all cited above, make indispensable
reading for every student of Nigeria 1966. For a critical survey of the events of 1966–70
written in immediate retrospect, see the author's 'The War of A Thousand Days',
Blackwood's Magazine, March 1970, pp. 193–207.

COUPS AND AFTERMATH

JANUARY 1966—JULY 1967

THE identification of such steps on Nigeria's primrose path to threat-ened disintegration in 1966 allows us to introduce the first items of major documentation in this verbatim record of crisis and conflict since that fateful 15 January. How have Nigerians and Biafrans themselves assessed the root causes of their escalating tragedy and sought to ex-plain the reasons for the bloody *coups d'état* in that year of the long knives? Apart from allusions in some of the 1967–70 war and peace speeches included later on in these pages, judgements made nearer the event are of special importance and may be read in support of the diagnosis of political dystrophy propounded above. Writing within three weeks of the coup, the widely-read, outspoken Nigerian columnist Tai Solarin followed up his colleague's important attempt to explain to posterity why it all took place, Peter Pan's 'Letters to a grandchild',[1] with his own conclusion that the civilian leaders had wanted to run before they had learned to walk.

Before this country gets back a civilian government again a few million words are going to be written by Nigerians and friends of Nigerians as we analyse and synthesize the corpse of our first republic. Any school boy of ten would tell anybody why our first experiment failed. The school boy would, invariably, give two reasons.

He would, for the first reason say there was bribery and corruption and for the second, he would mention rigging of elections.

But the fault lay not with our stars but with our leaders:

Immediately you think, as a leader, that you are special, from that very minute you have lost your place in the hearts of the people. The leader in a republic is not a special man. He, like all his fellowmen, is a plebeian. All he has which the others have not got, is a special opportunity for a unique service. If that leader is any good he will continue to identify himself with the tears and laughters of the people.

His fingers he must keep on the public pulse all the time. Once he breaks this contact and takes to his ivory tower and flanks himself with wine, women and song and, probably, too, with an armoury—as did a few of our erstwhile rulers—from that moment he becomes a misfit.

Like millions of other Nigerians, Tai Solarin saw military rule as alone offering the hope of salvation:

Under three weeks ago, I still sang Ebenezer Elliot's 'The People's Anthem'.

> When wilt thou save the people?
> O God of mercy, when?
>   The people, Lord, the people,
>   Not thrones and crowns, but men!
> God save the people; thine they are
>   Thy children, as Thine angels fair:

[1] Peter Pan, *Daily Times*, 24 and 25 January 1966.

> From vice, oppression, and despair,
> God save the people!

Now we have been saved—and we want to stay saved.[1]

Nigeria's intellectuals also asked themselves why their governments had been overthrown and why they fell at the particular moment they did, and they came up with an answer that placed most of the blame on the N.P.C. and its pressurizing of the central government:

The national politicians who took over from the British were lawful and indigenous rulers. Unfortunately power went to their heads. They took for granted that control over parliament gave them total control over political activity in the country. They equated parliamentary majorities with an effective power majority. . . . It was [the] sense of constitutionalism that the ruling class destroyed. . . . The use of federal power in 1962 to crush the Action Group alienated the West. The reversal of the Privy Council decision showed that the government was not going to respect the courts. The courts themselves were discredited by some strange decisions and by the systematic withdrawal of charges against government supporters. The use of the Western Electoral Commission to fabricate results was one of the last decisive steps towards convincing many persons that they had nothing to gain from law or from abiding by the rules of the game. When the federal government under Sir Abubakar supported this last piece of law-breaking (and there were only occasional whimpers of dissent from its patronage-seeking N.C.N.C. members) it was telling many people that they had nothing to expect from elected government. . . .

Had the Northern-dominated federal government ruled with efficiency and integrity, it might have conciliated the Southern intelligentsia—after all, the latter did not greatly love their own politicians. But whispers of corruption grew into shouts. Convictions grew that ministers, even when they devoted time to their work, were not able men. People became convinced that there was no political group to whom they could tell their frustration or ask to rebuild their hopes.

In short, the rulers used power that they held constitutionally to do unconstitutional things. In the process they destroyed themselves. Nigeria had censuses that were not censuses, elections that were not elections, and finally governments that were not governments.[2]

Two of the most blackening indictments of the First Republic come from the successor Federal and Mid-Western Military Governments, whose categorization of maladministration reads like a handbook to the art of unstable government:

Among the most important causes which affected the stability of the Nigerian Federation soon after independence, are:

---

[1] 'They Ran Too Far Ahead', Tai Solarin, *Daily Times*, 3 February 1966. Tai Solarin was to be no less critical of Government maladministration in the aftermath of civil war.

[2] Editorial, 'The Last Hurrah', *Nigerian Opinion* (University of Ibadan), February 1966. A further analysis of the reasons for parliamentary collapse was made by Tam. S. David-West in the same journal a year after the civil war had started: 'Towards the New Nigeria', ibid., July 1968.

(*i*) The existence at the Centre of a very powerful executive which weakened the Central Legislature in its role of safe-guarding the interests of component units of the Federation.

(*ii*) The abolition of the Judicial Service Commissions, the precipitate termination of appeals to the Judicial Committee of the Privy Council in London, and the surbordination of Public Prosecutions to political control.

(*iii*) The restrictions imposed on the emergence of truly national political parties and the refusal of regional authorities to accept or work with political parties with roots in other regions.

(*iv*) The electoral systems which left the control of elections to machineries dominated by politicians who could and did manipulate elections to the advantage of their supporters.

(*v*) The abuse of powers such as the power to control the Police Forces and the use of Courts and appointments of Judges for political ends.

(*vi*) The ineffectiveness of Parliaments in the discharge of their functions and the misuse of the powers of Parliament.

(*vii*) The avoidance of public accountability and public examination by Ministers.

(*viii*) The division of powers between the Federal and Regional authorities, which in certain cases left vital areas of conflict between them and, in others, failed to allocate to the Federal authority functions which would have promoted national unity.

(*ix*) The absence of codes of conduct for public functionaries and the absence of democratic traditions.

(*x*) The collapse of normal safeguards against misrule, in particular:
   (*a*) the right of public protests;
   (*b*) free Press and radio;
   (*c*) free public discussion;
   (*d*) the ultimate sanction of the threat of an alternative government.

(*xi*) National traits of sycophancy and deference support.

(*xii*) The psychological impact of coups in neighbouring African States.

(*xiii*) Tribalism, tribal discrimination, nepotism and corrupt practices, particularly in appointments to public offices and in the distribution of amenities.

(*xiv*) The desire of ethnic and linguistic groups for separate states within the Federation.

(*xv*) The continued economic and ideological interests of, and intrigues by, the old colonial regime and other foreign countries in Nigeria.

(*xvi*) The slow pace of social integration among the various population groups.

(*xvii*) The problem of the Army:
   (*a*) the dichotomy in social origins between the majority of the rank and file and the majority of officers;
   (*b*) political interference with the role of the Army as guardians of legitimacy;
   (*c*) the unanswered question of the peace-time role of young, educated, politically conscious officers.[1]

---

[1] Federal Ministry of Information, *The Struggle for One Nigeria* (1967).

The Mid-West Region, born from dissent and up to 1966 apparently destined to remain the Cinderella of the Federation, was in a peculiarly effective position to diagnose the root causes of the nation's malady, and accused the 'dominant ethnic groups' of showing more concern for the maintenance of the *status quo* than for finding permanent solutions to the continuing constitutional crises. This led to the minority groups' leaders developing a sense of insecurity and dissatisfaction, so that before long 'internecine rivalry of the Regions and tensions characterized our political system.'[1]

While the early interpretations of January 1966 by the Nigerians themselves are the more important,[2] those made at the time by some of the most influential English-language newspapers abroad are impressive by the accuracy of their own confirmatory assessments.[3] 'Nigeria in Peril' ran the first leader in *The Times* on 17 January:

The mutiny which has shaken Nigeria has its roots in the tribal, regional, religious, and personal conflicts which the Federation was designed to bridge. The assassination of the Sardauna of Sokoto, the Northern Region Premier, and of Chief Akintola, Premier of the West, provides one clue to its motives. These two combined to maintain the hegemony of the Muslim and conservative North over the basically anti-northern West. This combination infuriated all the southern regions and indeed some of the non-Muslim tribes of the North itself. . . .

What is at stake is Nigeria's unity. It is not yet clear if the young officers, who are reported largely to be Ibos from the Eastern Region, are bidding for political control or are mainly prompted by the widespread public dissatisfaction with the politicians. This anger with ineffective politicians, all too often highly corrupt, is now characteristic in Africa.

Yet, whatever the Government's mistakes, to make them a reason for destroying Nigeria's unity would be a disaster. It would not solve any real problems. It would shatter the hopes placed everywhere in Africa's largest state. It would be bad for Nigerians, bad for Africa, bad for the Commonwealth. Through unity alone is Nigeria likely to develop the great potential strength (including oil) which can overcome poverty in time. Four little states would do much worse. In the world at large a break-up of the Nigerian Federation would be taken as another sign that Africans mismanage government and are incapable of union or of the brotherhood they proclaim. The voices of all African leaders would be less regarded.

This tone was matched by that of the *Scotsman*, 'Nigeria in Turmoil', and by the *Guardian*'s assessment of what it saw as 'the twofold occasion for revolt', analysed by its correspondent under the gloomy heading 'A Democracy that Failed':

[1] *Understanding the Nigerian Crisis* (Benin, July 1968).

[2] It is worth noting that on 4 December 1965 the *Nigerian Outlook*, doubtless disturbed by the military coups in the Congo (Kinshasa) and Dahomey, carried an editorial on such military takeovers and mentioned the word 'coup' in a Nigerian context.

[3] All references are to the issues dated 17 January 1966.

The dispossession of the Yorubas and the sheer weight of numbers by which the North has dominated the politics of the Federation have been one element making for revolt. But there is another, of which no visitor to Nigeria can remain for very long unaware. The transition from colonial to indigenous rule has nowhere been so smooth, and this, the young men of Lagos and Ibadan will say, is the trouble. Nothing has changed except the colour of the rich man emerging from the back seat of his car. Independence has not brought any social reforms of consequence. Even universal primary education in the southern regions was begun some years before the British moved out. In spite of all the talk of African socialism from Dr. Azikiwe and Chief Awolowo before independence, Nigeria's economy is capitalist in an extreme form.

It is also corrupt. Corruption has its open defenders. They describe it as the African Welfare State. And, indeed, if a Minister or civil servant is expected to keep and educate an extended family running perhaps into dozens of distant cousins is his 5 per cent on a contract to be regarded as corrupt or as merely prudent? Yet almost the first words to be broadcast by the rebels who gained control of the radio were directed against the corruption and nepotism with which so many young Nigerians have associated their Federal Government. Many a young man would gladly exchange some of the political freedom and immunity from arbitrary arrest which Western democracy has given him for a redistribution of wealth and a sense of national purpose infused into political parties grown fat on Nigerian free enterprise. . . .

The concentration of ebullience in the South is not explained solely by the more volatile temperament of the Southerners or the conservatism of the Moslems in the North. In the mid-1950s the two Southern regions embarked on a huge programme of universal primary education which met the popular clamour at the time but created serious social problems which were predicted then but have ripened only in the last few years. By providing universal education before they had had their industrial revolution the southern regions of Nigeria created an army of educated unemployed and an underpaid labour force both in clerical and manual jobs. The North has been more reactionary, or more careful. It deliberately delayed an expansion of education until there was a guarantee of jobs for the school-leavers to go to. Nigeria's National Plan, which envisaged the creation of many more thousands of jobs between 1962 and 1968 has hit the snag common to most national plans in underdeveloped countries—that foreign generosity was overestimated and the time allowed to do the job was too short.

The *Daily Telegraph* editorialized on the 'Explosion in Nigeria'. The *Financial Times* described the whole concept of Nigeria's federation as an enormous gamble and talked of the 'fatal division' of the South as having guaranteed the political supremacy of the North. In the same vein, a report in the *Scotsman* placed the blame on the Lagos Government:

The attempted military coup in the Federal Republic of Nigeria—whether it finally succeeds or fails—has focused world attention on the Achilles heel of the administration of the captive Prime Minister, Alhaji Sir Abubakar

D

Balewa. It had allowed public corruption to flourish almost with official approval and it had failed to assess with sufficient seriousness the attitude which this was breeding among the emerging radical youth in the universities and other places of future leadership.

This wealth of judgement may be advantageously complemented by two short but instructive summaries put forward by the Federal Military Government to explain the public's approval of the first coup:

(a) Unfortunately that government [the 'broad-based' 1965 Federal cabinet] included many personalities who had been discredited by a large section of Nigerian public opinion. The public was equally restless with the widespread corruption and abuse of office by highly placed persons. It was in this climate of general disillusionment with the political ruling class [that the coup was organized]. . . .[1]

(b) Firstly, some people saw in it [the coup] an attempt to end Northern domination. Secondly, some regarded it as an attempt to remove corruption in Government. Thirdly, others hoped it would introduce an honest and just programme to correct the structural imbalance in the Federation. No one quarrelled with these aims.[2]

From these retrospective reflections and from the coda of political crescendo identified in this prelude to Nigeria 1966, we now turn to the chronological record from January onwards.

In Lagos, mid-January 1966 saw the centre of attention momentarily shifted from the frightening breakdown of law and order in the Akintola-imposed Western Region to excited pride[3] in Sir Abubakar Tafawa Balewa's triumph in arranging for Nigeria to play host to the first meeting of Commonwealth Prime Ministers ever to be held outside London.[4] But it was only momentarily. On the very day the conference ended, an U.P.G.A. front-bencher startled the House of Representatives by alleging 'this country is on fire . . . we are sitting on a tinder-box'.[5] Outside the Western Region, indifference to the gravity of the situation found expression in the callously laconic headline of the *New Nigerian* reporting the official statement made to Parliament by the Minister of State for Police Affairs—not, significantly enough, by the Prime Minister as the situation might have expected: 'Only 153 people killed in West',[6] and again in the anodyne leader of the Government-sponsored *Morning Post* which had greeted the new year with the unfortunate judgement that 'Many thought the Federation would have broken up;

[1] *Government Statement on the Current Nigerian Situation* (Lagos, 1966), paras. 3–4.

[2] *The Collapse of Ojukwu's Rebellion and Prospects for Lasting Peace in Nigeria* (Lagos 1968), p. 4.

[3] *The Times* of London carried an editorial on 10 January headed 'Salute to Nigeria'.

[4] It was suggested in some quarters, e.g., *Sunday Telegraph* of 16 January, that the spectacular conference had been arranged for Lagos by the Prime Minister so as to divert Nigerians' attention from the crisis in their own country. Cf. Okoi Arikpo, *The Development of Modern Nigeria* (1967), p. 150.

[5] *Morning Post*, 12 January 1966. Headlines in the U.K. press over this period reiterated this fear.

[6] *New Nigerian*, 15 January 1966.

others even averred there were going to be tribal wars; it did not seem to occur to them that the glue holding this Federation together is diversity itself.'[1] On 13 January the Prime Minister moved back from the Federal Palace Hotel, where he had stayed for the conference, to his Onikan residence, and the Premier of the North returned from his pilgrimage to Mecca. Twenty-four hours later the Western Premier flew to Kaduna.

But if, in the terse phrase of the press statement on the Western Premier's hurried journey northwards, 'the purpose of the visit was not disclosed',[2] there has been no lack of speculation as to the object of the meeting held at State House, Kaduna, on that Friday between the Sardauna and Chief Akintola.[3] Rumour, eagerly believed at that emotion-loaded time, insisted that the Sardauna was planning to bring the deteriorating situation in the West to an end by sending in the army for 'a ruthless blitz'. A booster had been given to an atmosphere already charged with apprehension by the Northern press allegedly urging the Sardauna to 'have a go' in the West, a call that did not pass unnoticed in the East.[4] Like so many incidents in the crisis months to come, what was true or not now began to matter less than the fact that the assertions were believed as truth and were acted upon. The Eastern Government subsequently claimed the capture of a document purporting to show that the 15 January coup had forestalled a Northern coup scheduled for 17 January.[5] Whether in fact, there was one coup, two coups, or coups within coups,[6] is so far unconfirmed; all that we can be certain of is that the New Year period of 1966 witnessed the culmination of coup kites flown ever since the perilous days of constitutional confrontation at the previous New Year. Nor has the confusion surrounding the inferred purpose of the Northern colonel who flew down from Kaduna to Lagos on that night brought any more light on to what really took place in Kaduna on 14 January. It may well be that now, with the death of the principal *dramatis personae*, including four of the five officers[7] recognized as having master-minded the military coup of 15 January, the whole truth will never be satisfactorily established. For this reason if no other, the police inquiry undertaken much later in the year may assume a unique status [DOC 1].

[1] *Morning Post*, 1 January 1966.

[2] *New Nigerian*, 15 January 1966.

[3] *Africa Research Bulletin*, p. 446, and *January 15*, p. 13, enlarge upon these rumours of what was in the air that week-end.

[4] This was the headline splashed over the *West African Pilot* on 14 January 1966. In the event, the editorial of the *New Nigerian* on 11 January was far less positive and simply pointed out that the West was one of the problems that the Sardauna would have to face on his return, maybe in consultation with Akintola.

[5] *January 15*, pp. 13–14.

[6] The 'coup within the coup' is a theory on which M. J. Dent has been working.

[7] 'We were five in number'—Nzeogwu, in an interview published in *Africa and the World*, May 1967, p. 15. The Federal Government lists many more names, but the five ringleaders would seem to have been Ifeajuna, Okafor, Anuforo, Nzeogwu, and either

Fact returns to the story in the shooting that broke out in Lagos about 2.00 a.m., soon after the guests had left a big party at Brigadier Maimalari's, and in the brutal abduction of the Prime Minister and his Minister of Finance. In Kaduna, the Premier had been murdered in a full-scale military assault on his house at 2.00 a.m., undertaken on the pretext of a training manoeuvre—sustained until the last, mortar-crackling, minute—and senior officers were shot in their beds. In Ibadan, Chief Akintola was killed in his house when soldiers burst in. In Enugu and Benin, the blow was far less dramatic: troops merely threw a cordon round the Premiers' and Governors' residences, though not until 10 o'clock in the morning in Benin. The fact that, whether by design or accident, the Premiers of these two Regions escaped the fate of their colleagues in the other parts of the country, was to rankle for a long time to come and to fester in the Northern mind. Lagos, its sleep disturbed by the night's alarums and excursions, woke to hear an unidentified voice announcing a military take-over on the radio.[1] The citizens of Kaduna's first realization of trouble was the blazing residence of the Sardauna. Hard news becomes tantalizingly scarce for Nigerians listening in to their radios throughout the morning. Then, at noon,[2] Major Nzeogwu broadcast a statement from Kaduna 'In the name of the Supreme Council of the Revolution of the Nigerian Armed Forces', declaring martial law in the North and promulgating ten decrees (among them a remarkable collection of offences) henceforth punishable by death [DOC 2]. During the afternoon, the national radio network carried, in two instalments, a bulletin covering the single statement issued by the Council of Ministers. Its contents were palliative but uninformative to a population eager for news:

In the early hours of this morning, 15 January 1966, a dissident section of the Nigerian Army kidnapped the Prime Minister and the Minister of Finance and took them to an unknown destination. The G.O.C. and the vast majority of the Nigerian Army remain completely loyal to the Federal

---

A. or O., all majors (see DOC 1 including note, and DOC 8). The forthcoming publications of M. J. Dent and R. Luckham on the military in the political process and on the Nigerian officer corps respectively should shed more light on this. It is interesting to note that the Federal Government, in its account *Nigeria 1966*, perpetuates the non-Hausa form 'Exercise Damissa' for the plot in the North and mistranslates it as 'Exercise Tiger'.

[1] I have not traced any record of this other than the news item broadcast from Brussels in French on 15 January that 'an anonymous man had spoken over Lagos radio announcing that the army intended to end the nepotism and corruption prevailing in Nigeria' (B.B.C. Monitoring Service ME/2063/ii. In further references to B.B.C. Monitoring Service reports only the initials B.B.C. will preface the reference number.) The *Sunday Telegraph* of 16 January quoted a report from Cotonou radio that a 'rebel pirate radio in Nigeria said the Army had taken power "to bring an end to gangsterism and disorder, corruption and despotism".' According to *West Africa*, in its diary 'A weekend that shook the world' (1966, p. 105), the message ended with the words 'My compatriots, you will no longer need to be ashamed to be Nigerians'.

[2] Not, according to many versions, in the afternoon or evening. The Emir of Kano, at the invitation of the Commanding Officer of the 5th Bn., Lt.-Col. Ojukwu, broadcast over the local N.B.C. station there.

Government and are already taking all appropriate measures to bring the situation under control. All essential public services continue to function normally. The Federal Government is satisfied that the situation will soon return to normal and that the ill-advised mutiny will be brought to an end, and that law and order in the few disturbed areas of the country will soon be restored. All public buildings and establishments in the Federal Territory are being guarded by loyal troops.[1]

As was to be the case too often, and on occasions tragically,[2] during the next few months, Nigerians first learned of events in their own country from tuning in to foreign broadcasting stations. Abroad, the evening papers of that Saturday hinted at civil unrest as one cause of the cut in cable service with Lagos, while firmer details were given to those awaiting the arrival of the mid-afternoon V.C.10 from Nigeria to London when B.O.A.C. announced that the aircraft had been unable to leave Kano that morning because the airport was 'under insurgent control'.[3] In compensation, as it were, on Sunday the world press, and the Nigerian newspapers rather more restrainedly, gave front-page coverage to what information they had been able or allowed to glean about the coup. By now, all the signs were that it had succeeded, at least if its aim had been to topple the political régime: 'It had been a dream of a coup. "Bang, bang, you're dead!"—a satisfying infantile aggression fantasy.'[4]

In Lagos itself, Saturday had seen the adjournment of Parliament (only one Minister, appointed the previous day, and 33 out of 312 members were present) and two rump cabinet meetings at Police Headquarters under the chairmanship of the senior remaining Minister, Alhaji Zanna Bukar Dipcharima,[5] with General Ironsi and, apparently,[6] the British High Commissioner, in attendance. At the second meeting it was decided to send a special messenger ostensibly from the Prime Minister (despite the earlier announcement of his abduction) to Dr. Azikiwe, then convalescing in London. A communiqué was issued under embargo to the effect that 'The Minister of State for Commonwealth Relations, the Hon. Senator Dan Ibekwe, will leave Lagos for London this morning to deliver a special message from the Prime Minister, Alhaji Sir Abubakar Tafawa Balewa, to His Excellency Dr. Nnamdi Azikiwe, the President of the Federation of Nigeria. (Not to be published or broadcast before 7.00 a.m. on Sunday 16 January 1966.')[7]

---

[1] Federal Ministry of Information Press Release No. 94/1966.

[2] e.g., in the reports from Dahomey Radio of the killing of Northerners in the East during the last few days of September 1966.

[3] *Sunday Telegraph*, 16 January 1966. *The Times* of 17 January carried a full report by one of the B.O.A.C. captains on the West African run.

[4] W. Schwarz, *Nigeria* (1968), pp. 198–9. See also his account in the *Observer*, 23 January 1966.

[5] 'Balewa's chair was respectfully kept vacant', Schwarz, op. cit., p. 197.

[6] As reported in *West Africa* (1966), p. 105.

[7] Federal Ministry of Information Press Release No. 89/1966. It is possible that this

Interviewed at his Surrey hotel, Dr. Azikiwe said he would return to
Nigeria if he could [DOC 3]: as father of his people, 'all I am interested
in is restoring peace.'[1]

Ironsi's request for the whole Cabinet to meet and appoint a Deputy
Prime Minister able constitutionally to give orders to the army brought
no agreement on who this should be, and Ironsi is believed eventually
to have warned the rump of the Council Ministers that the loyalty of the
army could be guaranteed only if power was granted to him.[2] This legal
fiction of a constitutional handing-over of the reins of Government to
the army was maintained in the careful phrasing of the speech announcing a military administration, made to the nation by the acting
President shortly before midnight on 16 January:

> I have tonight been advised by the Council of Ministers that they had come
> to the unanimous decision voluntarily to hand over the administration of the
> country to the Armed Forces of the Republic with immediate effect.
>
> All Ministers are assured of their personal safety by the new administration.
>
> I will now call upon the General Officer Commanding, Major-General
> Aguiyi-Ironsi, to make a statement to the nation on the policy of the new
> administration.
>
> It is my fervent hope that the new administration will ensure the peace and
> stability of the Federal Republic of Nigeria and that all citizens will give them
> their full co-operation.[3]

It was again to the fore in General Ironsi's broadcast acceptance of this
'invitation',[4] without any reference to imposition of martial law, in his
first public statement [DOC 4].

The following day, 17 January, General Ironsi finalized the policy
that he had outlined on the radio the previous night by issuing a prepared seven-point programme to newsmen crowded into the Senate
House. In this he gave little more information than an elaboration of
the administrative changes listed in his broadcast over the national
network. It is therefore to the General's extempore answers to questions
put to him by the press that we must look for fresh indications of his
thinking at that time. Ironsi confirmed that Major Nzeogwu had now
offered his loyalty to him but was unable to throw any light on the
whereabouts of the kidnapped Prime Minister and Federal Finance
Minister. Asked whether it was correct to say that there had been a

---

message may have concerned the appointment of a Deputy Prime Minister, without
whom, as the 1964 electoral crisis had shown, the President or his deputy was unable to
give the army the orders that General Ironsi may well have wanted at that moment.

[1] *Daily Telegraph*, 17 January 1966. In the event, Dr Azikiwe was not invited to return to Nigeria by General Ironsi for nearly two months; and then in a private capacity.
The former President was ignominiously described in the passenger-list as 'journalist'.

[2] Schwarz, op. cit., p. 198.   [3] Government Notice No. 147/1966.

[4] Lawyers like E. A. Keay have pointed out that Ironsi did not say who had 'formally
invested' him with the authority of Head of the Federal Military Government. See
'Legal and Constitutional Changes in Nigeria under the Military Government', *Journal
of African Law*, vol. 10, no. 2, p. 94, note.

mutiny, he replied 'There was a general disorder in the Army.' He repeated that he did not intend to remain in power once law and order had been restored and a new constitution prepared in accordance with popular wishes had come into effect. He refused to be specific on whether Chief Awolowo might be released and concluded by once more defining the legality of his position: 'In order to bring law and order to all parts of the country, the former Federal Government decided to invite me to take over the administration.'[1]

These first declarations of policy were supplemented by a special order of the day addressed to all ranks of the Nigerian armed forces [DOC 5], listing various matters on which Ironsi called for action; by a directive requiring all military officers who had left their posts to resume normal duties at once;[2] changes in civil service nomenclature; a warning that the new government would not hesitate to use the army in order to halt the disturbances in the West;[3] and the issuance of a decree lifting the ban on the circulation of newspapers in any part of the country, such as had operated on the *Daily Times* in parts of the Eastern and Western Regions, the *Morning Post* and *Daily Sketch* in the East, and the *West African Pilot*, the *Nigerian Tribune*, and two vernacular papers in Ibadan.[4] Although Decree No. 1 [DOC 6], promulgating the suspension and modification of the constitution, was retroactive to 17 January, it was not signed by Ironsi till 4 March.[5] In lay terms, it legalized the policies adumbrated in the General's first broadcast.

Ironically, it was in Kaduna, the 'super-emirate' bastion of the *nordisme* which had been one of the chief targets of the plot, that the coup, in the hands of an Ibo major, had its greatest measure of success. The Northern press was already demanding to know how 'Kaduna came to be termed a rebel stronghold for three difficult and uncertain days'.[6] Major Nzeogwu's confident press conferences[7] and his insensitively flamboyant TV interview [DOC 7], subsequently shown in England where it was the cause of much disgust,[8] were quickly overtaken by his decision, once he grasped the folly of marching on Lagos and completing the coup that elsewhere had seemingly gone off at half-cock, to make his own terms for accepting General Ironsi's request for his surrender. These conditions were:

[1] A prepared statement was handed to the press at the conference. Questions and answers are taken from Federal Ministry of Information Press Release No. 96/1966.

[2] Quoted in *Daily Times*, 19 January 1966. The situation was described in the Government statement as now 'returning to normal'.

[3] The directive was reproduced in *Daily Times*, 19 January 1966.

[4] Decree No. 2 of 1966. See Arikpo, op. cit., p. 153.

[5] For a discussion of the legal consequences of this Decree, see Keay, op. cit. An even greater timelag occurred with the official dissolution of parliament, which was not gazetted until Decree No. 12 of 1967 was published on 12 May 1967.

[6] *New Nigerian*, 18 January 1966.

[7] The fullest accounts are to be found in *New Nigerian*, 17, 18, and 20 January 1966.

[8] e.g., letter from Sir Bryan Sharwood Smith, former Governor of Northern Nigeria, printed in the *Daily Telegraph*, 25 January 1966.

1. Safe conduct for himself, his officers and all the men who carried out the coup on the night of January 15.

2. A guarantee of freedom from legal proceedings, now, or at any time in the future, for officers and men who took part.

3. An assurance that the 'people we fought to remove will not be returned to office'.

4. Compensation to be paid to the families of all the officers and men who lost their lives in Kaduna, or other parts of Nigeria.

5. All officers and men arrested in the West to be released.[1]

On 19 January he was flown to Lagos under escort but with a guarantee of safe conduct.

Nzeogwu's controversial role in the Nigerian crisis, from his Brutus-like[2] role in the coup on Kaduna through his controversial detention without a court-martial[3] to his death in action and the military honours accorded to him,[4] along with all the facts and fantasies that have become associated with his story, is yet another dimension in the Nigerian era of crisis that may never be fully known. It does, however, render a case-study of Major Nzeogwu an early priority for research, and it is for this reason that the autobiographical statements attributed to him in a major interview are included here [DOC 8].

Two more aspects of those first few days of the violent overthrow of the First Republic retain continued importance. One is the immediate reaction of Nigeria's public opinion as expressed in the ebullient editorials, correspondence, and report columns of the daily press. The *Morning Post* carried on its front page on 18 January reports of congratulations pouring into Lagos from all over the country and quoted the National Union of Nigerian Students (N.U.N.S.) as having 'whole-heartedly welcomed the take-over' by the armed forces: 'We are happy that this salvation has come.'[5] The *West African Pilot* of the same date led with the headline 'Varsity Students Rejoice of Army Rule', quoting from the placards paraded by Lagos students 'To Hell with Tribalism' and 'This is the Birth of Real Nigerian Freedom.' The *Daily Times* editorial discussed the abuses of the old politicians and welcomed the military régime with characteristic colloquialism: 'About time, too!'[6] To decry the past and enthuse over the present was both sure and safe

---

[1] See *New Nigerian*, 18 January, and *The Times*, 20 January 1966.

[2] I am grateful to J. H. Smith and M. J. Dent for this epithet.

[3] This was to be a vital factor in the North's disenchantment and disaffection in the months ahead.

[4] He was killed in action shortly after the outbreak of the civil war. There are reports of his mutilation, and others of his wish to surrender to the Federal army. General Gowon paid a tribute to Nzeogwu on learning of his death, a gesture which did not earn him unmitigated approval in the North. Nzeogwu was buried in Kaduna. See *New Nigerian*, 2 and 3 August 1967.

[5] Government clerks in Lagos were heard to greet each other on their first Monday after the coup with the salutation *e ku 'new era'-o!*

[6] All quotations from the issues of 18 January 1966.

at that moment; those who might have thought otherwise were too wise to speak up in disagreement. In the words of the Nigerian Current Affairs Society, whose organ has seldom been effusive or hypocritical, written within a week of the coup, 'One of the most fascinating elements after the military take-over was the relief with which ordinary citizens felt that they were again free. . . . The outburst of enthusiasm in the Southern parts of the country and the concealed delight in most parts of the North showed how eager people were for a change.'[1] In particular, given the Northern violence of its 'reaction to conquest' four months later, the editorial welcome by the *New Nigerian* and its vernacular sister-newspaper as well as from the emirs[2] takes on added interest.

The other point to which attention may be drawn is the goodwill messages from the various political parties, whose dream-world had now broken round their ears. A former Minister of State, Alhaji Hashim Adaji, signed a statement on behalf of the N.P.C. in Lagos which declared that:

> The party regards the transfer of authority as the only solution to the many recent problems facing this country. The party gives its unqualified support to the military régime and to the Major-General in particular.
>
> We call on all our party members and supporters to co-operate with the military régime and to give the new administration unflinching support in its great task of bringing peace and stability to Nigeria.
>
> We believe and acknowledge that the paramount task of the new military régime is the welfare of all the peoples of Nigeria, and it is in this spirit that we call on all the peoples of Nigeria irrespective of tribe, origin or political persuasion to rally round the new military government so as to make easy its great and noble task.
>
> We pray that the Almighty God may help Major-General J. T. U. Aguiyi-Ironsi, in the execution of the difficult national duties thrust upon him by the present circumstances.[3]

Effusively welcome messages in the same vein were issued by the Zikist Movement,[4] by Mr. Richard Akinjide on behalf of the N.N.D.P.,[5] and by Alhaji Dauda Adegbenro for the A.G., all pledging support for Ironsi. For the N.C.N.C., Chief Kolawole Balogun declared:

> This is the only logical sequence of events and we hope that every true citizen of Nigeria will regard this decision as a turning point in our national life.
>
> The independence of this country was won by blood, sweat and tears by the masses and it is only fair that the principles for which they fought namely:

[1] *Nigerian Opinion*, vol. 2, no. 2, p. 14.

[2] Particularly in their calls for co-operation with the Ironsi régime contained in their Sallah messages. The Emir of Kano spoke of the Military Government's intention 'to eradicate all forms of corruption, bribery and nepotism in our society'. See *Morning Post*, 26 January 1966.

[3] Reproduced in *Daily Times*, 19 January 1966.

[4] ibid.   [5] *Daily Times*, 20 January 1966.

parliamentary democracy, the rule of law and respect for human dignity should prevail.

The Army, as the bulwark and the sanction of any civil government have come in to safeguard these principles. It is the binding duty of every citizen of Nigeria who believes in real independence for the country to rally round the new régime and give it active support.[1]

Lest too much be read into these welcomes, especially from such a basically antipathetic party as the N.P.C., it is well to recall the comment attributed to Zanna Bukar Dipcharima at this time: 'It is better to survive.'[2] The same belief that Nigeria 'now had a chance to take on a new lease of life'[3] was echoed in the foreign press. With regrets heard for only one among the dead politicians, the sole shadow on the week's sunny mood was that cast by fears about the fate of the widely respected Alhaji Sir Abubakar Tafawa Balewa. Exactly one week after the coup, these fears were realized in the emotion-drained announcement by the Military Government (its tone reflecting their anxiety at the inability to postpone this news, pre-empted by Tass, beyond the coincidence of *Id-el-Fitr* and its possible triggering-off of a Moslem uprising) that the Prime Minister's body had been discovered, at Mile 27 on the Lagos-Abeokuta road:[4]

The Federal Military Government announces with deep regret the death of Sir Abubakar Tafawa Balewa, former Prime Minister of the Federal Republic of Nigeria. Following the discovery of his remains on Friday, the 21st of January, burial will take place in his hometown in Bauchi today [22 January].[5]

In a pan-African context Dr. Nkrumah's waspish obituary on Sir Abubakar [DOC 9], which was cleverly turned back on him by Nigeria's High Commissioner in Accra when Ghana's own fall came within the month,[6] stands in contrast with the Nigerians' and the world's feelings that here was a life that might not have been intended as part of the price.[7] Hence, too, the last interview granted by the Prime Minister to a journalist, only 24 hours before his brutal abduction, assumes an added historical importance.[8]

[1] ibid.

[2] Private communication. He later died in an air crash. Of relevance in this context are the concluding paragraphs of Chinua Achebe's *A Man of the People* and its explanation of how 'overnight everyone began to shake their heads at the excesses of the last régime, at its graft, oppression and corrupt government. . . . Everybody said what a terrible lot; and it became public opinion the next morning. . . . And these were the same people that only the other day had owned a thousand names of adulation, whom praise-singers followed with song and talking-drum. . . .' pp. 166–7.

[3] *West African Pilot*, 16 January 1966.

[4] Amnesty International had sent out a mission to investigate the Prime Minister's death. Their report was never published.

[5] Federal Ministry of Information Press Release No. 112/1966.

[6] Personal communication from the late Alhaji Isa Wali, Nigerian High Commissioner to Ghana.   [7] Editorial, *New Nigerian*, 25 January 1966.

[8] With Bridget Bloom: *West Africa* (1966), pp. 113–14.

The announcement by General Ironsi of the composition of his Supreme Military Council[1] and the names of the four Military Governors along with their civilian advisers (the former Regional Governors), accompanied by a special summary of his Government's intentions circulated to foreign diplomats by Nigeria's delegation to the United Nations and her embassies abroad [DOC 10], meant that the process of depoliticization of authority could now be initiated at the provincial level too. In the North, Major Hassan Katsina outlined his Region's philosophy in a short press conference summoned at Brigade Headquarters as soon as his appointment as Military Governor to replace the rebel Major Nzeogwu (by whom he was, in fact, introduced) was announced [DOC 11]. Three days later he named his new Cabinet[2] and used the opportunity of an early official visit to impress on the army the North's new path.[3] In the East, Lieutenant-Colonel Ojukwu, who had commanded the Kano battalion during the events of 15 January, made a rousing appeal in his first policy speech, devoted to the theme of 'away with the old Guard' [DOC 12], while the Western[4] and Mid-Western [DOC 13] Governors made their policies known through broadcasts and press conferences. In the light of what was to take place in May, Lt.-Col. Ejoor's second press conference has extra significance because of its clear signposting, illuminated in its handling by the Government's own newspaper, towards a unitary form of government.[5] The three Southern governors went on to issue a number of edicts, but in the North Major Hassan preferred to restrict his first policy reforms to a series of explanatory, executive broadcasts.[6] One at least struck deep at the North's most cherished Native Administration institutions [DOC 14], yet Hassan clearly was carrying a lot of public opinion with him. In an editorial entitled 'Hurrah for Hassan!', the *New Nigerian* praised his plans to reform the Native Courts and N.A. Police forces as something long overdue, at the same time reassuring the powerful Native Authorities that this would in no way reduce their effectiveness or authority as the foundation of the North's local administrative system.[7] At the end of January, General Ironsi once more addressed the heads of diplomatic missions in reassuring and, as regards foreign policy, *status quo* terms.[8] The U.K. High Commissioner now felt able to send an 'all clear' letter to the several thousands of British nationals in Nigeria [DOC 15]. Then,

[1] Federal Ministry of Information Press Release No. 110/1966.
[2] *New Nigerian*, 22 January 1966.
[3] Northern Ministry of Information Press Release No. 57/1966.
[4] Western Ministry of Information Press Release No. 120/8/1966.
[5] The official *Morning Post* of 31 January 1966 carried the front page headline of 'We'll go back to Unitary System' and attributed the assertion that 'it is now certain Nigeria will return to the old system of unitary government' to an official hint from Ejoor. See also the article in *Morning Post*, 27 January 1966.
[6] e.g. (live) broadcast from Kaduna, 6.30 p.m., 5 February 1966.
[7] *New Nigerian*, 14 February 1966.
[8] Official hand-out at the press conference held in Lagos on 28 January 1966.

taking the pace of the nation from memoranda submitted by the trade unions, the left-wing Socialist Workers' and Farmers' Party,[1] and the new Nigerian University Students' Association,[2] as well as from his personal advisers, Ironsi spelled out on the evening of 28 January his government's overall programme of reform and reconstruction in a nationwide broadcast [DOC 16].

The month of February was devoted to implementing General Ironsi's objective of sweeping away 'loyalties and activities which promote tribal consciousness and sectional interests' so as to lay a solid foundation for a policy of one Nigeria, and to cleaning up the stables so fouled by many (but not all) of the discredited politicians. Such a programme was welcomed by the Lagos press in their editorials, one of which achieved immortality by its vernacular headline of '*Chop-chop— e don die-o*'.[3]

Just as, in the dusk of the colonial days, it was not difficult for a nationalist (be he politician, student union officer, or mere rabble-rouser) to sugar any pill and rally his audience by an appeal, however irrelevant to the advertised theme of protest, to help him overcome 'the wickedness of the imperialists', so in these opening months of 1966 did the Military Government find in a condemnation of the evils, attributable to the erstwhile national sport of regional politics as played under Nigeria's exuberant and extravagant rules, an easy way to divert attention from the long-term implications of its radically unificatory policies and elicit support for its progressively harsher decrees.[4]

An impression of momentum was created.[5] At the national level, Ironsi cut off the salaries of political office-holders, ordered them to repay their outstanding loans, and reduced the number of Ministries.[6] Decrees were passed to handle national security[7] and were quickly invoked to detain seventeen political figures in the West and another seven from the East. That which authorized the suppression of disorder enabled Ironsi to constitute any area where there had been widespread disturbances, such as the Tiv Division and the Western Region, a military area and thus subject to martial law. At the centre, too, Ironsi took the next step in killing the spirit of regionalism which he saw as the curse of the previous régime. Selecting another press conference to announce further major administrative reforms, he promised

---

[1] Part of their manifesto is quoted in *The Times*, 26 January 1966.

[2] Extracts from several students and trade unions are given in *Daily Times*, 21 January 1966.

[3] i.e., an end to bribery and corruption in public office. See *Morning Post*, 27 January 1966.

[4] For instance, the introduction of the death penalty for the not uncommon custom of taking hemp.

[5] Arikpo, op. cit., pp. 154–66, gives a good idea of the scope of the proposed reforms. Their record of implementation is less convincing.

[6] *Morning Post*, 2 February 1966, gives full details of the Federal reshuffle.

[7] Notably Decrees No. 3, with its subsequent extensions, and No. 4.

to set up a number of study groups to 'submit working papers on constitutional, administrative, and institutional problems in the context of national unity' [DOC 17]. Several such working parties soon received their terms of reference [DOC 18], and in course of time these were followed, after the issuance of the enabling Decree, by the establishment of a large number of tribunals, first by Ironsi and then by his successor under the same authority, to inquire into the maladministration of some of the institutions of the First Republic [DOC 19]. Over the succeeding months, General Ironsi and the Military Governors were able to supplement the terms of reference of the study groups in a number of addresses to their members, in each instance emphasizing the 'one Nigeria' aspect of their commissions [DOC 20]. In the event, two of these appointments—and, given the coming events of May, one was to be overridingly the most influential—antedated the General's policy statement of 21 February. The first was the appointment of the Nwokedi Commission on 12 February to consider the establishment of an administrative machinery for a United Nigeria and the implications of unifying the five public and judicial services. Because of the sensitive, and eventually explosive, nature of this one-man commission, its terms of reference and initial reception in the local press are worth keeping in mind. They were to study and report on:

(*a*) the establishment of an administrative machinery for a united Nigeria;

(*b*) unification of the five public services and judicial services.[1]

Lagos Radio gave the Nwokedi commission a more than fair wind[2] and, let it be noted in view of the directly consequent events of May in the North, the *New Nigerian* wished the commission good luck in a special editorial at the same time as it commended to its attention the long dormant Hudson proposals of 1956 proposing the creation of Provincial Authorities.[3] The other decision was the decree bringing all N.A. prisons under the operational control of the Federal Director of Prisons.[4]

At the Regional levels, too, this was a period of considerable reformatory activity. In the North, on paper the pace of reform set by Hassan Katsina showed no sign of slackening off. The House of Chiefs was dissolved, the Northern Chiefs' Council was revised,[5] and committees of inquiry were set up to probe the activities of the quasi-government Marketing Board and the Housing and Development Corporations.[6]

---

[1] From a confidential source that I cannot identify here, I understand that early in April Nwokedi's terms of reference were altered, on instructions in a letter from the Secretary to the Federal Military Government, to include the actual commission to 'examine the feasibility of unifying the Public Services in Nigeria'.

[2] B.B.C. ME/2089/B/1.

[3] *New Nigerian*, 15 February 1966.

[4] Decree No. 9 of 1966.

[5] See *New Nigerian*, 24 February 1966 for its new composition.

[6] See *New Nigerian*, 16 February 1966 for the names of the committee members.

The Military Governors of the East,[1] West,[2] and Mid-West[3] made further policy announcements, largely of tightening up the previous lax administrations, and dissolved their local government councils (East) and native courts (West).[4] Thus towards the end of February General Ironsi was able to call home Nigeria's ambassadors for consultation and outline to them the progress made in his policy of a unified Nigeria.[5]

Ironsi was riding the wave of public approbation. The army officers were too extended by administering to pause and wonder what it was all leading to; the civil servants—and also the traditional rulers, who had seen themselves steadily cut down to second place before the political commissioners—were relieved to have politicians no longer breathing down their neck or capriciously reversing the bureaucratic process; the intellectuals, the students, and the unions were delighted at being at last able to abuse the corruption and nepotism that they had hitherto been careful to condemn within the privacy of club, class-room, or hostel; and by and large the masses were either immediately untouched by the change (echoing the situation on the advent of the British in Kano in 1903) or else welcomed the promises that never again would the new Government allow graft, injustice, and squandermania to flourish. In such an atmosphere of achievement through riddance, the return of one of the Old Guard, Dr. Azikiwe, to Nigeria on 25 February, was deliberately played down to the point of discourtesy,[6] though his subsequent open letters announcing his return to journalism[7] and welcoming the military régime,[8] followed by his protest at his abrupt dismissal by the new Eastern Government from his office as Chancellor of the University of Nsukka [DOC 21] attracted enough publicity for the Northern press to begin anxiously to speculate on 'Just What is Zik up to?'[9]

As in October 1960, the land of promise again seemed to be within reach of the man in the street. Yet the question must be put of how much of this moralistic upsurge was more than superficial relief and reaction to a period of accustoming corruption and duress. The North, at any rate, declined to commit itself to a full and immediate participation in the enthusiasm manifest in the South's response to Ironsi's programme for creating one Nigeria. No politicians were detained in Kaduna, none called to account for misdemeanours almost masochistically denounced in the South. True, in the national press and in

[1] Eastern Ministry of Information Press Release No. OT/8/1966.
[2] Broadcast from Ibadan, 5 February 1966.
[3] See *Morning Post*, 18 February 1966, reporting a press conference held at State House, Benin.
[4] *West Africa* (1966), pp. 222 and 303.
[5] *Morning Post*, 22 February 1966.
[6] See the description in *West Africa* (1966), p. 281.
[7] *New Nigerian*, 30 March 1966.
[8] Statement issued at Nsukka on 14 April.
[9] *New Nigerian*, 16 April 1966.

meetings of intellectuals and élites-in-the-making there continued a fervent debate on the kind of constitution the country should have when the Second Republic came into being; nor did the North's educated elements shirk from proclaiming in public forum their advice to Ironsi to hasten slowly.[1] But there is evidence, so far not public, to show that the North knew how—and was already beginning in its leadership circles—to apply the brake to Southern acceleration.

Nigeria without political controversy would not be Nigeria at all. Ironsi found it necessary to remind political parties of the ban on meetings, warning that 'we cannot afford to continue with sterile political strife and mutual recriminations',[2] appealing to the press to emphasize in their approach the concept of 'one Nigeria', and to co-operate in cleansing national life of 'that rigid adherence to regionalism [that] was the bane of the last régime and one of the main factors which contributed to its downfall'.[3] Next, he invited the Sultan of Sokoto—doyen of the country's natural rulers, who in the North, were now enjoying a return to power unknown since self-government and filling the political vacuum as the Government's sounding board and only link with the hugely peopled hinterland beyond Carter Bridge—to visit Lagos and address the troops, reported to be restive about the delay in bringing to book the acknowledged mutineers and murderers of their popular Northern officers. The Sultan called on the army to co-operate with the new Government, adding significantly:

We are confident that it is the intention of the Military Government to preserve and protect our good customs. . . . It is our determination to ensure unity throughout the Federation and I am confident this will be achieved so long as we continue to respect each other's views.[4]

About the same time the Military Governor of the North, in a dawn broadcast welcoming a group of distinguished guests to the opening in Kaduna of the headquarters of the Islamic Congress (an international organization of which the late Sardauna had been Vice-President) warned that opposition to 'the good aims of the present government' could lead to the death penalty prescribed under the Suppression of Disorder decree.[5] His subsequent entanglement with the Lagos press over what he saw as an attempt to embarrass him on the delicate issue of Northernization—'I don't know anything like Northernization' was the remark attributed to him on the Lagos front pages[6]—and his out-

---

[1] Editorial, *New Nigerian*, 1 March 1966.

[2] Federal Ministry of Information Press release No. 225/1966.

[3] Meeting with press and radio representatives in Lagos, 21 February 1966.

[4] From Federal Ministry of Information Press Release No. 257/1966. The speech, which was barely a hundred words and was in Hausa, was made at State House, Lagos, on 12 March.

[5] The text was broadcast from Kaduna at 5.40 a.m. on 11 March 1966.

[6] e.g., *Morning Post*, 15 March 1966.

of-the-way references in his Id-el-Kabir broadcast to the Northern people to his 'birth or what they have chosen to call my aristocratic connections'[1] can, however, be interpreted as a hint of treading water if not actual back-tracking. It was in this light that it certainly earned the warm approval of the Northern press.[2] Had closer, or more serious, attention been paid to the rumblings of discontent in the North, not all of it covert, perhaps the disastrous consequences of Ironsi's forcing the pace of unification, culminating in his precipitate and maladroit Decree No. 34, could have been foreseen and forestalled.

The good intentions of the 1966–7 unified financial estimates, whose historical significance was rightly underlined by General Ironsi in his broadcast explaining to the nation how 'for the first time since the formation of Regional blocs our fiscal, economic and industrial proposals are being considered and directed by one central authority,'[3] were quickly overtaken by increasing demands to abandon the idea of a unitary government and retain the administrative autonomy of regional government. Such an opinion was expressed in unequivocal terms in the English and vernacular press of the time. Reference to samples of this protest [DOC 22], which gathered momentum in March and April, at once confirms the subsequent Biafran allegation[4] that the opposition to the plans for the unification of the civil service was spearheaded by Northern students—a charge readily conceded by the Federal Military Government in their own anatomy of the May disturbances in the North.[5] Yet the Nigerian press could without qualms indulge in an effusion of praise—some of it justified, but ominously not all—for the first 100 days of the Ironsi régime, with but one ear in Lagos [6] and one at Ibadan University [DOC 23] alert enough, or bold enough, to interpret the radar warning of how the majority of Northern elements viewed the anniversary. Unblinded, or undaunted, by proximity, the astuter foreign correspondents discerned too many cracks in the façade of smiling unanimity to allow them to swell the fulsome chorus.[7] Before

---

[1] Broadcast from Kaduna, 1 April 1966.

[2] 'Press Misleads Public on Northernization'—Northern Ministry of Information Press Release No. 381/1966; 'The Right Attitude', editorial in *New Nigerian*, 18 March 1966.

[3] Broadcast from Lagos, 31 March 1966. See also Federal Ministry of Information Press Release No. 348/1966.

[4] *January 15*, p. 34.

[5] *Nigeria 1966*, p. 8. Among the key documents for this educated resistance are the vernacular press, for example, the editorial 'Discipline these insolent Ibos living in the North' in *Gaskiya ta fi Kwabo*, 28 March 1966, and the two outspoken articles carried in the *New Nigerian* on 5 and 7 April 1966, by H. A. Sani and Mustafa Dambatta respectively.

[6] Peter Pan's two exceptional articles, 'To the Battlements, My General!' *Daily Times*, 27 and 29 April 1966.

[7] See Walter Schwarz, 'Nigeria Takes Stock of its 100 Days', *Guardian*, 29 April 1966. He accurately saw the unsatisfactory lack of official action towards the mutinous majors as an ominous sign given the uncertain temper of the Northern-dominated soldiery. Cf. *The Times*, 26 March 1966, which reached the same conclusion. This was indeed to prove

the local congratulations were even off the press, the Military Government was obliged to follow up the Cabinet statement about soaring food prices,[1] issued only a week earlier to quieten discontented public opinion, with the sudden introduction of austerity measures. In the South, the press attributed this 'rocketing' of staple prices not to any economic factors but to 'organised sabotage' of the army régime.[2] While the Northern columnists continued to urge the retention of the administrative system they knew and liked[3] and their students, exceptionally, demonstrated in the streets of London against a unitary government, the Southern leaders made strong attacks on what they held as nothing more than tribalism, and a hindrance to the orderly progress of the Republic:

We have been told 'what the North must tell the South' as if the North is the only section of the Federation which must lay down the law. This expression of course is a refined version of the once crude and arrogant expression 'we of the North'. What we will ask is, 'when do we want to speak as Nigerians?'

The Government has a duty to call a halt to this incitement. Only a few days ago, those responsible for the release of some gramophone records were called for questioning by the police. On any showing, these records are less dangerous to the body politic than a number of articles being published regularly and with impunity by the New Nigerian.

We want to believe that in the new nation we are building, privileges and favouritism are things of the past. All citizens and institutions must be treated equally regardless of their origin or location. There shall be no First and Second Class citizens. . . .

Is it true that only Northern officers died on the fateful January 15? We know Yoruba as well as Ibo officers died too.

Let us have the answers to this and other questions and face the consequences. This country cannot be run by calculated blackmail.[4]

Even the appointment of the Oba of Benin as Chancellor of the North's Ahmadu Bello University (where there was student agitation for a change of name) and of the Emir of Kano as Nsukka's Chancellor—a ceremony subsequently marked by one of the first 'national' speeches of Lt.-Col. Ojukwu [DOC 24]—seemed hollow symbolism in the face of the North's suspicions about the motives for the much-paraded merits of a single administration and a unitary constitution.[5]

And so simmering April turned into bubbling May. On the evening

to be Ironsi's graveyard: whatever he did with them, he offended either the North through not punishing mutineers or the South through court-martialling those who were to many the heroes of the revolution.

[1] Issued on 19 April 1966. *Daily Times*, 20 April 1966, reproduced the statement in full.
[2] *Daily Times*, 13 April 1966. See also B.B.C. ME/2141/B/1.
[3] e.g., Mustafa Lantaiwa, 'Unitary System Not For Us', *Morning Post*, 9 May 1966; editorial in *Gaskiya ta fi Kwabo*, 18 April 1966, 'Leave the North as it is.'
[4] 'Whither Nigeria?' editorial from *Nigerian Tribune* reproduced challengingly by *New Nigerian*, 23 May 1966, under the leader 'The Path of Reason and Tolerance?'
[5] See the *Guardian*, 25 June 1966.

E

of the 24th, the pot was brought to the boil[1] when General Ironsi sprung upon the nation his proposals for a new constitution, using the radio to dissolve all political parties [2] and to promulgate his now celebrated Decree No. 34 [DOC 25]. If in immediate practice, the decree changed little but nomenclature, the key message in his milestone broadcast [DOC 26], 'The former Regions are abolished. . . . Nigeria ceases to be what is described as a federation, it now becomes simply the Republic of Nigeria,' was ominous enough to confirm the suspicions of the North on the honesty of Ironsi's motives. Had not its spirit already been bruised by two promotion lists in both of which Ibo names out-shone the rest? Had not its mind been troubled by an ugly incident over recruitment to the Air Force, when Northerners (admittedly of doubtful qualifications) had been dismissed to make way for Souther-ners? Were there not plausible grounds for mistrusting the designs of the closely knit group of Ibo advisers who alone seemed to have the Supreme Commander's ear?[3] Editorial comment[4] was now either short-sighted or far away in dream cuckooland. But the nation was rapidly to be jerked back to harsh reality.

Within 72 hours reaction came, in the form of savage violence on a scale hitherto reserved for 'Congo' behaviour in Nigerians' vocabulary. From Kano the riots spread to Kaduna and Zaria, and thence to Katsina and the Plateau mining towns of Jos and Bukuru, all centres of Ibo concentration and *sabon gari* settlements. Slogans of *a raba*, 'Let us secede', and 'Down with Ironsi' were shouted as Ibo shops were looted and their owners slaughtered (even within the sanctuary of the N.A. police-station, it was reported from Katsina,[5] one of the worst areas, where the curfew was not lifted till 13 June). The crowds, swelled by the gangs of thugs never far from a palm-crossing summons in political-party Africa, felt that the anti-North intent of Decree 34 had at last revealed the Ibo in his true, take-over colours. The North, hurt beyond measure at the lack of consultation and at the perfidy of pre-judging the Nwokedi report on the unification of the civil services before its actual submission, had reacted as a frightened people are wont to do.

[1] Hassan Katsina's metaphor was 'the egg will break' when reporters at Kaduna air-port asked him what the General's national broadcast would contain. See *New Nigerian*, 24 May 1966. The *Daily Times* of 23 May had hinted that the contents would concern food hoarding.

[2] Decree No. 33 of 1966.

[3] 'Unfortunately the General abused the opportunities of 15 January by allowing prominent Ibo leaders . . . to advise him on national matters to the exclusion of other ethnic leaders.' Public Statement by the Mid-West State Government, July 1968.

[4] e.g., *Daily Times* and *New Nigerian*, 26 May 1966, both of which interpreted the two decrees as a new charter for unity, 'free from the blunders of the past' (Kaduna), and the historical culmination of 'the nation's political purpose of the last fifteen years' (Lagos).

[5] *Daily Telegraph*, reports by David Loshak for the last week of May 1966. He was subsequently deported by the Ironsi régime. His figure of over 600 killed in the North compared with the official figure of 92 deaths.

With strict censorship imposed on the press (the Lagos *Sunday Times* and Kaduna's *New Nigerian* appeared with blank pages as an angry protest at the Government's ban on all references to the riots), it was once again the radio that came into prominence. Lt.-Col. Hassan cut short a tour of the provinces to hurry back to Kaduna and broadcast an important message to the people on 29 May, explaining the true import of the unification Decree [DOC 27]. Ironsi attributed the outbreak to foreign incitement[1] and Hassan again went on the air to warn the rioters of what it would mean if martial law had to be imposed in the North.[2] With the situation becoming even worse, Hassan now changed his mind about not sending in troops and ordered them to move into Kaduna, with instructions to shoot on sight.[3] Ironsi, too, issued a general warning and threatened to proclaim the trouble centres a military area.[4] Meanwhile, the Military Governor of the East had broadcast a special message to reassure his kinsmen in the North [DOC 28].

Then, as peace began to return to the riot-stricken North, General Ironsi addressed the nation yet again, denying rumours about another Ibo-inspired take-over bid and announcing that the Northern Chiefs would be summoned to advise on the unrest.[5] Acting quickly on one of the bones of contention, namely the arrogant flaunting of wall photographs of a smiling Nzeogwu and the circulation of an article accompanied by a picture depicting the late Sardauna stretched out at the feet of an Ibo, Ironsi ordered the arrest of anyone displaying provocative photographs or singing offensive songs likely to incite tribal feeling.[6] From Lagos, an inspired radio campaign now took up the theme of foreign involvement in fomenting the disturbances in the North,[7] a charge which the U.K. High Commissioner (the assumed scapegoat) promptly refuted [DOC 29]. Lt.-Col. Hassan summoned the Northern emirs and chiefs to Kaduna for consultation on 1 June; a conference seen by the Northern press as the most crucial meeting in the constitutional history of the Republic of Nigeria. There the Military Governor addressed them [DOC 30] before a working committee went into private session. The chiefs presented to the Governor a secret memorandum, containing their view on how to prevent the recurrence

[1] Statement issued in Lagos on the night of 29 May and published in the *New Nigerian* on 31 May 1966.
[2] Statement issued in Kaduna on 30 May and published in *New Nigerian*, 31 May 1966.
[3] Statement issued in Kaduna on 30 May and published in *New Nigerian*, 1 June and in *Morning Post* (predominantly a Lagos circulation) on 31 May 1966.
[4] Issued in Lagos on 30 May and published in *New Nigerian*, 1 June 1966.
[5] Broadcast from Lagos on the night of 31 May 1966.
[6] Order issued simultaneously in Kaduna and Lagos on 1 June 1966. The text is given in *New Nigerian*, 3 June 1966. An example of such provocation was the issue of *Drum* magazine for June 1966, where an article on the late Sardauna caused grave offence by its tone and its illustration. Despite talk of other photographs of this nature, none has yet been forthcoming. The subsequent decree banning such pictures was extended to songs, among which 'Machine Gun' had been particularly resented in the North.
[7] Talk given over Lagos Radio, 1 June 1966.

of the May riots, for onward transmission to General Ironsi. Though its contents have never been published, there are good grounds for believing that they took the form of an ultimatum to Lagos on its bulldozing tactics to impose a unitary system of government and administration. As the chiefs departed for their emirates, the Sultan of Sokoto made a statement on behalf of the conference.[1]

Lt.-Col. Hassan flew to Lagos to introduce the emirs' memorandum to Ironsi at a specially summoned meeting of the Supreme Military Council on 7 June. This body now found itself back uncomfortably close to square one, involved in confrontation with the very problem of political apartheid and social incompatibility that had long bedevilled the efficacy of its antecedent Council of Ministers.[2] Besides issuing a somewhat woolly but would-be firm statement on the situation [DOC 31] and announcing its decision to set up a commission of inquiry to probe the events in the North [DOC 32], the Supreme Council also drafted a reply to the emirs. In Lagos, Ironsi reassured Nigeria's recalled diplomats that all was well with the state of the nation.[3] The Northern Governor was still uncertain of his people's reaction to the statement from the Supreme Council and to the establishment of a public tribunal. He warned against current rumours that a special fate was being 'cooked up' in Lagos for the North[4] and followed this up with the launching of a special public enlightenment campaign to explain to the people the immediate intentions of the Military Government as well as mounting flag marches under the general aegis of his 'Operation Vigilant'.[5] In Ibadan, Lt.-Col. Fajuyi also broadcast reassurances on the communiqué issued by the Supreme Military Council.[6] In Kaduna, the chiefs were recalled and on 16 June Lt.-Col. Hassan Katsina addressed them in yet another important speech, on the long-term implications of the recent rioting [DOC 33]. Then, in private, he delivered General Ironsi's reply. When the emirs dispersed next day, the Sultan broadcast (in Hausa) to the people of the North [DOC 34]. Meanwhile, the Federal Military Government deported two journalists[7]—one of whom then had no hesitation in revealing how Ironsi was reviving the old ethnic bitternesses,[8] a diagnosis amply confirmed by Nigeria's peak fever six weeks later—and declared an expatriate member of the administrative

[1] Northern Ministry of Information Press Release No. 723/1966.

[2] Cf. *New York Times*, 10 June 1966.

[3] Speech opening a three day conference of Nigeria's heads of missions in Africa, held at State House, Lagos, 11 June 1966.

[4] Statement issued in Kaduna on 12 June 1966.

[5] Ministry of Information Press Release No. 758/1966 and report on Radio Kaduna, 11 June 1966.

[6] Broadcast from Ibadan, 9 June 1966.

[7] Legal Notice No. 49 of 1966.

[8] Walter Schwarz, 'General Ironsi's trust in his friends leads Nigeria back to tribal strife', *Guardian*, 25 June, and his 'What's gone wrong in Nigeria', *Observer*, 26 June 1966.

staff of Ahmadu Bello University—a favourite focus of Eastern hatred[1]
—a prohibited immigrant.[2] Lagos also issued decrees[3] detaining several
Northerners suspected of complicity in the May flare-up, among them
the editor of the Hausa vernacular newspaper and the former Minister
of Information in the North, and, from the East, the editor and car-
toonist of the *Pilot*.[4] With the appointment of the Brett tribunal[5] and
the passing of a decree delegating to the Military Governors power to
impose a curfew in their 'groups of provinces' (as they were now re-
styled in order to get away from the regional complex), Ironsi, with
Hassan's help, seemed at least to have halted the killing with the same
characteristic élan he had shown in regaining control of the army on
that mutinous morning of 15 January. Many, however, wondered to
what extent the dangerous Northern situation could really be said to be
in hand: what calm there was was a disturbingly uneasy one.[6]

With the North nominally quiet, the General could take stock.
Among his first moves back at the national level were the naming of
more tribunals to investigate the activities of former statutory corporations, a decree to investigate the assets of public officers,[7] a robust
'Operation Clean-up',[8] a tightening up on lax civil servants by the army,
and the formation of an Orientation Committee to consolidate the 'tell
the people' campaign already under way under the directions of a new
National Government Liaison Officer.[9] Ironsi next intensified his
attacks on tribalism, hammering away at the theme of 'no room for
tribe' in addresses such as that to the Obas of the West on the proper
growth of Nigerian society. In it, the Supreme Commander said anyone
who preached tribalism should 'quickly get out of this habit . . . because
he is a sick man and there is no room for him in this society. . . . The
fact that tribal unions have been banned does not mean you cannot say
you come from one town and as such contribute to the development of
that town. But the moment I hear that any of these town unions is
operating on political platform, there will be trouble.'[10] Support came,
too, in speeches by two leading intellectuals. Dr. Okigbo, speaking at
Convocation at Nsukka, blamed Nigeria's intelligentsia for having

[1] *January 15*, p. 35 and p. 81.
[2] Legal Notice No. 50 of 1966.
[3] Decrees No. 47 and 52 of 1966.
[4] Decree No. 40 of 1966. The cartoon, captioned 'The Dawn of a New Day', showed
the Ironsi Government as a large cock (the symbol of the banned N.C.N.C.) crowing
'One Country, One Nationality'. It was published to mark Ironsi's broadcast of 24 May.
Both men were released at the beginning of July.
[5] For the terms of reference, see DOC 32.
[6] See *New Nigerian*, 11 June and 27 July 1966, and *The Times*, 13 June 1966.
[7] Decree 51 of 1966. A lengthy explanatory statement was issued by the National
Military Government in Lagos on 8 July 1966 giving the reasons for the urgent imposition of the new measures aimed at restoring 'high standards of public morality'.
[8] For a layman's guide to Decree 51, see *Daily Times*, 18 July 1966.
[9] *Morning Post*, 9 July 1966. Increase Coker was appointed to the post.
[10] Quoted in *Daily Times*, 15 July 1966.

condoned the divisive policies of the old régime by remaining silent when they should have spoken up in protest.[1] Dr. Dike, in an address at Ibadan, castigated the intellectuals in even more astringent terms:

> It must be said to our shame that the Nigerian intellectual far from being an influence for national integration is the greatest exploiter of parochial and clannish sentiment. And they exploit local prejudices not for the national good but for their selfish ambitions. You will be no credit to this University if you leave us to join the band of educated advocates of tribal division and strife and worshippers of tribal gods. . . . The worst pedlars of tribalism in this country are the educated Nigerians.[2]

Yet whether General Ironsi ever really understood,[3] or believed, the depth of the North's feelings against a unitary government, it was now imposed without a referendum, embodying the glaring insult of an arbitrary decision to unify the civil services blandly announced over the radio, and prejudging the deliberations of the administrative and constitutional Commissions set up to examine those very issues back in February. This doubt is increased by the fact that no sooner had the brouhaha in the North caused by Decree 34 quietened down than on 13 July the General inopportunely announced his intention to rotate the Military Governors and appoint area prefects.[4]

Further dismay in the North at this plan to have governors serve outside their region of origin, welcomed by the Southern press[5] but largely ignored in Kaduna, was forestalled by the coinciding news that the Supreme Commander was about to undertake a nationwide tour.[6] There had for some time been signs of discontent at the way General Ironsi remained in Lagos,[7] where it was increasingly felt he was, if not the prisoner, certainly the tailor's dummy of a tight in-group of influential and persuasive Ibo officials.[8] Now not only would he be able to meet the people, but also, in the minatory undertones used by the *New Nigerian*, 'reassure any doubts they might have about the effectiveness

[1] Convocation address to the University of Nigeria, Nsukka, 26 June 1966, by Dr Pius Okigbo, Economic Adviser to the National Military Government.

[2] Address by the Vice-Chancellor of the University of Ibadan, Dr K. O. Dike, on Graduation Day, 1 July 1966.

[3] Cf. Nzeogwu's comment, 'He joined the army as a tally clerk and was a tally clerk most of the time'—DOC 8.

[4] Announcement made in Lagos, 14 July 1966. It was warmly welcomed by the Lagos press in their issues of 15 July. The Federal Government has since revealed that this plan had been previously discussed by the Supreme Military Council and rejected as untimely—*Struggle for One Nigeria*, p. 10.

[5] e.g., *West African Pilot*, 15 July 1966.

[6] The route was to be Abeokuta, Ibadan, Kano, Kaduna, Zaria, Jos, and Benin. From there he would return to Ibadan for a special meeting. He was due to return to Lagos on 29 July before starting a tour of the Eastern Provinces in early August.

[7] The same criticism was levelled at his disinclination to leave Lagos during his famous Hundred Days.

[8] Schwarz, op. cit., p. 204, has an interesting paragraph on how Ironsi was being pulled all ways in his futile attempts to please everybody and appear to be above tribal considerations.

of recent Government legislation.'[1] After a big welcome in Kaduna, Ironsi went on to address Kano N.A. and the student body of Ahmadu Bello University,[2] an institution that he regarded as instrumental in fomenting opposition to his policies. This was later alleged even more bitterly by the breakaway Government of Biafra. The climax of this nationwide tour was to be Ironsi's address to a Natural Rulers' Conference at Ibadan on 28 July, representative of chiefs from all over the country [DOC 35]. A well-fed press gave full treatment to the fundamental importance of this assembly of the nation's natural rulers in this 'their finest hour',[3] and the import of Ironsi's speech was carefully —but, in the event, inopportunely—prepared by a release from the National Liaison Officer listing the Federal Military Government's development plans for the future [DOC 36]. Ironsi's speech was greeted by the chiefs' obligatory singing of the national anthem. Alas! this was more like Ironsi's swansong, for 24 hours later he was dead and the unity of the nation was once again in fragments.

It is as yet no more possible to trace the hour-by-hour happenings of the July coup[4] than it is to be certain of all those of the January one.[5] Both stories must await the opening of the national archives to uncommitted scholars, an event unlikely to be witnessed in the near future. In subsequent attempts to place the blame, both the Federal and Eastern Governments agreed[6] only on the fact that the mutiny started when Northern troops shot three Ibo officers of the Abeokuta detachment on the night of 28 July. At Ibadan, General Ironsi and his host, Lt.-Col. Fajuyi, were arrested in Government Lodge, taken off and killed (though it was another six months before their death was officially announced). In Lagos, troops mutinied in the Ikeja barracks and, seizing the international airport, ordered a B.O.A.C. captain to fly Northern soldiers' families to Kano before returning to pick up his commercial passengers bound for London.[7] There had been grapevine talk as far afield as England that something was planned for early August, but this was the first clue as to who was at whose throat this

[1] *New Nigerian*, 16 July 1966.

[2] *Morning Post*, 21 July 1966; *New Nigerian*, 22 July 1966.

[3] Radio talk from Lagos by Increase Coker, Liaison Officer to the National Military Government, 25 July 1966.

[4] The *New York Times* at first interpreted Ironsi's downfall as a second southern coup, this time engineered by more young Turks, who were reportedly dismayed by the way Ironsi had sold out to the Moslem North—31 July 1966.

[5] Information at any level, including the personal one, is much harder to come by for the events of 29 July than for the mutiny of 15 January. It is doubtful whether even the opening of official archives will result in the full story being told, for the impression is given that in the July mutiny personal memory will be of greater importance than the written record. The fullest accounts so far available are, besides the partisan ones from the Federal and Eastern Governments required for the propaganda war, those given at the time in *West Africa* (1966), p. 901, and by Frederick Forsyth in Chapter 4 of his *The Biafra Story* (London, 1969). The semantics of 'coup' or 'mutiny' are not at issue here.

[6] *Nigeria 1966*, p. 9; *January 15*, p. 44.

[7] Interview in the *Guardian*, 1 August 1966.

time: it was now clear that this coup was Northern-led. In Kano and Kaduna, rebel elements shot their Ibo officers and took control of their battalions, but there was no mutiny in the unit stationed in Enugu. Lt.-Col. Gowon, dispatched by the Chief of Staff, Brigadier Ogundipe, to restore order, was taken prisoner by the soldiers. A convoy sent out by Ogundipe to recapture Ikeja airport was ambushed and shot up. Ogundipe issued a communiqué relayed at 2.30 p.m., proclaiming a state of emergency in the Lagos-Abeokuta-Ibadan conclave and adding the hope that he would be able to 'restore peace and tranquility very soon'.[1] Later that evening he broadcast to the nation reassuring them that things were under control and that there was 'no cause for alarm'.[2]

Meanwhile discussions between Ogundipe, accompanied by three or four senior Northern advisers from Lagos, and the rebels continued throughout the night.[3] They were reported to have turned on the latters' refusal to share barracks any longer with their Ibo brothers-in-arms, and their demand either for secession by the North or for a repeal of the unification decree with a return to the *status quo ante* 15 January under a civilian government.[4] When Brigadier Ogundipe declared himself unable to accept these proposals, the rebels asked Lt.-Col. Gowon, whom they had earlier released to take part in these negotiations, to assume command of the army. This he did. Ogundipe now relinquished his command and reportedly retired to the sanctuary of an Elder Dempster boat offshore.[5] In a broadcast on the morning of 1 August [DOC 37] Lt.-Col. Gowon brought the nation's suspense to an end by describing what had happened and announcing that he had assumed responsibility for filling the dangerous political vacuum. In a vital and much-quoted passage from this seminal speech (said by some to have been altered at the last moment on the intervention of the British and American diplomatic leaders to dissuade him from announcing the North's secession from the Federation),[6] Gowon declared 'As a result of the recent event and the other previous similar ones, I have come to strongly believe that we cannot honestly and sincerely continue in this wise, as the basis for trust and confidence in our unitary system of government has been unable to stand the test of time. Suffice to say

[1] Nigeria House Press Release, 29 July 1966. This announcement was broadcast on all the Nigerian radio stations between 2.30 and 8.30 p.m. on that day.

[2] A reference, but no verbatim text, appeared in *Daily Times*, 30 July 1966. The B.B.C. Monitoring Service also carried only a résumé of the broadcast, made from Lagos at 11.00 p.m.

[3] *Africa Research Bulletin*, p. 571.

[4] The Biafrans claim that the Northern troops flew their improvised secessionist flag of the Republic of the North over the Ikeja barracks but this has not been confirmed by any other source. Cf. Schwarz, op. cit., p. 212.

[5] At Aburi later, Ojukwu was to say that he had assured Ogundipe by telephone that if he were to go on the air and announce that he had taken over the Government, Ojukwu would have at once come out in support.

[6] Forsyth is explicit on this accusation, op. cit., pp. 58 and 144.

that putting all considerations to test, political, economic as well as social, the base for unity is not there, or is badly rocked not only once but several times.' He promised that a new decree would be drawn up to prevent Nigeria from drifting to destruction. Editorials of the day reveal Nigeria's reaction to yet another traumatic coup as many asked themselves whether Nigeria could survive this further bout of naked tribalism.[1]

Events now moved swiftly. On the very same evening came a radio retort by the Eastern Governor [DOC 38], claiming that Gowon's announcement was but a breathing-space before negotiations on the country's future shape could begin. Ojukwu thus set a pattern of broadcast and counter-broadcast that was to become so familiar in the vigorous oral confrontation between Gowon and Ojukwu over the succeeding months. Gowon's reply, promising that no constitutional changes would be effected without taking the Nigerian people into full confidence and denying that troops were moving on the East, was released the next day,[2] along with a strong warning against rumour-mongering[3] and a denial by the Governor of the North that his Region was planning compulsorily to repatriate all Southerners.[4] Then came speeches from the new Governor of the West [DOC 39] and from the Mid-West [DOC 42] in support of the new régime. The Northern emirs took this opportunity to point out to 'the new man in Lagos' that the previous government had come to grief because their views had been ignored.[5] In a shrewd concession to the South, Lt.-Col. Gowon rapidly released a number of political detainees (with certain remissions of unexpired prison sentences), including Chiefs Awolowo[6] and Enahoro, and later Dr. Okpara, as well as persons imprisoned after the Tiv riots of 1964 [DOC 40]. The amnesty elicited a brief welcome for Okpara from Ojukwu who said that 'a time like this demands the services of men like you';[7] personal statements from Awolowo who spoke about his philosophical reflections while in gaol,[8] and from Enahoro,[9] made amid wild jubilation in Lagos; and congratulations from the new Military Governor of the West, Colonel Adebayo, who looked to Awolowo as having

[1] e.g., the analytical article by J. D. F. Jones, *Financial Times*, 2 August 1966.

[2] Statement issued in Lagos on 2 August 1966.

[3] Issued in Lagos on 2 August and reproduced in *Daily Times*, 3 August 1966.

[4] Statement issued in Kaduna on 2 August and published in *Daily Times*, 4 August 1966.

[5] See *New Nigerian*, 6 August; also report from Radio Kaduna, 3 August 1966. Similar appeals for co-operation with the new Military Government, contained in their Sallah messages at the end of January 1966, were of immense importance to the Ironsi régime in Lagos, uncertain of what leadership the emirs would give the North.

[6] Gowon greeted Awolowo with the remark 'We need you for the wealth of your experience.' See the description in *Daily Times*, 4 August 1966.

[7] Broadcast from Enugu, 4 August 1966.

[8] 'A new testament—a new philosophy', Chief Awolowo, speaking at Ikenne on 4 August 1966. See also *Daily Times*, 5 August 1966.

[9] Published in *New Nigerian*, 4 August 1966.

more to contribute towards the rebuilding of Nigeria.[1] A few days later Awolowo was to make an important speech [DOC 41] in reply to his acknowledgement of the optimistic title of 'Leader of the Yorubas'—a people whose long history of division had been cruelly scarred by the internecine political feuding of the past few years. Given the decisive position of the Yoruba,[2] in whose hands the fate of the Federal Government was to remain during the delicate days ahead and never more so than in their reaction to Ojukwu's appeal almost exactly a year later to join forces with him and complete the South's liberation from alleged Hausa-Fulani domination, this speech takes on added importance in the history of the conflict.

On 4 August Gowon held his first press conference since he had 'had the responsibility thrust on' him [DOC 43]. In it he announced his intention of appointing an Advisory Committee to guide him on the main matters of national interest. This he followed up with another major broadcast to the nation on 8 August, announcing the abolition of centralism by repealing Decree 34 and a three-stage programme for returning to civilian rule [DOC 44]. After the slaughter of senior army officers in January and again in July,[3] the close administration of a country the size of Nigeria by the military alone was an impossible task. The strain had already begun to show in the Ironsi régime, which had relied heavily on a competent but small cadre of top civil servants. Gowon may well have realized that the potential disintegration of the army after the collapse of discipline and murder of officers and men in July made some civilian participation, however nominal, a matter of sheer necessity to prevent a total breakdown of the country's administration. Recent events could augur badly for the nation's reaction to military rule. The next day, nominees of the Military Governors met in Lagos to consider ways of 'easing the difficult situation arising from the events of 29 July and the resulting bitterness, and preparing grounds for further action by the leaders of the country.'[4] They made five recommendations [DOC 45].

In the Regions themselves co-opted 'Leaders of Thought', as they had come to be known, were summoned to debate the issues involved in the constitutional review referred to by Lt.-Col. Gowon in his policy statement of 8 August. In the North Lt.-Col. Hassan had called the chiefs to an emergency meeting immediately after Gowon's assumption of leadership and made his general attitude known.[5] The emirs and

---

[1] Broadcast from Ibadan, 4 August 1966.

[2] Gowon's immediate release of Awolowo was aimed at enlisting Yoruba support in the crisis that was obviously blowing up with the East. Though by no means a military power to be reckoned with at this time, in 1966 and again in August 1967, the fate of the Lagos Government lay unwillingly at the mercy of the West whether they would remain in or opt out of the Federation. Thus the Yoruba, devoid of positive military power, were to prove a key to political events: everything hung on which way they went.

[3] The names are given in *Nigeria 1966*, p. 17.   [4] Terms of reference of the meeting.

[5] Northern Ministry of Information Press Release No. 1009/1966.

chiefs made it clear that much of the blame for the recent events must be laid at the feet of the central government who had ignored their advice and views. The meeting concluded with the issuing of a lengthy but unspecific communiqué[1] and the Sultan again stressed the responsibility of the natural rulers for law and order.[2] The addresses of the Military Governors to the private meetings of their respective leaders of thought throughout the months of August and the subsequent resolutions of these *ad hoc* assemblies as they began to draw the lines for their regional stands at the forthcoming constitutional review conference can offer further guidance to understanding the shocked political thinking of the period. The exact nature of this new phenomenon in Nigerian political life was clearly defined by the Military Governor of the North:

A little under a fortnight ago when you assembled here I acquainted you with the background information of the situation in Nigeria. I did the same with the last conference of Chiefs and further went on to afford them opportunity of discussing the matter and to consider the best lines, in their opinion, the North should adopt in finding a solution to the problems of the country.

The Chiefs deliberated on the issue and arrived at a decision which they conveyed to me. I am again convening another meeting of Chiefs on Monday to acquaint them with the result of your meeting.

At your first meeting, I mentioned that you would be required to convene again for a discussion on the future of Nigeria and what best form of association should be recommended for the country.

Now is your opportunity to study this problem and to make your own recommendations in this matter. I must, however, make it quite clear to everyone, very emphatically, that your gathering here is not a political one, nor is it concerned with selecting a future civilian leader for the North or intended for raising purely political issues.

You will have ample opportunity for all these and more when the time comes. Your present meeting, I repeat, is purely and simply to decide on solutions to our problems and to recommend the form of association the various component parts of Nigeria should have with one another.

In considering this question, you will no doubt be guided by what the country has been through in the past seven months. The events which span this period have brought to the surface the grave problems which the association of the various units of administration in Nigeria have been facing in the last 10 years or so.[3]

In the East, to where tens of thousands[4] of frightened, harassed, and

---

[1] Northern Ministry of Information Press Release No. 1012/1966. The chiefs also recommended the names of those to represent the North at the Ad Hoc Constitutional Conference called by Colonel Gowon in Lagos.

[2] Northern Ministry of Information Press Release No. 1014/1966.

[3] Opening address to the Northern Leaders of Thought at Lugard Hall, Kaduna, by Hassan Katsina, 25 August. Northern Ministry of Information Press Release No. 1093/1966.

[4] The *New York Times* of 18 August gave a figure of 300,000: *The Times* of 19 August 1966, half a million. There were also several thousands of refugees leaving the East, especially the Hausa communities.

often molested refugees were making their way in what was the start of a massive exodus from the North, the Government announced that it had set aside £1m. for their resettlement.[1] By now the regional radio stations were locked in a battle of alleged and denied charges of hardship meted out to each other's nationals, accusations of Northern troops abducting an Ibo officer from the Kaduna military hospital,[2] and an Eastern lawyer having been beaten up by armed Hausa thugs in Makurdi,[3] being countered by allegations that Ibo highway robbers were terrorizing travellers on the Oturkpo road.[4] Attention to the possible political plans of the East was renewed when Lt.-Col. Ojukwu gave an interview to two foreign journalists, declaring that 'Ibo and Northern soldiers can no longer live together in the same barracks,' accusing the North of plotting his murder, and concluding with the grave assertion: 'This is a pogrom. This is intended as the Northerners' final solution to end what they call the "Eastern menace".'[5] He was also quoted as saying the fact had to be faced that the national unity which the army above all had sought to forge was now an illusion.[6] Ten days later, however, he gave a categorical assurance to a meeting of oil company executives held in Enugu that the East had no wish to secede: 'The people of the East have all along demonstrated restraint and discipline. . . . The East is anxious to ensure peace in the country and she does not wish for secession. In fact she has continued to make concessions in the interest of peace and unity. But we recognise that the factors that make for true federation no longer exist.'[7] This assurance came at a time when there was growing talk of the need for a parting of the ways[8] and an open advocacy of the weasel-word 'confederation' [DOC 46]. The denial was one that Ojukwu was to repeat a month later when, at the height of the constitutional review talks in Lagos, he reassured the foreign diplomatic representatives in an important statement at Enugu that any talk of his Region's secession was 'grossly mischievous' [DOC 47]. The same affirmation of no secession was reiterated in an exclusive interview with a Lagos journalist.[9] In Lagos and the West, public opinion remained certain of one thing: that, to quote the slogan used by the Provost of Lagos Cathedral in a sermon delivered at this period, 'we perish if the Old Brigade gets in'.[10]

Towards the end of August the Federal Executive Council met for the

[1] *Sunday Post*, 28 August 1966.

[2] Broadcast from Enugu, 2.00 p.m., 31 August 1966.

[3] Broadcast from Enugu, 5.00 p.m., 31 August 1966.

[4] Statement issued by the Office of the Military Governor, Kaduna, 27 August 1966, denying allegations made by the *Nigeria Outlook* and E.N.B.S.

[5] Interview with Harold Sieve, *Daily Telegraph*, 9 August 1966.

[6] Interview with Lloyd Garrison, *New York Times*, 12 August 1966.

[7] *Daily Times*, 19 August 1966.

[8] See the open letter from an Ibo published in *New Nigerian*, 23 August 1966, urging that Gowon should 'let each Region goes its own way' in order to resolve the impasse.

[9] *Daily Times*, 17 September 1966.

[10] Excerpts quoted in *Daily Times*, 22 August 1966.

first time under Lt.-Col. Gowon, but without Ojukwu. The National Military Government found it necessary to issue an explanatory note reassuring the country that the meeting was nothing special.¹ Almost at once the East increased tension by a broadcast from Lt.-Col. Ojukwu in which, echoing Gowon's sentiment of 1 August,² he gave his opinion that, 'there is in fact no genuine basis for true unity in the country' [DOC 48]. He went on to declare 29 August a day of mourning for the dead 'in view of the significance of the events of the last two months'.³ At this time Ironsi's death had still not been officially announced. Predictably, this gesture was at once countered by a statement from Lt.-Col. Gowon deprecating the decision as 'most unhelpful'.⁴ On the last day of the month Lt.-Col. Gowon signed the edict abolishing Decree 34 and reinstating Nigeria as a Federation [DOC 49]. Simultaneously, Ojukwu summoned the 145-man Eastern Region Consultative Body, the parallel to what the other Regions had called leaders of thought, to address them on the current situation.⁵ They gave him the mandate he sought [DOC 50], the first of many such warrants of leadership during the months ahead. At home, the Nigerian press made its assessment of the gravity of the hour.⁶ The Military Governors of the North and of the West once more broadcast to their people to inform them of the opinions on constitutional reform that their delegates would be taking to Lagos in mid-September, the former adding that he now intended to resuscitate the pigeon-holed Hudson proposals for the establishment of provincial authorities as a measure of the devolution in which he believed⁷ and the latter commenting on the remarkable achievement of the Yoruba people in actually having adopted a single leader for the first time in their history.⁸ Hassan Katsina also broadcast on the implications to the North of the reversion to a regional form of government.⁹ Abroad President Tubman called for O.A.U. assistance in solving Nigeria's crisis, a move now hailed by Lagos as 'a brotherly but premature gesture'¹⁰ in contrast to the brusquer treatment meted out to such appeals a year later.¹¹

¹ Statement issued in Lagos, 26 August 1966.

² 'The base for unity is not there.' It has since been argued that this must be read as a rider to the preceding sentence and that the lack of unity refers simply to that over accord on a unitary system of government: 'the basis for trust and confidence in our unitary system of government has been unable to stand the test of time.' See DOC 37 for full text. Gowon was quick to correct Ojukwu on this point at Aburi.

³ See *Daily Times*, 30 August.

⁴ Statement issued in Lagos by the National Government Liaison Officer, 28 August 1966.

⁵ Speech made at Enugu, 31 August 1966, and repeated to the Advisory Council of chiefs and elders at their meeting on 7 September 1966. See *Crisis '66*, pp. 33–7.

⁶ Press review broadcast by N.B.C., Lagos, 30 August 1966 (B.B.C. ME/2253/B/2).

⁷ Broadcast from Kaduna, 1 September 1966.

⁸ Broadcast from Ibadan, 1 September 1966.

⁹ Broadcast from Kaduna, 3 September 1966.

¹⁰ Text of talk over Lagos Radio, 6 September 1966 (B.B.C. ME/2260/B/1).

¹¹ e.g., the broadcast talk contained in B.B.C. ME/2435.

Despite the East's hesitation to send its delegation to Lagos without what it deemed sufficient guarantee against molestation or worse, the telephonic dialogue between the two brother-colonels was encouraging enough to allow Gowon to go ahead and convene an *ad hoc* Constitutional Conference. Its function was to consider the resolutions of all the regional leaders of thought as entrusted to their respective delegations. These comprised just fourteen delegates all told and an equal number of advisers.[1] On 12 September the conference met, undeterred by a terrorist exploding a bomb in the Federal Palace Hotel[2] the previous night despite the biggest security operation ever mounted in the capital. In his keynote opening address, Lt.-Col. Gowon put to the conference the four alternatives that were open to them in their search for the framework of a satisfactory constitution [DOC 51]. The agenda included as its only other item consideration of what interim arrangement would be necessary to tide the country over the period until the implementation of whatever future form of political association was agreed in broad outlines could be effected. (In the event, only the Western and Lagos delegations applied themselves [DOC 52] to the second item on the agenda at this stage, though the Mid-West came up with proposals [DOC 53] when the conference resumed in late October.) Typically, Ojukwu chose the very same day to make a dawn broadcast, assuring the people of the East that he had done all he could to secure the safety of their delegation.[3] Hassan, too, had broadcast a stern warning about good behaviour in the North during the talks.[4]

No communiqués were issued during the first week of the Lagos talks. The East's delegation stated its position, urging a union of four virtually independent regions.[5] The Northern delegation tabled a similarly oriented proposal for 'autonomous states', attaching as an annexure a complete description of the structure of the Central African Joint Services that it had in mind as a model. The West's proposal for eight states and a strong central government was in contrast to Awolowo's own memorandum calling for eighteen states, drawn on a linguistic basis, and to the Mid-West's demand for twelve states with a relatively weak government at the centre. The Lagos delegation, too, published its own wish for a multi-state federal structure. To this con-

---

[1] The names of the delegates are given in *Nigeria 1966*, p. 18. Each Region sent three delegates, with two from Lagos.

[2] Details of further planned sabotage with explosives are listed in *Nigeria: 12 State Structure the Only Way Out* (Lagos, 1966), p. 7.

[3] Broadcast from Enugu, 12 September 1966. The full text is given in *Crisis '66*, pp. 29–32.

[4] Broadcast from Kaduna, 10 September 1966.

[5] Documentation of the conference is taken from the Federal Government's *Memoranda submitted by the Delegations to the Ad Hoc Conference on Constitutional Proposals for Nigeria* and the Eastern Government's *The Ad Hoc Conference on the Nigerian Constitution*. The latter was released more than a year before the former record was officially published for the Federal Government, though short extracts had been carried in the national press in 1966.

troversy on the creation of more states, the intellectuals' Nigeria Society
aired its views in an open appeal not to split Nigeria into unviable
'micro-states'.[1] There was soon enough public unease about the leaked
implications of the North's proposals for the leader of its delegation to
issue on 16 September a brief statement on where the North stood on the
crucial issue of more states [DOC 54]. The East's delegation also sought
to classify its attitude thereon [DOC 55]. After five days, the conference
suddenly adjourned and the Northern delegates flew to Kaduna. The
gravity of this possibly last chance for Nigeria to hold together was not
lost on the press, whose editorials warned the country that the fateful
hour had struck.[2]

To the campaign for more states already conducted by minority
leaders outside the conference hall, and the snowballing rumour that the
popular Tiv leader, J. S. Tarka, did not go along with the rest of the
Northern delegation's caution over the early creation of new states
(despite a specific recommendation therefor from the leaders of thought
deliberations in Kaduna), and their preference for retaining the present
Regions, albeit within a confederal context, there was now apparently
added some even stronger pressure. This was said to have been exercised
by Middle Belt elements, notably Tiv, in the army, physically outside
the conference hall or personally at a higher level, and to have at least
included the approval of Lt.-Col. Gowon, himself a Northern minority
man. With the former 'out'-group now dominating the Northern delegation and the army manned by a strong pro-states element, there was
little reason to expect the Middle Belt minority leaders to let slip this
chance to secure that recognition of status denied to them during the
years of parliamentary opposition, political persecution, nugatory
alliances with southern parties, and open resistance that had been their
lot over the previous decade. Be this rumour as it may, when the Conference reassembled on 20 September, the Northern delegation recast
its position on states and secession [DOC 56], though it was later at
pains to argue that this was not the volte-face[3] that others ascribed to
it [DOC 57]. On 24 September, the conference's steering committee,
made up of the heads of delegations, met the Supreme Commander and
handed him an interim report [DOC 58] on the following day. This included a clear recommendation on the creation of new states. A summary of this was then issued as a statement by the Federal Military
Government rather than by way of a release from the Conference itself
[DOC 59]. A tabular summary of the views of the different delegations
on the seventeen headings discussed was attached to the report from
the Conference's working committee [DOC 60].

[1] Release issued in Lagos over the signature of Dr. L. A. Fabunmi, President of the
Nigeria Society, in mid-September 1966.
[2] See, for example, *Sunday Post*, 11 and 18 September 1966.
[3] The term used by the leader of the Northern delegation to explain its further
thoughts was 'a modification of our stand as indicated in the original memo'. See DOC 56.

The Conference now adjourned, till 24 October, for the usual celebrations of Independence Day. Ignoring the primary security situation that had already begun to manifest itself in parts of the country, the regional leaders of the North[1] and East[2] made the customary patriotic broadcasts to mark the anniversary, and the Supreme Commander delivered a national message in general terms of unity.[3] Exceptionally, however, and after news of the massacres in the North had reached him, Gowon also broadcast a special message to the people of the North in which he referred to the fact that 'God, in his power, has entrusted the responsibility of this great country of ours, Nigeria, to the hands of another Northerner'.[4] Lulled by such a plenitude of pious hopes and honest wishes, the country prepared to relax for its annual holiday.

But this time the festivities broke with tradition; abruptly, and brutally too. It was to be a week-end of sorrow rather than celebration, of murder and maiming in place of merriment. Tragically, only a few days earlier Lt.-Col. Gowon had, in an effort to stem the paralysing flight of the Ibo civil servants, issued a directive instructing them to return to their posts or face termination of employment.[5] For the Northern Government had accused the East of purposely striving to sabotage its administration by recalling the Ibo technicians on whom its utilities and services largely depended:[6]

It is unfortunate to note that some employees in the Government service, including the statutory corporations, have found it necessary to desert their work on a flimsy excuse of exaggerated allegations of threats and hostility against workers of particular ethnic group.

It is clear from the enquiries made so far and the reports received from various parts of the Region that there is a plan by some people to paralyse the efficiency of the public services and to disrupt the cordial relation that had existed between the diversified peoples of the Region.

The plan is meant to lead some workers to believing that they should leave the region. Acts of intimidation and molestations are some of the means of executing the plan.[7]

Ironically, as it turned out, the Government's own newspaper, leading with an appeal for calm as the Constitutional Conference ended its third week of deliberation, had prefaced its editorial—typical of the press at this moment—on the eve of National Independence Day with the reflection that 'tomorrow, whatever happens, will be a turning point in

---

[1] Broadcast recorded from Kaduna on the evening of 30 September 1966.

[2] B.B.C. ME/2280/B/5 and 2281/B/2.

[3] Text reproduced in *New Nigerian*, 4 October 1966.

[4] Broadcast over Radio Kaduna at noon on 1 October 1966. The printed text in *New Nigerian*, 3 October 1966, differs somewhat from the recorded version of the broadcast.

[5] Report over Lagos Radio, 23 September 1966.

[6] For a contemporary view of the effects on the North's administration and economy, see the two articles in *West Africa*, 'Exodus from the North' (1966), pp. 1287 and 1317.

[7] Statement issued in Kaduna, 26 September 1966.

our history'.[1] Sadly for some the morrow was destined to prove an appalling point of no return.

The organization or the spontaneity of the riots (official blame[2] was subsequently laid by the North on Radio Cotonou for broadcasting inflammatory reports of Hausas being killed in the East,[3] which was then repeated over Radio Kaduna in English and the vernacular programmes: the East has never doubted the planned instigation of the massacre)[4], the incidents of inter-tribal asylum as well as the catalogue of retaliatory savagery, and the thousandfold[5] tally of the holocaust that rocked Nigeria over Independence week-end—monstrously the worst riots in the history of any former British or French colony—are neither yet fully established nor our concern here. Testimony of wanton murder is available from both sides. Mr. Isaac A. Ogbonnaya of Arochukwu was a catering clerk at Ahmadu Bello University, Zaria; he narrates:

On 8th September, Mr. I. E. Ubani, an Umuahia man, and clerk in the Ministry of Agriculture informed me and one Yoruba man that 'operation No. 3 to finish the Easterners' would be carried out on 28th September. . . . At mid-night of 28th September I heard a big and continuous noise at the Agriculture quarters about one-quarter of a mile away. I then woke up my inmates. . . . Observing that our lives were in danger we escaped into the nearby bush. Under cover of the bush we could see a mob break open the house of Mr. Ezima and his brother both of whom came from Umuahia (Eastern Nigeria) and drag their bodies out after killing them. Then at about 2 a.m. one of the roving mobs spotted us and gave chase. We all ran down to the river valley nearby where the grass was so thick that we escaped our

[1] Front page comment, *Morning Post*, 29 September 1966.

[2] 'Let us briefly examine the cause of last weekend's disturbances. The Government's release pinpointed the cause. It attributed it to exaggerated reports of a mass massacre of people of Northern origin in Eastern Nigeria. The reports were broadcast by a neighbouring radio station.' Radio talk from Lagos (B.B.C. ME/2284/B/2).

[3] Radio Cotonou emissions included the following reports of attacks on Hausas:
(i) 'Travellers returning from Enugu have reported that many Northern Nigerians resident in the Eastern Region were killed during the last weekend. The names of the victims were not given. According to a witness resident in Enugu, a surprise attack was made on the Enugu meat market and lorry park. The report adds that cattle dealers were attacked. The Military Governor of the East has appealed to the people to remain calm, adding that he will ensure that all Nigerians resident in the East are protected. These incidents were reported in today's issue of the Ibadan newspaper, *Daily Sketch*, under the following front-page headline: Ibo-Hausa clashes in the East.'
(ii) 'Bloody clashes were reported yesterday in Nigeria between the local people and the Ibos working at the Kainji Dam site. Several people were reported killed and 170 injured. Further north at Kaduna, Zaria, Jos, Minna and Maiduguri, where clashes because of racial hatred broke out between Hausas and Ibos, 150 people were killed and hundreds of others injured. The Military Governor has been trying to restore peace.' (B.B.C. ME/2277/B/2 and 2281/B/4.)

[4] Some of the most accusatory statements are to be found in its publication *Pogrom*, but the theme is a recurrent one throughout the following months, especially as a justification for secession.

[5] Estimates have ranged from 5,000 to 50,000 dead.

F

chasers. There we parted and I hid myself inside a culvert. At 7 a.m. the following day, Thursday, I came out when I saw some policemen passing. I decided to go back to my house to see if I could get any of my things. On my way to my house one fellow worker, Mr. Stephen Onuoha, a native of Okigwi (Eastern Nigeria), saw me and started to hail at me. His calls attracted the attention of a group of Northerners working at a building site. They chased and caught him and beat him to death with hammers and sticks. When they killed him they carried away his portmanteau. Then they turned and chased me but being already far from them I was able to out-run them. As I ran towards the senior service quarters in the campus I met Mr. J. O. Arukwe of Arochukwu (Eastern Nigeria) and Mr. Philips of Asaba (Mid-Western Nigeria Ibo), both of them Executive Officers in the University. Both were driving in their cars to work. I stopped them and warned them that there were violent disturbances in the campus. They reversed their cars and drove back to their quarters. I ran up to the house of a Yoruba lecturer and took shelter. As the lecturer lives near Mr. Arukwe and Mr. Philips I was able to see Mr. Arukwe join Mr. Philips in the latter's house. I also later witnessed an attack on Mr. Philips' house and I saw Mr. Arukwe dragged out dead from the house. . . .   (Enugu.)

And again:

I ran into the room of one Yoruba man and hid inside the ceiling of the building. I stayed there from 7 a.m. to about 7 p.m. They went into my room and looted all my belongings after which they came into the Yoruba man's room and asked whether there was any Ibo man hiding there. They were told that no Ibo man was there. They left saying that they would come back again and that if they discovered that the Yorubas were hiding anybody they themselves would be in danger of losing their lives. They said they knew I had not gone to work and that I was hiding somewhere as they were sure I had not escaped. I heard all these things from my hiding-place in the ceiling. At about 7 p.m. I left the yard and sought a way out. I entered the bush and ran until I came out on a tarred road. Just as I was looking to see if I could get a lorry to take me I saw some Hausas and they were the very people who were looking for me. I ran in the opposite direction but unfortunately I came upon a road block and many soldiers were there with their guns. The soldiers caught me and started beating me. Judging from the way they handled me I believed that I was a dead man. But they left me half dead. I called on them to come and take my life but they refused and said that they would leave me there to suffer and die in agony. . . .   (Enugu.)

Nor was such behaviour confined to the North:

In Enugu, the attack on Northerners started on the 15th of August. Ibo soldiers led the attack. About 630 Northerners were killed in the province while twenty-seven were seriously wounded. A Northern boy, seven years old, was publicly slaughtered in the street by uniformed Ibo soldiers in the presence of another Northerner who was dressed like an Ibo and was thus able to escape detection.

In Onitsha Province, thirty Northerners were killed and six seriously injured.

In Owerri too, where Northerners had lived for long and inter-married with the Ibos, they were attacked and killed in cold blood despite assurances from the 'Ibo Elders'. One Northerner who escaped from Owerri was Alhaji Sabo who was born there, his father having settled there seventy years ago. His father, chief of the Hausa community in Owerri had been a customary court judge there for thirty-seven years. He was killed at the beginning of the organised attack on Northerners in the presence of the son who later managed to escape to Kaduna.

In September, a very large number of those Northerners who had managed to reach Obolo Afor on their way to the North were murdered. This atrocity was witnessed by some foreigners on the Oturkpo-Onitsha road on their way to Western Nigeria and these eye witnesses are believed to be one of the sources of information for the foreign broadcasts of the atrocities. . . .

In Port Harcourt, a house with a large number of Northern women in hiding was attacked. The women were raped and beaten to death. Ibos singing war songs slaughtered every Northerner they could find in the street, and a number of those who were in hiding were killed quietly by their neighbours.

During the evacuation, a train driven by an expatriate, carrying about 2,000 Northerners from Port Harcourt was stopped at Imo River by Ibo soldiers. Suddenly Ibos armed with deadly weapons rushed out from the bush and attacked the passengers. Every adult male Northerner on the train was killed and the body thrown into the river, while children and the young women were captured and taken into slavery. The few survivors were eventually admitted into Oturkpo and Makurdi Hospitals.   (Kaduna.)

Suffice it to say that the grisly evidence of bestial butchery[1] which reached its Grand Guignol nadir in the bloodbath of Kano airport[2] and provided the springboard for Ojukwu's subsequently exploited theme of a pogrom, constituted a milestone on the road to Nigeria's imminent disintegration and remained a demonstrable point of no return in any discussion. Because of the importance attached in many quarters, outside as well as inside Nigeria, to the persistent accusations made by the East during the months ahead that neither Gowon nor Hassan ever expressed regret for the appalling events of this lost weekend, the former's emotional and overtly human address of 3 October to the constitutional review delegates [DOC 61] and the North's prompt setting-up of a court of inquiry into the mutiny of the troops in Kano,[3] furnish evidence deserving closer examination before such judgement is accepted. In our archival role, we must pass beyond the record of massacre so adequately set out in the contemporary press and subsequent propaganda to note the attitudes taken by the nation's vehicles of public opinion during the atrocities of that notorious week-end in

---

[1] The testimony of the Eastern victims is found in their Governmental publication *Pogrom* (illustrated). That of Northern victims in the East is contained in the publication *The Nigerian Situation* issued under the imprint of the Current Issues Society, Kaduna. Typical of the revolting evidence therein are the above extracts.

[2] Amply covered in the world press of 1–3 October 1966.

[3] Report on Lagos Radio, 3 October 1966.

Nigeria's history.[1] With Ojukwu ordering non-Easterners to quit the Region and harassed Ibos fleeing from all corners of the Federation back to their homeland, memories of the mass *Völkerwanderung* of Indians and Pakistanis in August 1947 came unhappily to mind, substantiated by the same grim attacks on the refugee-filled trains and the army running amok in Gboko. The exodus had assumed a biblical intensity.[2] It was against this background of bloodshed and confusion that Lt.-Col. Gowon called a press conference in the National Hall to clear the air and reaffirm his faith in 'the continued existence of Nigeria as constitutionally one country'.[3] Ojukwu's reaction was inflexible. His accusations[4] of military moves against the East and allusions to having intercepted instructions from Kaduna for the recruitment of mercenaries from Chad and guerrilla warfare brought sharp denials from Kaduna.[5]

While attention in Lagos now shifted to recent service promotions and changes and directives in the Federal civil service on the absorption of refugee officers,[6] the familiar pattern of the Military Governors reacting to a crisis by taking soundings from their recognized leaders of thought once more began to take shape. In Enugu, Ojukwu delivered on 4 October a comprehensive address to a second meeting of the Consultative Assembly, now swollen to over 300 members. Having summarized the events of the past two months, he turned to the issue of new states, seen by him as the central theme of this special assembly:

Nobody in this Region is opposed to the creation of states for healthy objectives. All right thinking persons, who believe in a Nigeria governed and run on sound democratic principles, have advocated this. The creation of states has in the past been advocated as a means of founding a true federal country where no one or two sections could use their size and numbers to dominate and hold the rest of the country to ransom. The ills of the first Republic had direct relevance to the fact that this country did not have such an arrangement. We shall fall for any arrangement about the creation of states based on sound principles of democracy. I will loathe to be a party to any discussion about the creation of states on the poisoned principles of HATE, FEAR, and SPITE, because that would mean laying foundations for a worse country than anything we have so far known. It would be an open betrayal of the trust and pledges of the Militray Government.

[1] The reaction of the Nigerian press is particularly significant. See the editorial round-up carried by N.B.C., Lagos, on the morning of 4 October 1966 (B.B.C. ME/2284/B/2).

[2] For example, Edun Akenzua's article 'Exodus' in the *Morning Post*, 4 October 1966, and the strongly worded editorial 'Genesis of the Exodus' in the *New Nigerian*, 28 September 1966.   [3] Press conference in Lagos, 8 October 1966.

[4] Quoted in his address to the Consultative Assembly, Enugu, 4 October 1966.

[5] Statement issued by the Military Governor's Office, Kaduna, on 6 October 1966.

[6] The Acting Secretary to the Federal Military Government issued a long circular to all Permanent Secretaries in Lagos with instructions on how to proceed on absorption and the procedure for filling vacancies caused by the exodus of civil servants. This was reinforced by talks over the radio, such as those broadcast from Lagos on 14 and 19 October 1966 (B.B.C. ME/2292/B/7 and 2296/B/2).

Our enemies and detractors, aided and abetted by people with an axe to grind or with selfish ambitions, have done their worst during the past few weeks to undermine the position of this Region over this issue. Our delegates to the Lagos talks have been denied the sympathy and understanding which they need in the discharge of their delicate and difficult task. They have been maligned, misrepresented and misinterpreted. . . .

The Eastern delegation wanted first things considered first. There was nothing in the statement to show that the Eastern delegation was opposed to the creation of states. If anything, nothing would gladden them more than to see the giant North broken up. As far as the East is concerned, they left here with the firm and honest impression that we of this Region had reached an internal agreement satisfactory to all.

It is now clear that all that the North is prepared to concede in this issue of states, and that because of great and understandable pressure, is the creation of a Middle Belt State, an exercise which has been long overdue. They do not want the Moslem North with its over twenty million souls touched!

Let us look at this matter from another angle. Chief Awolowo's philosophy is that of creating states based on tribal, linguistic or ethnic groupings. Would states created on such basis ever make for stability and harmony in the country? Considering the fact that the North would not want its Moslem section touched, the fact that some tribal groupings would be extremely large as compared with very small tribes as exist, for instance, in this Region, and the fact that the Army is likely to be based on Regions or states of origin, would that make for a truly federal country where no one group or a combination of groups could use their size and numbers to dominate others?

I have spoken to you at this great length, because I consider it my duty to place all the facts before you. I have done my best to keep this Region together as one people, which they are. But I am not out to impose my will on anyone. If in spite of all these facts, you want this Region to disintegrate, I shall be disappointed and sad. But history will know whom to blame. No one, who is honest and fair, will at any time accuse me of dereliction of duty. No one with unbiased and objective mind, will doubt my sincere and genuine efforts and intentions.[1]

After considering the report from their delegation to the Lagos talks they advised in a policy resolution [DOC 62] that the East should take no further part in the Lagos talks until such time as the Federal Military Government implemented the decisions reached at the meeting of 9 August[2] and until compensation was paid for the lives and property of Easterners lost in the disturbances. This Ojukwu followed up by holding a press conference on 11 October at which he once more denied rumours of any plan to secede [DOC 63]. During the aftermath of murder, leaders of thought were also summoned in the North [DOC 64], West [DOC 65], and Mid-West [DOC 66] to answer the question 'Where do we go from here?' The Supreme Military Council, meeting for only the second time since the July coup and still without Ojukwu, issued a communiqué announcing that civilians would soon be associated with

---

[1] 4 October 1966. Full text in *Crisis '66*, pp. 45–62.   [2] See DOC 45.

the government and that Regional Governments would be financially helped in rehabilitating their refugees.[1] This the East dismissed as 'accompanying music to a funeral march'.[2]

A few days before the Constitutional Review Conference was due to resume, the Federal Government issued its official report on the nine months of crisis [DOC 67]. This was glossed as being preparatory to a White Paper[3] covering the complete events of January and July 1966 which would enable the general public to 'know the various roles played by some civilians and the principal actors in the Nigerian Army'. Ojukwu allowed his Adviser, Sir Francis Ibiam, to rebut the Government Statement's implication that the January coup was an Ibo military affair, while he himself wrote a personal letter, subsequently leaked, to his fellow Governors, discussing the breakdown of the army's discipline and inviting them all to a conference in Calabar or Port Harcourt [DOC 68]. On 22 October he made a broadcast setting forth three terms for the East's continued participation in the Lagos talks:

(1) That memoranda of the different delegations on issues on which there was no agreement be exchanged for study and consultation as agreed by the conference before adjournment. (2) To ensure the security of our delegates and provide an atmosphere of free and useful discussion, as well as of movement, all Northern troops now present in Lagos and the West be posted to their barracks in Northern Nigeria in accordance with the unanimous decision of the representatives of the Military Governors on 9th August 1966, and as unanimously advised by the enlarged Consultative Assembly of Eastern Nigeria in their resolution to which I have already referred. (3) The police should be used in maintaining law and order in Lagos, at least for the duration of the conference. If proposals (2) and (3) above cannot be accepted or implemented, then the resumed meeting of the ad hoc conference should be held outside Nigeria, and the following places are suggested: Addis Ababa, Liberia, Switzerland.

I must say this. Our delegation feels so strongly about these conditions that they have made it quite clear to me that they will not be able to proceed to Lagos unless the innocuous and absolutely reasonable requests made for the fulfilment of fundamental agreements already reached are met.[4]

Gowon responded by immediately confirming that the conference would nevertheless resume on 24 October, at the same time dismissing the major pre-condition that the East had stipulated on the withdrawal of Northern troops from Lagos and the West, and warning Ojukwu against 'secession brinkmanship.'[5] This reference to secession evoked a strong

---

[1] The communiqué, issued on 15 October, was published in *New Nigerian*, 17 October 1966.

[2] *Nigerian Outlook*, 17 October 1966.

[3] This had still not been published at the time of writing [February 1970].

[4] Broadcast from Enugu, 22 October 1966.

[5] Statement issued in Lagos on 22 October 1966. See also radio talk from Lagos, 21 October 1966, discussing Gowon's 'timely' warning on the foolhardiness of secession (B.B.C. ME/2299/B/3).

retort in the Eastern press on the theme of Gowon being 'haunted by ghosts'.[1] At the same time, the East initiated its publication *Crisis '66*,[2] and at its launching ceremony Dr. Azikiwe took the opportunity to appeal to the 'seasoned elders' of the country to abandon their passivity and mediate in the national catastrophe [DOC 69].

The Ad Hoc Committee duly met on 24 October, noting 'with concern' the absence of any representative from the East, and the Supreme Commander delivered a message to them. In it he said:

It is a matter for regret that your colleagues from the Eastern Region are not here with you today but I assure you that everything is being done to see that they rejoin you as soon as possible. Unfortunately, I have been unable, in spite of strenuous efforts, to contact the Military Governor of Eastern Nigeria since he made the announcement that the Eastern Region delegates will not be resuming with you.

I would like you, both collectively and individually, to see if you can contact your counterparts in the Eastern Region and convince them of the need for them to come and join you and complete this important assignment. Certainly, from your own knowledge you can assure the Eastern delegates of the present improved atmosphere in Lagos and the other parts of the country from which you have come. I need hardly add that you can confidently convey again the assurance I have already given that all delegates attending the Constitutional Talks will be fully protected.

Once again, I thank you and wish you continued success in the efforts to find answers to our country's problems.

Yours in God and one country.[3]

After a week's deliberations, the Committee issued its own communiqué. Though it was then meant to be an interim one, in the event it became their final communiqué:

During the week the Heads of Delegations in Lagos held several meetings with the Supreme Commander and Head of the Federal Military Government to discuss the absence of the Eastern Nigeria Delegation and its effect on the work of the Committee. At these meetings, suggestions were made regarding an alternative venue for the Ad Hoc Committee, in an effort to meet one of the objections of the Military Governor of Eastern Nigeria to continue participation by the Eastern Nigeria Delegation in the Conference. The alternatives included Akure, Benin and a Nigerian warship outside Lagos harbour. The Committee learnt with regret that none of these suggestions has so far proved acceptable to the Eastern delegates. It is however learnt that the Military Governor of Eastern Nigeria is making efforts to persuade the delegates to agree to one of these alternatives including also an offshore oil rig.

[1] Editorial, Eastern Nigeria *Guardian*, 22 October 1966.

[2] Radio report from E.N.B.S., Enugu, 23 October 1966 (B.B.C. ME/2299/B/5). There were in the end seven volumes in this series *Nigerian Crisis 1966*. They provide valuable data for the Eastern viewpoint in 1966–7. One or two volumes have now acquired a certain rarity value.

[3] Full text in *Nigeria 1966*, p. 23.

After a final discussion with the Supreme Commander and Head of the Federal Military Government this morning by Heads of Delegations, the Ad Hoc Committee adjourned till Thursday, 17th November, in the hope that efforts which are still being made to bring the Eastern Nigeria Delegation to the Committee will prove fruitful.[1]

More revealing than the communiqué itself were the two appendices attached thereto, appealing to the Eastern delegation to rejoin the Conference [DOC 70] and citing the reply received [DOC 71]. Having noted the failure of the top-level emissaries[2] to mediate in Enugu and the rejection of the alternative venues of Benin, Akure, or a Nigerian naval vessel[3] proposed as a concession to the East's repeated fears for the safety of their delegation anywhere within Nigeria, the Ad Hoc Committee adjourned for a fortnight on 2 November. But any hope of agreement was by now nothing more than wishful thinking, and on 17 November the Federal Military Government decided to adjourn the Conference indefinitely, promising an early announcement of 'proposals for lessening tension and for constitutional reforms'.[4] This move was irritatingly interpreted by Ojukwu, who denied that he had ever been consulted over what he called the 'dismissal' of the Ad Hoc Committee, as a plot by Gowon to impose a constitution on the country [DOC 72], an accusation which the Supreme Commander lost no time in refuting by giving in detail his reasons why he had been constrained to adjourn the conference *sine die*. Dismissing one by one the 'somewhat dishonest statements' reported from Enugu, he declared it to be quite untrue that the adjournment had been decided on without prior reference to all four Military Governors:

The Supreme Commander denies this allegation categorically and declares that, in fact, he spoke to the Governor of the East over the telephone on several occasions before the announcement of the adjournment. Besides the Regional Military Governors, he consulted members of the Federal Executive Council based in Lagos. He also recalls that according to the report of Western Obas who visited Regional headquarters recently, suggestions for adjournment were made at Benin and Enugu. He did not, therefore, 'dismiss' or abandon the conference as claimed by Lt.-Col. Odumegwu-Ojukwu; what he did was to postpone the meeting indefinitely, and this he did for two reasons. Firstly, in order to leave enough time for all concerned to find a meeting point of minds; and secondly, so that the interim may be utilized in successfully persuading the Eastern delegation to rejoin the conference.

Gowon was quite specific on where he considered the blame lay:

[1] From the official record of the conference. There are errors of date in the Federal version given in *Nigeria 1966*.

[2] The names of the delegation are given in *Nigeria 1966*, pp. 25–6.

[3] See editorials in *Morning Post* and *New Nigerian*, 7 and 9 November 1966. The *New York Times* of 3 November contained a reference to the use of an offshore rig.

[4] Statement issued in Lagos on 16 November 1966. Full text in *Nigeria 1966*, p. 26.

It is pointed out that the major cause of the breakdown of the Constitutional Talks was the conditions demanded by the Eastern delegation as regards personal security and safety. In spite of all assurances given by the Supreme Commander, the East insisted on conditions which, in effect took no notice or cognisance of the fears of delegations from other sections of the country.

As regards a commonly acceptable venue for either the resumed Constitutional Conference or a meeting between the Supreme Commander and the Governors of the East, the Supreme Commander declares that the plans for going outside Nigeria has always been the pet idea of Lt.-Col. Odumegwu-Ojukwu. Besides the Eastern Governor, nobody has ever accepted the unpatriotic suggestion that the Conference be held anywhere outside Nigeria soil. The rest of the country still maintains this stand. . . .

As regards the search for a venue for the Constitutional Conference, the alternative of a naval ship at sea was proposed by the Supreme Commander but was rejected by Lt.-Col. Odumegwu-Ojukwu. Benin as a possible venue was at one stage accepted by the Eastern Governor, but he later demanded as a condition that all Northern troops must be repatriated from the West if the East must come to Benin. This in turn raised fears amongst delegations from other Regions about their security even in Benin. These argued that, after all, Benin is much nearer Enugu than Ibadan, or Lagos. Akure was offered but the East turned it down just as the other delegates turned down Port Harcourt and Calabar. All delegations turned down the suggestion to meet on an offshore oil rig.[1]

Although this Constitutional Review Conference thus came to naught, the memoranda presented to its resumed meetings in October are still major documents and the summary of the new proposals submitted to the October reconvening [DOC 73] may be compared with the positions of the delegations at their first sessions in September.[2]

On the same day as the final adjournment, the Military Governor of the West announced the discovery of a plot to overthrow his Regional Government.[3] Lagos Radio took the line that to be forewarned is to be forearmed.[4] Hardening his anti-Northern Old Guard attitude, Adebayo went on to appoint a commission under Mr. Justice Piper[5] to investigate the conduct of civil servants in the grossly mismanaged Western Regional election of October 1965. The North's 'inept' attempt to inter-

---

[1] Statement issued in Lagos on 21 November 1966. Full text in *New Nigerian*, 23 November 1966.

[2] See DOC 60.

[3] Announcement made during Colonel Adebayo's address to Western and Lagosian leaders of thought at Ibadan, 16 November 1966.

[4] Talk over Lagos Radio, 18 November 1966 (B.B.C. ME/2322/B/7). Wondering whether Nigeria was not on the way to becoming 'another Latin American state' because of the frequency of its coups and rumours of coups, the speaker went on to identify the possible plotters, among whom he found 'a class of people who may not like the unanimous election of Chief Awolowo as the leader of the Yorubas—Colonel Adebayo himself hinted this.'

[5] For details, see *West Africa* (1966), p. 1279. The Commission did not complete its inquiry till two years later, having heard over 1,500 witnesses.

fere in this decision, reputedly exacerbated by Lt.-Col. Hassan's subsequent public statements in Ibadan on the presence of Northern troops there which caused a furore in the Western press and obliged Adebayo to extricate his brother-officer from the embarrassing situation, now precipitated Western leaders to join the East in calling for the withdrawal of Northern troops from the West and Lagos, thereby putting Lt.-Col. Gowon in an impossible position.[1]

Lt.-Col. Ojukwu now took his problem to the Consultative Assembly and gave them another extensive survey of the impasse at their third meeting, held on 23 November.[2] In accepting their renewed mandate of his leadership [DOC 74], Ojukwu delivered a further policy speech, in which he introduced a White Paper on a new system of provincial administration proposed by his Arikpo Commission and, reviewing the memoranda submitted by the different regional delegations to the Ad Hoc Constitutional Conference, outlined the East's stand on the Lagos conference.[3] He also called for a unified army—a volte-face from his speech of 1 August and the belief of many officers that, at least for the foreseeable future, Ibo soldiers could not coexist in the same barracks as their Hausa comrades-in-arms.[4] Then, in a major broadcast on 30 November [DOC 75], Lt.-Col. Gowon rejected confederation as unworkable and outlined his views on more states as well as his pledges for building a new Nigeria. Reaction in the East was predictably hostile, with mass disturbances at the University in Nsukka. Placards proclaimed 'the push is complete' (a reference to Ojukwu's promise that the East would not secede unless it was pushed out) and a prepared protest note was distributed to reporters declaiming 'We are apprehensive of the dogged determination of the Gowon Government in Lagos to overrun, subjugate, and annihilate the people of the Eastern Region.'[5] Elsewhere there was relief that here, once again, Nigeria seemed to acquire from the promises in Gowon's message to the nation the much-needed chance to start afresh. This sentiment was summed up in one of the editorials of the day, 'Let us begin from here.'[6]

Apart from a front-page report of gun-running by the East, occasioned by the discovery of incriminating evidence after a plane had

---

[1] The West having virtually no troops of its own.

[2] Eastern Region Ministry of Information Press Release No. 75/1966. This time the 10,000-word speech ended with the sort of dramatic invocation that was to become common in the months ahead: 'May God not destroy our souls with the wicked, nor our lives with men of blood.'   [3] Delivered on 30 November 1966.

[4] Ojukwu returned to this belief at Aburi: 'Men from Eastern Nigeria would find it utterly impossible to stay in the same barracks, feed in the same mess, fight from the same trenches as men in the army from Northern Nigeria.' However, the *Morning Post* of 23 December 1966 quoted Colonel Hassan Katsina as saying that he thought soldiers of Northern and Eastern origin might in the near future 'eat and drink together in the same mess', even though at the moment this was improbable.

[5] See report from Radio Enugu in *Africa Research Bulletin*, p. 661, and *Nigerian Outlook*, 2 December 1966.

[6] *New Nigerian*, 2 December 1966.

crashed in Cameroon;[1] the sustained war of words between the *Nigerian Outlook* in Enugu and the North's information media; an exclusive press interview in Enugu at which Ojukwu now openly referred to the secretly active idea of the East's seceding from the Federation;[2] and the moves of all the Regions to devolve power upon some form of provincial authorities,[3] the next step towards a constitutional rapprochement came in the middle of December. A report from Benin told of a secret midnight meeting between Ejoor and Ojukwu on the bridge over the Niger.[4] Speculation on the likelihood of a summit meeting of all the Military Governors, occasioned by a meeting of the five Secretaries to the Military Governments in Benin, was confirmed by an announcement in Lagos on 14 December that such a conference would be held very shortly, either in Nigeria or abroad.[5] The probability was brought much nearer by a five-hour meeting between Gowon and the four civilian advisers to the Military Governors held in Lagos just before Christmas.[6]

The year ended with revealing reviews of the shattering events of 1966 incorporated into the traditional New Year messages of the *dramatis personae* still living, notably Gowon,[7] Hassan, and Ojukwu. Political memories of the North's struggle for equality in the early 1950s were evoked by Hassan's announcement that the Northern Self-Development Fund was to be reopened:

Now my last appeal is to every one of us. During their last meeting the chiefs of Northern Nigeria advised me to revive the fund known as the Northern Self-Development Fund, which was started in 1950. The chiefs gave me this advice because of their realisation that the North must wake up in many affairs and it must work hard if it is to catch up with other developing countries. The chiefs realised that although it is possible to obtain assistance from our friends and well-wishers abroad, our salvation lies squarely in our own hands. If we do not work ourselves to build ourselves into a strong nation, no one else will do it for us. But we will stagnate and cease to be a factor to be reckoned with. These considerations which led the chiefs to advise me are strong. I appeal to every Northerner who wants to protect the integrity of the North and to see it prosper to give full support to this fund when it is launched, and this I will soon do. You can render no better service than to assist the North.[8]

[1] See the Nigerian press for the last week of October 1966. The incident was taken up at an international level.
[2] Interview with A.F.P. (by courtesy of the Overseas Press Service).
[3] In the North, the Hudson proposals of 1957 were momentarily revived and a commission appointed to consider their relevance. *West Africa* carried several articles on these local government reforms during January 1967 (pp. 8–9 and 46). Ojukwu introduced his measures in a speech broadcast from Enugu on 9 December (B.B.C. ME/2340) and gazetted them in Edict No. 33 of 1966.
[4] *West Africa* (1966), p. 1469.
[5] Radio Nigeria, 14 December 1966.
[6] *Africa Research Bulletin*, p. 676, and Lagos Radio, 23 December 1966.
[7] Full text in *Nigeria 1966*, pp. 60–1.
[8] Broadcast from Kaduna at 11 p.m., 31 December 1966.

Unlike his fellow leaders, Ojukwu turned his New Year message into a vehicle for introspection and recollection of what he called 'a tragic and treacherous year':

> Of its tragedy we have heard and known enough and I shall not dwell on it since in this broadcast I want to look into the future in relation to the past. Of its treachery we need only recall the great hopes and confidence which the advent of what was to be a corrective Military Regime generated right through this country and beyond on the 15th of January, 1966. Those hopes and confidence were subsequently quickly betrayed by sordid events of immense dimensions. . . .
>
> The people of Eastern Nigeria have been the unjust victims of an organised pogrom. The offenders have shown no remorse for what they have done— indeed if anything, they feel very satisfied and proud of it all. Their own idea of settlement is a condonation or approval of their bloody acts, and if the country is to remain together, then it must be on their own terms. For this reason they have done everything to make a realistic settlement impossible and have no qualms in going back on or withdrawing from agreements which do not exactly serve their aims and sectional interests. They make sure that moves which are not likely to land the country exactly where they want are stultified. Time is running out, while the ship of state is drifting and wallow- ing on the confused and deceptive sea of fantasy. . . .
>
> It has been argued or claimed that a confederal system will push Nigeria further and further apart. Members of this school of thought do not appear to have been very well or objectively informed about the constitutional forms of other countries. Since experience has shown that too close an association for the country now can lead to friction threatening mutual destruction, the sensible thing is for the Regions to move a little further apart and develop in their own ways, at least for a period. That is how America came to be a great, strong and united country. It is better that people should pull a little further apart and survive than that they should pull too close together and perish in the collision.[1]

This theme, of treachery and tragedy, became the lead-in to the East's multiple charge-sheet of 23 promises allegedly unfulfilled by the Federal Government.[2] In the retrospective mood associated with the passions of the old year, an evaluation of the motivations of the Regional Governments at the close of 1966 as presented in a synthesis of the thinking of Nigerian intellectuals at the University of Ibadan [DOC 76], and the impression made on one of the more perceptive foreign corres- pondents,[3] ease an understanding of the transfer into 1967 of the un- resolved and hazardous crisis of leadership: in brief, whether Nigeria would be allowed to be or not to be.

[1] Full text in *Eastern Spotlight*, 4 January 1967.

[2] The complete charges are set out, in question and answer form, in the special supple- ment to the *Spotlight*, 11 January 1967.

[3] 'North More Trouble than the East?', *Financial Times*, 30 November 1966.

1967

THE new year opened in a spirit of hope: despite months of abuse and virulent charges of perfidy, Nigeria's leaders were at least still speaking to each other. Thanks to General Ankrah, head of Ghana's military government and a comrade-in-arms who had already shown himself willing to mediate in the nugatory bickering of his neighbour's leaders, and also to the 'unknown and unsung' efforts[1] of Mr. Malcom Macdonald operating at the Commonwealth level, a meeting of the Supreme Council was arranged outside Nigeria, thereby allaying the fears about the safety of delegates expressed by Ojukwu. It was held at ex-President Nkrumah's luxurious week-end retreat of Peduase Lodge in Aburi, just outside Accra, on 4 and 5 January. This was the first meeting of the Supreme Military Council attended by Lt.-Col. Ojukwu since the events of 29 July; it was also to be the last time Lt.-Col. Gowon and he talked face-to-face.

A last-minute quarrel over the holding up at Lagos airport of Ojukwu's new executive jet[2] almost sabotaged the talks. Though all the delegates returned to Nigeria on the night of the conference's first day and then flew back to Ghana the following morning, thereby ruling out the precious chance of fruitful off-the-record and out-of-context personal discussions among erstwhile brother-officers,[3] the verbatim tape recording of the talks is noteworthy for, *inter alia*, the many moments of jocular camaraderie and good humour in this cards-on-the-table confrontation which must have lent strength to hopes of an agreed settlement. It is impossible to listen to the debate without being as impressed by the first-name mutual affection of these brother-officers, with their straightforward Sandhurst-style[4] standards of right and wrong and their proto-African readiness to dissolve into gusts of easy laughter, as by the skilful histrionics and superior intellectual adroitness of the only one who came to the conference table with a clear-cut idea of exactly what he intended to achieve—Ojukwu.[5] There can, inciden-

---

[1] The phrase was used by Mr. Whitlock in the House of Commons debate on Nigeria, 12 August 1968. This was the first public hint of Mr Macdonald's role as a mediator. His name was urged in this role by Sir Alec Douglas-Home in a later debate on Nigeria, 17 July 1969.

[2] *Guardian*, 3 and 4 January 1967.

[3] The same criticism has been levelled at the hotel apartheid observed by the two delegations at the Kampala conference in May 1968.

[4] This is not to imply that all the military governors and senior police officers were Sandhurst, but that the tone set was that of military academy ethics and *mores*.

[5] Cf. Schwarz: 'Ojukwu got his way with little effort, by being the cleverest. He was the only one who understood the real issues. Step by step the others came to acquiesce in the logic of Ojukwu's basic thesis—that to stay together all the Regions had first to

tally, be fewer summit conferences whose record has been more fully or more rapidly made available to the public; its very profusion makes our task here more difficult. To a large extent, too, this massive documentation—exceeding even the literature attached to the abortive Lagos Constitutional Conference of 1966—denotes another hightide mark: subsequent publications of 1967–1969, for all their fulsomeness and frequency, began to assume more and more the tones of partisan propaganda, too often characterized by the accusations and half-truths inseparable from wartime publicity and, in some cases, degenerating into nauseating exaggeration, abusive character-assassination, and jejune nonsense. No such charge of inadequacy or irksome hyperbole can be levelled against the record of Aburi.

At the first meeting on 4 January an agenda was drawn up [DOC 77] and in the evening a brief communiqué was issued to say that the talks had been cordial and that they included 'a declaration renouncing the use of force as a means of settling the present crisis'. Hopes were raised further by Gowon's comment to reporters as he left Accra that it had been 'an excellent conference which achieved what we came for—Nigeria will definitely remain united.'[1] Small wonder that, outside Nigeria too, the international press expressed its relief at the breakthrough with editorials captioned 'Nigerians on Speaking Terms' and 'Nigeria: Back on Course'.[2] Nor is the authenticity of the final communiqué [DOC 78] or its annexures [DOC 79] in dispute. It is on the divided interpretation and the implementation of the understanding beyond the minutes that the agreement apparently reached at Aburi was destined to be undone. The Federal and Eastern Regional Governments both released early a document giving the official minutes [DOC 80]. When arguments subsequently arose about what exactly was said, including the vital matter of the right to secede, the Eastern Government decided to base its case of charging Gowon with bad faith on a full publication of the verbatim discussions at Aburi. This it did, in print and on gramophone, leaving the Federal Government no option but to publish its version of the Aburi record as an adjustment to its abbreviated minutes and press statement of 26 January which had purported to set out the decisions reached.[3] With over 50,000 words as documentary evidence of a prime nature, it is possible only to be selective in this book; the passages quoted [DOC 81] have been grouped around half a dozen of the main themes of the meeting. The verbatim report has been

---

draw apart. Only Ojukwu understood that this meant, in effect, a sovereign Biafra and the end of the Federation,' op. cit., p. 221. A Federal spokesman was later to say that Ojukwu alone came to take, not to give.

[1] Quoted in most of the Nigerian press, 6 January 1967.

[2] Respectively the *Guardian*, 7 January and *New York Times*, 8 January 1967.

[3] In comparison to the official record, these were 'a mutilated and truncated version of the official minutes of the meeting', according to Ojukwu. Preface to *Aburi: The Verbatim Report* (1967).

given wide circulation so that further abridgement would not seem necessary in this volume.

Aburi resulted in a potential resolution, agreed personally by the five military leaders, of the major issues of discord and distrust that had brought Nigeria to the threshold of disintegration. In brief, they agreed on 'back to 14 January'. It was at least enough to rouse the leaders from their mutually antagonistic stalemate and offer them a valid spring-board for moving constructively forward rather than a mirror for glancing recriminatingly backwards. Ojukwu's eventual charge of Gowon's bad faith is less fair than his assertion that the civil service advisers to the Federal Government found the agreement by these soldiers so out of touch with legal and economic actualities that it was impossible to implement the letter of the Aburi agreement, however willing the spirit was. There is also room for assuming that the Federal Permanent Secretaries would have been justified in negativing the perilous trend of the Aburi agreement reached by the military leaders on political as well as technical grounds. An analysis of the vast documentation over the ensuing months gives an idea of where the differences in interpretation lay.[1]

We may therefore, in the absence of other evidence so far not open to us, accept that the reason for both the delay and the difference in making public the decisions was in all probability connected with the need to reconcile the items of agreements reached personally by the Military Governors with the feasibility, legality, and maybe desirability, of their assumed implementation as assessed by their respective law officers and by the able Federal Permanent Secretaries. Without the go-ahead at this bureaucratic level, any accord by the Military Governors might be little more realistic than pipe-dreams. This train of civil service consideration was at once set in motion by Gowon on his return to Lagos. The Solicitors-General of all the governments met in Benin on 14 January to make their recommendations on what changes would be required in the current standing decrees, setting these out in a form that would 'expedite the drafting of the Decree intended to give effect to certain of the Accra agreements.' They noted how their efforts were, however, 'handicapped by the fact that no authentic copy of the Accra agreements as such were available, and in fact some of the law officers came to Benin either on purely verbal instructions or with very sketchy instructions in writing'.[2] Their report was naturally a classified document, but when it was evident that the East intended not to honour this convention, an official résumé was carried by the N.B.C., some seven weeks after the event, and a full record was eventually released

---

[1] In this respect, Ojukwu's mammoth speech of 26 May 1967 to the Consultative Assembly is an encapsulation of the recent political history. See DOC 110.

[2] From their covering letter, signed by all six law officers. The report is included in the Federal Government's version of the Aburi Conference.

by both Governments.[1] Next, the Federal Permanent Secretaries met in Lagos and drew up their considered 'comments on the "Accra Decisions" of the meeting of the Supreme Military Council'.[2] This report [DOC 82], too, is another unchallenged top secret document (cf. the demi-official letter attributed to the Permanent Secretary, Federal Ministry of Finance, urging his Northern counterpart to impress on the military leaders that only war could stop the economic disaster facing Nigeria once Biafra seceded[3]) subsequently leaked by the Eastern Region. Its release had strong propaganda aims of discrediting the supposedly sinister influence of the Federal civil service in adopting a *non possumus* attitude to what had been accepted at Aburi. A meeting of senior army officers was also held in Benin on 24 January, attended by representatives from all the Military Governments, to discuss the division of the armed forces and their ancillary services into Area Commands as agreed at Aburi.

In the meantime, the work of drafting a decree to reconcile the views expressed at these three top-level, authority-invested, pan-Nigerian exchanges with the decisions reached personally by the Military Governors at Aburi had in no way been helped by a series of inopportune and, on occasion, intemperate press conferences and comments pre-empting the official release of the heads of agreement reached there. Within twenty-four hours of his return from Ghana, Ojukwu had unilaterally issued a statement to the press summarizing what he regarded as the decisions reached there and announcing how the Regions would move further apart [DOC 83]. His verbatim answers to the supplementary questions, though omitted from the official text, are also important. Ojukwu's stand met with approbation in the local press of the East, where the circulation of the Federal Government's newspaper *Morning Post* and the independent *Daily Times* was now banned. Nor, it must be conceded, did the Federal Government help in keeping tension and tempers relaxed when, on the anniversary of the first coup, it published a booklet narrating Lt.-Col. Gowon's 'efforts at finding a suitable and popular solution to Nigeria's problems in her greatest hour of need'.[4] Not only did this contain a strong innuendo of Lt.-Col. Ojukwu's complicity in the allegedly Ibo-masterminded coup of January 1966, which he found libellous, tendentious, and calculated to 'inflame passions and cause disaffection within the country',[5] but it also coincided with the first

[1] Broadcast from Lagos on 5 March 1966. See also pp. 71–85 of the Federal Government version of the Aburi record, and pp. 37–54 of the Eastern Government's version.

[2] From the covering letter issued from the Cabinet Office on 20 January 1967. See DOC 82 for its top secret nature.

[3] Reproduced in *Focus on Biafra*, New York, issue dated 20 May 1968. Yet another leakage of civil service minutes in Lagos occurred in April, when Radio Enugu gave details of a memorandum alleged to have been presented to the Supreme Military Council by General Gowon dealing with military, economic, and diplomatic measures against the East; or again, see p. 81 and DOC 92.

[4] Radio comment from Lagos in describing the publication, *Nigeria 1966*.

[5] Eastern Nigeria Official Document No. 5 of 1967, p. 9.

official announcement by the Government that Major-General Ironsi and Lt.-Col. Fajuyi had been killed in the mutiny of the previous July. (The phrase 'owing to the situation prevailing in the country at the time' to explain the absence of an announcement in July echoed the caution exercised by the Ironsi régime in delaying the news of Sir Abubakar Tafawa Balewa's death in January.) Besides listing the plotters of 'Exercise Damissa', the Federal Government's anniversary pamphlet *Nigeria 1966* named the leading civilians and the nine army officers killed in the 'mutinous activities' of 15 January, but gave no details of the 29 July counter-coup casualties beyond again promising that a full account would be set out in an eventual White Paper.[1] Two months after this, the Eastern Regional Government published its own report[2] of the two mutinies, including a shocking list of military personnel allegedly put to death in the 'bloody massacre of 29 July–September'.[3] They also published lists of 334 Eastern officers and men said to be either held in detention outside the Region or posted as missing, and a charge sheet accusing 144 individuals in the North (including Europeans) of complicity in the murder.[4] While flags were flown

[1] Not yet published [February 1970].

[2] *January 15: Before and After.*

[3] The summarized figures put out in the East's casualty list were:

Officers	East	Mid-West	West
Major-General	1	—	—
Lt.-Cols.	1	1	1
Majors	9	2	—
Capts.	11	—	—
Lts.	8	2	—
2/Lts.	3	2	2
Total	33	7	3

Other Ranks	East	Mid-West	West
WOs. I	3	—	—
WOs. II	8	1	1
S/Sgts.	12	6	2
Sgts.	30	4	—
Cpls.	25	2	—
L/Cpls.	22	1	—
Ptes.	53	—	—
Total	153	14	3

	East	Mid-West	West
SUMMARY OF TOTALS	186	21	6

'The over-all list of other ranks killed during this bloody massacre [July 1966] is estimated at 200. Other names particularly those newly trained or single soldiers are not easy to get at owing to the fact that official documents are not presently accessible.' *January 15: Before and After*, Appendix III.

[4] ibid., Appendices I and II. Appendix IV quotes the Lagos casualty list for comparative purposes and finds it 'far from complete in regard to casualties of Eastern Nigeria origin'. Like the figures for those who died in the May or September/October massacres of 1966, none has yet been authoritatively proved or its claim disproved.

G

at half-mast in Lagos out of respect for the late Supreme Commander, in the East, where Ironsi was buried with full military honours,[1] Ojukwu broadcast an obituary and spoke of the General having died 'in search of a greater and better Nigeria'.[2] The North converted the Federal declaration of 15 January as a day of national mourning into a Northern Nigeria Dedication Day and marked it with a *laudator temporis acti* speech by the Military Governor [DOC 84].

On 26 January Lt.-Col. Gowon released to a press conference in Lagos his account of what had transpired at Aburi and of what his Government's plans were to solve the constitutional impasse of the previous six months [DOC 85]. The Military Governor of the East, whose view of what had been agreed was very different [DOC 86], made his reaction to this announcement very plain in a speech given at a dinner arranged in Port Harcourt by the African Continental Bank the following day, in which he referred to the Bank's role in helping to resettle the Region's refugees and spoke of the East's aim as turning 'what appeared to be a misfortune or a setback into a blessing'.[3] The same message was apparent in Ojukwu's good wishes sent to the inaugural meeting of the Eastern Nigeria Students' Union at Nsukka, encouraging its growth as a bulwark against alleged discrimination by the Federal Government towards students of Eastern origin:

> I am hoping, therefore, that the great events of 1966 will cause a great revolution in the East which will bring out the best that we have both in natural and in human resources. I look upon our institutions of higher learning as centres where the kind of renaissance which I envisage will forment [*sic*] and radiate.[4]

In the same vein, too, Ojukwu told the leaders of thought in Port Harcourt that any going back by the Federal Government on the Aburi agreement would 'block the way to the return of peace and concord in the country.'[5]

Meanwhile, in the North the emirs and leaders of thought were re-called to hear from Hassan Katsina an outline of an Aburi-derived policy. High among its changes was the setting up of a consultative committee, drawn from prominent Northerners in all walks of life, to advise on how to strengthen 'unity and cohesion' in the Region. This would embrace members from the present leaders of thought assembly

[1] For a description, see Eastern Ministry of Information Press Release No. 99/1967.

[2] Full text of the funeral speech is to be found in Eastern Ministry of Information Press Release No. 98/1967.

[3] Speech at Port Harcourt, 27 January. Full text in Eastern Ministry of Information Press Release No. 104/1967.

[4] Message to Nsukka Students' Union delivered by Colonel Imo on behalf of the Military Governor, 27 January. Full text in Eastern Ministry of Information Press Release No. 105/1967.

[5] Report of press conference and addresses in Port Harcourt broadcast by E.N.B.S., Enugu (B.B.C. ME/2380/B/1).

as well as emirs and chiefs.[1] The week-long meeting concluded its session by recommending the creation of eleven states in Nigeria,[2] a significant resolution in view of later suggestions from some quarters that Gowon imposed the 12-state structure on the country with as little consultation as Ironsi appeared to have had in announcing his Decree 34. This 'political revolution' in Northern thinking was confirmed by two more decisions of a socio-administrative revisionist nature, the abolition of Grade A (holding the power to pass a sentence of death) Native Authority Courts,[3] and the even more radical act of banning N.A. employees from simultaneously holding political office once civilian rule was restored.[4] Here was a blueprint for as thorough a restructuring of the political make-up of the North as the subsequent States decree was to be for reshaping the administrative conceptualization of Nigeria.

At the end of January the Federal Military Government issued statements [DOC 87] attributing the delay in the implementation of the Aburi proposals to the 'administrative circumstances' of the country, 'some of [which] were unforeseen at the time the decisions were made.' It also expressed disappointment at the uncooperative attitude shown by the East and the 'misleading impression' given by Ojukwu in his premature press conference of 6 January [DOC 83]. An enabling decree in draft was circulated to all the Regional Military Governors for them to submit comments on for consideration by Lagos. The actual draft first decree has not been made public, though we have on record the East's denunciation of where it and its successor fell short of their interpretation of the Aburi agreement [DOC 88]. Thus, because of the intricacies involved in producing a watertight decree that would 'forestall controversy and meet the requirements recommended,' the Secretaries to the Military Governors reassembled in Benin on 17 February to consider a revised draft. No communiqué was issued, but a fortnight later a long official précis was carried on the N.B.C. and Radio Enugu provocatively announced that the Permanent Secretaries were still opposed to a constitution embodying the Aburi proposals.[5] At about the same time, Ojukwu sent a personal letter to Gowon (later made public) [DOC 89] expressing his anxiety at the deterioration in the

[1] Address to leaders of thought, Kaduna, 25 January, reported by N.B.C. Kaduna, (B.B.C. ME/2376/B/9).
[2] *Morning Post*, 28 January and 4 February 1967. The creation of states was the first item on the 'Programme of Action' communiqué issued by the Supreme Military Council on 22 April. See DOC 102.
[3] Statement issued in Kaduna on 21 February 1967. The full text is given in *New Nigerian*, 22 February 1967. See also *New Nigerian*, 25 April 1967.
[4] For comment, see talk over Lagos Radio, 24 February 1967 (B.B.C. ME/2403/B/12).
[5] Broadcast over Lagos Radio on 5 March 1967 (B.B.C. ME/2412/B/1). The meeting had been held some weeks earlier, on 17–18 February. The Federal Government later included the official minutes of this meeting in its record of the discussions held at and subsequent to Peduase Lodge (Aburi), but no such document is included in the Eastern version of the Aburi record.

situation consequent on what he saw as a stalemate over the implementation of the Aburi agreements.

Then, in a dawn broadcast on 25 February [DOC 90], he spoke publicly. Stirring his people with a jingoistic promise that 'it is not our intention to be slaughtered in our beds: we are ready to defend our homeland, we are prepared to crush any aggressors,' he threatened that unless the Aburi agreements were fully implemented by 31 March, he would feel free to give effect to them unilaterally. He also released a number of Aburi documents as part of his mounting campaign towards making 'a final stand against a régime which cannot honour agreements voluntarily arrived at'.[1] In a manner recalling Marshall Pétain's stubborn motto at Verdun of *ils ne passeront pas*, Ojukwu coined for the East the slogan 'On Aburi we stand: there will be no compromise.' Three days later the Supreme Military Council met in Lagos (again without the Governor of the East) and reaffirmed their faith in the continued existence of one Nigeria.[2] Colonel Adebayo now referred for the first time to the Aburi meeting, in a broadcast explaining the Western Region's determination to keep Nigeria together [DOC 91]. On 1 March Lt.-Col. Gowon invited the diplomatic representatives of foreign governments in Lagos to a private meeting at which he briefed them, in confidence,[3] on the post-Aburi impasse [DOC 92]. On the very same day, Lt.-Col. Ojukwu addressed a gathering of foreign heads of mission in Enugu and, reaffirming his refusal to recognize Gowon as Head of the Federal Military Government,[4] advanced his own assessment of the Lagos moves [DOC 93].

The first two weeks of March brought such a marked tensening of the situation that many were forced to wonder when exactly would be the breaking-point. Radio Enugu's campaign of vilification was by now in full spate, but often its accusations were returned, with interest, by the information media of Kaduna. Mutual recriminations of an arms build-up were followed by the North claiming that the East was holding up the evacuation of its produce and recountered by the East's sardonic question over a rail accident in the North asking when would the Hausa learn that 'trains do not understand the language of force.'[5] The East embarked on a long spiel of how Gowon was secretly plotting its downfall. Abroad its students bought expensive (manifestly beyond their own financial resources, if their unions' continued requests for more funds were genuine grievances) advertising space in the leading

---

[1] Statement issued in Enugu on 7 March 1967, accompanying the publication of the East's *Meeting of the Supreme Military Council (Aburi)*.

[2] *New Nigerian*, 2 March 1967.

[3] See the reference to this breach of confidence in Gowon's address to diplomatic representatives in Lagos on 24 April 1967—DOC 103.

[4] In a broadcast from Enugu. See also *Financial Times*, 3 March 1967.

[5] The radio vilification campaign of this period can be assessed in a study of the B.B.C. Monitoring Service bulletins ME/2384–94.

Eastern Ministry of Information poster

newspapers of Britain and the United States to publicize the Eastern
Region's version of 'Nigeria's Last Hope' [DOC 94]. Lt.-Col. Hassan
pushed the temperature several degrees nearer boiling-point when he
declared that if need be the East could be crushed in a matter of hours,[1]
a touch of chauvinism that drew from Ojukwu a solemn retort that 'I
feel we have crossed the line'[2] and a challenge to substantiate the boast.
Ojukwu went so far as to attack the role of the Federal Civil Service,
who in an unprecedented move, and with Cabinet support, publicly
refuted the charges.[3] At Nsukka, a seminar held to discuss the East's
refugee problem was addressed by the chairman of the rehabilitation
committee, Mr. Ihenacho, on the problems and work of his organization
[DOC 95]. The Eastern Region Information Service put out a large
number of loyal addresses presented to Lt.-Col. Ojukwu by the chiefs
and elders of various 'non-Ibo' provinces in the East,[4] emphasizing how
they too suffered in the indiscriminate Northern massacres and calculated to indicate apparent pan-Eastern solidarity even among the
minority peoples of the Region. Meanwhile, in Enugu, posters were on
display as early as March calling on the people to 'Be Vigilant', 'Be
Prepared and Avoid Panic', and, that depicting a soldier on guard,
asking 'This Man is Ready: Are You?' [DOC 96]. Enugu now revealed
an advanced state of *ante-bellum* preparedness against invasion, and
signs of a siege mentality, not known to Britain till the middle of its
war with Germany.

It was in such an atmosphere of public recrimination and open sabre-
rattling that the Supreme Military Council (still without Ojukwu)
gathered in Benin in the middle of March to discuss the draft decree
for implementing the Aburi heads of agreement. In its communiqué the
Council announced that it had adopted the Aburi minutes 'after some
amendments' and had agreed on a draft decree 'reflecting the Aburi
decisions', which would shortly be published.[5] Ojukwu's reply was
stubbornly to reaffirm to a conference of diplomats and journalists
summoned on 13 March that he felt the Rubicon had now been crossed
and he would therefore proceed with his plans by the end of the month
to 'decentralize Nigeria'; both his address and, particularly at this
conference, his replies to questions put by the world press [DOC 97] are
important for gaining an understanding of the East's sense of grievance

[1] *New Nigerian,* 9 March 1967; *Guardian,* 10 March 1967.
[2] Quoted in *The Times,* 10 March 1967.
[3] The statement was issued by the Cabinet Office on 16 March 1967. It may be compared with the equally significant (for an understanding of how the powerful Federal
Civil Service viewed its role in these months of potential administrative breakdown)
speech by Mr Alison Ayida, Permanent Secretary, to the Nigerian Institute of Management in Lagos on the theme 'The Permanent Secretaries' Committment to the Concept
of One Nigeria'. While admitting the immense authority of the civil services in the crisis
months of 1966–7, few would deny that without such strength and competence all the
military governments would have been in dire straits.
[4] e.g., Press Releases Nos. 135–9/1967.   [5] *New Nigerian,* 13 March 1967.

at what it held to be the Federal Government's breach of faith over Aburi and of the Region's 'expectations for the future'. The Governor of the North contemptuously wrote off Ojukwu's heavily publicized press conference as 'only a repetition of his effort to display what English he knew,' repeating his earlier claim that 'if the Supreme Commander gives the word to go, it would only take a few hours to subdue [the East] and remove the cause of friction in this country.'[1] This resurgence of jingoism was gleefully repudiated by the Eastern Ministry of Information in a no-holds-barred personal attack on Lt.-Col. Hassan:

> In the context of the crisis, such a statement is ominous. For there is a clear implication here that the rest of the country has been crushed and that the only thing which stands between the North and the complete domination of Nigeria is the failure of the North to crush the East. If that is the case, then it is up to the West and the Mid-West to say whether they have in fact been crushed; and if the North is planning to attack the East, then it needs a leader who can show greater fortitude. [Abuse of Hassan and Gowon follows].[2]

The attack was sustained by Lt.-Col. Ojukwu at a public rally on 10 March.[3] Ojukwu's public stand thus underlined his point-of-no-return belief expressed in a private interview on the eve of this declaration of policy,[4] while his shock at the belligerent utterances[5] of the Northern Governor was subsequently to be exploited in a significant, hotted-up broadcast urging the 'Middle Northerners' not to be led astray by the Hausa/Fulani elements [DOC 98]. Already the propaganda war was abusively under way.

Ojukwu's remarks were interpreted by the national press generally in the vein that the East must be prepared to face the consequences of such intransigence.[6] Gowon called a press conference on 14 March, at which he warned Ojukwu against making 'a laughing-stock of the constitution and the Federation',[7] and announced that another meeting of the Supreme Military Council would be held even though Ojukwu would probably refuse to attend on the grounds that Northern troops were stationed in Lagos.[8] Two days later, the Eastern Government published

---

[1] These remarks to reporters at Kaduna airport on 8 March are recorded in B.B.C. ME/2412/B/5.

[2] Talk over Enugu Radio by Christian Ofodile, Head of Research and Evaluation in the Eastern Ministry of Information, 13 March 1967.

[3] Reported in B.B.C. ME/2414.

[4] 'We really have come to the line of no return—and crossed it'—interview with Thomas Sterling, *Sunday Times*, 12 March 1967.

[5] Further cited in the *Guardian*, 14 March 1967.

[6] Daily editorials quoted in Lagos Radio round-up (B.B.C. ME/2418/B/4). Ojukwu's press conference was reported in the *Daily Times*, 14 March 1967.

[7] Quoted in *Morning Post*, 15 March 1967.

[8] Held in Lagos on 14 March 1967. A summary is given in B.B.C. ME/2418/B/3, quoting Radio Kaduna.

its White Paper on the Aburi meeting of the Nigerian Military Governors,[1] and within 24 hours the Federal Government promulgated, on 17 March, Decree No. 8 of 1967, designed to implement the measures of decentralization resulting from the views expressed at Aburi [DOC 99].

One of the basic causes of the East's total rejection of this Decree was the provisions of the amendment to section 70 of the 1963 Constitution which now vested in the Supreme Military Council the power to declare a state of emergency in any part of the country where it seemed necessary. Yet in the view of the vociferous minority communities of Calabar and Ogoja, this Decree 'was still another major concession to the Military Governor of the East. . . . It also satisfied the desire for more power by some other Military Governors. . . . The Decrees conferred more authority on the Regional Governments than the civilian Premiers exercised at the peak of their powers. . . . The Central Government was completely emasculated.'[2] The Lagos independent press felt, indeed, that Gowon had carried the process of decentralization too far.[3] The Northern Military Governor now defined his attitude towards the East at a long news conference held on his return from the Supreme Military Council meeting in Benin, declaring that the quarrel was no longer between the East and the North but between 'one ambitious man and the rest of the country' [DOC 100]. The world press took a more alarmingly positive view of the Nigerians' own scepticism and the headlines over this week were in the vein of 'The Slow Slide to Secession',[4] 'A Timebomb Ticks in Nigeria',[5] 'Nigeria's Young Colonels Bring Country To The Brink'.[6]

There was now hardly a hope that the East would do anything other than reject Decree 8; and this it did, flatly.[7] With a fortnight to go before Ojukwu's threatened unilateral action to implement his view of the Aburi agreement, the country was activated by a flurry of mediatory missions bent on persuading an obdurate Ojukwu to modify his stand on Aburi. A Ghanaian team took a message from General Ankrah and Ojukwu flew to Accra on 26 March (Gowon had visited Ankrah on the fifth, but reports of his meeting Ojukwu there were denied by the Lagos Information Ministry and the E.N.B.S.[8]) and gave an undertaking not to take unilateral action 'provided Lagos paid its debt to us before 31

[1] Official Document No. 5 of 1967.
[2] *Minorities, States and Nigerian Unity* (Lagos, 1967), p. 25.
[3] Editorial, *Daily Times*, 18 March 1967.
[4] *Financial Times*, 17 March 1967.
[5] *New York Times*, 18 March 1967.
[6] The *Observer*, 19 March 1967. In this connection, it should be noted that *The Economist* argued strongly against this Aburi outcome (19 March 1967).
[7] B.B.C. ME/2418.
[8] There appear to be reasonable grounds for supposing that an Aburi No. 2 summit was frustrated by the attempted counter-coup in Accra at this time.

March.'¹ This 'debt', according to a White Paper from the Eastern Government, amounted to over £11 million.² The civilian advisers to all four Regional Governors, including Sir Francis Ibiam of the East, met in Benin on 26 March, and the next day the Military Governor of the West accompanied the Commander of the Nigerian Navy and the Deputy Inspector-General of Police on a visit to Lt.-Col. Ojukwu in Onitsha. On his return Lt.-Col. Adebayo admitted 'My mind is clearer after [this] meeting about his 31 March ultimatum. Tension has gone down considerably. . . . We have all agreed to keep Nigeria together.'³ Ojukwu subsequently maintained that this delegation undertook to persuade Gowon to do two things: 'First, to make sure the debt owed to the East was paid by 31 March; secondly, either to suspend Decree No. 8 or to repeal those sections which were obnoxious to the East. It also suggested that the North should express public apology to the East for their atrocities.'⁴

From as far afield as the United States, the Civil Rights leaders—among them Dr. Martin Luther King—privately volunteered their services as mediators, a gesture that prompted a wordy reply from among the business stranger community in Lagos,⁵ tracing the causes of the crisis as one minority group saw them. Enugu's only identifiable reaction to this succession of goodwill offers was to institute a series of would-be situation reports called 'weather reports', carried in the *Eastern Spotlight* and broadcast over the E.N.B.S. as an indication of the political barometer. They included flashes such as 'West: not taken in' and 'East: damning it all',⁶ and, significantly on the day Ojukwu's ultimatum expired, the formula of 'Lagos: fiddling. West: breaking the fetters. Mid-West: reassessing. Northern North: scared stiff. Middle North: slipping away. Eastern Nigeria: counting down.'⁷ Perhaps the most memorable 'weather report' from Enugu was that brazenly forecast on the day after the East's breakaway had been declared: 'Lagos: overcast with intrigue. West: it is Oduduwa. Mid-West: marooned. Northern North: having political stroke. Middle North: crushed. Biafra: happy birthday.'⁸

Lt.-Col. Gowon was now to pay his first visit to the North since the July military coup brought him to power (he had remained in Lagos

---

¹ Ojukwu's speech of 26 May 1967 (DOC 110). He also had personal discussions with Colonel Adebayo, Commodore Wey, Mr. Omo-Bare, and Lt.-Col. Ejoor, during this tense period. See also *West Africa* (1967), p. 396.

² This was calculated at: oil royalties £4,140,000; current accounts £1,574,000; military expenditure £1,020,000; provident fund £4,097,000; and debts and reimbursable expenditure totalling £499,000 incurred by the Railway Corporation, Coal Corporation, and the Nigerian Airways Corporation. For further discussions of the fiscal implications of the Aburi agreement as interpreted by the East, see *The Meeting of the Supreme Military Council* (Enugu, 1967), pp. 13–14.

³ *West Africa* (1967), p. 449.   ⁴ Speech of 26 May 1967 (DOC 110).

⁵ *Nigerian Crisis: The Root Cause* (Lagos, 1967).

⁶ Quoted in B.B.C. ME/2424.   ⁷ B.B.C. ME/2429.   ⁸ B.B.C. ME/2481.

even longer than the censured Ironsi) and address the initial batch of officer-cadets to be commissioned at the military academy in Kaduna. On his return to Lagos Gowon made a crucial speech to the nation on 25 March [DOC 101]. The same day, an edict was published in Enugu giving Ojukwu emergency powers to declare the Region a disturbed area. The meeting of the Supreme Military Council scheduled for 29 March was postponed by twenty-four hours to allow the Regional senior law and finance officers to meet in Ghana in accordance with General Ankrah's undertaking to Ojukwu to bring all such officials together there.[1] Then, at the eleventh hour, the Supreme Council met briefly in Lagos on 30 March: Ojukwu stayed away. Elaborating the slim communiqué issued, Lt.-Col. Ejoor told reporters in Benin that they had narrowed the gap and gave his word that the Federal Military Government did not intend to use force on any Region that wanted to secede.[2] This promise was later reaffirmed by the Chief of Staff, Lt.-Col. Akahan.[3]

Came Ojukwu's D-Day: the East did not secede nor did Lagos wake up on April Fool's Day to the brittle snap of rifle fire or the drone of bombers. Instead, there was precipitated another crisis, one which seemed to many merely to postpone, not eliminate, the likelihood of an armed showdown. In a Revenue Collection Edict issued on 31 March, Ojukwu peremptorily ordered all revenues derived from the Eastern Region to be diverted from the Federal authorities in Lagos and paid instead into his Regional treasury. The objects and reasons for this far-reaching edict were given as follows by the Eastern Government:

(1) At Aburi it was unanimously agreed that those civil servants and corporation employees including daily-paid workers who fled their places of work and returned to their regions of origin and who have not found alternative employments must be paid their salaries and wages up to 31st March 1967. This agreement was not carried out by the Federal Government corporations in relation to Eastern Nigeria and the Government of the region was compelled by circumstances to pay the salaries and wages involved.

(2) Other expenses properly chargeable to the Government of the Federal Republic of Nigeria have been borne by the Government of Eastern Nigeria.

(3) The events of July 1966 and after have caused a big shift of population. As far as Eastern Nigeria is concerned this shift is irreversible. As a result, the Government of Eastern Nigeria now has some 1,800,000 displaced persons to cater for and rehabilitate.

(4) The Federal Government has been delaying in turning over to this region its statutory share of revenues centrally collected despite the fact that those statutory shares represent only a fraction of the revenues derived from the region.

---

[1] See *Guardian*, 30 March 1967.
[2] Remarks made in Benin on 31 March 1967 (B.B.C. ME/2429/B/1).
[3] Remark made by Lt.-Col. Joseph Akahan when addressing the 3rd Battalion in Ibadan on 5 April 1967 (private information).

(5) The Federal Government is also withholding monies due to this region from other sources. The total amount due and unpaid from the federal authorities is well over £10,000,000.

This Edict is intended to enable the government of Eastern Nigeria to collect and retain what is owed to it and prevent further indebtedness to it by the Federal Government.[1]

This gave the East virtual control of the railways, airports, harbours, coal, electricity, and postal communications situated within its borders. Some such move might have been expected, for back in March the East had publicized its claims for a revision of the revenue allocation and demanded an extra £10 million necessitated, in particular, by the fact that the forced repatriation of Easterners from the North had destroyed the original base of inter-Regional fiscal relations. Naturally, this claim was rejected by the Federal Government as exorbitant; Lagos also saw it as dishonest:

It is well known that the Eastern Nigeria Government has of late been incurring additional unbudgeted expenditures. This makes it all the more absurd to suggest that the Federal Government owes about £10,000,000 of payment to the East. The dishonesty of this claim is demonstrated by the fact that at the Benin meeting of finance officials on 23rd March 1967, the figure of the alleged indebtedness was put at £4,000,000. This was raised to £5,600,000 a few days later in Ghana and subsequently escalated to £12,600,000 by 31st March 1967. It is significant that the Eastern Nigeria Government has been unable to publish the composition of the so-called debt.[2]

Gowon at once issued a strong personal statement, lamenting that Ojukwu should have been so precipitate and accusing him of economic sabotage:

It is regrettable that the Eastern Military Governor has embarked on this unfortunate course of action at the time when the whole country was expecting an early solution to the Nigerian crisis. As a matter of fact, at the most recent meetings in Benin and Ghana of senior officials from the Federal Government and all the Regions, it was agreed that the Supreme Military Council should authorise an early review of the revenue allocation system by an independent commission.

The Federal Military Government therefore considers that the action of the Military Governor of the East is not really a revenue matter but a calculated attempt to subvert existing Federal institutions by unilateral action.[3]

This view was shared by the press outside the East, with the North bluntly describing the edict as an act of secession. In the event, Ojukwu was not to stop at this, for in the next three weeks he issued the rest of his quartet of what he termed the East's 'Survival Edicts.'[4] Meanwhile,

---

[1] From the explanatory notes to the Revenue Collection Edict, 1967. The edict came into force with effect from 1 April.

[2] Statement issued by the Cabinet Office, Lagos, on 6 April 1967.

[3] Statement issued in Lagos on 1 April 1967. Full text in *New Nigerian*, 3 April 1967.

[4] These were the Revenue Collection, the Legal Education, the Statutory Bodies, and the Court of Appeal Edicts.

on 2 April he followed up his seizure of Federal revenues by setting forth, at a rally in Aba, the three conditions under which the East would consent to take part in any future negotiations. These were that the North should show 'remorse' for the 'atrocities they have perpetrated against the Easterners, that they should make some formal gesture of recompense towards the East, and that the agreements reached between the military governors, notably those at Aburi, should be implemented at once'. He characterized the struggle as one between good (the East) and evil (the Northerners). He ended by calling for a summit meeting to be held in Enugu and requesting a half minute's silence from the assembly at Aba for the Region's 'dead heroes'.[1]

In Lagos the first retaliatory measure was to suspend all Nigerian Airways flights to the East; additional sanctions were to await the next meeting of the Supreme Council. In retrospect, it seems that the experts in Lagos may have been no less optimistic, and no less incorrect, in their assessment of the effect of economic measures than their counterparts had been in London 18 months earlier in advising the British Government on the potential effect of sanctions imposed against Rhodesia.

The Supreme Council meeting took place in Lagos on 20 April. The very important communiqué issued on 22 April showed that its deliberations had extended beyond the authorization of stern economic measures should Ojukwu continue his illegal actions, for it presented the Federal Government's package plan for a 'programme of action' to preserve the unity of the Federation as well as outlining a phased return to elected civilian rule by 1969 [DOC 102]. Immediately after this announcement, Lt.-Col. Gowon once again took the heads of diplomatic missions into his confidence [DOC 103]. Lt.-Col. Ojukwu had done the same thing for foreign diplomats in Enugu as soon as the Supreme Military Council's communiqué was released, assuring them of his determination to refrain from any 'use of force provided nothing is done by anyone to impair the integrity and corporate existence of the Federation.'[2] Complementary to this declaration is a talk over Enugu Radio by Cyprian Ekwensi, Director of the Eastern Ministry of Information, in which he clearly set out the limits beyond which the East would feel itself as having been pushed into secession:

In the present situation, in very precise terms, the East would only secede if she were attacked and an attack could be in two ways—physical military attack or economic blockade. That pronouncement was made by the Military Governor of Eastern Nigeria, Lt.-Col. Odumegwu Ojukwu, in answer to a question during a recent world press conference.

Another question has been in the air since Lagos began a series of frantic

[1] Report broadcast from Enugu on 1 April 1967 (B.B.C. ME/2433/B/2).
[2] Speech made at Enugu, 22 April 1967, to foreign diplomats (B.B.C. ME/2448/B/3, quoting Radio Enugu summary).

and suicidal actions against Eastern Nigeria. That question is: when will the push be complete? Daily the catalogue of military and economic actions against the East lengthens. The new policy in Lagos seems to be: if you cannot shoot the East or knife the East, do the next best thing—strangle the East. The result will be the same—death. A misguided policy indeed. How

else can you explain all the unilateral actions? . . . Daily the catalogue lengthens; daily the situation gets more and more intolerable. Are there really any remaining ties to hold this country together or will the slide plunge us all into an abyss? Only a dramatic step now can arrest the push. That dramatic step is simply a meeting of the full and only Supreme Military Council outside Nigeria and in the presence of H.I.M. Haile Selassie, Gen. Ankrah of Ghana, Col. Nasser of the U.A.R. and President Tubman of Liberia. These Heads of State, all members of the O.A.U., have offered to mediate in the crisis and could bring about a family settlement. Failing this, there is absolutley no other hope that any force will reverse the action already taken or stop Lagos from completing the push. Then, it will not be a matter of meeting to discuss association, but of meeting to share the assets of what was once Nigeria.[1]

The East was stung into making a rejoinder to Gowon's unambiguous warning that the corollary to secession by the East would be 'a clear

[1] Radio talk by Cyprian Ekwensi, 13 April 1967 (B.B.C. ME/2442/B/6).

signal . . . to create a C.O.R. state for the protection of the minorities in Eastern Nigeria whom [*sic*] we know do not want to part from the rest of the country [and] this action . . . will be backed by the use of force if need be,'[1] and called this boast 'the funny tale of Alice in Wonderland'.[2] In defence of the threat of severe economic sanctions, Ojukwu now proceeded to introduce his 1967/8 budget and spoke once more of the Region's need to withstand the bulldozing tactics of 'the Lagos military junta'[3] and 'accept the challenge to take the destiny of our lives into our hands'.[4] The broadcasts emitting from E.N.B.S. again provoked Radio Kaduna into a sustained attack on the East's information media:

> The information media in Eastern Nigeria have become a laughing-stock in other parts of the Federation, particularly in the North, because they disseminate false reports, particularly of events in Northern Nigeria. They have failed to realise, and the events of last year have not taught them a lesson, that the North cannot be hoodwinked by a common enemy seeking to cause confusion among its people. The rock-like foundation of unity of various sections of the Northern Nigeria community cannot be shaken or broken by any form of propaganda, no matter how cleverly carried out. Both the Eastern 'Nigerian Outlook' and the E.N.B.S., as well as the Zik group of newspapers, have resorted to yellow journalism by publishing stories which only existed in their imagination about happenings in the North. The brains behind this vicious propaganda against the North have failed to realise that, if there was an iota of truth in their reports, this could have been confirmed by foreign news agencies, for there is no censorship of news in any part of the country except in the East.[5]

In the critically-situated Mid-West, the Governor warned his people of the crisis ahead.[6]

To this confusion the uncertain politics of Yorubaland once more made their own contribution. Just before the Ad Hoc Constitutional Committee was due to reassemble in Benin, in accordance with Gowon's declared programme for stage I of the return to civilian rule,[7] Chief Awolowo not only announced his resignation from the committee in a letter to the Military Governor of the West (it was followed by the resignation of the Northern and Lagos leaders) but let off another bombshell by telling the leaders of thought gathered in Ibadan that if

---

[1] Speech of 24 April 1967. See DOC 103.

[2] Radio Enugu broadcasts quoted in B.B.C. ME/2451 and 2455.

[3] From here on one notices the beginnings of an exercise in pejorative terminology, with Lagos seen as a 'junta' and its troops (especially the Northern ones) as 'vandals', while Enugu becomes the stronghold of a 'rebel clique' and, after July 1967, its leader is pointedly downgraded to 'Mister' Ojukwu.

[4] Reported by Enugu Radio on 27 April 1967. B.B.C. report ME/2448 contains a remark attributed to Ojukwu that 'The path open to the East is clear, and I should have no alternative but to take it.'

[5] Talk over Radio Kaduna, 26 April 1967 (B.B.C. ME/2453/B/6).

[6] Broadcast from Benin, 14 April 1967.   [7] See DOC 102.

the East were to secede, the West and Lagos should also withdraw from the Federation [DOC 104].[1] The following day, Lt.-Col. Adebayo urgently broadcast to the people of the West[2] denying that his Region was in collusion with the East but affirming that force was not the answer. These resignations at once brought about the indefinite postponement of the resumed meeting of the Constitutional Conference. Nevertheless, the Regional meetings of leaders of thought continued their deliberations on constitutional advance within Lt.-Col. Gowon's timetable, with particular reference to the question of creating more states, and important resolutions were adopted. In the North, the Military Governor made a major policy speech [DOC 105]; in the Mid-West, Lt.-Col. Ejoor restated his determination not to allow the buffer Region 'to be used as a battleground in a conflict born of revenge and aimed at the acquisition of naked power', at the same time warning against subversive elements within its borders working to make it 'an appendage of another Region';[3] in Lagos the traditional chiefs declared their opposition to a loose central federation and dissociated themselves from any demand for the recall of non-Yoruba troops from the city;[4] and in the West six policy resolutions were passed, echoing the Awolowo thesis that secession by one Region must entail secession by all. These included:

1. We hereby resolve that the West stands for a peaceful solution to the present crisis and will not be a party to any attempt to impose a military solution or to the use of force.

2. Noting that the West does not subscribe to the view that the way out of the present crisis in the country is either to impose a solution by force on the East or to annoy the East out of the Federation; We hereby resolve that every peaceful effort must be made to keep the East in the Federation on a basis which recognises the mutual interests of all the Regions even if this means a constitutional arrangement that is looser than hitherto.

3. Noting that the Federation of Nigeria consists of the Eastern, Mid-Western, Northern and Western Regions and Lagos, it follows that in the event of any of the component units seceding or being forced out, the Federation as we know it shall cease to exist. Our earnest hope is that this eventuality shall not come to pass, but if it does, Western Nigeria shall automatically become independent and sovereign.

4. Considering the existing circumstances in the country; it is hereby resolved that Western Nigeria shall:
   (*i*) not participate in the work of the Ad Hoc Committee on Constitutional proposals;
   (*ii*) not comment on the programme of the Supreme Military Council.[5]

---

[1] Chief Awolowo reaffirmed this stand in an open letter to the Lagos press during the middle of the war, *Sunday Times* (Lagos), 30 March 1969.

[2] Broadcast from Ibadan, 3 May 1967.

[3] Address to opening session of the Mid-West representative assembly in Benin, 19 May 1967.

[4] Lagos Radio report, 8 May 1967 (B.B.C. ME/2463/B/1).

[5] Passed in Ibadan on 3 May 1967. Full text in *Peace and Solidarity* (Ibadan, 1967).

The Federal Military Government now tightened its grip on the East's economy, suspending postal and money-order transactions and cancelling passports issued to over thirty prominent citizens.[1] Simultaneously, civilian leaders joined to form a National Conciliation Committee and dispatch a delegation under Awolowo to confer with Ojukwu in Enugu.[2] On 6 May Ojukwu presented them with his proposals for effecting a rapprochement [DOC 106]. Not surprisingly, the Committee failed to convince Lagos of the validity of these demands (Ojukwu was later to refer to Awolowo's mission as 'an ill-conceived child'),[3] but, reconstituted later in the month, it met with more success and did persuade Lt.-Col. Gowon to accept its proposals for a *détente*.[4] These, however, were rejected by the East, where the *Nigerian Outlook* demanded that they be looked on with suspicious care 'in the light of Gowon's past record'.[5] Once again Enugu Radio did not pull its abusive punches:

The Nigerian crisis is still very much there. The lifting of the sanctions is a wrong first step, but it is neither strange to the East nor surprising to it, knowing the group involved. The real crux of the matter—the removal of Northern troops—is conveniently muffled. Why does Western Nigerian security have to depend on Hausa-Fulani armed regiments when the most senior officer in the Nigerian Army is the Governor of the West? Today there are the hateful Hausa soldiers in Kaduna and Makurdi, rightly enough; but they are also in Akure, Oshogbo, Ondo, Ibadan and Lagos—unruly reminders that the North has seized power and means to keep that power against the wishes of the South and against all realistic proposals for a peaceful solution. This is all to the good. The East wishes for nothing better than North for North, West for West, East for East, and Nigeria for us all. Let Gowon go back to his mountains. Hassan is already in his desert.[6]

And the threat of secession was no longer muted: 'Let the Democratic Republic of Biafra emerge as Easterners are now busy demanding all over Eastern Nigeria!' was a radio slogan.[7] Gowon humanely ordered an immediate relaxation of the economic blockade of the East. This measure was, in its turn, assailed by the East's radio, in another of its stinging assaults on Nigeria's integrity, as provoking 'contempt, apathy, and levity'.[8] The resolution of a joint meeting of Nigerian members of university teaching staffs also failed to bring the two governments any closer.[9]

[1] Government Notice No. 710 of 1967.

[2] The inaugural meeting was held at the Nigerian Institute of International Affairs, Lagos, on 4 May 1967. The convenor was Sir Adetokunbo Ademola, Chief Justice, and there were 20 other distinguished members. They included Sir Francis Ibiam and Sir Louis Mbanefo from the East.   [3] *Nigerian Outlook*, 22 May 1967.

[4] Report by Lagos Radio, 20 May 1967 (B.B.C. ME/2472/B/2).

[5] *Nigerian Outlook*, 17 May 1967.   [6] Talk over Enugu Radio, 23 May 1967.

[7] Quoted in B.B.C. ME/2475.   [8] ibid.

[9] Communiqué issued in Ibadan on 7 May 1967 after a meeting attended by 24 senior academics from all five of the country's universities. The communiqué was phrased in anodyne general terms, adding that the political programmes with bite to them as

The Supreme Military Council, which had now delegated most of its functions to the Federal Executive Council established by Decree 8, meanwhile met again on 8 May in rump form (neither the Western nor the Eastern Governors would attend) and passed a £76m. budget.[1] Ten days later Gowon announced that the search for a safe meeting-ground for a meeting of all the military leaders included, among the possible venues, a British naval vessel or a neutral zone to be demarcated at the Oil-Palm Research Institute in Benin by a company of British troops [DOC 107]. This sparked off denouncements and demonstrations against the United Kingdom in the Eastern Region, including a telegram from Ojukwu to Gowon impudently dubbing the plan 'British invasion of Mid-West',[2] and the British High Commissioner had to issue a denial that any troops had been asked for [DOC 108]. In an interview with a British journalist,[3] Ojukwu confided that 'I think we are now rolling downhill . . . we are very close, very very close,' while in an address to Eastern University students he warned that 'the East can no longer move back'.[4] The East's exuberant youth was by now truly on the move. At a huge rally of 50,000 people gathered in Enugu Sports Stadium, there were calls for a declaration of independence and placards were produced proclaiming 'We hail the Republic of Biafra' and 'Operation Secession'.[5]

The Western Region's Military Governor also took offence at the possible presence of British troops and, after banning the circulation of the Federal Government's official newspaper *Morning Post*, repeated his request for the removal of Northern troops from the West. Reversing the previously reported decision of Gowon that security considerations ruled this out, the Inspector General of Police issued a statement on 25 May that troops of non-Western origin would, after all, be evacuated from Ibadan and Abeokuta.[6] As Ojukwu was quick to point out, there was no reference to withdrawing what he called 'the Northern army of occupation' from Lagos or Ikeja.[7] Hassan flew down to address the Northern troops stationed in the West, but his explanation of the decision to withdraw them, given in a major personsl interview [DOC 109], seemed to add fuel to the Western Region's fire and elicited an appeal from Brigadier Adebayo for 'absolute calm and dignity' during the forthcoming redeployment of the army.[8]

---

adopted by the meeting had been forwarded to the Nigerian military authorities. The text is to be found in *New Nigerian*, 8 May 1967.

[1] Radio Enugu broadcast on 17 May a leaked version of preparations for war allegedly discussed at this meeting. The communiqué issued in Lagos on 9 May said nothing of importance. (Full text is given in *New Nigerian*, 10 May 1967.)

[2] Quoted by Ojukwu in his speech to the Consultative Assembly on 26 May 1967. (See DOC 110.)   [3] *Guardian*, 17 May 1967.

[4] Speech made at the Enugu campus of the University of Nigeria, 18 May 1967.

[5] Report of Youth Rally at Enugu, 12 May 1967, broadcast by E.N.B.S. (B.B.C. ME/2467/B/3).

[6] Statement by Alhaji Kam Selem to a news conference held in Lagos on 25 May 1967.

[7] Quoted in a broadcast from Enugu Radio on 26 May 1967.

[8] Reported by Ibadan Radio on 26 May 1967 (B.B.C. ME/2477/B/9).

H

When the Eastern Region's Consultative Assembly met jointly with the Advisory Committee of Chiefs and Elders, on 26 May, Lt.-Col. Ojukwu centred his marathon and milestone address on the theme of 'The East is at the crossroads'. Dramatically reading out a telegram received from Lagos during the session,[1] he presented his Region's leaders with three alternatives for the future. The final one was that of 'ensuring the survival of our people by asserting our autonomy' [DOC 110.]

Even as Ojukwu spoke, Gowon was preparing the final draft of another watershed policy decree. On the night of 27 May, broadcasting to the nation [DOC 111] Gowon declared a state of emergency throughout Nigeria and announced a new decree to abolish the four Regions by creating twelve states in their place.[2] Four days later he addressed nine of the new Military Governors on their responsibility:

I wish to emphasise that this is a temporary job which you are being called upon as good Soldiers and Police Officers to perform. We are all to re-establish a new Nigeria and go back to the barracks. My advice is that you should not approach your new jobs as politicians but as professional Soldiers.

Your duty as Military Governors of the new States is to establish the nucleus of the administration in your States and to function as the Head of the Government to be established in the State. . . .

Each State is an autonomous unit within the Federation of Nigeria. Each State is equal in all respects to other States. You as Military Governors, therefore, have full powers over all constitutional responsibilities allocated to the States. No one Military Governor is subordinate to another in the discharge of his constitutional responsibilities.

I am aware that there has been some concern over the establishment of the Administrative Council for the new States created out of the former Northern Region. This administrative committee is not a Council of the States in the Region, as reported in some newspapers.[3]

(Later some of these made inaugural speeches: those of the South-Eastern[4] and Rivers[5] States, because of their imminent engulfment into Biafra, and of the long-clamant Lagos State,[6] may be of special interest.) Thus, with the repeal of the short-lived 'Aburi' Decree 8, on the grounds that 'Executive authority in Eastern Nigeria has been so exercised as to prejudice the executive authority of the Federation in circumstances such that it is expedient and necessary to make other

[1] It contained the sentence 'earnestly appeal to you to co-operate to arrest further drift into disintegration' and expressed the belief that 'it is not too late to commence measures to resolve crisis without bloodshed.'

[2] The Federal Government was later at pains to emphasize how this decision was but the just culmination of a 'long history of movement for the creation of states'. *The Collapse of a Rebellion* (Lagos, 1968), p. 9.

[3] Delivered at Dodan Barracks, Lagos, on 31 May 1967. Full text from Federal Ministry of Information hand-out.

[4] Lt.-Col. Esuene. Full text reproduced in *A Clarion Call for Action*, Ministry of Information, South-Eastern State, 1967.

[5] Lt. Diete-Spiff, broadcast from Lagos on 2 June 1967.

[6] Major Johnson, broadcast in Lagos, 4 June 1967.

provisions for the continuance of federal government,'[1] and the promulgation of Decrees 13 and 14,[2] Gowon did more than bring into being
the very states whose creation had been at the centre of the political
quarrels of the First Republic:

By this stroke of the pen . . . he also brought to an end a way of administrative, political and fiscal life that had endured since 1900, had received confirmation in 1914, and had, despite the political tremors of the 1950s caused
by threats of fission and refusion, remained apparently sacrosanct in the
vocabulary of both colonial and independent Nigerian administrative
thought.[3]

Ironically, the creation of the very states in the North demanded by the
East's leaders throughout the political decade was now rejected by the
East. For it saw in the dismemberment of the *soi-disant* Biafra into three
states, two of which comprised non-Ibo majorities and contained the
oil installations as well as Port Harcourt and access to the sea, a ploy to
strike at the very concept of a viable, sovereign Biafra and reduce it to
nothing more than an impoverished, landlocked, over-populated Ibo
province. Gowon's shrewd move to block secession turned out to be the
final pressure on the trigger releasing the explosion.

Late that same day of 27 May, the Joint Meeting in Enugu gave
Ojukwu its mandate for secession [DOC 112]. The final issue of the East's
own 'thunderer', *Nigerian Outlook* (to reappear as *Biafran Sun* in the
immediate Biafranization of institutions east of the Niger) headed its
editorial of 29 May 'The Moment has Arrived'. The Eastern Ministry of
Information, discussing the Region's 'stunned amazement [at] the
ominous and disastrous announcement of Gowon proclaiming himself
the Dictator of Nigeria', interpreted the States Decree as a 'one man
coup d'état'[4] and warned that the East stood firm and prepared to meet
the challenge [DOC 113]. At that moment, the East's view was that she
was 'neither a part of the Nigerian Federation nor a nation in her own
right—a state of affairs which the 14 million people of Eastern Nigeria
could not continue to suffer.'[5] On 30 May, after summoning the U.K.
and U.S. chargés d'affaires at 3 o'clock in the morning to inform them
of his intention, Lt.-Col. Ojukwu broadcast a dawn message declaring
Eastern Nigeria a sovereign independent state and proclaiming the
birth of the new 'Republic of Biafra' [DOC 114]. In its flag, the stripes
were described as red for the blood of the people, black for mourning,
and green for progress, with the central sun symbolizing the emergent

[1] Federal Government statement quoted in *West Africa* (1967), p. 716.
[2] These are the administrative and fiscal enabling decrees, published in the *Nigerian Gazette*, 27 May 1967.
[3] A. H. M. Kirk-Greene, *Lugard and the Amalgamation of Nigeria* (London, 1968), p. 33.
[4] Cf. Walter Schwarz: '27 May had been, in a real sense, the third coup—the coup of the minorities. It was the profoundest revolution of all.' *Nigeria* (1968), p. 231.
[5] *Case for Biafra* (Enugu, 1967), p. 4.

nation. Not for nothing had Ojukwu chosen the date of 30 May,[1] for this was the anniversary of the bloody riots against the Ibo in the North which Biafra now regarded as the first of the intimidatory moves to cast her bodily out of the Nigerian Federation.

In a prompt statement, Gowon castigated Ojukwu's 'ill-advised secession as an act of rebellion which will be crushed'.[2] In Lagos, the Ministry of Defence announced the promotion of Lt.-Col. Gowon to Major-General[3] and advanced the Military Governors of the West and Mid-West to the ranks of Brigadier; *en revanche*, Enugu reported that Lt.-Col. Ojukwu (subsequently to be stripped of his army rank by the Federal Government and discharged with ignominy[4]) was to be invested with the new title of *okaome*, 'Man of his Word',[5] and it promoted its own general and brigadiers in the Biafran army.[6] General mobilization was ordered throughout the Federation. All army leave was cancelled, officers abroad on courses of instruction were recalled and new commissions offered, ex-servicemen were re-enlisted, the navy was put under sailing orders, and economic sanctions were tightened up to include the closing of the new Niger bridge at Asaba and a total maritime blockade of the East's ports. Overseas reaction to Biafra's declaration of independence demands special attention when it is viewed against the attitudes of certain African and European powers towards Biafra just a year later.

Yet for all this prelude to war[7] and despite this brutally forced parturition of Nigeria which left the Federation with its flank ripped open, General Gowon preferred to put his trust in diplomatic negotiation rather than an immediate deployment of force to bring the undisputedly rebel East to heel. In Lagos, the wings of the gathering hawks and protestant doves were heard fluttering excitedly. Abroad, secession posed a tricky problem to the Ibo members of the hitherto unified Foreign Service as well as to students enjoying Federal Government grants: in both cases geographical 'Biafrans' were, sooner rather than later and quite understandably, invited to sign a declaration affirming that they were loyal 'Nigerians'.[8] On 3 June twelve civilians, one from each state (the names for men from the three states now within Biafra were not announced immediately) were appointed to the Federal

---

[1] Shrewdly, the *Financial Times* had earlier pinpointed this as the likely date for secession. *Financial Times*, 18 May 1967.

[2] Statement issued in Lagos on 30 May 1967.

[3] *Nigerian Gazette*, 1 June 1967.

[4] *Nigerian Gazette*, 1 July 1967.   [5] B.B.C. ME/2480.   [6] B.B.C. ME/2489.

[7] The breathtaking succession of events during the crisis months of April–June 1967 are well catalogued in the series of aide-mémoires and chronological diaries carried in the pages of *West Africa*. The journal also carried useful summaries of the reaction of world opinion to Biafra's declaration of independence, notably at pp. 772 and 806. The monthly *Africa Research Bulletin* is also valuable for assessing international reaction.

[8] For an intimate account of Brigadier Ogundipe's directive within the High Commission in London, see *Guardian*, 1 June 1967.

Federal Ministry of Information Poster

Executive Council. A similar process was to follow at the State Executive Council level. Observers were quick to interpret the appointment of Chief Awolowo to such high office after his recent exercise in rocking the Federal boat as an earnest that he was no longer intent on leading the West into secession. On 12 June General Gowon addressed the inaugural meeting of the reconstructed Federal Executive Council [DOC 115] and Chief Awolowo replied with a flourish of metaphor:

Nigeria's ship of State is now in the midst of a very heavy storm. That we have been invited by you at this time to lend a hand in piloting the ship, safe and whole, to the happy haven of our dreams is at once a tribute to our reputed competence and a challenge to our skill. . . . As I see it, we have been invited by you to assist in doing a rescue operation—to do such repairs and close such holes as are necessary in the process, but certainly not to rebuild the ship. Otherwise our ship of State might be irretrievably wrecked by the sheer and unduly prolonged buffetings of the storm.[1]

In the States, several of the new Military Governors made important maiden speeches, of which those from the 'occupied' South-East and Rivers states are again among the most meaningful.[2]

Newspapers in Lagos now began to blazon the new Federal slogan of 'To keep Nigeria one is a task that must be done.' Student support vociferously followed 'Nigerian' and 'Biafran' lines according to the location of the institution, those at Ibadan and Lagos urging the Federal Government to topple the 'traitorous and Tshomberian'[3] régime of Ojukwu while their erstwhile brothers at Nsukka called on their government to arm them. An editorial in the influential *New Nigerian*, echoing the apparent Gowon preference for economic sanctions rather than military action to break Ojukwu's rebel régime, was vigorously rebuked by the new Administrative Council of the Northern States which dissociated itself from such a plea:[4] appeasement was clearly 'out' in Kaduna. Telling propaganda talks over the Nigerian broadcasting systems were countered by no less astringent replies from the new-named Voice of Biafra. While Kaduna jeered:

Is the Ibo Easterner likely to see through the campaign of deceit and see Ojukwu and his clique as cowards who ought not to be allowed to escape? You cannot fool all the people all the time. Sooner or later, and sooner rather than later, the Iboman's eyes will be opened. When this happens I shudder to think what treatment will be meted out to Ojukwu, his clique, and his minions. The day is not far off. When that day comes, the East and indeed the whole of Nigeria can celebrate the downfall of the Nigerian Tshombe.[5]

[1] Federal Ministry of Information Press Release No. 1300/1967.
[2] For example, that of Esuene on 29 June and that of Spiff on 6 July, both broadcast from Lagos (B.B.C. ME/2506/B/3 and 2511/B/2 respectively).
[3] Quoted in *West Africa* (1967), p. 837.
[4] *New Nigerian*, 7 June 1967.
[5] Talk over Radio Kaduna, 2 May 1967.

and Lagos pontificated on how:

In the hands of a true and sincere Nigerian patriot, the situation would
have provided an effective tool to shape the dawn of a glorious era for Easterners, and to give to them all that will enable them to forget the past, and live
henceforth in harmony with their fellow Nigerians. But, for a power maniac,
the situation supplies a very tantalizing bait and a spring-board to the goal
of his ultimate ambition—absolute power. Very unfortunately for Nigeria
generally, and the East in particular, Lt.-Col. Ojukwu belongs to the latter
category. Having swallowed the bait, hook, line and sinker, he sees through
his vista a mighty empire whose founder he can easily claim to be, and over
which he can, therefore, preside for as long as he lives.

Lt.-Col. Ojukwu thus pursues the achievement of the empire of his dream
with certain definite assumptions. He assumes the full support of Westerners
because, at certain times, leaders in that part of the country have found it
necessary to speak with frankness and candour on the Nigerian crisis; he
interprets this as a decision to team up with him. With the support of Westerners, including Lagosians, in hand, he assumed that whatever may be their
attitude, the Mid-Westerners cannot, for obvious reasons, constitute a problem. These two assumptions produce yet a third—the assumption that
Southern Nigeria is solidly behind him, and that secession by the East will
only be the first stage of the disintegration of Nigeria, ending in the entire
South coming into an agreement under his leadership, to confront and subdue
the North.[1]

Enugu depicted the Lagos administration as a modern Dracula:

How low will a depraved government sink? For how long will the civilised
world watch with horror the daily violations of all the canons of decency and
law by the Government of Nigeria? This week the Nigerian Government
added one more item to its already long list of international crimes. According to reliable reports the soldiers and agents of the Government have now
begun to ambush all Biafrans returning from Lagos and compelling them at
gunpoint to donate blood for the blood bank of the tottering Federation.
Reports say that the donation of blood has become the passport for a free
passage from Nigeria to neighbouring Biafra. Biafran travellers who refused
or demurred have the official reply with butts of the gun.

For little children and friends of fairy tales, these reports will bring back
memories with brutal vigour of the blood-chilling story of the adventures of
Dracula. Dracula is a malicious ghost which feeds on the blood of the living.
His fabled mischief has been a source of nightmares to children. With its
new action, the Lagos Government has turned itself into the modern Dracula.[2]

and its radio delivered another personal attack upon Gowon:

This intensely ambitious Gowon had three obsessions soon after he mutinied against General Ironsi. First, to become a Major-General; second,
under the guise of creating a Middle Belt state, to carve up the East while
retaining the North as one bloc; third, to become dictator of Nigeria. He has

[1] Talk by Felix Ani, 'The Assumptions of a Rebel', broadcast from Lagos.
[2] Broadcast from Enugu, 8 June 1967.

now nearly achieved all his ambitions, and so it is time to call in puppets to give some flimsy support to his hypocrisy. Ambitious Gowon, not even rank-ing seventh in line of promotion in the Nigerian Army, suddenly shot up to the post of Major-General. The promotion, he explained, being necessary for him to put Ironsi's ghost to bed. But Ironsi's ghost still drags his chains about Gowon's nightmares. Gowon can never be equal to the internationally recognised distinguished soldier.[1]

Biafra made no secret of the real focus of its enmity:

Biafrans are sick and tired of the endless Northern Nigerian permutations and combinations which have only one result in view—continued domination of all Nigerian affairs by the Hausa-Fulani illiterate oligarchy. In the words of Dikibo, Administrator for Degema Province: The new republic of Biafra is founded on a rock, and the gates of Gowon's hell can never prevail against it.[2]

The no-holds-barred language of Radio Kaduna and the Voice of Biafra may be seen from these excerpts from the propaganda war of words that emanated from the Regional capitals and complemented the external programmes now stepped up by both Nigeria and Biafra.

Roving emissaries from both sides, whose lobbying and press con-ferences were to become such a feature of the next two and a half years, began to turn up in a round of the sensitive capitals of the world in search of support for their respective causes. In a radio interview, Ojukwu gave his views on the all-important question of Biafra's chances of recognition,[3] while Gowon warned the O.A.U. that Nigeria would regard such recognition by any member-state as a grave affront and a breach of diplomatic relations.[4] It was at one of the several interviews granted to foreign correspondents at this period that Ojukwu wrote off the Federal army as an 'untrained rabble' of 40,000 men.[5] But above all this concern with recognition, troops, and economic sanctions, there loomed the matter of oil. For here was the common factor for Nigerian, Biafran, British, French, and American alike. Already the inflammatory issue of whether the oil royalties due to the Government of Nigeria on 1 July would be paid, and if so where, was under urgent discussion, and notice was taken of the cautious reply by the Secretary of State for Commonwealth Relations when asked in Parliament whether there was any effective *de facto* diplomatic contact with Biafra.[6] Small wonder that at the beginning of June the *New York Times* felt compelled to sum up the Nigerian situation under the headline 'Hell Bent for Dissolution'.[7]

Back in Nigeria, the sabre-rattling reached a climax when Biafra announced, in a dawn news flash over the radio on 10 June, an invasion

[1] Radio talk on Voice of Biafra, 15 June 1967. [2] ibid.
[3] Quoted in B.B.C. ME/2483. [4] Report in *Egyptian Mail*, 3 June 1967.
[5] *Daily Telegraph*, 3 June 1967.
[6] Reply in the House of Commons, 6 June 1967.
[7] *New York Times*, 4 June 1967.

of the Obudu area by Northern troops.[1] This was denied by Lagos, though one of its Permanent Secretaries did concede that a reconnaissance patrol of the kind that 'puncture the frontier from time to time' had crossed near Ogoja and been fired on by Eastern troops.[2] More news conferences were held in London, where Anionwu and Mbu answered questions on the Biafran platform[3]—their reply to a query on oil royalties echoed the earlier Federal warning that 'If the oil companies were to resort to the device of paying into a suspense account, they would be making a big mistake.'[4] Indications of the lines of thinking of the military leaders at this critical period are to be found in the foreign television interviews given by Ojukwu and Hassan[5] (seen by some observers as a hawk already in flight),[6] and in the significant statement made by Ejoor to the press emphasizing the Mid-West's policy of non-involvement.[7] General Gowon now allocated portfolios to his civilian commissioners. Methods for the crushing of the rebel East were outlined to the foreign press at a special briefing session held in Lagos on 17 June, at which the Federal Government spokesman warned that 'This is the final stage of the showdown, there will be no more concessions.'[8]

And still war did not come. Had military Nigeria perhaps after all not lost its political gift of bringing itself to the edge of the most appalling abyss and then withdrawing at the very last moment? Did it, then, still retain its skill in that perilous art of brinkmanship, defined by the Federal Government itself as 'a game that has come over the years to form part of [our] national character'?[9] True, military movements continued on both sides; students called for arms; decrees were issued touching on such prelude to conflict as territorial waters, exchange control and security measures; and the radio stations of Enugu and Kaduna engaged in cannonades of mutual acrimony that were at no pains to camouflage their depth of passion. None the less, days became weeks and May turned into June, then July; and still the crunch did not come nor some overzealous commando perpetrate a frontier incident (though the Obudu raid of 10 June came close to it).

Indeed, it may not be too fanciful a metaphor to say that while the tinderbox was that of the Nigeria-Biafran confrontation, the actual ignition was sparked off by the final response of the international oil

---

[1] Radio Enugu, 10 and 11 June. *The Times* reported that this message was relayed by Radio Dahomey, a statement that recalls the events of September 1966 in this context.

[2] *West Africa* (1967), p. 806.   [3] *West Africa* (1967), p. 838.

[4] Press conference by Messrs. Asiodu and Ogbu, *Financial Times*, 15 June 1967.

[5] Interviews granted to the B.B.C. on 13 and 15 June 1967 respectively. Unfortunately the B.B.C. has not been able to provide any transcripts. There are references in *West Africa* (1967), p. 836, and in B.B.C. ME/2492–3.

[6] *New York Times*, 14 June 1967.

[7] Reported from Radio Benin, 16 June 1967. In it he laid stress on how the Mid-West would never 'allow its soil to be used as a battleground'.

[8] *The Times*, 19 June 1967.

[9] *Major-General Yakubu Gowon: A Short Biography* (Lagos, 1968), p. 3.

combines to the mounting pressure by both régimes to pay into their respective treasuries the royalties due in July, notably the £7 million payment expected from Shell-B.P. Whether Shell-B.P. paid Ojukwu a token sum or not, and if so whether voluntarily or under duress,[1] the belief in Lagos that they had made such a payment was to be the immediate *casus belli*. The intricate negotiations, diplomatic as much as commercial, of the oil magnates in June 1967 have yet to be disclosed in full. What is already clear, however, is that, with both Lagos and Enugu

OIL   DIPLOMACY

By kind permission of the *New Nigerian*

opposed to any stalling tactic of the oil companies by paying their mid-year royalties into a suspense account, it was Ojukwu who made the first move by ordering on 21 June that all revenue derived from oil exploitation in Biafra, 'whether directly or indirectly' was to be paid into the State Bank of Biafra.[2] Troops were moved to guard the installations at Port Harcourt and Bonny and an ultimatum was issued to the companies that part payment of the biannual oil revenues of some £7m. was expected within ten days.[3] Lagos, reassured by the receipt of its royalty from Gulf Oil but disturbed by Shell-B.P.'s silence, retaliated by issuing its own Petroleum Control Decree. Caught between the devil and the deep blue sea, Shell-B.P.'s international board hesitated in a desperate search for a compromise. As the deadline grew nearer for the payment, a campaign against the company was mounted by the Federation's public information media. Hints of Federal action were backed up by an

[1] See the reports in *Financial Times* 5–7 July 1967. Also that of 29 December 1967.
[2] Radio Enugu, 21 June reported in *West Africa* (1967), p. 872.
[3] *Financial Times*, 1 July 1967.

organized boycott-threat of their products by transport workers and an inspired press attack.[1] Contractually, there was little room for argument against the semi-annual instalments being paid to Lagos; but *de facto* the bulk of the oil exploration and the massively-invested installations were in territory controlled by a militant Biafra. It was reported[2] that oil companies meeting in New York had decided on a compromise by paying to Enugu 57·5% of any royalties, rents and profit taxes derived from operations in Biafra, and the balance into a suspense account.

In New York,[3] as in London, Chief Enahoro was putting the Federal Government's case against secession as an awful precedent for disintegration in the present delicate state of so many African countries' political health. This he followed up with a news conference in which he gave a hint of further stern measures planned against the East and a warning to the oil companies not to pay royalties to Ojukwu.[4] Nor, as it happened, did Shell-B.P.'s sitting-on-the-fence bring any more joy when war broke out, for first the Federal Government threatened them with loss of their concessions in the event of non-payment of royalties,[5] then troops occupied their Bonny terminal, and finally their general manager was held captive in Enugu for ten days apparently as a hostage to royalty payment.[6] Another Federal emissary, hurriedly dispatched abroad as the sands of time ran out, was Dr. Arikpo, commissioned to put the Nigerian case to the East African leaders who, on the initiative of pro-Biafran Zambia, had planned their own summit meeting to work out a solution to the dangerous impasse.[7]

At home, the Federal Executive Council met on 26 June. Armed Service Chiefs saw General Gowon on the following day and Colonel Hassan Katsina, accompanied by two States Governors and senior army officers, flew to Lagos amid hawkish speculations. The Assistant Under-Secretary in charge of the West African desk at the Commonwealth Relations Office hurried out to Lagos, in a manner reminiscent of the none-too-welcome visit of October 1966, to assess the situation.[8] But in none of these cases was any communiqué issued. On 29 June General Gowon released a code of conduct [DOC 116] for his troops for what he described as the 'now inescapable'[9] battle with the East. Radio Nigeria, besides elaborating the army's new code of conduct,[10] put forward

[1] B.B.C. ME/2514, 2515, 2519, and 2524, and Nigerian daily press.

[2] The *Observer*, 25 June 1967.

[3] *New York Times*, 30 June 1967, and *West Africa* (1967), p. 873.

[4] *West Africa* (1967), p. 904.   [5] *Financial Times*, 19 July 1967

[6] He was released on 6 August. See *Financial Times*, 28 July 1967.

[7] *The Times*, 17 June; *West Africa* (1967), p. 873; *Africa Research Bulletin*, p. 797; *Financial Times*, 5 July 1967.

[8] It is not unfair to infer that at this stage straight political considerations were coloured by the overtones of the politics of oil. Symptomatic of the 'oil dilemma for Britain' interpretation (*Guardian*, 8 July 1967) was the *Daily Telegraph*'s warning on 7 July of probable petrol rationing in Britain.

[9] Quoted in the *Guardian*, 30 June 1967.

[10] Talk by John Kumolo, reprinted in *Towards One Nigeria*, vol. 3 (Lagos, 1967).

compelling arguments why there should be no international recognition
of the dangerous phenomenon called 'Biafra' and warned that 'every
single African country, with the possible exception of Somalia, is
plagued by tribal problems' and so had its own built-in Biafran disease.[1]
In a radio talk from Enugu, the commentator warned the East's people
of the Ides of June, for it was, he pointed out, the twenty-ninth of the
month that the Northerners delighted in choosing for their pogroms.[2]
On 30 June Ojukwu gravely broadcast his final warning [DOC 117]:
'Fellow countrymen and women, we have arrived at zero hour.' In reply,
a patient Federal Government set out its five conditions for a negotiable
settlement to welcome Biafra into the Federation [DOC 118]; but as this
offer included Biafra's renunciation of secession and was somewhat discounted by stripping Ojukwu of his military rank and accusing him of
treason, it was unlikely to appeal to bellicose Biafra as an olive branch.
On the expiration of his ultimatum, Ojukwu was reported to have personally sought a token payment of oil revenues from Shell-B.P.[3] At an
interview in Enugu on 6 July,[4] Ojukwu claimed he had indeed won
assurances from the oil companies that taxes and royalties on the
Biafran operations would be paid to his treasury and that a token
payment of £250,000 had already been made by Shell-B.P.[5] But if
Enugu was 'insulted' by this sum, Lagos was infuriated by the report.
Even as Ojukwu spoke, reports reached Enugu of heavy artillery firing
by Federal forces against Biafran troops on the Northern frontier. Civil
war had come to Nigeria.

Although the fighting started in the early hours of 6 July, it was not
until the following day that an official communiqué confirming this was
issued. It stated that fighting had broken out between the Nigerian
army and the rebel forces of the three Eastern States, when the former
were fired on in their defensive positions along the border between the
Benue-Plateau and East-Central States. The communiqué went on:

> The Federal troops immediately returned the fire. The Commander-in-
> Chief of the Armed Forces has since issued orders for the Nigerian Army to
> penetrate into the East-Central State and capture Ojukwu and his rebel gang.
> Already Federal troops have taken Obudu in Ogoja and Obolo near Nsukka
> and inflicted heavy casualities on the rebel forces. Orders have also been given
> for the Nigerian armed forces and the Nigeria Police to take adequate
> measures to safeguard the security of the citizens in the Rivers, South-
> Eastern, and the East-Central States. The Federal Military Government
> recalls that on Friday, June 30th, Ojukwu boasted to the whole world that
> he will wage total war against the people of Nigeria. He immediately un-
> leashed terrorist activities in Lagos and other parts of Nigeria.

[1] Quoted in B.B.C. ME/2504.
[2] Radio talk on the Voice of Biafra, 28 June 1967 (B.B.C. ME/2504/B/8).
[3] *The Times*, 3 July and *West Africa* (1967), p. 904.   [4] *The Times*, 8 July 1967.
[5] *The Times*, 3 July 1967. This was denied by Shell-B.P. (*Daily Telegraph*, 7 July
1967).

Bruno Barbey-Magnum

The rebel régime in Enugu had earlier committed acts of provocation by blowing up the Igumale Bridge in Idoma Division and attacking several villages on the northern side of the border. The villages terrorised included Ofante, Akpanya, Ibale, Ogurugu in Igala Division. The rebel forces have since been cleared from these areas.

For the past six months, while Ojukwu was planning his secession, he and his collaborators carried out unprecedented acts of terrorism and intimidation against the innocent minority people of the Calabar, Ogoja, and Rivers areas for wanting their own States within the Federation of Nigeria. These acts included wholesale murders, pillage, arson, unlawful imprisonment, and the seizure of personal properties and money.

The Federal Military Government appeals to the general public to remain calm and alert and to give their full support to the civil defence organisation in their areas.[1]

The communiqué ended with the slogan that had now established itself as a rallying cry: 'To keep Nigeria one is a task that must be done.' While Lagos radio did not broadcast its first battle bulletin until 9.00 p.m. on 7 July, Enugu gave its announcement that the war had started at 3.00 p.m. that afternoon in the following terms:

Biafran soldiers have beaten off and inflicted heavy losses on troops of the Nigerian Army who early yesterday opened a four-front attack on the Northern frontiers of Biafra. The enemy offensives, led by white mercenaries, were launched on Biafran troop positions at Gakem, Obudu, Nyonya and the Enugu-Ezeke areas in Ogoja and Nsukka provinces.

In all the encounters, troops of the Biafran army repelled the attack and the enemy retreated with heavy casualties. Many Nigerian soldiers were killed in the fighting at the Nsukka border. In this encounter, Biafran soldiers knocked out the enemy offensive position with heavy mortar fire, pushed the Northern Nigeria army back more than five miles into Northern Nigeria, and held the town of Okpo. Intercepted enemy messages indicate that during the battle leading to the capture of Okpo towns, six Nigerian army officers were killed and a whole company of Nigerian soldiers lost. Biafran army casualties were mainly injuries, and the wounded are being treated in hospitals.[2]

Within twenty-four hours, Federal reports were talking of the troops' instructions from the Commander-in-Chief to 'capture Ojukwu and his gang'.[3] The Governor of Lagos broadcast a message warning the Ibo population of the city against throwing in their lot with Ojukwu.[4] A special press briefing was given to the large number of journalists now in Lagos on 8 July (they were not allowed to go to the front),[5] but the main opportunity came when General Gowon held his first wartime press conference on 13 July [DOC 119]. It was here that he emphasized

[1] Statement issued in Lagos on 7 July 1967, to the first wartime press conference. It was reproduced in most of the Nigerian newspapers the following day.
[2] Announcement from Voice of Biafra, 7 July 1967 (B.B.C. ME/2512/B/1).
[3] Radio report from Lagos, 8 July 1967 (ibid.).
[4] Broadcast in Lagos on 7 July 1967 (Full text in B.B.C. ME/2513/B/3).
[5] *West Africa* (1967), p. 911.

the 'police action' nature of the operations,[1] echoing the very term used by the Government of India to explain its march into Hyderabad State in September 1948. From Enugu, Ojukwu called for revenge, urging

that 'for every one of the 30,000 of our people who perished in the Nigerian pogrom, every Biafran with a weapon owes it as a duty to their memory to claim ten Northern Nigerian heads.'[2] In New York, Biafra's special representative issued the first of his many press releases, naïvely laying the blame at the door of Gowon and the Moslem North and calling on the world to denounce the Federal aggression:

To the traditionalist society of the Muslim North, the sword has been the answer to all problems of Nigeria's national development. During 1966, Northerners killed 30,000 Eastern Nigerians living in the North and forced almost 2 million others to fall back into the then Eastern Region of Nigeria. Today they resort again to the sword. General Gowon hopes to subjugate the economic and political development of Biafrans to the traditionalist Muslim society of Northern Nigeria. It cannot work.

[1] 'This is not civil war. This is police action against Ojukwu and his rebel gang.' An editorial in *West Africa* (1967, p. 910), written after a week of war, justified this description: 'The size and nature of the forces engaged make General Gowon's description of the fighting as a "police action" appropriate.' However, the phrase was already in use in the Lagos press as early as 9 July. See also DOCS 92 and 97 for its introduction in March 1967.

[2] Quoted on Voice of Biafra, 6 July 1967 (B.B.C. ME/2511/B/4).

Heads of State of many African governments have repeatedly offered to mediate the differences between Biafra and Nigeria but General Gowon consistently shunned such offers preferring instead the use of force. Whatever the results of today's battle, General Gowon cannot solve the problems of Nigeria and Biafra through the killings and bloodshed of war. He will only help make permanent the open wounds that have existed so long among the national groups of the former Nigerian Federation.

It is hoped that the governments of the world will not condone this route of carnage by giving support to General Gowon's actions. Only by denouncing such brutality can an atmosphere of peace be restored in which the common problems of Nigeria and Biafra can be solved.[1]

The outbreak of the fighting coincided with the arrival of Mr. George Thomson, Minister of State at the Commonwealth Office, to have talks in Lagos on the oil blockade and what was labelled 'the Nigerian oil dilemma for Britain'.[2] There he had to deny a charge by a Federal spokesman that the British Government had been involved in Shell-B.P.'s reported decision to make some form of royalty payment to Biafra.[3] Immediately on his return the House of Commons was plunged into a debate on the oil issue, a topic which over the next two years was to be replaced by an increasingly controversial series of parliamentary debates on the supply of arms. At this juncture, however, H.M. Government deferred a decision on whether to allow Nigeria to purchase arms on a commercial basis.[4]

But Nigeria, having made its name better known in eighteen months of newspaper coverage—not always of the most welcome kind—than it had in sixty-five years of empire and independence, suddenly found its civil war swept off the headlines of world interest almost as soon as it began. A full-scale, nuclear-armed war between Israel and the Arab countries was unarguably of far closer import and of far greater danger to the Western world, because of its higher escalatory and inter-nationalizing potential, than an 'outburst of querulous scrapping between two tribes in Black Africa':[5] the more so when, for all the shout-

---

[1] Issued in New York on 8 July 1967, by Mr. Aggrey K. Oji from his new office as Special Representative of the Republic of Biafra.

[2] *Guardian*, 8 July 1967. See also *Financial Times*, 7 July 1967.

[3] *The Times*, 10 July 1967. The *Financial Times* of 15 July 1967 carried a major article on the crucial ramifications of the oil problem in its political setting. The Nigerian Government's view on the validity of its oil stand is to be found in *Morning Post*, 11 July 1967.

[4] The view held in the United States is that the British Government held up the decision to implement its total arms agreement to Nigeria until it became clear, in August, that the U.S.S.R. was more than willing to provide ample armaments to Lagos—cf. *The Nigeria-Biafra Conflict* (Center for Strategic and International Studies, Georgetown University, Washington D.C., 1969), pp. 20–3.

[5] This became the theme of several *parti pris* articles emanating from America, e.g., Charles Sanders 'The Bloody War between Blacks that Nobody Cares about', *Jet* (Chicago, 27 July 1967), and Dr. Conor Cruise O'Brien's contention that 'the indifference to the tragedy is in part a racial one'—*Pan-African Journal*, vol i, no. 1, 1968 (reproduced from the *New York Review of Books*, 21 December 1968).

ing and the shooting, the military spokesmen of the bigger army had brushed aside the incident as a 'police action' and one of its senior force commanders had confidentially predicted a blitzkrieg requiring 'only a few hours'.

Yet those who read beyond the headlines and between the lines knew better. So, too, in their realistic moments, did the two parties now involved in this most traumatic of all military horrors, a civil war. Clausewitz's maxim of war being the pursuit of political ends by other means was about to be played out to its bloody consummation in Nigeria; only in this instance the war was not to be the traditional one of rallying national cohesiveness through external aggression but rather to take the disintegrating form of internal fratricide. The uncompromising politics of ethnicity and winner-takes-all[1] had now achieved their awful destiny. In angered sorrow, Nigeria's leading poet, Wole Soyinka, allotted to one of the most moving pieces in his collection *Massacre October '66* the terrible title of 'Harvest of Hate', as he surveyed the possible holocaust of the nation's past and future:

> Now we pay forfeit on old abdications,
> The child dares flames his fathers lit;
> And in the briefness of too bright flares
> Shrivels a heritage of blighted future.[2]

Nor was he alone in the years ahead in asking

> That lone question—
> Do you, friend, even now, know
> What it is all about?[3]

---

[1] Achebe has used the concept of the politics of primitive loyalty in his highly apposite novel *A Man of the People*, published fortuitously at the same time as the January 1966 coup. Of these personal politics in action he gives a neat vignette at the end of Chapter 3.

[2] Wole Soyinka, *Idanre and Other Poems* (London, 1967).

[3] 'Civilian and Soldier', ibid.

I

DOCUMENTS

JANUARY 1966—JULY 1967

1.
Special Branch Report of the Events of 15 January 1966[1]

For a List of Documents see Volume II

1. Due to unforeseen circumstances it has not been possible so far, to inform the nation fully of events which took place in the Federation on 15th January 66 at Lagos, Ibadan, and Kaduna, events which were directly responsible for further military action on the 29th July 66.

2. It will be appreciated that events of this nature require prolonged, painstaking investigation. It is realised that the absence of legitimate information on this subject has produced a flood of undesirable rumours and speculation. It is, however, pointed out that without thorough investigation, the wisdom of any premature releases, unsupported by fact, was questionable.

3. Investigations have not yet been completed but it is now possible to put the nation, and the world, in possession of the facts so far collected. The civilian involvement and influence in the whole affair is not, as far as possible, included in this report.

4. It has been established that sometime during August 1965, a small group of army officers, dissatisfied with political developments within the Federation, began to plot in collaboration with some civilians, the overthrow of what was then the Government of the Federation of Nigeria. The plan which eventually emerged from their deliberations was that, on a date not yet decided at the time, the following action would be taken by troops from selected units, led by the ringleaders of the plot:

1. The arrest of leading politicians at Lagos, Ibadan, Kaduna, Enugu and Benin. The plan stipulated that wherever resistance was encountered, the individuals concerned were to be killed.

2. The occupation of key points such as radio and TV stations, telephone exchange and other public utilities, police headquarters and signal installations, by carefully selected troops who were not, however, to be informed in advance of the true nature of their operations.

3. The movement of troops and armoured fighting vehicles to Jebba and Makurdi to hold the Benue and Niger bridges with a view to preventing the movement of any troops, opposed to the plotters' aims, to and from the North.

4. The assassination of all senior army officers known to be in a position to foil, successfully, the conspirators' efforts to topple the governments of the Federation.

5. The eventual take-over of the machinery of government by the rebels.

5. Although the original plan stipulated that the action intended by the plotters should take place, simultaneously, in all the Regional capitals, no arrangements were made to implement these intentions in Benin and Enugu.

6. The date on which the plot was to be put into execution was decided by several factors. These include the return of the Premier of Northern Nigeria from Mecca and the Commonwealth Prime Ministers' conference held at Lagos between the 11th and the 13th January 1966. An additional factor was the possibility that details of the plotters' intentions might have leaked out

necessitating early implementation of the plot. In this manner, the night of 14th–15th January was finally selected.

7. The action, which was well planned and conducted like a military operation was, in its first stages, efficiently carried out.

8. Immediately before 'H' hour, which had been set for 2 a.m. on the 15th January, a number of junior officers were taken into the confidence of the ringleaders of the plot. It is known that a number of these were reluctant to comply with the wishes of the plotters. Confirmed information indicates that it was made clear to those junior officers that those who were not with the conspirators would be regarded as being opposed to them and might suffer death as a consequence.

9. Non-commissioned ranks involved in the night's activities at Lagos, Kaduna and Ibadan, were given no previous information of the true nature of the action in which they were about to be engaged.

10. The activities of the rebels, commencing at 2 a.m. on 15th January 66, resulted in the deaths of the following personalities [names follow]. . . .

13. Details of the events are as follows:

In August 1965 Major Okafor, Major Ifeajuna and Captain O., who were already dissatisfied with political developments in the Federation and the impact of those developments on the Army, held series of discussions between them about the matter and set about the task of searching for other officers who held views similar to their own and who could, eventually, be trusted to join them in the enterprise of staging a military coup d'etat.

14. In September 1965 Major C. of Nigerian Army Headquarters, Lagos, was persuaded to join the group of conspirators, followed in October 1965 by Major C. I. Anuforo also of the Army Headquarters. Major C. K. Nzeogwu was brought in around that time through the efforts of Major Anuforo, an old friend of both Majors Nzeogwu and Okafor. Major Nzeogwu in turn secured the support for the plan of Major A. . . .

15. By early November the recruiting activities of the group were completed and an inner circle of conspirators emerged, consisting of the following officers: Major C. K. Nzeogwu, Major C., Major A., Major D. Okafor, Major E. A. Ifeajuna, Capt. O., Major C. I. Anuforo.

Planning for the execution of the plot started in earnest in early November 1965 at a meeting of the inner circle which took place in Major Ifeajuna's house in Lagos.

16. The plan which eventually emerged from their deliberations was broadly as follows [Here follow the five objectives already set out in para. 4.] . . .

17. Amongst the civilian VIPs scheduled for arrest, the following have been named: (1) The Prime Minister of the Federation, (2) The Federal Finance Minister, (3) The Premiers of Northern, Western, Mid-Western and Eastern Nigeria.

18. Additional personalities scheduled to be arrested in Lagos were the following:

(1) K. O. Mbadiwe	(6) Ayo Rosiji
(2) Jaja Wachuku	(7) M. A. Majekedunmi
(3) Inuwa Wada	(8) Mathew Mbu
(4) Shehu Shagari	(9) R. A. O. Akinjide
(5) T. O. Elias	(10) Waziri Ibrahim

19. Other ranking politicians were to be placed in house arrest pending a decision as to their disposal and eventual fate.

20. Events have shown that other political figures including the Deputy Premier of Western Nigeria, the Finance Minister and the Governor of Northern Nigeria were scheduled to be arrested.

21. The conspirators further decided that the following senior army officers represented a threat to their plans and must be killed during the first hours of the rebellion:

(1)	Brigadier Z. Mai Malari	Lagos
(2)	Brigadier S. Ademulegun	Kaduna
(3)	Colonel K. Mohammed	Lagos
(4)	Colonel R. A. Shodeinde	Kaduna
(5)	Lt. Col. Largema	Ibadan
(6)	Lt. Col. Unegbe	Lagos
(7)	Lt. Col. Pam	Lagos

Note: Lt. Col. Largema was the CO of the 4th Battalion NA stationed at Ibadan. On 15th January '66, however, this officer was on temporary duty at Lagos, staying at the Ikoyi Hotel.

22. For the actual execution of the plan three commanders were nominated, namely:

(1)	Northern Nigeria	Major C. K. Nzeogwu
(2)	Lagos Area	Major E. A. Ifeajuna
(3)	Western Nigeria	Captain N.

23. The latter officer was not a member of the inner circle and was not approached until either the 13th or 14th January 66. He was, however, well known to the conspirators who were certain that, when the time came, he could be relied on to co-operate.

24. The execution of the plan was to take place in three areas only, i.e. Kaduna, Ibadan and the Lagos Area, although many of the participants believed the insurrection to be nation wide. It is a matter of established fact that no violent action took place in either Benin City or Enugu. It has been suggested that these areas were spared because the plotters found it impossible to recruit reliable co-conspirators in these regions. None of the officers has indicated under interrogation that any efforts to recruit collaborators in either Benin or Enugu were made. . . .

25. For the purposes of this report, the execution of the plan is dealt with in three main sections namely Lagos Area, Ibadan and Kaduna. [Only Lagos is included here.] Each section is divided into incidents, showing the identities of officers and men involved. [Not revealed here. See note, p. 124.]

LAGOS AREA

26. The execution of the plan commenced by the calling of a meeting late on 14 Jan 66 of the Lagos members of the inner circle and, for the first time, of junior officers previously selected to take an active part. A number of those present had attended a cocktail party that very evening in the house of Brigadier Mai Malari in Ikoyi. The following attended this meeting which was held in the Apapa house of Major Ifeajuna:

(1) Major E. A. Ifeajuna	(3) Major D. Okafor
(2) Major C. I. Anuforo	(4) Major A.

(5) Major C.	(10) 2/Lt. N.
(6) Captain O.	(11) 2/Lt. I.
(7) Captain A.	(12) 2/Lt. W.
(8) Lieut. E.	(13) 2/Lt. I.
(9) Lieut. O.	

27. Major Ifeajuna addressed the meeting on the subject of the deteriorating situation in Western Nigeria to which, he contended, the politicians had failed to find a solution. He added that as a result the entire country was heading towards chaos and disaster. He next acquainted the junior officers with the inner circle's plans and asked them if they were prepared to assist to put an end to this state of affairs. Major Ifeajuna claims that all present pledged their support for his plans with the exception of Capt. A. who was, however, later persuaded to join. It was made clear to these junior officers that those who were not with the conspirators would be regarded as being opposed to them and might suffer death as a consequence.

28. When, at the end of the meeting it was clear that all present were in support of the rebellion, tasks and targets were issued as follows:

(1) Abduction of the Prime Minister and the Federal Finance Minister
- 2/Lt. O.
- Major E. A. Ifeajuna
- 2/Lt. E.

(2) Killing of Colonel Mohammed and Lt. Col. Unegbe
- Major C. I. Anuforo
- 2/Lt. N.

(3) Killing of Brig. Mai Malari
- Major D. Okafor
- Capt. O.
- 2/Lt. I.

(4) Killing of Lt. Col. Pam
- Major C.
- 2/Lt. O.

(5) Occupation of the Control Room at FT Police HQ, Lion Building
- 2/Lt. W.

(6) Occupation of the P & T Telephone Exchange
- Lt. O.
- 2/Lt. A.

(7) Occupation of the N.E.T. Building
- 2/Lt. N.

But there were apparent last minute change of the plans as will be shown later in this paper. . . .

30. The Federal Guard Officers' Mess at Ikoyi was named as the rallying point for all teams on completion of their tasks.

31. All other officers and other ranks to be involved, either consciously or unconsciously, in the operations were called out for alleged Internal Security operations between midnight and 0100 hours to allow time for the issue of arms and ammunition and the provision of the necessary transport. With the exception of other ranks of the Federal Guard, they were all ordered to report to Headquarters of No. 2 Brigade NA in battle order, with their arms. Ammunition was issued to them by Lieut. O., assisted by Major Ifeajuna. . . .

32. Officers and men moved off to their various assignments at around 0200 hours as planned.

Abduction and Assassination of Alh. Sir Abubakar Tafawa Balewa

33. The party charged with the abduction of the Prime Minister (PM) left HQ 2 Bde at approximately 0200 hours. The following have been identified as members of that group.

    Officers
    (1) Major E. A. Ifeajuna   In command
    (2) 2/Lt. E.
    (3) 2/Lt. O.

    Other Ranks [twenty-two names follow] . . .

34. The small convoy reached the Onikan roundabout at approximately 0230 hrs. and halted near the PM's residence. Major Ifeajuna ordered all troops to leave their vehicles and divided them into 3 groups [details of division follow]. . . .

35. The latter group was given the task of stopping and turning back all vehicles approaching Onikan road. There is no record concerning their instructions as to what action they were to take in the event of any of the drivers refusing to obey the order to turn back.

36. The Major knocked on the gate and was answered by a policeman who was on guard inside. The Major identified himself as an Army officer whereupon the PC granted them access. The Major asked the PC how many men were on guard with him and was told that there were six. The Major then ordered the PC to show where they could be found. The PC agreed whereupon the Major seized his rifle and passed it to one of his men. The PC then led the group to round up the remaining members of the police guard. At the back of the house, i.e. at the creek side, they found a PC armed with a rifle, and accompanied by a police dog. The Major ordered the PC to surrender his rifle, which he refused to do. He was then hit in the face by Sgt. O. whereupon he capitulated and surrendered his firearm. Major Ifeajuna ordered Sgt. O. and Cpl. O. to stand guard over the PC and his dog with orders to shoot both if they made an attempt to abscond or raise the alarm. All the other members were disarmed and taken to the main gate where they remained guarded by Sgt. I. and 3 others. They were all informed that they would be shot if they attempted to escape or raise the alarm.

37. Major Ifeajuna and a few of his men then approached the back entrance to the Prime Minister's residence having secured the police orderly and the stewards under arrest, and broke into the lounge and thence to the Prime Minister's bedroom. A voice from the inside asked who was there. The Major replied by kicking the door open, entering the room and pointing his gun at the Prime Minister and thereafter led out the PM wearing a white robe with white trousers and slippers. The PM was then led away by Major Ifeajuna along Awolowo Road where Ifeajuna had parked his car adjacent to the Onikan Swimming Pool.

Abduction and Assassination of F. G. Okotie-Eboh

38. On arrival at the Onikan roundabout, at approximately 0230 hrs on 15

Jan 66, Major Ifeajuna divided his force into three groups as shown in para 34 of this report. Major Ifeajuna and his group proceeded towards the PM's residence and 2/Lt. E. took his men to the compound of the Finance Minister. When they arrived at the front gate, they found this locked and were compelled to gain access by jumping over the wall. Inside they found a number of civilian guards, about 5, who were armed with bows and arrows. These offered no resistance and were disarmed and placed under guard. At least one policeman was encountered in the compound. He too was disarmed and escorted to the 3-ton truck. . . .

39. 2/Lt. E. then attempted to open the front door but found this also to be locked. He broke one of the panes of glass in the door with his SMG but even then failed to open the door which he finally broke down by kicking it with his boot. He then entered accompanied by the following other ranks [five names follow]. . . .

Before entering 2/Lt. E. ordered his men to walk quietly and to make no noise, a rather superfluous caution considering the noise which must have been made when the door was broken open. They mounted the stairs to the first floor. Arrived there, the 2/Lt. posted one man on the balcony and 3 on the landing.

40. The officer then shouted twice 'Okotie-Eboh, come out'. When this met with no response he entered a bedroom where he found the Minister dressed only in a loin cloth. He ordered the Minister to precede him down the stairs, and the Minister was escorted to the 3-ton lorry. Rumours that the Minister was beaten and otherwise ill-treated on the way to the vehicle have been stoutly denied by all who took part in the operation.

41. Whilst the Finance Minister was being loaded into the 3-tonner, the PM was escorted from his house and placed into Major Ifeajuna's car. 2/Lt. E. joined Major Ifeajuna whilst the ORs re-entered their respective vehicles. The convoy then moved off to the Federal Guard Officers' Mess, stopping en route at a point in Ikoyi where Major Ifeajuna and [another officer] killed Brig. Mai Malari. [See para. 65.]

42. Meanwhile Major C. I. Anuforo, assisted by 2/Lt. N. and the following other ranks [six names follow] . . . proceeded in the two private cars of Anuforo and N. to No. 1, Park Lane Apapa, the residence of Colonel K. Mohammed. This was then being guarded by unarmed nursing orderlies of a Field Ambulance, stationed in Apapa.

43. On arrival Major Anuforo ordered all his party to leave the cars, which had stopped some distance from the house. They then advanced towards the house led by Major Anuforo. They were challenged by Pte. O., then on sentry-go. Major Anuforo told the sentry to 'shut up' and to put up his hands. The Major then gave orders that the sentry and the other 3 members of the guard be banded together in one place in the custody of Pte. U. who, although a member of a medical unit, was then bearing arms.

44. Major Anuforo then went to the front door of the house and knocked. It would appear that he received an answer, because he was heard shouting 'You first come out and see who is knocking'. With the Major at this stage was O. When he received no further answer to his knocking, Anuforo ordered his men to cock their weapons. He then kicked open the door and entered accompanied by [three N.C.O.s].

45. The house was searched until the Colonel was found, in night attire, in his bedroom. The colonel was forced out of the house by Major Anuforo, and the other ranks who had accompanied him, and put into Anuforo's car. It is believed that before being put into the car, the colonel's wrists were tied with a rifle sling which was still in place when later his body was discovered along the Abeokuta road.

46. Before leaving, Major Anuforo instructed the colonel's guard to return to their unit and not to discuss what they had seen with anyone. . . .

47. On arrival at Lt. Col. Unegbe's house Major Anuforo entered the house alone. They heard SMG fire inside the compound and were later ordered to bring out the dead body of the Lt. Col.

48. Whilst the men were inside collecting Lt. Col. Unegbe's body, Col. Mohammed was compelled to leave the car by Major Anuforo. The latter told the Colonel to say his prayers as he was going to be shot. The Colonel did not plead for mercy or remonstrate in any other manner, but quietly prayed until he was shot in the back by Major Anuforo, using his SMG.

49. Col. Mohammed's corpse was stowed into the boot of Major Anuforo's car while the body of Lt. Col. Unegbe was placed on the floor in the back of the car. Anuforo and his men then entered the vehicle which was driven straight to the Federal Guard Officers' Mess. At the Mess the two bodies were unloaded on the ground.

50. Major C. assisted by 2/Lt. O. and [five] other ranks: [names follow] had then accomplished the arrest of Lt. Col. J. Y. Pam and was being guarded inside a landrover in the Mess premises. Majors C. and Anuforo held a brief discussion after which both Majors entered the landrover. The driver was ordered to proceed into Ikoyi.

51. At a point inside Ikoyi the landrover was stopped and both Majors descended. Major Anuforo ordered Lt. Col. Pam to leave the vehicle, which he did. Major Anuforo then spoke to him and told him that he was going to be killed and would do well to say his prayers first. Lt. Col. Pam pleaded but Major Anuforo remained adamant stating that he was carrying out orders. Then without warning Major Anuforo fired a burst from his SMG into Lt. Col. Pam's body, killing him on the spot.

52. Major Anuforo then ordered the NCOs in the landrover to come down and load the dead body into the vehicle. The men, who were shocked and frightened by the killing, were reluctant to comply with this order and refused to leave the vehicle until Major Anuforo pointed his SMG at them and threatened to kill them unless they did as they were told. They then obeyed and loaded the corpse. The party then drove back to the Federal Guard Officers' Mess where the body was off-loaded and placed alongside the bodies of Col. Mohammed and Lt. Col. Unegbe.

53. The assassination of Brigadier Z. Mai Malari as originally conceived in the conspirators' master plan failed.

54. Major D. O. Okafor and Captain O. were present at HQ 2 Bde when troops were being mustered and issued with arms and ammunition. When these arrangements had been completed, these two officers entered Major Okafor's personal car. . . .

55. They drove direct to the Federal Guard Unit in Dodan Barracks, Ikoyi, where, in the meantime, Lt. E. and 2/Lt. I. had roused additional troops and

arranged for the issue of arms and ammunition. By the time the troops were ready for the alleged IS operations Major Okafor and Capt. O. had arrived at the barracks and were at the unit guardroom. . . .

58. The party drove direct to the house of Brigadier Z. Mai Malari at 11 Thompson Avenue, Ikoyi. This is a corner house. . . . On arrival at their destination, the troops were dismounted and divided into three sections.

59. The reserve section under Sgt. U. was ordered to take post in a dark place opposite the house. The three officers followed by their men then entered the compound which was guarded by NCOs and men of 2 Battalion NA. Major Okafor ordered the sentry to call the Guard Commander whom he informed that the situation was bad and that he, Okafor, had come to take over the guard. He instructed the Guard Commander to assemble his men and to take them back to his unit. The Guard Commander, according to some of the ORs interrogated, replied that he could not obey this order as he had received no instructions to that effect. Major Okafor and Capt. O. overruled the Guard Commander's objections and entered the compound.

60. Whilst Major Okafor was pre-occupied with the guard, the telephone in the downstairs lounge of the Brigadier started to ring. Some of the men present, including 2/Lt. I., have stated that the Brigadier came down stairs to answer the telephone. No sooner had he picked up the receiver than a burst of SMG fire was heard in the compound. This was Captain O. firing at a member of the Brigadier's guard. . . .

61. Brigadier Mai Malari, alerted to the presence of Major Okafor's force in his compound by Capt. O.'s burst of fire, dropped the telephone and, followed by his wife, was observed running into the boys' quarters. From there he escaped into the road and, it is thought, tried to make his way to the Federal Guard Barracks.

62. According to the ORs interrogated, Major Okafor flew into a rage when he discovered that the Brigadier had escaped and bitterly blamed the men of the Federal Guard for not shooting the Brigadier when they saw him running towards the boys' quarters. He then ordered all present that the Brigadier must be shot on sight.

63. Major Okafor then jumped into the landrover. . . . He informed 2/Lt. I. that he was going to get 'that man' and to arrange for more troops to come to the Brigadier's house. He drove around the area for some time but failed to find the Brigadier. By the time he returned to 11 Thompson Avenue, Major A. and Capt. A. had arrived there. . . . Major A. had already informed that the Brigadier had been killed and that he had seen his body at the Federal Guard. Capt. O. was overheard telling Okafor that 'the Jack had been killed'. It is presumed that by 'the Jack' O. meant the Brigadier. Major Okafor then informed the troops with him that Brigadier Mai Malari had been killed by men from another unit.

64. The time, by then, was nearly 0400 hrs. Capt. O. was ordered by Major Okafor to proceed to 2nd Battalion in Ikeja to check the situation here.

65. As stated elsewhere in this report, Major Ifeajuna and his convoy, after the abduction of the PM and the Finance Minister, drove towards the Federal Guard Officers' Mess where he made a brief stop and then proceeded towards Ikoyi Hotel, still with the PM in the car. At a point in the Golf Course, adjacent to a Petrol Station, Brigadier Mai Malari was walking towards the

Dodan Barracks when he saw Major Ifeajuna's car. The Brigadier recognised his Brigade Major, Ifeajuna, and shouted and beckoned him to stop. Then Ifeajuna stopped the car and accompanied by [another officer] went towards Brig. Mai Malari and killed him.

66. After the Brigadier had been killed, his body was loaded into the 3-tonner and driven to the Federal Guard Officers' Mess.

67. Although not initially allotted to Major Ifeajuna as a target for assassination, Major Ifeajuna proceeded to Ikoyi Hotel to kill Lt. Col. Largema. On arrival at the hotel Major Ifeajuna told the receptionist on duty that he had an urgent message for Lt. Col. Largema of Room 115. The time was between 0330 and 0400 hrs. He then asked the hotel receptionist to supply him with the master key which can open all doors in the hotel but was told that this was not available. He then ordered the receptionist to lead him to the room in which Lt. Col. Largema was staying, warning the receptionist on the way that he would be shot if he refused to comply with whatever he might be ordered to do.

68. On their arrival on the first floor Major Ifeajuna, accompanied by [another officer], instructed the hotel receptionist to knock on the door of Lt. Col. Largema and to inform him that he was wanted on the telephone. It should be pointed out here that rooms in this hotel have no telephones. These are situated in small alcoves in the corridors. In the case of Room 115, the telephone alcove is only a few paces away.

69. Lt. Col. Largema responded and came out dressed in pyjamas and slightly dazed by sleep. In the meantime the two armed soldiers had stepped back into the corner near the lifts from where they could not be observed by Lt. Col. Largema when he came out of his door. The Lt. Col. then picked up the receiver which was off the hook. At this moment both the soldiers near the lift opened fire with their SMG. Lt. Col. Largema fell down and died.

70. The killers went downstairs and called the third man to come up. Between the three of them they then carried the dead body down the stairs and deposited it on the floor. They then called yet another soldier from the Mercedes car who helped the other three to carry the body to the car. The whole party then drove off.

71. When Major Ifeajuna and party returned to the Federal Guard Officers' Mess he learnt that the GOC was in town and was organising 2nd Battalion NA at Ikeja to attack the rebels. He was then joined by Major Okafor and they drove off together in Major Ifeajuna's car. At the Yaba Military hospital they dropped [another officer] who had been wounded in the encounter with Brigadier Mai Malari. The time then was about 0400 hrs. Major Ifeajuna drove away on to the Abeokuta road. On the way they stopped and Major Ifeajuna asked PM out of the car whence he shot and killed him. When he and Okafor became certain that the PM was dead they left the body in the bush at a point beyond Otta on the Lagos to Abeokuta road. They then opened the boot of the car and dropped the body of Lt. Col. Largema near that of the PM. They then drove on to Abeokuta. On the way after Abeokuta the other two soldiers in the car were dropped and told to find their way back to Lagos whilst Ifeajuna and Okafor proceeded to Enugu. They arrived Enugu at about 1415 hours and proceeded to the Premiers Lodge where they held discussion with Dr. M. I. Opara, then Premier of Eastern Region, after which

they separated and went into hiding. Ifeajuna eventually escaped to Ghana where he was received by the former President Kwame Nkrumah who sent him to Winneba. . . .

72. At the Federal Guard Officers' Mess the corpses of Brigadier Mai Malari, Col. Mohammed, Lt. Col. Pam, and Lt. Col. Unegbe were loaded into a 3-tonner lorry in which was sitting Chief Okotie-Eboh still alive. The time was then about 0330 hours.

73. By this time Major A. and Major C. I. Anuforo were present on the mess premises. Major Ifeajuna having departed, these two officers took command of his men and vehicles. They mounted into Major Anuforo's Peugeot car accompanied by 2/Lt. I. Major A. entered the car.

74. On the instructions of Major Anuforo, the little convoy moved off with Anuforo leading. They traversed Lagos and went along the Abeokuta road. At a given point, unidentifiable by the men interrogated, Major Anuforo stopped the convoy and he, 2/Lt. I. and Major A. left their vehicles. They came to the tailboard of the 3-ton truck and detailed a number of men to take up position in front and to the rear of the convoy with instructions to stop and turn back all approaching traffic.

75. Major Anuforo then ordered the four corpses to be unloaded into the road. The bodies were then carried into the bush on the left hand side of the road. Major Anuforo then observed F. S. Okotie-Eboh still seated in the truck and asked the question, 'Who is that man?' which leads to the belief that, until then, Anuforo was unaware of the presence of Okotie-Eboh in the truck. The Finance Minister replied 'I am Okotie-Eboh'. Major Anuforo then ordered the Minister to step down. The latter complied whereupon Major Anuforo informed him that he was going to be shot. The Minister commenced to plead for his life. This met with little or no response from Anuforo who is reported as having confined himself to stating that he was acting under orders. The Minister was then forced to go into the bush, pushed along by Major Anuforo and Major A . . . to the spot where the bodies of the 4 senior officers had been deposited. Arrived there, without hesitation Major Anuforo killed Okotie-Eboh with a short burst from his SMG.

77. Major Anuforo then returned to the road followed by the others but leaving 2/Lt. I. [and 3 N.C.O.s.], on guard over the five bodies.

78. The convoy drove off and returned later. . . . Four spades were brought out from the landrover and used to dig graves for the burial of the corpses. . . . When this task had been completed they all boarded their respective vehicles and drove off to Lagos. . . .

---

[1] *This is an extract from a very full report which seems to have been prepared by the Lagos Special Branch. This report (which circulated in a highly restricted way outside Nigeria in 1969) later came into the hands of an official of the Co-ordinating Committee for Action on Nigeria/Biafra. This Committee decided to arrange for the publication of the report (see The Times, 6 November 1969). The excerpts here are reproduced by courtesy of the Committee's Secretary, but concern for the career of certain officers named in the original has persuaded the editor of this volume to reduce to rank and initial the names of all officers other than those reliably reported to have been killed since the events of January 1966. For other names, see Nigeria 1966 (Lagos, 1967).*

It is likely that this report [see para. 3] may have been the basis for the White Paper on those events promised by the Federal Government in October 1966 (see DOC *67) but in the event never published as such. The pamphlet* Nigeria 1966 *is not styled a White Paper.*

2.
Nzeogwu Announces Martial Law in the North and Promulgates Ten Decrees[1]

In the name of the Supreme Council of the Revolution of the Nigerian Armed Forces I declare martial law over the Northern Provinces of Nigeria. The Constitution is suspended and the Regional Government and elected assembly are hereby dissolved. All political, cultural, tribal and trade union activities together with all demonstrations and unauthorised gatherings, excluding religious worship, are banned until further notice.

The aim of the Revolutionary Council is to establish a strong, united, and prosperous nation, free from corruption and internal strife. Our method of achieving this is strictly military, but we have no doubt that every Nigerian will give us maximum co-operation by assisting the regime and not, repeat not, disturbing the peace during the slight changes that are taking place. I am to assure all foreigners living and working in this part of Nigeria that their rights will continue to be respected. All treaty obligations previously entered into with any foreign nations will be respected, and we hope that such nations will respect our country's territorial integrity and will avoid taking sides with enemies of the revolution and enemies of the people.

My dear countrymen, you will hear and probably see a lot being done by certain bodies charged by the Supreme Council with the duties of national integration, supreme justice, general security, and properties recovery. As an interim measure all Permanent Secretaries, Corporation Chairmen, and similar Heads of Departments are allowed to make decisions until the new organs are functioning, so long as such decisions are not, repeat not, contrary to the aims and wishes of the Supreme Council. No Minister or Parliamentary Secretary possesses administrative or other forms of control over any Ministry even if they are not, repeat not, considered too dangerous to be arrested.

This is not, repeat not, a time for long speech making and so let me acquaint you with ten proclamations in the Extra-Ordinary Orders of the Day which the Supreme Council has promulgated. These will be modified as the situation improves.

1. You are hereby warned that looting, arson, homosexuality, rape, embezzlement, bribery or corruption, obstruction of the revolution, sabotage, subversion, false alarm, and assistance to foreign invaders are all offences punishable by death sentence.

2. Demonstrations, unauthorised assembly, non-co-operation with the revolutionary troops are punishable in the very manner of death.

3. Assistance to wanted persons, attempting to escape justice, and failure to report anti-revolution activities are punishable in the very manner of death.

4. Refusal or neglect to perform normal duty or any task that may of necessity be ordered by local military commanders in support of the change will be punished by any sentence imposed by the local military commander.

5. Spying, harmful or injurious publications, and broadcasts of troop move-

ments or actions will be punished by any suitable sentence deemed fit by the local military commander.

6. Shouting of slogans, loitering, and rowdy behaviour will be rectified by any sentence of incarceration or any more severe punishment deemed fit by the local military commander.

7. Doubtful loyalty will be penalised by imprisonment or any more severe punishment sentence.

8. Illegal possession or carrying of firearms, arms smuggling, or attempts to escape with documents, valuables including money or other assets vital to the running of any establishment will be punished by death sentence.

9. Waivering or sitting on the fence and failing to declare open loyalty for the revolution will be regarded as an act of hostility punishable by any sentence deemed suitable by the local military commander.

10. Tearing down an order of the day or proclamation, or any other author-ised notices will be penalised by death.

This is the end of the Extra-Ordinary Order of the Day which you will soon begin to see displayed in public.

My dear countrymen, no citizen should have anything to fear as long as that citizen is law abiding and if that citizen has religiously obeyed the major laws of the country and those set down in every heart and conscience since 1 October 1960. Our enemies are the political profiteers, swindlers, the men in the high and low places that seek bribes and demand ten per cent, those that seek to keep the country divided permanently so that they can remain in office as ministers and VIPs of waste, the tribalists, the nepotists, those that make the country look big for nothing before international circles, those that have corrupted our society and put the Nigerian political calendar back by their words and deeds.

Like good soldiers, we are not, repeat not, promising you anything mira-culous or spectacular, but what we do promise every law-abiding citizen is freedom from fear or other forms of oppression, freedom from general in-efficiency, and freedom to live and strive [?reach the sky] in every field of human endeavour both nationally and internationally. We promise that you will no more be ashamed to say that you are Nigerian. I leave you with a message of good wishes and ask for your support at all times so that our land watered by the Niger and Benue between the sandy wastes and the Gulf of Guinea, washed in the south by the mighty Atlantic shall not, repeat not, detract from Nigeria from gaining sway in great aspects of international en-deavour.

My dear countrymen, this is the end of this speech. I wish you good luck, and I hope you will co-operate to the fullest in this job which we have set for ourselves of establishing a prosperous nation and achieving solidarity.

Thank you very much and goodbye for now. [National anthem]

[1] *Broadcast over Radio Kaduna at midday, 15 January 1966. Several of the texts in cir-culation are corrupt, and the one recorded by the B.B.C. (ME/2064/B/1-3) is totally un-reliable on account of poor reception from Kaduna at that hour. The text used here is as near accurate as can be ensured in the absence of the original (removed from the Broadcasting Company of Northern Nigeria office in Kaduna, on Ironsi's orders, according to personal*

information received from a senior official in the news section) and is taken from a verbatim diplomatic signal checked against a taped recording of the broadcast made privately at the time.

3.
Statement made by Dr. Azikiwe to the Press in England, 16 January 1966 [1]

Violence has never been an instrument used by us, as founding fathers of the Nigerian Republic, to solve political problems. In the British tradition, we talked the Colonial Office into accepting our challenges for a *tête-à-tête* to debate the demerits and merits of our case for self-government.

After six constitutional conferences in 1953, 1954, 1957, 1958, 1959, and 1960, Great Britain conceded to us the right to assert our political independence as from October 1, 1960.

None of the Nigerian political parties ever adopted violent means to gain our political freedom and we are happy to claim that not a drop of British or Nigerian blood was shed in course of our national struggle for a place in the sun. This historical fact enabled me to state publicly in Nigeria that Her Majesty's Government has presented self-government to us on a platter of gold. Of course, my contemporaries scorned at me, but the facts of history are irrefutable.

I consider it most unfortunate that our 'Young Turks' decided to introduce the element of violent revolution into Nigerian politics. No matter how they and our general public might have been provoked by obstinate and perhaps grasping politicians, it is an unwise policy.

I have contacted General Aguiyi-Ironsi, General Officer Commanding the Nigerian Armed Forces, who I understand, has now assumed the reins of the Federal Government. I offered my services for any peace overtures to stop further bloodshed, to placate the mutinous officers, and to restore law and order. As soon as I hear from him, I shall make arrangements to return home.

As far as I am concerned, I regard the killings of our political and military leaders as a national calamity. . . .

[1] *By courtesy of Dr. Nnamdi Azikiwe, from among his private papers. Excerpts from his impromptu replies to questions at the press meeting, which was held in the Burbridge Hotel at Boxhill, near Dorking, Surrey, are to be found in the reports carried in the* Sunday Telegraph, *16 January,* The Times, *17 January, and the* Morning Post (*Lagos*), *19 January 1966.*

4.
Statement by Major-General Ironsi in Lagos on 16 January 1966 [1]

The Government of the Federation of Nigeria having ceased to function, the Nigerian armed Forces have been invited to form an Interim Military

K

Government for the purposes of maintaining law and order, and of maintaining essential services.

This invitation has been accepted, and I, General J. T. U. Aguiyi-Ironsi, the General Officer Commanding the Nigerian Army, have been formally invested with authority as Head of the Federation Military Government, and Supreme Commander of the Nigerian Armed Forces.

SUSPENSION OF CERTAIN PARTS OF THE CONSTITUTION
The Federation Military Government hereby decrees:

a. the suspension of the provisions of the Constitution of the Federation relating to the office of President, the establishment of Parliament, and of the office of Prime Minister;

b. the suspension of the provisions of the Constitutions of the Regions relating to the establishment of the offices of Regional Governors, Regional Premiers and Executive Councils, and Regional Legislatures.

APPOINTMENT OF REGIONAL MILITARY GOVERNORS
The Federation Military Government further decrees:

a. that there shall be appointed a Military Governor in each Region of the Federation, who shall be directly responsible to the Federation Military Government for the good government of the Region;

b. the appointment as Adviser to the Military Governor of the Region, of the last person to hold the office of Governor of the Region under the suspended provisions of the Constitution.

THE JUDICIARY, THE CIVIL SERVICE AND THE POLICE
The Federation Military Government further decrees:

a. that the Chief Justice and all other holders of judicial appointments within the Federation shall continue in their appointments, and that the judiciary generally shall continue to function under their existing statutes;

b. that all holders of appointments in the Civil Service of the Federation and of the Regions shall continue to hold their appointments and to carry out their duties in the normal way, and that similarly the Nigeria Police Force and the Nigeria Special Constabulary shall continue to exercise their functions in the normal way;

c. that all Local Government Police Forces and Native Authority Police Forces shall be placed under the overall command of the Inspector-General.

INTERNAL AFFAIRS POLICY
The Federation Military Government announces, in connection with the internal affairs of the Federation:

a. that it is determined to suppress the current disorder in the Western Region and in the Tiv area of the Northern Region;

b. that it will declare Martial Law in any area of the Federation in which disturbances continue;

c. that it is its intention to maintain law and order in the Federation until such time as a new Constitution for the Federation, prepared in accordance with the wishes of the people, is brought into being.

EXTERNAL AFFAIRS POLICY

The Federation Military Government announces, in connection with the external affairs of the country:

a. that it is desirous of maintaining the existing diplomatic relations with other States; and

b. that it is its intention to honour all treaty obligations and all financial agreements and obligations entered into by the previous Government.

CITIZENS TO CO-OPERATE

The Federation Military Government calls upon all citizens of the Federation to extend their full co-operation to the Government in the urgent task of restoring law and order in the present crisis, and to continue in their normal occupations.

[1] *Federal Ministry of Information Release and Government Notice No. 148/1966.*

5.
Special Order of the Day from the Supreme Commander of the Nigerian Armed Forces (General Ironsi) to all ranks, 17 January 1966[1]

Order of the day from Supreme Commander Nigerian Armed Forces to all ranks. As you all know I have been formally invested with authority as Head of the Federal Military Government and Supreme Commander of the Nigerian Armed Forces. In pursuance of this authority, I have suspended certain parts of the Constitution particularly those which provide for the establishment of Parliament, Offices of the President and Prime Minister and Offices of Regional Governors, Regional Premiers, Executive Councils and Legislature. I have decreed as follows:

There shall be appointed Military Governor in each Region of the Federation who shall be directly responsible to the Federal Military Government for good government of the Region.

The appointment as Adviser to the Military Governor of the Region of the last person to hold the office of the Governor of the Region under the suspended provision of the Constitution.

The Chief Justice and all other holders of Judicial appointments within the Federation shall continue in their appointments and that the Judiciary generally shall continue to function under their existing statutes.

That holders of appointments in the civil service of the Federation and of the Regions shall continue to hold their appointments and to carry out their duties in the normal way and that similarly the Nigeria Police Force and Nigeria Special Constabulary, shall continue to exercise their functions in the normal way.

That all local Government Police Forces and Native Authority Police Forces shall be placed under the overall Command of the Inspector General.

I have further announced that in connection with the Internal Affairs of the Federation, the Federal Military Government is determined to suppress the current disorder in the Western Region and in Tiv area of the Northern Region.

That the Federal Military Government will declare martial law in any area of the Federation in which disturbances continue.

That it is the intention of the Federal Military Government to maintain Law and Order in the Federation until such time as a new Constitution for the Federation prepared in accordance with the wishes of the people is brought to being.

That in connection with the External Affairs of the country, the Military Government of the Federation is desirous of maintaining existing Diplomatic relations with other States.

That it is the intention of the Military Government of the Federation to honour all treaty obligations entered into by the previous Government and that it is its intention to honour all financial agreement and obligation entered into by the previous Government.

To this end I order that all ranks support the Head of the Federation Military Government and Supreme Commander of the Nigerian Armed Forces loyally and honestly.

I further order that the rebellion be stopped at once, all troops must move into Barracks immediately; all Arms and Ammunition must be checked and accounted for and any losses and damages reported to Army Headquarters at once.

I further order that Ex-Ministers and Politicians must not repeat not be molested.

Every citizen including Non-Nigerians must move about in complete safety any where in the Federation.

[1] *By courtesy of a Nigerian army officer.*

6.
Decree No. 1, 1966. Constitution (Suspension and Modification) Decree 1966 [1]

DECREE NO. 1

Commencement.

[*17th January* 1966]

THE FEDERAL MILITARY GOVERNMENT hereby decrees as follows:

Suspension of some, and modification of other, provisions of Constitution of Federation. 1963 No. 20.

1. *1.* The provisions of the Constitution of the Federation mentioned in Schedule 1 of this Decree are hereby suspended.

2. Subject to this and any other Decree, the provisions of the Constitution of the Federation which are not suspended by subsection (*1*) above shall have effect subject to the modifications specified in Schedule 2 of this Decree.

2. *1.* The provisions of the constitution of each Region which are mentioned in Schedule 3 of this Decree are hereby suspended.

   2. Subject to this and any other Decree, the provisions of the constitution of a Region which are not suspended by subsection (*1*) above shall have effect subject to the modifications specified in relation to that constitution in Schedule 4 of this Decree.

3. *1.* The Federal Military Government shall have power to make laws for the peace, order and good government of Nigeria or any part thereof with respect to any matter whatsoever.

   2. The Military Governor of a Region—
   a. shall not have power to make laws with respect to any matter included in the Exclusive Legislative List; and
   b. except with the prior consent of the Federal Military Government, shall not make any law with respect to any matter included in the Concurrent Legislative List.

   3. Subject to subsection (*2*) above and to the Constitution of the Federation, the Military Governor of a Region shall have power to make laws for the peace, order and good government of that Region.

   4. If any law—
   a. enacted before 16th January 1966 by the legislature of a Region or having effect as if so enacted, or
   b. made after that date by the Military Governor of a Region, is inconsistent with any law—
   i. validly made by Parliament before that date, or having effect as if so made, or
   ii. made by the Federal Military Government on or after that date, the law made as mentioned in paragraph (*i*) or (*ii*) above shall prevail and the Regional law shall, to the extent of the inconsistency, be void.

   5. Nothing in subsection (*2*) of this section shall—
   a. preclude the Military Governor of a Region from making provision for grants or loans from or the imposition of charges upon any of the public funds of that Region or the imposition of charges upon the revenues and assets of that Region for any purpose, notwithstanding that it relates to a matter included in the Exclusive Legislative List; or
   b. require the Military Governor of a Region to obtain the consent of the Federal Military Government to his making such provision as aforesaid for any purpose notwithstanding that it relates to a matter included in the Concurrent Legislative List.

   6. The question whether a law made by the Military Governor of a Region with respect to a matter included in the Concurrent Legislative List was made with the consent required by subsection (*2*) (*b*) above shall not be enquired into in any court of law.

   7. In this section 'the Exclusive Legislative List' and 'the Concurrent Legislative List' have the same meanings as in the Constitution of the Federation.

Side notes:

Suspension of some, and modification of other, provisions of constitutions of Regions.

Powers of Federal Military Government and Regional Military Governors to make laws.

1963 No. 20.

4. *1.* The power of the Federal Military Government to make laws shall be exercised by means of Decrees signed by the Head of the Federal Military Government.

2. The power of the Military Governor of a Region to make laws shall be exercised by means of Edicts signed by him.

3. A Decree or Edict may be made known to the public by means of a sound or television broadcast, or by publication in writing, or in any other manner.

4. In so far as a Decree published on any date in the Federal Gazette makes provision with respect to the same matters as a Decree which—

a. was made known to the public on or before that date; but

b. has not been published in the Federal Gazette,

the Decree published in the Federal Gazette shall prevail.

5. In so far as an Edict published on any date in the Gazette of the Region to which it applies makes provision with respect to the same matters as an Edict which—

a. was made known to the public on or before that date; but

b. has not been published in that Gazette,

the Edict published in the Gazette shall prevail.

6. Any decree made by the Military Governor of a Region before 16th February 1966 shall, notwithstanding anything in this section (but subject to section 3 of this Decree), be deemed to be, and to have taken effect as, an Edict; and references to an Edict shall be construed accordingly.

5. *1.* A Decree is made when it is signed by the Head of the Federal Military Government, whether or not it then comes into force.

2. An Edict is made when it is signed by the Military Governor of the Region to which it applies, whether or not it then comes into force.

3. Where no other provision is made as to the time when a particular provision contained in a Decree, Edict or subsidiary instrument is to come into force, it shall, subject to subsection (*4*) below, come into force on the day when the Decree, Edict or subsidiary instrument, as the case may be, is made.

4. Where a provision contained in a Decree, Edict or subsidiary instrument is expressed to come into force on a particular day, it shall be construed as coming into force immediately on the expiration of the previous day.

5. In this section 'subsidiary instrument' means any order, rules, regulations, rules of court or byelaws made in the exercise of powers conferred by a Decree or Edict.

6. No question as to the validity of this or any other Decree or of any Edict shall be entertained by any court of law in Nigeria.

7. *1.* The executive authority of the Federal Republic of Nigeria shall be vested in the Head of the Federal Military Government and may be exercised by him either directly or through persons or authorities subordinate to him:

Provided that nothing in this subsection shall prevent any

authority having power to make laws from conferring functions on persons or authorities other than the Head of the Federal Military Government.

2. The executive authority of the Federal Republic of Nigeria shall extend to the execution and maintenance of the Constitution of the Federation, as modified and supplemented by this or any other Decree, and to all other matters whatsoever throughout Nigeria. 1963 No. 20.

3. Without prejudice to subsection (*1*) above, the Head of the Federal Military Government may either conditionally or unconditionally delegate to the Military Governor of a Region executive functions falling to be performed within that Region in relation to any matter.

4. Subject to subsection (*5*) below, all executive functions which immediately before 16th January 1966 were vested in or exercisable by the Governor or any officer or authority of a Region by virtue of section 86 or 99 of the Constitution of the Federation shall be treated as having been delegated under subsection (*3*) above to the Military Governor of that Region as from 17th January 1966.

5. Any delegation effected under subsection (*3*) above (including any delegation which in accordance with subsection (*4*) above is to be treated as having been effected under subsection (*3*) above) may be varied or revoked by the Head of the Federal Military Government at any time.

6. Any executive function which by virtue of any such delegation as is mentioned in subsection (*5*) above is exercisable by the Military Governor of a Region may, subject to any conditions imposed under subsection (*3*) above, be exercised by him either directly or through persons or authorities subordinate to him.

8. *1*. There shall be for Nigeria a Supreme Military Council and a Federal Executive Council. Establishment of Supreme Military Council and Federal Executive Council.

   2. The Supreme Military Council shall consist of—
   a. the Head of the Federal Military Government, who shall be President of the Supreme Military Council;
   b. the Head of the Nigerian Army;
   c. the Head of the Nigerian Navy;
   d. the Head of the Nigerian Air Force;
   e. the Chief of Staff of the Armed Forces;
   f. the Chief of Staff of the Nigerian Army;
   g. the Military Governors of Northern Nigeria, Eastern Nigeria, Western Nigeria and Mid-Western Nigeria; and
   h. the Attorney-General of the Federation.

   3. The Federal Executive Council shall consist of—
   a. the Head of the Federal Military Government, who shall be President of the Federal Executive Council;
   b. the Head of the Nigerian Army;
   c. the Head of the Nigerian Navy;
   d. the Head of the Nigerian Air Force;
   e. the Chief of Staff of the Armed Forces;

f. the Chief of Staff of the Nigerian Army;

g. the Attorney-General of the Federation; and

h. the Inspector-General and the Deputy Inspector-General of the Nigeria Police.

4. Each of the Councils established by this section may regulate its own procedure and, subject to its rules of procedure, may act notwithstanding any vacancy in its membership or the absence of any member.

Powers of Head of Federal Military Government, Supreme Military Council, Federal Executive Council and Military Governors to delegate functions conferred on them by laws.

1963 No. 20.

9. *1.* The Head of the Federal Military Government may, subject to such conditions (if any) as he may think fit, delegate any function conferred on him by any law (including the Constitution of the Federation or the constitution of a Region) to the Federal Executive Council or to any other authority in Nigeria:

Provided that this subsection shall not apply to the function of signing Decrees.

2. The Supreme Military Council may, subject to such conditions (if any) as it may think fit, delegate any function conferred on it by any law (including the Constitution of the Federation or the constitution of a Region) to any of its members.

3. The Federal Executive Council may, subject to such conditions (if any) as it may think fit, delegate any function conferred on it by any law (including the Constitution of the Federation or the constitution of a Region) to any of its members or to any officer in the public service of the Federation.

4. The Military Governor of a Region may, subject to such conditions (if any) as he may think fit, delegate any function conferred on him by any law in force in the Region (including the Constitution of the Federation and the constitution of the Region) to any member of the public service of the Region:

Provided that this subsection shall not apply to the function of making and signing Edicts.

5. Any function of the Head of the Federal Military Government or of the Supreme Military Council or of the Federal Executive Council or of the Military Governor of a Region may be exercised respectively by the Head of the Federal Military Government or that Council or Governor notwithstanding any delegation of that function for the time being in force under the foregoing provisions of this section.

6. References in this section to functions conferred by a law do not include references to executive functions conferred by section 7 of this Decree.

Execution of instruments made by certain authorities.

10. *1.* Where a power to make an instrument is conferred on the Head of the Federal Military Government or the Supreme Military Council by any law, then, without prejudice to the exercise of the power by the Head of the Federal Military Government in person or by the Supreme Military Council itself, as the case may be, any instrument made in exercise of that power may be executed under the hand of the Secretary to the Federal Military Government.

2. Where a power to make an instrument is conferred on the Federal Executive Council by any law, then, without prejudice to the exercise of the power by the Council itself, any instrument made in the exercise of that power may be executed under the hand of the permanent secretary to the department of government of the Federation responsible for the matter to which the instrument relates, or under the hand of the Secretary to the Federal Military Government.

3. Where a power to make an instrument is conferred on the Military Governor of a Region by any law, then, without prejudice to the exercise of the power by the Military Governor in person, any instrument made in the exercise of that power may be executed under the hand of the permanent secretary to the department of government of that Region responsible for the matter to which the instrument related, or under the hand of the Secretary to the Military Government of that Region.

4. Section 23 of the Interpretation Act 1964 (which is superseded by subsection (*1*) above) is hereby repealed. *1964 No. 1.*

11. *1.* There shall be an Advisory Judicial Committee which shall consist of— *Establishment of Advisory Judicial Committee.*

    a. the Chief Justice of Nigeria, who shall be chairman;

    b. the Chief Justices of Northern Nigeria, Eastern Nigeria, Western Nigeria and Mid-Western Nigeria, and the Chief Justice of Lagos;

    c. the Grand Kadi of the Sharia Court of Appeal; and

    d. the Attorney-General of the Federation.

2. The Solicitor-General of the Federation shall act as secretary of the Advisory Judicial Committee.

3. The Advisory Judicial Committee may, with the consent of the Head of the Federal Military Government, by regulation or otherwise regulate its own procedure and, subject to its rules of procedure, may function notwithstanding any vacancy in its membership or the absence of any member.

12. *1.* Subject to this and any other Decree, all existing law, that is to say, all law (other than the Constitution of the Federation or the constitution of a Region) which, whether being a rule of law or a provision of an Act of Parliament or of a Law made by the legislature of a Region or of any other enactment or instrument whatsoever, was in force immediately before 16th January 1966 or having been passed or made before that date came or comes into force on or after that date, shall, until that law is altered by an authority having power to do so, have effect with such modifications (whether by way of addition, alteration or omission) as may be necessary to bring that law into conformity with the Constitution of the Federation and the constitution of each Region, as affected by this or any other Decree, and with the provisions of any Decree or Edict relating to the performance of any functions which are conferred by law on any person or authority. *Modification of existing law.* *1963 No. 20.*

2. It is hereby declared that the suspension by this or any other Decree of any provision of the Constitution of the Federation or of the constitution of a Region shall be without prejudice to the continued operation in accordance with subsection (*1*) above of any law which immediately before 16th January 1966 was in force by virtue of that provision.

3. Any function which is conferred by any existing law within the meaning of subsection (*1*) above on the President or on the Prime Minister or any other Minister of the Government of the Federation or on the Council of Ministers, the House of Representatives or the Senate shall, until other provision in respect of that function is made by an authority having power to do so, vest in the Federal Executive Council:

1964 No. 5.

Provided that this subsection shall not apply to any function conferred by the National Honours Act 1964.

4. Any function which is conferred by any existing law within the meaning of subsection (*1*) above on the Governor of a Region or on the Premier or any other Minister of the Government of a Region or on the Executive Council, the House of Assembly or the House of Chiefs of a Region shall, until other provision in respect of that function is made by an authority having power to do so, vest in the Military Governor of that Region.

5. Any function which is conferred by any existing law within the meaning of subsection (*1*) above, or by the constitution of a Region, on the Provincial Commissioner or Provincial Administrator of a province shall vest in the Provincial Secretary of that province.

Saving for existing offices, appointments, etc.

13. *1.* Subject to this and any other Decree, any court of law, authority or office which was established, any appointment which was made and any other thing whatsoever which was done before 16th January 1966 in pursuance of any provision of the Constitution of the Federation or of the constitution of a Region, being a provision that—

a. is not suspended by this or any other Decree; but

b. is modified by this Decree,

or which was deemed by virtue of any such provision to be so established, made or done before that date, shall be deemed to have been duly established, made or done in pursuance of that provision as modified by this Decree.

1963 No. 20.

2. The suspension by this Decree of section 98 of the Constitution of the Federation (which relates to the constitution of offices and the making of appointments thereto) and of the corresponding sections of the constitutions of the Regions, shall not affect any office which was constituted under any of those sections before 16th January 1966 or any appointment to any such office which was made before that date.

Succession to property, etc.

14. *1.* Without prejudice to the generality of section 12 of this Decree, all property which, immediately before 16th January 1966, was

held by the President or any Minister of the Government of the Federation on behalf of or in trust for the Federation shall on 17th January 1966, by virtue of this subsection and without further assurance, vest in the Head of the Federal Military Government and be held by him on behalf of, or as the case may be on the like trusts for the benefit of, the Federal Military Government.

2. Without prejudice as aforesaid, all property which, immediately before 16th January 1966, was held by the Governor or a Minister of the Government of a Region on behalf of or in trust for the Government of that Region shall on 17th January 1966, by virtue of this subsection and without further assurance, vest in the Military Governor of that Region and be held by him on behalf of, or as the case may be on the like trusts for the benefit of, the Government of that Region.

3. Without prejudice to the generality of section 12 of this Decree or of the other provisions of this section, any contract or other arrangement entered into before 16th January 1966 by any person or authority on behalf of the Government of the Federation or the Government of a Region shall as from 17th January 1966 be deemed to have been entered into on behalf of the Federal Military Government or the Government of that Region, as the case may be.

4. Without prejudice to the generality of section 12 of this Decree or of the other provisions of this section, all promissory notes, stock, bonds and debentures issued under the General Loan and Stock Act, the Local Loans (Registered Stock and Securities) Act or the Government Promissory Notes Act 1960 before 17th January 1966 by the Minister of the Government of the Federation responsible for finance, or by any person acting on his behalf, shall, so far as any liability of the Government of the Federation in respect thereof remained undischarged immediately before that date, be deemed— Caps. 74 and 111.

1960 No. 6.

a. to have been duly issued under the Act in question by the Federal Executive Council; and

b. to have been so issued on the date on which (and with the date of redemption with which) they were actually issued;

and the principal sums and interest represented or secured thereby shall accordingly continue to be charged on the Consolidated Revenue Fund.

5. Subsections (*1*) and (*2*) above shall, with the necessary modifications, apply in relation to rights, liabilities and obligations arising out of a contract or other arrangement as they apply in relation to property.

15.   Without prejudice to the generality of section 12 of this Decree, the Interpretation Act 1964 (except section 2 thereof) shall apply in relation to a Decree as it applies in relation to an Act of Parliament; and accordingly any reference in that Act (except in section 2 thereof) to an enactment shall include a reference to any provision of a Decree. Application of Interpretation Act 1964 to Decrees. 1964 No. 1.

16.   In this Decree, and in any other law—

'Decree' means an instrument made by the Federal Military Government and expressed to be, or to be made as, a decree;

'Edict' means an instrument made by the Military Governor of a Region and expressed to be, or to be made as, an edict;

'the Head of the Federal Military Government' means the Head of the Federal Military Government, Supreme Commander of the Armed Forces of the Federal Republic of Nigeria.

17. *1.* This Decree may be cited as the Constitution (Suspension and Modification) Decree 1966 and shall apply throughout the Federation.

2. This Decree shall be deemed to have come into force on 17th January 1966.

3. Where a power to delegate a function is conferred by this Decree, that power includes—

a. power to delegate the function to a limited extent only; and

b. power to delegate the function to different persons or authorities for different purposes, or in respect of different matters or different parts of Nigeria.

4. In this Decree 'functions' includes powers and duties.

5. For the avoidance of doubt it is hereby declared that any power to make laws conferred by this Decree includes power to make laws having extra-territorial operation.

[1] *Supplement to Federal Republic of Nigeria Official Gazette Extraordinary no. 20, vol. 53, 4 March 1966, Part A. The Schedules are not given here.*

7.
Television Interview with Major Nzeogwu [1]

Nzeogwu: Well, when we went in there [Sardauna's house in Kaduna], there were a lot of guards, policemen and some of us . . . Naturally they tried to shoot us so we shot them first.

B.B.C.: Were there many casualties?

N: Oh, not very many no.

B.B.C.: Can you give me an idea?

N: I don't know. On our side, yes, one . . .? and our injured . . . and the number of policemen I think about three or four have been killed.

B.B.C.: Did the Sardauna himself attempt to fight?

N: Well, no, we didn't see him until the time we actually shot him. He ran away from his house when we fired the first few shots from anti-tank gun into the building, the whole roof was blown off and the place was still alight. Then we went into the rear of the house and there searched it from room to room until we found him among the women and children hiding himself, so we took away the women and children and took him.

B.B.C.: Were the women and children safe, or did they die?

N: Oh, they were safe. No problems at all. We didn't bother much with them. We had to get them out in the front because they tried to surround him and protect him. They were mostly the women of his harem and his children.
B.B.C.: There was one report of one of his wives died. Is this true in fact?
N: Oh, that is possible because we fired many shots, yes, and in the darkness, you know, accidents are bound to occur, yes.

[1] *Transmitted on B.B.C. Television News, 22 January 1966.*

8.
Interview with Major Nzeogwu[1]

Ejindu: I am glad to meet you, Sir. How would you feel if you knew that you are being regarded as a hero?
Nzeogwu: Very pleased naturally. But the truth is that I am not a hero. If there was any famous Major Nzeogwu, I have never heard of him. . . .
E: It is rumoured that you have just finished writing a book, what is it like?
N: Good gracious! Ninety-nine per cent of all the stories you hear in this country are false. I have not written any book because there was nothing to write about. You can only write about a finished job. It would have been a useful means of warding off boredom though, but one did not do it for the fear that the authorities might seize the papers. However I had enough time to make detailed notes on what happened, and one might use them if in future there was any need to write something.
E: Before you went into prison, the cloud was so clear above this country that one could see very far into the future. Now that you are out, what do you see?
N: A job very badly done. If I may borrow your metaphor, the atmosphere is admittedly somewhat cloudy. But I don't think there will be rain. Indeed if you look steadily up you will find that the sun is not yet set and might still peep through. The trouble is that people generally can't tell which is a rain cloud and which is not, and as a result they tend to be confused. As you know there is too much bitterness at present in the country, and in the past people had imagined that they could conveniently do without one another. But the bitterness will clear in the end and they will find they are not as self-reliant as they had thought. And they will long to be together. . . . The same applies to the Northerners. It may take ten or fifteen years for them to come together again but there is no doubt, as far as I can see, that they will. You see, in this world of imperfection, it is sometimes very difficult to capture the ideal. But we can, at least start with the second best.
E: What is the second best?
N: A Confederation.
E: Before I come back to that, may I take you back to January, 1966. What exactly happened at Nassarawa Lodge (the premier's residence at Kaduna) on the night of the 14th?
N: No, no, no; don't ask me anything about that, I don't want to remember it.

E: All right. A lot has been talked and written about the January coup. But how tribalistic was it really in conception and execution?

N: In the North, no. In the South, yes. We were five in number, and initially we knew quite clearly what we wanted to do. We had a short list of people who were either undesirable for the future progress of the country or who by their positions at the time had to be sacrificed for peace and stability. Tribal considerations were completely out of our minds at this stage. But we had a set-back in the execution. Both of us in the North (himself and Major T. C. Onwuatuegwu) did our best. But the other three who were stationed in the South failed because of incompetence and misguided considerations in the eleventh hour. The most senior among them (possibly Major Emmanuel Ifeajuna) was in charge of a whole brigade and had all the excuse and opportunity in the world to mobilize his troops anywhere, anyhow and any time. He did it badly. In Lagos, even allowing for one or two genuine mistakes, the job was badly done. The Mid-West was never a big problem. But in the East, our major target, nothing practically was done. He and the others let us down.

E: You must have anticipated that Gen. Ironsi would let you down in the end. Why did you surrender to him the way you did?

N: I was being sensible. The last thing we desired was unnecessary waste of life. If I had stuck to my guns there would have been a civil war, and as the official head of the Army, he would have split the loyalty of my men. Again, you must remember that the British and other foreigners were standing by to help him. Our purpose was to change our country and make it a place we could be proud to call our home, not to wage war.

E; It has been said that Gen. Ironsi set out to complete your job for you. Was there anything you did not like in his administration?

N: Yes, everything. First he chose the wrong advisers for the work he half-heartedly set out to do. Most of them were either mediocre or absolutely unintelligent. Secondly, he was tribalistic in the appointment of his governors. Thirdly the Decree 34 (which nullified the federal constitution and established a unitary government) was unnecessary, even silly. In fact . . .

E: But you wanted a unitary government?

N: No. Not a unitary government as such. We wanted to see a strong centre. We wanted to cut the country to small pieces, making the centre inevitably strong. We did not want to toy with power, which was what he did.

E: Tell me, what do you think of him as a soldier?

N: I am afraid I cannot tell you that. But I will say that as a person he was very well liked and as the Supreme Commander, his orders were promptly carried out.

E: If he joined the Army as a gunner, he must have progressed as a military strategist?

N: Yes, if he had, he could have done so. But he actually joined the Army as a tally-clerk and was a clerk most of the time.

E: From the present chaos, what type of Nigeria do you envisage?

N: In the first place, secession will be ill-advised, indeed impossible. Even if the East fights a war of secession and wins, it still cannot secede. Personally, I don't like secession and if this country disintegrates, I shall pack up my things and go. In the present circumstances, confederation is the best answer as a temporary measure. In time, we shall have complete unity. Give this country a confederation and, believe me, in ten or fifteen years the young men will find it intolerable, and will get together to change it. And it is obvious we shall get a confederation or something near it. Nothing will stop that.

E: Do you think there will be any war?

N: No. Nobody wants to fight. The East which is best equipped and best prepared for war, does not want to attack anybody. The North cannot fight. And Lagos cannot fight now. If they had attacked the East in August or September, they would have had a walk-over. Today, I think they will be ill-advised to try.

E: An Englishman said to me the other day that the best thing Ojukwu can do is to take over Lagos. Do you think he can do it even if he wanted to?

N: Yes, I think the East is strong enough to do it if they want to. But it will serve no useful purpose. It can only serve to destroy life and property. You see, the effective power does not lie in Lagos but in Kaduna, and if you remove Gowon somebody else will take his place. If you capture the South against the North, all you can achieve is civil war, disintegration and border clashes.

E: Finally, let me come to the controversy over your release. Much as it has been a popular action you have been released by the East government against the wish of the Federal government. What do you say to that?

N: All I can say is that I am happy and grateful to be out. We feel grateful to the Nsukka students for their persistent demand, and to the boys in the barracks for their pressure on the authorities in the East. And to the Nigerian public in general for their concern over our welfare.

[1] *Dennis Ejindu*, Africa and the World, *May 1967. This interview took place soon after Major Nzeogwu's release from prison and shortly before the war started.*

9
Nkrumah's Broadcast on the Death of the Nigerian Prime Minister [1]

Barely two months ago Sir Abubakar Tafawa Balewa was our honoured guest here in Accra. Today he is dead. He died a victim of forces he did not understand and a martyr to a neo-colonialist system of which he was merely the figure head.

Deeply religious, honest and sincere in his personal dealings, striving valiantly to master a situation which was beyond his capacity, he has fallen in a struggle whose nature he never understood.

It is right that we should mourn him. It is right that we should honour his memory. But it is equally important that we should understand the factors which brought about his death.

His early life was spent in Northern Nigeria where neo-colonialism in its earliest form of indirect rule had been developed and perfected since the beginning of this century.

Subconsciously, the ruling classes of Northern Nigeria came to look upon

British imperial power as the source of their authority and they considered independence merely as a method of continuing indirect rule over a larger area by other means.

Here it was that the inherent inconsistencies and contradictions of neo-colonialism showed themselves.

Those who inherited power in Nigeria assumed that they had only to copy the British Parliamentary system in every detail to ensure freedom and justice in Nigeria.

In fact by so doing they only transferred to the parliamentary stage the underlying contradictions of Nigeria as colonially constituted.

What Sir Abubakar and his Government succeeded to was an artificial state created to suit the needs of early twentieth century imperialism.

Nigeria became an entity not because of affinity of its peoples but because the rivalry between France and Britain at the turn of this century made it necessary for Britain to control the Niger and its hinterland.

The subsequent unity of Nigeria was a product of the railways, roads and ports developed by the imperial power which compelled peoples of different ethnic origins and traditions to co-operate irrespective of the fact that bigger ethnic groups that make up Nigeria had closer historical and cultural connections with the surrounding peoples now lying outside Nigeria than they had with each other.

The retiring colonial administration in Nigeria, as in Ghana, insisted on having the final responsibility for the constitution adopted at independence. In Nigeria as in Ghana the State was divided into regions, each region so drawn as to create an ethnic minority problem.

In Ghana, if we had allowed this system to continue we should have had as many political parties as we had regions.

In Nigeria this is precisely what has occurred. A Federal Constitution was imposed upon Nigeria. To make things worse the Federal Government was left with the shadow of authority, but real power rested with the regions.

Behind this facade of different forms, imperialism sought to perpetuate its interests. Sir Abubakar and his Government therefore faced an impossible task. . . .

The tragedy of Sir Abubakar was that he never realised that for Nigeria the choice was either immediate political unification of Africa or Nigeria's disintegration. He scoffed the idea of African unity. Thus he was destroyed by those very pressures and forces which only a continental union government could have eased.

The Federal system resulted in dispersed power and a weak Central Government. Thus each organ of government in the federation in its turn became the prey of neo-colonial interests. Independence widened instead of closing the gap between rich and poor; and, in the circumstances of the imposed Nigerian Constitution opened the door to every type of corruption, bribery and nepotism.

Remarkably honest himself Sir Abubakar was unable to control the forces of evil generated by the system over which he ruled. His failure sprang from the fact that he supposed, if his Government copied all the outward attributes of British political life, all would be well.

He failed to realise that he was being manipulated by neo-colonialism. He was deluded perhaps, despite his personal modesty, by the applause of Western countries who lauded Nigeria as the one true democracy of Africa.

In fact they meant by this that Nigeria was, from their point of view, the easiest of all to influence. However this may be, Sir Abubakar never examined scientifically the basis of the society over which his Government governed. . . . May he rest in peace.

[1] *The* Ghanaian Times, *24 January 1966.*

10.
Policy Statement of the Federal Military Government issued by Nigerian Embassies Abroad, January 1966 [1]

The Military Government of the Federal Republic of Nigeria wishes to state that it has taken over the interim administration of the Federal Republic of Nigeria following the invitation of The Council of Ministers of the last government for the Army to do so.

For some time now there have been escalating political disturbances in parts of Nigeria with increasing loss of faith between political leaders themselves. This crisis of confidence reached a head during the elections in Western Region in October last year. There were charges by the opposition parties of rigging of the elections and general abuse of power by the regional government, in the conduct of the elections. Riots, arson, murder and looting became widespread in Western Nigeria since October. The situation deteriorated and certain army officers attempted to seize power.

In the early hours of the morning of 15th January, 1966 these officers kidnapped the Prime Minister and the Minister of Finance and took them to an unknown destination. The revolt was widespread throughout the country and two regional Premiers and some high-ranking army officers were killed. The vast majority of The Nigerian Army under the command of The General Officer Commanding The Nigerian Army remained completely loyal to the Federal Government and immediately took steps to control the situation.

The Council of Ministers of the Federal Government met and appraised the problems confronting the government. They appreciated the immediate need to control the serious situation which threatened the Federation. They also saw quite clearly a possible deterioration of the situation in the light of developments on Saturday 15th January, 1966. On Sunday 16th January, The Council of Ministers unanimously decided to hand over voluntarily the administration of the country with immediate effect, to the Nigerian Army. This was formally done the same day by the Acting President of the Federation.

Suspension of the certain parts of the constitution
a. Suspension of the provisions of the constitution of the federation which provide for the establishment of the office of President, the establishment of parliament, and of the office of Prime Minister;

L

b. Suspension of the provisions of the constitution of the regions which provide for the establishment of the offices of Regional Governors, Regional Premiers, Executive Councils and Regional Legislatures.

Machinery of Administration of Federal Military Government
a. The Functions of the Federal Military Government shall be exercised by a Supreme Military Council and an Executive Council, details of which will be announced later.

b. The Permanent Secretaries in charge of Federal Ministries shall continue in their office carrying out the normal functions of government and they shall be directly responsible to the Federal Military Government when constituted.

Appointment of Military Governors
a. Outside Lagos, there shall be Military Governments under a Military Governor, assisted by an adviser who is the last person to hold the office of Regional Governor. The normal functions of government shall be carried on by the Permanent Secretaries and they shall be directly responsible to the Military Governments there.

b. The following Military Governors have been appointed: North—Major Hassan Katsina, P.S.C., East—Lt. Col. C. Odumegwu-Ojuku, J.S.S.C., West—Lt. Col. F. A. Fajuyi, M.C., B.E.M., Mid-West—Lt. Col. D. A. Ejoor, P.S.C.
They will be directly responsible to the Federal Military Government and Supreme Commander of the Armed Forces, Federal Republic of Nigeria.

The Judiciary, The Civil Service and The Police
a. The Chief Justice and all other holders of Judicial appointments within the federation shall continue in their appointments, and the Judiciary shall continue to function under their existing statutes.

b. All holders of appointment in the civil service of the federation and of the regions shall continue to hold their appointments and to carry out their duties in the normal way, and similarly the Nigerian Police Force and the Nigeria Special Constabulary shall continue to exercise their functions in the normal ways.

c. All Local Government Police Forces and Native Authority Police Forces shall be placed under the overall command of the Inspector-General.
    The Federal Military Government has also made the following announcements:

Internal Affairs Policy
a. That it is determined to suppress the current disorders in the Western Region and in the Tiv area of the Northern Region,

b. That it will declare martial law in any area of the Federation in which disturbances continue,

c. That it is its intention to maintain law and order in the Federation until such time as a new constitution for the Federation, prepared in accordance with the wishes of the people is brought into being.

External Affairs Policy

a. That it is desirous of maintaining existing diplomatic relations with other states.

b. That it is its intention to honour all treaty obligations entered into by the previous government.

c. That it is its intention to honour all financial agreements and obligations entered into by the previous government.

d. That it welcomes all honest and genuine businessmen who are prepared to invest in the country in mutually beneficial projects, and

e. That it re-affirms the assurances given by the previous government that there are no plans to nationalise industries, and that there should be no doubt in the minds of entrepreneurs that Nigeria will provide adequate compensation in the event of any industry being nationalised in the future.

The Federal Military Government wishes to state that the voluntary transfer of powers from the last government to the Federal Military Governments has been popularly accepted by the people of Nigeria. All political parties in the country have similarly acclaimed this transfer. Natural rulers, leaders of religion, trade unions, student and other voluntary organisations have sent messages of congratulations to the Military Government.

The Federal Military Government wishes to assure all friendly states that its foreign policy will continue to be based on non-alignment, respect for the sovereignty of all states and friendly relations with all countries.

[1] *By courtesy of a Nigerian Foreign Affairs official. The document is dated 23 January 1966.*

11.
Major Hassan Katsina's First Press Conference as Military Governor of the North, 18 January 1966 [1]

Fellow country-men and women. I, Major Hassan Usuman Katsina, having been appointed by the Supreme Military Commander as the Military Governor for the Northern Provinces of the Republic of Nigeria wish to address you all on the responsibilities falling on all of us and the new philosophy we intend to follow.

It is our intention to build the nation on the foundation of honesty and hard work and to bring about unity among all Nigerians living in whatever part of the country with respect, love and understanding towards one another. Everyone must realise that we are one nation irrespective of the tribe from which each of us originates. At our present stage of development we need not be divided by tribal unions, political parties or trade unions. It is our experience in the past that such bodies had not worked for the common good but for sectional interest. I do not need their greetings or congratulations as this is not the time for jubilation or flattery but for hard work and selfless service. This is the way to reach our goal in satisfying the aspirations of the common man.

My assumption of Office does not change the administrative structure, and the machinery set up by my colleague, Major Nzeogwu at the end of the last Government. Civil Servants will continue to run the civil administration under my authority. I warn them however that they must be honest and show in everything they do concern for the rights of the common man. They are not masters but servants of the public.

In local administration the Native Authority system will continue but reform will be introduced. Native Authorities must cut down on unnecessary expenses, do away with redundant staff and use public funds correctly and efficiently. Misuse of authority will not be tolerated. Administrative Officers who are charged with advising Native Authorities in the Provinces and seeing to it that Government directives are carried out must wake up to their duty with vigour and zest.

The new Government will support private initiative in industry, commerce and agriculture. However we must wipe away immediately the attitude of the past when it was regarded that Government money could be borrowed with no intention of repaying. In future the Government will only help businessmen who are serious and honest. The Government will also see to it that past debts arising from loans by public corporations are repaid according to the terms of the loans. Those who refuse to pay will have to face the consequences. Public funds must be spent wisely and honestly. The new Government has no intention to be vindictive but it will at the same time watch closely the activities of people who had in the past engaged in corrupt practices. Any subversive activity on their part will be severely dealt with. The Military Command will maintain vigilance.

I said at the beginning that I need your support. I expect this from those in the public services whether Government or Native Authorities or the private sector but what I particularly pray for is the support of the ordinary private Nigerian citizen.

Jama'a Allah shi ba mu alheri. [May God be merciful to us.]

₁ *Northern Ministry of Information Release 49/1966.*

12.
'Away with the Old Guard'—First Speech by Lt.-Col. Ojukwu, Military Governor of the East, 25 January 1966[1]

This is a crucial moment in the history of our country—the dramatic culmination of ten wasted years of planlessness, incompetence, inefficiency, gross abuse of office, corruption, avarice and gross disregard of the interests of the common man.

The financial institutions and statutory corporations have been completely misused for the self aggrandisement of a number of adventurers in positions of power and influence.

Under the system, mediocrities were transplanted overnight from situations of obscurity into positions of affluence and corrupt power.

Key projects in the National Development Plan were not pursued with necessary vigour. Instead of these, palaces were constructed for the indulgence of ministers and other holders of public offices—men supposed to serve the interest of the common man.

Expensive fleets of flamboyant and luxurious cars were purchased.

Taxpayers' money was wasted on unnecessary foreign travel by ministers, each competing with the other only in their unbridled excesses.

This has disrupted the economy, depressed the standard of living of the toiling masses, spiralled prices and made the rich, richer and the poor, poorer.

Internal squabbles for parochial and clannish patronage took the place of purposeful co-ordinated service in the service of the people.

Land, the basic heritage of the people, was converted into the private estates of rapacious individuals who, thus trampling on the rights of the people, violated their sacred trust under this system, the public service was being increasingly demoralised.

Nepotism became rife, tribalism became the order of the day in appointments and promotions mere lip service was paid to honesty and hard work.

Under the system, efficiency inevitably declined.

All this led inevitably to the complete loss of moral and political authority by the former regime.

You are aware of the dramatic events of the past few days which led to the self-liquidation of the Federal Government and its abandonment of power to the Armed Forces.

You are also aware of the immediate steps taken by the Supreme Commander to set up an effective administration and to repair the damage done to the country by gangster politicians, and to set the country on the path of true progress and greatness—the creation of the Supreme Military Council, the appointment of Military Governors to administer the former regions under the direction of the Supreme Commander and Head of the Executive Council.

In the Eastern Provinces, all executive powers are now vested in the Military Governor. In the day-to-day business of government, I have appointed an Executive Committee which will assist me. The Executive Committee will be composed of:

1. The Military Governor, 2. The Commanding Officer of the Army in the Eastern Provinces, 3. The Commissioner of Police, 4. The Chief Law Officer, 5. The Chief Secretary, 6. The Permanent Secretary, Ministry of Finance.

All other permanent secretaries will be co-opted to participate in the discussions of the business of their respective ministries.

It is our intention to stamp out inefficiency, corruption and dishonesty in all facets of public life, to create the consciousness of national unity and to lead the citizens of Nigeria as one disciplined people in a purposeful march to maximum realisation of the country's potential.

The citizens of Nigeria must, therefore, realise that we are determined to turn our back forever on the unproductive drift of yesteryears. To this end, the following will come into immediate effect:

All the powers and functions formerly vested in or exercised by the former

Governor, Premier and Ministers have been vested in and will be exercised by the Military Governor. The Regional Public Service Commission shall no longer be responsible for the appointment and promotions of senior staff in the public service of the Eastern Provinces.

In future, the Public Service Commission will act in an advisory capacity to the Military Governor in relation to the appointment, promotion and discipline of senior members of the public service of the Eastern Provinces.

All Provincial Assemblies in Eastern Nigeria are abolished.

The former Regional Governor, Premier, Ministers, Provincial Commissioners and Parliamentary Secretaries shall, if they have not already done so, vacate their former official residences and surrender any Government property, including cars in their possession forthwith.

The post of Agent-General for Eastern Nigeria in the United Kingdom is abolished.

All photographs of the former President, Prime Minister, Regional Governors, Premiers and Ministers shall be immediately removed from all public buildings in the Eastern Provinces.

These photographs shall be replaced with the photograph of His Excellency, the Head of the Military Government and Supreme Commander of the Nigerian Armed Forces, Major-General J. T. U. Aguiyi-Ironsi.

No person in the Eastern Provinces, except the Military Governor, shall fly any flag on cars and private residences.

The salaries of all members of boards of statutory corporations and companies solely owned by the Government of Eastern Nigeria not exercising executive or administrative functions are hereby suspended until further notice.

They will, however, be entitled to their present sitting allowances.

All debtors to Government or Government sponsored financial institutions are warned in their own interests to liquidate such debts without delay in order to avoid the use of drastic measures in their recovery.

The public is hereby warned against bribery, nepotism and other forms of corruption in public life. This warning is directed particularly to the holders of public offices in the Police Force, Civil Service, Judiciary (including Customary Court judges), local government bodies, statutory corporations and trade unions.

All doctors, pharmacists, nurses and other workers in hospitals are reminded of their responsibility for the health of the members of the public.

The Military Government will not tolerate acts of irresponsibility, dereliction of duty and corruption in Government hospitals, maternities, health centres and dispensaries.

The Military Government will deal firmly with any case that comes to its notice.

The public is warned against careless talk, acts and gestures contemptuous of all sections of the public, calculated to incite or cause disaffection among any section of the community.

Such acts will be deemed to constitute an offence against public order and will be dealt with summarily with firm measures.

The activities of the regional and provincial scholarship boards are suspended until further notice. In future scholarships will be awarded purely on the basis of merit to enable us solve our urgent high-level manpower needs.

The law establishing the University of Nigeria, Nsukka, will be reviewed to ensure that matters academic are left entirely in the hands of the academicians subject to the overall direction of the country's manpower needs as recommended by the National Universities Commission.

The appointment of chairmen and members of statutory corporations will be reviewed and any future appointment or re-appointment will be based entirely on qualifications and merit.

I hereby call on all citizens, whether working in Government or private organisations to give to the Military Government both loyalty and hard work.

The Military Government will regard disloyalty, inefficiency, bribery, corruption, nepotism, abuse of public office, and squandering of public funds as acts of sabotage against the regime and will not hesitate to invoke summary measures against any offenders in any position.

Finally, I thank you for your widespread expressions of goodwill and support. Fellow citizens, I shall count on you.

[1] Daily Times, *26 January 1966;* The Role of the Federal Military Government of Nigeria Today (*Yaba, 1966*), *pp. 18–20. The speech was broadcast live by Enugu E.N.B.S. at 7.00 p.m. on 25 January 1966.*

13.
First Speech of the Military Governor of the Mid-West (Lt.-Col. Ejoor), 26 January 1966[1]

I have now had time to examine the various administrative agencies operating under the previous Government, both at Headquarter level and at the level of Local Government Councils. I have also looked into the machinery for the administration of Boards and Corporations in Midwestern Nigeria. I now record the following observations and Decree as hereunder:

a. I decree that here, in Midwestern Nigeria, there shall be an Executive Committee presided over by myself, as Military Governor. Subject to, and under the Supreme Council, this Committee constitutes the final authority and power in respect of decisions affecting Midwestern Nigeria.

b. In addition to myself as its President, the composition of this Committee will be as follows: The Chief Law Officer, The Second Senior Military Officer in station, Secretary to the Military Government, Permanent Secretary, Ministry of Finance, Permanent Secretary, Ministry of Economic Development, Permanent Secretary, Ministry of Establishments, and The Commissioner of Police. Additionally, the Permanent Secretary whose submissions are at any particular meeting being discussed will, for the purpose of that discussion, be coopted as member of the Committee.

I further decree:

a. that the decisions of the Public Service Commission will now be in the form of recommendations to me. I propose, however, to delegate to the Commission power to take final decisions in respect of certain categories of appointments.

b. I further decree

that the following powers shall be vested in a Recruitment Committee:

  i. The power to appoint (including appointment on promotion transfer or secondment) to any post whether established or unestablished the initial basic salary of which is less than £240 per annum.

  ii. The power to appoint (including appointment on promotion or transfer) daily-rated employees.

  iii. The power to confirm or terminate the probationary appointment of any officer whose initial basic salary is less than £240. . . .

c. I also decree:

that all recruitments shall be initiated by means of open advertisement which, in the case of recruitments by the Recruitment Committee shall issue from the Ministry of Establishments, on behalf of all Ministries/Departments.

I further decree that:

the Midwestern Nigeria London Office will be closed, and the responsibilities and duties it now carries will be taken over by the Nigerian High Commission. Immediate steps will be taken to wind up the Agency-General.

In place of elected members, all local government councils in the Region have Management Committees. These comprise persons selected because of their political affiliation. I am convinced that this arrangement is not in the best interest of the development of local government in the Region. Little wonder that a majority of these councils are either impotent or grossly inefficient.

I decree that all Management Committees of Local Government Councils will be abolished with immediate effect. In place of these, Administrative Officers of experience will be selected and be posted as Sole Administrators.

[The Local Authorities] comprise Local Education Authorities, Joint Water Boards, Land Trustees, and Town Planning Authorities [and each] has a body of officials who operate the organisation with expert advice from the appropriate ministries. Over and above these officials, there is in each case an appendage of politicians, who have converted the function of determining the political implication of the organisation's actions into a full time job.

I now decree that all these groups of politicians in these Institutions be suspended. The officials of the Institutions, with supporting advice and guidance from the appropriate ministries, will carry on the work of the Institutions.

I am not satisfied that political affiliation is a fair yard-stick for the composition of Tax Assessment Committees. The existing Committees have been got together on that basis. A machinery for fiscal purposes cannot function efficiently with such composition.

I hereby suspend all existing Assessment Committees. In due course a Tax Assessment Machinery able to generate confidence and to alert all and sundry to their responsibility to pay tax will be set up. . . .

I further decree:

that all Chairmen, Executive Directors and Members of all Boards and Corporations will henceforth cease to have any day to day functions in respect of these organisations. Instead, they will meet not more than once monthly to deliberate on the basis of agenda presented to them by the General-Manager or Secretary of these organisations, after clearance with the

Permanent Secretary of the relevant Ministry. Accordingly, all Chairmen, Executive Directors and Directors cease with immediate effect to be entitled to salaries, but will be eligible for sitting fees and expenses in respect of transport to place of meetings.

that each Corporation, Board and Commission shall operate under the detailed guidance of the Permanent Secretary of the Ministry under whose aegis such Corporation, Board or Commission functions. For this purpose I propose to inject officials and experts in business into each organisation to assist so as to enhance its performance.

I further decree:

that all political functionaries suspended will now be checked out of Government quarters, if this has not already been done. All government properties in those quarters shall be taken on charge by the Ministry of Works.

I decree also:

that only the National Flag may be flown on public buildings in Midwestern Nigeria. No flags of any description may be flown on private buildings, premises or cars, excepting that the Commissioner of Police may fly the Police Flag on his official car. The only vehicle that may fly the National Flag is the Military Governor's Car.

For the avoidance of doubt I want to make it clear that the above decrees do not relate to the Regional Tax Board, the Board of Education, and the Scholarship Board. I propose at a later date to deal with these.

At a later date I will issue an appropriate decree concerning Customary Courts.

All debtors to the Midwest Government and its agencies are advised to maintain their repayment agreements. Any defaulters will have themselves to blame.

[1] *Mid-West Ministry of Information Release 70/1966.*

14.
Policy Statement by the Military Governor of the North, 11 February 1966 [1]

Fellow country-men, when I spoke to you recently I told you that the new regime proposed to introduce certain reforms for the good government and interest of all our people. Since my first broadcast to you I have visited all thirteen provinces in Northern Nigeria in order to explain to the people through Government and Native Authority channels the new order to dispel rumours and so ensure that people live in peace and happiness and without fear. Twice in the three weeks since the setting of the new regime, I have also had to join my colleagues in the Supreme Council at Lagos to discuss matters of importance to our country. In the time available, I and my advisers have given thought to the many urgent matters which face us including the reforms which are necessary to be made.

It is our view that there is a number of fundamental reforms which we must tackle with urgency. For example we have the Native Courts System, the Native Authority Police and Native Authority Prisons. These three important departments affect the lives of all of us. Upon the efficiency and impartiality of these organs depend the happiness and welfare of all of us and so it is important for us to begin our reforms with them.

After very careful consultations I have decided that the following reforms will be made:

Firstly, all Native Courts will be taken over from the hands of the Native Authorities and merged with the Judiciary so that they will become independent of the influence of both the Government and the Native Authority. As a first step towards this, I am placing the Office of the Commissioner for Native Courts under the supervision and control of the Chief Justice.

Secondly, the Native Authority Police Forces will remain under the operational control of the Inspector-General of Police as already announced by the Supreme Commander. Steps are being taken to integrate them with the Nigeria Police in due course.

Thirdly, arrangements will be made for all Native Authority Prisons to be handed over to the Federal Government.

These changes will enable the Native Authorities to concentrate their energies and resources on the provision of Social Services which are closer to the life of the citizen.

Now I turn to the Government Agencies which need immediate review. I am referring to Corporations and Boards like the Marketing Board and the Development Corporation. The political appointees to these Boards have been dismissed. The membership of these Boards will be reconstituted as soon as possible, but it is necessary to examine the past activities and methods of these Boards and Corporations in order that a more efficient and honest system of operation will be introduced. I have, therefore, decided that teams of experts will be set up to examine their activities as is necessary and to make recommendations to me for desirable reforms.

Fellow country-men, apart from the changes I have mentioned, there are others under consideration. Decisions on them will be announced in due course. I now expect both Government and Native Authorities to work with increased vigour and efficiency. I hope that every man and woman will respond by participating readily in the spirit of self-help whenever called upon to do so.

I started this broadcast by informing you that I have completed my visits to all Provinces. I would now like to tell you how very impressed I have been with the warmth and simplicity of the reception I have received everywhere. What is more important, I have been most impressed by your calm and responsible behaviour. It is clear that there are hopeful expectations for a better future everywhere. I have no doubt that with your cooperation we shall be able to satisfy our aspirations.

I end by thanking you all most sincerely for the support and encouragement you have given me thus far. I ask you again to continue to give me this support so that together we can build a happy and prosperous nation, free from fear, free from hate. With your support and the guidance of God, I have no doubt, Nigeria will succeed.

[1] *Northern Ministry of Information Release No. 140/1966. The speech was broadcast from Kaduna on the evening of 11 February 1966.*

15.
Letter from the British High Commissioner, Lagos, sent to all British Nationals in Nigeria[1]

The authorities in the period immediately following the events of 15 January, took vigorous measures to maintain law and order and restore conditions to normal. In the subsequent week there has been complete calm throughout the Federation. The disturbances in the West have come to an end, and travel has become safe again on roads that have long been dangerous. The North, East and Mid-West have been tranquil with life proceeding as usual. The Federal and Regional departments are functioning normally and the new machinery of government seems to have slipped into gear smoothly without disruption. You will have observed what widespread and hearty applause and support has been given to the new regime throughout the country. If the Military Government succeeds in its object of proceeding effectively and quickly with economic and social development with attention to the needs of the under-privileged, it is likely to retain great popularity.
2. The Military Government has emphasised its desire that relations with Britain should be maintained on the usual cordial basis, and the British Government reciprocate this wish. We can therefore all proceed on the basis that business will be as usual, and that the value of the contribution of expatriates in the life of Nigeria will continue to be recognised.
3. The Military Government have indeed on several occasions emphasised the value that Nigeria continues to attach to the contribution of expatriate interests to the economy. And the Government's appreciation of the services of expatriates in other fields remains unchanged. Business and other expatriate interests will benefit from the achievement of the Government's policies of eliminating abuses and the authorities can justifiably look to us for all possible support. The British Government for their part will continue to give all possible backing to the Nigerian Development Plan. It is helpful that the transition should come at a time when economic conditions are fairly buoyant, the danger of loss of the cocoa crop in the West having been averted.
4. I hope that relatives of yourself and members of your staff and of your wives have not been made unnecessarily anxious by some of the more sensational press reports that appeared at home. I arranged for the B.B.C. to broadcast that there had been no attack on expatriates, and the C.R.O. has been giving general reassurance in reply to enquiries.
5. We are fortunate in Nigeria in the friendly and relaxed relationship which expatriates enjoy with Nigerian citizens; I know that you will agree that this legacy of the good relations of the past underlines our obligation to take special care not to offend susceptibilities in any way by careless talk.
6. Now that conditions are restored to normal, it is no longer necessary to restrict journeys. There are still a number of road blocks to help in the apprehension of wanted persons: and care should continue to be exercised to comply with the requests of those manning them.

[1] *By courtesy of the British High Commission, Lagos. The letter was dated 28 January 1966.*

16.
Policy Broadcast by General Ironsi, 28 January 1966 [1]

Fellow Citizens

When I assumed office, I appealed to you for your co-operation in restoring law and order. I am happy that you have responded magnificently. To-night I wish to outline the policies and programmes of my Government for the Federation. All Nigerians want an end to Regionalism. Tribal loyalties and activities which promote tribal consciousness and sectional interests must give way to the urgent task of national reconstruction. The Federal Military Government will preserve Nigeria as one strong nation. We shall give firm, honest and disciplined leadership. There are a number of urgent problems now facing us. In solving them I shall count on your continued cooperation and hard work.

The Federal Military Government will stamp out corruption and dishonesty in our public life with ruthless efficiency and restore integrity and self-respect in our public affairs. In the public service efficiency and merit will be the criteria for advancement. The Government will study very carefully the questions posed by those who recklessly abused their public offices through the acquisition of state lands and financial deals.

The Federal Military Government will introduce administrative reforms. It will also restore the laid-down procedures for tenders and awards of contracts so as to eradicate corrupt practices and ensure maximum benefit from the expenditure of tax payers' money.

The Government realizes that a few unscrupulous foreign and Nigerian business men and contractors have contributed their own share to the tragic plunders and waste of the past. There will be no place in the new order for such profiteers and adventurers. The Government, however, reassures all honest business men and genuine investors who are in the majority and who can contribute to the country's development that they are most welcome.

An end will be put to extravagance and waste in public expenditure. I have already reduced the number of Federal Ministries and I have ordered the Military Governors to take similar steps in their areas. I have abolished the offices of Agents-General in London. Overseas tours by officials in Government, public corporations and other public bodies will be drastically curtailed. In future only essential tours will be undertaken by such officials.

Public corporations all over the country have been a source of public waste. As a first step towards reforming these statutory bodies and state-owned companies, all political appointees and other non-official members of their boards shall cease to be members as from the 31st of January, 1966. The Boards will be reconstituted to ensure that each statutory body and state-owned company is properly managed.

The major challenges facing us are the rapid development of the Nigerian economy and the problem of unemployment. The Government will pursue with vigour the implementation of the Six-Year Development Programme and see to it that key projects like the Iron and Steel Complex are started without undue delay. Prestige projects such as fanciful office buildings and palatial residential quarters will be discontinued. . . .

We will ensure that objective economic criteria are used in determining the policies of all the Marketing Boards in the country to ensure more effective contribution from the Marketing Boards to the funds available for development. Government will take appropriate steps to increase food production and bring prosperity to the rural areas.

We realize the important role of industrialization in the rapid development of the economy. We will ensure that industrial development is co-ordinated on a national basis to avoid wasteful duplication of industrial projects. Where Government is a partner in an industrial venture, it will ensure that it is profitable and that it promotes genuine development. We also recognize the important role of private investment. To this end the Government is revising the legislation relating to incentives in order to assist genuine private business men wishing to establish projects of benefit to the economy.

Every effort will be made to increase revenue and to observe strict control in the disbursement of public funds to increase the funds available for development.

The Government will give priority to the construction of adequate modern housing for the low-income groups in urban areas. Work will proceed immediately on the long delayed low-cost housing scheme for workers in the Lagos area. Government houses occupied by former Ministers, Chairmen of statutory bodies and other political appointees will now be utilized in the public interest.

The Government will re-appraise educational policies to ensure high and uniform standards throughout the country. Our Universities will be re-orientated to serve the genuine needs of our people. As regards health, the Government will ensure efficiency in the management of hospitals and check abuses by doctors, pharmacists and other health workers.

I stress once again the need for hard work and honesty from all Nigerians. Flattering messages, political jobbery and such corrupting activities have no place in the new Nigeria. As regards political activities, we cannot afford to continue with sterile political strife and mutual recriminations. I have therefore ordered that there shall be no display of party flags or symbols and no shouting of political slogans. Fellow citizens, this is a unique opportunity to build a strong united Nigeria. We are determined to succeed and with your support we shall succeed.

[1] *Federal Nigeria, vol. ix, nos. 1–4, 1966, pp. 3–4. The speech was broadcast by the N.B.C. on the evening of 28 January 1966.*

17.
Ironsi's Press Conference of 21 February 1966 [1]

Gentlemen of the Press,

I have requested this meeting in order to have the opportunity of speaking to you about matters of great importance to all of us, concerning the welfare and progress of our country.

You will appreciate that since the Military Government assumed office on

January 17, it has not been an easy task either for you as moulders of public opinion, or for us as trustees of the nation. We are all faced with the problems of national reconstruction, which involves a re-examination of the principles on which our national edifice was based.

In this transitional period, we seek, and we have been assured, of the co-operation of all sections of our community, including the Press. In order that we may accomplish our task with minimum friction and with maximum efficiency, we solicit the co-operation of all our people.

In this connection, the Federal Military Government will, in particular, expect maximum co-operation from the Press in reporting the activities of Government. You are all aware of the need to create a favourable image of Nigeria both at home and overseas. This is important for our economic development which, in a large measure, depends on foreign investments.

There is a calculated attempt by some sections of the foreign press to misrepresent the circumstances which have brought the Military Government in control of the affairs of this country. Deliberate misrepresentation of the Federal Military Government cannot help Nigeria. In the foreign press it is deplorable; in the Nigerian press it is unpardonable. The Federal Military Government should be given the time to accomplish the great tasks before it.

The masses of the people have welcomed the new regime. It will be the duty of the Press to prevent its publications being used as a medium to revive unwelcome associations of the past order.

This meeting is therefore summoned to appeal to you once again to exercise a sense of loyalty, responsibility and restraint in the performance of your duties. You should avoid reports in your newspapers which are likely to incite one section of our people against another. You should also avoid the dangerous practice of rumour-mongering which is so much in evidence in our country today. On this point, it might be necessary to sound a note of warning. While it is not the intention of Government to muzzle constructive press comments on matters of public interest, it should be realised that it is the duty of any responsible Government to ensure that confidential matters of State are not being made the subject of sensational press speculation; especially, where such matters have not been officially cleared for release to the public. Whenever in doubt about anything, you should always check up your facts from the Ministry of Information, who will either furnish you with the correct answers, or make enquiries from the proper quarters on your behalf. . . .

I would therefore wish to take this opportunity to emphasise the need for your co-operation in tackling our gigantic and urgent problems of economic and social development within the framework of national unity in the concept of 'One Nigeria'. The public would like to know the kind of administrative reforms we intend to undertake and the organs we propose to establish in order to attain our objectives. As a first step, administrative reforms are essential in order to lay a solid foundation not only for the present but for the future as well. Here the Press should reflect the thinking of the people and provide a forum for public discussion and constructive suggestions. The country needs a sort of nerve centre which will give the necessary direction and control in all major areas of national activities, so that we will be in a position to plot a uniform pattern of development for the whole country.

Matters which were formerly within the legislative competence of the Regions will need to be reviewed, so that issues of national importance could be centrally controlled and directed towards overall and uniform development in the economic and social fields; effective liaison and co-ordination should be established between the Federal authority and its provincial counterparts, if we are to avoid the pitfalls of the recent past and make a more significant impact both internally as well as externally. The works programme of the Supreme Military Council and the Federal Military Government will necessarily include the establishment of certain essential organs which are indispensable for accelerated development in some major and sensitive areas where proper planning has been neglected, haphazard or unco-ordinated. We are undertaking a review of commercial and industrial development, details of which will be announced shortly.

Other equally important problems requiring early attention are: the formulation of an educational policy related to the needs of a developing country such as Nigeria; manpower training tailored to meet the demands of the country; unemployment and its attendant social evils. The solution to these problems, you will admit, cannot be effected overnight. The new regime should be given time to tackle the heavy programme of work it has been called upon to shoulder. We need maximum co-operation from all sections of the country and we need to apply our energies and resources to the utmost in order to lay a proper foundation for the present as well as for the future.

On the question of the political future of the country, the experiences and mistakes of the previous Governments in the Federation have clearly indicated that far-reaching constitutional reforms are badly needed for peaceful and orderly progress towards the realisation of our objectives. I have already touched on some of the major issues involved in my recent broadcast to the nation. It has become apparent to all Nigerians that rigid adherence to 'Regionalism' was the bane of the last regime and one of the main factors which contributed to its downfall. No doubt, the country would welcome a clean break with the deficiencies of the system of Government to which the country had been subjected in the recent past. A solution suitable to our national needs must be found. The existing boundaries of governmental control will need to be re-adjusted to make for less cumbersome administration.

We are determined that constitutional changes, which are pre-requisite to the re-establishment of parliamentary system of Government, will be undertaken with the consensus of various representatives of public opinion. Proposals for constitutional changes will involve careful and detailed analysis, so that the nation will eventually have a system of Parliamentary government best suited to the demands of a developing country in modern times. We expect that when the system of Government acceptable to the people of Nigeria has been formulated, all elections to Parliament will be by universal adult suffrage. It will be necessary to review also the method of selection for future Ministerial appointments, in order that the destiny of the country will be placed in the hands of men capable of shouldering the heavy responsibilities of modern Government; capable of commanding the respect and admiration of their fellow citizens and capable of reflecting a proud image of Nigeria outside her borders. In the new order of things, there should be no place for Regionalism and tribal consciousness; subjugation of personal service to personal aggrandisement, nepotism and corruption.

The Military Government has no political affiliation or ambition; nor did it come into power with the fiat of any political party. It has no desire to prolong its interim administration of Government longer than is necessary for the orderly transition of the country to the type of Government desired by the people. Study Groups are being set up, details of which will be announced shortly, to study and submit working papers on constitutional, administrative and institutional problems in the context of national unity. A constituent assembly will in due course examine constitutional proposals followed by a Referendum before the new Constitution comes into being. In this transitional period, all citizens have a useful part to play in shaping the destiny of our country, and the Press which serves as one of the important media of public opinion also has a responsible and constructive role to play. The measure of confidence which the Military Government reposes on the Press will in turn depend upon the confidence inspired in the Government by the Press.

[1] *Federal Ministry of Information Release No. 188/1966.*

18.
Terms of Reference of the Constitutional Review Group[1]

a. To identify those faults in the former Constitution that militated against national unity and the emergence of a strong central government.
b. To ascertain to what extent the powers of the former Regional Governments fostered regionalism and weakened the Central Government.
c. To ascertain to what extent the structure and, in particular, the territorial divisions of the country under the former Constitution contributed to the deficiency of the former regime.
d. To suggest possible territorial division of the country.
e. To consider the merits and demerits of—
  i. a unitary form of government
  ii. a federal form of government,
    as a system of government best suited to the demands of a developing country like Nigeria in modern times and most likely to satisfy local needs without hampering the emergence of a strong united democratic Nigeria.
f. To examine the Electoral Act, the Voting System and the Revision of Voters' Register.
g. To consider the merits and demerits of—
  i. One-party system,
  ii. Multi-party system, as
    a system best suited to Nigeria.
h. To determine to what extent party politics fostered tribal consciousness, nepotism and abuse of office.

i. To determine to what extent professional politics contributed to the deficiencies of the past regime.

j. To determine the extent to which regionalism and party politics tended to violate traditional chieftaincies and institutions and to suggest possible safeguards.

[1] *Government Notice 863/1966.*

19.
Instrument Constituting the Nigerian Ports Authority Tribunal of Inquiry[1]

. . . The Tribunal shall with all convenient speed inquire into the administration, management, staff and financial policy of the Nigerian Ports Authority for the period 1st October 1960 to 31st December 1965:

And in particular, it shall—

a. inquire into whether the Authority has at all relevant times performed its duties and functions in accordance with the enactment under which it was established and in the best interest of the State or as the case may be, the general public;

b. inquire into the procedure generally applicable to contracts awarded by the Authority, with special reference to the procedure from inviting tenders up to and including the award of any contract;

c. inquire into all matters (contractual or otherwise) relating to—

  i. the Wharf Extension at both Apapa and Port Harcourt,

  ii. the award of Dock Labour contracts at both Apapa and Port Harcourt,

  iii. Bonny Bar and River Dredging,

  iv. Upstream Development;

d. inquire into any contract or other matter whatsoever which, during the hearing by the Tribunal, may appear to the Tribunal to require further inquiring into its ramifications;

e. inquire into the extent to which land of the Authority (including any leasehold or being held, owned, occupied or possessed by the Authority) has been acquired or disposed of by or on behalf of the Authority and the manner of its acquisition or disposal and whether such acquisition or dispositions are justified or could be justified as being in the public interest;

f. inquire into the recruitment, grading and deployment of the staff of the Authority;

g. inquire into the irregularities (if any) committed by any member of the Authority, by members or any member of its staff, or by any other person ostensibly on behalf of the Authority, which may come to the notice of the Tribunal at any time in the course of the Inquiry and which the Tribunal may consider sufficiently serious to require probing; and

h. make such recommendations, including the future organisation and management of the Authority as the Tribunal may think fit.

[1] *Legal Notice 113/1966.*

M

20.

Address by General Ironsi to the National Working Party on Higher Education[1]

Gentlemen,

I am glad to be able to meet all of you, the Vice-Chancellors of Nigeria's five Universities, this evening. As you are no doubt aware, my Government is currently engaged in a detailed re-examination of our public policies, with a view to bringing them into line with the national needs and aspirations of the people of Nigeria. No aspect of the public effort is more important for national unity than the contribution of the universities to our national life. This country depends on her universities not only for the high-level manpower which is essential for accelerated economic development, but also for the intellectual and moral leadership without which no country can be truly great.

The Universities are already providing the country with many top administrators, doctors, engineers and other categories of professional manpower. But I am sure you will agree that not enough of these graduates are coming off the University 'pipe-line' to meet our national needs; worse still, many of the vital fields are being neglected. We need technologists and scientists urgently. We cannot afford the expensive luxury of unnecessary duplication of facilities for professional education which would be wasteful of both capital and recurrent funds, and of scarce teaching personnel. In the recent past our universities have, owing to political pressure, tended to compete with rather than complement, each other. In the new nation which we are trying to build we expect the universities to work together as partners not rivals in the service of the nation.

My Government recognises the traditional freedom of Universities to seek and disseminate truth as they see it and is determined to preserve this tradition; but you will all agree that as public institutions, universities owe a duty to the Nation. It is because I believe that our universities have an important role to play in the development of our nation that I have directed that you the leaders of the Universities should constitute a Working Party on higher education to examine those problems which must be solved if we are to confer maximum benefits on the masses of the people of this country. Your terms of reference enjoin you:

1. To make proposals for the establishment of a national university system designed to meet the growing high-level manpower needs for the country.

2. In the light of (1) above to assess the facilities now available in Nigerian Universities and to advise on how best to remedy the deficiencies, if any, that may exist.

3. To make proposals for the maximum utilization of higher educational resources, including human and physical resources, in order to promote accelerated economic growth.

4. To make proposals for an expanded programme for post-graduate and technological training for Nigerians.

5. To review the facilities provided by the Extra-Mural Departments of Nigerian Universities and submit proposals for the most effective use of

these facilities to advance the professional and vocational competence of Nigerian workers.

6. To submit comprehensive recommendations in the light of the Working Party's examination of the above issues.

I have further directed that your Working Party shall be served jointly by the Secretariats of the National Universities Commission and the National Manpower Board. You are at liberty to invite any expert or group of experts to assist you in your task. I am confident you will all give the nation the benefit of your accumulated experience.

[1] *Delivered in Lagos on 16 May 1966. Federal Ministry of Information Press Release No. 574/1966.*

21.
Dr. Azikiwe Issues a Statement in Defence of his Role as Chancellor of Nsukka[1]

On my return from convalescence after a prolonged treatment abroad for a lung ailment, I was completely demoralised when I learned of certain unfounded and fantastic rumours about my relationship with the University of Nigeria, particularly in respect of the use of ten hostels under the auspices of the Nnamdi Azikiwe Foundation.

This was not the first occasion I have had justifiable reason to condemn the Nigerian mortal for his lack of faith in man's innate goodness and philanthropy.

But the allegations which imputed improper motives and impugned integrity to the utter exclusion of any room for altruism in my make-up shocked me beyond description and nearly drove me to the breaking point of being misanthropic.

What were these rumours which made even university students, in spite of their vaunted intellectual development and academic acquisitions, to be blind to reason and become easy preys of cunning, petty and evilly-disposed persons?

First, it was freely circulated that I was so mercenary that, in addition to my personal emolument of £7,150 per annum, as President of the First Federal Republic of Nigeria, I also earned £5,000 per annum as chancellor of the University of Nigeria, and another £5,000 per annum as chairman of the Council of that university, excluding an additional £1,500 per annum, which was alleged to be paid to me as perquisites and fringe benefits. That is, a total of £11,500 per annum from the university.

My answer to this first allegation is that it is grotesque and completely false.

The truth is that since April 1960, when I became Chairman of the Council of the University of Nigeria to the date when I read in the Eastern Nigeria Gazette (after previously hearing the news over the wireless) that I had ceased to have any connection with that university, either as chancellor or as chairman, I never drew one penny either as salary or as an allowance. My witnesses are the bursar of the University of Nigeria and his accounts staff, who are in position to correct me if my statement is false.

The second allegation was that the money voted by the Federal and Regional Governments, for building halls of residence in the University of Nigeria, was diverted by me for maintaining other services of the university to enable me, selfishly to populate hostels, in which I have vested interest, with the students of the university.

This allegation did not take into consideration that the chairman of the Council of the University of Nigeria has no over-riding powers as far as that body and the budget of the university were concerned.

My answer to this second allegation is that the suggestion is absurd. It is completely abstruse and wickedly false for the following reasons. Since 1964, neither the Federal Government nor the Regional Government, to my knowledge, has given the University of Nigeria any subvention specifically earmarked for building halls of residence.

The university usually makes provision in its capital budget for constructing halls of residence, but having spent all that was provided for the building of halls of residence, and having no immediate prospect of receiving capital grants from the Federal or Regional Government for this purpose, it is impossible for the Council of the university to proceed to build any more halls of residence outside its budget. We had no funds.

That is why no new halls of residence have been built at the Nsukka or Enugu campus for some time for the last two years. My witness is the Chief Secretary to the Government of the Eastern Provinces at Enugu.

To infer that I or the Foundation took initiative to divert university funds to my pocket or to the funds of that body is defamatory because such an innuendo would be false and malicious.

To insinuate that I or the Foundation collected the rent of £24, paid by each student residing in the hostels for selfish purpose and personal aggrandisement or for any other purpose for that matter is libellous because this is utterly a lie.

If any body stands to gain from this transaction, it is the University of Nigeria which retains £15 out of the £25 it collects from each student and not the Foundation, which is a licensed non-profit making body, or any other person connected with it. My witness is the vice-chancellor of the University of Nigeria.

[1] *Statement made at Nsukka. See* Daily Times, *22 April 1966.*

22.
'Federalism *is* Good for Nigeria'[1]

Since the Army assumed control in Nigeria much has been said about the merits of the change and the future constitution Nigeria should have. One surprising aspect, however, is that no-one has been bold enough to point out the demerits of the manner of the change. More surprising is the attitude of silence and indifference to what is happening in the country on the part of the indigenous sons of the North.

I feel duty bound to say that our silence is neither born out of fear nor is it born out of lack of views to present. But as one writer put it in the *New Nigerian* of April 7, it is partly born out of shock.

The shock that even if the Military regime demanded the lives of those politicians who allegedly spoiled this country, how could such a bloody consequence be restricted to a particular part of the country?

The shock that never in the history of military coup had it occurred that the lives of innocent army leaders (from a particular part of a country) should also be claimed along with those of the politicians. One is bound to ask why and what is the attitude of those who now guide our destiny.

The shock that though the Supreme Commander of the Armed Forces admitted that there was an Army mutiny in the country on Saturday, January 15, those who subsequently assumed power have so far failed to do anything to the mutineers and, possibly, the alleged civilian brains behind such a mutiny.

Those shocks are some of the reasons that kept us quiet, not to mention the mad rush of application letters for jobs pouring into the North from the other parts of the country. Nor to talk of newspaper editorials which shamelessly went all out to condemn the masters that brought them into being, especially those recalled to the country.

And now about the constitution and the various study groups, appointed by the Military Government. With regards to the constitution, much has been written on the dangers and disasters brought on us by Federalism, and the few who have the privilege to write to the papers have even gone to the extent of forcing 'Unitary' Government on us without ascertaining the wishes of the people.

Why should they place the cart before the horse?

One sad fact which these journalists as well as some of the Military top advisers refused to admit is that a Nigerian unitary government does not necessarily unite the people of Nigeria. Especially if one views critically the events that led to the introduction of that desired unitary government.

Unitary government will only be justly accepted in this country when we Nigerians learn to respect one another's views, when we are able to tolerate and respect each other's background, and when some few arch tribalists realise the fault in their belief that it is their right to dominate this country.

In fact, I could advise that in writing our new constitution, a phrase be included which would allow for the breaking up of the Federation.

Whether this decision is accepted or not, I say bluntly that nothing short of 'Federalism' is good for Nigeria. The Federation may be modified, but it must remain.

It is also our wish that Mr. Francis Nwokedi will tell the real fact about the impracticability of unifying the Nigerian Civil Service, especially with our out-moded communications, and environmental factors.

Again we must not lose sight of the fact that much has been spent by the erstwhile Governments to establish civil service headquarters in the regions. The money spent was derived from taxpayers and to render such projects of no use now means a gross disservice to these taxpayers.

As Mustafa Danbatta put it,[2] we in the North must speak up. But I have to point out that most of the steps taken so far both on the part of the Government and of the Press are so disheartening and full of unfavourable speculations, that we are bound to wait and see. We are, however, still convinced that the problem is yet to be solved. To force a unitary type of government on people without an impartial referendum is setting the clock backward.

[1] *Sulemanu Takuma*, New Nigerian, *19 April 1966. When the full story of the North's resistance to Ironsi's unification programme, especially of the public services, is written, it will be found that this letter played a key role in alerting the North's middle grades of civil servants and new intelligentsia.*

[2] *Writing in* New Nigerian, *7 April 1966. This is another key article.*

23.
Ironsi's 100 Days: 'Smouldering Fires'[1]

Within a hundred days of assuming power, the military government has succeeded in restoring law and order all over the country, and it has been duly been credited for this. Also, the old political class have been removed from office. But they have not gone from the political scene and, unlike their Ghanaian counterparts, they are being little investigated or dispossessed of their ill-gotten gains. Various commissions have been set up to investigate ways and means by which national unity and economic growth can be ensured. In many respects we should all be, and are, grateful for what is being done. But there is a haunting feeling about in the country that things are not fully right. People expected changes but the conviction is gradually growing that all that we have had is a change in the personnel of government, more rational government, and not much after that.

The provincial governments still continue to be run from the 'regional' capitals. The East reduced taxation on incomes under £60 unilaterally and has gone on, like the other provinces, to call for foreign investment in the region. The West is to introduce administrative changes by creating eight 'provinces' in place of the existing six without a comparable change occurring elsewhere. In the North the Emirs are back in power, in some cases with a status not dissimilar to that of the old Sole Native Authority, and some Northern civil servants (like some Western ones) are building a federalist lobby and are trying to give the impression that all Northern sentiment is united in that direction. The announcement of the items in the capital budgets of the provincial governments shows the same repetitiveness and unnecessary competition which was characteristic of the old regime. There is little evidence of any attempt at rationalisation and also little evidence of effective co-ordination of plans.

At the centre, some decisions have been taken arbitrarily. Decrees have been issued with, it seems, little thought having been given as to how they are to be carried out. The decree on rents, for example, is a gesture of good will. But good intentions are simply not enough when the administrative problems involved are ignored or overlooked. A rule which cannot be enforced is hardly worth the paper on which it is written or the effort taken to declare it. The same argument can be made about the seemingly inhuman punishment to be meted out to growers of Indian hemp. Capital punishment has not prevented people from committing homicide, let alone growing hemp, which can more easily go undetected. With a ratio of one policeman to some 2,500 Nigerians, about 70 per cent of whom live in the rural areas, we have not even got the manpower to deal with the overall problem of criminality. Increasing the level of punishments for specific crimes is not a substitute for dealing with the socio-economic factors which make for criminal behaviour.

There are however, far weightier grounds for feeling uneasy at the moment. Firstly, the sentiment is fast developing that the military government's sympathies are more those of the middle class than of the farmers and the working class. This is tending to make the workers belligerent. The increase in the prices, and shortages, of foodstuffs have not contributed to alleviating the growing dissatisfaction of the workers nor the misery of the rural population. The army might be able to deal with a lot of things in a 'military way'. One thing they cannot so deal with is a general strike, as the old regime found to its cost in June 1964. Another is the current food shortage. In any case, the country can least afford now, more than at any other time, the economic breakdown associated with a general strike.

This becomes even more important when it is related to recent speculations about the state of discipline in the army itself. While we can concede that such statements are either unfounded or, at the worst, exaggerated, few can deny that the tendency to appoint army officers to many commissions and committees of one type or another cannot but adversely affect the general level of discipline, particularly when it is realised that even before the coup the commissioned ranks of the army were under-staffed. These men serve little purpose on such bodies. They should be quietly withdrawn.

Secondly, there is the general problem of the civil service. Two few Permanent Secretaries are engaged in doing too many things. There does not seem to be enough willingness to delegate authority. Most people were willing in the immediate post-coup period to see top civil servants take a more direct part in decision-making. But the point surely has been reached when these men are being overworked. This has two implications. The first is that with so much concentration of authority, not enough time is being given to individual problems. The result at best is improperly thought out advice; at worst, bad advice. The second is that the civil service is, by tradition and nature, a cautious service. In a context where novel and daring solutions are sought, to have civil servants involved in so much decision-making may be more of a liability than an asset. There should be a deliberate attempt made by the military government to introduce rapidly a much stronger non-civil service element into the decision-making process.

Thirdly, there is the question of the 'majors'. Whatever may be said about them, one fact we cannot deny: Nigerians have been offered a new opportunity in the effort at nation building by their risk-taking and courage. Surely a better solution can be found for their case than to leave them indefinitely languishing in 'protective custody'? We should not in any event allow them to be used as a scape goat to appease the fears and sentiments of certain groups.

The problems confronting the nation are challenging. The proliferation of commissions is not going to solve them. The experience of the first hundred days does suggest that while much has been done, much remains to be done. The opportunities are there. Either we seize them or it will be 'the fire next time'. We have no alternative to the Army at the moment. We want them to succeed.

[1] Nigerian Opinion, *May 1966.*

24.
Ojukwu's Speech Welcoming the Installation of the Emir of Kano as Chancellor of the University of Nigeria, June 1966 [1]

I am sure that I shall be expressing the minds and feelings of all who are gathered here, when I say that we are extremely happy to have in our midst, as the guest of honour tonight, His Highness Alhaji Ado Bayero, the Emir of Kano. His Highness and I have been old friends. We met some five years ago under rather different circumstances—His Highness was then a Chief of Kano Native Administration Police and I, a young Major in the Brigade Headquarters in Kaduna. We met again soon after my arrival in Kano in January, 1964 as Commander of the 5th Battalion of the Nigerian Army. It was during this period, through constant official and social contacts that our acquaintance blossomed into what I am proud to call firm friendship. Unfortunately when the time came for me to leave Kano the circumstances were such that it was impossible for me to take leave and to thank him for his great sympathy and charity. I was in command at Kano during the crisis of January 15th and I judge it a great tribute to our friendship that in close co-operation, Kano was kept insulated throughout from the turmoil and bloodshed of those days. I therefore feel honoured and privileged to be able to say both welcome and thank you to an old and trusted friend.

Your Highness, may I start by offering you once again our heartiest congratulations and very best wishes on your appointment as the Chancellor of the University of Nigeria, in which office you were installed with appropriate pomp and dignity yesterday. You must yourself have sensed the unfathomable depth of goodwill generated and transparently shown for you by the people on that occasion.

The University of Nigeria is a young but great institution, full of hope and promise for this country. So also, if I may be permitted to say so, are you as a person. At your early age of thirty-six (or is it thirty-five?) you have distinguished yourself as an individual, independently of your birth and heritage. A prince though you were, you chose early in life to tread the path of the ordinary man, and this is now helping you, as one of the powerful potentates of this country, to have the right insight into, and understanding of, the needs and aspirations of the commonalty of this country. This understanding and insight have made you one of the most highly respected figures in this country and beyond. . . .

Here, Your Highness, I must extend to you and the people of your Emirate the sympathy of the people of this Group of Provinces on the sad and tragic events of recent weeks, events which erupted in parts of the Northern Group of Provinces including your area of authority. I know that those events have greatly distressed you as they have done all well-meaning Nigerians and friends of Nigeria.

We must thank Providence that the situation has been brought under control. The Military Government has already reaffirmed its reliance on the good sense and mature leadership of the Emirs and all traditional rulers of the country to ensure that that sort of episode is never allowed to occur again.

Meanwhile, we must accept the sad events as a challenge to all who have dedicated their energies to the tasks of unity for the country. No doubt, enemies and cynics have taken false comfort in those events. It is for the forces of construction and unity to go on marching to the promised land of brotherhood and oneness for the country.

Lives and property have been lost; many have been made homeless; others have been bereft of their loved ones; confidence has been shaken; fear has replaced faith in one towards the other. These are sad reflections which must remain a source of guilt and shame for all who, by deliberate acts and insinuations were responsible, directly or indirectly, for them. We cannot restore the lives which have been lost nor the blood which has been shed. But we should not ignore the fact that they have been valuable lives and blood. It must, therefore, be our prayer that the innocent blood thus shed will be accepted as the supreme purchase price for the solid and everlasting unity of this country, and that the events which had led to the situation will for ever be the worst that this country should experience. . . .

The aims of the Military Government have been repeatedly stated in clear and unmistakable terms. Those aims conform with the statement of a great American philosopher who said: 'The purpose of military rule is to provide time for moral ideas to take root; the ideas of justice; the ideas of fairness; the ideas of merit; the ideas of unity and solidarity.' The Military Government is in power in Nigeria today because the nation needed a corrective force which would foster and enthrone those ideals—ideals which were being desecrated, debased and virtually destroyed.

It is the place of the Armed Forces to protect and defend the country, and not its place to govern or rule. But when it is necessary for them to assume political power, it is always for definite objective which they must allow nothing to stand in their way of achieving. Those objectives for us are those of fairness and fairplay, of justice, of merit and of unity and solidarity.

Ours is to 'provide time for these ideas to take root'—or, at least, to provide the necessary conditions for those ideas to grow and thrive. As military men we do not claim to have cut and dried answers to all the problems now confronting the nation. It is therefore totally unfair and unjustified for anyone to fear that the Army is out to impose permanent arrangements on the people. Any such fears must be dislodged and destroyed from any minds where they may be lurking.

As Nigerians, we naturally have ideas of the areas from which the national ills and ailments have in the past emanated. In order to find out and provide the right remedies, we have set up many expert committees and commissions to have a detached and objective look into these areas and suggest remedies which will make them cease to be sources of discomfort for the nation. When they have finished their work their recommendations will be placed before the people for consideration before adoption. Let me repeat and emphasize that everyone will be involved, and expected to participate, in that final exercise. Meanwhile it is the duty of everyone to give the expert bodies and commissions, now engaged on the essential groundwork, every co-operation. I have said that fairness and national unity and solidarity are among our objectives. . . .

I have talked of ensuring maximum productivity through the deployment of trained and experienced personnel according to need. That is the sole motive behind the National Government's unification of the civil service. Far from this being done in order to place any person or group of persons at a disadvantage, it is to help ourselves by utilizing to the full what we have. What is the sense of allowing schools in some areas to starve of trained teachers while some areas are having enough and even to spare? What is the sense in going overseas to beg for help without first exhausting what we have? Why restrict the varying experience of the civil service to compartments when the best could be made of it in an open and common pool?

I now come to the objective of national unity and solidarity. For years this country has striven for unity. In this they have met and passed many hurdles. All the danger points of disintegration have been passed. The common generality of the people of this country have come to regard one another as brothers and sisters. The conscious and unconscious apostles of disunity are not the common men and women of this country. They are the few with vested interests, selfish and inordinate ambition for power and wealth, men who fear losing their positions and privileges, who care more for self than for the nation and the common good. These men have tried to exploit our differences to the detriment of the country, when they should be expected to work for the removal of those differences. They have tried to make unhealthy capital of our diversity, when a healthy perception of our diversity could be turned to our national advantage as a source of strength—diversity of culture, of background, of outlook, of experience, of our education, of our up-bringings. . . .

That we should, after having gone this far, still be talking of lack of unity shows that there is something basically wrong with what has been our system thus far. We must find out what that is, and correct it. It may be something requiring more than the mere administration of oral medicine or panacea. It may require some surgical operation. I am personally convinced that it is a surgical operation that is required. Surgical operations are usually painful and uncomfortable when conducted, and may be for sometime afterwards. But once the patient is able to survive the operation and after pains, he is able to survive as a healthy and strong individual. And the success of a surgical operation depends on the promptness, decisiveness and courage of the doctor—otherwise it may be too late.

Let us be true to ourselves. Nigeria is now having its last chance to make permanent arrangements for lasting unity. That chance may never occur again. Our very survival is through unity; without it we shall perish. Without it our people will remain weak and poor. We shall lose our chance of influence in a shrinking world. Let us not forget that we have been blessed with a number of things which have rightly been the envy of many, ready to cash in when they can.

We must be prepared to approach this issue of unity and national solidarity realistically, selflessly, and fearlessly. We must be prepared for sacrifices in the spirit of give and take. We must overcome old prejudices and entrenched interests.

It is the aim of the Military Government to uphold, protect and strengthen our traditional institutions. We respect the position and influence of traditional rulers who must increasingly be recognized as the healthy arms of government. Through a process of modernization and evolution, we want to preserve our special identity as a race and people. Unfortunately, the politics of the last regime did not allow anything to stand in its way and rode roughshod over our traditional institutions, even halting the growth of natural industries in certain areas as a political reprisal. All this the Military Government is committed to eradicate.

We in this country are a deeply religious people. The two principal religions, Islam and Christianity, have a lot in common for the general good. They both believe in the brotherhood of man, they believe in truth and justice, they believe in love and humility, they believe in self-sacrifice. They are both outward looking, with a deep concern for others and their needs. They seek the right human understanding as a means of service to mankind.

All these are what have brought us so far. We must not do anything which would be a betrayal of these great ideals. . . .

I apologize for the length of this speech but I consider this visit perhaps the best and most significant act of faith in the unity of this country, the oneness of our people, and the singularity of our purpose.

¹ Crisis '66 (Enugu, 1966), pp. 13–20.

25.
The Unification Decree: No. 34 of 1966 ¹

DECREE NO. 34

[24*th May* 1966]   Commencement.

THE FEDERAL MILITARY GOVERNMENT hereby decrees as follows:

1.   Subject to the provisions of this Decree, Nigeria shall on 24th May 1966 (in this Decree referred to as 'the appointed day') cease to be a Federation and shall accordingly as from that day be a Republic, by the name of the Republic of Nigeria, consisting of the whole of the territory which immediately before that day was comprised in the Federation.

Nigeria to be a Republic.

2. *1.* As from the appointed day—

   a. the Federal Military Government and the Federal Executive Council shall be known respectively as the National Military Government and the Executive Council;

   b. the Federal territory shall be known as the Capital territory;

Consequential changes.

c. the provinces, including Kaduna capital territory, in schedule 1 of this Decree which immediately before the appointed day were respectively comprised in Northern Nigeria, Eastern Nigeria, Western Nigeria and Mid-Western Nigeria shall be known respectively as the Northern group of Provinces, the Eastern group of Provinces, the Western group of Provinces and the Mid-Western group of Provinces;

d. for the purposes of administration each group of provinces shall subject to the authority of the Head of the National Military Government, be under the general direction and control of a Military Governor appointed by the Head of the National Military Government;

e. Act No. 20 of 1963 (that is to say the Constitution of the Federation) may be cited as the Constitution of the Republic.

2. Without prejudice to section 8 of this Decree, the person who immediately before the appointed day holds the office of Military Governor of a Region shall be deemed to have been appointed by the Head of the National Military Government as Military Governor of the corresponding group of provinces with effect from that day.

3. The National Military Government may either conditionally or unconditionally delegate to a Military Governor of a group of provinces power to make laws by edict for the peace, order and good government with respect to any matter specified in the delegation in relation to that group of provinces.

4. Subject to this and any other Decree, a Military Governor of a group of provinces may exercise by way of edict or, as the case may be, by regulation, order, or instrument the powers and functions vested in the Executive Council of the Government of a former Region, or of the Governor, Premier, or Minister (except in relation to criminal prosecutions) of a government of a former Region under any existing law with respect to that group of provinces; and accordingly sections 3 (*2*), (*3*), (*5*), (*6*) and (*7*) and section 4 (*6*) of the Constitution (Suspension and Modification) Decree 1966 (in this Decree referred to as 'the principal Decree') shall cease to have effect.

1966 No. 1.

5. Subsection (*4*) shall be without prejudice to section 8 of this Decree, and the repeal by that subsection of any provision of the principal Decree shall not affect the operation of that provision in relation to any time before the appointed day.

6. Any Edict made by the Military Governor of a Region which is in force immediately before the appointed day shall, as from that day, have effect as a Decree applying only to the group of provinces which corresponds to that Region; and references to a Decree shall be construed accordingly.

In this subsection 'Edict' includes a decree made as mentioned in section 4 (*6*) of the principal Decree.

7. Notwithstanding section 1 of this Decree, on and after the appointed day—

a. the provisions of the constitution of each former Region which are not for the time being suspended shall, in relation to the corresponding group of provinces, have effect as modified by the combined operation of the principal Decree, as amended, and this Decree; and

b. the constitution of each former Region may be cited as the Constitution of the Northern, Eastern, Western or Mid-Western group of Provinces, as the case may be, and references to the constitution of a group of provinces shall be construed accordingly.

3. *1.* As from the appointed day all offices in the service of the Republic in a civil capacity shall be offices in a single service to be known as the National Public Service; and accordingly all persons who immediately before that day are members of the public service of the Federation or of the public service of a Region shall on that day become members of the National Public Service: Unification of the public service.

Provided that this subsection shall not apply to the office of the Attorney-General of the Republic or of a group of Provinces.

2. As from the appointed day— 1963 No. 20.

a. the Public Service Commission established under section 146 of the Constitution of the Republic shall be known as the National Public Service Commission, and references in that section and elsewhere to the Public Service Commission of the Federation shall be amended accordingly;

b. all Regional Public Service Commissions established under the appropriate provisions of the Constitutions of the Regions shall be known as the Provincial Public Service Commissions, and references to the Public Service Commissions created under the Constitutions of the Regions shall be construed accordingly.

3. Notwithstanding anything contained in the Constitution of the Republic or of a group of Provinces, the members of the Public Service Commission of the Federation and of the Regions who, immediately before the appointed day hold office, shall continue in office until the appointments expire or are sooner revoked, and fresh appointments are made.

4. *1.* Subject to the provisions of this section, power to appoint persons to hold or act in offices in the National Public Service (including power to make appointments on promotion and to confirm appointments) and to dismiss and exercise disciplinary control over persons holding or acting in such offices shall, as from the appointed day, vest in the National Public Service Commission. Appointment, etc., of officers in National Public Service.

2. The National Public Service Commission may, with the approval of the Head of the National Military Government, either conditionally or unconditionally delegate any of its powers under subsection (*1*) above to any person or authority in Nigeria.

3. Subject to subsections (*4*) and (*6*) below, all the powers of the National Public Service Commission under subsection (*1*) above in respect of any office in the National Public Service carrying an initial salary not exceeding £2,292, shall be treated as having been

delegated to the appropriate Provincial Public Service Commission.

4. Any delegation effected under subsection (2) above (including any delegation which in accordance with subsection (3) above or subsection (6) below is to be treated as having been effected under subsection (2) above) may be varied or revoked by the National Public Service Commission with the approval of the Head of the National Military Government.

5. Subsection (1) above shall not apply in relation to any of the following offices—

   a. the office of any judge of the Supreme Court, the High Court of Lagos, the High Court of a group of provinces or the Sharia Court of Appeal;

   b. the office of economic adviser to the Republic;

   c. except for the purpose of making appointments thereto, the office of the Director of Audit of the Republic and the office of the Director of Audit of a group of provinces;

   d. the office of Magistrate and Justice of the Peace;

   e. any office in the Nigeria Police Force;

   f. any office to which section 148 of the Constitution of the Republic applies.

6. Without prejudice to subsection (4) above or to section 8 of this Decree, any delegation effected under section 147 of the Constitution of the Federation, or under the corresponding section of constitution of a Region, which is in force immediately before the appointed day shall, as from that day, be deemed to have been duly effected by the National Public Service Commission under subsection (2) above.

7. The provisions of this section shall be subject to the provisions of section 5 of this Decree.

Appointment, etc., of permanent secretaries and other public officers of equivalent rank.

5. 1. Power to appoint persons to hold or act in the office of permanent secretary to any department of government of the Republic or any other office of equivalent rank in the National Public Service, and to remove persons so appointed from any such office shall, as from the appointed day, vest in the Supreme Military Council.

2. Before appointing any person by virtue of this section, the Supreme Military Council shall consult the National Public Service Commission.

3. Subsection (1) above shall not apply in relation to any of the offices mentioned in section 4 (5) of this Decree.

Appointment, etc., of members of Police Service Commission.

6. As from the appointed day the members of the Police Service Commission shall be appointed by the Head of the National Military Government; and accordingly in the entry in Schedule 2 of the principal Decree relating to section 109 of the Constitution of the Republic, for the words 'Federal Executive Council' in both places where they occur, there shall, as from the appointed day, be substituted the words 'Head of the National Military Government'.

7. *1.* As from the appointed day, the provisions of the Constitution of the Republic mentioned in Schedule 2 of this Decree shall be suspended.

   2. As from the appointed day—
   a. the provisions of the constitution of each group of provinces which are mentioned in Schedule 3 of this Decree shall be suspended; and
   b. Schedule 4 of the principal Decree shall have effect subject to the amendments specified in Schedule 4 of this Decree.

Consequential suspension of some and modification of other constitutional provisions.

8. *1.* As from the appointed day the principal Decree, as amended, shall have effect with such modifications (whether by way of addition, alteration or omission) as may be necessary to bring it, and through it—
   a. the unsuspended provisions of the Constitution of the Republic and of the constitution of each group of provinces; and
   b. all existing law within the meaning of subsection (*1*) of section 12 of the principal Decree, so far as in force immediately before the appointed day; and
   c. all other law which would be existing law within the meaning of the said subsection (*1*) if the references in that subsection to 16th January 1966 were references to the appointed day;
   into conformity with this Decree.

   2. Without prejudice to the generality of subsection (*1*) above, section 13 of the principal Decree (which makes provision for the saving of existing offices, appointments, etc.) shall, with such modifications as may be necessary in consequence of this Decree, have effect in relation to the appointed day in like manner as it has effect in relation to 16th January 1966.

   3. Nothing in this Decree shall affect the validity of anything done before the appointed day.

Transitional and saving provisions.

9. In this Decree, and in any other law—
   'enactment' includes any provision of a Decree;
   'group of provinces' means the Northern Group of Provinces, the Eastern Group of Provinces, the Western Group of Provinces or the Mid-Western Group of Provinces;
   'the Military Governor', in relation to a group of provinces, means the Military Governor of that group of provinces;
   'the Northern Group of Provinces', 'the Eastern Group of Provinces', 'the Western Group of Provinces' and 'the Mid-Western Group of Provinces' have the respective meanings assigned in section 2 (*1*) (*c*) of this Decree.

Meaning of certain expressions in Decrees and other laws.

10. Every Decree made on or after the appointed day shall apply throughout Nigeria except in so far as the contrary intention appears therein.

Extent of Decrees.

[1] *The Constitution (Suspension and Modification) (No. 5) Decree 1966, Federal Republic of Nigeria Official Gazette no. 51, vol. 53, 24 May 1966, A153. The Schedules have beenomitted here.*

26.
'The Regions are Abolished': Ironsi's Broadcast to the Nation
banning Political Parties and introducing Decree No. 34, 24
May 1966[1]

Fellow Nigerians:

During the past two weeks I presided over meetings of the Supreme
Military Council and the Central Executive Council at which many important
state matters were considered. . . .

It is now three months since the Government of the Federal Republic of
Nigeria was handed over to the Armed Forces. Now that peace has been
restored in the troubled areas it is time that the Military Government indicates clearly what it proposes to accomplish before relinquishing power. The
removal of one of the obstacles on the way is provided for in the Constitution
(Suspension and Modification) Decree (No. 5) 1966 which was promulgated
by me today and comes into effect at once.

The provisions of the Decree are intended to remove the last vestiges of the
intense regionalism of the recent past, and to produce that cohesion in the
governmental structure which is so necessary in achieving, and maintaining
the paramount objective of the National Military Government, and indeed
of every true Nigerian, namely, national unity.

The highlights of this Decree are as follows:

The former regions are abolished, and Nigeria grouped into a number of
territorial areas called provinces. . . .

Nigeria ceases to be what has been described as a federation. It now becomes simply the Republic of Nigeria.

The former Federal Military Government and the Central Executive
Council become respectively the National Military Government and the
Executive Council. All the Military Governors are members of the Executive
Council.

A Military Governor is assigned to a group of provinces over which and
subject to the direction and control of the Head of the National Military
Government, he shall exercise executive power. In order to avoid any major
dislocation of the present administrative machinery, the grouping of the
provinces has been made to coincide with the former regional boundaries.
This is entirely a transitional measure and must be understood as such. The
present grouping of the provinces is without prejudice to the Constitutional
and Administrative arrangements to be embodied in the New Constitution in
accordance with the wishes of the people of Nigeria.

The National Military Government assumes the exercise of all legislative
powers throughout the Republic subject to such delegations to Military
Governors as are considered necessary for purposes of efficient administration.

The public services of the former federation and regions become unified
into one national public service under a National Public Service Commission. There is a provincial Service Commission for each group of provinces
to which is delegated functions in respect of public officers below a given rank.
This rather drastic change will probably involve a reconstitution of the

existing commissions, and the National Military Government reserves the right to do so in the manner stipulated in the Decree. Until this is done, the present Commissioners continue to act in their posts. Every civil servant is now called upon to see his function in any part of Nigeria in which he is serving in the context of the whole country. The orientation should now be towards national unity and progress. I expect all civil servants to co-operate and to consult at all levels, vertically and horizontally, between groups of Provinces and between Provinces and the Centre.

People are aware that Study Groups have been set up to look into various aspects of governmental activity. One of them is concerned with problems relating to the Constitution. This Decree is without prejudice to their activities and their reports will be given proper consideration by the National Military Government in formulating the proposals for a future civilian government.

In my nation-wide radio broadcast of January 28, 1966, I said, among other things: 'We cannot afford to continue with sterile political strife and mutual recriminations. I have therefore ordered that there shall be no display of party flags or symbols, and no shouting of political slogans.'

On March 3, I caused a press release to be issued calling attention to the fact that political meetings were, in spite of my order, being held in certain parts of the country, and warned the public and the press to cooperate with the Federal Military Government in its task of national reconstruction.

In spite of these warnings, political party activities still continue, either directly, or through various tribal societies and organisations. The National Military Government owes it as a duty to the people of this country to remove the ills which infested the former regime, to restore the faith of our people in their fatherland and its institutions, so that when the time comes for the civilian government to return, a healthy body politic would have emerged, and last vestiges of bitter factionalism removed.

The National Military Government having committed itself to this task is firmly resolved to conclude it, and will not be diverted from, or obstructed in, the fulfilment of this objective by the activities or political manoeuvres of any society, party, union or association. Part of our task is the removal of politics based on tribal affiliations which, as everybody knows, have manifested political intrigues, or have been used as bases for party-political propaganda. This leads me to the removal of the second obstacle on the way for which provision has been made in the Public Order Decree 1966, which I have signed today and which comes into operation forthwith, dissolving all organisations of the type scheduled therein, and banning any manifestations of their political purpose. These organisations have been dissolved and will be buried along with the tribal, sectional and regional bitterness which they engendered. Certain types of associations and organisations are unaffected, and will remain so, only for as long as they do not engage in any political activity. It is the cardinal aim of my Government to foster the growth of town development unions, membership of which should be open to all inhabitants of the particular town irrespective of their tribal origin. This does not mean for instance that Efiks residing outside Calabar should not contribute towards the development of Calabar development union but it does mean that a Tiv or a Hausa residing in Calabar should be eligible for membership

N

and should be allowed to participate fully in the development of that town.

This Decree also prohibits the formation of new political parties. I must emphasize however that the ban on the formation of new political parties is of limited duration and is designed to enable this corrective government to get on with its task especially at this initial stage. At the appropriate time provisions will be made outlining the procedure for the formation of new political associations.

I want however to leave no doubt in the mind of anybody, that the provisions of this decree will certainly be enforced. This is a Military Regime and soldiers do not allow themselves to be diverted from or obstructed in the fulfilment of their objectives. With us the objectives will be pursued with supreme determination and vigour. In this we need not only the co-operation but the discipline of every Nigerian.

I wish to make it clear that the prohibition of the formation of new political associations has no sinister motive. The limitation period until the 17th of January 1969 may be reduced if the Military Government accomplishes its aims before then. Our determination is that until the two decrees I have signed today are abrogated, every individual should be preoccupied with the task of national reconstruction, not as ex-politician or politician, but simply as a Nigerian with faith in his country's destiny.

Malicious rumours designed to mar our national reconstruction continue to be carried about by certain individuals in spite of my repeated warnings. Cases of impersonation of officers of the Armed Forces are still reported. I have to warn again those who indulge in these criminal acts to discipline themselves forthwith and not to provoke us into taking very drastic measures which may otherwise become necessary.

In pursuance of its policy for achieving national unity, my Government is setting up a body to review all the existing Government-sponsored newspapers in the context of national unity. This body will also recommend the most effective organisation for running the Information, Broadcasting and Television Services in the country and the financial implications involved.

I must not end this broadcast without pointing out a recent development which, if not checked, will adversely affect the morale of the Civil Service and thereby hamper our national reconstruction. By this I mean the unnecessary criticisms recently being levelled against the Civil Service by certain sections of the Press. It is common knowledge that civil servants are expected to tender advice to Ministers but it was not obligatory on the part of the former Ministers to accept advice so tendered. It will therefore be wrong to blame civil servants for mistakes made by their Ministers who in many cases did not accept the advice given to them by these officers.

I have to make it abundantly clear to everyone that my Government will continue to use the services of the present civil servants. However, my Government believes in maintaining the highest standard of efficiency in the Civil Service and will not hesitate to do away with anyone found guilty of inefficiency, nepotism, tribalism and corruption.

I therefore wish to appeal to all newspaper editors and columnists to look for a more profitable pastime and desist from criticising civil servants unnecessarily especially as they realise that because of the tradition of their calling, civil servants are barred from defending themselves on the pages of newspapers. Such attacks will certainly not help the Military Government and is sure eventually to demoralise members of the Public Service who are rendering such noble service to this nation under difficult conditions. If any member of the public has any genuine case against any civil servant, he or she should make a report to the appropriate quarters.

We are determined to accomplish the main tasks we have set ourselves. The various problems involved are being studied by the various working parties which I have set up. Whilst these studies are in progress my Government cannot remain at a standstill and must therefore forge ahead in the meantime. As a corrective regime we must ensure that the fatal maladies of the past are cured before we relinquish power. We propose as a last act to give the country an accurate count as well as a Constitution which will guarantee unity, freedom, and true democracy to all Nigerians everywhere. Investigations are proceeding in respect of ex-politicians of the former regime. Any of them found guilty will be dealt with according to Law irrespective of their position in the community. My Government will then consider utilising the services of those who have not been found wanting and who are prepared to serve in the context of national unity.

Nigerians must understand and respect one another in the new national spirit. Those ex-politicians in different camps who previously regarded one another as enemies should now forget the past and work together for the common good.

With the dissolution of political parties and tribal unions I want all Nigerians everywhere in Nigeria to regard one another not as strangers but as Nigerians with common nationality irrespective of their tribe or place of origin. From henceforth no reference to tribe or place of origin will appear in any official document. . . .

Finally, I appeal to all Nigerians and friends of Nigeria to co-operate with the Military Government in the difficult task of national reconstruction.

[1] *Federal Ministry of Information Press Release No. 610/1966. The speech was broadcast over the national radio on the evening of 24 May 1966.*

27.
Broadcast by Military Governor of the North, 29 May 1966[1]

I must apologise to you for being late after you heard the broadcast saying that I am going to speak to you at 8 o'clock tonight. I am sorry for being late. However, what I am going to say to you tonight is of serious tone, and you must listen carefully and understand.

Good evening fellow citizens. I found it necessary to cut short my tour of the provinces. The National Military Government is fully aware that, within the last few days, certain Nigerians, in collusion with certain foreign nationals are inciting law-abiding Nigerians to dissatisfaction and are misinterpreting the honest intentions of the Government in its work of reconstruction. I understand that, as a result, some disturbances are taking place in a few portions of these provinces over the recent decree abolishing the regions and unifying the civil services of the country.

It is my intention tonight to dispel any doubt you have been led to entertain on the policy of the national government. The aim of the Military Government is to bring about a better understanding between Nigerians of all tribes. It is the intention of the Military Government that, as soon as such understanding has been brought about, the administration should be handed over to the civilians. No soldier wants to rule. Our normal function is not to govern but to protect the integrity and safety of the nation. We shall be much happier doing that than governing. But, as you all know, things went wrong in the last few years with the civilian administration, and it became necessary for the Army, at the request of the civilian government, to step in and restore the country to normalcy. We in the armed forces believe in discipline. We believe that Nigerian society cannot be brought together so that every member of it, irrespective of tribe or religion, respect one another without discipline. The armed forces also believe in fair play. We cannot manage a society with some members dominating others. We believe whenever people have to live together, there must be a spirit of give and take. It is for this reason that the unification decree was introduced.

The unification decree is not intended to give advantage to any section of the community. Its aim is to treat all Nigerians alike. But we do realise that it is difficult to treat everybody alike. Some areas are more advanced than others. It is our intention that the National Government shall give massive assistance to the less developed areas so that they can catch up as soon as possible with the more developed areas. In this way all fears of domination can be ended and all Nigerians will be able to compete with one another on an honest competitive basis.

I also want to remind you, fellow citizens, that the Supreme Commander has made it perfectly clear that the measures introduced are interim and temporary until civilian administration is once again restored. We in the Army have got a unified command and it is the method we are used to. We believe that, if we are to carry on this holding operation until the return of civilian rule, we have got to work with the method we are used to. The Supreme Commander has said that this is an interim arrangement merely for the army to work under methods it is used to. The permanent arrangements for the government of Nigeria cannot be made without the fullest consultations with the people. As you all know, the Government has appointed a number of study groups to make recommendations on various aspects of government. These study groups are still working and our decisions on the future of the government and its institutions will depend on the recommendations of these bodies if they are found to be acceptable to the people. We will not for one moment impose a permanent system which is not acceptable to the majority of the people.

Now, I want to touch on a vital issue, many people are concerned about the question of employment. Naturally, all of us Nigerians want to see that employment is based on merit, but at the same time we must recognise that if the merit system alone is the only criteria, certain areas of the country, which are educationally backward, will suffer. For this reason the national government intends to give special consideration to the more backward areas.

We shall continue the special training programmes and introduce new ones so that all areas of the country will continue to be fairly represented in government service, industry, and commerce. More important, the national government will give special attention to the rapid development of education in areas lagging behind. I pressed this in Lagos and I am glad to say that I have got the support of the Supreme Commander and my colleagues, the other Military Governors.

I want to appeal to everyone, whether in authority or not, to keep calm and to study the proposals of the Government. I can assure you that neither I nor my colleagues will support any proposal that is aimed against any section of Nigeria. We are working for the country as a whole, and we cannot allow sectional interests to deviate us from our path. We shall support merit but we shall also protect the weak. I appeal to you all to avoid provocations. The Military Government is not for any one section. It is for the whole of Nigeria. Anyone who tries to show that the Military Government is for him alone is clearly mistaken.

I am soon calling a conference of all the chiefs of the provinces, and I shall explain to them the true position with regards to the new measures. I shall listen to the advice of the chiefs and shall convey it to my colleagues in the Supreme Council. I am confident that the chiefs of these provinces have implicit confidence in me and the Government. I implore you to keep calm and await the results of the discussions I am going to hold with the emirs and chiefs who are respected by all of us. We must all give a chance to these leaders to put across their views to the Government and give the Government a chance to study them and reach a decision.

I must stress before I finish that it is not in the interest of anyone to disturb the peace. . . . If things deteriorate further, the Government shall not hesitate to declare any area of disturbance a military area which involves many restrictions and hardships on the ordinary citizen. If this happens, things could be very difficult. It is not my wish to do this. The life and property of every Nigerian are dear to me. I once again appeal to you to co-operate with me so that we all together can work out our problems in peace. God be with you. Good night.

[1] *Broadcast over Kaduna Home Service on the evening of 29 May (B.B.C. ME/2174/B/8).*

28.
Ojukwu Appeals for Calm among Easterners in the North [1]

In the past twenty-four hours there have been disturbances in certain parts of the Northern Provinces. These disturbances are a sequel to the promulgation on national unity which the Head of the National Military Government and Supreme Commander made a few days ago. Many of you will no doubt have heard the statement of the Supreme Commander yesterday in which he stated that these disturbances are being caused by a few misguided Nigerians in collusion with foreign nationals whose objective is the sowing of discord among sections of the population. You will also no doubt have heard the broadcast of the Military Governor of the Northern Provinces in which he stated that active steps were being taken to contain the situation.

Since its assumption of office five months ago, the National Military Government has been making strenuous efforts to create an atmosphere in which Nigerians can live and work together as brothers. It is a matter for deep regret that some people by their ill-considered actions are trying to set the hands of the clock back. The Military Government is committed to the forging and maintenance of national unity and cannot be diverted from these objectives by these events.

I wish to assure all of you that the National Military Government is taking all necessary steps to bring the situation back to normal. The steps taken so far have had a salutary effect. Those Nigerians who are fomenting these disturbances will face the consequences of their actions, and their foreign backers will be dealt with in an appropriate manner.

I wish also to assure all of you, especially those of you who have relatives in the disturbed areas, that there is no cause for panic or alarm. All necessary action will be taken by the Military Government. No one must take the law into his own hands or use this as an opportunity of starting other troubles in these Provinces. Everyone must go about his or her business peacefully and rest assured that the Government has the situation well in hand.

Finally, I must repeat my earlier warning against careless talk and rumour-mongering. In times like this, these can only exacerbate the situation.

Thank you.

---

[1] *The message was recorded by the Military Governor of the East and broadcast by the E.N.B.S. in the late afternoon of 30 May 1966.*

29.
British High Commission Denies Complicity in Northern Disturbances, June 1966 [1]

I have been glad to know that official sources are reported to have dis-associated themselves from suggestions that there have been improper British activities in relation to recent events. Nigeria's domestic affairs are nothing to do with the British Government: Britain has always strictly respected the principle that one Commonwealth nation does not interfere in the domestic affairs of another. Recent allegations that the British have been in some way meddling in Nigeria's internal matters are, of course, sheer nonsense. As a friend and partner of Nigeria within the Commonwealth the British Government deplores any action that threatens the stability of Nigeria. Britain wants Nigeria to continue to build up her strength in order that she may continue to make her valuable contribution to Commonwealth and international relations, and develop her great resources with the maximum speed. Most of the British men and women working in Nigeria are here to contribute towards the expansion of development and trade, education and social progress. They cannot do their work in conditions of disorder, and

I speak for them all in expressing the hope that the peaceful conditions of law and order now restored will enable British personnel to make the fullest contribution to Nigerian progress in all parts of the Republic.

¹ *By courtesy of the U.K. High Commission, Lagos, and the Foreign and Commonwealth Office.*

30.
Hassan Addresses Northern Emirs and Chiefs, 1 June 1966 ¹

Sultan, Emirs and Chiefs:

I wish to welcome you to Kaduna on your first official visit to the Capital since the administration of the country passed into the hands of the Armed Forces. It had been my intention to invite you Chiefs to Kaduna periodically for consultation so that the Government can have the benefit of your varied and mature experience in planning the administration and economy of the country. In fact I had intended that the first meeting would take place this month. I regret very much that we had to meet earlier than planned under rather sad circumstances.

As you have all heard the National Government has unified the country by abolishing the former Regions and providing for one National Government. A Decree to this effect came into force on the 24th of May, 1966. Among the provisions of this Decree is the transfer of all the powers of the Military Governors to the National Military Government, of which all the Military Governors are members. The Military Governors however still retain the power to make subsidiary legislation which were formerly exercised by the Regional Executive Councils, the former Governor, the former Premiers and Ministers. The Decree also provides for the unification of all the Civil Services under the new name of the National Public Service. This means all Government Officers of whatever rank are employed by the National Military Government. Service matters such as appointments, promotions, transfers and discipline are under the control of the National Public Service Commission. There will however be Provincial Public Service Commissions to which the National Public Service Commission can delegate its functions concerning appointments. The Decree itself has already provided that the power to make any appointment to any office carrying an initial salary not exceeding £2,292 is to be treated as having been delegated to the Provincial Public Service Commissions. The Provincial Public Service Commissions will therefore still retain considerable powers in matters of appointment since the vast majority of Civil Servants are in the categories for which appointment will be made locally. Those officers of Government on salaries exceeding £2,292 are the minority of senior officers at the top. It is also at the level that unification is most significant since even under the old Government it was at this level that contact between officials of different Governments took place. If unification has to have any meaning the higher levels of Government Officers have to be brought closer together since they more than other levels help to share Government Policy. One other effect of unification is that appointment to posts in the Departments of the former Federal Government situated in the former Regions such as the Posts and Telegraphs or Ministry of Labour will be made by the Provincial Public Service Commissions, provided that the salary attached to the post does not exceed £2,292 a year. As I pointed out before, the bulk of appointments in Government Service fall within this range.

Since the announcement of the Decree there have been grumblings and rumours which indicated that the measures adopted have not pleased certain people. Everybody knows that it is not every time that measures adopted by Government please everybody. In any sensible society when Government action displeases any group or interest there are established ways of so informing the Government. It is the right and duty of every citizen to let the Government know if he thinks any of its actions are wrong or unduly against his interests. There are constitutional and well established channels of doing this. The citizen can express his views in the press or he can address petitions direct to the Government. As far as I am aware in this case there has been little attempt to use these well-tried methods which any Government which has the interest of the people at heart is bound to pay attention to. Certainly as far as I am concerned I have received no representations from anyone stating clearly what his grievances are. Instead over the last week-end disturbances broke out in some centres of these Provinces. Some of these disturbances were serious. Innocent lives of Nigerian citizens who had nothing to do with the introduction of these measures were lost. Property of innocent citizens was destroyed and hardship inflicted on many people.

For everybody this has been a shock since the people of these Provinces have acquired a reputation for their love of peace and solving their problems by discussion using the intelligence which God has given them. You will all recall the behaviour of our people after the events of January 15th. The facts that our reaction was calm and mature after those sad events was an indication that our people do not panic and want to settle problems facing them in a peaceful and civilized manner. Now the good reputation which we have rightly earned by our behaviour stands in danger of being shattered.

When I assumed duty as Military Governor my first official action was to visit all the Provinces in order to meet the Chiefs and discuss with them the broad outline of our plans. I then informed you all that no permanent changes would be adopted without consultation with you and the people. We are still keeping to our word. The future constitution of Nigeria and the administrative machinery of Government are by no means settled. As you are aware the Government has appointed a number of Study Groups to make investigations and submit recommendations to it. The members of some Study Groups have already visited some of you to obtain your view before formulating their recommendations. When their recommendations are received there will be the widest possible consultation before they are adopted either in whole or in a modified form.

The Head of the Military Government has made it quite clear that the measures newly introduced are purely temporary to enable the Armed Forces to put through major reforms which will pave the way for more permanent constitutional arrangements. The role of the Armed Forces is to hold the ring and provide the correct atmosphere for Nigerians to reshape their constitution free from the conflicts and rivalries of the political era. It is not the intention of the Military Government to force a Constitution of its own choice on the people. The people will be given the opportunity to decide what is the best constitution for the country. But the Military Government feels if it is to play its role well it must remove all sources of conflict and have the whole nation working with a singleness of mind.

Now even if these transitional measures are considered in any way un-workable for the limited duration which has been announced by the Head of the Military Government, those who think them defective should state their case. It is the duty of every citizen and every authority within the country to advise Government on any of its action. Although the Military Government is not an elected Government it wants at every stage to meet the wishes of the people. The wishes of the people should be expressed through the various media available to us—the press, correspondence, leaders such as Chiefs and officials. The Government must be given the opportunity to look into representations made to it. To express our wishes through the methods of violence is a practice unworthy of our people.

It is the duty of all leaders of opinion, particularly our Chiefs, to enlighten the public about their civic responsibilities. They should know the oppor-tunities which are now open to them if they bring their intelligence to bear on the problems facing us and produce constructive proposals in the search of a better life for all of us. When I toured the Region immediately after my assumption of Office I stressed to the Chiefs and all those I saw that we must look forward to the future rather than the past. It is only by what we do in the future that we can secure for the people under our charge an honourable position in the scheme of things in Nigeria. It is necessary for us to have a new awakening, to face up to our responsibilities like men. In the past we had tended to wait for everything to be done for us. This attitude of idleness and fatalism has, let us face the facts, made our people backward and weak. We now all realise that this is a competitive world and unless we can stand on our feet squarely we shall find ourselves even far behind than we are now. We have failed to make any real effort to prepare ourselves for competition. This is particularly so in the field of education where the vast majority of these Provinces have failed to make any significant contribution through voluntary effort. Without increased effort these Provinces cannot catch up with the rest of Nigeria and will remain perpetually behind. I can assure the Chiefs and people that the Military Government is determined to mount a crash programme for education and training in these Provinces, so as to enable their peoples to have their fair share in the manning of the services of the country, now and in the future. Nevertheless this must be backed up by determined voluntary effort so that these Provinces can catch up with the rest of Nigeria in the shortest possible time. We all realise the value of edu-cation and training. They are the most important tools today. Why should we wait until they are given to us? It is the duty of our leaders, particularly the Chiefs, to train the minds of our people in these constructive ways. Let the people of these Provinces show to the world that they too can make con-structive and positive contribution to the development of the country. It will be sad indeed if the impression gains ground that in these Provinces we have only enthusiasm for destroying what hardworking citizens have built.

If we are to survive we must, each one of us, show more hard work and more effort than we have so far shown.

I call on all Chiefs and all leaders of opinion to weigh carefully the points I have made. It is now time for us to take a stock of things and to adopt a new attitude to life. We should use the constructive powers which God has given us in order to secure for all of us a position of equality with all the other peoples of Nigeria. Only through the methods of hard work and effort can we attain such position. Defensiveness and violence cannot take us anywhere. They will only lead to suffering to our people.

I therefore appeal to all leaders of opinion particularly the Chiefs to discourage all acts of lawlessness. The present situation must be brought to normal in the areas affected and must not be allowed to spread elsewhere. It is the duty of everyone of us to protect the interest of all the people under our care no matter from what area they come. This is a duty enjoined on both Muslims and Christians. At all costs we must prevent violence. We must educate our people to think and work constructively. This is particularly so when the bulk of the population is engaged in producing the food on which we all depend. If normal business is disrupted then I can foresee a long period of suffering which we must all avoid. Then, of course, if violence continues the Government will have no alternative but to meet force with force. Our duty is to keep the peace so that the ordinary citizen can go about his lawful business. We must give him the assurance that we are determined to do so. The Government will not hesitate to declare as Military Area any area in which violence persists. To live in a Military Area will not be easy for anyone. It will entail hardship. If we want to avoid it we must let the Government know our wishes through peaceful means rather than by violence.

I have spoken to you at length because the situation warrants it. I know that you will all do your best when you return home to see that law and order are maintained. You will also do your best to see that those with any views and ideas to put forward bring them up constitutionally and peacefully. I hope also that you will awaken the spirit of effort and endeavour in all our people. This must be a continuous effort and not once for all. I now leave you in case you wish to discuss among yourselves and bring forward any suggestions to me.

I pray Allah to help us in all our good deeds and intentions.

[1] *Special meeting of the Northern Chiefs in Lugard Hall, Kaduna, 1 June 1966. Northern Ministry of Information Press Release No. 716/1966.*

31.
Statement Issued by the Supreme Military Council on 8 June 1966 [1]

The Supreme Military Government met in Lagos on Tuesday and Wednesday 7th and 8th June, 1966 to consider reports on the recent disturbances in certain areas of the Northern Provinces and to take measures to bring the situation under control in order to ensure that peace is restored to the whole country. In this context, the Supreme Military Council also considered the memorandum submitted by the Conference of Emirs and Chiefs of the Northern Provinces. The Council took note of the points raised in this memorandum and a suitable reply will be sent to the Emirs and Chiefs. As a matter of urgency, the Council took the decision to set up a Commission to enquire into the causes of the disturbances and to make recommendations. This is without prejudice to the law running its course. Steps are also being taken to improve information media to ensure that the policy of the Government is properly interpreted to the public as the Government is satisfied that the decree on the regions and public services has been grossly misinterpreted.

For the benefit of the public the Supreme Military Council hereby reiterates its position that the Military Government did not come to power by leave of any political party or any section of the country. The Military Government is not an elected Government and must not be treated as such. It is a corrective Government designed to remove the abuses of the old regime and to create a healthy community for return to civil Government.

The Military Government has not imposed and does not intend to impose any permanent constitution of the people. In fact, steps have been taken to set up study groups to identify the problems in the various aspects of Government activities and to submit proposals. . . .

The Military Government stands by its word. It has not deviated from [its declared] policy, but the public must not be led to confuse Military Government with government by civilian regime under a constitution approved by the people. Nobody will expect the present Military Government to cease to function until the new constitution has been approved or to be compelled to operate the old system of Government with its obvious weaknesses.

It cannot be too seriously emphasised that the Military Government while in office can only run the Government as a Military Government under a unified command. It cannot afford to run five separate governments and separate services as if it were a civilian regime.

A great deal of confusion has been generated on the latest decree on the regions and the civil services. The Supreme Military Council wishes to reassure the entire nation that this decree was designed to meet the demands of the Military Government under a unified command and to enable it carry out its day to day administration. It has in no way affected the territorial divisions of the country. The provincial Public Service Commissions continue to exercise the same functions as before except in regard to few posts in Group 6 and above. Final decision on the territorial structure of the country and the Public Service will be matters for the constituent assembly and the referendum.

The Supreme Military Council wishes to dispel any fears of domination by any section of the country. The decree is not intended to give advantage to any section of the country. The aim is to treat all Nigerians alike but it does realise that it is difficult to treat everybody alike. Some areas are more advanced than others. It is the intention of the National Military Government to give massive assistance to the less developed areas so that they can catch up as soon as possible with the more developed areas. In this way all fears of domination can be ended and all Nigerians will be able to compete with one another on an honest competitive basis.

The Supreme Military Council takes this opportunity to warn against any temptation to resort to violence as a means of compelling the Military Government to change its policy or as a reprisal. This Government will not succumb to pressure from any quarter and will no longer tolerate disturbances in any part of the country and will not hesitate in future to declare any disturbed area a Military area which will involve many restrictions and hardships on ordinary citizens. The Military Government has so far refrained from taking this drastic step because it is very conscious of the hardships this will entail. In this connection, the Military Government warns against impersonation of Military personnel and will treat any person or group of persons making such attempt according to Military law. As no person should now be left in doubt as to the intentions of the Military Government any further disturbances can only be attributed to other causes.

[1] *Federal Ministry of Information Press Release No. 686/1966.*

32.
Setting up of the Northern Group of Provinces Tribunal of Inquiry
See p. 187.

[The Notice given here is that widely advertised in the press during June and July 1966. The original is to be found in Legal Notice 56/1966, Supplement to Federation of Nigeria Official Gazette Extraordinary no. 65, vol. 53, 24 June 1966, Part B. The inquiry was never held.]

33.
Hassan Addresses Meeting of Northern Chiefs in Kaduna, 16 June 1966 [1]

Sultan, Emirs and Chiefs:
    I must begin by thanking you and all men of goodwill under your jurisdiction who have helped in restoring peace and calm throughout the Northern Group of Provinces. The disturbances which have taken place have been

PUBLIC NOTICE

THE NORTHERN GROUP OF PROVINCES

TRIBUNAL OF INQUIRY 1966

His Excellency Major-General J. T. U. Aguiyi-Ironsi, Head of the National Military Government and Supreme Commander of the Armed Forces, by an Instrument dated the 24th of June 1966 and by virtue of the powers conferred on him by Section I of the Tribunal of Inquiry Decree, 1966, has constituted and appointed a Tribunal to be called 'the Northern Group of Provinces (Disturbances) Tribunal of Inquiry', to inquire into the recent disturbances in the Northern Group of Provinces.

2.   **Terms of Reference:** The Tribunal shall, with all convenient speed:—
   (i) inquire into the causes of the recent disturbances which broke out on or about the 29th May 1966 in the Northern Group of Provinces;
   (ii) determine the areas affected by these disturbances and the sections, classes or groups of persons directly involved therein;
   (iii) ascertain the extent of loss of life, and personal injuries, as a result of these disturbances;
   (iv) frame a scheme for payment of compensation for loss of and damage to property;
   (v) determine whether any section or class or group of persons shall be held liable to pay any part of the compensation in view of their conduct during, and involvement in, the disturbances;
   (vi) have regard to the causes of the disturbances, and suggest measures designed to promote peace and harmony among the various sections of the communities involved.

3.   The Tribunal will open its meeting in Lugard Hall Kaduna, on the 2nd of August 1966 at 8 a.m. and thereafter adjourn to the 6th of September 1966 in the same venue from which date sitting will commence at 9 a.m. (unless otherwise decided by the Tribunal). All persons who wish to give evidence before the Tribunal should forward to the Secretary, Northern Group of Provinces (Disturbances) Tribunal of Inquiry, c/o Lugard Hall, Kaduna, their Memoranda giving the substance of the matter about which they wish to testify. Such memorandum which should bear the writer's full name and address should be submitted to reach the Secretary to the Tribunal not later than Tuesday 6th of September, 1966.

4.   The terms of reference of the Tribunal do not include pronouncing on individual claims for loss of or damage to property and the Tribunal will not receive evidence in support of such claims. If any such claim is sent to the Tribunal it will be preserved and transmitted with the Tribunal's report.

most unfortunate. They have been a serious set back to our economy and onward march to progress. I do feel most sincerely that the protest should not have taken this form. I am sure that every man of goodwill must feel the same way. However, I shall not dwell too long on this theme.

You all recall that on the 1st and 2nd of June you met here to consider the causes of disturbances which had broken out from the 28th of May in some areas of these Provinces. After your deliberations a memorandum was presented to me by a delegation headed by the Sultan for delivery to the Supreme Commander and Head of the National Military Government. I am glad to inform you that I have delivered your message. The Head of the National Military Government considered the contents of the message of so great importance that he promptly called a meeting of the Supreme Council in order to give immediate consideration to it. The Supreme Council duly met on the 7th and 8th of June. As a result of the deliberations of the Council certain conclusions were reached on the points raised in your memorandum and these have been embodied in a memorandum which I am to deliver to you shortly.

Before delivering the reply of the Supreme Council to you, I want to say a few words. I think that it is necessary for all of us to reflect calmly and soberly over the events of the last few weeks and over the position of our people in the scheme of things in Nigeria in general. Clearly the people of these Provinces have been left far behind and have a feeling that they are not yet in a position to compete on equal terms with their counterpart from the other Group of Provinces. This has naturally produced fears and suspicion of the intentions behind the measures introduced by the National Military Government. I want to assure you that the National Military Government is determined to protect the rights of every citizen irrespective of his place of origin. No decent man will take part in a Government whose aim is to oppress one section for the benefit of another.

If our reflections lead us to honest and true conclusions we are bound to realise that a number of things are lacking in us. The first is a basic lack of realisation that in the modern race for progress we must do things for ourselves if we are to keep abreast with the times. This requires personal effort from everyone of us. Many people have taken part in violence and destruction—and no doubt there are people who are always inclined to destructive thinking. However the man that will be remembered by history and who will deserve the gratitude of generation after generation, will be the man who can rouse our people from the slumber and spur them to a new upsurge of effort in the interest of themselves and their country. To do this requires courage, foresight and wisdom. But where better to search for these qualities than among you, the trusted and experienced leaders of your peoples?

I want to remind you that you have a duty to see that your own people, from every Emirate, have a positive and constructive contribution in every aspect of development. Many of them however think that everything must be done by Government and the Native Authorities. This notion must be erased from everybody's mind. Other people in Nigeria are ahead of the North because they are doing many things for themselves, particularly do they organise education for their children quite apart from what the Government is doing. If we are not to remain for ever behind we must cultivate the spirit of self-help and I think that it is incumbent on you, as leaders of your people to give them a lead in this matter. I am glad that the Sultan has opened the way by organising an education fund for Sokoto Province. I earnestly urge every Emir and Chief to follow this example. This is a very serious matter and we must all take it seriously. A new spirit of self-help and personal endeavour must be infused in our people and this duty squarely devolves on you. Unless we act now it will be too late and the future will be dismal.

I want to draw your attention to the serious and painful set back which recent disturbances have brought about. Many businesses have been disrupted and many people have no hand in formulating the measures objected to have suffered. They are leaving their livelihoods. We must show our maturity and tolerance by arresting these sad events. In particular we must do everything to arrest a large scale movement of people. We must do this by restoring the confidence of everyone living in these Provinces irrespective of his tribal origin. The people of these Provinces have always been known to be hospitable and tolerant. They must not abandon these qualities in the heat of emotion. I appeal to everyone to assist in restoring confidence particularly among those who are leaving the Provinces. The way to protest to Government is not through attacks on fellow citizens but through discussion and reasoned argument as you Emirs and Chiefs have shown.

Emirs and Chiefs are part and parcel of the machinery of Government. Not only have you the duty of seeing that law and order are maintained but you carry on the day to day business of administration which ensures the peace and welfare of everyone in the community. Your work therefore brings you in close touch with the people and no one is more aware of the movements of their opinion than yourself. This interim Government intends to consult public opinion before reaching major decisions and, in the absence of party political activity, I can see no better body to inform the Government of the wishes of the people than yourselves. This is why the Supreme Council has decided that in future periodical Conference of Chiefs should be held to enable you to discuss matters of importance and to give advice to the Government.

Representatives of Chiefs from all the Groups of Provinces will also go to Lagos from time to time for the purpose of giving advice to the National Military Government on national issues. I intend that the first Conference in Kaduna will take place towards the end of September. In the meantime I want the present meeting to appoint a number of committees which can meet from time to time and make recommendations to you on various subjects before you advise me.

Now I am handing over the message of the Supreme Council to the Sultan. I think that it deserves to be considered carefully and I know that you will treat it in that way. If after reading it you wish to have discussions I trust that they will result in forward looking sober and constructive proposals.

Lets all think of our future and that of our children and produce ideas for the betterment of our country. May God guide you in your thoughts and deeds.

[1] *Northern Ministry of Information Press Release No. 762/1966.*

34.
Translation of Broadcast in Hausa by the Sultan of Sokoto to the People of the North, 17 June 1966 [1]

Peace be upon you, people of the North. I am very pleased to have the opportunity to inform you that all of us, Emirs and Chiefs of the North, have once again gathered here in Kaduna at the call of the Military Governor of the Northern Group of Provinces, Lt.-Col. Hassan Usman Katsina, as you no doubt have already been aware.

We have gathered in order to receive reply to the memorandum which we addressed to the Head of the National Military Government. We have now received this reply and have carefully studied and noted its contents.

The reply touches on all the fears and grievances which led to the recent disturbances. We consider the explanations and assurances given therein by the Head of the National Military Government sufficient to allay our fears and anxieties.

I wish therefore to assure you on behalf of my brother Emirs and Chiefs that there is no longer any cause for fear or anxieties. I am also pleased to inform you that committees of chiefs have from the first day of our meeting been appointed in order to advise Government on matters of policy on the various important aspects affecting the well-being of the community.

I assure you that we Emirs and Chiefs will never subscribe to any decision which is not aimed at the common good of all. I also assure you that the Military Government has no intention whatsoever of imposing a permanent pattern of Government or administration for the benefit of a particular section of the country.

It is my earnest prayer that you will give us your increased support and have faith in what we consider to be trustworthy, just as you responded to my appeal for the discontinuance of the recent disturbances.

I wish to reassure you that we are in no doubt that no permanent pattern of Government will be imposed on the country without the consent of the people to be ascertained by a freely conducted referendum.

Therefore, let there be no longer any apprehension, fear or rumour. You should all return to your normal daily pursuits without fear of molestation or discrimination on grounds of tribe or religion. You should forget about the recent disturbance.

Whenever you are in doubt about the implication of any public policy you should seek explanation from your elders and leaders.

The Military Government is your Government; and is determined to work for the best interest of all the people as they have promised upon assumption of power.

We are conscious of our traditional hospitality. I therefore appeal to all those people from other Provinces who are now preparing to leave, to remain and those who have already left, to return.

[1] *Broadcast from Kaduna on the evening of 17 June 1966. See also* New Nigerian, *20 June 1966.*

35.
Ironsi's Address to the National Conference of Traditional Rulers, Ibadan, 28 July 1966[1]

I greet you and welcome you to this conference which is the first of its kind since the present Military Government was handed the administration of the Republic by the former Federal Council of Ministers.

You are all aware of the events leading to the handover. For some time before January 1966, law and order had all but broken down in certain parts of the country: the ordinary people were not free to move about: political leaders found it impossible to meet: life and property were not safe and there was utter bewilderment, frustration and despair. Today the reverse is the case and ordinary people can now move about.

The situation at the material time called for men imbued with true patriotism and the courage to uphold and proclaim the truth in the interest of the nation. Unfortunately, our former leaders jointly and severally failed the country in its hour of need.

Partisan interest became equated with the public interest and men were ranged implacably in warring camps, pointing accusing fingers at one another.

It is regrettable, indeed painful to recall that some traditional rulers pitched their fortunes with one or the other of those warring camps and so did much to bring the institution of chieftaincy into ridicule and contempt. . . .

The first aim of the Military Government was to restore law and order where these had broken down. Calm and peace has now returned to all parts of the country despite the recent disturbances in the Delta Area and in some parts of the Northern Group of Provinces.

The administration's basic task now is to maintain peace and good Government throughout the Republic. Law and order are the essential ingredients of a stable society and we must do everything within our power at all levels to see that they are reserved.

You the traditional rulers of the country have a great part to play in its survival and development. You hold a revered position in the Nigerian community and it is in the belief that, in this period of national reconstruction, you can contribute immensely to the stability of the country that I have summoned this conference.

You will, I am sure, wish to know what contribution you can usefully make. The National Government does not expect you to take the place of the disbanded politicians. Your exalted position as father to all your people precludes you from fulfilling such a role.

But you can set a good example in the community in which you live and provide effective leadership.

As chiefs and traditional rulers you are expected to co-operate wholeheartedly with the Police and local administration in the maintenance of law and order in your domain.

You are expected in the performance of judicial functions either as customary court judges or justices of the peace to dispense justice impartially according to the merits of the case.

More than anything, you are expected to reflect in your conduct all that is

o

good in the community over which you have been appointed to be traditional rulers.

But you cannot fail in your eminent positions to form your own impressions on what may be done to enable the republic to live down its recent unhappy past and to return once more to the path of prudence, rectitude, discipline and honour.

This conference affords all of us taking part in it an excellent opportunity for a frank exchange of views. Nigerians are noted for their respect for constituted authority; for their cherished traditions and culture and for their chieftancy institutions.

In my view, every Nigerian should regard the Obong of Calabar as his Obong; the Ovie of Oghara as his Ovie: the Emir of Argungu as his Emir; Oni of Ife as his Oni; the Obi of Onitsha as his Obi and the Oba of Lagos as his Oba.

In response each and every natural ruler should see to it that no Nigerian suffers by accident of his origin. Nigerians, wherever they reside, expect the natural ruler to be the fountain of justice and leader of all inhabitants in his area of authority.

I should fail in my duty however if I do not also point out that it is equally important that those who reside in other than their normal domicile should respect the feelings of those among whom they sojourn. They should not be selfish in their dealings, seeking merely to advance only the cause of themselves and their relations to the detriment of the common people among whom they live.

The National Military Government would therefore welcome such suggestions as you may wish to make for a better and more enduring foundation for the future administration of this country.

I will not on this occasion recount in detail the steps which the National Military Government has taken to create a healthier climate for genuine and honest investors in Nigeria.

I wish to assure you however, that the Government is actively engaged with the formulation of plans for a 5-year development programme which will ensure rapid industrialisation, increased food production, increased diversification of the economy and a more equitable distribution of income.

I wish to take this opportunity to reiterate that it is the policy of the National Military Government to hold adequate and full consultation with the public before any major and fundamental changes affecting the constitution or their civic rights are introduced.

Maximum publicity will be given to all future measures which the Military Government intends to pursue.

Their true implications will be explained to the people through every possible known mass communications media so as to ensure that the people are fully aware of the purpose of such measures.

The National Military Government believes in the free expression of views by the people provided that such views are not libellous or slanderous and they do not tend to foster disunity.

In conclusion, I wish to state clearly that the National Military Government has implicit confidence in the ability of the traditional rulers as custodians of our cherished traditions to give our people the correct type of leader-

ship which will ensure that this great country of ours strides into the future
proud and united.

[1] Morning Post, *29 July 1966.*

36.
National Military Government Announces its Plans for the Development of the Economy[1]

Since the National Military Government came into office on January 17,
1966, individuals and various organisations have made suggestions and requests in the Press on how to reconstruct the nation.

These have been given careful, sincere and honest consideration by the
National Military Government.

Those which are realistic and practical are receiving immediate attention
by the Government.

Some are useful but impractical at the moment.

Therefore, to make the public aware of the plans of the Government, the
National Ministry of Information is putting out in series 'Guide to the National
Military Government Plans' which will not only be devoted to putting forward the plans of the Government but will also analyse and answer the suggestions and requests from the public.

The National Military Government is a corrective government which is
prepared to receive suggestions, requests and constructive criticisms. . . .

The National Military Government has been asked to take steps to reduce
house rents in the Capital Territory to a minimum of £1 10s. a room without
modern amenities; £2 10s. for a room with modern amenities and £10 per
month for each wing of flats containing four rooms with individual amenities;
£12 10s. for a self-contained flat with modern amenities i.e. two bed-rooms,
sitting room, dining room, boy's quarters and garage, or £20 per month for a
self-contained flat with four bed-rooms.

On Rent Decree the National Military Government is asked to amplify and
tighten up the Rent Decree to counteract the exploitation of poor tenants by
landlords.

On Rent Control, the policy of the Military Government has been enunciated in Decree No. 15 on Rent Control and recently amplified by an amendment Decree and by Regulations under that Decree.

Briefly, rent will be fixed such that investment in housing together with
recurrent expenses can be recovered with reasonable profit over a period of
not less than ten years.

The rent chargeable per room will therefore depend on the cost of buildings,
the level of rates chargeable in the area and the level of profit which the land-
lord wants to make.

In order to ensure a fair deal, rent tribunals are being set up in four
tribunal districts in the Lagos area.

The figures quoted as rent in various suggestions on this subject cannot be
accepted unless they conform with the general policy stated above.

With regard to payment of rent in advance, the Rent Control Decree has laid down a maximum of one month as the period over which a demand may be made in advance. . . .

The suggestion that the National Military Government should make it compulsory for the National Public Service Commission to interview and employ university graduates early in July instead of August yearly, so as to end the frustration which has been usually the lot of newly qualified graduates can best be viewed from the Government's stand; that there is no set policy that graduates must be interviewed in August every year.

However, every effort is made to interview graduates for employment as soon as the results of the final year students in all the five universities are known.

On the view that the National Military Government should set up a Compulsory National Military Service to inculcate in every Nigerian a sense of discipline.

The National Military Government is aware that this question received the attention of the former Federal Government on a number of occasions.

The then Government examined the suggestion very closely but discovered that in spite of some seemingly attractive arguments adduced in its favour, the proposal was in fact not necessary in Nigeria.

This is, firstly because compulsory national service is normally introduced in countries where there is difficulty in recruiting adequate numbers of volunteers to serve in the Armed Forces.

No such difficulty exists in this country at present.

There are more volunteers than the Armed Forces are in a position to recruit having regard to the size of the Armed Forces.

In fact up to the present moment the number of those absorbed into the Armed Services represents a very small fraction of the total number of volunteers.

Secondly, as recruitment into the Armed Services must be highly selective and adequate training facilities have to be provided very little advantage would be gained from recruiting larger numbers than necessary into the Armed Forces.

The size of the Armed Forces must be determined in the light of the needs of our national defence and internal security.

Besides, unless the question is carefully considered it may be difficult to find jobs for the demobilised youths at the expiration of their national service.

Another factor which weighed considerably with the Government at the time was the question of costs.

The expense of setting up compulsory national service would be enormous as the recruits have to be paid, equipped and provided with accommodation.

Unless there was threat of external aggression such heavy expenditure could hardly be justified at a time when the Government was trying to ensure that the best use was made of the limited available resources.

The present National Government has not given any further consideration to this matter since the conditions which militated against the setting up of a compulsory national service in the past are still present today.

A large number of highly placed and experienced service officers are, under the present Government, being engaged in duties other than pure military service.

To introduce compulsory national service now, would burden the Armed Forces with a large number of recruits for whom there are not enough experienced service officers available to provide the necessary training.

The policy of the Government has been to encourage the establishment of cadet units in secondary schools throughout the country as a means of stimulating interest in manly pursuits and encouraging qualities of leadership among the youths.

No change from that policy is considered either necessary or practicable.

On the question of the National Military Government investigating the various 'white elephant' projects organised by the previous Governments and scrapping such projects which, it considered, will yield no profit; The National Military Government is already looking into this matter with the main aim of protecting the long-term interests of both the Government and the people of Nigeria.

It should be emphasised however that some of the projects which appear to be 'white elephants' are desirable, although they are over-burdened with technical, financial and administrative problems.

The previous Governments had already sunk so much money into some of them that a realistic solution to the problems created by them might not necessarily lie in having them scrapped.

Steps are being taken to identify these problems, draw up conclusions and put up recommendations to the Governments. . . .

In making its stand clear on the call by the public for the National Military Government to probe the question of unemployment in the country;

The National Military Government wishes to assure the public that the question is receiving urgent attention.

The National Manpower Board is collecting the necessary information to enable it to recommend solutions to the problem of unemployment.

Various suggestions have been made to the National Military Government on matters concerning Labour Unions.

These are:

the introduction of compulsory arbitration and establishment of industrial courts to facilitate a speedier settlement of trade disputes which may otherwise have resulted in strikes;

issuing of stern measures towards the promotion of labour unity in the country;

banning of all existing labour unions since they are a source of disunity in the country. . . .

On the above suggestions, the National Military Government has recently approved proposals designed to regulate the procedure for dealing with trade disputes and for the establishment of an industrial court.

It is hoped that a Decree embodying these proposals will be issued in the near future.

The National Military Government has also approved proposals for the regulations of the organisation and development of trade unions.

A Decree embodying these proposals is under preparation and when promulgated its provisions should assist in the promotion of Labour unity.

---

[1] *Statement issued in Lagos on 26 July 1966.*

37.

'No Trust or Confidence in a Unitary System of Government': Lt.-Col. Gowon's Broadcast on the Assumption of Office, 1 August 1966 [1]

This is Lt.-Col. Y. Gowon, Army Chief of Staff, speaking to you. My fellow countrymen, the year 1966 has certainly been a fateful year for our beloved country, Nigeria. I have been brought to the position today of having to shoulder the great responsibilities of this country and the armed forces with the consent of the majority of the members of the Supreme Military Council as a result of the unfortunate incident that occurred on the early morning of 29th July 1966.

However, before I dwell on the sad issue of 29th July 1966, I would like to recall to you the sad and unfortunate incidents of 15th January 1966 which bear relevance. According to the certain well-known facts, which have so far not been disclosed to the nation and the world, the country was plunged into a national disaster by the grave and unfortunate action taken by a section of the Army against the public. By this I mean that a group of officers, in conjunction with certain civilians, decided to overthrow the legal government of the day; but their efforts were thwarted by the inscrutable discipline and loyalty of the great majority of the Army and the other members of the armed forces and the police. The Army was called upon to take up the reins of government until such time that law and order had been restored. The attempt to overthrow the government of the day was done by eliminating political leaders and high-ranking Army officers, a majority of whom came from a particular section of the country. The Prime Minister lost his life during this uprising. But for the outstanding discipline and loyalty of the members of the Army who are most affected, and the other members of the armed forces and the police, the situation probably could have degenerated into a civil war.

There followed a period of determined effort of reconstruction ably shouldered by Maj-Gen. J. T. U. Aguiyi-Ironsi but, unfortunately, certain parties caused suspicion and grave doubts of the Government's sincerity in several quarters. Thus, coupled with the already unpleasant experience of the 15th January still fresh in the minds of the majority of the people, certain parts of the country decided to agitate against the military regime which had hitherto enjoyed country-wide support. It was, unfortunately, followed by serious rioting and bloodshed in many cities and towns in the north.

There followed a period of uneasy calm until the early hours of 29th July 1966, when the country was once again plunged into another very serious and grave situation, the second in seven months. The position on the early morning of 29th July was a report from Abeokuta garrison, that there was a mutiny and that two senior and one junior officers from a particular section of the country were killed. This soon spread to Ibadan and Ikeja. More casualties were reported in these places. The Supreme Commander was by this time at Ibadan attending the natural rulers' conference and was due to return on the afternoon of 29th July. The Government Lodge was reported attacked and the last report was that he and the West Military Governor were both kidnapped by some soldiers. Up till now, there is no confirmation of their whereabouts. The situation was soon brought under control in these places. Very shortly afterward, at about the same time, there was a report that there were similar disturbances among the troops in the North, and that a section of the troops had taken control of all military stations in the North as well. The units of Enugu and the garrison at Benin were not involved. All is now quiet and I can assure the public that I shall do all in my power to stop any further bloodshed and to restore law, order and confidence in all parts of the country with your co-operation and goodwill.

I have now come to the most difficult part, or the most important part, of this statement. I am doing it, conscious of the great disappointment and heartbreak it will cause all true and sincere lovers of Nigeria and of Nigerian unity both at home and abroad, especially our brothers in the Commonwealth.

As a result of the recent events and the other previous similar ones, I have come to strongly believe that we cannot honestly and sincerely continue in this wise, as the basis of trust and confidence in our unitary system of government has not been able to stand the test of time. I have already remarked on the issues in question. Suffice to say that, putting all considerations to test —political, economic, as well as social—the base for unity is not there or is so badly rocked, not only once but several times. I therefore feel that we should review the issue of our national standing and see if we can help stop the country from drifting away into utter destruction. With the general consensus of opinion of all the Military Governors and other members of the Supreme and Executive Council, a decree will soon be issued to lay a firm foundation of this objective. Fellow countrymen, I sincerely hope we shall be able to resolve most of the problems that have disunited us in the past and really come to respect and trust one another in accordance with an all-round code of good conduct and etiquette.

All foreigners are assured of their personal safety and should have no fear of being molested.

I intend to continue the policy laid down in the statement by the Supreme Commander on 16th January 1966 published on 26th January 1966.

We shall also honour all international treaty obligations and commitments and all financial agreements and obligations entered into by the previous government. We are desirous of maintaining good diplomatic relationships with all countries. We therefore consider any foreign interference in any form will be regarded as an act of aggression.

All members of the armed forces are requested to keep within their barracks except on essential duties and when ordered from SHQ.[2] Troops must not terrorise the public, as such action will discredit the new National Military Government. Any act of looting or sabotage will be dealt with severely. You are to remember that your task is to help restore law and order and confidence in the public in time of crisis.

I am convinced that with your co-operation and understanding, we shall be able to pull the country out of its present predicament. I promise you that I shall do all I can to return to civil rule as soon as it can be arranged. I also intend to pursue most vigorously the question of the release of political prisoners. Fellow countrymen, give me your support and I shall endeavour to live up to expectations. Thank you.

[1] *The speech was broadcast from Lagos on the morning of 1 August 1966. The printed*

texts contained in the Federal Military Government's publications Nigeria 1966 and The
Struggle for One Nigeria *contain minor textual variations—including in one instance the
omission of the key word 'not'—and so the version used here is the actual recording of the
verbatim broadcast. See B.B.C. ME/2229/B/1.*
  [2] *Supreme Headquarters.*

38.
Statement by Ojukwu, 1 August 1966 [1]

Fellow Countrymen,
  I have considered with my Executive Committee the very grave events in
some parts of the country regarding the rebellion by some sections of the
Nigerian Army against the National Military Government, which resulted in
the kidnapping of His Excellency the Head of the National Military Govern-
ment and Supreme Commander of the Armed Forces, Major-General J. T. U.
Aguiyi-Ironsi, and the cold premeditated murder of officers of Eastern
Nigeria origin.
  In the course of this rebellion, I had discussions with the Chief of Staff,
Supreme Headquarters, Brigadier Ogundipe who, as the next most senior
officer, in the absence of the Supreme Commander, should have assumed
command of the Army, my colleagues the other Military Governors, and the
Chief of Staff, Army Headquarters, Lt.-Col. Gowon. During these discussions
it was understood that the only conditions on which the rebels would agree
to a ceasefire were:
i. that the Republic of Nigeria be split into its component parts;
ii. that all Southerners resident in the North be repatriated to the South, and
all Northerners resident in the South repatriated to the North.
  In spite of the fact that the only representations made at these ceasefire
negotiations were those of the rebels and their supporters in the North, and
notwithstanding that the views of the people of the Eastern Group of
Provinces had not been ascertained, it was agreed to accept these proposals
and stop further bloodshed.
  The public is aware of the wanton and deliberate massacre of several people
of Eastern Nigeria origin in last May's disturbances in parts of the Northern
Group of Provinces. In view of the very strong feelings aroused amongst the
people of the East at that time as to whether their membership in the
Nigerian nation was desirable, I appealed to the Chiefs and leaders of the
people to use their influence to stop any retaliation or precipitate action in
the hope that this would be the final act of sacrifice Easterners would be
called upon to make in the interest of Nigerian unity. However, the brutal
and planned annihilation of officers of Eastern Nigeria origin in the last few
days has again cast serious doubts as to whether the people of Nigeria, after
these cruel and bloody atrocities, can ever sincerely live together as members
of the same nation.
  I have noted the action taken to stop bloodshed in the country, and now
consider that the next step would be to open discussions at the appropriate
level to allow other sections of the Nigerian people to express their views, as

their Northern compatriots have recently done, as to what form of association they desire for themselves in accordance with the ceasefire terms.

As a result of the pressures and representations now being made to me by the Chiefs, Leaders and organizations in the Eastern Group of Provinces, I am arranging for Representatives of Chiefs and organizations in these Provinces to meet and advise me.

Meanwhile, I appeal to our people of these Provinces not to give expressions to their feelings in any violent form, but to co-operate with the law enforcement authorities in the assurance that your rights of self-determination will be guaranteed.

I have further conveyed to the Chief of Staff Supreme Headquarters, my fellow Military Governors and the Chief of Staff Army Headquarters, my understanding that the only intention of the announcement made by the Chief of Staff Army Headquarters today is the restoration of peace in the country whilst immediate negotiations are begun to allow the people of Nigeria to determine the form of their future association.

Goodnight and thank you.

[1] *Broadcast from Enugu on the evening of 1 August 1966. Text taken from* Crisis '66, *pp. 22–3.*

39.
Military Governor of the West (Colonel Adebayo) Declares for the New Régime[1]

My dear people. I am Colonel Adebayo. It has fallen to my lot to address you this evening as the new Military Governor appointed by the National Military Government to look after the affairs of the Western Group of Provinces. We are all aware of the circumstances which necessitated this appointment.

As revealed in the statement made by the new Supreme Commander and Head of the National Military Government, a few days ago, Lieutenant-Colonel Adekunle Fajuyi, the former Military Governor of this group of Provinces, was kidnapped together with the former Supreme Commander and the Head of the National Military Government, last Friday.

Up till now, nothing is known of the whereabouts of either the Supreme Commander or the Military Governor.

I know how deeply touched the people of Western Provinces feel about the disappearance of Lt.-Col. Fajuyi, who had endeared himself so much to every citizen of the provinces, through his hard work, his vision and devotion to the cause of progress in the provinces.

We do hope that both the former Supreme Commander and Lt.-Col. Fajuyi are still alive and that they will soon be returned safely to continue their services to the nation, but whatever happens, I am sure that Lt.-Col. Fajuyi's record as a great soldier and able administrator is one which will be long remembered in this group of provinces and throughout the Republic of Nigeria.

As many of you will have noted, the announcement of my appointment coincided with another event which is of momentous importance to all Nigerians.

Here I refer to the release from prison of Chief Obafemi Awolowo and other Nigerian leaders, which was announced by the National Military Government last Tuesday.

The release of Chief Awolowo has, for some time, been the burning desire of most of our people in Nigeria.

I am sure, therefore, that you all share a feeling of gratitude to the National Military Government for its gesture in this respect.

Chief Awolowo is one of the architects of Nigeria's independence and one who still has a lot to contribute towards the building of the new Nigerian nation which is the aspiration of many Nigerians. I personally wish him many more years of useful service to Nigeria.

One important point to which I want to invite your special attention in this address is the question or unity. You have every right to say that this is not a new point, as it has been emphasised several times in the past by several people.

But I would like to raise this question with you in a special way tonight, because I regard unity as one of the main objectives of my administration.

I consider it most important that the people of Western Provinces should forget the recriminations and differences of the past and form a united front in order that they as a people might succeed in bringing about the political, economic and social progress of the Western group of Provinces in particular and of the Republic of Nigeria in general.

Charity, it is said, must always begin at home, and unless we in Western Provinces learn to live together as brothers forgiving one another, whatever injuries or offences we might have committed against one another in the past, it will not be possible for us to make that great contribution which other groups of provinces in the Republic have a right to expect of us in the affairs of the nation.

I therefore call upon all our people: our obas, chiefs, elders, intellectuals and other leaders of thought, farmers—and indeed every Western Provinces citizen—to let us bury the hatchet and enlist with me in this 'operation unity' —unity for our immediate progress and well-being as people of the Western group of Provinces and unity for the advancement of the Republic of Nigeria.

I trust we have all learnt the necessary lesson from the regrettable events of the last few days. They serve to remind us of the need to reconsider a number of political, economic and social issues confronting our nation.

They also serve to bring home to all of us the potential destructive consequences of parochialism, intolerance and lack of mutual affection not only between one Nigerian and another, but also between groups in the nation.

Now that a calm atmosphere has been restored I believe everyone of us will devote their energies and resources towards ensuring that the unhappy situation is never repeated in the history of our nation.

I enjoin every man and woman in the Western group of Provinces to carry on his or her normal duties and endeavour to practise in his or her dealings with other citizens in the community the spirit of tolerance and mutual respect.

I commend the action of church leaders in Nigeria in calling for special prayers for peace and unity in the nation. In pursuance of this, I have specially requested that today be set aside for special prayers in all mosques, throughout the Western group of Provinces for unity in the provinces, and peace and progress throughout the Republic.

A similar request is being made to all Christian churches of all denominations throughout the Western group of Provinces, for the observance of next Sunday as a day of special intercession in all the churches in the Western group of Provinces.

Before bringing this address to a close, I would like to assure all our people that I have come here to serve and to give of the best service I am capable of in the interest of our beloved nation.

I do not regard myself as belonging exclusively to any sections or groups. I belong to all and wish to be able to count upon the co-operation of everyone of our people—whatever his past attachments or leanings and irrespective of his place of origin or position in life—to ensure the success of this great task which it has pleased Providence to entrust unto me (and unto all of you) at this time and stage in the history of our country.

May God bless you all and give us all the necessary wisdom, strength and courage to serve the best interest of our nation and generation. Good night.

[1] *Broadcast from Ibadan, 4 August 1966*; Daily Times, *5 August 1966*.

40.
Instrument of Pardon—Chief Awolowo, 2 August 1966 [1]

By His Excellency Lieutenant-Colonel YAKUBU GOWON, Head of the National Military Government, Supreme Commander of the Armed Forces of the Republic of Nigeria.

WHEREAS Chief Obafemi Awolowo, having been duly convicted of the offences of treasonable felony, conspiracy to commit a felony and conspiracy to effect an unlawful purpose, and sentenced to imprisonment for ten, five and two years respectively on all three counts:

AND WHEREAS the said Chief Obafemi Awolowo, having served a portion of the sentence originally imposed on him in September 1963:

AND WHEREAS the Supreme Military Council after reviewing his case, is pleased to remit the sentence and to grant a full pardon:

NOW THEREFORE, in exercise of the powers conferred by section 101 (1) of the Constitution of the Republic and of all other powers enabling it in that behalf, the Supreme Military Council do hereby remit the unexpired portion of the sentence imposed on the aforesaid Chief Obafemi Awolowo and grant him a full pardon.

GIVEN UNDER my hand and the Public Seal of the Republic of Nigeria at Lagos this 2nd day of August, one thousand nine hundred and sixty-six.

[1] *Government Notice No. 1507/1966.*

41.

Awolowo's Speech to the Western Leaders of Thought on accepting the title of 'Leader of the Yorubas', August 1966 [1]

It gives me much pleasure to address this gathering of Western Nigeria leaders.

The times in which we live are very difficult and most trying. There is disaffection everywhere in the country and, in most parts, there is pronounced bitterness. The emotion for revenge wells high in almost every heart and our potentially great country now stands perilously on the brink of disintegration and chaos. Though the first scene in the first act of this prolonged tragedy was performed here in the West, the actual performances and dramatis personae of this belong, at present, to the other parts of the Republic. It would be criminal folly, however, for us in the West to rejoice at the misfortunes of our fellow-citizens for the happiness of Nigeria are indivisible and so are their misfortunes and adversities. There are two things which we must seek to do immediately. Firstly, we must seek to arrest the process of Nigeria's disintegration and reunite the country. Secondly, we must put an end to the prevailing internecine hostilities, and we must reorganise our affairs in such a manner as to prevent a recrudescence of these hostilities.

In the task of preserving the unity of the whole country, those of us who are gathered here have an important role to play. We must endeavour with all our might, to stamp out from our midst in Western Nigeria, every factor or element which may tend to keep our people asunder and at daggers drawn. I say this in the firm belief that unity and harmony among the people in this part of the Republic, apart from doing our provinces good, is bound to have uniting and beneficial effects on the Republic as a whole. It is my humble opinion that the search for unity, be it for Western Nigeria or for the entire Republic need not elude us. It need not elude us, provided the leaders of thought throughout the land are prepared to forget our unedifying past, and devote our full attention to selfless service to our people by promoting their welfare and happiness, recognise that revenge, naked self-interest, and injurious self-aggrandizement are obstacles to unity, and we must resolutely eschew them.

During the past four years, Western Nigeria has been strife-torn and the victim of self-inflicted wounds. The same thing goes for the whole of the country since last January. We must now bend our energies towards the ending of the strife, and the healing of the wounds. These we can achieve (1) by abjuring revenge (2) by cultivating the spirit of benevolence and goodwill towards one another and (3) by making the welfare and happiness of the mass of our people our exclusive and overriding objectives.

The unity which we seek today must be unity based on selfless service to our fellowmen. This kind of unity can never fail. The bloody hostilities which we have witnessed in recent times are political not personal. We must therefore seek political solutions to them. In this connection, it is imperative that we make an intensive as well as objective re-appraisal of our constitutional problems. We must also set for ourselves normative social objectives which are rationally and scientifically orientated.

It is extremely sad to note that some leaders of thought in the country are seriously suggesting that the so-called four component units of the country should go their own separate ways as so many sovereign states. Those who advocate this course of action are invoking terrible, unknowable and unpredictable disasters and catastrophes on the heads of the 56 million innocent people of this country. In any case, these advocates must be reminded that there are more than four component parts in Nigeria. There are 10 major component parts as follows: (1) Hausa/Fulani—13·6 million; (2) Yoruba— 13 million; (3) Ibo—7·8 million; (4) Efik/Ibibio—3·2 million; (5) Kanuri— 2·9 million; (6) Tiv—1·5 million; (7) Ijaw—·9 million; (8) Edo—·9 million; (9) Urhobo—·6 million; (10) Nupe—·5 million. There are 41 minor component units. Thirty-two of these are in the Northern Provinces, while nine are in the Eastern Provinces. I give these data in order that those who are insisting on the breaking-up of the country may appreciate, before it is too late, the magnitude of the unspeakable calamities which the success of their advocacy is sure to import.

In a nutshell, the problems which confront the nation in general and Western Nigeria in particular are the same. We all fervently desire unity and peace. If this meeting can evolve formulae for unity and peace in Western Nigeria, it would have taken a big and decisive step towards the achievement of unity and peace for the entire Republic. It takes two to make friends. Until we know exactly the settled attitudes of our fellow citizens in the North and East towards the future of the Republic, it would be sheer waste of time for us to embark on the detailed consideration of a new constitution for the country. In the meantime, therefore, I suggest that we confine ourselves to two things. Firstly, we should here and now evolve a formula for unity amongst us in Western Nigeria. Secondly we should define in precise terms our own attitude to the future of Nigeria.

May success attend our deliberations here.

[1] *By courtesy of a Western civil servant.*

42.
Mid-West Military Governor's Speech in Support of the New Régime [1]

Barely one week ago, the people of the Mid-Western Group of Provinces had the honour and privilege to receive Major-General J. T. U. Aguiyi-Ironsi as Head of the National Military Government and Supreme Commander of the Armed Forces. The reception accorded him was such that he felt reassured of unflinching support for the National Military Government.

I was shocked to hear that within 24 hours of his departure from the Mid-West for a conference of traditional rulers at Ibadan, he and his host, Lt.-Col. F. A. Fajuyi, Military Governor of the Western Group of Provinces, were kidnapped by a section of the Army and taken to an unknown destination.

It is gratifying however, that, despite these unfortunate and gruesome incidents, the people of the Mid-Western Group of Provinces have remained calm and have refrained from violent reactions.

This is no doubt because they are noted to be generally peaceful and law abiding, especially in times of crisis. I trust that these qualities will be maintained, whatever the situation, and that law and order will continue to be preserved in this area. I personally intend to do everything in my power to see that the balance is maintained.

Although I am deeply touched by the events of the last few days, I am resolved not to allow what has happened to becloud my sense of responsibility to the Republic as a whole and to the people of the Mid-West in particular. A new Military Government, led by Lt.-Col. Gowon, has been announced and we should do our utmost to co-operate with it.

I am convinced, however, that it is idle and unpatriotic to pretend that all is now well with the nation. Frankly, the position, as I see it, is still tense and all true lovers of the country, especially those in positions of trust and authority, must take all necessary measures firmly to arrest the situation. Time may well be against us. . . .

It seems that most Mid-Westerners are giving serious thought to the following questions:

Are we to have a unitary state with powers centralised at the national capital?

A federal state with strong Central Government and relatively weak regional or provincial Government?

A loose Federation with strong Regional (or provincial) Government and a relatively weak Government at the centre responsible only for limited common services? Or

Should the country be broken up into several new and independent states?

The questions posed above raise fundamental issues to which the right answer must be found without delay, not by bullets but by mutual and friendly discussion.

This is a challenge from which we must not flinch.

I hope that the Head of the new National Military Government will accept it and arrange in the next few days for a conference to be attended by representatives of all parts of the Republic and at which serious and objective attempt would be made to help determine the future of the country.

[1] *Speech made in Benin, 3 August 1966;* Daily Times, *4 August 1966;* New Nigerian, *5 August 1966.*

43.
Gowon's First Press Conference, given at the National Hall, Lagos, 4 August 1966[1]

Gentlemen of the Press,

I welcome this opportunity of addressing myself to you, as new Head of the National Military Government and Supreme Commander of the Armed Forces of the Nigerian Republic. You are all aware of the circumstances of the country in the past week-end which brought me into this office. I had the responsibility thrust upon me, and I had to accept it in the national interest. It is a responsibility whose gravity and sheer weight form the main motive behind my desire to meet you gentlemen of the Press, radio and television with a view to making an urgent appeal for your co-operation.

In my maiden statement last Monday, I hastened to assure the people of Nigeria that plans would be laid on for an early return to civilian government. I wish to repeat this undertaking once again. I wish to add that, meanwhile, no major constitutional or other changes will be effected without the fullest consultation with the people. To this end, I propose to appoint an Advisory Committee dealing with the main issues of national interest. The aim is to fill part of the vacuum created by the ban on all political organizations. This committee will be composed of independent and respectable Nigerian citizens drawn from various sections of the community. It is my intention to seek their advice from time to time on matters affecting the national interests and the welfare of our people.

The National Military Government under my headship will be a continuing effort. As I indicated in my maiden broadcast of last Monday, it is my intention to continue the policy laid down in the statement by the former Supreme Commander on 16th January, 1966. We shall also honour all international treaty obligations and commitments and all financial agreements and obligations entered into by the previous Government. We shall maintain good diplomatic relations with all countries. All foreigners in Nigeria are assured of their personal safety and should have no fear of being molested. We shall continue with vigour the policy of providing a climate conducive and attractive to foreign investors. They are assured of the protection and goodwill of my government. In view of the foregoing, it is the stand of my government that foreign interference in any form will be regarded as an act of aggression.

All public officers at the national level and in the various Groups of Provinces will continue in their office carrying out the normal functions of government. Public corporations and other statutory bodies as well as local government councils will continue to function under their appropriate Ministries. All existing laws, regulations, orders and official instructions remain in force, unless and until either modified or abrogated by the National Military Government.

Arising from the events of the past week the whole atmosphere is heavily charged with false and tendentious rumours. Thus the circumstances of the Republic at present call for a maximum and judicious use of all the media of publicity with a view to enlightening the people and clearing the suspicions and anxieties generated by these rumours. The public outside Nigeria must also be enlightened about the true position of things. They must not be allowed to form grossly exaggerated notions about this country.

It is for these reasons that I wish to make a special appeal to the Press and Radio, local and foreign, for their co-operation with the National Military Government. We have no intention of curtailing in anyway the freedom which the Nigerian Press has enjoyed up to this time. But we appeal to them to exercise such freedom with a deep sense of national duty, loyalty and responsibility.

Further, we appeal for the sympathy and understanding of the Foreign

Press. Let them be honest and constructive in their reporting and interpretation of the Nigerian scene. We know our circumstances too well and do not ask for a rosy and unrealistic picture of Nigeria. Let them take and present us for what we are—a newly independent African State struggling against great odds of history, geography, ethnography and the evil effects of imperialism, to build a nation in less than one-fiftieth of the time it took European states to build theirs.

Thank you, one and all.

¹ *Reproduced from* Nigeria 1966, *pp. 34–5.*

44.
Gowon Announces his Government's Policy for Return to Civilian Rule, 8 August 1966¹

In my recent statement to the Nation, I stressed that the events of the past few days had proved beyond doubt that a Unitary system of Government had not stood the test of time in our country and that, with the general consensus of all the Military Governors and the other members of the Supreme and Executive Councils, I intended to issue a new decree detailing the proposals for the building of a sound foundation for national unity, in a manner which would prevent our country at daytime drifting away into utter destruction. I ended the statement with a promise that I would do all that was possible for a return to civilian rule as soon as it could be arranged.

Since then, as you would have probably gathered from the Press and other media of information, the Military Governors, of the Eastern, Mid-Western, Western and Northern Provinces have all agreed with me that there is urgent need for discussions, at the appropriate level, to pave the way for the people to express their views as to the form of association they desire for themselves. Consultations at Provincial level are going on right now to ascertain the wishes of all sections of the people and I sincerely hope that these will be constructive and fruitful in the overall national interest.

The basic point which has emerged from recent events is that, we as a people, are quite aware that this great country of ours has much to benefit in remaining a single entity in one form or another. Our difficulties in the past have been how to agree on the form which such association should take and the task of my Government is to provide facilities for the widest and fullest consultations at all levels, on all vital matters of national interest before a decision is taken. In the past we have been too presumptuous and have acted on such presumptions. Too often we presumed that we know best what the people desire. In one or two cases, hasty decisions were taken without sufficient consultation. To ensure an effective implementation of the basic policies of my Government, I intend to carry out the following immediately:

a. A three-stage plan for return to civil Government, starting with the immediate modification or nullification of any provision of any decree which assumes extreme centralization. This will ensure a rapid return to the former

Federal structure of the Constitution as a basis for further constitutional review.

b. An immediate meeting of the already proposed Advisory Committee to follow up the deliberations which are currently in progress and to which I made reference earlier. This Committee will include nominees of the Military Governors. One of the first tasks of the Advisory Committee will be to arrange and pave the way for a Constitutional Review Assembly reflecting all shades of opinion throughout the Republic. The Constitutional Review Assembly will, when established, make recommendations as to the form of constitution best suited to Nigeria.

c. The recommendations of the Constitutional Review Assembly will then be subjected to a referendum.

The newly elected bodies, as provided by the peoples' constitution, will assume political control of the nation and my Government would fade away after having carried out its task of laying a firm foundation for our national unity. It is not possible for me at this stage to lay down a firm time-table for the handing over of the reins of Government to the people as this will depend upon innumerable factors which have not yet been worked out in detail. For the interim period, however, my Government intends to take action which will ensure complete stability and the maintenance of law and order throughout the Republic. It is absolutely necessary, at every stage, that no more blood is shed and that everybody within the Republic enjoys complete sense of security.

I have already said that the basis upon which we can forge a new national unity is a return to the position before 24th May, 1966. Accordingly, with the concurrence of all the Military Governors, a new Decree will be issued to repeal Decree No. 34[2] and return to the *status quo*. The Central Executive Council will, however, be enlarged to include citizens of outstanding merit who will assist the Military Government in the work of National reconstruction during the transitional period.

I would like to repeat what I said in my recent warning, that politicians should refrain from making statements which are likely to create an unfavourable atmosphere at this critical stage of our national reconstruction. One point which I had not hitherto made abundantly clear is that my Government is very determined to stamp out corrupt practices and to bring to book all persons, including those recently released from detention, against whom there is evidence of improper practice and criminal acts. At this stage of our economic development, I should like to reiterate my recent statement at the Press conference, that my Government welcomes genuine investors and will do everything in its power to encourage and protect their interests.

Efforts are being made to preserve and strengthen confidence within the Army. My Government wants to make it abundantly clear that, as the Nigerian Army has never participated in politics in the history of our country, I am determined to keep politics out of the Army and the Army out of politics.

Arrangements have been made to ensure continued maintenance of law and order throughout the Republic, and I hope and trust that life among the civilian population will continue as before.

Finally, I should like to express my sincerest hope that the people of this great country will co-operate with me fully in carrying out the policies which

P

I have just announced. As a military man, I have no political ambitions. My task is not to impose any form of government on the people but to pave the way for the people to determine the form of government they wish for, ensuring the stability and unity of the country. Thank you.

[1] *Broadcast to the nation 8 August 1966. Taken from* Nigeria 1966, *pp. 35–7.*
[2] *See* DOC 25.

45.
Recommendations made by the Representatives of the Regional Military Governors Meeting in Lagos on 9 August 1966 [1]

The meeting was declared open by the Head of the Federal Military Government and Supreme Commander of the Armed Forces at 12 noon.

In his opening address, the Supreme Commander referred to the difficult situation arising from the events of July 29 and the resulting bitterness on all sides and implored the meeting to give consideration to ways of easing the situation and preparing ground for further action by the leaders of the country. In particular he referred to his policy statements in which he stressed his intention to abrogate Decree No. 34 and to modify or nullify any enactments that assumed extreme centralization in order to pave the way to return to civilian administration and national unity.

The meeting, after the Supreme Commander had taken leave of the delegates, unanimously chose Sir Kashim Ibrahim as its Chairman and the Eletu Odibo of Lagos as his supporter.

In an effort to arrive at an Agenda for the meeting, members considered at some length the speech of the Supreme Commander and the proposed repeal of Decree No. 34 and similar enactments and finally agreed that the theme of the discussion should be the present situation in the country and ways and means of avoiding a recurrence. In this regard, the meeting unanimously agreed that the greatest problem at the moment was the sense of insecurity within the Armed Forces which had hitherto been the greatest unifying force in the land. It agreed that a situation should exist where the Army should be entirely harmless to itself. It was accordingly agreed to recommend that:

i. as far as possible the Army personnel should be posted to barracks in their Regions of origin with immediate effect as an interim measure;

ii. having regard to its peculiar position, the question of maintenance of peace and security in Lagos should be left to the Supreme Commander in consultation with the Military Governors.

Having dealt with the fears in the Army, the meeting tried to consider some grievances between the leaders of the country.

A. Discussion then took place on the need to expedite consultations on future constitutional arrangement so that decision can be reached as soon as possible. Most members agreed that these subject matters were of considerable urgency and that any procrastination might lead to more dangers. The meeting, however, found itself unable to proceed with the detailed discussions especially as the Governor of the Western Provinces had not completed consultations with Chiefs and leaders of thought. The meeting noted that such consultations had taken place in the North, East, Mid-West and Lagos. The Committee accordingly agreed to adjourn for a short time, say one week, to enable the Western Provinces to complete their consultations. *B*. Thereafter this Committee or an enlarged body should meet to recommend in broad outlines the form of political association which the country should adopt in the future. Meanwhile, every possible step should be taken to ensure that the situation in the country improves, and the Supreme Commander should be advised to make conditions suitable for the Supreme Military Council to meet at the earliest opportunity as a further means of lowering tension.

The meeting accordingly agreed to make the following recommendations:
1. Immediate steps should be taken by the Supreme Commander to post military personnel to barracks within their respective Regions of origin.
2. Having regard to its peculiar position the question of maintenance of peace and security in Lagos should be left to the Supreme Commander in consultation with the Military Governors.
3. A meeting of this Committee or an enlarged body should take place in a week's time to recommend in broad outlines the form of political association which the country should adopt in the future.
4. Immediate steps should be taken to nullify or modify any provisions of any decree which assumes extreme centralization.
5. The Supreme Commander should make conditions suitable for a meeting of the Supreme Military Council urgently as a further means of lowering tension.

[1] *Summary taken from* Nigeria 1966, *pp. 16–17.*

46.
'Whither Nigeria—Federation or Confederation?'[1]

NIGERIA: TO BE OR NOT TO BE?

Nigeria, yesterday and today. Where do we go from here?

Until 1900, there was virtually no Nigerian nation.

By 1914, there was an amalgamation of the southern and northern provinces of a geographical area called Nigeria. . . .

By 1946, we had started to talk of 'one Nigeria' when elected and nominated representatives of the country met for the first time in a legislative assembly in Lagos.

By 1960, we raised our flag and the bunting also went up in celebrating The Federation of Nigeria, an independent, sovereign state.

The Federation was sick at birth and by January, 1966, the sick, bed-ridden babe collapsed.

By May, 1966, a diagnosis indicated the cause of the collapse and 'physicians' proclaimed that the babe would have to be a unitarian.

Three months after, to this day, the babe is sitting on the brink of an abyss.

It may fall one side to its abysmal perdition. A calamity which all Nigerians and their well-wishers pray should never happen to a country with such a rich background, such rich potentialities; a country that was once seen by observers as the only one that could exercise a salutary, stabilizing influence in a continent that inherited a colonial heritage of under-development and political imbalance; a nation that has served on several occasions as a source of inspiration and support to her neighbours.

It may very well fall the other side and regain its glory.

Whither Nigeria?

Leaders of thought in Lagos, Ibadan, Benin, Enugu and Kaduna have been meeting or are meeting soon to find a way of helping this sick babe to regain its health and vigour.

The talks are 'top secret' which is not a bad exercise in ordinary circumstances and in a small country. Confidential talks allow men to speak their minds freely and to avoid saying things which they might otherwise consider their supporters enjoy.

But we are not under ordinary circumstances now and Nigeria is not a small country, in size and population.

Let the leaders discuss in privacy but every Nigerian should realise that they are deciding his or her future. And the ordinary people have a right and indeed, a duty to speak aloud on how they wish to be governed.

So, let's talk it over now in the open. Whither Nigeria?

The questions which our leaders have been pondering over and which will be agitating their minds in the coming weeks are:

Should Nigeria continue as a federation? If so, what amendments should be made to the suspended constitution?

How should powers be divided between the Regions and the Federal Government?

Should the operational control of the Army and the Police be in the hands of the Regional or the Federal Government; and is it desirable that the men serving in the Army and Police in one Region should be indigenes of that Region?

And should the continuance of the Federation rest on the condition that more states will be created so that, in the words of John Stuart Mill, 'there should not be any one state so much more powerful than the rest as to be capable of vying in strength with many of them combined' for 'if there be such a one, and only one, it will insist on being master of the joint deliberations; if there be two, they will be irresistible when they agree; and whenever they differ everything will be decided by a struggle for ascendancy between the rivals.'

The alternative to federation is confederation, a word which is fast entering the political dictionary of the country.

The implication is that the existing Regions will become almost sovereign states, with their own army, police and most of the powers of a sovereign state, leaving perhaps matters like railway, airways, currency, diplomatic representation to a confederate council of all the states' representatives in Lagos. . . .

Countrymen, federation or confederation? That is the question which you have all got to settle down and study now—the implications and complications; devoid of the emotion and sentiments that becloud the thinking in many minds now.

[1] Editorial, Daily Times, 25 August 1966.

47.
Ojukwu Reassures the U.K. Deputy High Commissioner and the American Consul: No Secession[1]

I have had a recent telephone call from Lt.-Col. Gowon who, after surprising me with what he considered confirmed rumours of the intention of the East to secede on the 1st of October this year, informed me that he had called in the British and American representatives and explained the position to them. I have considered it necessary to call you in and explain our position.

I consider any talk about the East's intention to secede as grossly mischievous, to say the least. It is probably a question of giving a dog a bad name in order to hang it! I have been aware that, because of the lack of proper appreciation of our position, wild rumours, based on fear and suspicion or borne out of malice, have freely circulated among our friends and foes against the East.

Easterners have been the greatest believers in one Nigeria, and have spearheaded all movements to that end. It is this deep and absolute belief in one Nigeria that has led Easterners to adopt any place they find themselves in Nigeria as their home. Wherever they have been, they have contributed their utmost to the development of the area. The Easterners have contributed most for what Nigeria is today, and would no doubt lose something if Nigeria ceased to exist as a political and economic unit. Nobody is more conscious than ourselves of the problems that would be created by Easterners who have, all their lives, lived and worked in other parts of the country—some of whom have never before been to the East—returning home for resettlement. . . .

I consider Lt.-Col. Gowon's statements on the 1st and 8th of August, to which I have referred, as realistic and courageous.[2] We have in the past been working and living on assumptions. It is unfortunate that we should have waited until tragic events made us face realities. But it is better late than never. We are unshaken in our belief that Nigeria should remain together, but it must be a Nigeria free of hate and distrust among the different communities. We must have a constitution which will remove all areas of conflict, without destroying the basis of the country's existence as one. After studying the different memoranda submitted by the different delegates to the current conference in Lagos, I can say, with all humility and sincerity, that our approach to the current issues are the most realistic.

Recent history has shown that most of the troubles and conflicts among the Regions have arisen from a struggle to control the Centre, and this has in turn been the direct offshoot of suspicion and fear, buttressed by ambitions for power. Our delegation in Lagos have been given the mandate to work on the following broad principles:

i. The fact of very deep-rooted differences in religion, culture, attitude, outlook and rate of development existing in the country should be recognized and accepted.

ii. The necessity of allowing each Region to develop in its own way and at its own pace should also be recognized and accepted.

iii. Since the control of the Centre has ever been the main cause of friction and tension between the different Regions, thereby threatening national solidarity and integrity, the distribution of functions between the Regions and the Centre should be reviewed and so arranged that only such subjects and functions as will engender the minimum of suspicion and friction among different groups are allowed in the hands of the Federal Government.

iv. The composition of the organs of the Federal Government should be so arranged as to give no one Region an advantage over the other.

v. The subject of representation and the method of selecting such representatives should be carefully gone into. We would like to see the practice of Federal General Election abandoned.

The acceptance and application of the above principles will inevitably, if regrettably, lead to a looser form of association than anything we have known before. We believe that there is no other course to adopt, but we hope that with time Nigerians managing their affairs separately will come to learn how profitable it is to live together in peace, oneness and brotherliness. That is why our delegation will also insist that whatever constitution ensues from the present discussions, has a clause for its automatic review after a stipulated period.

I have earlier on in this statement mentioned the Army. Does anyone honestly think that the present members of the armed forces, consisting of people from different Regions and tribes, will ever live and operate together as comrades without fear and suspicion which may again lead to internal feud? And yet there cannot be a strong and effective central government without a coherent and confident Army.

I now understand that instead of the previous agreement to consider first the form of association suitable for Nigeria and in spite of Lt.-Col. Gowon's statement to the opening session of the Conference outlining the types of association to be discussed, the issue of the creation of states has since been introduced to obstruct the work of the Conference. I want to assure you that the East believes in self-determination for all groups, and cannot therefore be opposed to the creation of more states, provided the basis for such is mutually agreed upon. We do not here in the East wish for, neither have we worked for, secession! If, however, circumstances place us outside what is now known as Nigeria, you may be certain then that we should have been forced out.

---

[1] *Speech made in Enugu, 22 September 1966. Text from* Crisis '66, *pp. 39–43.*
[2] *See* DOCS *37 and 44.*

48.
Ojukwu's Broadcast of 27 August—'No Genuine Basis for True Unity'[1]

I last spoke to you on August 1, following the unfortunate and tragic events of July 29.[2] I am sure that you all have since followed through the Press and radio the sad turn of events. One thing has come out very clearly from this, the proceeding and subsequent events, that is, that there is in fact no genuine basis for true unity in the country.

The people of Nigeria have gone through one crisis after another in the last year. Serious as these have been, we have tended to gloss over them and to find compromise in political settlement, leaving the fundamental issues unresolved.

The present crisis therefore, becomes significant because the people of Eastern Nigeria, as I have learnt from my meetings with, and correspondence from them, are determined that a permanent solution must now be found.

For us in this area, it has become a struggle for survival and there is need above all things else for solidarity amongst all people of Eastern Nigeria.

Let us make no mistake about it. This tragedy has befallen all the people of Eastern Nigeria origin.

Those who have attacked them in the last two months in their barracks, in cities or in hamlets, have not discriminated between groups in our community. The attacks have been directed against all of us.

With apparent lack of control shown by those who should protect life and property, Eastern Nigerians have no choice but to maintain vigilance.

Our people have demonstrated great calm and discipline in face of provocations and dangers, a discipline which the world has not failed to note. By this we have established beyond doubt that Eastern Nigeria is stable and our peoples civilised and mature. I call upon you to continue to keep calm.

Indeed, great sacrifices have to be made by each and every one of us in the times ahead and I am confident that with your firm resolve, the present difficulties will be surmounted and that the people of Eastern Nigeria would emerge vindicated in their effort to ensure their rights of self determination.

I have been in continuous consultation with chiefs and elders, representatives of groups and interests, leaders of thought and professional organisations, in the past four weeks and I shall continue this exchange of views.

I have today established a consultative body for this Group of Provinces. This will consist of representatives drawn on an equal basis of four members from each of our large towns, and two members each from the smaller towns.

I have selected representatives for the following interests: The legal profession, the medical profession, the chambers of commerce, women's organisations, trade unions, and the teaching profession.

I will consult this body on current developments in the country and hope the members will give full expression to the views of all groups within Eastern Nigeria so that when we speak at the constitutional conference in Lagos our delegates will be voicing the concerted views of the entire people of this region.

I will also establish soon an advisory council of chiefs and elders whose mature and detached advice, I am sure, will have a most establishing influence in our present circumstances.

Further, I intend to reconstitute my executive committee in order to bring in some of our distinguished and public-spirited men to advise me.

I had said earlier that we in Eastern Nigeria are determined that a permanent solution must be found now to the problems of Nigeria.

The people of Nigeria must decide and agree amongst themselves as to what form of association they desire themselves.

In view of the importance of this question. I have set up a constitutional committee made up of distinguished Eastern Nigerians, representatives of all shades of opinion under the chairmanship of my Attorney-General, Mr. Nabo Graham-Douglas, to study this vital matter and to present a report to me without delay. The members of this committee will be as follows: [names] . . .

This committee will review the political situation in Nigeria, determine the place and role of Eastern Nigeria in any future constitution and suggest a form of future association which would eliminate the difficulties and dangers of the past, ensure the security of life and property, remove suspicion and distrust amongst various components of the country and in particular. assuage the fears of minority groups wherever they may be.

All families in Eastern Nigeria have experienced some bereavement and the sad return of some of their kinsmen and women who had put in several years of useful service in other parts of Nigeria and who are now coming home without clothing, property, sometimes without their husbands and parents.

In order to minimise this suffering, I have established a high powered commission for the resettlement of these people under the distinguished chairmanship of Mr. F. O. Iheanacho.[3]

The sum of £1,000,000 is being made immediately available for this task and this sum will be augmented from time to time as and when it becomes necessary.

All government and non-government organisations, voluntary agencies and commercial enterprises are requested to co-operate with the Government of Eastern Nigeria in order to minimise the hardship for these people and accelerate their absorption into suitable appointments and eventual rehabilitation.

I have already issued directives to the Ministry of Education to expand enrolment in all our education institutions to ensure that all students returning to Eastern Nigeria are found places.

All our other refugees have been requested to report to their district officers who are maintaining a register for this purpose.

I am happy to announce to you that I have succeeded, with the co-operation of Lt. Colonel Gowon, in repatriating the wife and family of the Supreme Commander, Major-General J. T. U. Aguiyi-Ironsi.

Finally I know that I speak for all of you when I call for mourning and dedication for all our sons and daughters who lost their lives as a result of the tragic events of May 15 and July 29.

In view of the significance of the events of the last few months I hereby declare Monday, August 29, a day of mourning for all our dead.

All flags will fly at halfmast.

One minute's silence will be observed at 12 noon, and religious services will be held at 6 o'clock in the evening on the same day in their memory.

My fellow countrymen and women, the least honour we can do these our sons and daughters now dead is to ensure that their blood would not have been shed in vain and that out of this tragedy will emerge a solution which will bring to an end the indignities, molestations and atrocities directed against the people of Eastern Nigeria.

I know I can count on your sympathy and support in this regard.

In our hour of travail, may God be our guide. Thank you.

¹ *Eastern Ministry of Information Release, printed in* Sunday Times *(Lagos)*, *28 August 1966.*
² *See* DOC *38.*   ³ *See* DOC *95.*

49.
Gowon Abolishes Decree 34 and Reinstates a Federal System[1]

In fulfilment of the undertaking given on his assumption of office by Lt.-Col. Yakubu Gowon, Head of the National Military Government and Supreme Commander of the Armed Forces, a new decree has been signed by him today and come into effect tomorrow taking back the Republic to the position it was prior to May 24, 1966.

By this decree, the Federal System of Government has been restored throughout the country. The Military Government becomes the Federal Military Government, the Groups of Provinces are to be known once again as Regions, the Capital Territory of Lagos becomes the Federal Territory of Lagos, the National Public Service Commission reverts to its former title of Federal Public Service Commission, and with it, the various Regional public service commissions to their former positions.

Decree No. 34 of May 24 is thus repealed by this new enactment. But two other decrees are also superseded. The first is Decree No. 14 by which the Attorney-General of the Republic was empowered to institute criminal proceeding against anyone in respect of any law anywhere in Nigeria whenever he considers it desirable.

The second is decree No. 36 which empowered the Supreme Military Council, after consultation with the Advisory Judicial Committees, to appoint persons to hold or act in the office of magistrate or registrar of a court under law enacted and enforced anywhere in Nigeria.

By this Decree, the Supreme Military Council also has power to confirm, dismiss and exercise disciplinary control over all persons so appointed.

The effect of the repeal of Decree Nos. 14 and 36 will be two-fold.

Firstly, the Federal Attorney-General will henceforth be concerned only with Federal matters through the Federal Ministry of Justice, while Regional matters will be left as before in the hands of Regional Attorneys-General.

Secondly, the power to appoint, confirm, dismiss and exercise disciplinary control over magistrates and registrars, henceforth reverts to the Federal

Public Service Commission in case of the Federal Territory and to the Regional Public Service Commissions in the case of regions.

The significance of the new Decree is further underlined by yet another aspect, that is in respect of the exercise of the prerogatives of mercy.

By this enactment, Decree No. 1 of March 4, 1966, which took effect from January 17, 1966, has been modified in respect of the exercise of that power.

This Decree vested in the Supreme Military Council the exercise of the prerogatives of mercy in respect of offences committed under any law in Nigeria.

The position henceforth is that a Supreme Military Council retains this power, but only in respect of offences under Federal Law.

In respect of offences under Regional Laws, this prerogative is now vested in the Military Governors of the various regions.

[1] *Statement issued in Lagos on 31 August 1966. The enabling Decree was No. 59 of 1966.*

50.
Ojukwu's Mandate from the People of the East, 31 August 1966[1]

Be it resolved as follows:
1. We, the representatives of the various communities in Eastern Nigeria gathered in this Consultative Assembly, hereby declare our implicit confidence in the Military Governor for Eastern Nigeria, Lt.-Col. Odumegwu Ojukwu, in all the actions he has so far taken to deal with the situation which has arisen in Nigeria since May 29, 1966.
2. In view of the grave threat to our survival as a unit in the Republic of Nigeria, we hereby urge and empower/advise him to take all such actions that might be necessary to protect the integrity of Eastern Nigeria and the lives and property of its inhabitants.
3. We advise constant consultation by His Excellency with the Consultative Assembly.
4. In view of the gravity of the present situation we affirm complete faith in and urge the need for solidarity of Eastern Nigeria as a unit.
5. In view of the present situation of things no delegates be sent to Lagos for any constitutional talks unless the safety of the delegates is guaranteed.

[1] Proclamation of the Republic of Biafra (*Enugu, 1967*).

51.
'The Moment of Truth': Gowon Opens the Ad Hoc Constitutional Conference in Lagos, 12 September 1966[1]

Gentlemen,

I welcome you to this conference which will perhaps go down as the most important of its kind in our history. We are now faced with greater difficulties and harder decisions than any we have faced as a nation in the past years. I trust that you have all come here with open minds and that in a spirit of give and take you will help to build a better future for Nigeria.

The result of your deliberations will not only be crucial to the future well-being of the fifty-five million people of this country but will also be of great concern to other African countries and all friends of Nigeria the world over. I say this because I do know and respect the yearnings of the great majority of the people of this country to live in peace together; not to talk of the hopes entertained throughout the world of Nigeria emerging as the most influential African country in world affairs.

We must not look for scapegoats for the ills that have beset our efforts towards nation-building. The truth is that there is so much pretence in our society, so much posing. We like to appear better than we are, but we do not always work hard enough to be better.

Eighteen days from today it will be the Sixth Anniversary of Nigeria's Independence. Let us recall the emotions at the solemn ceremony in the square just across the road. Let us not forget that we joyfully decided to take our country's destiny into our own hands.

No realist had ever overlooked the long-term dangers of the rivalry of personalities and the differences in cultural and social outlook in this country. But it was one of the hopes that these differences should be played down in the course of time. Yet, after nearly six years of independence we seem to be farther away than ever from the goal of national solidarity. And we have failed either to provide honest administrations or to create an atmosphere conducive to rapid economic growth—our economic potentialities as one unit notwithstanding.

This is the moment of truth. It may not be appropriate to indulge in acrimonious retrospection but it is expedient to have self-examination and take serious note of some of the things we have done individually and collectively to bring threats of disintegration to the country since we first hoisted our national flag and lustily sang:

> Though tribe and tongue may differ,
> In brotherhood we stand,
> Nigerians all, and proud to serve
> Our Sovereign motherland.

As a direct result of the actions and behaviours of those who were expected to steer our ship of State, we have been plunged into a series of avoidable crises since the past four years. After politics had been thoroughly debased and commercialized, a Census affair became an exercise involving a tussle for political power. This was followed by two elections which led to actions constituting grave threats to the stability of the country. As if the situation was not bad enough, then came the events of January 15th with its repercussions in the incidents of July 29th. It should be remembered that we have always found political solutions to our problems until the first callous military intervention in January, 1966.

Now, 'where do we go from here?' This is the real question you are here to answer as the representatives of the various communities in this country.

In spite of all that has happened, which is not peculiar to Nigeria in the history of the world, we must not minimize the advantages that will derive from our remaining together as one strong political and economic entity. It will be to our eternal glory, therefore, if we can find ways and means of eliminating fear and restoring trust and confidence as well as mutual love and respect among our people.

This meeting is a follow-up of a former meeting of representatives held here in Lagos on the 9th of August.[2] To those representatives we owe a lot of thanks. It was agreed then to call this meeting to consider and 'recommend in broad outlines the form of political association which the country should adopt in the future'. It is not for me to make any prescriptions for curing the ills of the country, but there are certain facts which you must bring to bear on your deliberations, *viz*:

a. After many years of Constitution-making exercises, it was eventually agreed to adopt a Federal system of Government, which the former politicians failed to make workable.

b. Discounting the experience of pre-independence days, the incidents of May last in Northern Nigeria following the tendencies to extreme unification during the period after January 17 points to one and only one thing. That a country as big as Nigeria and comprising such diversity of tribes and cultures cannot be administered successfully under a unitarian form of Government—unless such a Government is to be enforced and maintained by some form of Dictatorship.

It is very clear to me that it will be economically and politically suicidal to harbour any idea of a complete break-up of the Federation. Therefore, we seem to be left with the alternatives of—

a. a Federation with a strong central Government;

b. a Federation with a weak central Government;

c. a Confederation.

On the other hand, it may be that through you deliberations which commences here today, we may be able to devise a form of association with an entirely new name yet to be found in any political dictionary in the world but peculiar to Nigeria.

Depending on the choice that you eventually recommend you may later have to consider such matters as—

a. the distribution of powers as between the regional Governments and the central Government;

b. the territorial divisions of the country; and

c. the system for selecting representatives to the legislatures.

I sincerely hope that whichever way we choose to go, we will not overlook the facts of geography and the paramount interest of the absolute majority of our people: that is, to have the basic necessities for a happy life in a modern society. It is our duty to find the most practical solutions to our problems, and we must therefore throw away theories which have not helped us in the past and will not help us now or in the future.

I trust that after a careful and dispassionate look at our problems, you will be able to find the proper answer to the big question 'where do we go from here?' In any case, if we should fail to raise, once again, the sincere hopes of a united Nigeria emerging as economically and politically the strongest and most stable country in Africa, it would be best for us not to do anything for which we would be cursed by future generations. It is therefore vital to make such political arrangements as will prevent the recurrence of the bloody incidents of January, May and July this year, which can easily degenerate into civil war.

I pray that you do find a formula for our continued association in a condition whereby we can hand down to our children and their own children a structure upon which they will be able to improve. We must do nothing to jeopardize their own chances of building a great African nation that can command the respect of the whole world.

Let us not allow our country generally referred to as 'the giant of Africa' to become a flop!

In conclusion, and by way of summary, I call upon you all to help me and your Military Governors whose lot it is at the present time to hold the reins of government to search for proper solutions to the urgent problems. You are therefore required to find what form of political association this great country should adopt. You will need to analyse, in the light of Nigerian circumstances, all the arguments for and against all the various types of political arrangements. Two things for the present exercise I feel should be ruled out, *viz*:

a. complete break-up;

b. a unitary form of Government.

I therefore put before you the following forms of Government for consideration:

a. Federal system with a strong central Government;

b. Federal system with a weak central Government;

c. Confederation; or

d. an entirely new arrangement which will be peculiar to Nigeria and which has not yet found its way into any political dictionary.

You must however bear in mind that your efforts should be directed towards healing the present wounds and guaranteeing that there will not be repeats of experiences of the past twelve months. Above all, our children must be given the chance to do better than we of this generation have in the task of nation building.

I thought it inadvisable to impose upon you a Chairman of my own choice but I wish to suggest that the chairmanship should rotate among the Regional delegates in the following order: North, East, West, Mid-West.

I am sure that by the grace of God your deliberations will be crowned with success. Good luck and good hunting.

[1] *Reproduced from* Nigeria 1966, *pp. 37–40.*
[2] *See* DOC *45.*

52.
Proposals from the West and Lagos Delegations for an Interim Administration pending a New Constitution[1]

It is possible that it might take a few months, perhaps about three, before the new constitutional arrangements can be fully put into operation. For immediate and practical purposes, however, it is considered that interim arrangements could be effected along the following lines:

a. The Supreme Commander may issue a Decree to give interim effect to the new constitutional arrangements agreed at the Conference.

b. The Decree may also set up in the centre an interim body comprising mainly civil servants drawn equally from the Regions, to carry on meanwhile the functions of the Council of States under the new constitutional arrangements; a few public men might be required to advise this body as and when necessary and the Government in the centre would of course remain a Military Government with the Supreme Military Council as the final authority.

c. Similarly, in the Regions, the existing Executive Committees could be vested with the functions of the State Governments under the new constitutional arrangements and here also a few public men might be required to advise the Committees as and when necessary. The Regional Military Governor would of course remain the Head of the Military Government in the Region.

d. It would be the responsibility of the body to be set up in the centre and also of the Executive Committees in the Regions, among other things, to make arrangements for the following:

   i. the smooth exchange of personnel in the public and statutory corporations' services in accordance with any decision that civil servants and others engaged in the operation of the Common Services should now be employed in the public services of their respective Regions of origin;

   ii. the reshuffling of the Armed and the Police Forces so that the members thereof could now be stationed in their respective Regions of origin where they would form the nucleus of the new Armed and Police Forces;

   iii. an equitable division among the Regions of the existing stores, ordnances, equipments and other materials of the Armed and Police Forces;

In the Regions it would be the responsibility of the interim State Governments to reorganize the Armed and the Police Forces as necessary, carry out recruitment of fresh personnel as well as procure for them all necessary stores, ordnances, equipments and other materials.

e. The interim Governments in the Regions would arrange for the holding of general elections in their various areas after taking such action as they may respectively consider to be necessary preludes to the holding of such elections. The last Voters Registers, to be revised for the purpose of eliminating errors therein which have been disclosed as a result of the recent elections, would have to be used for the purpose of the proposed elections and so also the last delimitation of Regional constituencies.

f. After the holding of the proposed elections, a new civilian Government for each Region would be formed and the new Legislative House or Houses of the Regions as may be appropriate in each case would then form the Constituent Assembly to draft a new Constitution for the Region according to the wishes of their peoples.

g. The new State Governments would take such action as may be necessary for the purpose of establishing, on a permanent basis, the various authorities for the Centre agreed to be established under the new constitutional arrangements for Nigeria.

[1] *Submitted to the Ad Hoc Constitutional Conference held in Lagos, September 1966. From the Federal Government record.*

53.

Proposals from the Mid-West Delegation for an Interim Administration pending a New Constitution[1]

The Supreme Commander and Head of the Federal Military Government has announced his desire for an early return to civilian rule. In the view of the Mid-West Delegation, the following factors, among others, would appear to govern the length of time it might take for the country to return to complete civilian rule:

i. the situation in the Army;

ii. arrangements leading to the emergence of new regions, in the light of the Northern Delegation's proposals for the creation of new states, and

iii. the time required for the process of bringing the new constitution into being.

2. The events of the past nine months have created a crisis of confidence amongst military personnel and affected public confidence in the Nigerian Army. This confidence must be restored quickly if the Army is to resume its proper place and role in national life.

3. It would appear to be beyond question that the Army stands in need of reorganization if it is to cease to be a house divided against itself, and if it is to provide adequately for the future prospects and careers of all officers and men, particularly those officers and men most intimately affected by the events of the last nine months and especially those officers who, since the events of January 1966, have been burdened with politico-military responsibilities.

4. This is a major task and it does not appear on present evidence that a purely internal solution by the Army itself is possible or likely. The Mid-West Delegation suggests therefore that a Committee of Military and Civilian Leaders should be set up to examine the problem.

5. It is suggested that:

i. the Committee should consist of:

(*a*) Supreme Commander and Head of Military Government, (*b*) Army Chief of Staff, Heads of Navy and Air Force, (*c*) Inspector-General of Police, (*d*) Regional Military Governors and Administrator of Lagos, (*e*) Heads of Delegation to Ad Hoc Committee, (*f*) Two Christian and two Moslem Religious Leaders.

ii. the Committee could be served by a Subcommittee consisting of:

(*a*) Supreme Commander and Head of Military Government, (*b*) Army Chief of Staff, (*c*) Regional Military Governors, (*d*) Heads of Delegations.

iii. since the subject under consideration is essentially an Army problem, the Committee could be composed as at (*ii*), dispensing with the need for a Subcommittee.

6. Among the solutions, which the Committee might consider are:

i. whether or not an external agency should be invited to advise upon, and assist in, reorganization of the Army; if so,

ii. whether such external agency should be:

(*a*) a Commonwealth country or countries; (*b*) the Organization for African Unity; or (*c*) the United Nations Organization.

7. The argument in favour of the association of civilian leaders with the military in the reorganization of the Army also favours inviting the assistance of an external agency in this task. No considerations of false national pride should deter the Committee from seeking such assistance.

8. As to the alternatives in paragraph 6 (*ii*), the Mid-West Delegation fears that the necessary machinery for invoking multinational assistance would be slow and cumbersome, whether the external agency concerned is the U.N.O., the O.A.U. or the Commonwealth. In addition, there is some danger that multinational assistance may lead to other problems affecting Nigerian Unity and national security, and may create an opening for undesirable political interference in Nigeria's affairs. For these reasons, the Mid-West Delegation suggests that the Committee of Military and Civilian Leaders should seek assistance from only one country. Obvious practical considerations would seem to favour a Commonwealth such as Canada or Britain.

9. The reorganization suggested at paragraph 3 must take some time and if any sizeable section of the Army or any Region were unfortunately reluctant to associate itself fully with the reorganization, the delay might be longer still.

10. The Northern Delegation has suggested that a subcommittee of the Ad Hoc Committee should draw up proposals for submission to the Supreme Commander and Head of Military Government on the question of the creation of new States, that the proposals should include a suggestion for the appointment by the Supreme Commander of a Special Commission to ascertain the wishes of the inhabitants of 'the areas concerned,' and that the subsequent creation of new States (involving the whole process of bringing new States, their Constitutions and Regional Governments into existence) should be accomplished before a complete return to civilian rule. Clearly, such operation would take some time.

11. If the Ad Hoc Committee agrees on new constitutional proposals, as the Mid-West Delegation earnestly hopes it will, the proposals will have to be embodied in a new constitution and submitted for the people's approval in a referendum. This operation will also take some time.

12. Therefore, in considering how soon the country might return to civilian rule, account must be taken of the three major causes of delay set out in paragraphs 9 to 11 and of the fact that they are of such character that it is impossible at this stage to set a definite date for the military authorities to hand over power to elected civilian administrations throughout the country.

13. In the interim period, however, the Mid-West Delegation believes that it is desirable that civilians should be associated with the military in the administration of the country, as a first step towards a return to civilian rule. In view of the decision to include civilians in the Federal Executive Council and Regional Executive Committees taken by the Supreme Military Council at its most recent meeting, the Mid-West Delegation does not wish to submit proposals on the manner of such association.

14. At a date to be agreed now, however, the Supreme Commander and the Regional Military Governors should assign executive responsibility in respect of ministries to the Civilian Members of the Federal Executive Council and the

Regional Executive Committees, as an intermediate stage to a return to civilian rule.

15. Apart from the day-to-day functions of government, the responsibilities of the reconstituted Federal Executive Council should include supervising and effecting arrangements for:

   i. civilian co-operation with the Military in the reorganization of the Army;
   ii. the creation of any new regions which may be agreed upon and bringing new interim regional administrations into being;
   iii. elections in all regions on a given date;
   iv. Federal elections;
   v. bringing the new constitution into being; and
   vi. civilian co-operation with the Military in the formal transfer of power to new elected civilian administrations.

16. Consideration will of course have to be given to the question of the stage at which normal political activities, which are at present banned, may be resumed. On the one hand, enough time must be afforded for the organization of political parties and for campaigns leading to elections which will usher in new civilian administrations. On the other hand, the obvious dangers of intense political activities over a protracted period must be avoided. To meet both needs, the Mid-West Delegation suggests that the ban on political activities should be lifted three months before the military are due to hand power over to elected civilian administrations.

17. Although it is suggested at paragraph 12 that it is impossible at this stage to set a definite date for complete return to civilian rule, there is an obvious advantage in declaring a target date. Bearing in mind the problems set out at paragraphs 1 (*i*), (*ii*), (*iii*), 9, 10 and 11, it is suggested that a realistic date would probably be 15th January, 1968, which may have public appeal as the second anniversary of the original intervention by Army personnel in public affairs.

18. There has been considerable disruption of life in Nigeria within the last nine months. Any programme for a return to civilian rule must take account of this disruption and provide a means of solving the problems which it has raised. To this end, the Mid-West Delegation proposes;

   i. that arrangements should be made for the rehabilitation of persons forcibly displaced from their normal places of abode and employment in consequence of the events of January, May, July and September, 1966.
   ii. that there should be a crash training programme in respect of the Northern Region to provide staff to fill those vacancies inside and outside the Public Services which have been caused by the exodus of persons from other regions.

19. It is obvious that such a massive programme is at present beyond the capacity of the country's resources, and that external assistance would be necessary. In the view of the Mid-West Delegation, this is an appropriate field in which to seek multinational assistance. It is suggested that assistance should be sought from the U.N.O. and from the Commonwealth through their respective Secretariats.

[1] *Submitted to the Ad Hoc Constitutional Conference on its reassembly in Lagos, October 1966. From the Eastern Government record.*

54.
Statement by Sir Kashim Ibrahim on the Northern Delegation's Stand on the Creation of States[1]

On behalf of my Delegation, I should like to draw the attention of the Conference to the misrepresentations and distortions in the Nigerian Press on the stand of the Northern Delegation regarding self-determination. Some Nigerian newspapers have carried news that the Northern Delegation, like the Eastern Delegation, is opposed to the creation of more States in Nigeria.

This is completely untrue. Whereas the Eastern Delegation has no proposal about the creation of more States, the stand of my Delegation on this all important subject is contained in our Memorandum submitted to this conference.

By way of amplification, I should like to point out most emphatically that the Northern Delegation stands in favour of creation of more States anywhere in Nigeria if the majority of the people directly concerned express such a wish.

What we, as a Delegation, do not stand for is for some people from outside coming to dictate that certain areas must be carved out or readjusted and made into States, when the people of the areas concerned have not expressed such a wish or demand.

As the Nigerian Press have given prominence to these distortions and misrepresentations, probably as a result of hints from sources close to this conference, or perhaps directly from some delegations, I should like the secretariat of this conference to publicise in full the text of this statement in order to clarify our stand.

[1] *Issued to the press in Lagos, 16 September 1966. The version given by the* West African Pilot *omitted the final paragraph, which has been restored here.*

55.
Statement by Dr. Njoku on the Eastern Delegation's Stand on the Creation of States[1]

The Eastern Nigerian Delegation does not believe that the splitting up of the country into more States at this stage is what we need in order to normalize conditions of life in this country and provide a sense of security for its inhabitants.

At the moment the country is in the grip of fear, suspicion and mistrust. We believe that in order to save the existence of the country before it is too late, immediate constitutional arrangements for the country as a whole should be made on the basis of the existing Regions.

To split up the country into more States now will involve a long-drawn-out process of inquiries, commissions and plebiscites, taking up many months or even some years which we cannot afford under the present crises.

From the experiences of the recent past it is not in the interest of harmony and peace of the country to have a strong central Government. The splitting up of the country into new States will automatically have the effect of trans-ferring functions which the smaller States cannot be expected to execute with their limited resources. This would, once again, engender inter-regional rivalry and political warfare to control the centre. This we must avoid.

Since it is the proposal of the Eastern Delegation that the Armed Forces should now be regionalized, it is in the interest of the country and of the efficiency of the Armed Forces that it should be organized on the basis of the existing Region rather than on smaller units.

In a society such as ours, it is impossible to devise any political arrangement which will be devoid of minority problems. It is the view of the Eastern Nigerian Delegation that these problems can be best contained and satisfied within larger Regional units.

Consultations in the East have shown that the various cultural and linguistic groups, while recognising the principle of the creation of more States as a means of allaying fears, feel satisfied that such exercise should be the responsibility of the Eastern Regional Government.

In this connection, there are agreed arrangements in the proposed Regional Constitution vesting in suitably defined units certain legislative and executive functions.

The points raised above notwithstanding, it should be provided in the future Constitution of the country that any Region can agree to split into more states which may be accepted into the future Nigerian association on equal terms as the existing Region if the people of such an existing Region and the areas concerned so desire.

In conclusion, we hold that the issue of the creation of new States is an internal responsibility of the Region. The initiative for the creation must come from the Region within which the State is to be created.

[1] *Issued to the press in Lagos, 16 September 1966.*

56.
Northern Delegation's Supplementary Constitutional Proposals following the Resumption of the Constitutional Conference, 20 September 1966[1]

When my delegation supported the adjournment of our meeting last Friday it was because we felt that the proposals put forward by the various delega-tions as well as the appeals made for a careful re-thinking of the stands of all delegations needed thoughtful consideration. My delegation is conscious of the need for this conference to work fast and put forward suggestions to the Government on the country's future with as little delay as possible. We felt, however, that we had no right to decide the future of 56 million people hastily without weighing carefully what sort of fate we are likely to land the country in. We felt we should not sacrifice a fair and just decision for speed.

My delegation is convinced that Nigeria should not be allowed to disintegrate. No Nigerian has anything to gain on the long run if this nation disintegrates. We shall all be losers.

My delegation therefore believes that there must be an effective Central Government that the world and the people of this country can recognize as the Government of Nigeria. The Conference may wish to note that this represents a modification of our stand as indicated in the original memo.

The existing Regions should be constituted into states with increased powers over their own affairs. Subjects which had caused friction in the past should as far as possible be made the responsibility of each state.

To embody the right of secession of any part of this country from the rest is to invite a break-up of the country. Secession should therefore not be allowed under the Nigeria Constitution. Accordingly, the relevant section in our memo is therefore withdrawn.

In order to allay the fears of domination by sections of the country, the principle of creation of states must be agreed. A system of ascertaining the wishes of the people of areas where demands for creation of states have been made should be devised and these wishes should be ascertained and states created in the areas concerned before the administration of this country is returned to civilian hands.

In this connection, my delegation recommends very strongly that a subcommittee of this conference should be set up to draw up proposals which this conference can submit to the Federal Military Government on what machinery should be adopted in the light of present Nigerian circumstances for ascertaining the demands for the creation of more states. My delegation will suggest that the Military Government should at some stage and during their tenure of office, consider the establishment of a Commission on which representatives of neutral bodies could serve to assist the assessment of genuine desire in areas concerned for the creation of new states.

PROPOSALS

PRESIDENT AND HEAD OF STATE

1. There shall be a President and Head of State to be provided by States in rotation. His term of office shall be four years. The State whose turn it is to provide a President shall nominate three persons endorsed by that State's Legislature. An electoral college consisting of all State Legislatures and the Federal or Central Parliament shall elect one of the three nominees.

2. *Functions*

a. He shall receive Foreign Missions and on the advice of the Prime Minister appoint Nigerian Ambassadors and High Commissioners.

b. He shall be ceremonial Commander-in-Chief of Armed Forces.

c. He shall authorise the Prime Minister to form his Government. Provided that portfolios shall be assigned to Ministers representing each State on the basis of a formula to be worked out in a manner which will ensure a fair distribution of Ministries amongst all the States; portfolios should be reshuffled occasionally, say halfway, through the 4-year term of the Cabinet.

d. He shall confer honours and award titles and decorations on the recommendation of the Prime Minister.

e. Whenever the President is temporarily incapacitated or unable to perform his function or is temporarily outside the country, the Governor of his State shall act as President and Head of State.

f. In the event of death, or permanent incapacity, resignation or removal of the President during his term of office, the State Government which recommended his appointment shall submit the names of three persons from whom one shall be appointed as set out earlier to be President for the remaining period. Meanwhile the Governor of the State concerned shall act until such appointment is made.

g. He shall assent to Laws of the Parliament.

h. He shall exercise Prerogative of Mercy on the advice of the Advisory Committee of the Prerogative of Mercy.

i. He shall appoint the Chief Justice of the Federation, as well as the Judges of the Supreme Court on the advice of the Judicial Service Commission.

j. He shall formally appoint the Federal Public Service Commission on the advice of the Prime Minister.

3. PRIME MINISTER AND HEAD OF GOVERNMENT

He shall be nominated every four years in rotation by the States. The State government whose turn it is to provide the Prime Minister shall, with the consent of its State Assembly nominate from amongst the representatives returned whether by election or nomination by that State to the Federal Parliament. The Head of State who shall appoint who-so-ever is nominated by the State concerned shall present the Prime Minister designate to the Federal Parliament for formal acceptance. In the event of the Federal parliament rejecting the Prime Minister designate the President shall advise the State which nominated him to re-consider its recommendation.

Functions

a. He shall be responsible for the nation's security.

b. He shall be responsible to Parliament.

c. He shall name his Cabinet who shall be appointed formally by the President.

The Formula for appointment or election to the posts of President and the Prime Minister should be so arranged that where the Prime Minister or the President for the meantime comes from one particular State, the holder of the other post shall in no circumstance come from the same State.

4. CABINET

a. The designation 'Minister' for members of the Cabinet should be discontinued. The designation 'Secretary of States' should be adopted.

b. States shall be represented in the Cabinet on equal basis. In putting up candidates to the President for appointment as 'Secretaries of State' the Prime Minister shall consult all State governments.

c. Secretaries of State shall not be members of Parliament. Where a Member of Parliament is appointed Secretary of States he shall resign from Parliament.

d. Secretaries of State shall be ex officio members of Parliament to which they shall also be responsible; he shall be removable from office if a motion to that effect is passed by a two third majority of the whole House. No Secretary of State shall be removable merely at the instance of a State Government or Assembly.

e. In the event of death, resignation or removal of a Secretary of State during his term of office, the Prime Minister shall consult the government of the State concerned in respect of a replacement.

f. Decisions on major issues—the nature of which shall be defined in advance shall be by unanimity of the Cabinet.

5. PARLIAMENT

a. There shall be a unicameral Federal Parliament to which each State shall elect equal number of members. The life of Parliament shall be four years.

b. The first Federal Parliament to which the Military Government shall hand over shall consist of persons who are not members of State Legislatures nominated on the basis of personal merit by State Governments and approved by State Legislatures.

The question of elections and popular representation should be re-examined at the end of this Parliament.

c. Members of the first Federal Parliament shall not be liable to recall at any time by the Government of the State from which they were chosen but shall be free to resign their seats.

6. CITIZENSHIP

There shall be a common Nigerian Citizenship.

7. DEFENCE COUNCIL

Slight amendment on Items agreed by the Conference to be on the Exclusive Legislative List.

a. Army

The composition of the Defence Council agreed in paragraph 11 (7) of the progress report by the Conference should be enlarged to accommodate the Inspector-General of Police. Its composition should therefore be as follows:

    i. The Head of State of Nigeria
    ii. The Head of Central Government
    iii. The Heads of Regional Governments
    iv. The Chief of Staff
    v. Regional Commanders
    vi. The Minister of Defence
    vii. Inspector-General of Police

8. GARRISONING OF FEDERAL CAPITAL

The North reserve its position on this item because of the peculiar position of Lagos. The North suggests very strongly that a garrison composed of personnel drawn from all State Units should be stationed in Lagos. The fear of possible friction between the Units can be eliminated by providing separate barracks for each unit. The question of joint command can be left to the Army to work out.

9. LAGOS

Lagos as Federal Capital Territory. It is our view that Lagos will continue to be the political capital of Nigeria. The argument that Lagos should be constituted to a State because it has been neglected cannot be supported against the background of the enormous development which has taken place in Lagos in the past ten years. To say that the welfare of its citizens has not received adequate attention has not been borne by facts for example:

a. The Federal Government spends on Lagos, the best part of £6 million which it votes annually on health facility alone for Lagos—a territory with a population of ·6 million; as compared with £3 million spent by the North on a population of 29 million. This disparity will be true also vis-à-vis other Regional Governments.

b. Lagos has always been represented on the Federal Cabinet and has eight members of Parliament.

c. The Administration of Lagos has always been left in the hands of its people.

d. Millions of pounds have been sunk on land reclamation alone in Lagos.

e. Furthermore Lagos has for many years been developed by the Central or Federal Government for this purpose. And to alter its position will certainly result in such expenditures that the country can hardly afford.

The arguments advanced for the so called neglect of Lagos can be put forward by most administrative capitals. Indeed any place chosen as the future capital of Nigeria can put forward the same kind of arguments to prove neglect.

10. EXTERNAL AFFAIRS

External Affairs should remain an Exclusive Legislative subject. The North now wishes to withdraw its reservation on proviso (iv) of item 15 of the Progress Report. It now agrees that it should be possible for States to negotiate treaties and agreements with foreign powers on matters which are purely of trade and commercial interests. States should therefore be in a position to appoint Commercial Attache or Counsellor to a Nigerian Mission abroad if they so wish. He should be regarded as a member of the Mission.

The North would like to maintain its reservation on proviso (i) which advocates appointments to foreign missions on a quota system based on equality of representations amongst the Regions. Since appointments into foreign missions are appointments into the Federal Public Service recruitment should be on population as in the case of item 36 of the Progress Report.

11. HIGHER EDUCATION

The Higher Educational Institutions listed in item 17 of the Progress Report should continue to remain on the Exclusive Legislative List. Conscious effort should be made however to ensure that staff and student population in these institutions come from all the States. In view of the close proximity of the two Teaching Hospitals in Lagos and Ibadan and in view of the importance of a Teaching Hospital one of them could be transferred elsewhere.

12. MARITIME SHIPPING AND NAVIGATION

Maritime Shipping and Navigation should continue as an item on the Exclusive Legislative List. In fact North will like to withdraw its reservation on item 22 of the Progress Report concerning the amendment which reads as follows 'existing ports and such new ports as may, with the agreement of the Regional Government concerned be declared by Parliament to be Federal

Ports (including the constitution and powers of Ports Authorities for federal ports).' In order to ensure that no state will be legally able to hold the rest of the country to ransom over a given port, the agreement of the region in which the port is situated should not be made a condition precedent for declaring a port as a federal port.

13. METEOROLOGY

The North supports that meteorology should continue as a Federal subject but that where a State intends to establish and maintain its own meteorological service the consent of the Federal Government should first be obtained.

14. MINES AND MINERALS, INCLUDING OILFIELDS, OIL MINING, GEOLOGICAL SURVEYS AND NATURAL GAS:

The right to all mines and minerals was, before the handover of power in that regard, vested in the Crown. This right was derived from the Crown's prerogative of being the owner of all minerals attaching to the land. The right was accentuated by the provision in our laws laying down that the entire property in and control of all minerals and mineral oils in, under or upon any lands in Nigeria and of all rivers, streams and water-courses throughout Nigeria, was and should be vested in the Crown.

Upon handover of power the right was transferred to the Federal Government which has to date been exercising it. In this regard the Federal Government continues to hold the right among other things to legislate on mines and minerals, including oilfields, oil mining, geological surveys and natural gas as provided in the Constitution. This right, of course, is being exercised for the benefit of the Country as a whole. The Constitution of the Federation for example provides for a fair distribution of revenue obtained from mining royalties and rents between the Regions in so far as such revenue is in respect of minerals obtained from inland.

In these circumstances the Northern Delegation does not see how this item can be removed from the Federal to the Regional Legislative List.

It is noteworthy that at one time the country's main sources of revenue from Mines and Minerals came from tin and columbite of the North. And throughout such time there was never an objection raised from any quarter as regards Central and later Federal Control of mines and minerals.

It is interesting to note that now that we have, for the meantime, the main sources of revenue coming from oil from East, Mid-West and possibly West the other delegations at the Conference should raise an objection to what has in effect been the usual practice purely and simply in order to enrich their respective regional governments at the expense of the overall national interest.

On the other hand since it agreed that Nigeria should have an 'effective Federal Government' it is vital that the Federal Government should have an independent source of revenue.

15. CREATION OF STATES

The North has suggested both in its original memo and the statement made by the leader of the Northern Delegation on the issue of States[2] methods by which the areas demanding States can be ascertained and States created. The North would like the suggestion of the North discussed and formally adopted and recommended to the Supreme Commander.

The North has grave doubts about the wisdom of creating States based on 'ethnic and linguistic affinities'. In any arrangement based on this principle, there are bound to be large numbers or small pockets of minor ethnic and linguistic groups who will necessarily find themselves grouped uncomfortably with larger and dominant ethnic groups. Whilst in the past, such tiny tribes were undisturbed within large units not based on tongues they are most likely to develop genuine fears of tribal domination in any political arrangement based on the principle of language. Most of the smaller ethnic and linguistic communities have co-existed peacefully without any ill feelings towards their bigger neighbour only because they and their neighbours belong to a larger political entity.

The Northern Delegation hopes therefore that the dangers inherent in the division of Nigeria on bases of language and tribe would be fully appreciated and viewed dispassionately.

The North will want to reiterate its position that in the exercise of ascertaining the wishes of the people for the creation of States as well as the actual creation of States, no Region except the Mid-West should be left out of the operation.

16. INTERIM ARRANGEMENT
The North notes with satisfaction the decision of the Federal Supreme Council to bring in civilians into their Administration. It is essential that such civilians should be people of repute whose integrity have not been in doubt or questioned in the past and should be given some responsibility.

17. COURTS
North supports the idea of having an intermediate court of appeal to which appeals should be lodged before reaching the Supreme Court; but it does not support the proposal contained in Chapter ix paragraph 2 of the Memo MND (6) of the Mid-West. There are two ways of establishing such an intermediate Court of Appeal:

i. As proposed in paragraph 3 of the same Chapter—the enlargement aiming particularly to bringing in men learned in Muslim and other customary laws to enable the court to deal with appeals in such laws. This will remove the present unsatisfactory procedure of having appeals to end at the Sharia Court of Appeal in the North; or

ii. Every Region should establish an appeal Court to which all appeals from the High Court and (in the case of Northern Region) the Sharia Court should be made before passing on to the Supreme Court.

[1] *None of the three sources so far available for a record of the proposals submitted by the five delegations to the two sessions of the Ad Hoc Constitutional Conference, convened in Lagos on 12 September and resumed on 20 September, fully discloses the nature of the North's supplementary proposals. From a composite examination it emerges that:*

(1) The North's memorandum, circulated in 13 September, is reproduced in the Federal record Memoranda submitted by the Delegations to the Ad Hoc Conference on Constitutional Proposals for Nigeria, December 1967, pp. 5–16; in the East's record The Ad Hoc Conference on the Nigerian Constitution (Enugu, 1966), pp. 1–11; and in the official release

to the Nigerian press, carried in the Daily Times, *1 December 1966, pp. 11–13. There is no major disagreement, omission, or cutting here.*

(2) The North's supplementary memorandum, circulated after the resumption of the conference on 20 September, is to be found under this heading in the Federal record (above), pp. 18–20, without para. 9 being marked and stopping at para. 10. This memorandum is given in the Daily Times *(above), which also includes a discussion on Mining Royalties under the rubric of the Northern delegation, which the Federal record published separately on pp. 122–3, dating it 25 October. The Eastern record (above) contains the Mining Royalties argument but not the supplementary proposals referred to above. Instead, it carries a similar (but by no means identical) 17-point memorandum attributed to the Northern delegation, on pp. 71–5. This is also given in the* Daily Times *(above), pp. 14 and 24, but with no heading to differentiate it from the other version of the North's supplementary proposals. In the absence of the original record it may be provisionally assumed that the 10-point memorandum is the one attached to the North's Statement (see* DOC 57*) on the resumption of the conference and that the 17-point version is its post-discussion shape by the time the conference adjourned on 3 October. Since it is the earlier (*Daily Times*) version and not the year-later Federal record that contains the North's opinion on the creation of states, this is the source used for this Document.*   2 *See* DOC 54.

57.
North Denies Volte-face on Creation of States [1]

The statement attributed to Lateef Jakande which was carried on the NBC news yesterday concerning the stand of the North on certain issues at the last Constitutional Conference contains distortions which require correction.

The report attributed to Jakande that the East and North deviated from the previous agreement reached at the conference is totally untrue in respect of the North. If the truth must be told it was only the North and the Mid-West delegations who advocated in their memoranda an effective centre with sources of revenue independent of states or regions.

Lagos, in one of the three memoranda they submitted jointly with the West, advocated a very loose federal government which shall be financed by subventions contributed in equal amounts by each region.

On the issue of states, it is mischievous for anyone to have reported that the North had changed its position on the creation of states. The relevant portion on the subject in the Northern Memorandum to which Jakande referred reads as follows:

'The North has suggested both in its original memorandum and the statement made by the leader of the Northern Delegation on the issue of States methods by which the areas demanding states can be ascertained and states created. The North would like the suggestion of the North discussed and formally adopted and recommended to the Supreme Commander.

The North will like to reiterate its position that in the exercise of ascertaining the wishes of the people for the creation of states as well as in the actual creation of states, no region, except the Mid-West, should be left out of the operation.'

The North had earlier suggested that a system for ascertaining the wishes of the people in areas where demands for the creation of states have been

made should be devised and that these wishes ascertained before the administration of the country is returned to civilian hands.

The North also suggested that a sub-committee of the conference should be
set up to draw up proposals to the Federal Government on what machinery
should be adopted to ascertain the demands for states in the light of the present circumstances of the country.

The North even went further to suggest that the Federal Military Government should, at some stage, establish a commission on which representatives
of neutral bodies could serve to go into the issue of states.

How these suggestions can be interpreted to mean opposition to the
creation of states is difficult to understand. Difficult to understand also is the
Lagos Delegation support for the creation of states and at the same time
their advocacy of a central government financed by subventions contributed
in equal amounts by the regions or states.

On the issue of the creation of a Lagos state, the stand of the North has been
quoted out of context to give the impression that the North was outright
opposed to the creation of a Lagos State.

What the North refuted in its memorandum was the argument which based
the case for the creation of a Lagos State purely on the grounds that Lagos
had been neglected and that the welfare of its peoples had not received adequate attention.

On the issue of the offices of President and Prime Minister, the North was
not alone in the suggestion that the offices should be held in rotation between
states. The suggestion was intended to allay fears of domination particularly
at the interim period.

Lagos made exactly the same recommendation and it is completely untrue
as was reported that the North proposed that members of the Federal
Cabinet should have veto power.

The conclusion one is tempted to draw from recent utterances and Press
statements is that there are people who wish to see Nigeria dismembered, but
who wish to pass the blame and odium of its break-up to others. The affairs of
Nigeria deserve more objective and selfless treatment than this.

The nation's interest should not be subordinated to the interest of a group.
Nigeria can no longer afford misunderstanding between its leaders and
utterances which give cause for suspicion or which look like attempts to gain
political advantage over others should be avoided.

[1] New Nigerian, *22 November 1966. The release was signed by J. S. Tarka, on behalf of
the Northern Delegation to the Conference*

58.
Progress Report of the Constitutional Conference Committee submitted to the Supreme Commander, 30 September 1966[1]

Following the Supreme Commander's address delivered in the National Hall,
Lagos, on September 12, 1966, the *Ad Hoc* Committee adopted the following
Agenda:

i. consideration of the form of association best suited for Nigeria in the future;
ii. interim arrangements.
Plenary meetings were held on 12, 13, 14, 15, 16, 20, 21, 23, 28, and 29 September, 1966.

2. After a general debate on the form of association during which the various Delegations submitted Memoranda, the *Ad Hoc* Committee appointed a Sub-Committee consisting of two members of each of the five Delegations, to consider subjects to be allocated to the Central Authority on the basis of existing Legislative Lists in the Schedule to the Constitution of the Federation.

3. After considering the Lists drawn up by the Sub-Committee up to September 23, the plenary session authorized it to include consideration of:
  i. the structure of the Central Government, and
  ii. the question of the creation of more States in Nigeria. . . .

5. The areas of agreement and of disagreement in respect of the Exclusive and Concurrent Legislative Lists are set out in sections 'A', 'B' and 'C', while section 'D' deals with the structure of the Central Government and 'E' with the question of the creation of new States. . . .

7. The *Ad Hoc* Committee proposes to adjourn on Monday, October 3, 1966, for three weeks, in order to enable Delegates report back and have consultations in the Regions and Lagos on the progress so far made, and to exchange and study detailed Memoranda dealing, in particular, with the areas of disagreement as well as other aspects of the new Constitution which have not so far been considered.

A. ITEMS AGREED TO BY THE AD HOC COMMITTEE TO BE ON THE EXCLUSIVE LEGISLATIVE LIST

1. Accounts of the Government of the Federation and officers, courts and authorities thereof, including audit of those accounts.

2. Archives, other than the public records of the Governments of the Regions since the twenty-third day of January 1952.

3. Aviation, including airports and safety of aircraft, provided that the Government of a State may establish and maintain aerodromes and landing strips and operate aircraft either by itself or through any person or authority for civil purposes.

8. Copyright.

10. Customs and Excise duties, including export duties. (The Committee agreed to defer consideration of this item until revenue allocation has been dealt with).

11. Defence—Army:
  1. There shall be a Nigerian Army which shall be organized in Regional units composed entirely in each Region of personnel indigenous to that Region.
  2. The operational control of the units in each Region will be the responsibility of the Regional Commander.
  3. Directions with respect to the maintaining and securing of public safety and public order within the Region or any part thereof may be given to the

Regional Commander by the Security Committee in the Region and the Regional Commander shall comply with those directions or cause them to be complied with.

4. The composition of the Security Committee shall be as follows:
    i. The Governor of the Region;
    ii. The Head of the Regional Government;
    iii. The Regional Commander;
    iv. The Commissioner of Police;
    v. The Minister in the Region responsible for public order.

5. Training facilities, Ordnance Depots and other army stores shall be organized on regional basis. Recruitment shall be the responsibility of the Regional Commander acting in accordance with the policy laid down by the Security Committee.

6. At the national level there shall be a Defence Council which shall be responsible for—
    a. laying down military policy which should include the strength of military personnel in each Region, types and quantities of weapons, equipment, minimum standards of recruitment, promotion, discipline, etc.;
    b. overall operational control of the Regional units in the event of—
        i. external aggression;
        ii. inter-Regional conflict; and
        iii. the Regional Security Committee requesting the Council for military assistance to cope with any security situation within the Region beyond the capability of the Regional unit.
    c. the control of Defence Industries.

7. The Defence Council will consist of—
    i. The Head of the State of Nigeria;
    ii. The Head of the Central Government;
    iii. The Heads of the Regional Governments;
    iv. The Chief of Staff;
    v. Regional Commanders;
    vi. The Minister of Defence.

8. The office of Chief of Staff shall be held in rotation by the Regional Commanders for fixed periods not exceeding twelve months.

9. The Defence Council shall be served by a Defence Secretariat under the Chief of Staff. The personnel of the Secretariat shall be drawn from Regions in equal numbers.

Navy and Air Force
Same arrangements as for the Army with the expansion of the Defence Council to include the Regional Commanders of the Navy and the Air Force.

Police
1. There shall be a Nigeria Police Force which shall be organized in Regional units composed entirely in each Region of personnel indigenous to that Region.

2. The operational control of the units in each Region shall be the responsibility of the Regional Commissioner of Police.

3. Training facilities, depots and stores shall be organized on a Regional basis. Recruitment shall be the responsibility of the Regional Commissioner of Police acting in accordance with the policy laid down by the Regional Government.

4. At the national level there shall be a Police Council which shall be responsible for—

   a. laying down general policy which should include the strength of police personnel in each Region, types and quantities of equipment, weapons, minimum standards of recruitment, promotion, discipline, etc;

   b. overall operational control of the Regional units in the event of the Regional Governments requesting the Council for police assistance to cope with any actual or threatened security situation within the Region beyond or likely to be beyond the capability of the Regional unit; provided that a Regional Commissioner with the consent of the Head of the Regional Government may request the Commissioner of another Region for police assistance in an urgent situation and that such request shall not be granted or refused except with the approval of the Head of the Regional Government concerned.

5. The Police Council shall be served by a Secretariat under the Inspector-General of Police. The personnel in the Secretariat shall be drawn from the Regions in equal numbers.

6. Five years after the new Constitution has come into effect, all local authority police forces shall cease to exist, and in the meantime there should be a progressive reduction in those local authority forces.

12. Deportation of aliens, subject to the approval of the Defence Council.

16. Extradition, save that no person shall be extradited for political offences.

18. Immigration, including visas, provided that visas and entry permits shall be issued if requested for by a State government and provided further that there shall be a branch of the Immigration Office in each Region.

21. Legal proceedings between the Government of the Federation and any other person or authority or between the Governments of Regions.

27. (*See* under item 11 above).

28. Nuclear energy, provided that it shall be controlled and administered by the Defence Council and provided further that the Government of a Region, with the permission of the Defence Council, shall have power either by itself or through any person or authority to harness nuclear energy for peaceful uses.

29. Emigration, including passports and travel certificates, provided that passports and travel certificates shall be issued to Nigerian citizens as of right to all parts of the world and provided further that there shall be a branch of the Passport Office in each Region.

30. Patents, trade marks, designs and merchandise marks.

31. Pensions, gratuities and other like benefits payable out of the Consolidated Revenue Fund or any other public fund of the Federation.

32. Posts, telegraphs and telephones, including post office savings banks; provided that the Government of a Region shall have power to establish and

maintain, either by itself or through any person or authority, the foregoing services within its Region, provided further that a Regional Government shall have no power to print postage stamps, postal orders and money orders.

33. Powers, privileges and immunities of each House of Parliament and its members, provided that no law of any legislature within the Federation may grant absolute privilege to members of such a legislature in respect of anything said or written by them inside or outside the legislature.

35. Public relations of the Federation.

37. Railways, including ancillary transport and other services; provided that the Government of a Region shall have power to establish and maintain, either by itself or through any person or authority, the foregoing services within its Region.

39. Tribunals of inquiry with respect to all or any of the matters mentioned elsewhere in this list.

40. Federal highways, that is to say, the construction, alteration and maintenance of such highways as may, with the consent of all the governments of the Regions, be declared by Parliament to be Federal Highways.

41. Water from such sources as may be declared by Parliament to be sources affecting more than one territory.

42. Weights and measures.

44. (Not dealt with.)

B. ITEMS ON WHICH THE AD HOC COMMITTEE DISAGREED

4. Bills of exchange and promissory notes.

5. Borrowing of moneys outside Nigeria for the purposes of the Federation or of any Region, other than borrowing by the Government of a Region for a period not exceeding twelve months on the security of any funds or assets of that Government held outside Nigeria.

6. Borrowing of moneys within Nigeria for the purposes of the Federation.

7. Control of capital issues.

9. Currency, coinage and legal tender.

14. Exchange Control.

North, West, Mid-West and Lagos agree that these items should be on the Exclusive List, subject to the recommendations of the Committee of experts in their paragraphs 1 to 21. The East reserves its position on paragraphs 13, 14, 15 and 17 of the experts report.

34. The public debt of the federation.

North, West, Mid-West and Lagos agree that it should be on the Exclusive List. The East reserves its position.

11. *Army*

The Federal Capital shall be garrisoned in rotation for fixed periods by personnel drawn from the units of one Region at a time. (Northern Delegation reserves its position.)

Police

1. Directions with respect to the maintaining and securing of public safety

and public order within the Region or any part thereof may be given to the Regional Commissioner of Police by the Head of the Regional Government and the Regional Commissioner shall comply with those directions or cause them to be complied with; provided that before carrying out any such directions which may involve the use of arms the Commissioner may request that the matter should be referred to the Police Council for their directions.

The East proposes that the words 'Police Council' in the proviso to paragraph 3 should be replaced by the words 'Regional Security Committee' in order to bring it into line with the corresponding arrangement in the case of the Army.

The Mid-West reserves its position on the clause 'which may involve the use of arms'.

2. The Police Council shall consist of—
   i. The Head of the Federal Government;
   ii. Heads of the Regional Governments;
   iii. The Inspector-General of Police;
   iv. Regional Commissioners;
   v. The Minister responsible for police matters.

The North proposes the inclusion of the Chairman of the Public Service Commission.

3. The East and West propose that the Office of the Inspector-General of Police shall be held in rotation by the Regional Commissioners of Police for fixed periods not exceeding twelve months. The North and Lagos propose a period of three years and the Mid-West proposes that this should be held on permanent basis.

15. *External Affairs*

No unanimous agreement reached. West, Mid-West and Lagos propose that External Affairs should remain on the Exclusive List. The East proposes it should remain in the Exclusive List subject to the following four provisos:

i. Appointments to foreign Missions and appointments within their establishments should be on a quota system based on equality of representation among the Regions, as has been suggested by the East, and the Mid-West Delegations in the case of item 36: 'Public Service of the Federation'.

ii. All diplomatic and consular posts in the United Nations Organization, the Organization of African Unity, and in foreign and Commonwealth countries, should be held in rotation for fixed periods, as stated below, by suitable indigenes of the member Regions of Nigeria:

Head of Mission	2 years
Head of Chancery	
Counsellor	3 years
Heads of Division	
Other Staff	4 years

iii. The following Missions, namely, London, Washington, United Nations, New York, Bonn, Paris, Brussels, Rome and Moscow, should not be headed at the same time by more than two indigenes of any one Region, and any Region that has within the preceding twelve months had one of its indigenes as Head of Mission to one of these countries should not immediately be allowed to have another representative from such a Region to head such a Mission.

iv. The Regions shall have power to enter into treaties and agreements with foreign powers in the interest of trade and commercial development of the Region; any Region that so desires may appoint a commercial attache or counsellor to a Nigerian Mission abroad.

The North proposes that External Affairs should remain on the Exclusive List subject to Items (*ii*) and (*iii*) of the East's provisos above. The Mid-West reserved its position on proviso 1 and first sentence of proviso 4.

17. The following higher educational institutions, that is to say—the University of Ibadan; the University College Teaching Hospital at Ibadan; University of Lagos; the Lagos University Teaching Hospital; the West African Institute of Social and Economic Research; the Pharmacy School at Yaba; the Forestry School at Ibadan; the Veterinary School at Vom.

No unanimous agreement reached. The East proposes that Item 17 of the Exclusive List and Item 10 of the Concurrent List should be deleted. The North, West, Mid-West and Lagos propose that Item 17 on the Exclusive List and Item 10 on the Concurrent List should remain as at present.

19. Incorporation, regulation and winding-up of bodies corporate, other than co-operative societies, native authorities, local government authorities and bodies corporate established directly by any law enacted by the legislature of a Region.

No unanimous agreement reached. North, West, Mid-West and Lagos propose that item 19 should remain on the Exclusive List provided that there shall be a branch of the office of the Registrar of Companies in each Region. The East proposes that item 19 should either be Regional or retained on the Federal list but modified to read 'securing of uniform principles for the incorporation, etc.'.

22. Maritime shipping and navigation, including—

a. shipping and navigation on tidal waters;

b. shipping and navigation on the River Niger and its affluents and on any such other inland waterway as may be declared by Parliament to be an international waterway or to be inter-Regional waters;

c. lighthouses, lightships, beacons and other provisions for the safety of shipping and navigation;

d. such ports as may be declared by Parliament to be Federal ports (including the constitution and powers of port authorities for Federal ports).

No unanimous agreement reached. The East proposes that item 22 (*d*) should be deleted. The North, West, Mid-West and Lagos propose that item 22 should remain on the Exclusive List with the proviso that 22 (*d*) is amended to read: 'existing ports and such new ports as may, with the agreement of the Regional Government concerned be declared by Parliament to be Federal ports (including the constitutions and powers of ports authorities for Federal ports)'.

24. Meteorology; provided that the Government of a Region shall have power to establish and maintain its own Meteorological Service. (Position of the Northern delegation reserved in respect of the proviso.)

R

25. Mines and Minerals, including oilfields, oil mining, geological surveys and natural gas.

No unanimous agreement reached. East, West, Mid-West and Lagos propose deletion of item 25. North proposes retention as a Federal subject.

36. The public service of the Federation including the settlement of disputes between the Federation and officers in the public service of the Federation.

No unanimous agreement reached. East and Mid-West suggest that item 36 remain a Federal subject provided the appointments in the service shall be made from time to time on the basis of equality of numbers from the Regions and provided further that in making promotions to senior posts, regard should as far as possible in addition to other qualifications be had to the Region of origin of the candidate. North, West and Lagos suggest that recruitment into the Federal Public Service should be on population basis. The East, in addition, proposes that, in view of the likely injustice to the public servants in the proviso above, consideration should be given to the filling of the more senior posts in the Federal Service by secondment from the Regional Public Service.

43. Wireless, broadcasting and television other than wireless broadcasting and television, provided by, or at the instance of, the Government of a Region; allocation of wave lengths for wireless broadcasting and television transmissions. (Eastern Delegation reserved its position.)

THE CONCURRENT LEGISLATIVE LIST

The Eastern Delegation reserves its position on all the subjects on this list, on the ground that they should all be Regional subjects since, in its view, the concurrent list is a source of friction. The other Delegations agreed that those listed below should remain on the List.

2. Arms and ammunition.

4. Census.

6. Commercial and industrial monopolies, combines and trusts.

8. Such drugs and poisons as may with the consent of the governments of the Regions be designated by the President by order.

9. Finger-prints, identification and criminal records.

10. Higher Education, that is to say, institutions, etc., and other bodies offering courses or conducting examinations of a university, technological or of a professional character, other than the institutions referred to in item 17 of Part 1 of this Schedule.

11. Industrial development.

12. Labour, that is to say, conditions of Labour, industrial relations, trade unions and welfare of labour.

13. The legal and medical professions and such other professional occupations as may with the consent of the governments of the Regions be designated by the President by order.

14. National monuments, that is to say, such monuments in a Region as may with the consent of the Government of that Region be designated by the President by order as national monuments.

15. National parks, that is to say, the control of such areas in a Region as may with the consent of the Government of that Region be designated by the President by order as national parks.

16. Prisons and other institutions for the treatment of offenders.

17. Promotion of tourist traffic.

18. The maintaining and securing of public safety and public order; the providing, maintaining and securing of such supplies and services as may be designated by the President by order as essential supplies and services.

19. Quarantine.

20. Registration of business names.

21. Scientific and industrial research.

22. Service and execution in a Region of the Civil and Criminal processes, judgments, decrees, orders and other decisions of any court of law outside Nigeria or any court of law in Nigeria other than the Supreme Court, the High Court of that Region or any court of law established by the legislature of that Region.

23. Statistics.

24. Traffic on Federal highways.

25. Tribunals of inquiry with respect to all or any of the matters mentioned elsewhere in this list.

26. Trigonometrical, cadastral and topographical surveys.

27. Water-power.

28. The matters with respect to which Parliament is empowered to make provision by subsections (2) and (3) of section 76 and section 79 of this Constitution.

29. Any matter that is incidental or supplementary to any matter mentioned elsewhere in this list.

C. ITEMS AGREED TO BE DELETED FROM THE EXCLUSIVE LEGISLATIVE LIST

13. Designation of securities in which trust funds may be invested.

20. Insurance other than insurance undertaken by the Government of a Region but including any insurance undertaken by the Government of a Region that extends beyond the limits of that Region.

23. Marriages other than marriages under Moslem Law or other customary law; annulment and dissolution of, and other matrimonial causes relating to, marriages other than marriages under Moslem Law or other customary law.

26. Museums of the Federation, that is to say
    The Jos Museum.
    The Oron Museum.
    The House of Images at Esie.
    Any other museums established by the Government of the Federation.

38. Taxes on amount paid or payable on the sale or purchase of commodities except:

a. produce;

b. hides and skins;

c. motor spirit;

d. diesel oil sold or purchased for use in road vehicles;

e. diesel oil sold or purchased for other than industrial purposes.

ITEMS AGREED TO BE DELETED FROM THE CONCURRENT LEGISLATIVE LIST

1. Antiquities.

2. Bankruptcy and insolvency.

3. Chemical services, including analytical services.

7. Control of the voluntary movement of persons between territories.

D. STRUCTURE OF THE CENTRAL GOVERNMENT

The Committee considered the structure of the Central Government only in outline as follows:

1. Should there be a Federal Parliament?
   Yes, unanimously.

2. Should the Federal Parliament be bicameral or unicameral?
   West and Lagos propose bicameral. North, East and Mid-West propose unicameral.

3. What shall be the basis of representation in each chamber of Parliament?
   North, East and Mid-West propose equal representation in the single chamber. West and Lagos propose representation in proportion to population in the lower House and equal representation of the States in the Upper House.

4. Should members of Parliament be elected?
   West, Mid-West and Lagos propose direct election into Federal Parliament on the basis of universal adult suffrage throughout the Federation. The North and East propose selection of members on the basis of rules and procedure laid down by the State Government.

5. Should there be a Head of State?
   Yes, unanimously.

6. Should there be a Head of Government?
   Yes, unanimously.

7. Should there be a Federal Cabinet?
   Yes, unanimously.

8. Should the Judiciary remain as at present?
   No. It should not remain as at present.

Note: Subject to further discussion, the details of the answers to the above questions are contained in the memoranda submitted by the various delegations.

E. CREATION OF NEW STATES

The Committee considered the question of the creation of new states only in outline as follows:

1. Should more States be created in the country?
   Yes by North, West, Mid-West and Lagos.

2. Should there be a plebiscite to determine the wishes of the people in each proposed State?

East reserves its position in view of the impending Conference to be held in the Eastern Region to discuss the subject.

¹ *From the official record of the Conference issued by the Federal and Eastern Governments.*

59.
National Military Government Communiqué on Progress Report of the Ad Hoc Committee on Constitutional Proposals¹

The Ad Hoc Committee on Constitutional Proposals for the future of Nigeria has submitted an Interim Report on the progress of discussions at its meetings to the Supreme Commander and Head of the Federal Military Government.

The Committee hopes to adjourn shortly in order to enable the Delegates to report back and have consultations in the Regions and Lagos on the progress so far made, and to exchange and study detailed memoranda dealing in particular, with the areas of disagreement as well as other aspects of the new Constitution which have not so far been considered.

In the Progress Report, the Supreme Commander was informed that, after lengthy and exhaustive discussions, agreement had been reached on a wide variety of important matters; for example:

1. it was unanimously agreed, subject to further discussion and to the resolution of differences of detail expressed in the memoranda of various delegations, that

a. Nigeria shall continue as a political entity,

b. the structure of the central authority of Nigeria shall contain the following four elements: (*i*) a head of state; (*ii*) a head of government; (*iii*) a central or federal cabinet; and (*iv*) a central or federal parliament.

2. Fourteen of the items in the Exclusive Legislative List should still remain on the list.

It was also unanimously agreed that the following items, subject to provisos which would either permit the Regions to operate in these fields or otherwise safeguard Regional interests, should remain on the Exclusive Legislative List: Aviation, including Airports and safety of Aircraft. External Affairs. Immigration, including Visas. Emigration, including Passports and Travel Certificates. Posts, Telegraphs and Telephones, including Post Office Savings Banks. Railways, including Ancillary Transport and other services. Federal Highways.

It was unanimously agreed that there should continue to be a Nigerian Army, Navy, Air Force and Police Force; that the Armed Forces and the Police Force should be organized in Regional units composed entirely of personnel indigenous to each Region, and that the operational control of these forces shall be vested in their Regional head, subject in certain emergencies to overall control and deployment by central council including equal representatives of all the Regions.

It was unanimously agreed that the following five subjects, which were formerly items on the Exclusive Legislative List, should become Regional subjects:

Designation of Securities in which trust funds may be invested.

Insurance, Marriages, Museums, Taxes on Sale or Purchase of Commodities.

It was unanimously agreed that the following four subjects which were formerly items on the Concurrent List, should become Regional subjects:

Antiquities, Bankruptcy and Insolvency, Chemical Services, including Analytical Services, Control of the voluntary movement of persons between territories.

There was substantial, but as yet not unanimous, agreement that more States should be created in Nigeria and that there should be a plebiscite to determine the wishes of the people in each proposed State.

The retention in the Exclusive Legislative List of the following subjects on which a Committee of Experts have made recommendations to the Ad Hoc Committee will be further considered:

Bills of Exchange and Promissory Notes.

Borrowing of moneys outside Nigeria for the purposes of the Federation or of any Region, other than borrowing by the Government of a Region for a period not exceeding twelve months on the security of any funds or assets of that government held outside Nigeria.

Borrowing of moneys within Nigeria for the purpose of the Federation

Control of Capital Issues

Currency, Coinage and Legal Tender

Exchange Control.

Similarly the Concurrent List will be further discussed.

The Head of the Federal Military Government and Supreme Commander of the Armed Forces is referring the Interim Report of the Ad Hoc Committee to the Military Governors and the Administrator of Lagos for their views.

[1] *Issued in Lagos on 30 September 1966. Text taken from the Federal Government's official record of the Conference.*

60.
Summary of Proposals submitted by the Regional Delegations to the First Session of the Constitutional Conference, September 1966

See pp. 245–54.

[From the Eastern Government's Official Record. This summary is not found in the Federal Record.]

61.
Gowon's Address to the Committee on Constitutional Proposals, 3 October 1966 [1]

Gentlemen,

I requested that I should come and see you in order that, at least, I will be

Text continued on p. 255.

SUMMARY OF PROPOSALS

Subjects	North	East	West	Lagos	Mid-West
1. Form and Unit of Association	A weak centre with existing Regions remaining, at least for the time being, autonomous States delegating powers to a central authority for common services.	A loose association of states comprising the existing Regions, namely East Mid-West, North and West.	Federation with more States on linguistic basis and with Lagos as separate State. Failing that, a Commonwealth of Nigeria with existing Regions forming sovereign States and with Lagos as part of the West; the States shall delegate to a central authority to be known as a Council of States responsibility for agreed common services.	As for the West.	Federation comprising the existing Regions, i.e., North, East, West and Mid-West Regions with Lagos either as Federal Territory or as a separate Region.
2. Central Authority (a) Composition	A central Executive Council with equal representation from the constituent States. Chairmanship shall rotate annually. The Powers of the Central Executive shall be delegated by the constituent States except that powers connected with External Affairs and Immigration can be unilaterally withdrawn by a State government while all other functions delegated to the Central	There shall be a unicameral legislative body consisting of equal number of delegates from each of the constituent States. Chairmanship shall rotate from year to year. Laws passed by this legislature shall be subject to ratification by the State government. There shall be an executive body made up of equal membership. Chairmanship of the Executive shall rotate annually and shall autom-	Federal Parliament with a Federal Executive Council. Failing that, Council of States as mentioned above; the Council to have powers to make laws by Orders in Council and major decisions to be taken by unanimous agreement of the States which shall be equally represented on the Council. Chairmanship shall be rotational annually and Chairman shall be Head of State.	As for the West.	Federal Parliament with Federal Executive with equal representation from all Regions on both bodies.

Subjects	North	East	West	Lagos	Mid-West
	Executive Council can only be withdrawn by a State government after a unanimous decision by their representatives in the Central Executive Council.	atically be Head of State. This Executive will run certain agreed common services.			
(b) Functions (i) External Affairs	Central Authority.	Central Authority, provided that the regions shall have powers to enter into treaties and agreements in the interest of trade and economic development as long as such are non-political and not prejudicial to the security of other Regions. Provided also that war cannot be declared, nor peace concluded, without the consent of every Region, and if war is declared or peace concluded without such consent, the Region not consenting shall have the right to secede.	Position reserved on the allocation of functions under a Federal system. Failing which, Central Authority. Appointments to foreign legations and the most senior appointments within their establishments shall be on a quota system based on equality of representation among the States; diplomatic and consular posts in the United Nations Organization, the Organization of African Unity, and in foreign and Commonwealth countries shall be held in rotation for fixed periods of one to two years at a time by suitable nominees of the member States of the Commonwealth of Nigeria; provided that each	As for the West.	Position reserved on the allocation of functions between Regions and Central Authority.

Subject						
(ii) Immigration Emigration Passports and Visas	Delegation to Central Authority.	Should be handled by central authority, provided that the central authority shall issue passports to Nigerian citizens only on the recommendation of state of origin of applicant and provided also that no foreigner shall be admitted into a state without the approval of that state and no foreigner permitted to enter a state shall be prevented from doing so by the central authority.	State shall have the right to enter into direct relations with foreign and Commonwealth States and international institutions and to conclude agreements and consular representatives with them.	In the case of Federation, position reserved. Failing which, immigration only to the central authority, provided that each state shall be empowered to issue visas and entry permits which shall be valid within its own territory.	As for the West.	Position reserved.
(iii) Weights and Measures	Central Authority.	Central Authority.	Central Authority	Central Authority	Central Authority	Position reserved.
(iv) Central Banking currency and coinage	Over-all monetary policy and all instruments thereof such as exchange control, credit creation and maintenance of separate external reserve shall be vested in the central	Central authority subject to the appendix to memorandum.	Position reserved in the case of a Federal Constitution. Failing which, central banking to be vested with central authority, excluding exchange control but including bills		As for the West.	Position reserved.

DOCUMENT 60 (continued)

Subjects	North	East	West	Lagos	Mid-West
	authority. Details to be worked out by experts.		of exchange and promissory notes, currency, coinage and legal tender.		
(v) Railways	Central Common Service provided that the participation can only be withdrawn with the unanimous consent of all the States.	Maintenance of existing railways and co-ordination of the railways of the regions.	In the event of Federal Constitution, position reserved; otherwise, Central Common Service.	As for the West.	Position reserved.
(vi) Ports and Harbours	All Ports, present or future, to be under central authority.	Existing Ports and Harbours to be under central authority.	In the event of Federation, position reserved: otherwise Ports and Harbours to be under central authority.	As for the West.	Position reserved.
(vii) Shipping	Shipping under central authority.	Nigerian National Shipping Line under central authority.	In the event of Federation, position reserved; otherwise Shipping under central authority.	As for the West.	Position reserved.
(viii) External Telecommunications	Central Common Services.	Central Common Services.	In the event of Federation, position reserved; otherwise Central Common Services.	As for the West.	Position reserved.
(ix) Internal Posts and Telecommunications	Central Common Service provided that participation can only be withdrawn with the unanimous consent of all the States.	Co-ordination of services only to remain in the centre.	In the event of Federation, position reserved; otherwise Central Common Services.	As for the West.	Position reserved.

(x) Inland Waterways	All inland waterways to remain with the central authority.	Navigation on the Niger to remain with the central authority.	In the event of Federation, position reserved; otherwise silent.	—	Position reserved.
(xi) Territorial Waters	To remain with central authority.	—	In the event of Federation, position reserved; otherwise silent.	—	Position reserved.
(xii) Water Sources affecting more than one State	—	To remain with the central authority.	In the event of Federation, position reserved; otherwise silent.	—	Position reserved.
(xiii) Airways	To remain with central authority.	Existing Nigeria Airways to remain with the central authority.	In the event of Federation, position reserved; otherwise Central Authority.	As for the West.	Position reserved.
(xiv) Civil Aviation	To remain with the central authority.	Central authority only in respect of safety of aircraft and laying of aviation standards.	In the event of Federation, position reserved; otherwise silent.	As for the West.	Position reserved.
(xv) Meteorology	Central authority.	Central authority only in respect of co-ordinating of services to the centre.	In the event of Federation, position reserved; otherwise silent.	As for the West.	Position reserved.
(xvi) Niger Dams Authority	Central authority, provided that the participation can only be withdrawn with the unanimous consent of all the States.	—	In the event of Federation, position reserved; otherwise silent.	As for the West.	Position reserved.

Subjects	North	East	West	Lagos	Mid-West
(*xvii*) Central Public Service Commission	Central authority, provided that the participation can only be withdrawn with the unanimous consent of all the States.	Central authority subject to the rotation of Chairman.	In the event of Federation, position reserved; otherwise silent.	As for the West.	Position reserved.
(*xviii*) Foreign Trade	Central authority.	—	In the event of Federation, position reserved.	—	Position reserved.
(*xix*) Customs and Excise	Central authority.	For purposes of legislation, central. Collection and disbursement, State.	In the event of Federation, position reserved; otherwise Central Authority.	As for the West.	Position reserved.
(*xx*) Common Citizenship	Citizenship dual; central authority in respect of Nigerian citizenship; State citizenship to be under State authority.	Central authority.	In the event of Federation, position reserved; otherwise Central Authority.	As for the West.	Position reserved.
(*xxi*) External Publicity and Information	Central authority.	—	In the event of Federation, position reserved; otherwise silent.	As for the West.	Position reserved.
(*xxii*) Public Relations of the Centre	—	Central authority	In the event of Federation, position reserved; otherwise Central Authority.	As for the West.	Position reserved.
(*xxiii*) Other Functions of the Central	—	Accounts of central authority and Audit thereof, copyright; ex-	In the event of Federation, position reserved; otherwise future public	As for the West.	Position reserved.

Authority	tradition, Insurance undertaken by the central authority, legal proceedings between the central authority and the Regions and individuals or between Regions; patents, designs and trade marks, Tribunals of Inquiry with respect to matters within the competence of the Central Authority.	debt of Nigeria; Settlement of interstate disputes by mixed Arbitration Tribunals.			
3. Judiciary	Central Court of Appeal performing the same functions as the present Supreme Court.	Supreme Court at the centre having limited original and appellate jurisdiction.	In the case of Federation, position reserved; otherwise silent.	As for the West.	Position reserved.
4. Armed Forces and Police	State Army, Air Force and Police, Navy to be central with personnel recruitment on population basis. Central Defence Commission with a civilian head and heads of State forces as members to eliminate the danger of arms race. All States must sign a treaty to defend the country against external aggression.	State Army, Police, Air Force and Navy; for external defence, each State to contribute part or all of its forces as occasion demands. Suitable co-ordination arrangement to be worked out.	In the case of Federation, position reserved; otherwise State Army, Navy, Air Force and Police. Central authority to deal with inspectorate general of the armed forces (excepting their operational control) for the purpose only of ensuring by means of periodic meetings and inspections that the armed forces of each State are adequately maintained and equipped in the in-	As for the West.	Position reserved.

DOCUMENT 60 (*continued*)

Subjects	North	East	West	Lagos	Mid-West
			terest of defence of the Commonwealth of Nigeria; the Inspectorate-General would comprise representatives of State armed forces in equal numbers.		
5. Secession	Right to secede completely and unilaterally.	Right to secede.	In the case of Federation, position reserved; otherwise right to secede unilaterally.	As for the North.	Position reserved.
6. Other Financial Arrangements	Revenue from central authority to be allocated on principle of derivation.	As for the North.	As for the North.	As for the North.	Position reserved.
7. Financing of the Centre	—	By equal contribution from all the component States.	In the event of Federation, position reserved; otherwise as for the East.	As for the West.	Position reserved.
8. Assets and Liabilities	—	Existing Federal assets and liabilities to be determined and shared according to an agreed formula.	The existing national debt of the Federation should become the responsibility of the States on the basis of the location of the projects in respect of which the debts have been incurred. New National loans to be met by Council of States in direct proportion to the degree of benefit derived therefrom by each State.	As for the West.	Position reserved.

9. Pensions	—	Existing Federal pensions and pensions rights shall be central subject.	Retirement benefits payable to former Federal civil servants shall become the responsibility of their respective States of origin. In respect of non-Nigerians, all States shall contribute in equal proportion.	As for the West.	Position reserved.
10. Review of Constitution	—	Automatic review of constitution after ten years or earlier if parties agreed.	In the event of a Federation, position reserved; otherwise silent.	As for the West.	Position reserved.
11. Regional Constitution	—	The drawing up of Regional Constitution is the exclusive responsibility of the people concerned.	In the event of a Federation, position reserved; otherwise silent.	As for the West.	Position reserved.
12. Position of Lagos	Central Authority subject.	—	Lagos to comprise a separate State in the Federation otherwise to form part of Western Nigeria.	As for the West.	Lagos to constitute a region or remain Federal territory.
13. Seat of Central Authority	Lagos.	—	Lokoja.	As for the West.	Lagos as capital of Federation.
14. Fundamental Human Rights	Silent.	Fundamental human rights to be written into the constitution without any of the destructive	For Federation as for East.	As for the West.	For Federation, the constitution must assure democratic liberties and include an enforceable bill

Subjects	North	East	West	Lagos	Mid-West
		provisions inserted in the former constitution.			of rights.
15. Creation of More States	Right of self-determination guaranteed, subject to referendum and provided that implementation will not delay determination of the future of Nigeria.	See 11.	In the event of Federation, immediate creation of more States including creation of Lagos State; easier and more precise machinery for the creation of additional states in the future. Failing Federation, creation of more states envisaged.	As for the West.	Expert Commission to be appointed to study and report on the creation of more States, such expert Commission to be guided by the criteria set out at paragraph 23 of memo.
16. Central Appointments	Personnel shall be composed in proportion to the population of each State.	Appointments to the Central Civil Service, Commissions and Agencies shall be on an equal basis amongst the Regions.	In the event of Federation, position reserved; otherwise staff employed in operating the Common services shall belong to the State in which they are employed and also to the public service of that State.	As for the West.	

able to ask you to do one or two things for me when you go home. The arrangement was for the Leaders of the Delegations to come and see me before you adjourn, but I thought, after what has happened over the week-end, I should come here personally and tell you what the situation is at the moment. There is no cause for alarm. And this is what I would like to leave with you. There is no cause for alarm, I repeat.

After we met on Saturday evening and I got home, I received telephone messages about some disturbances in Kano. I was able to locate that it is only a small section of the army that went out of order and I was able to get those that remained loyal to round them up and get them back to barracks. This, I think, they were able to do during the early hours of Sunday morning. My last call to Kano was at about 3.30 a.m. I was able to send troops to Kano just in case the situation was out of hand but fortunately enough, there was no need to use the troops from Kaduna in order to put down the rioters in Kano.

Gentlemen, I will tell you this: certainly there has been a damage. I think that is what we never seem to admit when there is something like that. There is a damage and I am very, very sorry about it. I regret it and I am doing everything I can; honestly, there will be a difference this time. There will be a difference. Give me about a week and you will see: it is either I go or those people who normally do this sort of thing go.

The situation has now been brought back to normal, but for the safety of individuals—in case there are any riotous few the movement of people of Eastern origin back to the East is being carried out. The Governor of the East had said that because of this renewed violence, he had no alternative but to ask non-Easterners in the East to go back to their own homes. I think he is justified; I will tell you that.

However, as I said, there is no cause for alarm. The situation has been brought under control in Kano and we are doing the cleaning up at the moment. I think protection is being given to each and everyone remaining in in those areas. So, for God's sake, gentlemen, bear with me. I know this is a very hard time for us. I thought this meeting was going to adjourn when the atmosphere in the country would be such that people would say: 'Certainly they have done a good job; at least, the way the country is going on at the moment shows that things will be alright,' but it seems as though the week-end's happenings has certainly put a blot on this excellent work you have done. As I said, for God's sake, don't lose hope. If we are alive and if we are determined, we can get this country back to its proper shape. I am determined to do that even if it means my life. I give you my word for it.

Gentlemen, I will ask you, when you go back home, particularly those of us from the North, to waste no effort in going to each and every man, each and every village, and speak to the people. I think there are a few among us who just do not want to see anything good happening in this country and they are fanning up some of these ignorant people to do some atrocious things. Rumours are too rampant. For God's sake, I would like you to go and speak to each and everyone. Don't think these three weeks are going to be holidays; they are not. I think it is going to be a question of being more determined to reach at the people. I think you are not doing that enough. We just stay at our little Headquarters and we do nothing more than that. I request each

S

and everyone of you, when you go back to your Regions, please for God's sake, get people out and speak to them, ask them to calm down their nerves.

Give me a chance and see what we can do.

I think this country has seen enough of bloodshed. We have seen enough of bloodshed. For God's sake, let us try to stop all this. We can only do this if we are able to convince the local people. Even if some riotous soldiers do anything, at least, they can be rounded up and beaten in the best way. If we are able to get our local people to stop going mad, I am quite convinced that we can get somewhere. So, this is an appeal I am going to leave with you. For God's sake, when you get home, do whatever you can to get to the people. Give me a chance. I am quite convinced I will be able to do something. I think enough of blood has been shed in this country. The year 1966 is never to be remembered in Nigerian history any more. Let us try to stop it and I think we can start from here.

Gentlemen, honestly, if I tell you that I am the saddest man today in this country you may not believe it, but I have not had a wink of sleep because of worries and concern about what is happening and I say, particularly because I come from the North. I do not mind saying this. I may be trying to be parochial but I am being honest about this. Honestly, I am not happy about happenings in the country. As I said, I promise you that I am going to do something about it and something will be done. Thousands of people are being made homeless just like that. I think the Government also will have to do something about this.

To our Eastern friends, for God's sake, please don't lose hope. Let us try and see what we can do to mend up what has happened. Give me a chance and I am quite convinced I will be able to do something very shortly.

Well, I am very sorry to come and leave you departing with such a sad note. It is the realities of our days. As we are alive today, we can contribute to the future success of this country. Let us now go back and see what we can do. It is not a question of three weeks' rest but three weeks of determined action to see what we can do to salvage the country. As far as I am concerned, except for these very few dissident elements, I think I can assure you that the others are all loyal and I can really carry out a lot of work of reconstruction. So, may God help us in this new rededication.

Thank you very much.

[1] *Text from* The Struggle for One Nigeria, *pp. 40–2.*

62.

Resolution of Eastern Consultative Assembly, 7 October 1966 [1]

The Consultative Assembly and the Advisory Committee of Chiefs and Elders . . .

1. PLACES on record its deep gratitude to the Eastern Nigeria Delegation to the Constitutional Conference in Lagos for the diligent and faithful way in which, under conditions of severe strain, tension and fear, they carried out

the mandate given to them by the Consultative Assembly and the Chiefs
and Elders of Eastern Nigeria.

2. ENDORSES the stand of the Eastern Delegation at the Lagos Constitutional
Conference.

3. URGES that as an interim measure, a beginning be made to implement
those aspects of the recommendations as relate to the Armed Forces at least
to the extent of returning them to their Regions of origin and vesting the
operational control of the regional contingents in the respective Military
Governors.

4. RE-AFFIRMS its acceptance of the Report of the Committee on the
Pattern of Constitution for Eastern Nigeria within the Federation of Nigeria
and the additional suggestions proposed by the Graham-Douglas Constitutional Committee regarding the legislative and executive functions to be
devolved upon the Provincial Units, and urges that the Constitutional Committee should forthwith study the details of the scheme, with particular
reference to the number and size of provinces, the distribution of functions
between the Provinces and the Regional Government, financial arrangements
and the method and timing of implementation.

5. ENDORSES both the principle of the creation of more states in Nigeria and
the statement of the Eastern Delegation to the Lagos Constitutional Conference to the effect that the splitting up of the country at this stage is not
what is needed to normalize conditions of life in the country and provide a
sense of security for its inhabitants, and that immediate constitutional
arrangements for the country as a whole should be made on the basis of the
existing Regions in order to save the country from impending disintegration.

6. SINCE the issue of the creation of more states is a vital and inevitable item
on the Agenda of the Lagos Constitutional Conference, RECOMMENDS the
following as the conditions upon which the creation of states should proceed:

a. The basis for the creation of states must be mutually agreed upon beforehand and must be uniformly and consistently applied throughout the
country.

b. The creation of states must take place simultaneously throughout the
country.

c. The creation of any new state must be based upon the consent of the
people of the area which is to be included in the proposed state and
where two or more distinct tribal groupings are comprised within such area
the wishes of each such grouping must be separately ascertained and respected.

d. The population, area and economic resources of any new state which it is
proposed to create must be reasonably commensurate to the enormous
functions which the states will be expected to perform under the new
constitutional arrangements envisaged for Nigeria.

7. IN VIEW of the fact that the desire on the part of the minority groups for
self-determination is the active force behind the demand for the creation of
more states, and since in the context of present-day Nigeria minorities are
defined by reference to tribe, AFFIRMS its belief that the best hope for a
satisfactory solution to the problems of Nigeria lies in the recognition and
preservation of the separate identity of the various tribal or linguistic groupings and their right to develop each along its own line and at its own pace;

accordingly RECOMMENDS that the creation of states throughout Nigeria should be on the basis of tribal or linguistic groupings or mutual consent between the linguistic groupings.

8. ADVISES that, until the agreements reached by the personal representatives of the Military Governors on August 8 and 9 are fully implemented, and until immediate compensation is paid by the Federal Military Government for the lives and property of Easterners lost in the disturbed areas of Nigeria, the Eastern Nigeria Delegation should no longer participate in future Constitutional Conference.

9. SATISFIED that the interim report of the Constitutional Conference has been completely overtaken by the most recent events in the country, ADVISE that the only possible and logical solution to the problem of political association for Nigeria lies in the organization and running of common services.

[1] *Press Release issued to those attending the press conference on 11 October (see DOC 63).*

63.
Ojukwu's Press Conference in Enugu, 11 October 1966[1]

Gentlemen,

I heartily welcome you to Eastern Nigeria. I regard your visit as a reassuring effort on your part to get at the truth and present such truth to the world. There is no greater way of getting at the truth than coming as you have done, to find out facts on the spot. You have, I believe, already moved round Enugu and seen some of the people who have been victims to the callous and inhuman excesses of the people of Northern Nigeria. What you have seen tells only a small fraction of the story, but they represent a fairly accurate picture of the type of provocations and atrocities which the people of this Region have suffered in a country for which they have sacrificed and contributed so much to bring to the present stage.

Unfortunately, the world does not seem fully to appreciate our position. They do not understand our case. If anything, we have been misrepresented. Our sufferings have been played down and sympathy tends at times to be on the other side. Foreign Press and radio, either out of sheer ignorance, failure to take the trouble to find out the truth, or sheer mischief, have been putting out news which do not present the true picture about this Region.

It is my belief that the world should know the true facts in order to reach a fair and sympathetic assessment of the situation. To this end, I have decided that if the world does not want to come to us to find out the truth, we should go out to them to present our story, our case. I have accordingly decided that documentary evidence be compiled for widespread distribution. Luckily, the first of these documents which one could call the 'Curtain Raiser' has just been completed and you now have the privilege of being the first to see it before it is released to the public and the world. [*Crisis '66*—Ed.] . . .

What has baffled everybody, whether friend or foe, is the comportment and restraint of Eastern Nigeria in the face of the current cruel happenings. . . .

The reason for this restraint has been a mystery to all. Our enemies have been wondering, they have been conjecturing, and they have been speculating. The truth is that the moment this Region attempts to retaliate, what we now know as Nigeria will cease to exist. That is a fact which we ourselves know and which, I am sure, our enemies cannot mimimize. But the last thing that this Region would like to do is to help destroy the edifice which they have made more sacrifices, put in greater efforts and made far greater contributions than any other section to build. I have played my humble part in bringing this restraint about. In this I have enjoyed absolute confidence and co-operation on the part of the people. But there is always a limit to human endurance and it is now for all lovers of Nigeria, both within and outside the country, to do everything they can to make sure that we are not pushed to a position beyond which self-preservation and honour will not allow us to go without hitting back.

I hope to be answering your questions, but there is one recent action taken by this Government which I should explain to you a little further. As you know, I have been driven to a situation where I have lost confidence in the effectiveness of my ability to restrain the emotions of Eastern Nigerians against non-Eastern Nigerians resident and working in this Region. You have seen the horrible sights in hospital and at the airport. I believe you have also seen the Chairman or the Secretary of the Rehabilitation Commission. You have seen the facts and you have heard the stories.

The people you have seen lying in hospital—as I have said, they tell only a fraction of the story—are people who were living and working in other parts of the country and who had been subjected to the type of suffering and conditions which you yourselves have witnessed. It is quite possible that a relation or friend of any of these people or even some of those who have managed to escape without personal injury, although with total losses of all that they had, could lose his self-restraint and act rashly against a non-Easterner. Any such isolated action could lead to widespread reactions which I can assure you could not be restricted to this Region.

A day before I announced my decision, Eastern Nigerian students at the Enugu Campus who had just returned from their vacation and who had seen evidence of the sufferings of their fellow students who had to flee their universities in other parts of the country, reacted against the return of students of non-Eastern Nigeria origin to the campus. But for the prompt and effective intervention by the Police that incident could have led to serious disturbances which, probably, could not be confined to the Enugu Campus. That such should have happened amongst students who had been living and working together as colleagues seemed to me a pointer to what could happen elsewhere.

Painful as it was, the decision had to be taken, because I consider it my duty to give protection to life and property of all who are resident and working under my jurisdiction. It was with a heavy heart that I decided that non-Eastern Nigerians should temporarily leave this Region. I emphasize 'temporarily', because we shall welcome them back as soon as we are sure that they will be able to live and work in peace and harmony without molestations or even threat, either to their positions or persons. We are doing our very best to cool the tempers of the injured persons now returned. You have already heard of our rehabilitation programme being managed by a Commission which has been given an initial grant of one million pounds. There is already evidence that this grant may have to be augmented in the very near future. Private individuals and organizations are making sacrifices in order to raise money and material for the rehabilitation of the unfortunate victims of wanton fratricide. (We still regard those who have perpetrated these atrocities against us as 'brothers'.)

We do hope that with all these plans and activities on our part, a good number of those who have fled to this Region or have been repatriated, as they are now being done, will be suitably resettled and made to try to forget and to forgive. . . .

Question: Are you going to attend the next week's meeting of the Supreme Military Council in Lagos?

Ojukwu: I have said often enough that it is not a question of merely going to Lagos. It is a question of what guarantees I have that there is going to be some good sense and that faith will be kept. There is a second point, and that is, that I have said earlier before in a Press Conference such as this that unless the safety of myself and my team going to Lagos or anywhere else can be guaranteed there is no question of my leaving this Region for such a meeting. In any case, even if I wanted to, my people would not allow me. . . .

Q: (John Bulloch—*Daily Telegraph*) Do you acknowledge Gowon as your superior or as the Supreme Commander?

O: Militarily, Gowon is not my superior. Acknowledging him as the Supreme Commander, I think does not arise at this stage. I do not consider the post of Supreme Commander vacant yet. We had Major-General Aguiyi-Ironsi as the Supreme Commander; I am told he has been missing since the 29th of July. I have not even been told that he has been presumed dead. I do not know whether he has deposed and how. I am told that such a vacancy occurred in the Western Region and an acting Military Governor was appointed. So really, gentlemen, I do not think the question, whether or not I recognize him as the Supreme Commander, arises at this stage.

Q: (Donald Louccheim—*Washington Post*) In an early statement you declared that the East will insist upon payment of compensation as reparation to the victims of the North. Can you spell out exactly what you would expect as compensation?

O: What I really meant was that this to me was something we should be addressing our minds to at this moment. I feel that our meetings should be considering ways and means of reducing tension, ways and means of alleviating the sufferings of these people. I think first things should be taken first. That in my view, is what this country wants at the moment, rather than talking high-faluting political philosophy. It is not the form of association as such—I mean what political ideology Nigeria wants to adopt—that matters. I have always maintained that the first and foremost thing is to stop the killings. Secondly, do something about those who have suffered. And thirdly, find a *modus vivendi* between the various entities for the moment until we can in fact evolve something for a permanent solution. I do not know if you remember there was a Commission of Inquiry set up to deal with the Northern May Riots.[2] This now seems to have gone back into history. Nobody talks about it. Thousands of people have suffered deprivations. Rich men have suddenly left and come back to the East completely penniless, becoming liability to the society. We in the East are doing our best to keep these people, at least fed, given the basic necessities of life. I think the Federal Government and the Northern Government that perpetrated these atrocities have certain responsibilities towards them. They should show—demonstrate— their own good faith by contributing, by volunteering to contribute. This sort of thing generates confidence and confidence is so necessary for our continued discussions, for our continued negotiations.

Q: (Godwin Ironkwe—*Reuters*) May I know from information available to you, how many Easterners have been killed in the North?

O: I am always very wary about giving figures especially on this issue, because it is very difficult to really assess. I have not been to the North but from Police Reports I know that the May Riots claimed over 3,000 lives, indeed, the Police reports say 3,300—whatever that means. I know also that on the first night alone in Zaria of this last riot, 670 people were killed. I know also that in Kano on the same first day of the riot, they lost over a thousand. It will take us a long long time to find out the exact figures.

Q: (Walter Partington—*Daily Express*) I recently visited the North. I was told that there are one million Ibos still in the North. Can you confirm that this is correct?

O: I will answer the question this way. Before the troubles started in May this year, it was stated officially that there were some two million Easterners in the North. I know that not a million have yet returned. We might have had half a million back or more but perhaps there is a small likelihood that about a million still remain there, I do not know. But the significant thing about the Easterner has always been the way he gets absorbed into any society in which he lives. He becomes part of it and then gets very difficult to separate from the indigenes. I know there must be a lot of them still there going on with their business and people not knowing that they are Easterners.

Q: Having personally seen what people have been suggesting as the Constitutional solution to the problem in Nigeria, that is to say, Federation, Confederation and so on, what are your own views?

O: I will be very honest, I do not understand what the term federation means. A lot of terms have been handed around in the newspapers since this crisis began. They talk of federation, confederation, they talk of common services, they talk of customs union, so many of them. I personally do not think these are the important points for discussion. I think we should go deeper into the content of the terms to find out really what any group means. What I said to my team before they left for Lagos was this: that the difficulties in Nigeria have arisen primarily from the desire to control the central machinery and that therefore it was necessary at this stage to make the central authority weak enough to be unattractive to any sort of ambitious politicians. I have also maintained that these conflicts always come to the fore in positions within the central authority where the Easterner has, by the nature of his work, to be confronting his Northern counterparts. I do think that these points of friction should be removed, that the people should be kept so sufficiently apart that they do not come into friction. I think by so doing at least, for the foreseeable future, we would be able to live in peace. I have been stressing the fact that tempers are so high today in Nigeria, that no solution

we might find could be considered objective and dispassionate, that whateve⟨
solution we find should have written into it a period of automatic review, sa⟨
five years, when it would automatically have to be reviewed without anybod⟨
or unit even having the onus of initiating it. . . .

Q: (Colin Legum—*The Observer*) I wonder if I could check up some rumour⟨
because the difficulty today is that there are many rumours and your Regio⟨
is no exception. Rumour No. 1: that you are resisting making partition effect
ive for only two reasons: first, because you will like to have secession blame⟨
on the others, and second, because you are not militarily strong enough t⟨
enforce your secession. Would you like to comment?

O: I have said a number of times before that secession is not our aim in th⟨
East. Throughout my tenure of office right from January when I came her⟨
rather suddenly, I have been perhaps the foremost advocate of true unity fo⟨
this country. Even talked about it more than the General himself. I say thes⟨
things not as platitude but because I really believe the East does not believ⟨
in secession, our meetings have shown that. But there is a limit to our endurance and that is all. Militarily, I would like to take on anybody wh⟨
wishes to attack this Region. Indeed, sometimes one wonders whether i⟨
would not be a good thing to give to one's opponents a bloody nose to le⟨
them realize the difficulties of coming in here instead of talking about it
The question of blame, I think after the 29th September incident, should I
decide and declare that we have seceded, no right-thinking person in the
world could blame us. The facts are there for everyone to see. We had every
right to secede, but I refused. . . . I have in fact been talking to Gowon abou⟨
this for six weeks now. In a situation and in a country where people do no⟨
really understand military matters, such rumours are bound to be current,
particularly when the North insisted on amassing troops on the border. I
have said to Gowon that a prerequisite to the reduction of tension in thi⟨
country is for troops to get back to the barracks. I think the Northern troop⟨
should go back to Kaduna or to Kano where they belong and stay there an⟨
the unruly ones should be disarmed. As long as you have them patrolling
back and forth the frontier, of course, such rumours will come up and people
will believe them and then, of course, I do not think the troops there are s⟨
controlled that they do know exactly where the frontier is. There have been
incidents of some forty soldiers crossing into the Eastern border which in
normal circumstances and to all intents and purposes would be an invasion.
But with good sense here and calmness, we have been able to resolve these
things. I have got on the telephone to Gowon and informed him of the
situation and I must say this for him that once he knows that these things
have happened, he does take action to see that they are stopped. The only
trouble is that they happen so often and that he does not know about them
quick enough. Indeed, at a certain stage, I said to him that his men were not
telling him the truth about the situation. . . .

Q: (John Bulloch—*Daily Telegraph*) When I entered your Region the other
day the atmosphere here in the present situation and in the way people move
around amounted to *de facto* secession in everything except formal declaration.

O: One can read so many things into this but the fact simply is this, that I
am determined to protect my people from any mad attempt from outside to⟨

eliminate them. It is not *de facto* secession. Indeed, the only reason why the Federation continues today is because I have continued to pay for the federal services and the world knows that it is the East that pays for these services monthly. Indeed from Port Harcourt you see oil shifted to Lagos. If it is a secession I will keep it off and it will take only forty-eight hours to collapse the Federation.

Q: (Lloyd Garrison—*New York Times*) On these rumours that have been going on concerning the military position in the East,

    (*a*) that small arms have arrived in the East,

    (*b*) that you are training citizens in the camps,

    (*c*) that some of the officers who have been in custody since January have been released:

would you kindly comment on these points?

O: Would you like to meet the officers? It might be a good thing to let you see some of them where they are. That is one, we can talk about that later. Secondly, that we have been training people—one of the signals [paper handed over]; then you will find out who has been training people. Importation of arms: on the 18th of August the Gowon Government in Lagos received ammunitions, cost £8 million. There were 100,037 packages. Country of origin: No, I better not. Port of entry: Apapa, Lagos. They contain small arms, ammunition and ammunition for the 105 Hauiser [*sic*]. The East has not imported any arms. I know that even in the North it is said that I have here Supersonic Jet Fighters; it would be nice to have. I am told too that I have plans completed for bombing Kaduna. Indeed, I am accused of having bombed Lagos. But really, jokes aside, you all know the difficulties attendant upon such line of action: that unless one really has a full machinery of government functioning it will be very difficult to get arms of such significant quantity to make the sort of impact they are expecting.

Q: Have there been any recruitment or training of defence force in the East?

O: No, you can walk round the East. Indeed, I was hoping by your visit that you should meet people, talk to them, indeed follow any queue you find. I should be very grateful if you could lead me to any such camps in the East because as far as my government knows, or as far as I am concerned, there is no such thing.

Q: Following what you said earlier about defence and that the Federal Government has imported arms and ammunitions worth £8 million, is it not wise that you should get some arms in order to defend yourself against invasion?

O: I have not considered anything like that.

Q: It has been reported that Northern troops took a great deal of ammunition within the country back to the North and left you in a bad situation. Is this correct?

O: From Lagos they took a great deal. From here they took the arms which were allowed the Northern soldiers for their self protection on their way to the North; even though we had agreed that these arms would be returned to us we never got them. It leaves us in a weak position in the East militarily but then as I have always said, no nation, no people, can be entirely subjugated by the force of arms alone. Subjugation comes when you have captured the spirit of the people. The people of the East are determined and I do not think even the arms they have already seized, and those they have imported, could bring the East low.

Q: May I refer to the earlier question. While one expects the political will as expressed that Nigeria should have some kind of unity, one does get the impression that the men in this Region are in favour of secession. How long can one maintain the political will against the popular emotional demand for secession, so long as there is no evidence of any single authority for unity in this country?

O: This has been my problem of today. I have been saying this hence the urgency I attach to the finding of a solution. Lagos does not seem to understand the urgency of the situation. I do not honestly know how long I can keep the people of this Region restrained. . . . Indeed, it is for that reason that I have made a suggestion to Lagos that while we are all averse to foreign intervention in our domestic affairs, that is, foreign troops coming into Nigeria, that I personally, and the Eastern Region, would not be averse to troops from Commonwealth countries being stationed in Lagos alone to facilitate our movements in and out of Lagos, give Gowon himself protection in Lagos, to enable us meet and discuss our problems whilst at the same time he would be able to fulfil the agreements we have reached—which is that troops of Northern origin should go back to the North, troops of Eastern origin to go back to the East and so on. We cannot consider here in the East any part of Nigeria safe for anything as long as there are Northern soldiers present in that area.

Q: (*Life Magazine*) Who is in control in Lagos?

O: The sixty-four million dollar question! I wish I knew. I can tell you who is in control here. . . .

Q: Are you sending any emissaries of your people abroad to represent you? . . .

O: The word representative is rather wrong there. If you mean whether we are seeking ways and means of getting this literature out, of course, we are seeking ways of getting them out so that the world will know our case, but that does not presuppose sending out emissaries or having delegations out to meet Governments and things like that. We are certainly going to try to get all these out. I would certainly like the world to know . . .

Q: (Ironkwe—*Reuters*) It would appear that relationship between Enugu and Benin has been strained as a result of certain things. I do not know if you would like to comment.

O: Relationship between Enugu and Benin: I am certainly in the best of terms with David Ejoor. We talk to each other almost daily on the telephone. I know that there has been certain suspicion as a result of the declaration of the Ika Ibos, that is, Ibos of the Mid-West—the declaration of their solidarity with the East, but that in itself should not create difficulties. After all, everybody has taken this opportunity to voice their own views on the political future of this country. . . . No leader can ever hope to carry 100 per cent. of his people. I am glad that here in the East I think I have succeeded in carrying with me 98 per cent. I do not think that there is something really of major significance between . . . you know. There is no upset between the East and the Mid-West at the moment.

Q: If the Lagos Conference was reconvened in the Eastern Region, would you agree that the major issue is the creation of more states in order to stop domination of any one Region?

O: On the issue of the creation of more states, I have said that the East is not averse to such a creation, provided the criteria for the creation are mutually agreed by everyone, and that there is a simultaneity in the creation. Provided that is agreed, I go with it.

Q: (*Life Magazine*) Is genocide likely to continue in the North?

O: I wish I knew how they think there. I really do wish I knew, because right now, privately, what really worries me is my inability to find the reason for such a waste. I do not know; anything can happen.

Q: Are there still groups of Easterners in the North seeking to flee?

O: Ah! There are a lot. There was even a stage we reached four days ago when Easterners coming back to the East were stopped at Makurdi, eighteen coaches load of them, and then a telegram was sent to Enugu: 'Send us eleven wagons of petrol or else we will kill these people.'

Q: Have you any knowledge or any idea of what caused this last massacre?

O: The North says this came from a broadcast made by Radio Cotonou which said that there was some disturbance in the East and that Northerners had been killed. I have lived in the North for many many years and it is rather gratifying to know that they are now so sophisticated that they listen to Radio Cotonou. Further on, I understand that this report was rebroadcast by Radio Television Kaduna. Why that was necessary I do not know. But perhaps the most significant thing about this is that according to the Northern story, as soon as they heard this, they found their bows and arrows at their right hands and moved out immediately to look for Easterners. What I am saying is, it was indeed a planned operation. The reason for it I do not know. ... It makes me start wondering again in view of what happened on 29th September whether we should not review those things we had agreed upon.

Q: You said you wish you knew what the people of the North are thinking. Do you have any explanation, that is, is it organized or a panic reaction?

O: Well, when I say it was planned then obviously it must have been organized; that is one. But I think right at the bottom of our relationship is the difference in our system of thinking. The Easterner when he goes out to do this, he does it because he wants this or that. That I have been able to follow throughout in everything we do. The Northerner would appear, I say would appear, to do things because they just want to do this and then having done it, faced with the situation, they reconsider the next stage. ... It seems to me like this: they decide ah! let us go and kill these people. Now having killed them, they are faced with this mass movement. They do not seem fully to understand the reason for this mass movement.

Q: You have talked about killings and financial support which you give to Lagos. Why do you still talk about unity in the face of it all?

O: It is a very grave step to decide to part companies. This is the main reason and whilst we are seeking ways and means of solving our differences, I think one must support and help to keep together the few things that remain because these might be the start of our settlement. I think it is necessary. Somebody has used the word 'panic measures' in reference to the North. If I did stop subsidizing the Federal Government, it might lead them to further panic measures which would definitely destroy the Nigeria we know. I am not willing to destroy Nigeria. I am trying everything possible to hold together what is left of Nigeria.

Q: You said before that the East will only secede as a result of pressure. Do you still feel the pressure? Do you feel you are being pushed?

O: Everyday it becomes more difficult to see a solution to the problems with all these continued atrocities. Somebody asked what would be a sufficient push to make us break. Honestly I do not know, except that push in itself depends on the pressure. I maintain that they have started applying pressures. When it will be sufficient I do not know. I do not know because it is not my desire to move out. I did not plan it. I do not set limits to what they can do to push us out. . . .

Q: You mentioned that it was a plan. Do you suppose that the Northern Emirs had a hand in the plan?

O: I have not been to the North since January. I still have friends indeed amongst the Emirs. I find it difficult to see that some of them actively participate in this. I know that at a certain stage, Gowon did appeal to the Northerners, indeed, it was a most unfortunate appeal in that he stated quite clearly for the world to understand the policy of the North regarding Nigeria. You all know the statement which he made stating quite clearly that the people of the North should be happy in the knowledge that Allah in His infinite wisdom has once again entrusted the affairs of this country into the hands of another Northerner.[3] That tells the story. This is their approach to the Nigerian problem. Even before this final onslaught starting from 29th July, the Emirs met and decided in their wisdom that they had found a constitutional arrangement which would be suitable for the country. . . .

Q: Are you in touch with Hassan?

O: Yes.

Q: Did the Emir of Kano play sufficient role to prevent at least the Kano shootings especially in view of your personal relationship with him?

O: I do not know. Before this last onslaught, I was led to understand that he personally was distressed about the happenings.

[1] Ojukwu Talks to World Press (*Enugu, 1966*). *The full verbatim report did not appear in the Nigerian press* (e.g., Daily Times) *until 20 October*.
[2] *See* DOC *32*.   [3] *See p. 62*.

64.
Hassan Katsina Addresses Leaders of Thought in the North[1]

I welcome you again to this meeting, the third of its kind in recent months. Since your meeting here last August to discuss the situation in the country and to suggest the best possible form of association for the component parts of Nigeria, new developments have taken place, some of which, no doubt, have done great harm to our image both at home and abroad. It is with some mixed feelings, therefore, that I address you today.

The events of recent weeks in this Region were indeed unprecedented both in their nature and in their form. It is a matter for deep regret that the orderly progress of the Region should be disturbed on so large a scale and in this way. Whatever may have been the reasons or motives behind them they deserve to be severely condemned. I am sure all reasonable and decent people will agree with me on this. As you all know, during those disturbances, wanton destruction of life and property took place. Innocent people were killed and their property destroyed or looted.

It has been a matter of deep sorrow for the Supreme Commander and Head of the Federal Military Government and for me and indeed for all right thinking people that in spite of all the official efforts and appeals for calm and return to normality such ugly and senseless disturbances should have taken place at the very time when our delegates were engaged in talks on the future constitutional arrangements for Nigeria.

The most recent destruction, believed to have been motivated by rumours of alleged atrocities committed against Northerners elsewhere, were unjustifiable even if they were true. Two wrongs do not make a right and as civilized people we should on all occasions abide by the rule of law.

The authorities are there to assist the people when anyone feels aggrieved for any wrongs done. People should continue to turn to the authorities for redress rather than take the law into their own hands and resort to violence and other forms of lawlessness. The futility of violence as a means of solving a problem, or as a weapon for satisfying one's ambition or even righting a wrong where non-violent remedies are open is the clearest lesson which we should all have learnt from all the incidents from January this year.

If after violence, those engaged in it pause and ponder its futility becomes doubly apparent. . . .

I do not think I need to labour this point any further, vital though it is, since all decent people are only too aware of the risks involved for everyone and for Nigeria's future if disorderly behaviour in any form is not brought under control.

For my part, I declare solemnly that I shall exert all my influence and authority for the preservation of law and order and will spare no effort in using the forces of the law against trouble makers. . . .

Gentlemen, Nigeria today is at the cross-roads. Our economy has already suffered a great set-back and our onward march to economic, social and political progress has been retarded. Our good name and reputation have been smeared. Our prestige and dignity have suffered. The respect and sympathy which we have hitherto enjoyed have been partially lost. The confidence of our friends and well-wishers have been greatly shaken while our pride as a people and all that we have worked hard to achieve and stood for are in danger of being lost.

We must have calm and peace in which to resume our good work of progress, and restore the image of the country which had been a source of pride for us all. . . .

The willingness of our people to face hardship and to make sacrifices when called upon to do so in the interest of the country is not a new quality in us. I need hardly to appeal to you and to the Northern people as a whole on this score. We must all however adopt new attitudes and seek a new purpose for life. In the world today, the growing contacts amongst many races, the ever shrinking distances between nations and the inevitable meeting of cultures and mixing of ideas are introducing new values, new attitudes and new modes of living. In such a situation, to stick rigidly and uncritically to one's traditions, no matter what their past or historical merit, is to endanger the very best elements in those traditions worth preserving. In this context, isolation leads to decadence since a society that seeks to keep itself to itself must surely deprive itself of the vitalizing pollen necessary for growth. I cannot believe that we in the North are not clearly certain of this for when we reflect on our own situation we find that the North itself is a federation of many tribes of differing tongues, customs and background closely knit together by common ideals and the mutual acceptance of one another. We all are a product of this marriage from which we derive our culture and strength. Our association with other people of different background and culture provided it is founded on mutual respect and fair play can only result in mutual enrichment.

Gentlemen, I know that at this moment the hearts of our people are filled with emotion and it is not my wish to arouse any further feeling and passion among you. This much I will say as I feel, I owe it as a duty not only to the memory of many great leaders who served the North and Nigeria selflessly but to the men and women of our present generation. In recent weeks much has been said or written about the contributions which the people of the other Regions of the Federation have made in order to achieve and sustain the unity of the country. While the outstanding achievements of the North in this field are well-known and acknowledged by all, and while the occasion does not call for a recital of those achievements in detail, I make no apology for recalling the part played by the people of the North and their leaders in promoting the building of the Federation of Nigeria. It is incontestible that we in the North have been known for our willingness to make sacrifices and our disposition to compromise to the extent of modifying our cherished views and giving up our rights in order to promote and maintain the Federation of Nigeria. In their effort to promote this our leaders risked their lives, their popularity and their reputation. They risked in the interest of peace and unity of the nation the displeasure of their people. Even when undeserved abuses were heaped on them they exercised restraint. At the risk of being accused of weakness they overlooked past wrongs against themselves and tried selflessly to accommodate even their enemies and detractors. Theirs was a thankless effort, but history will show that these efforts were born of the purest, unalloyed motives and will not be in vain. In spite of the conveniently short memory of some sections of this country, in spite of the massive propaganda launched at home and abroad to confuse issues and paint us black, there is no doubt that when the history of our times comes to be written the contribution the North has made to Nigeria especially since independence, and the selfless service rendered by its leaders past and present, will be such that posterity can be proud of. It is our duty to resolve to continue to work nobly for the good of all where our leaders left off.

We should continue, no matter what the odds and whatever the provocations, to work genuinely and sincerely for better understanding which should lead to the progress of Nigeria. We know that only in unity can we render effective service to our people, to Africa and the world. We know that to achieve the lofty ideals we have set for ourselves we must first establish peace and stability, and no efforts should be spared in our determination to achieve them. We are by nature a peaceful people and we want to live at peace with everybody. We believe in discussion and reasoned argument in settling our differences with our friends and fellow countrymen. It is unfortunate that since the beginning of this year a new principle, alien to our nature—the principle of violence—was introduced in the settlement of differences. This is a principle which in the modern age gives satisfaction to neither the victor nor the vanquished. In consequence all parts of Nigeria have needlessly suffered. Now it is our duty to resume our example and continue to show our belief in the principle of discussion, in tolerance, in give and compromise. These are the principles which can ensure unity in any diverse community. Our union must be based on equity and fair play for all the sections of Nigeria, each contributing and receiving its share in the nation's efforts and its rewards.

It is in this light and for this reason that strenuous efforts are being made by all to keep Nigeria united in a Federation. This, too, is the conclusion reached by the Lagos Constitutional Conference as shown in their interim report to the Head of the Federal Military Government and the Supreme Commander of the Armed Forces. Most of you, no doubt, are already aware of the outline of the interim measures arrived at by the Conference before its adjournment. You will at this meeting study the report of the Conference and see what further measures may be pursued by the North in the interest of a truly federal state of Nigeria, and in order to safeguard the integrity of the country as a sovereign nation. The delegates who represented the Region at the Conference in Lagos have already undertaken extensive tours of the North in order to explain the recommendations in the report and their implications to the people. You, too, are expected to do the same thing when you return home. For it is important that the people should be sufficiently educated in these important matters if unfounded rumours and deliberate falsehood are to be avoided.

You will note from the report that some of the recommendations which you agreed upon at your last meeting in August have been modified. I am however, certain that you will appreciate why our delegates in Lagos found it necessary to alter their mandate in some aspects. For by the very nature of conferences on issues of this kind mandates should not be too inflexible: and in some cases, where necessary, delegates should be empowered to change their stand as circumstances compel.

My charge to you is that you should approach your task with objectivity, realism and open-mindedness. You should be honest and constructive, bearing in mind the heavy responsibility placed upon us all for the orderly development of our country both now and in the future. You must remember that upon you and other leaders will depend the prosperity, peace, happiness and the stability of the country. I must warn you against taking hasty decisions. This interim report should be considered very carefully and the implications of the recommendations made in it should be fully understood. You must not limit considerations of its content to the conclusions drawn from the recent past, but should take a long term view of the effect of your decisions. This is especially necessary if we are to bear in mind that what Nigeria needs is an enduring and just solution to her problems without which strife will never end and stability and progress will elude us. . . .

Before I close, Gentlemen, I wish to make one final appeal. Despite the dark clouds which hang over parts of our great country, there appear to be signs of peace and calm everywhere and a manifest desire for Nigerians to remain united in diversity come what may. This favourable atmosphere must continue if we are to discuss and solve the problems now facing us constructively. I know that it is the desire of every man and woman of good-will to see that this country is not again plunged into chaos and confusion. It is your duty as leaders of the people to educate them in these matters. . . . We have already suffered enough and cannot afford to suffer any more. We all in Nigeria must recognise that we have been following the wrong course since the beginning of the year and we must now go back to the path of honour, rectitude and duty.

To the families of those who lost their lives in these distressing times, be they Yoruba, Tiv, Efik, Ibo, Itsekiri, Hausa, Ijaw, Ibibio, Kanuri, Fulani or Edos I personally and on behalf of all the people of Northern Nigeria offer our deepest condolences. Our suffering and their suffering should not be in vain. They should be seen as the costly sacrifice that Nigerians have had to make to achieve mutual respect for one another irrespective of tribe or creed. If all sections of this country can learn from the events beginning from January that to depart from the normal peaceful means of settling differences or solving national problems and to resort to assassination of leaders or opponents is to invite incalculable violence, then those who have lost their lives would not have died in vain. If we can learn not to take one another for granted, and if we can learn that unity has to be worked for humbly and achieved after much pains rather than by decrees then the tragedies of the last ten months would have had in them some good results.

All our efforts should now be directed towards maintaining peace, order and good government and providing a calm atmosphere under which alone the problems now facing us can be amicably solved. Peace and stability are paramount and no sacrifice made to achieve them can be too great. I beseech all of you to heed this warning seriously. May God assist us all in our great endeavour, Amen.

[1] *Lugard Hall, Kaduna, 18 October 1966. Northern Ministry of Information Press Release No. 1323/1966.*

65.
Adebayo Addresses Leaders of Thought in the West[1]

My dear people. In one of my recent broadcasts to you I informed you of the arrangement made for delegates representing this Region to meet other delegates representing the Northern, Eastern and Mid-Western Regions and the Lagos Capital Territory at a conference to be held in Lagos on the future political association in Nigeria.

After about three weeks' meeting with occasional breaks, the conference adjourned last Monday for three weeks to enable the delegates to return to their respective Regions for further consultation and exchange of views on the points still outstanding.

Before adjourning however, the conference reached agreement on a number of issues, particularly on the subjects which should be the executive, federal and concurrent legislative lists in the future constitution for Nigeria.

Perhaps the most important outcome of the Lagos Conference is the unanimous agreement that Nigeria should continue as a single political entity even though there is yet no unanimity on the type of Government which should form the basis of such association.

Let us hope that the next three weeks will be devoted to a further examination of the outstanding issues and such exchange of views which will be designed to facilitate the deliberations of the conference when it resumes towards the end of October.

I would however like to say something to you all about certain recent occurrences. As disclosed in the address of the Head of the Federal Military Government and Supreme Commander of the Armed Forces to the Lagos Conference before it adjourned last Monday, there have been certain incidents in parts of Northern Nigeria as a result of which a number of persons of Eastern Nigeria origin have been killed or injured and still a large number have had their property destroyed.

It has also been observed in Lagos and in Western Nigeria, mass exodus of our Eastern Nigerian compatriots to the East as a result of a feeling of insecurity or what they believed to be actual threat and danger to their lives and property.

Added to these have been rumours and stories—some true, others untrue, and a number exaggerated—of alleged atrocities to Southerners living in Northern Nigeria and to Northerners and other non-Easterners living in Eastern Nigeria. Some of these incidents are most saddening and distressing.

I wish to make a special appeal to the people of Western Nigeria. First, I would like to express my personal appreciation of and gratitude for your patience and forbearance in the face of the temptations and provocations of the recent past.

Although most of the conflicts in the recent months have been largely between two other major ethnic groups in the country, quite a number of people of Western origin have lost their lives whilst a still larger number have had their business and property destroyed and they themselves have had to be uprooted from other parts of the country where they made their homes for many years.

It speaks for the sense of patriotism of the people of Western Nigeria and their sincere devotion to the cause of Nigerian unity that they have remained calm and co-operative with the Military Government in its efforts to establish order and stability out of the chaos and confusion into which the irresponsible actions of certain groups have thrown our dear country.

In the whole of the Federation, Western Nigeria is almost the only Region where members of all the ethnic groups in Nigeria can today feel safe without any fear of attack or molestation from the people among whom they live.

This is in the fine Yoruba tradition of hospitality to the strangers within our gates, and I appeal to you all to do everything you can to continue to live up to that tradition.

T

Many of you may have listened to the recent broadcast of the Military Governor of Eastern Nigeria in which he indicated that he had, as a result of the high tension in Eastern Nigeria, given orders for the repatriation of all non-Easterners from the East in the interest of their own safety.

I have been in touch with Lt. Col. Ojukwu on this and other national problems.

He has confirmed that the first batch of Western Nigerians repatriated are now on their way to Western Nigeria.

He and I have agreed that the Eastern Nigerians living and working in Western Nigeria should continue to do so unless there is evidence—which happily is not the case at present—that their lives are in danger.

I believe that I am speaking for you all when I say that we in Western Nigeria have no interest of molesting any of our brother Nigerians of any ethnic group living or working in our midst provided, of course, such people are themselves law-abiding.

As for the Western Nigerians who are being repatriated from the East, necessary arrangement is already in hand for their reception and re-settlement in Western Nigeria.

My Government will do everything possible to minimise the effect of this sudden change on the lives and prospects of those affected.

We all belong to Nigeria and Nigeria belongs to us all. . . .

[1] *Broadcast from Ibadan, 5 October 1966.* Morning Post, *6 October 1966.*

66.
Ejoor Addresses Leaders of Thought in the Mid-West[1]

Since I last addressed a meeting of this kind on 26th August, many things have happened in the country, some of them fraught with such disturbing implications that I have decided that it was time we met again in this forum.

As you will have observed, I have, in the light of the changing situation, invited certain dignitaries, including representatives of women's organisations and trade unions, to this meeting. I have done this because it seems to me essential, more than ever before, that all sections of the community should be aware of the position of the country so that no one is left in doubt about its gravity.

In a situation such as we in this country are passing through at the moment, it is all too easy for one side to point an accusing finger at another, either in cheap self-glorification or in a plain attempt to create mischief. But neither vanity nor mischief will get us anywhere. I myself have hitherto refrained from blowing the Midwest's trumpet because I did not think that this was the time to score points and to pat ourselves on the back. The role of the Midwest since the mutiny in the army on 29th July has, however, been so distorted and misunderstood that I consider that it may do some good if I now take this opportunity to disclose to the nation some facts which may help to put matters in their true and proper perspective.

I think that my other colleagues in the Supreme Military Council, including the Supreme Commander himself, will bear me out when I say that, without the fervent intervention by the Midwest, the country would have remained without a central government much longer than it did after the mutiny in the Army in July. The ensuing confusion would have been much greater and the first hopeful strides then taken towards a return to normalcy would have been impossible.

In my first public statement on the present situation in the country on 3rd August[2] I said, among other things: 'From the information at my disposal it seems that most Midwesterners are giving serious thought to the following questions: (a) are we to have a unitary state with powers centralized at the national capital?; or (b) a federal state with a strong central government and relatively weak regional (or provincial) governments?; or (c) a loose federation with strong regional (or provincial) governments and a relatively weak government at the centre responsible only for limited common services?; or (d) should the country be broken up into several new and completely independent states?'

I endeavoured in those words to echo the feelings of Midwesterners on this country's renewed effort in constitution making. When the Supreme Commander subsequently decided to set up an *ad hoc* committee for this purpose, the committee's terms of reference as outlined by him in his opening address on 12th September[3] turned out to be substantially the same as had been foreshadowed in my statement of 3rd August. The Midwest had again taken the initiative in the right direction.

Even before that stage was reached, it is on record that it was the Midwestern delegation at the talks in Lagos on 9th August[4] which proposed that, as a major step designed to prevent further bloodshed, army officers and men should be temporarily posted to their Regions of origin. That proposal has been partially implemented in the sense that army units in two Regions at least now consist wholly of personnel drawn from those Regions.

The Midwest has taken the steps described above, as well as others which need not be recounted here, for the sole purpose of helping to ensure that the crisis in the country is not permitted to get out of hand and that passions are not unduly inflamed. Whatever our detractors may think or say, I honestly believe that the Midwest is pursuing the correct policies in connection with the crisis, in conformity with its consistent policy of advocating what is right for Nigeria.

It is true that recent events have taken a heavier toll of lives and properties of persons from a particular Region. It is true also that people of that Region as a whole have shown conspicuous restraint in the face of reckless destruction of the lives and properties of their kinsmen. Speaking for myself, and for other well meaning Nigerians, they deserve nothing but praise for the calm they have, by and large, demonstrated in the midst of fearful odds. . . .

Let me deal first with the question of federation.

In the early stages of the Conference, the Northern delegation proposed that Nigeria should consist of a number of autonomous states which would be the present Regions; that the new union of states should have a central executive council, the chairmanship of which should rotate from year to year; that the chairman should, during his year of office, be regarded as the Head of State; that each state should have its own Army, Air Force and Police;

and that any member state of the union should reserve the right to secede completely and unilaterally.

The Eastern delegation proposed that there should be a central authority for the present Region but that all legislation by the central authority should be subject to ratification by the Regional Governments before they become effective; that the central authority should have an executive, the chairmanship of which should rotate annually from Region to Region; that the chairman, during his term of office, should be the Head of State; that members of the executive should be paid by their Regions and subject to recall by them; that each Region should keep its revenue and finance the central authority by equal contributions; that each Region should have its own Army, Air Force, Navy and Police; that the assets and liabilities of the federation should be shared out among the Regions; that each Region should issue its own currency notes and coins; and that each Region should be free to secede from the association.

The Western and Lagos delegations proposed that if a true federation according to a formula which would have produced eighteen states but which would have left control of the armed forces with the states were not created, then there should be a Commonwealth of Nigeria consisting of the present Regions as states (Lagos being merged with the West); that the Government of each state within the Commonwealth of Nigeria should be completely sovereign in all matters excepting a few which should be delegated to a Council of States; that each state should establish and operate its own armed forces and police; that the chairmanship of the Council should rotate from year to year among the states; that the chairman for the time being should be the Head of State; that the national debt of the federation should become the responsibility of the states on the basis of the location of the projects in respect of which each debt had been incurred; and that each state should have the right unilaterally to secede from the Commonwealth at any time of its own choice.

In contrast to these proposals it was, and continues to be, the position of the Midwest delegation that the causes of failure of Nigeria's first experiment in democratic federal government were numerous and varied and that the federation should continue whether or not new states were created at this stage.

The Midwest delegation therefore stood unequivocally for federation, and proposed that the form of association best suited for Nigeria was one which must provide for the continuance of federation; for a correction of past injustices; for the lowering of present tensions; for the resolution of basic conflicts; the reconciliation of the basic interests and the provision of the basic needs of the various communities in the country; and for the assurance of democratic liberties to the people; above all, that the new constitution must provide expressly that there shall be *no* right of secession by any Region. . . .

As regards the question of the creation of new Regions, there have been exaggerated accounts as to the importance which this matter has so far received in discussions at the Conference. The country should be told that so far there has been no full scale discussion of this subject at the Conference.

The attitude of the various delegations may be briefly stated as follows:

the Northern delegation has stated its belief in the creation of new Regions in the country and suggested that the Supreme Commander should appoint a special commission to ascertain the wishes of the inhabitants of the areas concerned so that the creation of new states is accomplished during the period of the Military Government.

The Eastern delegation has stated that it does not regard the present as an opportune moment for the creation of new Regions and in any case that this is a matter best left with the Regional Governments.

The Western and Lagos delegations have suggested that if states were to be created, the linguistic formula should be used in determining eleven such states and the rest of the country divided into seven other states.

The Midwest delegation has suggested that if new states were to be created in Nigeria, six criteria should be applied, namely:

(1) ethnic, linguistic and cultural affinity (*e.g.*, Yoruba, Ibo); (2) historical association (e.g., Hausa/Fulani, Efik/Ibibio); (3) viability, both of each state and of the nation as a whole; (4) geographical contiguity (i.e. no Pakistans in Nigeria separated by intervening states); (5) comparable populations, so as to remove the fear of domination of smaller states by larger states; (6) reciprocal self-determination (i.e. not only should a minority have the right to determine its future, but also that a majority must have the right to determine whether it is willing to associate with a minority seeking such association).

Before the Conference adjourned on 3rd October for three weeks, to resume on 24th October, the Northern, Western, Lagos and Midwest delegations agreed that more states should be created in the country and that there should be a plebiscite to determine the wishes of the people concerned. The Eastern delegation then stated that it wished to reserve its position on the matter.

It will be seen, therefore, that it is completely untrue either that the Midwest delegation has based its whole approach to the Conference on the creation of states or that the delegation has suggested that certain elements in the Midwest should be transferred to other Regions. The leader of the delegation will, I assume, have an opportunity of reporting confidentially to you at this meeting.

I believe that, both on the question of the survival of federation and on the issue of the creation of new Regions, the stand of the Midwest delegation has been realistic and objective. The Midwest does not seek special credit for its contributions to the solution of the country's problems, but I am certain that when the full story of the Conference, or indeed when the full story of these anxious times can be told, we will have no cause to regret the part which the Midwest has played in the whole episode.

As you are all well aware, Midwesterners have been affected in large numbers by the latest outbreak of disturbances in the Northern Region. Many of them have been obliged to return to the Midwest and every arrangement is being made for their reception and their comfort. A committee, consisting of non-officials and some civil servants, has been charged with the primary responsibility for taking care of the persons involved, whom, for lack of a better expression, we now call 'refugees'. As they arrive they are provided, at Government's expense, with transport to their homes and are encouraged to register themselves at registration offices already established in the respective divisional offices. They fall into four broad categories, namely, (*i*) civil servants or quasi-civil servants (i.e. employees of statutory boards and corporations); (*ii*) employees of commercial firms; (*iii*) self-employed persons (e.g., traders and shopkeepers); (*iv*) students and pupils.

I am in consultation with the Supreme Commander about the immediate position of persons in the first two categories specified above and I hope that it will be possible for him to announce shortly certain arrangements intended to ensure that their emoluments will continue to be paid by their respective employers until their future can be better determined. As for persons in the third category, this is, traders and shop-keepers, as well as similarly self-employed people, it is proposed to work out a suitable scheme for them after full information is available about them and the magnitude of the problem, in so far as they are concerned, can be securely assessed.

With regard to students and pupils, action has been taken at once to absorb the latter in several primary and secondary schools in the Region. They are therefore able to continue with their schooling without interruption. I am afraid that students, that is, those pursuing courses at universities and other higher educational institutions, are in a more difficult position, simply because of the absence of any of such institutions in the Midwest. Nevertheless, I will do my utmost to see that some satisfactory arrangements are made for them as soon as possible. I assure them that their difficulties are appreciated, that we sympathise very much with them and that the Government will do all that lies in its power to see that their studies are not too long interrupted.

I would like at this stage to mention the attitude of a particular Region to the Midwest, which appears to me, putting it at its mildest, to be unfriendly. If the problems now facing the Midwest were due solely to the upheavals in the areas affected by the incident of 29th July and by the latest disturbances in the Northern Region, I personally and, I think, most Midwesterners would have understood the position. But it is surprising, again putting it mildly, that, for no apparently justifiable cause, a deliberate attempt has been made to differentiate between those Midwesterners who are welcome in a particular Region and those of them who are not welcome there.

It is clear that, for no good reason, that Region is determined to interfere in the internal affairs of the Midwest in order, no doubt, to divide our people and to cause confusion and unrest within our Region. The campaign to this end is being persistently conducted not only in the highest official quarters in that Region, as recent official pronouncements emanating therefrom clearly show, but also through the press and radio controlled by them. . . .

Mr. Chairman, Ladies and Gentlemen, if I have accurately judged the essence and objectives of the present campaign of calumny and abuse directed against the Midwest, I must say plainly that it is both ill-conceived and futile. I believe that I speak for all Midwesterners when I say that the Midwest is a political entity in its own right in this country and that no self-respecting person in our community will like to see this Region exist merely as an appendage of another Region, devoid of any collective will of its own and incapable of giving determined and unfettered expression to its will on any given issue affecting its welfare in particular and the corporate existence of the Federation of Nigeria as a whole. We must demand and exercise the right to adopt, as we have hitherto done, an independent and objective approach to this country's affairs and I hope that you will make it clear before you rise that it is our determination to continue to do so.

I wish I could reach a wider audience as the need arises. The absence of the necessary facilities for doing so has never been so keenly felt as after the incident of 29th July. I refer, of course, to the absence of broadcasting facilities in this Region. Happily, however, thanks to the former and the present Head of the Federal Military Government, who have both taken a personal interest in the matter, the Federal Government has now decided to establish a broadcasting service. . . .

The Midwest does not intend to emulate the example of others and to compulsorily eject anybody from its area of jurisdiction. We do not intend to lose our heads, however depressing the general atmosphere may be, and we will continue to contribute our fair share in the search for sane decisions in the present anxious situation facing the country as a whole. We have given no cause for alarm and I appeal to you all, and through you to the wider communities outside this hall, to remain as calm as we have hitherto been. The Midwest itself is a miniature Nigeria and all Nigerians are welcome here as well as our friends from abroad.

Thank you very much indeed.

[1] *Benin, 10 October 1966. Statement made available to the press.*
[2] *See* DOC *42.*   [3] *See* DOC *51.*   [4] *See* DOC *45.*

67.
Supreme Military Council's Statement on the Events of 1966 [1]

The Military Government intend to issue a White Paper on the events leading to the change of government on January 15 and July 29 and the related disturbances in certain parts of the country. The general public will then know the various roles played by some civilians and the principal actors in the Nigerian Army. It is hoped that this objective presentation of the facts will go a long way to explain all the tragic events which have plagued Nigeria in 1966 and assist all concerned in the earnest search for a just and lasting solution. . . .

4. It was in this climate of general disillusionment with the political ruling class that certain officers in the Nigerian Army sought to use the army, created for the defence of the fatherland and the protection of the citizen, to attain purely political ends. Widespread violence followed the Western Region election crisis of 1965 believed by many honest Nigerians to have been rigged on a very large scale. But the revolt in the West only provided the occasion for some officers in the Nigerian Army to use the army to attain political ends. There had been a similar attempt during the 1964 Federal election constitutional crisis which was foiled by the prompt intervention of army officers who did not believe in the military seizure of political power from civilians. On

that and subsequent occasions, the army officers plotting to seize power were assisted by some prominent civilians, including politicians. It is to the credit of the former civilian Federal Government that in the interest of peace, no army officer or civilian was subsequently punished for the planned military coup of December 1964.

5. The tragedy in using the army to resolve purely political questions is that a military coup usually brings in its trail tragic episodes in which violence and cold blooded murder is the order of the day. The experience in Nigeria since January 15 has followed this familiar historical pattern which all men of goodwill are now trying to arrest. It is unfortunate that the pattern of killings both on January 15 and July 29 followed mainly tribal lines as will be shown in the proposed White Paper. This has therefore tended to heighten tribal distrust particularly as between the Ibos and the Northerners in the army. Some observers, particularly foreign commentators, have seen in this unfortunate pattern a kind of genocidal warfare. Just after the January 15 military uprising, these observers were trying to convince the whole world that there was an Ibo master plan to wipe out the Northern ruling class. After the July 29 army mutiny, these people now say that there is a Northern plan to kill all the Ibos. The Supreme Military Council has decided on measures which will convince every Nigerian wherever he may be in the Federation, that the armed forces of the Federation will henceforth protect him irrespective of his tribe or Region of origin. All well-meaning Nigerians should contribute to this most difficult task and do nothing, say nothing which will worsen the situation or aggravate the current mutual distrust between the major tribal groups brought about by the recent tragic events in our otherwise peaceful history.

6. Often in the recent past, the public has been fed with the partial truth that the present uncertain political situation in the country started as a result of the disturbances in the Northern Region in May this year. The real truth, based upon investigations the details of which will be published soon, is that as far back as August 1965, a small group of Army Officers of a certain ethnic group, dissatisfied with political development within the Federation, began to plot, in collaboration with some civilians, the overthrow of what was then the Government of the Federation of Nigeria and the eventual assumption of power in the country. On January 15, 1966 the plan was executed. Although the original plan stipulated that the action intended by the plotters should take place simultaneously in all the Regional capitals, all available information indicates there was in fact no intention to carry out the plan in Benin and Enugu. It has been established that the plotters brought in some junior officers and other ranks to assist in the execution of their plans, on the threat of death if they refused to collaborate; others participated as soldiers obeying command instructions although some joined the revolt of their own free will. The plan of the army officers appeared to have been successfully carried out in Kaduna but in Lagos the coup was foiled by the intervention of the bulk of the Nigerian army to whom the civilian government had to hand over power. The mutinous activities of January 15 resulted in the death of seven people in Lagos, including the Prime Minister and five senior Military Officers; the Premier of Western Nigeria; seven people in Kaduna including the Premier of Northern Nigeria and two senior officers of the Nigerian Army. For a period

of about seven months thereafter, every Nigerian hoped that the country
would go on to achieve greater progress in development generally.
7. But there was the vexed question of the fate of the plotters of the January
15 incident. Some Nigerians thought of them as heroes in leading the overthrow of the much hated politicians but their killing of innocent army officers
mainly from Regions other than their own inflicted a major wound on the
Nigerian army famous for its discipline. It is unfortunate that a decision one
way or the other was not promptly taken in this regard. When it was learnt
in some quarters of the army that those directly involved, although detained
in various prison establishments in the country were being paid their regular
salaries plus other allowances, the hitherto smothered feeling that those concerned should have been brought to book according to military tradition
apparently began to show expression in the impatience of a section of the
army. The already charged situation reached an explosive point when a very
strong rumour started circulating that there was a further plot to annihilate
army officers and civilians from the same Region as most of those who had
been killed in January. This was the immediate cause of the events of July 29.
8. After the 15th January, the Northerners who were mostly affected by the
change, adopted an attitude of 'wait and see' even though there were jubila-
tions that the politicians had been overthrown. In several parts, especially
Kano, Katsina and Zaria, some of the ex-Ministers of the former Government of Northern Nigeria were molested and jeered on their return to their
provinces. But the situation soon changed because of (*i*) newspaper articles
and comments from Lagos advocating introduction of measures which many
Northerners believed were inimical to their interests; (*ii*) the attitude of some
southerners living in the North who became less friendly and 'provocative'
by displaying pictures of Major Nzeogwu and the late Sardauna and commenting that the country is now in their hands and no more in the hands of
Northerners; and (*iii*) articles and comments in the *Gaskiya Ta Fi Kwabo*
reporting such incidents in (*ii*) adding here and there that as far as the North
was concerned the situation was 'hopeless'. Thus a feeling of resentment and
fear was created in the minds of the ordinary people. . . .
10. Meanwhile, in the North the local petty contractors and party functionaries whose livelihood depended solely on political party patronage became
active. Most of them like their counterparts in other Regions, were indebted
to either the Northern Marketing Board or the Northern Nigeria Development Corporation. They were the hardest hit by the change of government
especially as all those indebted to Marketing Board and the NNDC were
made to pay up their arrears. They resorted to whispering 'campaign',
rumour mongering and incitement, aided and abetted by other factors. They
are the elements most close to the ordinary people and they have utilised
that to create a public opinion which is very strong and potentially dangerous against the authorities.
11. When the Nwokedi Commission was appointed, most of the Civil
Servants in the Federation particularly in the North, were apprehensive and
convinced that there was a preconceived plan to 'bulldoze' the unification of
the Civil Service through—come what may. On the 24th of May the 'unification decree', a major constitutional and political step which had not been
widely discussed, was announced, along with the dissolution of political and

tribal parties decree. The key words in that announcement are: 'The Regions are abolished.'[2] In whatever way it was put, it was bound to give offence to those who had already made up their minds against unification. The May 29 disturbances in the North followed.

12. There was an uneasy calm after the May disturbances. There was political uncertainty as to the future of Decree No. 34[3] and widespread tension and mutual suspicion in the army. Regular channels of communications were being by-passed in the transmission of instructions. There was the sudden public announcement to rotate Military Governors and to appoint military prefects which further heightened tension and mutual distrust in the army. There were wildly circulating rumours that the uncompleted job of January 15 was to be finished by eliminating the remaining officers of non-Eastern origin. There were also rumours of a counter coup planned by some Northern elements in the army with the assistance of civilians. On July 28 there was strong evidence that one group or the other would attempt something but the details were not available to the senior officers in command headquarters. The Supreme Headquarters and the Army Headquarters took the normal military precaution of warning all units to remain alert. It appears from the preliminary investigations available, that an officer in Abeokuta went beyond the precautionary measure and armed some men drawn from southern rank and file. When those of Northern origin got wind of this they became apprehensive of such a move, thinking a repeat of 15th January, 1966 was in the offing. They also took their weapons. These latter men shot three of their officers on the spot and in-fighting within the Army spread to Ibadan, Ikeja and then the units stationed in the North followed. The disorder in the army continued all over the weekend after the former Supreme Commander Major-General Aguiyi-Ironsi and the Military Governor, West, had been kidnapped at the Government House, Ibadan. The details of all those killed during the events of January 15 and July 29 and the full circumstances as far as they can be ascertained, will be set out in the proposed White Paper. But it seems clear from the scanty evidence available so far, that it is mainly officers and men from Eastern Nigeria who lost their lives in the revolts in the various units, the exact opposite of what happened on January 15 when officers and men mainly of non-Eastern origin were killed. The various incidents and negotiations and the circumstances which led to the assumption of office by Lieutenant-Colonel Yakubu Gowon as Head of Government and Supreme Commander of the Armed Forces will also be set out in the White Paper when the investigations into the events of July 29 are completed in the near future. An honest attempt will also be made to put into proper perspective the incidents in Enugu, the bomb explosions and the network of organisers behind the tragic events of the October 1 weekend resulting in the regrettable loss of many civilian lives mainly of Eastern origin living in the North and finally of similar incidents in Port Harcourt resulting in the death of civilians of Northern origin living in the East. It is not generally realised that some army personnel of Northern origin lost their lives in the attempt to quell the mutinous troops and protect defenceless innocent civilians. At this point, it should be emphasised that had the incidents of January 15 not occurred the subsequent tragic events in the country would certainly have been avoided.

13. Following the recent unfortunate incidents of September and early

October, the country has now returned to relative peace and quiet. The question paramount in the mind of the average Nigerian to-day is 'where do we go from here?' One of the outstanding problems is the continued exodus of certain ethnic groups in private and public establishments partly out of genuine fear but in many cases in answer to frantic appeals from their people. The latter moves could be designed to dislocate essential services and paralyse the economy of the country and to perpetuate the already tense situation which the Federal Military Government is trying to restore to normalcy. In these circumstances, it is necessary to re-emphasise the basic policies guiding the Military Governments in the Federation so as to leave no doubt in the minds of the people.

14. Foremost, the Government condemn unreservedly all recent outrages and acts of violence and lawlessness in the country and would like to express its deep sympathy for the victims and their relatives. It is for this purpose that the Supreme Military Council has given definite instructions for funds to be set aside to assist the victims. The Government believe that, since in most cases evidence points to outbursts of violence resulting from built-up emotions, our energies should be directed towards constructive ends and preventing a re-occurrence. In these grave hours, the Government consider that no one person or group of persons should act in a manner which is likely to prolong the agonies of our people. The Government hold therefore that, any person or a group of persons involved in anti-social behaviour, would be dealt with severely.

15. The Supreme Military Council has decided that no physical means should be used to prevent people who, in answer to calls from their peoples have deserted their posts in these grave hours however misguided they may be since it is the primary object of the Government to seek a peaceful solution without further bloodshed. In order to ensure the continued growth of the economy and maintain the level of employment as well as reduce friction to the minimum, it is clear that discipline in our national life must be maintained. To this effect, the Supreme Military Council has directed that public officers and men who voluntarily vacate their posts without further cause will, with effect from a given date, cease to be paid their salaries and their appointments terminated. As regards the private sector, the Government expects normal commercial activities to be resumed soon. Shops and market stalls closed with the intention of paralysing the economy will have to be re-opened or reallocated after a reasonable period has been given to their owners to return to their trade.

16. The Government accepts the basic principle that the country is an integral and indivisible unit and that any attempt by any section to force a split or to secede will definitely be regarded as unpatriotic, unconstitutional and treasonable. The position in this respect is like that of the relation between the Republic of Congo (Kinshasa) and the then Katanga and its political leaders where attempts were made by military and other means to disturb the integrity of that country owing to the selfish motives of certain individuals and foreign interests. Any attempt by any foreign government to encourage the intention of a certain section of the Nigerian people in the direction of secession, will be regarded as an unfriendly act and shall be treated as such. The Supreme Military Council wish to make it clear that the

activities of such governments would be regarded as interference in the internal affairs of this country. . . .

18. The Supreme Military Council in furtherance of its fundamental belief in the organic unity and integrity of the country, wish to leave on record the continued close collaboration between the Federal and the Regional Military Governments. As regards the present attitude of some prominent persons in the Eastern Region, the Supreme Military Council is fully aware that by far the largest number of Easterners desire peace and a rapid return to normalcy. The Supreme Military Council has faith in the commonsense of the people of the Eastern Region, but would like to express its doubt on the integrity of the small group of people who hitherto have failed to see objectively Nigerian problems and the conflicting claims of various regional and ethnic groups throughout the Federation. The Head of the Federal Military Government and Supreme Commander, Lieutenant-Colonel Yakubu Gowon and the other Military Governors will maintain their continuing dialogue with the Military Governor East, Lieutenant-Colonel Odumegwu-Ojukwu in their mutual search for solutions to the pressing problems of the day. The need for early return to peace and political stability in the country with assured economic progress for all Nigerians, remains the preoccupation of the Supreme Military Council. The Federal and the Regional Military Governments sincerely hope that every true Nigerian and sincere patriot will co-operate.

¹ Government Statement on the Current Nigerian Situation, *Lagos, no date (? 22 October 1966). It was announced as a trailer to a White Paper, but in the event no such document was ever issued. See note to* DOC 1.

² *See* DOC 26.　　　　　　　　　　　　*See* DOC 25.

68.
Personal Letter from Ojukwu to Gowon, Hassan, Adebayo, and Ejoor[1]

After long and serious reflections, I feel compelled to address you this letter. I am doing this with a very heavy heart and deep sense of responsibility and duty, and have no doubt that you will share in full those feelings.

2. I write first as a Nigerian citizen who saw in the Army Government a source of good, of dedication, and of courage to do the best for the nation. The boundless feelings and expressions of joy and hope which pervaded every inch of this nation bear witness to this fact. Secondly, I write as a soldier who, like you and others, answered the call of duty and accepted positions of responsibility for bringing our beloved country back from the path of madness and ruin to that of sanity and progress.

3. The foremost duty of a soldier is to protect the integrity of his country. In the discharge of this duty, no price can be too high for him to pay. He is not trained to govern, but to defend his country. If, however, circumstances compel him to interfere with the Government of his country, he does so as a corrective duty. As a non-partisan member of his country's community his path of duty is expected to be clear and objective, free from encumbrance and extraneous distractions.

4. Let me come directly to the point. No matter how or what we may feel about the circumstances which brought the Army into power, we have committed ourselves to specific duties to the country. The country expects us to discharge certain responsibilities from which we cannot honourably escape. Our failure will be disastrous both to the Army and to the nation. It will be a betrayal of trust and a breach of faith.

5. I wonder how many of us have been able at times to take our minds from the pressing and tragic problems, which now make so many demands on us, to reflect, even for a few minutes, on the events of the past ten months in this country. It can be quite challenging to go back and read the feelings of the people as expressed through the different information media in the country, following the event of January 15. To read the newspapers of those days will pointedly remind us of our responsibility to this country and its people; it would bring us to the full appreciation of the hope and faith which the total generality of the people of this country placed in us; it will bring back their expectations and make us search our minds and examine our actions and attitudes to see whether we are really living up to the trust and the expectations of the people and the world.

6. Are we discharging our duty, keeping our faith, keeping our honour, and facing our commitments? If we can be misguided enough to think that we can honestly and honourably answer those questions in the affirmative, then it is high time we knew that the public cannot be, and have not been, deceived.

7. Unfortunately and tragically, we seem already to be showing the people who had reposed such extreme confidence in us, the world who saw the Army as a beacon of hope for a potentially great but politically betrayed country, that we are not equal to the task. We seem, consciously or unconsciously, to be re-assuring the corrupt and the bad, who had brought the country to the verge of destruction but for the transfer of power to the Army, that they will soon return to their former positions of power unscathed. Quite a number of them are already making arrangements to return—and with a vengeance!

8. The public is becoming apprehensive, frightened and disappointed. It appears to them that the Army, which they saw as their last source of hope and salvation, is not only shirking its responsibility but is in fact becoming apologetic for being given the honour of salvaging the nation. Our actions and public words seem to show that we shared and liked all the ills of the past which we are sorry to have been made to interrupt. The utterly discredited forces of the past seem now to be the powers influencing the Army and its actions behind the scenes. The Federal 'Government statement on the Current Nigerian Situation',[2] just recently published, virtually admits this. Even more clearly, and disappointingly to the public, we have been giving indications that our duty is not longer the avowed one of correcting past ills but of running away from a difficult situation and handing power to the very people whose avarice, greed and corruption had compelled the Army to abandon its natural duty of defending the nation for that of salvaging it. We are lending ourselves to the popular fear that we have allowed sectionalism, prejudice, lack of direction and inadequacy to take us off the path of duty and honour.

9. The attempted coup of January 15 was a failure. But in spite of what might have been the motives and aims of the leaders of the attempted coup the nation and the world welcomed, without reservations, the dethronement

of the civilian governments which at that moment of crisis suddenly realised their failings and handed over power to the Army which had remained loyal to them. The leaders of those Governments were among the first to wish the Army well in the needed and urgent task of national reconstruction. All sections of the country, collectively and individually (the displaced politicians not excepted), united in a single voice and pledged their loyalty and support for the Army.

10. It was against this background that the Military Government announced its programmes and intentions. Its early pronouncements were universally acclaimed, and the Army was held as the saving Messiah for the country. It is true that some of our programmes of reconstruction have been discredited and forcefully abandoned; for example, those set out in Decree 34 now repealed. Maybe that here the Army was a little overzealous or misguided—as any human organisation could be. But, that a mistake has been made in one direction, should not make us abdicate our responsibility and abandon the other programmes which we set ourselves to execute.

11. Such programmes included that of purging the country of corruption, of making sure that ill-gotten goods were disgorged, of making the public and those who abused their positions of trust to feel that such actions do not pay and of setting the country on the path of fairness and justice. To achieve these aims, we set up a number of commissions of inquiry and investigations into public institutions and completed plans for inquiries into private wealth in order to sweep clean the public life of this country. All these were done both at the Federal and Regional levels. A number of commissions of inquiry are still holding, their reports will have to be examined and implemented. In some cases work has not even begun but it is a work which the public does not expect us to abandon.

12. Apart from this there are other matters which had constituted the baneful ills of the past to which the Army ought, and the public expect it, to address itself. One has in mind the census issue. There are also the deep wounds and scars which have been caused to the Nigerian body politic as a result of events subsequent to January the 15th. These are legacies the Army cannot morally leave to someone else. To heal the wounds and cover the scars cannot be a matter of months; and yet we do not seem to show either by our words or actions that we are seriously considering these issues. Instead, we are giving the world and the public totally different impressions.

13. What do we mean by constantly repeating to the world and the Nigerian public that our main concern now is to return to barracks and hand over powers to the former politicians? By this, does it mean that we have completed our assignments? Does it mean that our duty is now different from what we claimed in January, to the relief and unbounded jubilation of men, women and children of this country, and to our friends both at home and abroad? Or, are we abdicating our responsibilities? If so, let the army state that and admit its failure and betrayal of trust to the people, and return at once to the barracks with eternal dishonour, contempt and shame.

14. I have so far been dealing with the general Nigerian problems; but there is an even much closer problem which concerns the Army. On the 29th of July, Major-General Aguiyi-Ironsi, Supreme Commander and Head of the National Military Government was reported kidnapped while on a visit to

Ibadan. With him was kidnapped Lt.-Col. Fajuyi, Military Governor of Western Nigeria, who was his host. Up to now no public announcement has been made about the whereabouts of these top Army officers, particularly of the Supreme Commander and Head of the National Military Government. An acting Military Governor has been appointed to the West. Lt.-Col. Gowon has assumed the title of Supreme Commander and Head of the Federal Military Government. It is not known whether he assumed this position in acting capacity or not. So long as the whereabouts of Major-General Aguiyi-Ironsi remain beclouded so also will the prestige and corporate body of the Army remain confused. The air must be cleared by announcing to the public what has happened to Major-General Aguiyi-Ironsi. If he is dead that should be announced and due honour given to him as the Head of State who died in active service. If it is considered that he does not deserve this honour then the Army should tell the world the reason. If, on the other hand, he is still alive, the world should be told whether he has resigned or has been deposed or has temporarily relinquished his post. When this is known, it will be possible to determine the chain of command within the Army and re-establish its prestige and orderly conduct. This will be done by taking into account the accepted hierarchy. If after all the facts are known—militarily speaking, and we do not need to reveal Army secrets to the public—we find it necessary that Lt.-Col. Gowon should occupy the position he now claims, it will become possible to know and define on what conditions he should hold that post, perhaps while the Army is in control of the administration of this country.

15. Even more important that what may be the interim arrangements, clearly defined and accepted by all, is the problem of what will happen when we return to barracks. We cannot expect to have an Army which has thrown to the winds all hierarchical principles about its control and administration. It is something that we must settle in advance if we are sincerely trying to keep and maintain whatever remains of the country as a corporate whole.

16. Returning again to the heavy role which Fate has thrown on the shoulders of the Army, it is important that all of us are agreed on what we are doing and where we are going. Unfortunately, circumstances in the country have made it impossible for me to attend a meeting in Lagos or anywhere else where there are signs of Northern soldiers. This is a situation in which no right thinking person will fail to appreciate as far as my position and that of Eastern Nigeria, which I have been called upon to serve, are concerned. But it is important that we should meet somehow, somewhere, and talk things over. I make this suggestion with all sincerity because I am fully appreciative of the sad consequences which are bound to arise if we allow ourselves to be drifting in the present abyss of confusion and uncertainty.

17. It is true that we send our representatives to meetings from time to time, but these are civilian representatives whose role cannot legitimately absolve us from ultimate responsibility as members of the Military Government now charged with the conduct of affairs in this country. We must meet and exchange views and consider all the implications of the present situation, as well as of our own responsibilities, and evolve common attitudes and methods of approach as members of the Military Force on whom now rest the ultimate responsibilities of what may happen during the tenure of our office, and be

able to know what directions to follow ourselves and what directives to give to our representatives.

18. To this end, I hereby extend to you all a cordial invitation to meet in the East. I propose that we meet in Calabar or Port Harcourt which everyone will accept is as safe a place as anywhere in the world. There are no soldiers there and we could travel and leave there in complete secrecy. I give you absolute guarantees for your safety and will ensure that nobody except the security officers will know of the date and time and of our movements in connection with the meeting until after we should have ended and returned to our stations and issued the release. I sincerely trust that you will accept this invitation in good faith and let us quickly agree on a date for such a meeting. If it is possible to have this meeting before our representatives meet again, this will go a long way to inspire confidence and help to rescue the waning and dwindling life of the country.

[1] *Signed in Enugu on 25 October 1966. This personal and private letter was subsequently leaked by the Eastern Government. Copies were addressed to Wey and Johnson for information, but the invitation in paragraph 18 was also extended to them.*

[2] *See* DOC *67.*

69.
Azikiwe calls on Nigeria's 'Seasoned Elders' to Intercede [1]

My dear compatriots, we have gathered here today in answer to a call which challenges us, as human beings, to be merciful to fellow Nigerians who have tasted the vinegar of persecution, experienced the gall of torture, and escaped from the jaws of certain death. It is an appeal to our humanitarian feelings so that we may demonstrate our sense of brotherhood.

The object of this rally is to entreat you to buy this booklet, entitled *Nigerian Crisis 1966: Eastern Nigeria viewpoint,* which is a collection of pertinent speeches made by the Military Governor of Eastern Nigeria on the present situation in our country. Its distribution should enable funds to be pooled from its sale and used to heal those who were wounded, reclaim those who were incapacitated, rehabilitate those who were displaced, and restore confidence to those who have lost their bearings in this tragi-comedy of life.

What is a crisis, and what is the crisis of 1966? One dictionary definition is that change in a disease which indicates whether the result is to be recovery or death. Another definition is the decisive moment or the turning point. Indeed, our beloved country is very sick, having been attacked by a virulent disease diagnosed as fratricide-cum-genocide. We are now at the crossroads of existence.

The crisis of 1966 is the crucial stage in our national history and the issue now is: To be or not to be? Since the beginning of this year, Nigeria has been involved in the throes of a series of sanguinary revolutions. Day by day we hear of violence and bloodshed, as we become chagrined spectators and living witnesses of the frightful sight of the tortured, the grisly spectacle of the maimed, the unsightly scene of the immolated, and the gruesome panorama of the slaughtered.

Under these circumstances, our political co-existence has disenchanted us to realise the danger of our people not being socially homogenous. But it will always be a sociological riddle why people of diverse cultures and languages who had lived together as a political entity for nearly a century should suddenly discover their inveterate hatred for themselves to such extreme that they manifest same in a shameful exercise which degenerates into a brutal immolation of innocent children, women and adults with all the unrestrained emotions of savagery and barbarism known to humanity.

In recent months, we have been rudely shaken by the slaughter of harmless Nigerians, the molestation of law-abiding citizens, the looting of property, and the apparent breakdown of law and order.

All around us, we have seen Nigerians harassed in their normal enjoyment of life, displaced from their regular employment, and dislodged from their usual habitations.

Far and wide, they have trekked the routes of the country by different means of transport in their bid to escape from the uncertainties of horror to the security of freedom. Our nation is now confronted with the refugee problem.

This is sufficient evidence to demonstrate that our people are living under a gloomy shadow of fear and uncertainty. Why shouldn't they? When they are not sure that their persons are safe? When they are apprehensive that their property may not be secure? When rumours and gossip of real and imaginary situations are the order of the day? And the fate of the nation swings like the pendulum of an erratic clock?

It is now imperative that there should be a restoration of peace. This calls for statesmanship of the highest degree and we can no longer afford to be complacent. In our African society, elders do not sit smuggly and watch their homes destroyed by fire. An English clergyman who flourished in the nineteenth century said: 'We hate some persons because we do not know them; and we will not know them because we hate them.' How can they know us who only know themselves? And how can we know them when we only know ourselves?

Under alien rule we lived together, influenced by common traditions and values inherited through our British connection. Hitherto, we had lived in peace under the panoply of the rule of law. Could we not at least emulate one British trait in time of national crisis, by abandoning the fixed bayonet for the round table? Commonsense dictates that the elder statesmen and women of this nation should now intercede because if we do not have peace within ourselves, it is vain to seek for it from external sources.

The time has come for our elders to mediate and save this country from ruin and shame. Not that the people of Eastern Nigeria, who have been extremely provoked, are incapable of defending themselves and their homes creditably; but it is prudent that, whenever possible, peaceful solutions should be employed to settle internal disputes before a last resort to extremities with their disastrous consequences.

The seasoned elders of this nation should now abandon their passive roles and be more active in the cause of peace in our beloved country. They should

U

no longer turn a blind eye on the fratricidal tragedy confronting us today. They should no longer turn a deaf ear to the wailings of those who have been victimised in the genocidal conflict now raging in our beloved nation. Acts of extreme provocation can test human endurance to its limits. Eastern Nigerians are no exception.

Let the tried and tested patriots of our country accept the challenge of statesmanship and mediate in the blood bath now engulfing our country so that brother may no longer slay his brother.

Let them give this nation the benefit of their rich experience and maturity by reconciling all sides now, so that Nigerians may drink together the milk of human kindness and realise the futility of the gun as an instrument for the reasonable settlement of disputes.

Without trying to be invidious, I would like certain leaders of Christian and Moslem thought, among others, to bestir themselves and mediate without further delay so as to calm the troubled waters of our national life. To remain unconcerned could lead to tragic repercussions the like of which we may not be able to envisage. The present lull is dangerous. Eastern Nigeria seethes. The nation perches on a tinder box. One can sense an impending cataclysm which could be averted. This has impelled me to make this appeal.

If the leaders of this nation could surmount the mutual fear and distrust whose sombre shadow has cast a pall of gloom over our beloved country; if our leaders could insist on doing what is right for Nigeria and forget about who is right in this bloody argument that has cost the nation enormous losses of lives and property; if our leaders could meet in an atmosphere of mutual confidence and goodwill to settle their honest differences, they should be able to establish a lasting peace that will bring joy to the hearts of many.

The Federal Military Government should now take positive steps to arrest the disturbances of the past nine months which have drained the nation of its most valuable human and natural resources. The conscience of the nation should be aroused to realise that rehabilitation is not only a localised responsibility but also a federal obligation. After all, the individuals who lost their lives or property were Nigerian citizens who inhabited a part of Nigeria when their persons were violated and their properties were outraged.

A federal rehabilitation policy should have been formulated since the January tragedy. All the regions have been equally affected and the Federal Military Government should now implement a practical programme for compensating those who lost their property, and for maintaining, educating and rehabilitating the dependants of deceased victims.

May I summarise and conclude? The grave issues confronting our nation require the matured judgment of experienced leaders of our people. The threat to the continued maintenance of law, order and good government is a fact which is indisputable. The wanton destruction of human life and property flares up capriciously. Tempers are escalating to the saturation point.

Therefore, it is a moral obligation for the tried and tested leaders of our country to use their good offices to mediate now, now, and stay the hands of violence so as to restore peace and mutual confidence. Such a restoration should be done with honour and our displaced citizens should be rehabilitated on a national scale.

Let us have peace with honour in our beloved nation. Let there be a moratorium on the wanton destruction of human life and property. Let the bitterness of the past be mollified by the sacred blood of Nigerians that was shed as a propitiation for the unity of our motherland. Let there be a change of heart on the part of all concerned in this mêlée.

Let the guns be silenced so that Nigerians may live in peace with one another without fear of their persons being molested and their properties being disturbed. Let a ceasefire be ordered and let the command be enforced so that the apprehensions and uncertainties which grip the nation shall be relaxed. Let peace return to give Nigerians faith for today and hope for tomorrow and secure for our citizens freedom from fear and freedom from want.

[1] *Speech made at Nsukka, 22 October 1966.* Daily Times, *24 October 1966.*

70.
Ad Hoc Committee's Appeal to Eastern Delegation to attend in Lagos [1]

Our Fellow Compatriot,

As agreed by all Delegations to the Ad Hoc Committee three weeks ago, the Committee resumed sitting yesterday in the National Hall, Lagos, to consider matters outstanding and subjects on which agreement had not been reached at the date of adjournment. The Delegations present yesterday noted with regret the absence of the Eastern Nigeria Delegation and requested us to communicate with you in order to reinforce other efforts which we are aware are being made to persuade the Eastern Nigeria Delegation to resume participation in the work and proceedings of the Ad Hoc Committee.

We note reports in the Press that one of the conditions required for the return of the Eastern Nigeria Delegation to the Conference is the exchange of memoranda on outstanding matters by all Delegations, in accordance with the decision of the Committee before it adjourned on 3rd October.

It is unfortunate that in consequence of tours of the Regions undertaken by Delegations at the personal request of the Supreme Commander and Head of the Federal Military Government, and in consequence thereafter of lengthy consultations by Delegations with their Advisory Committees in the Regions, the majority of Delegations including the Eastern Nigeria Delegation, were unable to prepare and circulate their memoranda before the Ad Hoc Committee resumed. In the case of the Mid-Western Nigeria Delegation which did submit memoranda on 20th October, this date proved too late for the memoranda to be circulated to other Delegations before their arrival in Lagos at the week-end.

Having considered this position, the Ad Hoc Committee agreed yesterday to adjourn until Thursday, 27th October, in order to enable Delegations now in Lagos to complete and circulate memoranda, and in the hope that the Eastern Nigeria Delegation too will by then have prepared and circulated its memoranda.

In regard to the other conditions reported in the Press as requirements for the return of the Eastern Nigeria Delegation to the Ad Hoc Committee's sittings, you are no doubt aware that they are not matters within the competence of other Delegations. We have, however, had discussions with the Supreme Commander and Head of the Federal Military Government, and it is our earnest hope that you will find the arrangements and assurances by him adequate and acceptable.

We need hardly say that Nigeria is today in the throes of violent convulsions, and we have a common duty to save our country from the unhappy consequences of recent events. We also have no doubt that you share the deep desire and concern of other Delegations, of all patriotic Nigerians and of Nigeria's friends abroad, not only that Nigeria shall survive as a strong, united country but also that the protracted convulsions should be brought to an end as soon as possible, so that our people may resume without further delay their peaceful progress which has been so violently interrupted.

For these reasons, we appeal to you and to the Eastern Nigeria Delegations, in the name of God and of our dear fatherland, to rejoin us as soon as possible and thus clear the way for the Ad Hoc Committee to fulfil the hopes of all peace-loving Nigerians for an early settlement of our most pressing problems.

[1] *Addressed to Dr. Eni Njoku in Enugu and signed by the heads of the other four delegations in Lagos on 25 October 1966. From the official record.*

71.
The East's Reply to the Ad Hoc Committee[1]

Dear Fellow Compatriots,

I have received today your joint letter addressed to me as Head of the Eastern Nigeria Delegation. I am greatly touched by the trouble you have taken to write to me and I wish to assure you that I share your hopes, the hopes indeed of all our countrymen and women, that the pressing problems of our country should be settled as soon as possible.

You will remember, however, that during the previous session of the conference I was at great pains to explain to you that the Eastern delegates were truly delegates, not plenipotentiaries, and have no independent existence except in so far as they are mandated as representatives by the Government and people of Eastern Nigeria. At present the position is that the East has not mandated a delegation to the resumed conference, and consequently I am not at the moment head of the Eastern Delegation. Arrangements for the preparation, circulation and study of memoranda relating to the resumed conference are being handled by the Secretary to the Government of the Eastern Region.

I cannot therefore write to you as head of the Eastern Delegation. But as a citizen of Nigeria and an Eastern Nigerian I can assure you that it is the wish of Eastern Nigerians that their delegates should continue to participate in the conference, in spite of all that has happened. You already know that under very trying circumstances the East still decided to send a delegation to the first session of the conference and you will yourselves bear witness to the determined efforts made by the Eastern Delegation to work for the success of the conference. During and since the first session of the conference events have taken place which have heightened tension and intensified the fears of the people of the Eastern Region about the safety of delegates they send to Lagos. If you were able to visit the Eastern Region and see things for yourselves I am sure that you would be convinced that these fears are real. The plain fact is that Eastern Nigerians do not now feel secure in any part of the country occupied by Northern troops, not only because of possible acts of indiscipline by these troops such as occurred in Lagos during the first session of the conference, but also because of the possibility of mutiny by the troops such as occurred in Kano while the conference was sitting in Lagos.

It is against this background that the representatives of the people of Eastern Nigeria at their recent consultative assembly decided on the conditions under which their delegates should continue to participate in the resumed conference. These are the conditions which were publicized by the Military Governor in his radio broadcast. In my humble opinion, those conditions are not unrealistic in the light of the most recent events in the country.

Although the more important of these conditions are, as you say, outside your competence, yet I hope that you will use your good offices to foster those conditions or appropriate alternatives so that the work of the conference can proceed in an atmosphere in which all delegates can feel free and fearless in making their contributions. I am sure that if you reflect seriously on the unfortunate situation of our country at present you will appreciate the position of Eastern Nigerians today. I appeal to you therefore to apply to this matter the full force of your joint endeavours so that Eastern Nigerian delegates can participate in the conference and work with you all in bringing back peace to our unhappy country.

[1] *Sent by Dr. Njoku from Nsukka on 26 October 1966. From the official record of the Conference. Only part of the letter is given in the Federal publication* Nigeria 1966.

72.
Ojukwu Accuses Gowon of having summarily dismissed the Constitutional Conference [1]

Fellow countrymen and women, I have found it necessary to make this broadcast today in order to bring you up to date on the position of Eastern Nigeria with regard to the problems besetting the country, with particular reference to the constitutional talks which were scheduled to take place in Lagos last Thursday, 17th November, but which were suddenly adjourned indefinitely by Lt.-Col. Gowon.

You will recall that after the last meeting of the ad hoc committee, attended by your delegates in Lagos, I made a similar broadcast to the nation on 27th October. Earlier, on 4th October, the Consultative Assembly had met in Enugu and heard the report of your delegates to the conference. At the end the Consultative Assembly agreed on certain lines of action and specifically laid down the conditions under which our men would participate in further discussions.[2] I naturally pondered over the Assembly's recommendations for several days, during which I was in constant touch with Colonel Gowon with a view to seeing whether we could be met somewhere in our demands. Apart from telephone conversations, I wrote a letter to him, with copies to the Military Governors, setting out clearly the position of this Region and conveying to him the conditions and proposals which the Consultative Assembly had made about future meetings.[3] The ad hoc committee was scheduled to resume on 24th October. The only reaction to my representations was a statement that the meeting would still be held, and it was indeed held without our participation. By 1st November, the other delegations, after consultation with Colonel Gowon, decided to adjourn the meeting until 17th November when it was hoped conditions would be created which would make it possible for all the delegations to attend the discussions in an atmosphere of freedom, conducive to personal safety.

In the course of my several telephone conversations with him, Colonel Gowon suggested Ghana or Fernando Po or any nearby country in Africa as a possible venue for the resumed conference. I readily agreed to this suggestion. He even returned to the question of Benin, which I had previously suggested. I agreed that the ad hoc committee should meet in Benin, subject to two qualifications: in the first place, I insisted that Northern Nigeria troops in the Western Region should be returned to the North. I was prepared to agree to the retention of a sufficient number of Northern Nigeria troops in Lagos for his own personal security; but, bearing in mind that early last August Northern Nigeria troops travelled from the West to Benin, broke into a prison, removed soldiers, detainees of Eastern Nigeria origin, and shot five of them, I could not but insist on the removal of these unruly soldiers from Western Nigeria to the North before our delegation could attend the conference. Colonel Gowon informed me that the Northern delegation would not come to Benin.

Regarding the alternative venues proposed by Colonel Gowon himself, the public will no doubt wish to know which Regions have refused to accept any of them. On Wednesday of last week, less than 24 hours before the time when the ad hoc committee was scheduled to resume its meeting, an announcement came out of Lagos dismissing the ad hoc committee. Since then, many of you in the East and beyond have got in touch with me and asked a number of questions. Uppermost in everyone's mind is the question: where do we go from here? It is this which has prompted me to broadcast this morning. I have also convened a meeting of the Consultative Assembly because it is my policy to keep you adequately informed and to receive your mandate in every move.

Before commenting on Colonel Gowon's statement dismissing the ad hoc committee, I should like to make it clear that I was at no time consulted before this action was taken, nor am I aware that the other Military Governors had prior knowledge of Colonel Gowon's intention. The only conclusion to be drawn from this anti-democratic, unilateral and dictatorial decision is that we are entering a new phase in the struggle for national existence.

Colonel Gowon's statement could mean a lot of things. One of these is that he has abandoned faith in negotiations as a means of settlement. This brings to mind a statement credited to a leading member of the Northern delegation to the effect that their aim was to settle the issues by negotiations—or otherwise. A request by this Government for a clarification of that statement has not been met up till now. We have wanted them to say what means they have in mind for settling our problems other than by negotiations. Colonel Gowon has surely stated that from the memorandums submitted by the different delegations no one can be left in any doubt that no useful purpose would be achieved by the continued sitting of the conference. It would be interesting to know what was the purpose of convening the conference in the first instance. Was it not in order to iron out differences? For why should one discontinue the conference mainly because the memoranda submitted by the different delegations contain different proposals? There would have been no need to meet at all if there were no differences of opinion, which it was the duty of the delegations to bring out in their different memoranda. This region did appreciate the fact that there must be some differences. Hence its insistence that regional memoranda should be circulated in advance, as previously agreed, in order that each delegation might be in a position to know the feeling of the others and go to the conference prepared to discuss and make necessary the concessions in the interest of all. I have myself read all the memoranda submitted by the different delegations. As far as I can see it is only the Northern memorandums which differ in substantial points from the rest. With the type of people of high integrity and responsibility which every Region has appointed as its delegates to the conference one should have thought that these people should be allowed to go to the conference table a d argue out the different points with a view to reaching agreement by means of necessary adjustments and concessions.

Now that it is no longer possible for the people's representatives to participate in the constitutional making process, I owe it as a duty to all of you to publish in full the proposals of the ad hoc committee. The people must not be kept in the dark and they have a right to know the full facts. I want to make it quite clear here that I cannot forget my position as a member of the military regime, which by its very nature is an interim administration and which has set itself a clear objective for performing specific duties for a nation in the grip of disaster.

I have, during the last few weeks, addressed important letters to Colonel Gowon and my other military colleagues at the helm of affairs in this distressed country. In one of those letters, dated 25th October,[4] I drew the attention of my colleagues to the heavy responsibility which the Army owes to the nation. The rest of that letter which was very long dealt with the position of the Army and ended with a suggestion for a meeting of the Military Governors with Colonel Gowon under guaranteed conditions. That letter was followed a week later by another one, dated 31st October, dealing with even more intimate problems about the position of the Army and its duty. In this last letter I made sincere and concrete proposals on how the Army could reorganise itself in a way which could put it in a position to discharge its responsibility to the nation. Up to this day, I have received no reply from Colonel Gowon to the above letters. I will also publish this correspondence very shortly.

Fellow countrymen, there can be no doubt that the Gowon Governmen does not fully appreciate the sense of urgency for which the present situatio in the country calls. It is difficult to explain such a destructive attitude in th face of the disintegration of the nation.

Last week, the country was shocked by the sad revelation by the Wester Nigeria Military Government of a plot to overthrow that Government. W must thank God that that bloody plot was uncovered in time because it success could have had wider implications and consequences than perhaps th plotter contemplated, or Lagos would be prepared to accept. We have bee told by the Military Governor of Western Nigeria, Colonel Abedayo, tha persons inside and outside the Western Region, including Lagos, were in volved in this plot. It is not for me to speculate on the master mind behind i nor on any possible connection between the plot and the dismissal of the a hoc committee. However, I have reason to believe that the assumption o dictatorial powers by Colonel Gowon is the first of a series of arbitrar measures taken unilaterally, which the country may expect in the comin months. Having now arrogated to himself the power to dictate a Constitution Colonel Gowon has accepted by implication the enormous consequences o this venture. Despite solemn assurances by the National Military Govern ment, headed by Maj-Gen. J. T. U. Aguiyi-Ironsi, that the Military Govern ment would never impose a Constitution on the people of this country an that that was entirely a matter which the people themselves must determine an assurance which the Military Governors and Colonel Gowon have re peatedly supported in so many deliberations, Colonel Gowon in complet disregard of this pledge and assurances now proposes to draw up a Consti tution without consultation.

The basis of the proposed Constitution is apparently no other than th discredited constitutional report which Colonel Gowon had accepted withou consulting the Military Governors, and despite the fact that Dr. Elias an other members of the committee had described the committee as defunct an overtaken by the events of 29th July, and the fact that the committee coulc not and did not tour the country as proposed in order to ascertain the wishe of the people. I can well understand Colonel Gowon's predicament in some of these matters. His particular interest in the creation of states is all to obvious. We wish him luck. We in this Region have made our stand clear on this issue. What is needed in Nigeria today is a return to normalcy before anything else. The extreme suffering and loss of life and property by Easter- ners dictate no other policy.

The constant practice in Lagos of taking decisions on national issues with- out reference to the Military Governors and the futile attempt to have such decisions implemented have set a new pattern. There would appear to be a calculated attempt in Lagos to isolate Regional Governors, indeed the people of this Region, from participation in decisions affecting the destiny of this country. Colonel Gowon now wishes to run the country with a clique of senior civil servants mainly drawn from officers of a certain ethnic group.

I will not end this broadcast without reference to our repeated demands for implementation of the unanimous agreement reached by the representatives of the Military Governors on 9th August[5] for the repatriation of troops to their region of origin and their confinement to barracks. The continued resistance of Colonel Gowon to implement this unanimous decision exposes him to a breach of faith. This is causing tension particularly in the West, and it is understood that strong representations made by the leaders of the West have not even convinced Colonel Gowon that an explosive situation is fast approaching and developing in that part of the country.

Fellow countrymen, be warned. It is my determination to protect this Region from confusion and anarchy. The period of negotiation seems now at an end. If it is the intention of Colonel Gowon to impose a constitution on the people of Eastern Nigeria we shall resist. I therefore call upon you to be resolute, to be vigilant and to be prepared to meet the challenge. Please God, spare us this madness. Thank you.

¹ *Live broadcast from Enugu at noon on 20 November 1966 (B.B.C. ME/2323/B/1).*
² *See* DOC *62.*   ³ *See* DOC *68.*
⁴ *See* DOC *68.*   ⁵ *See* DOC *45.*

73.
Summary of the Regional Memoranda submitted to the Second Session of the Constitutional Conference

See pp. 296–304.

[From the Eastern Government's Record of the Conference. These comparative summaries do not appear in the Federal version. Cf. DOC 60.]

74.
East's Consultative Assembly Endorses Ojukwu's Stand[1]

Recalling the atrocious murders of persons of Eastern Nigeria origin and other acts of barbarism and inhumanity committed against us in other parts of Nigeria by fellow countrymen among whom they lawfully resided;

Aware of the planned and determined effort to exclude Eastern Nigeria and her people from the public affairs and public offices of the Federal Republic of Nigeria;

Conscious of the attempt made and being made, by the Government and people of Eastern Nigeria, in spite of the wrongs done to Eastern Nigerians, to promote peace and salvage what is left of Nigeria and her honour;

Determined to protect and defend the integrity of Eastern Nigeria and the dignity of her people;

Confirming the mandate given by us to our Delegates to the *Ad Hoc*

Text continued on p. 305.

Document 73

MEMORANDA TO THE AD HOC CONSTITUTIONAL CONFERENCE
STAND OF THE DELEGATIONS

Subject	East	West and Lagos	Mid-West	North	Remarks
Regions	Existing Regions subject to our statement on creation of states.	(1) Creation of more States on linguistic and ethnic basis. (2) If not possible now, then existing Regions to remain with Lagos as part of West.	Creation of more States. No clear formula proposed.	Creation of States based not on language but on principle of self-determination, demand and referendum.	(1) West proposes eighteen States, population ranging from 13·8m to 0·6m. This destroys Mid-West Region. (2) North's stand has no logical basis for creation of States.
Lagos	Reserved.	(a) To be part of West if no new States are created. (b) If new States, to be one State.	Not specific.	Capital Territory.	(1) Stand of North is based on fact that it was built up with common funds. (2) West considers this argument applicable to the North also.
Lagos Garrison	To be garrisoned by soldiers from Region of Head of State.	By soldiers from Region of Prime Minister.	Silent.	By troops from all the Regions quartered in separate barracks.	
Legislature	Council of States. Unicameral, members nominated by Regions on basis of equality and liable to recall. Members to be paid by Regions. Tenure: four	Parliament. Tenure: four years. Unicameral; nomination by Regions of members on equal basis. Thirty from each Region. Liable to recall. To be	Parliament. Unicameral; equal numbers from Regions through direct national elections. Tenure: five or six years.	Parliament. Unicameral; equal numbers by nomination in Regions liable to recall except first Parliament. Tenure: four years; thirty from	Only Mid-West wants general elections and tenure of five or six years.

Head of Legislature	Chairman of Legislature to be Head of Government. Annual rotation.	Prime Minister drawn from majority party in power after general elections.	Silent.		Only Mid-West wants present position of having general elections and government of majority party.
Head of Government	Head of State and of Government in one and the same person. Annual rotation.	Prime Minister. Annual rotation and drawn from the Secretaries of State who shall be members of the Federal Legislature.	Prime Minister from the Party in power.	Prime Minister to be nominated by the Regions in rotation every four years.	(1) East's stand conforms with proposal that Council of States should operate both as Legislature and Executive. (2) Nomenclature 'Prime Minister' is inconsistent with policy of avoiding use of word 'Minister' in favour of 'Secretary of State'.
Procedure in Legislature	All laws to be consented to by Regions.	Unanimity votes of the Regions in issues declared by the Constitution.	As at present (by implication).	Silent.	Mid-West adopts decision by majority.
The Executive	Council of States. Regions equally represented and nominated. Liable to recall.	Cabinet drawn from members of Parliament. Equality of Regions. Liable to recall.	Federal Executive Council. Equal numbers from Regions to be appointed by party in power from among its party members in Parliament.	Cabinet appointed by Head of State on advice of Prime Minister. Equal number. No recall by Regions.	Mid-West's position impossible in view of inconsistency between majority rule and equality of representation. North's position envisages a Prime Minister who could choose anyone he likes.

DOCUMENT 73 (continued)

Subject	East	West and Lagos	Mid-West	North	Remarks
Head of State	Chairman of Council of States. Annual rotation.	President. Rotation yearly.	Constitutional President and Vice-President. Rotation every five or six years.	Ceremonial President. Rotation every four years.	Position of Mid-West and North involves intervention of other Regions and encourages 'ganging up'. This involves conflicts which must be avoided.
Selection of Head of State	Rotation among members of Council of States nominated by the Regions.	Region to appoint him outside the members of Legislature.	By electoral college consisting of retired presidents, present or past State Governors; Members of State and Federal Legislatures.	Region puts up three names. Vote by electoral college consisting of members of States and Federal Legislatures.	The stand of West, Mid-West and North, does not save us from the sort of crisis we had in 1964.
Powers of Head of State	Same as powers of other members of Council of States save for ceremonial functions during one year. Acts on unanimous decision of Council of States.	As in present Constitution.	As in present Constitution.	As in present Constitution. Appoints Prime Minister who is nominated by the Region concerned. Acts on advice of Prime Minister.	
Powers of Head of Government	Decisions of Council carried out in his name as Head of State.	Powers as at present. President and Prime Minister not to be from the same Region.	As at present.	President and Prime Minister not to be from same Region. Rotation every four years. Powers as at present. President to act only on his advice. He is to be in charge of Security.	Mid-West does not approve of the principle of rotation.
Members of Executive (or Cabinet)	Members of the Council of States each assigned to group of departments, agencies or Commissions	Secretaries of State; equal numbers from Regions drawn from Federal Legislature. Subject	Secretaries of State. Same powers as former Ministers. Appointments from ministerial Pool subject	Secretaries of State who are not members of legislature. Equal numbers from	Mid-West and North have tried to dress the devils in white clothes. Also,

Number fixed at five from each Region. Liable to recall.	recall. Stipulated portfolios to be shared. Total number fixed at twenty.	ment. Number fixed at eighteen.	former Ministers. No recall. All to be appointed by Head of State on advice of Prime Minister. (Former stand: Direct appointment by President of persons nominated by Region.)	principle of rotation.
Procedure in Cabinet Unanimity.	Unanimity in major issues to be stipulated in the Constitution.	Majority decision by party in power.	Unanimity in major issues to be stipulated in the Constitution.	The entire position of the Mid-West is the maintenance of the *status quo*.
Judiciary Supreme Court at Centre with original jurisdiction in disputes on Constitution of Centre, and appellate in fundamental rights and matters assigned by Regions.	Supreme Court. Appellate jurisdiction only.	New Court with original and appellate jurisdiction (matters not specified).	Supreme Court with appellate jurisdiction only.	Mid-West adopts *status quo*.
Composition Equal number of Judges from the Regions. Head shall be President, and shall rotate annually.	Silent.	Five Judges of which one, the President, must be a Nigerian and others from the Commonwealth. Present Supreme Court to be intermediate appeal court between High Court and the New Appeal Court, and to sit in Regions in panels of three.	Introduction of Muslim and Customary Lawyers in intermediate Court of Appeal of Region.	General view: present Supreme Court should be reconstituted.
Mode of Appointing By the Regions.	Judicial Service Commission.	Judicial Service Commission.	By President on advice of Prime Minister. (Later	A Judicial Service Commission is an anomalous

Subject	East	West and Lagos	Mid-West	North	
Judges				stated to be on advice of Judicial Service Commission).	body in the proposed set-up.
Conduct of Judges	A Judge of Central Court shall not be eligible for any other public or political office during or after his tenure of office. Also usual conditions.	Silent.	Code of conduct to be stipulated in the Constitution.	Silent.	
Public Service	Equal contribution by the Regions. A Public Service Committee to maintain discipline and standards.	Appointment on basis of equality, Staff of Railways, Posts, etc., should be indigenous to the site of the service.	Public Service Commission to manage appointment as of now.	Recruitment on population basis by Public Service Commission appointed by President on advice of Prime Minister.	West's position recognizes the factual position today and is strong reason for regionalizing those services.
Financial Provisions	(1) Fiscal Powers in Regions. (2) Centre to be run by equal contributions from Regions.	(1) Fiscal Powers in Regions. (2) Centre to operate on subventions by the Regions in equal amounts.	Assumes the present system, revisable every four years by Federal Government. Each new State to have £2 million from Centre to launch it. This should be retrospective from 1960.	Revenue from oil and minerals to be allocated by the Centre. (Stand on September twenty: Principle of Derivation.)	It appears that North wants only Revenue from Oil and mineral to be federally controlled, and others to be by derivation.
Existing Assets and Liabilities	(1) Assets to go to Region in which sited. Relevant loans to be paid by such Regions. (2) Other assets and liabilities to be shared ac-	(1) Existing assets and liabilities to be the responsibility of Regions where sited. (2) Future public debt to be Federal.	Public debt to be Federal.	Public debt to be Federal.	

The Armed Forces and the Police	Regional with co-ordination at centre for defence and emergency purposes as was agreed by the *Ad Hoc* Conference. Minor modifications.	Ditto. (Same as for East.)	Ditto. (Same as for East.)	Ditto. (Same as for East.)	The stand of the East is in fact the stand of the other Regions. Therefore the matter must be removed from the Legislative List of the centre and spelt out in the body of the Constitution. The reservations made by all the delegates clearly show a strong desire to remove the Police and Armed Forces from central control in peace time.
Inspector-General of Police	To rotate annually among Regions.	Silent.	Silent.	To be member of the Defence Council.	It can be assumed that West will opt for rotation if the matter did not escape her mind since it is obvious that no federal police is envisaged.
Higher Education (including Existing ones)	Regional.	Regional.	Federal.	Federal but one of the two Teaching Hospitals to be transferred elsewhere.	The North and the Mid-West do not tell us how all Southerners can go to a School in the North or work in Federal Agencies there.
Existing Corporations, Commissions and Agencies	Regional.	Regional.	Federal.	Federal.	
Future Corporations, etc.	—	—	Federal, but to be equitably distributed.	Federal.	

DOCUMENT 73 (continued)

Subject	East	West and Lagos	Mid-West	North	Remarks
Electoral Commission	No place in proposals.	No place in proposals.	To remain with named safeguards.	No place in present proposals.	Only Mid-West wants general elections and an Electoral Commission.
Fundamental Rights	To be in Constitution.	To be in Constitution.	To be in Constitution.	Silent.	
External Loans, Monetary Policy and Related Matters	Rejects proposals of Committee of Experts set up by the Conference. East to submit a paper.	Accepts proposals of the Committee.	Silent.	Silent.	Monetary Policy, fiscal powers, trade and commerce and related matters are tied up with the form of association.
Interim Government	The Military Government is interim and the proposed Composition of the Supreme Military Council should solve its difficulties.	Civil Servants (with some public men as advisers) to arrange: (a) transfer of personnel to regions of origin. (b) Ditto, Armed Forces and Police. (c) Division of existing Army stores, etc. (d) Elections in Regions. (e) Thereafter, the new Governments should form Constituent Assemblies to draft the Regional Constitution and establish the various authorities at the Centre.	Proposes: (1) The Supreme Military Council to which is added the Heads of the Ad Hoc Conference, two Christian and two Moslem Religious Leaders. (2) A sub-Committee of (a) Supreme Commander; (b) Chief of Staff; (c) Regional Military Governors; (d) Heads of Ad Hoc Conference—a total of eleven men. The Civilian members will have executive functions.	Approves the decision of the Supreme Military Council to inject civilians into the Military Government. First Civilian Government to be made of persons appointed outside Legislatures.	(1) Mid-West proposes external help in reorganizing the Army, though it expresses certain fears about this. (2) The stand of the West may have changed since the adjournment.

X Amendment of Constitution	Automatic every ten years or in five years if Regions agree.	Country to be re-established in stages and Constitution to be reviewed in four years' time.	(1) For new States, as at present. (2) In minor matters approval of Parliament and majority of Regions. (3) In others: by a referendum.	Silent.	
Powers of the Centre:					
(i) Archives	Regional.	As agreed in Progress Report.	As agreed in Progress Report.	As agreed in Progress Report.	
(ii) Aviation, etc.	Centre to lay down standards.	As agreed in Progress Report.	As agreed in Progress Report.	As agreed in Progress Report.	
(iii) Customs, Excise, etc.	Regional with arrangements for co-ordination.	Regional in view of stand on Revenue Allocation.	Not decided.	Not decided.	East stand agrees with her proposal relating to the fiscal powers of Regions.
(iv) External Affairs	Provides for: (1) appointments to Missions abroad to be on stipulated basis; (2) Regional Power to enter into trade agreements and have commercial attaches.	As by East.	As by East and West.	As by others except that she reserves position on question of appointment to Missions on equal basis and would rather have it on population basis.	North here departs from the equality principle it advocates in the organs of government.
(v) Maritime shipping, etc.	Laying down of standards.	As in Progress Report.	As in Progress Report.	As in present Constitution.	
(vi) Meteorological Services, etc.	Co-ordination only.	As in Progress Report.	As in Progress Report.	Federal but Region can establish its own with federal consent.	
(vii) Patents, Trade Marks, etc.	Central, but there must be an establishment in each Region with full powers to operate the laws.	As in Progress Report.	As in Progress Report.	As in Progress Report.	

DOCUMENT 73 (continued)

Subject	East	West and Lagos	Mid-West	North	Remarks
(viii) Pensions, etc.	Existing pensions, etc., only.	As in Progress Report.	As in Progress Report.	As in Progress Report.	East proposals envisage civil service to be paid by the Regions.
(ix) Posts, Telegraphs, etc.	Co-ordination.	As in Progress Report.	As in Progress Report.	As in Progress Report.	
(x) Powers, Privileges, etc., of Parliament, etc.	To be considered in relation to Council of States.	As in Progress Report.	As in Progress Report.	As in Progress Report.	
(xi) Railways, etc.	Co-ordination.	As in Progress Report.	As in Progress Report.	As in Progress Report.	
(xii) Federal Highways	Regional.	As in Progress Report.	As in Progress Report.	As in Progress Report.	

Constitutional Conference, and our confidence in them, and, having noted with regret the indefinite adjournment of the meeting of the *Ad Hoc* Constitutional Conference by Lt.-Col. Yakubu Gowon for alleged inability to agree upon the venue of the meeting as well as according to him, because of other difficulties which he has not named;

Observing that, even though the decision to appoint the *Ad Hoc* Constitutional Conference was a unanimous agreement of the Governments of the Federation, yet the adjournment was made without consultation with or consent by the Eastern Nigeria Government;

Having also noted the many acts of bad faith on the part of the Gowon Government and its inability to fulfil promises or implement agreements unanimously reached;

Finding now that there is a plot hatched up by certain civil servants and other officials with the active involvement of Lt.-Col. Yakubu Gowon to impose a constitution and certain other measures on Nigeria;

Re-affirming the implicit confidence of the people of Eastern Nigeria in His Excellency, Lt.-Col. Odumegwu Ojukwu and assuring him of the solidarity of Eastern Nigeria and their support and admiration for the way he has handled the present crisis facing Nigeria;

Also assuring His Excellency of the admiration of the people of Eastern Nigeria in the Military Government of Eastern Nigeria and their desire for its continued administration until it has achieved its objective of creating a new society in Eastern Nigeria;

We do hereby resolve that our Military Governor be advised as follows:

1. To take any measures he considers appropriate for the defence and protection of the integrity of Eastern Nigeria, the lives and property of its inhabitants.

2. To maintain utmost vigilance against subversion of the Government of Eastern Nigeria not only from outside the Region, but also from within and to deal ruthlessly with anybody, high or low, engaged in subversion.

3. To resist the imposition on the people of Eastern Nigeria of any constitutional, administrative or legislative measures taken without prior consultation and agreement.

4. To reject any solution which will undermine the economic and industrial progress and prosperity of Eastern Nigeria or which will tend to sow the seeds of future friction among the Regions of this Country.

5. To continue with the good progress made so far in the rehabilitation of refugees.

6. To speed up the implementation of Provincial Administration with legislative and executive powers, and the re-establishment of Customary Courts.

7. To spare no efforts at the right time to purge former holders of public offices of corrupt practices so as to set a shining example for the youths of this Region, and inculcate into the people the spirit of honesty, integrity, fair-play, mutual trust and a feeling of oneness which will provide the basis for our future progress.

8. To continue Your Excellency's efforts to bring about a meeting of Military Leaders and the reconvening of the *Ad Hoc* Constitutional Conference under conditions of adequate security satisfactory to Your Excellency.

9. To ensure that only men and women of integrity and merit are appointed to public offices in the Region and that a code of conduct for public officers be drawn up for Eastern Nigeria.

Lastly, we assure Your Excellency that no Eastern Nigerian, whether living inside or outside this Region, has the mandate or support of the people of this Region to speak for or represent them unless appointed with the recommendation and approval of Your Excellency acting on behalf of Eastern Nigeria.

[1] *Resolution passed on 23 November 1966.* Proclamation of the Republic of Biafra, *pp. 9–11.*

75.
'Towards a New Nigeria'—Gowon's Broadcast to the Nation, 30 November 1966 [1]

Fellow Countrymen,

I wish to speak to you this evening about the measures which the Federal Military Government will implement to save the country from disintegrating. You are all aware that the Ad Hoc Committee has been adjourned indefinitely. They had run into difficulties which made it impossible for them to meet. In those circumstances there was little hope of the Committee evolving reasonable solutions to our present crisis. I shall deal later with the conditions under which the Committee could continue the work it started so well. Our problems demand urgent solutions. The Federal Military Government has therefore worked out a clear and objective programme for saving Nigeria. Our non-partisan programme will not favour any particular group or groups.

The foremost preoccupation of the Federal Military Government is to lessen tension and maintain peace in the country. On the Military front, I am in constant touch with all the Military Governors and we are all confident that the Nigerian Army in conjunction with other Armed Forces and Police can still save this country. I do appreciate that the recent tragic events have shaken the basis of mutual confidence in the Army but my colleagues and I will gradually rebuild it. We can succeed with the help of honest Nigerians.

My long-term aim is the preservation of one Nigerian Army and one country. For a start, however and because of the general distrust and suspicion in the country, the bulk of the army in each Region must be drawn from the indigenous people of that Region. In furtherance of this aim, steps are being taken to recruit more Westerners into the Nigerian Army. I have already given instructions for recruitment to commence next week. Those who advocate the withdrawal of Northern soldiers from the Western Region admit that any immediate wholesale withdrawal of Northern soldiers from the Western Region is not practicable. Law and order and the entire national security arrangements in the Western Region will break down if the troops were withdrawn at once.

The seat of the Federal Government is in Lagos. The Head of the Federal

Government must therefore make special security arrangements for Lagos. This is not in dispute in all responsible quarters.

We are all aware, however, that Nigeria's troubles started from bitter political strife and inordinate ambition for personal power. We must therefore try to avoid such bitterness and selfish manoeuvres in our approach to national problems. Political activities will therefore remain banned. We must also discourage any attempt to revive tribal consciousness and worsen Regional animosities. I have received some co-operation from Nigerian leaders in this respect but there must be greater restraint in all quarters if we are to succeed in reducing tensions everywhere. The press, the radio and other mass communication media must exercise a greater sense of responsibility in what they publish in these difficult times.

I now come to the immediate political programme of the Federal Military Government. As soldiers, my colleagues and I are ready to go back to the barracks any day. But the work of national reconstruction must be completed. public confidence in our institutions restored; and civilian leaders demonstrate to the nation that they are ready to take over and project a better image of the country than it had just before January, 1966.

There are five main issues which the Federal Military Government will deal with in the course of national reconstruction. The first is the reorganization and long-term reintegration of the Nigerian Army. The second is the implementation of a nationally co-ordinated resettlement and rehabilitation programme for displaced persons. The third is the preparation of the Second National Development Plan. The fourth is to continue the fight against corruption in public life and the fifth is the preparation of a new Constitution for the country.

I have already spoken about my long-term aims for the Nigerian Army. For security reasons, I do not intend to discuss in public the internal affairs of the Armed Forces.

The Federal Military Government recognizes the need for a nationally co-ordinated resettlement and rehabilitation programme for displaced persons. I appreciate the valuable work done by the Regional Governments and voluntary organizations in providing emergency relief for displaced persons. Nevertheless, the Federal Military Government must do all it can to provide national leadership for tackling the problems of resettling these unfortunate persons as part of its efforts to restore normalcy in the country. The Federal Military Government will provide a fair proportion of the funds required for implementing the national programme to be worked out in consultation with the Regional Military Governments. This is a matter to which I attach the greatest urgency.

One of the major tasks of the Federal Military Government is to guarantee the safety of investment, foreign and Nigerian. Genuine investors therefore have nothing to fear from our current difficulties.

Every effort will be made to ensure that the Nigerian economy will continue to grow without serious interruptions. To this end, the Government will press on with the preparation of the Second National Development Plan. It is quite clear that in the next stage of our industrial development we shall enter such fields as iron and steel, petrochemicals, fertilizers and industries based on agriculture where the entire Nigerian market is almost too small.

This is one reason why we should preserve Nigeria as one economic unit on terms acceptable to ordinary Nigerians in every part of the Federation.

Regarding the eradication of corruption from our public life, the Federal Military Government will take appropriate action on the Reports of the Inquiries recently held into the Nigerian Railway, Electricity Corporation of Nigeria and the Lagos City Council. Similar inquiries will be held into the other Federal Corporations. The Decree on the declaration of assets will be implemented and the investigations into the assets and liabilities of those who held public offices from 1960 to 1966 will be continued. Those involved will include former Ministers, Chairmen of Statutory Corporations, Board Members, Permanent Secretaries and other Senior Civil Servants, General Managers and the top Executives of the Public Corporations. The Government has been handling these investigations in a quiet way because it does not want to give the impression of witch-hunting. Those found guilty of ill-gotten gains will be appropriately dealt with. There will also be a special administrative tribunal to inquire into the allocation of Federal State lands in Lagos and elsewhere.

Coming now to the Constitutional issue, I reiterate my previous statements that it is not the intention of the Federal Military Government to impose a Constitution on the country. It is obvious to the Government, however, that the general sentiment among most Nigerians is that the country must be preserved as one entity.

I should emphasize that the idea of a temporary confederation is unworkable. In a confederation there will be no effective central authority. Each Region as a virtually sovereign state can contract out or refuse to join any common service. For example, the Mid-West may not like to contribute to the Nigerian railways, the East may not want to use electricity from Kainji Dam, the North may not want to use coal or refined petroleum products from the East and the West may prefer to pull out of the Nigerian Airways and so the process of disintegration will be complete in a very short time. Once we adopt the so-called temporary confederation because of the current difficulties it will be hard to come together again. This is not the future to which our children are entitled and we have no moral right to commit future generations of Nigerians to this disastrous course.

I am confident that Nigerians can agree on a Constitution which will preserve the integrity or the country and satisfy the aspirations of the vast majority of our people. It is important that all shades of opinion should be given full expression. I therefore propose to summon a fully representative Constituent Assembly to draw up a new Constitution which will reflect the genuine wishes of all Nigerians as distinct from regional blocs, tribal groups and vested political interests. The Federal Military Government will announce the detailed machinery for selecting delegates to the Constituent Assembly. The assembly will consist of at least one person from each of the existing administrative divisions in the country and the representatives of special interest such as Trade Union, Professional Associations, Chambers of Commerce and Industries, and Women Organizations.

To facilitate the work of the Constituent Assembly, I am appointing a drafting committee to prepare the outline of the draft Constitution to be submitted to the Constituent Assembly. The drafting instructions to the committee will be based on the decisions of the Supreme Military Council which will soon meet to consider the findings of the various Constitutional groups including the agreed recommendations of the Ad Hoc Committee submitted to me in their Progress Report of September 30.[2] If all delegates to the Ad Hoc Committee can meet within Nigeria and agree to carry on from where they left off in early October, their further conclusions would assist the drafting committee in its task.

The draft Constitution will reflect the generally expressed desire for a stable Federation. It is quite clear that our common need in Nigeria is that no one Region or tribal group should be in a position to dominate the others. The new Federal Constitution must therefore contain adequate safeguards to make such domination impossible. In the stable Federation, no Region should be large enough to be able to threaten secession or hold the rest of the Federation to ransom in times of national crisis. This brings me to the major question of the creation of new States.

I wish to make it clear to the nation that honestly I personally have no vested interest in the creation of any particular state. But there is no doubt that without a definite commitment on the states question, normalcy and freedom from fear of domination by one Region or the other cannot be achieved.

The principles for the creation of new States will be:

i. no one State should be in a position to dominate or control the Central Government;

ii. each State should form one compact geographical area;

iii. administrative convenience, the facts of the history, and the wishes of the people concerned must be taken into account;

iv. each State should be in a position to discharge effectively the functions allocated to Regional Governments;

v. it is also essential that the new States should be created simultaneously.

All these criteria have to be applied together. No one principle should be applied to the exclusion of the others. To give an illustration of what I have in mind: given the present size and distribution of the Nigerian population and resources, the country could be divided into not less than eight and not more than fourteen States. The exact number of States will be determined through the detailed application of these criteria and will be fully debated in the Constituent Assembly.

Meanwhile, I am still taking steps to associate some civilians with the Federal Executive Council in carrying out the programme I have just outlined. They will be persons known to believe strongly in the continued existence of Nigeria as an effective Federation and they are to help me in projecting the national image. They will not be persons who were actively involved in the partisan politics which divided us so bitterly. They will be men of undoubted integrity and of independent character. I shall select men who have no intention to seek elective political office on the completion of this programme and who will not compete with professional politicians for office in the next civilian government.

Dear countrymen, I have outlined a programme which I trust will further reduce tension and enable us to proceed with the preparation of a new Constitution in a calm atmosphere. As I have promised on several occasions,

I shall do everything in my power and use the resources of the Federal Government to guarantee the continued existence of Nigeria as one political and economic unit.

As part of our deliberate policy to reduce tension, I have preferred to ignore certain unfounded allegations and provocative statements against me and the Federal Military Government. My studied silence should not be taken as a mark of weakness. My belief is the less we talk and the more we act honestly in the interest of the whole nation, the better for everyone. It is easy enough for me to mobilize enough forces to deal with any dissident or disloyal group. But I have always preferred peaceful solutions to our current crisis. We have had enough bloodshed in this country. But if circumstances compel me to preserve the integrity of Nigeria by force, I shall do my duty to my country.

I am aware that some Nigerians and their foreign collaborators have been engaging in illegal arms trafficking. I need not spell out the grave consequences of such actions. I warn such misguided Nigerians to desist from these criminal acts.

I want to take this opportunity to appeal to the people of Nigeria to remain law abiding citizens and help us to maintain peace. My main concern is with the personal safety of you all and you must not allow yourselves to be misled by ill-motivated persons. I appeal to all soldiers, sailors and airmen to remember that this is a Military Government and any unlawful act on your part is a discredit to your Government. Your discipline and loyalty must not be shaken. My appreciation goes to all of you and members of the Nigeria Police for maintaining the necessary calm which is so essential for the restoration of trust and confidence so vital at this time. I appeal to all Nigerian leaders from all walks of life to come forward and help us in saving this country from falling apart. If we fail, we will deny future generations the opportunity to do better than we have done. If we fail, the whole of Africa and the black race will not forgive us. So, help us God.

With the genuine co-operation of you all, I am confident that we shall carry out this programme successfully. We shall give the country a workable Constitution and the basis for a return to normal political life and rapid economic progress.

Long live the Federal Republic of Nigeria.

Thank you and good night.

[1] *Federal Ministry of Information Press Release No. 1821/1966.*
[2] *See* DOC *58.*

76.
Crisis 1966: The View of Nigerian Intellectuals[1]

It is a well known fact that the individual's perception of his self-interest inevitably influences much of his actions. This is not to suggest that such self-interests are always rationally calculated, or even if they are, that actions based on such calculations turn out to achieve the results intended, the well known 'unintended consequences' theorem. What is true of individuals is also true of groups of individuals and other collectivities such as regional governments. In the present debate over the future of Nigeria, there is something to be gained if we try to examine the underlying self-interests of the different regional governments, to understand their motivations. By doing this, we may come to understand each other and ourselves better. This is not an unfamiliar exercise with psycho-analysts.

The North
Having for some five years been in a position to dictate to the federal government, the North now finds she has lost that advantage. And from feeling that she was large enough to stand by herself, she now finds that to survive, she needs the federal government to continue. The problem for her has been how to keep a federation in which the North will not lose altogether the initial advantage which she had. But the difficulty here is that the North is no longer what it was. The old-guard traditional oligarchy of the North seems to have lost control to a new breed of more radical young men who now want to 'clean up' the North. The September ending killings and the exodus of Easterners that followed, and the disorganisation which has resulted, now threaten the whole of Northern society, particularly, the threat of in-fighting, now imminent in places like Jos and southern Zaria. Should this start, it could easily spread throughout the North and the trouble would be the absence of a stabilising force. Though the radical elements of the North seem to be in the ascendant, they are as yet probably not in control of the machinery of government. The result is a power vacuum with no one seemingly in a position to take over all decisions.

The East
It would be foolhardy to attempt to understand the East's position without at the same time recognising, and sympathising with, the traumatic experience which thousands of Easterners have gone through, an experience which has fostered a sense of personal and group insecurity. Their attitude finds expression in reiterated statements such as 'we are no longer wanted in the federation'. But it is a short step from this to the position of saying 'we no longer want a federation' and from this to the attitude of 'if we don't want it, then you cannot have it since you cannot have it without us'. It would seem that the East is not unprepared to take this step and therefore not unwilling to hold the rest of the country to ransom. And no amount of argument or assurance can avail against such an attitude. But at the same time, the East seems still to want a country in which freedom of movement, freedom to trade wherever the individual wants, to own property without molestation, etc., is guaranteed and by an authority which it nevertheless refuses to concede. There may not be much point in expecting or asking the East to forget, but we can at least ask them to forgive. And we can ask them to think again on what their intentions and interests are.

The West
While one can appreciate the positions of the East and the North, this is not so easy with the West. Yorubas seem to be motivated by the belief that they

have always been 'cheated'; that they have been the victims of the misuse and abuse of power in the old republic; that their territory has been dismembered and point to Lagos, Ilorin, Kabba and Akoko-Edo. From this arises the attitude that whatever problem there is in the country is essentially one between the North and the East who should be left severely alone to settle their differences. In the meantime what best could the West do but expect to pick up the mantle of leadership and use the stalemate to benefit themselves. Hence the fad of taking cues from others, of largely re-acting to situations and refusing to argue any proposals based on principles, except where such principles derive from the myths to which they have themselves contributed.

The Mid-West
Caught in the struggle for leadership between the 'big brothers', the Mid-West cannot but argue the continuation of the federation as a condition of its own existence, in effect then, a form of enlightened self interest.

The burden of the foregoing is to point out the limited and often inconsistent perspectives from which much of the negotiations now taking place have been conducted. The main flaw in much of the position being taken is that the federal authority is still being thought of in terms adequate only to the old republic, one in which the central government was largely a ploy of regional governments and their politicians. What most people seem to have ignored is the simple fact that for the first time, we now have had a central government which is in a position to take decisions on its own initiative. But instead of working to reinforce this new departure from past experience, the unfortunate fact is that the positions being taken only serve to plunge us back into what no one really wants: a central authority manipulated by strings tied to the regions.

¹ Nigerian Opinion, *November 1966, pp. 122–3.*

77.
Agenda for the Aburi Meeting¹

1. Opening address by the Head of State of Host Country.
2. Response by Head of the Federal Republic of Nigeria and Supreme Commander of the Nigerian Armed Forces.
3. Review of the Current Situation in Nigeria, with particular reference to:
a. Organization of the Nigerian Army;
b. Implementation of the agreement reached on 9th August, 1966, in regard to the disposition of Army personnel.
4. Resumption of talks by the *Ad Hoc* Constitutional Committee. Acceptance of unanimous recommendations in September, 1966.
5. Problems of displaced persons, with particular reference to:
a. Rehabilitation;
b. Employment;
c. Property.

6. Arrangements for future meetings of the Supreme Military Council and the Federal Executive Council.

7. Communiqué.

¹ *From the official record. The printing of the Lagos record has certain obscurities. This text is taken from the Enugu version.*

78.
Final Aburi Communiqué[1]

The Supreme Military Council of Nigeria resumed its meeting in Ghana on the 5th of January and continued and concluded discussion of the remaining subjects on the Agenda. The Council reached agreement on all the items.

On the powers and functions of the Federal Military Government the Council reaffirmed its belief in the workability of the existing institutions subject to necessary safeguards.

Other matters on which agreements were reached included the following:

i. Re-organization, administration and control of the Army.

ii. Appointments and promotions to the senior ranks in the Armed Forces, the Police, Diplomatic and Consular Services as well as appointments to super-scale posts in the Federal Civil Service and the equivalent posts in the Federal Statutory Corporations.

On the question of displaced persons the Supreme Military Council agreed to set up a committee to look into the problems of rehabilitation and recovery of property. In this connection the Military Governor of the East assured the Council that the order that non-Easterners should leave the Eastern Region would be reviewed with a view to its being lifted as soon as practicable. Agreement was also reached that the staff and employees of Governments and Statutory Corporations who have had to leave their posts as a result of recent disturbances in the country should continue to be paid their full salaries up to the end of 31st March, 1967, provided they have not found alternative employment.

The Council agreed that the Ad Hoc Committee on the constitutional future of the country should be resumed as soon as practicable and that the unanimous recommendations of the committee in September 1966, will be considered by the Supreme Military Council at a later meeting.

The Council unanimously agreed that future meetings of the Council should be held in Nigeria at a venue to be announced later.

The entire members of the Supreme Military Council express profound regret for the bloodshed which has engulfed the country in the past year and avow to do all in their power to ensure there is no recurrence of the unhappy situation.

The Members of the Supreme Military Council place on record their profound appreciation and gratitude for the constructive initiative and assistance rendered by the Chairman of the National Liberation Council, the Government and people of Ghana.

[1] *Signed at Aburi on 5 January 1967. From the official record.*

79.

Statement by the Supreme Council on the Reorganization of the Army, and the Approval of Senior Appointments, and its Declaration on the Use of Force[1]

I

The Supreme Military Council now meeting in Ghana has agreed on the following reorganization of the Army:

a. The Army is to be governed by the Supreme Military Council the Chairman of which will be known as Commander-in-Chief and Head of the Federal Military Government.

b. There will be a Military Headquarters on which the Regions will be equally represented and which will be headed by a Chief of Staff.

c. In each Region there shall be an Area Command under the charge of an Area Commander and corresponding with the existing Regions.

d. All matters of policy including appointments and promotions of persons in executive posts in the Armed Forces and Police shall be dealt with by the Supreme Military Council.

e. During the period of the Military Government, Military Governors will have control over their Area Commands in matters of internal security.

2. The following appointments must be approved by the Supreme Military Council:

a. Diplomatic and Consular posts.

b. Senior posts in the Armed Forces and the Police.

c. Super-scale Federal Civil Service and Federal Corporation posts.

3. Any decision affecting the whole country must be determined by the Supreme Military Council. Where a meeting is not possible such a matter must be referred to Military Governors for comment and concurrence.

II

We the members of the Supreme Military Council of Nigeria meeting at Accra on 4th day of January, 1967, hereby solemnly and unequivocably:

i. DECLARE that we renounce the use of force as a means of settling the present crisis in Nigeria, and hold ourselves in honour bound by this declaration.

ii. REAFFIRM our faith in discussions and negotiation as the only peaceful way of resolving the Nigerian crisis.

iii. AGREE to exchange information on the quantity of arms and ammunition in each unit of the Army in each Region, and also on the quantity of new arms and ammunition in stock. [Signatures of the nine leaders].

[1] *Issued as annexes to the Official Minutes of the Aburi Conference (DOC 80). The declaration on the use of force was signed at Aburi on 4 January 1967.*

80.
Official Record of the Minutes of the Meeting of Nigeria's Military Leaders held at Aburi[1]

The Supreme Military Council held its meeting in Ghana on the 4th-5th January. Those present were:

Lt-Col. Yakubu Gowon
Colonel Robert Adebayo
Lt.-Col. Odumegwu Ojukwu
Lt.-Col. David Ejoor
Lt.-Col. Hassan Katsina
Commodore J. E. A. Wey
Major Mobolaji Johnson
Alhaji Kam Selem
Mr T. Omo-Bare

SECRETARIES

Mr S. I. A. Akenzua	Permanent Under-Secretary, Federal Cabinet Office
Mr P. T. Odumosu	Secretary to the Military Government, West
Mr N. U. Akpan	Secretary to the Military Government, East
Mr D. P. Lawani	Under-Secretary, Military Governor's Office, Mid-West
Alhaji Ali Akilu	Secretary to the Military Government, North

Opening
The Chairman of the Ghana National Liberation Council, Lt.-General J. A. Ankrah, declaring the meeting open, welcomed the visitors to Ghana and expressed delight that Ghana had been agreed upon by the Nigerian Military leaders as the venue for this crucial meeting. He considered the whole matter to be the domestic affair of Nigeria, and as such, he refrained from dwelling on any specific points. The General, however, expressed the belief that the Nigerian problems were not such that cannot be easily resolved through patience, understanding and mutual respect. Throughout history, he said, there has been no failure of military statesmen and the eyes of the whole world were on the Nigerian Army. He advised that soldiers are purely statesmen and not politicians and the Nigerian Military leaders owe it as a responsibility to the 56 million people of Nigeria to successfully carry through their task of nation-building. Concluding, the General urged the Nigerian leaders to bury their differences, forget the past and discuss their matter frankly but patiently.
2. Lt.-Col. Gowon invited the Nigerian leaders to say a joint thank you to their host, and all said thank you in unison in response to Lt.-General Ankrah's address.
3. At this point the General vacated the Conference table.

Importation of Arms and resolution renouncing the use of Force
4. Lt.-Col. Ojukwu spoke next. He said that the Agenda was acceptable to

him subject to the comments he had made on some of the items. Lt.-Col. Ojukwu said that no useful purpose would be served by using the meeting as a cover for arms build-up and accused the Federal Military Government of having engaged in large scale arms deals by sending Major Apolo to negotiate for arms abroad. He alleged that the Federal Military Government recently paid £1 million for some arms bought from Italy and now stored up in Kaduna. Lt.-Col. Ojukwu was reminded by the Military Governor, North and other members that the East was indulging in an arms build-up and that the plane carrying arms which recently crashed on the Cameroons border was destined for Enugu. Lt.-Col. Ojukwu denied both allegations. Concluding his remarks on arms build-up, Lt.-Col. Ojukwu proposed that if the meeting was to make any progress, all the members must at the outset adopt a resolution to renounce the use of force in the settlement of Nigerian dispute.

5. Lt.-Col. Gowon explained that as a former Chief of Staff, Army, he was aware of the deficiency in the country's arms and ammunition which needed replacement. Since the Defence Industries Corporation could not produce these, the only choice was to order from overseas and order was accordingly placed to the tune of £$\frac{3}{4}$ million. He said to the best of his knowledge, the actual amount that had been paid out was only £80,000 for which he signed a cheque on behalf of the General Officer Commanding. The £80 million about which so much noise has been made was nothing but a typographical error in the Customs in recording the payment of £80,000. As to why these arms were sent up to the North, Lt.-Col. Gowon referred to lack of storage facilities in Lagos and reminded his Military Colleagues of the number of times arms and ammunition had been dumped in the sea. This was why, he said, it became necessary to use the better storage facilities in Kaduna. The arms and ammunition had not been distributed because they arrived only two weeks previously and have not yet been taken on charge. After exhaustive discussion to which all members contributed and during which Lt.-Col. Ejoor pointed out that it would be necessary to determine what arms and ammunition had arrived and what each unit of the Army had before any further distribution would take place, the Supreme Military Council unanimously adopted a Declaration proposed by Lt.-Col. Ojukwu, that all members:

a. renounce the use of force as a means of settling the Nigerian crisis;

b. reaffirm their faith in discussions and negotiation as the only peaceful way of resolving the Nigerian crisis; and

c. agree to exchange information on the quantity of arms and ammunition available in each unit of the Army in each Region and in the unallocated stores, and to share out such arms equitably to the various Commands;

d. agree that there should be no more importation of arms and ammunition until normalcy was restored.

The full text of the Declaration was signed by all members.

6. The Supreme Military Council, having acknowledged the fact that the series of disturbances since 15th, January 1966, have caused disunity in the Army resulting in lack of discipline and loss of public confidence, turned their attention to the question of how best the Army should be re-organised in order to restore that discipline and confidence. There was a lengthy discussion of the subject and when the arguments became involved members retired into secret session. On their return they announced that agreement had been

reached by them on the re-organisation, administration and control of the Army on the following lines:

a. Army to be governed by the Supreme Military Council under a chairman to be known as Commander-in-Chief of the Armed Forces and Head of the Federal Military Government.

b. Establishment of a Military Headquarters comprising equal representation from the Regions and headed by a Chief of Staff.

c. Creation of Area Commands corresponding to existing Regions and under the charge of Area Commanders.

d. Matters of policy, including appointments and promotion to top executive posts in the Armed Forces and the Police to be dealt with by the Supreme Military Council.

e. During the period of the Military Government, Military Governors will have control over Area Commands for internal security.

f. Creation of a Lagos Garrison including Ikeja Barracks.

7. In connection with the re-organisation of the Army, the Council discussed the distribution of Military personnel with particular reference to the present recruitment drive. The view was held that general recruitment throughout the country in the present situation would cause great imbalance in the distribution of soldiers. After a lengthy discussion of the subject, the Council agreed to set up a Military Committee, on which each Region will be represented, to prepare statistics which will show:

a. Present strength of Nigerian Army;

b. Deficiency in each sector of each unit;

c. The size appropriate for the country and each Area Command;

d. Additional requirement for the country and each Area Command.

The Committee is to meet and report to Council within two weeks from the date of receipt of instructions.

8. The Council agreed that pending completion of the exercise in paragraph 7 further recruitment of soldiers should cease.

9. In respect of item 3 (b) of the Agenda, implementation of the agreement reached on 9th August, 1966, it was agreed, after a lengthy discussion, that it was necessary for the agreement reached on 9th August by the delegates of the Regional Governments to be fully implemented.[2] In particular, it was accepted in principle that army personnel of Northern origin should return to the North from the West. It was therefore felt that a crash programme of recruitment and training, the details of which would be further examined after the Committee to look into the strength and distribution of army personnel had reported, would be necessary to constitute indigenous army personnel in the West to a majority there quickly.

Non-Recognition by the East of Lt.-Col. Gowon as Supreme Commander

10. The question of the non-recognition by the East of Lt.-Col. Gowon as Supreme Commander and Head of the Federal Military Government was also exhaustively discussed. Lt.-Col. Ojukwu based his objection on the fact, *inter alia*, that no one can properly assume the position of Supreme Commander until the whereabout of the former Supreme Commander, Major-General Aguiyi-Ironsi, was known. He therefore asked that the country be informed of the whereabout of the Major-General and added that in his view,

it was impossible, in the present circumstances, for any one person to assume any effective central command of the Nigerian Army. Lt.-Col. Ejoor enunciated four principles to guide the meeting in formulating an answer to the question of who should be Supreme Commander. These were the:

a. Problem of effective leadership;

b. Crisis of confidence in the Army;

c. Disruption in the present chain of Command;

d. Inability of any soldier to serve effectively in any unit anywhere in the country.

Lt.-Col. Gowon replied that he was quite prepared to make an announcement on the matter and regretted that a formal announcement had been delayed for so long but the delay was originally intended to allow time for tempers to cool down. He reminded his colleagues that they already had the information in confidence. After further discussion and following the insistence by Lt.-Col. Ojukwu that Lt.-Col. Gowon should inform members of what happened to the former Supreme Commander, members retired into secret session and subsequently returned to continue with the meeting after having reached an agreement among themselves.

11. At this point, the meeting adjourned until Thursday 5th January.

The Power of the Federal Military Government vis-à-vis the Regional Governments

12. When the meeting resumed on the 5th January, it proceeded to consider the form of Government best suited to Nigeria in view of what the country has experienced in the past year (1966). Members agreed that the legislative and executive authority of the Federal Military Government should remain in the Supreme Military Council to which any decision affecting the whole country shall be referred for determination provided that where it is not possible for a meeting to be held the matter requiring determination must be referred to Military Governors for their comment and concurrence. Specifically, the Council agreed that appointments to senior ranks in the Police, Diplomatic and Consular Services as well as appointments to super-scale posts in the Federal Civil Service and the equivalent posts in Statutory Corporations must be approved by the Supreme Military Council. The Regional members felt that all the Decrees or provisions of Decrees passed since 15th January, 1966, and which detracted from the previous powers and positions of Regional Governments should be repealed if mutual confidence is to be restored. After this issue had been discussed at some length the Council took the following decisions:

The Council decided that:

   i. on the reorganisation of the Army:

     a. Army to be governed by the Supreme Military Council under a chairman to be known as Commander-in-Chief of the Armed Forces and Head of the Federal Military Government.

     b. Establishment of a Military Headquarters comprising equal representation from the Regions and headed by a Chief of Staff.

     c. Creation of Area Commands corresponding to existing Regions and under the charge of Area Commanders.

d. Matters of policy, including appointments and promotion to top executive posts in the Armed Forces and the Police to be dealt with by the Supreme Military Council.

e. During the period of the Military Government, Military Governors will have control over Area Commands for internal security.

f. Creation of a Lagos Garrison including Ikeja Barracks.

ii. on appointment to certain posts:

The following appointments must be approved by Supreme Military Council:

a. Diplomatic and Consular posts.

b. Senior posts in the Armed Forces and the Police.

c. Super-scale Federal Civil Service and Federal Corporation posts.

iii. on the functioning of the Supreme Military Council: Any decision affecting the whole country must be determined by the Supreme Military Council. Where a meeting is not possible such a matter must be referred to Military Governors for comment and concurrence.

iv. that all the Law Officers of the Federation should meet in Benin on the 14th January and list out all the Decrees and provisions of Decrees concerned so that they may be repealed not later than 21st January if possible;

v. that for at least the next six months, there should be purely a Military Government, having nothing to do whatever with politicians.

Soldiers involved in Disturbances on 15th January, 1966 and thereafter

13. Members expressed views about the future of those who have been detained in connection with all the disturbances since 15th January, 1966, and agreed that the fate of soldiers in detention should be determined not later than end of January 1967.

Ad Hoc Constitutional Conference

14. The Council next considered the question of the resumption of the Ad Hoc Constitutional Committee and the acceptance of that Committee's recommendations of September 1966. After some exchange of views, it was agreed that the Ad Hoc Committee should resume sitting as soon as practicable to begin from where they left off, and that the question of accepting the unanimous recommendations of September 1966 be considered at a later meeting of the Supreme Military Council.

The Problems of Displaced Persons

15. The Council considered exhaustively the problems of displaced persons, with particular reference to their rehabilitation, employment and property. The view was expressed and generally accepted that the Federal Government ought to take the lead in establishing a National Body which will be responsible for raising and making appeal for funds. Lt.-Col. Ojukwu made the point, which was accepted by Lt.-Col. Katsina, that in the present situation, the intermingling of Easterners and Northerners was not feasible. After each Military Governor had discussed these problems as they affected his area, the Council agreed:

Y

a. On rehabilitation, that Finance Permanent Secretaries should resume their meeting within two weeks and submit recommendations and that each Region should send three representatives to the meeting.

b. On employment and recovery of property, that civil servants and Corporation staff (including daily paid employees) who have not been absorbed should continue to be paid their full salaries until 31st March, 1967 provided they have not got alternative employment, and that the Military governors of the East, West and Mid-West should send representatives (Police Commissioners) to meet and discuss the problem of recovery of property left behind by displaced persons. Lt.-Col. Ejoor disclosed that the employment situation in his Region was so acute that he had no alternative but to ask non-Mid-Westerners working in the private sector in his Region to quit and make room for Mid-Westerners repatriated from elsewhere. Lt.-Col. Ojukwu stated that he fully appreciated the problem faced by both the Military Governor, West, and the Military Governor, Mid-West, in this matter and that if in the last resort, either of them had to send the Easterners concerned back to the East, he would understand, much as the action would further complicate the resettlement problem in the East. He assured the Council that his order that non-Easterners should leave the Eastern Region would be kept under constant review with a view to its being lifted as soon as practicable.

16. On the question of future meetings of the Supreme Military Council, members agreed that future meetings will be held in Nigeria at a venue to be mutually agreed.

17. On the question of Government information media, the Council agreed that all Government information media should be restrained from making inflammatory statements and causing embarrassment to various Governments in the Federation.

18. There were other matters not on the Agenda which were also considered among which were the form of Government for Nigeria (reported in paragraph 12 above) and the disruption of the country's economy by the lack of movement of rail and road transport which the Regional Governors agreed to look into.

19. The meeting began and ended in a most cordial atmosphere and members unanimously issued a second and final Communiqué.[3]

20. In his closing remarks the Chairman of the Ghana National Liberation Council expressed his pleasure at the successful outcome of the meeting and commended the decisions taken to the Nigerian leaders for their implementation. Lt.-Col. Gowon on behalf of his colleagues thanked the Ghanaian leader for the excellent part he had played in helping to resolve the issues. The successful outcome of the meeting was then toasted with champagne and the Nigerians took leave of the Ghanaians.

21. The proceedings of the meeting were reported verbatim for each Regional Government and the Federal Government by their respective official reporters and tape-recorded versions were distributed to each Government.

---

[1] *From the official record. The Federal Government qualified its published text, which was published after the East's version, with the caveat that 'these official minutes are yet to be adopted by the Supreme Military Council at its next meeting.' Cf.* DOC 81.

[2] *See* DOC 45.   [3] *See* DOC 78.

81.
Attitudes at Aburi[1]

a. How the military looks at the politicians

General Ankrah (Ghana): I will not like to dwell rigidly on any point whatsoever because I feel this is a domestic affair of Nigeria and, as I have always said, it is not difficult for military people to understand each other. It is a saying that if Generals were to meet and discuss frontiers, wars or even go into the details to forestall war, there will never be any differences or discrepancies but unity and understanding. There will be no war because the two old boys will meet at the frontier and tell each other—'Old boy, we are not going to commit our boys to die, come on, let us keep the politicians out' —and that is the end. I am quite confident that having met here to-day, you will continue and achieve what you are here for.

What I want to stress is this, that through the annals of history we have not seen failures with military statesmen and when military personnel do take over the reins of Government they have proved their worth and, I am sure and confident that the Military regimes that have been saddled with the onerous responsibility of rebuilding and reconstructing the various countries in Africa will not let us down.

You are aware that in Nigeria now the whole world is looking up to you as military men and if there is any failure to reunify or even bring perfect understanding to Nigeria as a whole, you will find that the blame will rest with us all through the centuries. There is no gainsaying this whatsoever.

Whatever the situation we are soldiers and soldiers are always statesmen not politicians. They deal with a little bit of politics and diplomacy when the time comes but they are statesmen. The people first and they themselves second but if you think like the politicians do that they want fame or they want to be heard of and neglect your people then, of course, I am quite sure that we as soldiers will live to regret, even our future generations will live to regret. They will be blaming us whenever our names are called or mentioned. . . .

Major Johnson: Gentlemen, if I can start talking on this one, please do not think I am taking undue advantage. Quite honestly I think we all know what brought this country to where we are to-day and while talking yesterday Emeka [first name of Lt.-Col. Ojukwu] touched on a point of how, due to the situation, the politicians got what they have been waiting for to come in. While I very much welcome this Item 4 and while I know that definitely we are not going to be in Government forever, I will like to say that, please for the next six months let us leave everything that will bring the politicians back into the limelight out of the question. Let us go on on all these things we have been discussing since yesterday because this is on the basis at which we can get our country back on its feet. Once we can get the papers on these things out and we see them working then we can call the Ad Hoc Constitutional Committee to come and discuss but for now they are just going to confuse the issues more if you bring them out to come and talk anything again. I will say let the Military Government continue for now and after working for six months and we see how far we can go before we start thinking of calling these people back.

Commodore Wey: I 100% support what you have said. Candidly if there had ever been a time in my life when I thought somebody had hurt me sufficiently for me to wish to kill him it was when one of these fellows opened his mouth too wide. I think we should let them stay where they are for the moment. It was simply because we could not get together and handle our affairs. Now that we have established the basis under which we can work please let us leave them where they are and let us try and see how far we can work.

Lt.-Col. Ojukwu: On this statement, Gentlemen, a lot depends on what the Ad Hoc Constitutional Committee is. I agree indeed that regarding other Regions it was indeed a platform for politicians, in the East it was not. I did not send politicians to it but be it as it may, if we say we are going to continue then we must obviously get quite satisfied the terms of running this thing properly. We have got to be able to meet and I said it outside and I repeat it here, I, as the Military Governor of the East cannot meet anywhere in Nigeria where there are Northern troops.

b. *The events of 29 July and the issue of Supreme Commander: the Colonels speak*

Major Johnson: Sir, before we go on if I may say something. I am happy we have got to this point again. I had wanted to take this Conference back all along because as my people say—'If you still have lice in your head, there will still be blood on your fingers:' May I ask one question, Gentlemen, is there a Central Government in Nigeria to-day?

Lt.-Col. Ojukwu: That question is such a simple one and anyone who has been listening to what I have been saying all the time would know that I do not see a Central Government in Nigeria to-day.

Major Johnson: Thank you, Gentlemen. I think this is the crux of the whole thing and I think if I can take you back this can be a personality clash or something.

I am saying here to-day that this is the backbone of our problem. As far as the Governor of the East is concerned there is no central government in Nigeria. You say, Supreme Commander, but as far as he is concerned there is no Supreme Commander. I think this is where we must start from, Gentlemen. Why is he not accepting that there is a Supreme Commander and we accept there is a Supreme Commander.

This brings me to this Conference that was held in August. As was rightly said, this Committee was a Steering Committee. We are all Military personnel here and we know one thing. We have all been pointing accusing fingers at politicians that they used to take military decisions without military men.

The main problem now is that as far as the East is concerned, there is no Central Government. Why? This is what we must find out. I mentioned something about personality clash. I remember that there was a long letter written by the Governor of the East sometime ago referring to the hierarchy in the Army, the policy on seniority and things like that. He said among other things in the letter that if even Lt.-Col. Yakubu Gowon is Supreme Commander is he not right to ask whether it is for a period or something.

For all the East knows the former Supreme Commander is only missing and until such a time that they know his whereabouts they do not know any other Supreme Commander. These are the points that have been brought out by the East.

Gentlemen, we said this morning that we have come with open minds and we must hit the nail at the head. The East should tell us now what are their views, what are the conditions they want to demand before they can say that there is a Central Government in Nigeria. For all we know now, nobody has seceded, the East is still part of Nigeria, the West, the North and we know Nigeria as a Federation.

Lt.-Col. Ejoor: The Mid-West please.

Major Johnson: And Lagos. Nigeria is still a Federation and in a Federation there is a Central Government. Where is this Central Government and who is Head of this Central Government? Gentlemen, unless we clear this one, all what we are discussing will not be good enough. What are the conditions the East demand before they can recognise what the rest of us recognise as the Central Government?

Lt.-Col. Ojukwu: I agree with you in essence on what you have just said, Bolaji [First name of Major Johnson], but the last bit is badly put. If you will forgive me it is not—'What conditions do they demand before. . . .'

If the problem is that we are trying to see how to solve the problem of Government in the centre then I will come in. I will seek your indulgence as I go a little bit back into what a number of people would perhaps wish to call history.

At a certain stage, we all accepted General Ironsi as the Supreme Commander and Head of the National Military Government. During his regime we met or rather whilst he was about we met as often as it was practicable, and sat and jointly discussed and took decisions. When the decisions were good we all shared the kudos, when those decisions were bad it is only natural that we should all share the blame.

On the 29th of July, whilst he was visiting the Governor of the West, he was said to be besieged in that residence in Ibadan and later kidnapped, further abducted. Subsequent to that, it appeared in his absence the normal thing was whoever is the next senior person to manage the affairs of this country until such a time as he reappeared; or it was necessary he was deposed or if he had suffered certain accident, until such a time as the circumstances were made known. Which ever is the case, the question of the headship of the Government and the Supreme Commander of the Armed Forces would normally be subjected to a discussion and agreement unless, of course, one party felt he was strong enough to push everybody aside and get to the seat.

When this affair of the 29th July occurred, I remember for certain, the first 24 hours nobody thought it necessary to contact the East from Lagos. I made the contact later and I know the advice I gave Brigadier Ogundipe at that time. I said to him, 'Sir, the situation is so confused that I feel that somebody must take control immediately. Also, I would suggest that you go on to the air and tell the country what has happened and that you were taking control of the situation.' Then I was told about concern for the whole country. I knew that if this thing resolved itself into factions we would get ourselves into so much trouble that we would never or we would find it difficult to get out. I maintained and still do that the answer would have been for the responsible officers of the Army to get together thereby trying to get the Army together to solve the problem that we had on our hands. I said to him—'As soon as you have made your speech I guarantee you within 30 minutes, I needed time to write my own, in 30 minutes I would come on to the air in the East and say that I, the entire Army in the East and the entire people in the East wholeheartedly support you.' Forgive me, David [first name of Lt.-Col. Ejoor], that I have never said this to you, but I told him too that I was sure that within fifteen minutes you would say the same in the interest of the country as a whole. He told me that he thought it was a good idea but it did not seem likely that it would be accepted by the faction.

Very soon after, I had occasion to talk to you, Jack [nickname of Lt.-Col. Gowon], I did mention amongst other things, two things. The first one was this question of solving the problem and I thought the Army together should solve it. I said also that any break at this time from our normal line would write in something into the Nigerian Army which is bigger than all of us and that thing is indiscipline. How can you ride above people's heads and sit in Lagos purely because you are at the Head of a group who have their fingers poised on the trigger? If you do it you remain forever a living example of that indiscipline which we want to get rid of because tomorrow a Corporal will think because he has his finger on the trigger he could just take over the company from the Major Commanding the company and so on. I knew then that we were heading for something terrible. Despite that and by force of circumstance as we did talk on the telephone, I think twice, you brought up the question of supreme command and I made quite plain my objections, but despite those objections you announced yourself as the Supreme Commander. Now, Supreme Commander by virtue of the fact that you head or that you are acceptable to people who had mutinied against their Commander, kidnapped him and taken him away? By virtue of the support of Officers and men who had in the dead of night murdered their brother Officers, by virtue of the fact that you stood at the head of a group who had turned their brother Officers from the Eastern Region out of the barracks which they shared? Our people came home, there are other circumstances which even make the return more tragic. Immediately after I had opportunity to speak to you again, I said on that occasion that there had been too much killing in Nigeria and it was my sincere hope that we can stop these killings. I said then, and have continued to say that in the interest of peace I would co-operate with you to stop the fighting, to stop the killing but I would not recognise.

I would not recognise because as I said we have a Supreme Commander who is missing. I would not recognise and to underline the validity of that claim of mine you appointed another Officer, be he senior to you, Acting Governor in the West, presumably acting for the Governor who was then abducted and that I saw no reason why your position would not then be acting. From there I think we started parting our ways because it was clear that the hold on Lagos was by force of conquest. Now, these things do happen in the world, we are all military Officers. If an Officer is dead—Oh! he was a fine soldier—we drop the national flag on him, we give him due honours and that is all. The next person steps in. So, the actual fact in itself is a small thing with military men but hierachy, order is very important, discipline are *sine qua non* for any organisation which prides itself for being called an Army. So, the mutiny had occurred, the mutineer seemed in control of the North, the West, Lagos. By international standards when that does happen then a *de facto* situation is created immediately where whoever is in a position get a *de facto* recognition of himself in a position over the area he controls. In this situation, Nigeria resolved itself into three areas. The Lagos, West and North group, the Mid-West, the East. What should have been done is for us to get round to discuss the future, how to carry on in the absence of our Supreme Commander.

We could not get together because of the situation so we sent our accredited representatives, delegates of Governments and personal representatives of Governors to Lagos to try and resolve certain issues on bringing normalcy to the country. They met and unanimously agreed to certain points.

Bolaji, I think in fact from this, if nothing else you do know what I consider went wrong. Perhaps at this juncture I might stop for others to contribute otherwise I would go on and tell you what I consider to be my solution to the problem even now, irrespective of the amount of water that had gone under the bridge. I think there is still a solution provided we are honest with ourselves and we are really very serious about solving this problem. I agree with you it is vital, it is crucial, without it I do not think we can really go anywhere.

I leave it for the time being.

Col. Adebayo: I think Emeka has narrated what happened on the 29th July and thereafter. We have all agreed and I am sure you still agree that what we are looking for now is a solution for the future. I do not want us to go into the past anymore, we want a solution for the future. I will suggest with the permission of the other members here that we ask Emeka to give us his solution. Thereafter there might be some others too who would have their own solutions, then we can make a compromise from the solutions we get.

Lt.-Col. Hassan: Gentlemen, General Ankrah told us not to go back into the past, if we are to go back into the past we will sit here for two months talking. Let us forget the past and I agree with Robert [first name of Col. Adebayo] that we ask the East to tell us their solution. If their solution is quite acceptable then we adopt it, amend or whatever we think is good for the country for peace. We are not going to say ourselves what efforts we have put in individually; let us find peace for Nigeria. This is the major issue, unless this is done whatever we are going to discuss is not going to work out well.

Lt.-Col. Ejoor: I believe that before we start suggesting solutions we must examine certain principles *vis à vis* the Governors. To me, we should not go too far into history but there is one valid point which must be considered and that is the coups we have had so far. The January 15 one was a failure and the Army came in to correct it, the one of the 29th I personally believe was a mutiny to start with but it has now turned out to be a coup. If it is a coup we have to ask ourselves—is it a successful coup or is it a partial one? I believe it is a partial one, it is not a fully successful one. This is the main point which has brought us here, trying to negotiate as opposed to receiving orders from the Commander. I think we must bear this in mind in reaching a decision or a Resolution affecting the re-organisation of the Army. To-day, the Army is faced with four main problems.

Firstly, the problem of leadership;

Secondly, the crisis of confidence amongst Officers and amongst the soldiers;

Thirdly, the chain of command is badly disrupted; and

Fourthly, we cannot now have any Nigerian from anywhere serving in the same unit as an effective unit of the Army.

These are bare facts and whatever solution we evolve must go to solve these main problems.

I leave these basic principles and what solutions offered should be considered alongside these problems.

Lt.-Col. Hassan: David spoke on re-organisation but the current topic is on Bolaji's point which Emeka narrated. I think this is the major point.

Lt.-Col. Ejoor: When you consider leadership you have to tell us what happened to the former leader.

Commodore Wey: Gentlemen, I think I have been properly placed in this issue from the 15th of January up till now. Unfortunately, I do not put them down because I think I can carry quite a bit in my head. The whole issue is unfortunate, it has happened and it has happened. The truth now is that we want to repair, we do not intend to point accusing fingers at anybody.

When the trouble of the 29th July started I was present, you came and joined us, therefore, I can tell any other person better. I was there when you phoned Brigadier Ogundipe and I knew what you said. At one stage, it was even said that I carried him in my ship and took him out to sea.

I must say one thing that it is impossible for any man to expect to command any unit which he has not got control over. Bolaji would bear witness, he was there, he started it. He was the one who went out first and came back to say that a Private refused to take orders from him; it all happened in the Police Headquarters.

The Inspector-General complained, I went into it and I said if they cannot take orders from an Army Officer like themselves they will not take from a Naval Officer. I retired and called Brigadier Ogundipe. He went out and if an ordinary Sergeant can tell a Brigadier—'I do not take orders from you, until my Captain comes,' I think this was the limit and this is the truth about it. Therefore, it would have been very unfair to Ogundipe or any other person for that matter to take command and there is no point accepting to command a unit over which you have no control.

It was after that negotiations started, I do not know what conversation went on between Ogundipe and Jack. On the long run I was consulted and what I have just said now was exactly my advice. Bob was with me, I went out and we did not finish until two o'clock in the morning. Jack then came into the issue, how he got there I have got the story; he himself has never told me. I have been doing private investigations myself. I knew how he got into Ikeja and how it came about.

I want to repeat that if we did not have the opportunity of having Jack to accept, God knows we would have been all finished. If you remember, you dragged me out, things changed. I do not think people can appreciate the difficulty we were in, therefore, if anybody accepted to lead them candidly, I doff my hat for him, I accept it purely from the point of respect. If 55 million people can be saved let us forget everything about position and for God's sake because of our 55 million people let us forget our personal pride. Whether it was a coup or a mutiny let us forget it. If this man comes out and everybody accepts him, please let us accept him.

One thing I would like to repeat, I am a sailor and I want to remain a sailor. I do not see why you soldiers should not remain soldiers. We were not trained to be politicians, let us run the Government, draw up a Constitution, hand-over to the politicians and we get back into our uniforms.

Whatever people may say, I think I will take this advantage to tell you here that when all of you were appointed Governors I was one of those who sat and appointed you Governors but right does not come into this at all; please let us forget personal feelings. I know my rank but if it is the wish of the 55 million people, please let us put our hearts into our pockets and forget our personal pride.

Personally, I am 100 per cent in support that we should mention the where-abouts of Ironsi, even I have advised on this. When that has been done, he is a Head of State and he should be given the proper honour; thereafter, who-so-ever is in the Chair now let us help him to run the country peacefully, no more bloodshed, we have shed enough. We cannot create why should we destroy. If we can help to save please let us do so but we must say the whereabouts of Ironsi. He is a Head of State and we should give him his due respect as a Head of State. It is a temporary issue, four, five years, maybe I would have retired by then.

Lt.-Col. Ojukwu: It is all well and good, Gentlemen, but I will be vehement on this. The point is that if a room is dirty you do not sweep the dirt under the carpet because whenever you raise the carpet the dirt will be there. It is not so simple as all that. Indeed, on the very principle that you have enunciated here, it is a question of command and control. I like to know who will stand up here and tell me that he commands and controls the Eastern Army or the Army in the East.

Lt.-Col. Hassan: You alone.

Commodore Wey: I can tell you also here now that you are doing it illegally because when we had the first Government no Governor was supposed to have the command of any Army.

Lt.-Col. Ojukwu: You have started on the basis of the principles of command and control. If you control a group who will take orders from you, according to you, everybody doffs his hat, well done. Right, that person you doff your hat to cannot command and control those under him and indeed those of the East. What do you do to that?

Commodore Wey: That is why we are here.

Lt.-Col. Hassan: This is why we are here to solve the problem. You command the East, if you want to come into Nigeria come into Nigeria and that is that.

Lt.-Col. Ojukwu: I am not out.

Lt.-Col. Hassan: This is the problem but if we are to go into the basis of coup and mutiny we will be here for months. I have seen an Army mutiny in Kano and if you see me trembling you will know what a mutiny is. You were the first I rang and for two good days I saw a real mutiny when a C.O. of Northern origin commanding soldiers of Northern origin had to run away.

Please, we have all come not to raise issues of the past, let us forget the past and come to the problem. Say what you want to say, let us go into the matter and discuss it.

Mr. T. Omo-Bare: Before we ask Emeka to give a solution will it not be advisable that somebody should say what happened to Ironsi?

Major Johnson: I support him fully.

Alhaji Kam Selem: If I may just say a few words. I am not a military man, but at that time it was just impossible for anybody else to take command of the country. As far as I know even the present Supreme Commander had to be persuaded to take over the Government. The Senior Officers you are talking about could not possibly accept the leadership of the country at that time. What could we do in a situation like that and the country was kept for 48 hours and nobody knew what was happening. As far as I know he has no ambition to remain in this present post. As soon as the situation in the country returns to normal and the problems are solved he will resign. I associate myself with all the Governors who said we should give the present Supreme Commander the respect he deserves. I was present through the whole trouble from January 15 and most of the things took place in my office.

As other speakers said, if the Governor of the East has a solution let us hear the solution.

Lt.-Col. Ejoor: Before we hear the solution, we want to know what happened to Ironsi and Fajuyi.

Lt.-Col. Gowon: If a public statement is required I am prepared to make one now. I have never been afraid to make a public statement anywhere. Left to me it would have been announced the day I knew about it and immediately I took the people that should know into confidence. I have explained this to my Colleagues in absolute sincerity and honesty. I had wanted to make the announcement before this meeting but unfortunately I was unable to do so. In any case, I want to make this announcement very shortly, and if you require it now I will say it. If you wish I can give the information in confidence and we can work on that.

Alhaji Kam Selem: I think the statement should be made in Nigeria so that the necessary honour can be given.

Lt.-Col. Hassan: This was what happened after the January coup. We agreed to announce the names of all the Senior Officers killed but there was fear all over. Let us combine the whole story ready, do the whole thing respectably and solve the problem.

Commodore Wey: Gentlemen, I would like to suggest this. I do not think there is anybody sitting on this table who would say that until to-day he did not know about the situation. In short, it is a public statement that is required and now we are going to have it in the scribe's book. We know the position and an announcement will be made as soon as we get back home.

Lt.-Col. Ojukwu: On this question of announcement and as you have all diagnosed, a lot depends on the public statement. The longer it is kept everything would remain uncertain, so that it is necessary to determine here how we are going to make this announcement. When?

Col. Adebayo: The best thing is to tell us here now what happened to

Ironsi then when we get home and we issue our communiqué, we can make the public statement.

Lt.-Col. Gowon: There is a Head of State and at the moment we are all assuming something serious or tragic has happened to him. He is a Head of State, we cannot just sit down here and discuss it. As I said, it is my responsibility to make the announcement in due course and I will make it in due course. I have already made up my mind that this would be done within the next week or two.

Lt.-Col. Ojukwu: I am not trying to be difficult on the issue but perhaps you will agree that this issue affects the area I am governing more than any other area. If it is in due course that the announcement is going to be made I would respectfully suggest that a statement would be in due course. Let us decide, if we want the Secretaries to move out, they can move out. If we want everybody out, let them go out for five minutes, the microphones can be taken away or we can move down there.

Gentlemen, if even the circumstances mean quite a lot, we can move away from this table, have a quick chat and come back to continue.

Commodore Wey: I support that.

c. *The problem of the army*

Lt.-Col. Gowon: I think all of us have at one time or the other discussed the situation in the country with regard to the reorganisation of the Army. With reference to 3 (*b*)—the implementation of the agreement reached on 9th August—this is on the disposition of Army personnel, that they should go back to their region of origin. This recommendation was made by the Ad Hoc Committee which consisted of Secretaries to the Military Governors, advisers and representatives of Regional Governors. They did not have any mandate to decide anything other than to come and express their feelings and make recommendations. Their recommendations, of course, would be considered by the Regional Governors. I think the recommendation says:

It was accordingly agreed that as far as possible the Army personnel should be posted to barracks in their Regions of origin with immediate effect as an interim measure. Having regard to its peculiar position, the question of maintenance of peace and security in Lagos should be left with the Supreme Commander in consultation with the Military Governors.

This question of movement of troops to their Region of origin arose from the fact that at the time there was so much misunderstanding, so much clash and killings between troops of Northern origin and troops of Eastern origin. I discussed this on the telephone with Emeka and I told him that—'Honestly, my consideration is to save the lives of these boys and the only way to do it is to remove the troops back to barracks in their Region of origin.' Emeka also told me that there were a number of threats to his life and any moment the troops in Enugu of Northern origin could mutiny and his life and the lives of the people of Eastern Nigeria would be in danger. I agreed with him and said the best thing we could do was to send them back to their Region of origin and some of the boys were already escaping from their units. We agreed to repatriate all troops of Northern origin from the East and those of Eastern origin particularly Ibo speaking from the other major units because the clashes were severest within major units.

As far as I was concerned I did not think the problem was in other units because the feeling at that time was that it was the Northern versus Eastern boys as a result of some things that had happened in the past which had been with us for a long time. If you remember, Emeka, you said something about the boys in the services returning and I agreed to this relunctantly but as far as the major units were concerned, I thought that was necessary. If we can mix up a little now this will certainly be a good basis for future coming together. If we separate totally we will sort of probably get further and further apart and each Region may have an independent Army. I think I have said enough as far as the review of the current situation with reference to the organisation of the Army is concerned and the implementation of the agreement of 9th August.

I think we can now discuss this point and later on come to some sort of agreement on the subject. . . .

Lt.-Col. Gowon: I think we can now go to the question of the organisation of the Nigerian Army. There was a Committee that was set up in August or September to think on the re-organisation of the Nigerian Army and I think they produced a paper which we sent to all Military Governors to comment upon and from that we will work out the question of re-organisation. This is something on a nation's security and I think we should be very careful about it. This is the truth about defence in the world to-day.

If I can say something about my idea for the re-organisation of the Army. I will be very brief. I think that the Nigerian Army to-day probably would not be able to remain exactly as it was before January 15 or July 29. There has been so much fear generated between ourselves as a result of events since the beginning of 1966 that there is something to be said towards the modification of the present stand. There are two extremes on this. One sort of saying that we remain exactly as we were before January 15 and the other which says, we go completely on Regional basis. I think those are the two extremes.

In the middle of course, you have got the possibility of having an Army predominantly people of that Region in their Region.

If I can express my own view or if you like you can call it my philosophy. As far as the Nigerian Army is concerned we cannot get everybody to where he was before January 15 or July 29. If we want to go to the other extreme of having Regional Armies we are trying to have the beginning of the arms race which is what we are trying to do away with. These Regional Armies will turn into private armies and before we know what we are doing we will start having internal troubles within the private armies and, of course, the whole country will be in flames. My thinking is that I do not feel that the basis of trust and confidence has been completely broken, it has been disrupted, it has been shaken but with little mixing and jingling we have got between people, I am quite convinced that it would form the basis of probably a more realistic mixing together in the future. If every Region wants to go its own way and think one day we will meet again, I feel that it may not work properly. . . .

On immediate re-organisation, one would like to see first of all proper command and control. Secondly, we all agreed that most of the soldiers in each Region should come from that Region.

The East and the Mid-West are lucky they have all their people there, unfortunately in the West, I have not got enough Westerners in the place and the people in the West are very afraid now because a lot of their own people were killed during January, July and August. I have tried to clear the fear from them but still they insist on having more Yorubas than they have at the moment. I know there are not enough Yorubas in the Army and those who are there are mostly tradesmen. I do not want to disrupt other units, but from what I said when we last met in Lagos, we can find an immediate solution to the Yoruba problem. That is, try and continue on the normal quota business which we started in Zaria and as a crash programme we should use Abeokuta area as a crash programme training centre for Westerners, for Mid-Westerners who cannot go to Zaria and possibly for the Easterners who cannot go to Zaria at the moment.

I still feel very strongly about this, this is the only way to clear the problem of the Yorubas and this is the only way we can get the confidence of the people of the West because they feel they are the only people now being helped because there are not enough Yorubas in the Army. The moment we can clear this side and we get command and control properly established, I do not think there will be any more problem. That is the immediate re-organisation which I would like now but the long term one is on the paper given to us by the Committee which was appointed. It is a very good paper and I am still commenting on it.

d. *The information media blamed*

Lt.-Col. Gowon: On the Government Information Media, I think all the Government Information Media in the country have done terribly bad. Emeka would say the *New Nigerian* has been very unkind to the East—

Lt.-Col. Ojukwu: And the *Post* which I pay for.

Lt.-Col. Gowon: Sometime I feel my problem is not with anyone but the *Outlook*.

Lt.-Col. Ojukwu: All the other information media have done a lot. When the Information Media in a country completely closed their eyes to what was happening, I think it is a dangerous thing.

Major Johnson: Let us agree it is the situation.

Lt.-Col. Ejoor: All of them have committed one crime or the other.

Lt.-Col. Hassan: The *Outlook* is the worst of them.

Lt.-Col. Ojukwu: The *Outlook* is not the worst, the *Post* which we all in fact pay for is the worst followed closely by the *New Nigerian*.

Mr. T. Omo-Bare: Let us make a general statement on all of them, no distinction.

Lt.-Col. Gowon: I think we agreed that all Government Information Media should desist from making inflammatory publications that would worsen the situation in the country.

e. The administrative arrangements for the future

Lt.-Col. Gowon: I personally think Decree 34[2] is worth looking into. I agree that the Supreme Military Council should sit on this, I think even in one of my addresses I said I would do away with any Decree that certainly tended to go towards too much centralisation and if you feel strongly about this, very good, they can be looked into. I think we will resurrect this one when we go back home and take decisions on them.

Lt.-Col. Ojukwu: We will not discuss the details but I am anxious that we find solutions. Whatever we do here we set a time for because there has been so much going on. What I am bringing up at this meeting are the things which generate the sort of suspicion we are trying very hard to avoid. If we can set a time limit I would be agreeable that all the parts of Decrees and Decrees that assume overcentralisation will be repealed.

Commodore Wey: Will be looked into, supposing it is a good one?

Lt.-Col. Ojukwu: Centralisation is a word that stinks in Nigeria to-day. For that 10,000 people have been killed. . . .

Lt.-Col. Hassan: We are not going back on the question of Government. I think we better make it clear what form of Government because up till now Emeka has been saying he does not recognise the Federal Government of Nigeria. This is the main point. Let us make it clear, is the East agreeing to the present Federal Government? If not what is the East thinking should be the form of Federal Government?

Lt.-Col. Ojukwu: I have said that a Government by a Council run perhaps the same as we have to-day with a Chairman with limited powers and we limit the powers here. . . .

Col. Adebayo: I do not think we should flog this thing too much. I think quite rightly a lot of powers of the Regions have been taken from them by centralising most of them, this was by some of the Decrees made by Lagos before 29th July. I think this must be looked into, the Decrees repealed and the powers must go back to the Regions.

Mr. T. Omo-Bare: Why not use the word, reviewed. We can hold a meeting when we get back home and review these Decrees.

Col. Adebayo: Can we then say that all our Solicitors-General get together and discuss these Decrees?

Lt.-Col. Ojukwu: Let us go through the points we know, we know we had a Federation before 15th January, the powers go back to the Regions and from there we try to put things right. All this talk about review, review and for the next six months they will not be reviewed.

Commodore Wey: As far as I am concerned this Government is known as the Military Government and all the Decrees produced so far were produced by the Army, therefore, let us not blame ourselves, let us look into the Decrees and find the ones we can send back. You were in the Council when we made these Decrees.

Alhaji Kam Selem: I think the point he made is good but it is not a matter for us to decide. We have to look into these things. Let the Solicitors-General meet, bring their lists and put up recommendations.

Lt.-Col. Ojukwu: The 'legal boys' have looked into it and said—repeal. If some 'legal boys' in some regions refuse to work it is not my fault. These are the things that cause a lot of trouble.

Col. Adebayo: Let us give them a date when they should meet. . . .

Mr. T. Omo-Bare: The Governors should go back and tell their men to meet at Benin on a certain date.

Lt.-Col. Hassan: The Ministry of Justice in Lagos—

Lt.-Col. Ojukwu: He will give the instruction in Lagos and I will give the instruction in Enugu.

Lt.-Col. Hassan: Lagos is the one to say let us meet at such and such a date.

Col. Adebayo: We are giving them instruction from this meeting.

Lt.-Col. Ojukwu: It is not Lagos. This is the crucial point about this Government.

Lt.-Col. Hassan: Let us take this question honestly, the East has not recognised the Federal Government, I think you better secede and let the three of us join together.

Lt.-Gen. Ankrah: There is no question of secession when you come here.

Col. Adebayo: What he is saying is that let this meeting decide on the date they are meeting somewhere and when we get back home we will tell our Solicitors-General that they are meeting at such and such a date.

Major Johnson: We can take a date here but I see what Lt.-Col. Hassan is getting at. Usually anything you do in a Federal Government, instructions come from the nerve centre and that nerve centre for all we know is Lagos. It is Lagos that will tell the Regions—You send your Solicitors-General to meet at Benin at so and so date. . . .

Personally, I feel we have a duty to the people, we should forget about ourselves at the moment. We must put behind our minds that we are all soldiers and we are all likely to go back to the Army after this. All we need now is to find a solution to the problem of Nigeria and that solution must be a sincere one. . . .

I know the Ghana system is working well; if we had started with that system from the beginning it would have been a different thing. There is nothing wrong with our own system, only the timing is bad, it will be bad if we change it now and I think we must make our own organisation workable. . . .

Lt.-Col. Ojukwu: I have to come in again. I do not agree with 90 per cent of what you have just said. I have used the analogy of sweeping dirt under the carpet, I again used the question of the ostrich posture burying our heads in the sand and hoping everything is all right. The fact remains that in the year 1966, Nigeria has gone through a turmoil and as Jack himself said, the basis for real unity in this—

Lt.-Col. Gowon: Unitary system of Government, please, not the question of unity.

Lt.-Col. Ojukwu: You made an important and realistic declaration in which you said—

Our difficulties in the past have been how to agree on the form which such an association should take and the task of my Government, meaning yours, is to provide facilities for the widest and fullest consultations at all levels on all vital matters of national interest before a decision is taken. In the past we have been too presumptuous and have acted on such presumptions. Too often we presume that we know what the people desired. In one or two cases hasty decisions were taken without sufficient consultation.

Based on that and knowing what has gone, therefore any government set up now in Nigeria that does not take into cognisance Regional loyalties is complete eye-wash. The Federal Government or support of Gowon or support of anybody, or of Emeka, whatever it is, is neither here nor there. What we want is that certain things were wrong, what are they, let us put them right. When I said Chairman, you can call him Chairman and still call him Governor. The fact still remains, it is really a nomenclature on functions and this is the crux of the matter. On the basis on which he assumed the position in Lagos, it is not possible for the East to accept blindly the leadership from Lagos. For this we have fought, we have struggled for in the past few years. For this the East will continue to struggle and fight if necessary, but thank God we have said there will be no force.

Lt.-Col. Gowon: You can thank God but your attitude is what will say.

Lt.-Col. Ojukwu: The point I am making is that this Council of ours whoever we decide should sit on the Chair would have limited functions and only act with our agreement. This was what caused the last downfall. We all know it, there were so many times that we quarrelled about this, argued about this, a number of things went down and not fully understood elsewhere. After all, we were all there when Decree No. 34 was made. The point was, amongst the Governors and senior officers, we knew, and we saw it and left it. The people did not, they felt it and re-acted, so we are told. If we are not going to fall into that trap again let us here agree that whoever sits on the chair can only act after consultation . . . and his action would, of course, be limited by our own agreement. . . .

The question of Government, Gentlemen. It would be entirely unrealistic not to take into full cognisance what has happened in the country. There was a mutiny in the Army on January 15, Army leaders from all parts of the country got together halted it and set up a Government. Until May there was a massacre which the Army leaders in their entirety regretted; based on the good faith generated by the realistic way in which the Army or the Armed Forces tackled the problem, it was possible for populations to continue to go back to their areas of domicile and continue living side by side with one another.

Come July, there was another mutiny in the Army as a result of which Jack assumed the title Supreme Commander. This title certainly is contrary to my own views as a member of the Supreme Military Council. . . . By September the molestations and the killings of Easterners had assumed such large proportions that Easterners everywhere outside the East lost complete faith in a Federal Government that could not offer the basic need to their citizen, that is to offer the citizen protection. The citizens from the East, therefore, sought that protection within their ethnic groups in the East. Contrary to sentiments and all advice, everybody thought the East was going to revenge.

I will say this here because it is no boast that but for my own personality in the crisis the East would have thrown itself completely into a revenge. I halted it because I foresaw that anybody that started an inter-tribal civil war would never be able to control it. I was absolutely certain that once we get into civil war it would take us at least 25 years to sort out.

Contrary to all expectation I sent our delegates from the East to the Ad Hoc Constitutional Conference. During this, contrary to what should have been indeed the Military Government's way of doing things, I think a genuine mistake, politicians found themselves for the first time in the fore-front of national discussions and, as usual instead of facing the problem be-fore them sought to gain personal triumphs and advantage. The East at the Conference was not doing very well, the molestations continued, the gory details I will spare you. . . .

In this case unfortunately, Gentlemen, Officers and men of Eastern Nigeria origin who had moved from other parts of the country know the names, the faces of individuals who perpetrated these atrocities. Mention a name, we know who killed him, mention somebody we know who at least hounded him out of his barracks. So, Gentlemen, for as long as that situation exists men from Eastern Nigeria would find it utterly impossible to stay in the same bar-racks, feed in the same mess, fight from the same trenches as men in the Army from Northern Nigeria, they would find this impossible because we know it.

My policy has been that of ensuring the prevention of further killing. If we do not take cognisance of all these and we put our men together and mix up we write in Gentlemen, vendetta into our Armed Forces and once it becomes vendetta it becomes extremely difficult for us to solve because they will stay by force in the same barracks but each Commanding Officer will never be sure when his day will come.

For these basic reasons, separation of the forces, the separation of the population, I, in all sincerity, in order to avoid further friction and further killing, do submit that the only realistic form of Government to-day until tempers can cool is such that will move people slightly apart and a Govern-ment that controls the various entities through people of their areas. It is better that we move slightly apart and survive, it is much worse that we move closer and perish in the collision. Therefore, I say no single one person to-day in Nigeria can command the entire loyalty of the people of Nigeria. People can command loyalties of various groups and, therefore, to save the suspicion, to enable us settle down it is essential that whatever form of Government we have in the centre must be limited and controlled by a consensus which we all agree. It is easier for people at the top to be reason-able, it is a different thing for people lower down and it is that that makes me say that Nigeria wide content should be at the highest possible level until such a time as tempers have cooled and tensions have come down. This is the basic principle, if we are agreeable on it then we go into the matters of detail.

Lt.-Col. Hassan: I do agree basically with the principles that have been mentioned by Emeka, but starting from May, I think, in his statement and in what you mentioned earlier, we that are here to-day know what we have done and we know what we have been doing to console and to stop the killings of the people of the East. On the other side, you may not know that all of us here on this table have done so much also, risking our lives and, as you mentioned, the whole thing is at the lower level. If you know how much it is at the lower level and how much we have tried to console the people to stop all these movements and mass killings, you will give me and others a medal tonight.

z

However, I do agree that at the moment the confidence at the lower level has to be restored and it will take time to get confidence because it is a known fact that the confidence now both in the East and in the North is not yet there. We have tried our best to see that the ordinary man in the street understands the difficulties as already mentioned by Emeka that may face the country, a complete civil war. However, we have done our best and we will continue to do our best but all the same I agree that whatever form of association we are to discuss has to be at the top; to make me believe that tomorrow a Northern soldier will stay in the same barracks within the next few months with an Eastern soldier, the confidence is just not there. With the civilians I would agree because there are so many that have written to us, we have so many from the East who still want to come back but I cannot really say to them— It is true, go and reside in such and such a place—because if he comes back and something happens to him I will have the feeling that it is my responsibility to save the life of that individual and I told him to come back and he has been killed.

Lt.-Col. Ojukwu: The Easterner who wanted to come back to the North I tried actively to stop because I know the Easterner, I know what he is going to do when he goes back to the North and I would be grateful if you discourage him.

Lt.-Col. Hassan: I encouraged some and discouraged some because I feel it is my responsibility. This was what made me face the mutiny in Kano, soldiers were ready to shoot me but all the same it is my responsibility to save lives and I did it. However, I feel that on the civilian side we can do it gradually but at the Army level that will give us great difficulty. I feel we should concentrate now on the form of association we want at the higher level not promises that an Eastern soldier and a Northern soldier can mix together tomorrow, the chances of their mixing together is about 35 per cent but not up to 45 per cent yet. I think that the form of Government that we should have should be discussed at the higher level and then we can try within our territories to bring confidence back gradually. We may say that the confidence is there but right at the bottom it is not there and I am sure Robert will agree. Even right now we have divisions within the Regions in the North, the West, the Mid-West, even in the East, the Rivers people want to go. Therefore, we better try to keep the big groups together at the moment and gradually we start mixing together.

Lt.-Col. Ejoor: I do not think I will recount the details which have been mentioned but the salient point which we want to consider is that since there is no one person that has absolute control of the Armed Forces, it is now difficult for us to accept one authority and I think this is the main point which Emeka has tried to make.

We can tackle it in two ways. First, by removing the subject of objection in the lower group, that is by separating the soldiers in the mean time to build confidence until we can bring them together.

Secondly, since we are working in good faith among ourselves we have to repose the responsibility for each group of the Army on those personalities until we are in a position to merge together. With this progression from a Federal set up it only means we have to look very closely into the central powers which are supposed to be those of the Supreme Commander and see how best we can limit these in such a way that the actions are acceptable to the various Regions. I would like this body to be maintained, the Supreme Military Council must be maintained but we have to reconstruct the duties or the powers of the Supreme Military Council in order to give effect to the other functions that will restore confidence within the various Regions and then in general. I do not think our answer here is to start re-organising the Council but to look into the functions and to specify very definitely what it can do and what it cannot do. If we do that we would go a long way in restoring confidence within the Regions. When this is restored we hope gradually we shall build up, it will be a matter of time and it will come automatically but we will want a strong centre. . . .

Col. Adebayo: I think I should come in here. Two points have been made, one on the Government side and the second which is inter-related to the Government side, the Army. This is a Military Government or Military rule and as such we are military people and must get ourselves together first. If we do not sort ourselves out I cannot see how we can confidently rule the country. I agree entirely with Emeka, Hassan and David. I think it will be simpler on the Government side if we can restore the confidence of the population which we have not got at the moment. Even in the West the Yorubas are afraid of moving around with the Northern troops because they feel—Well, they have done something to the Easterners may be it is our turn next. . . . I think I would agree with the majority here that our association should be tightened up at the top and see whether we can bring that association down to the ground when the time comes, when the troops have more confidence in themselves. As Jack and myself have always said, we do not want to break the Army completely into pieces because it will be very very dangerous to any one of us if we break the Army into pieces. If we can tighten up the Army on top then those who are on top will gradually have the confidence of the troops back but I agree entirely that we must separate these troops. ,

If there are areas where some people can work together, we can go into detail on that but in general I think one should agree that there should be separation from the bottom but not on top.

On the Government side, the problem has been half resolved. We agreed yesterday that our Solicitors-General should get together on the 14th and see what part of the Decrees we can repeal later on and submit their recommendations. I think if we can go back as at 14th January, 1966, I think half of the problem on the Government side is resolved. Then if we want to go through the functions of the Supreme Commander and see what the Regions can take on it will be all right. But, personally, I would say we only repeal those Decrees that were passed after 15th January, 1966 but I think we should revert to what the country was as at 14th January, 1966, that is Regional autonomy.

Lt.-Col. Ejoor: On that point, the implication is that the Civilian Government will have to come back.

Col. Adebayo: What we are doing is that we are trying to get a solution for us Military people to rule, the question of civilians coming back is a different exercise altogether. You repeal all the Decrees made that affected some of the powers of the Regional Governments.

In fact Decree No. 1 is one of them, there are certain parts of Decree No. 1

which should be repealed. . . . We can go through all the Decrees that have been passed, that will solve our problems and bring the Regional powers back to the Regions. . . .

If we agree on that I see no reason why we should go through the functions and the powers of the Supreme Commander because at the Supreme Military Council a joint decision is always made but unfortunately we could not meet since July 29 and there are areas in which the Federal Executive Council in Lagos could meet without the Regional Governors but on things affecting the Regions the Regional Governors must either attend the meeting or be consulted before passing it into law. If we all agree that we repeal Decrees that affect Regional powers and leave the Supreme Military Council to continue and the Federal Executive Council to continue I think half of our job is done.

Lt.-Col. Ojukwu: Again, whilst I agree with Bob I think what he has said has not gone far enough. It has not gone far enough in that before January 15 certainly the Armed Forces were one. These are crucial to whatever we decide to do and, therefore, whilst I agree that the Supreme Military Council should stay, I feel that here we must write it down in our decisions quite categorically that the legislative and executive authority of the Federal Military Government shall be vested in the Supreme Military Council because previously it had been vested in the Supreme Commander.

Col. Adebayo: No.

Lt.-Col. Ojukwu: The actions have been such.

Col. Adebayo: Actions, yes.

Lt.-Col. Ojukwu: If we are not going to get ourselves into another friction, I think this must really be spelt out, so that, what I envisage is that whoever is at the top is a constitutional chap, constitutional within the context of the Military Government. That is, he is the titular head but he would only act when we have met and taken a decision. It is in fact for that reason that I suggested yesterday, so as not to get it confused ever again, that whoever we choose should be the Chairman of a Military Council. Indeed, I have gone on to say or rather I would like to say that he should again be a Titular Commander-in-Chief of the Armed Forces and that he shall perform such functions as are performed by a Constitutional Head of State. By so doing we have limited the powers, by so doing our people will have the confidence that whatever he says must at least have been referred to us all and that we are doing it in the best interest of the entirety rather than saying that this chap is there he is a Northerner and suspect every action of his, this chap is there an Easterner, he must be pushing only Eastern things for the Eastern good. If we spell it out as I have just said I think we would go a long way.

I will go further and I will give you the papers of what I suggest—

Papers passed to Members of the Supreme Military Council

Major Johnson: Before we go into the details of this, I would like to add one or two points. . . . We must first of all face the social problems in our country.

What you have just enumerated, I am sure, in principle has been the intention of the Federal Military Government since January. General Ironsi, all of us will remember, used to say—'Look, it is easy to be a dictator but it is not easy to try not to be one.' There are several occasions when he would say—Look, we all take these decisions—even at Council meetings and putting his hand down he would say—any comments. I am sure this has been the

genuine intention of everybody in the Military Government, nobody wants
to be a dictator. I know there could be technical hitches, that in practice we
have deviated from it but from what you have said I am sure it is the intention of every military member here, nobody has got any personal aspiration, we are all just longing to get this country back on its feet. So, the
decisions being taken jointly I am sure is everybody's welcome.

The nomenclature now is something different. Again, I tie this one up with
social. This is why I believe, let us remain with the nomenclature we have got.
Supreme Military Council, Federal Executive Council, Regional Executive
Council, these are what we are talking about but it is within us. We have said
now that we must start this thing from the top. If we know we want unity
eventually which we know cannot be built now it is from the top and if we
do not show the genuine intention right from the top I do not see what we are
going to pass on to the lower people. Those of us here now should know how
we want it to be functioning. We know we have agreed, we are going to put
it down there that Supreme Commander you will be the man in Lagos to
do normal day to day things that were done by the Ministers and this should
be carried out with Members of the Executive Council in Lagos. He never
takes any decision by himself for all I know although there could be some
hitches as I have said and things to include the Regions the Regional Governments will come in and if it is not important they send a memo for them to
comment. We say this is what we have agreed upon and it goes on. I do not
think we should deviate from this. . . .

Gentlemen, it is not anybody's intention to remain head-up in Nigeria, it is
not anybody's ambition that he wants to be Governor. It has come on us and
we are doing national service now for our country. When they talk about the
history of Nigeria because after all 10 years in our lives is a long time but in
the life of a nation it is a very small time. We are going to pass away one day
but what are we going to give to posterity, that is what we should think about
now. Personal ambition, what this man should be or that man, we must forget
it.

I welcome what Col. Ojukwu said, we take a joint decision, that is what we
have been doing but the nomenclature I say, let it remain. . . .

The only thing I would like to add is because of the state of the Army itself
to-day I would like to see an effective Commander of the Army. I would like
to have an effective Commander and on top of that I would like to see that
we break the command of the Army into Area commands. I hate to use
Regional commands, I would say Area commands and have effective command
on the Area commands and then an effective command for the Army itself.
That will assist the Supreme Commander himself from going into detail on
Army matters. He can still be the Head of the Armed Forces but that will
assist him in going into detail on Army problems. I do not think personally
that the Chief of Staff (Army) is effective. He is the Staff Officer, I was Chief
of Staff, you were Chief of Staff and you all know that we want somebody
who can really command, go to the ground everytime and see that the
Officers and the troops are doing the right thing. That is what I would like to
add to what I said before but I think the nomenclature should remain.

Lt.-Col. Ojukwu: I will object completely to that last one. We started by
agreeing that nobody can effectively command the entire Army. Any attempt

to put somebody and say he commands the entire Army is—eyewash—it does not work, not in the present circumstances. Therefore, we must accept that the Army would be Regionalised whether we like the name or not we all understand what we mean by that.

I do not think what we need at the moment is Supreme Commander because Supreme Commander does involve commanding. I think what you need is a Commander-in-Chief who is just titular so that people will take orders from people, at least, they have confidence in. Whoever you put in Lagos, I say this, will not command the loyalty of the East if that person is not acceptable to the East, this is the fact of to-day. So many things have happened and we do no longer trust each other.

Lt.-Col. Hassan: This is taking us back on the whole issue of Nigerian history. . . .

Lt.-Col. Ojukwu: I said there should be a co-ordinating group to which each Region would send somebody but just for the façade of Nigeria there should be a titular Commander-in-Chief not a Supreme Commander which involves and which means somebody who commands over and above the various entities. Perhaps after we have created and generated certain confidence we could again have a Supreme Commander but it is not feasible to-day this is what I am saying.

Lt.-Col. Hassan: With respect, to summarise the whole thing the Eastern Region will not recognise whoever is the Supreme Commander in the form of association we are now in and it means a repetition of the whole history of Nigeria when the politicians were there, to strive to put either a Northerner or an Easterner at the top. It must be an Easterner for the Easterners to believe or a Northerner for the Northerners to believe. To summarise, the Eastern people will not recognise anybody in Lagos unless he is an Easterner.

Col. Adebayo: I do not think we should put it that way.

Mr. T. Omo-Bare: I would like to make a statement. I would like to request with respect that we adjourn to private session and iron out this matter because there is a lot involved in it. We cannot sit here on this round table and divide Nigeria because the talks are moving towards Regionalisation of everything and I do not think it is safe and we are right to divide Nigeria up on this table. If we retire into private session we might be able to thrash it out there. We will be able to say everything in our minds and then come back with a Resolution.

Lt.-Col. Gowon: If that is agreed we can retire then.

[1] *Selected according to topic from the Federal record* Meeting of the Military Leaders held at Peduase Lodge, Aburi, Ghana (*Lagos, 1967*).   [2] *See* DOC *25.*

82.
Comments by the Federal Permanent Secretaries on the Decisions reached at Aburi[1]

INTRODUCTION

1. The implications of the decisions of the Supreme Military Council meeting held in Accra recently are commented upon *seratim* [*sic*] in this paper.

2. REORGANISATION OF THE ARMY

a. *The Title: 'Commander-in-Chief'*

Objections are raised to the use of 'Commander-in-Chief' which the Accra meeting agreed should be the new title for the Chairman of the Supreme Military Council and Head of the Federal Military Government on the grounds that:

1. It would be a subtle way of either abolishing the post of Supreme Commander or declaring it vacant, to be filled by the *unanimous* decision of the Supreme Military Council; if the latter, there would be considerable instability caused by political and military manoeuvres to fill the post.

2. The Accra decision transfers the Executive Authority of the Federal Military Government from the Head of Federal Military Government and Supreme Commander, (in accordance with Decree No. 1) to the Supreme Military Council. The implication of this is that the Commander-in-Chief would have no powers of control or dismissal over the Military Governors; a situation which is incompatible with Military administration.

b. *Establishment of Military Headquarters*

It is considered:

1. that the establishment of Military Headquarters with equal representation from the Regions headed by a Chief of Staff amounts to confederation.

2. that there is a need for clarification on the term 'Military Headquarters' as distinct from 'Supreme Headquarters'.

c. *Creation of Area Commands*

It is considered that the creation of Area Commands has the following implications:

1. dividing up the Nigerian Army into regional ones, without links with or effective unified control over the army by the 'Supreme Commander'.

2. since area command would be under the control of Military Governors who can use the army for internal security, there is the serious political implication in respect of the creation of States in which the status of minorities cannot be guaranteed by the Supreme Commander.

3. since under the constitution the operational control of the army is vested in the Prime Minister (and after January 15, 1967, in the Supreme Commander), the acceptance of the Accra decision would require the amendments to the Armed Forces Acts and the Constitution.

4. no authority is vested with the power for the use of the army, for external attacks on Nigeria.

d. *Matters of Policy, etc. in the Armed Forces and Police vested in Supreme Military Council*

It is considered that the acceptance of this decision dispenses with the Army and Police Councils.

e. *Creation of Lagos Garrison:*

If the Lagos Garrison is intended to be the same status as 'Area Commands', it would imply that Lagos is regarded as another 'Area Command'. The Commander-in-Chief might not have direct control over any group of soldiers in any 'area'—a very vulnerable situation. Otherwise, the Lagos

342 Crisis and Conflict in Nigeria 1

Garrison can only be interpreted as the Commander-in-Chief's 'Body Guard'.

f. Preparation of Statistics by Military Committee;

This can be regarded as a useful exercise as long as there is unfettered and free inspection of all military operations in the regions.

3. APPOINTMENTS TO CERTAIN POSTS

There appears to be need for clarification as to the specific categories of officers for the appointment of whom the Supreme Military Council will like to be responsible. It is observed that:

a. whichever category of officers is meant, the effect of this decision will tend to paralyse the functions of the Federal Public and the Police Service Commissions.

b. if Regional Governors leave power to appointments, the loyalty of Federal Officers would be to their regions of origin—meaning in effect that there will be no Federal Civil Service.

c. the acceptance of this decision would also require, as the law officers have reported, amendments to those sections in the constitution dealing with appointment to Nigeria Police, Federal Public Service Commission and sections of various acts dealing with appointment in Federal Statutory Corporations;

d. furthermore, it is observed that while Military Governors will have power to appoint, or approve appointments of Federal Government Servants, there is no corresponding power of the Supreme Military Council to even influence the appointments to senior posts in the Regional Public Services. This clearly makes the Federal Military Government subordinate to the Regional Governments.

4. POWERS OF THE FEDERAL MILITARY GOVERNMENT

It is considered that the vesting of the legislative and Executive Powers in the Supreme Military Council and the introduction of the element of Regional Military Governors' consent in the Federal Legislation will leave the Federal Executive Council with virutally no functions, and the powers of the Federal Military Government vis-à-vis the Regional Military Governments no longer exists. This view has been clearly expressed in the Report of the law officers meeting held recently in Benin. . . .

The questions raised are quoted:

i. Whether it is the intention of the Accra agreement that a meeting of the Supreme Military Council will not be properly constituted and so cannot properly be held unless all the Military Governors are present.

ii. Whether where all the Military Governors are present at a meeting of the Supreme Military Council decisions of the Council can properly be taken only with the concurrence or unanimity of all the Military Governors, *or* by a majority of the Military Governors, *or* else by a majority of all the members present.

iii. Whether where one or more military Governors are present at any meeting of the Supreme Military Council their concurrence in decisions taken at such a meeting will still be necessary before such decision can be implemented.

iv. Whether all Decrees (whether affecting the whole country or not) are to be formerly approved by the Supreme Military Council before they are signed by the Head of the Federal Military Government.

v. In what manner should the concurrence of the Military Governors in the making of Decrees (in their capacity as members of the Supreme Military Council) be signified, that is, for instance, whether it will be enough for this to be signified orally in the course of a meeting of the Supreme Military Council *or* by writing under their respective hands *or* whether there should be a column in the Decree for the appending of signatures.

In the light of the implications of the Accra decisions as quoted above:

a. the recommendations of the law officers should be adopted, i.e. the powers and functions of the Federal Government as contained in the Exclusive and Concurrent Legislative Lists should be restored;

b. the law officers should confine themselves to only those decrees which tend to over-centralise the administration.

5. COMPOSITION OF THE FEDERAL MILITARY GOVERNMENT

The decision that the civilians should not be associated with the Federal Military Government for the next six months is incompatible with the various promises which the Supreme Commander has made to the Nation in this regard. Civilians including ex-politicians are closely associated with Military Governors in the running of the Regional Military Government. There is, therefore, a clear need to associate reputable Nigerians with the Federal Executive Council as previously recommended in the summary:

a. A provisional Federal Government should be established immediately comprising:
    (1) the Supreme Commander of the Armed Forces (Chairman).
    (2) The Head of the Navy, Army, Air Force, Police.
    (3) Three civilian members each from the East, Mid-West, North, West and one from Lagos.
    (4) Attorney-General of the Federation.

b. The civilians must be people who were not actively involved in politics in the past five years, of undoubted integrity and independent character.

c. They will, on oath and by their instrument of appointment, be debarred from seeking political office for at least five years.

d. They will be appointed by the Supreme Commander and the Head of the Federal Military Government himself.

e. The civilian members will be assigned Portfolios as Commissioners.

6. SOLDIERS IN DETENTION

It is considered that the determination of the fate of the soldiers in detention should be done after assessing the possible reactions of the rank and file in the Army. This is necessary to avert any adverse repercussions.

7. AD HOC CONSTITUTIONAL CONFERENCE

It is considered that the 'Accra Decisions'—in so far as they tend towards strengthening the regions at the expense of the Federal Government and hence towards the setting up of a Confederal system of Government—are incompatible with the unanimous decisions of the Ad Hoc Constitutional Conference. It seems more advisable, therefore to stick to previous recommendations and advice to the Supreme Commander, viz:

a. that the Ad Hoc Constitutional Conference should stand adjourned indefinitely;

b. that the immediate political programme announced to the nation on 30th Nov 66 by the Supreme Commander should be implemented and the country must be so informed.

8. PROBLEMS OF DISPLACED PERSONS

It is suggested that:

a. when the meeting of Permanent Secretaries of the Ministries of Finance resumes, the principle of revenue allocation should not be discussed as it was not mentioned in the minutes of the Accra Meeting.

b. the decision to continue to pay salaries till the end of March, 1967 does not take into consideration economic factors which are linked with it. For instance, the railways are not fully running and cannot earn enough revenue with which to pay their servants who are not working. The P & T is in the same plight and the Federal Ministry of Finance has indicated its inability to make additional financial provision for this purpose. Secondly, it does not make sense to include daily paid workers among those whose salaries should continue to be paid. The decision should therefore be reconsidered.

c. that there is no reason to leave out the Military Governor of the North from sending representatives to discuss the problem of the recovery of property because Northerners who left the East also left their property behind.

9. SUMMARY OF CONCLUSIONS AND RECOMMENDATIONS

a. If the adoption of the title Commander-in-Chief declares the post of Supreme Commander vacant, serious instability would result from political and military manoeuvres to fill the post.

b. The creation of Area Commands without any unified and effective Central control of the Nigerian Army has serious political implications: internally, because of the vulnerable position of the Commander-in-Chief or Supreme Commander and the status of minorities; externally, because no single authority is vested with the power to use the Army for defence against external aggression. Acceptance of the Accra meeting's decision would require amendments to the Armed Forces Acts and the Constitution.

c. To avert possible repercussions, the determination of the fate of soldiers in detention should be done after assessing the possible reactions of the rank and file of the Army.

d. The decision to appoint or approve appointments of Federal Public Servants, will not only paralyse the Federal Public and Police Service Commissions but will also create Regional loyalties among Federal Public Servants.

e. the decision that displaced persons should continue to receive their salaries till the end of March, 1967, should be reconsidered for economic reasons;

f. the vesting of executive powers of the Federal Military Government on the Supreme Military Council with the introduction of the element of consent of the Regional Military Governors makes the Federal Military Government subordinate to the regional Military Governments and this amounts to accepting Confederation. The powers of the Federal Government as contained in the Exclusive and Concurrent Lists should be restored as recommended by the law officers;

g. the Ad Hoc Constitutional Conference should stand adjourned indefinitely and the immediate political programme announced by the Supreme Commander to the nation on 30th November, 1966 should be implemented.

h. there is a clear need to associate reputable civilians with the Federal Executive Council as previously recommended and the nation should be so informed;

j. if the intention of the Accra decision is to restore to the regions the Constitutional powers which were taken from them before January, 1966, the Supreme Commander should instruct the law officers to list the relevant decrees for repeal.

[1] *This document, marked 'Top Secret', was leaked by the Eastern Government. It was dated 20 January 1967 and issued from the Cabinet Office over the signature of the Secretary to the Federal Military Government. Its authenticity has not been denied. It is included in the East's version of Aburi but does not appear in the Federal one.*

83.
Ojukwu's Press Conference on his Return from Aburi on 6 January 1967[1]

You are already aware that we have just ended the meeting of the Supreme Military Council in Ghana. This meeting began on Wednesday the 4th and ended yesterday.

It has come to my notice that the public are anxious to have more details of decisions taken. They are entitled to these details which I shall now give as far as public policy allows.

The meeting opened with a joint declaration by all of us, the Military leaders, renouncing the use of force as a means of settling the present crisis in Nigeria and holding ourselves in honour bound by that declaration. That declaration also re-affirmed our faith in discussions and negotiations as the only peaceful means of resolving the Nigerian crisis.

Having regard to the great fear and suspicion on all parts about the use of force, we thought that this declaration should precede any other business; and I am sure that all Nigerians will welcome it as a source of real relief.

The next important matter discussed, and upon which a lot of other things hinged, was the organization of the Nigerian Army. Let me say here that our discussions right through went on in a calm atmosphere, understanding and realism. We in the East have always felt that realism and understanding had been lacking in the past in the approach to our problems, and it was very

encouraging that our meetings on the two days showed the sincere determination by all to find realistic solutions to our problems.

On the organization of the Army, it was agreed that the Army will hence-
forth be governed by the Supreme Military Council, the Chairman of which
will be known as Commander-in-Chief and Head of the Federal Military
Government. There is to be a Military Headquarters on which the Regions
will be equally represented and which will be headed by a Chief of Staff.
There shall be an area command in each Region under the charge of an Area
Commander—the Regions corresponding to the existing ones. There will be a
Lagos garrison which will include Ikeja. For the duration of the Military
Government, Military Governors will have control over their area commands in matters of internal security. All matters of policy including appointments and promotions of persons in the executive posts in the Armed Forces
and the Police shall be dealt with by the Supreme Military Council. Any
decision affecting the whole country must be determined by the Supreme
Military Council and where a meeting is not possible, such a matter must be
referred to the Military Governors for comments and concurrence.

Subject to the above arrangements, we felt that the existing governmental
institutions, namely, the Supreme Military Council and the Federal Executive Council, as well as Regional Executive Councils, are workable, and
should be retained.

On the question of public appointments it was agreed that the Supreme
Military Council must collectively approve appointments to the following
offices:

a. Diplomatic and Consular posts.

b. Senior posts in the Armed Forces and the Police.

c. Super-scale Federal civil service and Federal Corporation posts.

This particular decision was made as a means of removing friction, it
being our unfortunate experience that friction and misunderstanding had in
the past bedevilled these appointments. What it means is that no one person
will have the right and power to make these appointments alone in the future.

Politically, it was unanimously agreed that it was in the interest of the
safety of this nation that the Regions should move slightly further apart than
before. As a prelude to this, it was decided that all Decrees and parts of
Decrees promulgated since the Military Regime, and which detracted from
the previous powers of the Regional Governments should be repealed by the
21st of this month. Once this is done and the agreements, which I have already described on the procedure and functions of the Supreme Military
Council, are implemented, the aim of allowing the Regions to operate more
independently and of ensuring fairness to all will be achieved.

The question of displaced persons was exhaustively discussed. As regards
civil servants and employees of Government Corporations who had to flee
their places of work as a result of the current situation, it was decided that
such people will be paid their full salaries up to the end of March this year,
unless they have found alternative employments.

On the question of other displaced persons, it was decided to set up a
Committee to look into the problems of rehabilitation and recovery of
property. I took that opportunity to repeat my assurance last given in my
New Year message, that those non-Easterners who had to be ordered to leave

the Region in the interest of their own safety, would be welcome back as soon as conditions become more normal. To this end I undertook to review that Order with a view to lifting it as soon as practicable.

There were other matters discussed the details of which it would not be in the public interest to disclose here. Such matters involved the military events of January the 15th and July the 29th of 1966.

I have hurried to make this statement to you because of the misgivings which I understand are prevalent in this Region as a result of this meeting. I recall that just before my departure, when the public did not even know that our meeting was so close, students and other groups of individuals issued resolutions, advising me against attending any meeting with my counterparts. You will now be convinced that this meeting was more than necessary and worthwhile. Our duty is to reduce or remove tension, in order to leave ourselves free to tackle the most urgent and constructive tasks of economic and social development, which cannot be possible in a state of tension and fear. I have no doubt that all of us who participated in the last discussions are determined to implement the agreements reached. Once this is done, we shall have gone a long way to relieving tension and banishing fear among us. It is our plan to meet again soon, this time in Nigeria, to consider other matters arising from our last discussions and those which were not touched.

I want here to place on record my personal indebtedness to the Government and people of Ghana for making a plane available to convey me to and from the meetings on the two days, and for making other arrangements to make this meeting possible. Provided our aims are achieved, we in this country will have cause to remain eternally grateful to Ghana for their constructive initiative.

For our part in this country, we must keep calm and avoid actions or words which might create difficulties for our progress in the solution of our problems.

God will certainly rescue this nation from collapse and perdition.

Question: (Herbert Unegbu, N.B.C.) Your Excellency, what you have explained has sort of taken the wind out of some of our questions but I will begin by referring to yesterday's official statement on the powers and functions of the Federal Military Council, and the reaffirmation by the Military Council of its belief in the workability of the existing institutions subject to necessary safeguards. Does this mean that the East accepts that the Federal system will succeed? The impression since the crisis has been that the confederal system is the answer to the present problem and this is what the East stands for.

Ojukwu: In my opening statement I did mention those federal institutions which we believe are workable. I will repeat, the Supreme Military Council, the Federal Executive Council and the Regional Executive Councils. We believe that these can work provided, as we have said, that all decisions that would affect the country must be taken by the Supreme Military Council of which, as you all know, the Governors are members, and where a meeting is not possible then the papers will be sent to the Governors to obtain their concurrence. Another thing I feel I might explain at this time is the real object of this meeting. Nobody thinks that the entire problems besetting Nigeria can be solved in 48 hours, far from it. The first thing is for the

Military leaders to get together and take control of the situation in order to find a solution. And what we agreed at this meeting gives us something workable to enable us go ahead and find our long-term solution to our problem. You all know that prior to this meeting things were just drifting away. We have now a sort of agreement which I am confident that if everybody keeps his side of the bargain, we will have something workable. The East believes in confederation. I believe that that is the only answer. I have not moved from that neither am I likely to move from that point of view. What is confederalism? Is it not a large measure of autonomy for the existing units? Is not that what we have been understanding it to be in this Region? We have gone a long way towards that as a result of this meeting.

Q: The second question is again on yesterday's statement about appointments and promotions in certain federal services. Since a large number of Easterners have left Lagos, and assuming that at your meeting you worked out a quota arrangement, I do not know whether key Easterners who have left Lagos will have to go back ultimately, that is to say, assuming that you worked out a kind of quota arrangement.

O: Right through the Eastern stand has always been that we will contribute to maintain the federal services. That is contributing in money and manpower on a quota to be agreed; nothing has detracted from that stand. But in the meantime, I think probably at the next meeting of the Supreme Military Council we would go into such details as you mentioned now. What we have got are general agreements.

Q: (National Press) Would Your Excellency say that from the last meeting of the Supreme Military Council, a quick solution of the country's crisis is forthcoming?

O: I do not think that there is a quick solution to the country's crisis. What I have said or indicated from my opening statement is that we are now taking the first steps to solving our problems or shall I say, the first realistic steps to solve our problems.

Q: (Eastern Nigeria Guardian) Did the Military Council reach any mutual agreement on what should be paid to the victims or individuals who sustained losses as a result of the brutal and bloody massacre in the Northern Region?

O: I like to answer this by putting the question back to you. Do you really or can you envisage such a meeting as ours, sitting for two days, arriving at a decision on the amounts to be paid to victims? No. No.

Q: (E.N.B.C.) Why was there no mention of any fiscal arrangements in the communiqué?

O: We started discussing fiscal arrangements and decided that they were rather intricate. I do not think any of us there was really competent to discuss matter of financial policy. What we agreed, and we gave a time limit for the considerations bearing in mind the end of the financial year or of the start of a new financial year, was that each Region would send three people to be named, I think, within the next fortnight, to discuss these details and in fact they were mandated to report back to the Supreme Military Council by the end of the month period for us to take urgent decision on it.

Q: (E.N.B.C.) The members of the Supreme Military Council vowed to do all in their power to ensure that there is no recurrence of the bloodshed of the past year. Can we place any reliance on this assurance? Can we, Sir, place any reliance on such promises? We have had them before even after the May incident and what followed was the September pogrom.

O: We wait and see, but my advice is that people of this Region must continue to be vigilant.

Q: (Outlook) What is the nature of the administration and promotion you envisage in the Army; will the nature of the administration and promotion envisaged affect in any way the constitutional arrangements of the whole country?

O: I would find it extremely difficult to answer the first part of your question because it borders on security. But whatever changes we envisage, I think, will eventually reflect and form another change in the constitutional arrangements. It must, it must.

Q: (Outlook) Who now represents the Air Force in the Supreme Military Council? Was there any representative of the Air Force at the Aburi meeting of the Council? If not, why?

O: At the moment, or rather at that meeting, nobody represented the Nigerian Air Force. Indeed this is one of the matters we would be discussing at a later stage at a subsequent meeting. After the events of July, we must obviously consider the reconstitution of the Supreme Military Council. It is a point. . . .

Q: (Eastern Star) If it is reviewed that non-Easterners who have so far left the region should return to their previous places of residence, do you think our refugees from the North would still go back to that region?

O: I doubt it very much. . . .

Q: (National Press) In the last communiqué issued after the second day's meeting, it is said that there has been a unanimous agreement on holding the second Supreme Military Council meeting in Nigeria. Does it then follow that Your Excellency has abandoned the idea of insisting that Northern soldiers who are now stationed in Lagos and the West be repatriated to the North?

O: No, I have not abandoned my stand on that. You will notice that it is not a stand but a matter of security for that venue; and this matter, of course, we discussed a great deal, and you will notice that in having area commands already we are on the way to solving that problem.

Q: (Outlook) You mentioned in your statement about the acceptance of the members that you have reached a stage where the different Regions will have to move further apart than in the past. In view of what had happened before this meeting, would Your Excellency say that that was likely to strengthen the unity of the country or whether it would actually be to fix definite decisions on the part of the component parts that will make it impossible in future to talk of one Nigeria?

O: We have always believed in one Nigeria. Our problem has always been that of finding a realistic form of association within that one Nigeria. You know the view of the East in this matter and I think it is the only answer in the present circumstances. I will be very surprised if eventually those views are not universally accepted. I do not think it would weaken Nigeria, indeed I believe that such an association as we envisage will strengthen Nigeria.

[1] *Eastern Ministry of Information Press Release No. 97 and 102/1967.*

84.

Speech by Military Governor (Lt.-Col. Hassan Katsina) on Northern Nigeria Dedication Day, 15 January 1967 [1]

Exactly one year today Nigeria, and this Region in particular, witnessed the most tragic and shocking event in the history of its existence. For on the 15th of January, 1966—that fateful day—the Prime Minister of the former Federal Republic of Nigeria, the Right Honourable Alhaji Sir Abubakar Tafawa Balewa, the Honourable Sir Ahmadu Bello, Sardauna of Sokoto and Premier of Northern Nigeria along with other illustrious and beloved sons of the Region in the Nigerian Army and some of their friends and colleagues from other parts of the country were murdered. May their souls rest in peace. They lost their lives in the hands of a group of conspirators in a bid to seize political power and impose the domination of the rest of Nigeria by a section. Today we mourn not only the passing away of those heroes and leaders but we also are taking stock of the past and looking to the future with more confidence. Let us hope and pray that their sacrifices will not be in vain and that their shining examples and all that they worked and stood for in their lifetime will for many years continue to guide this Region and Nigeria on the march to progress and enlightenment.

It is said to judge revolutionary heroes one must watch them at close range and judge them at great distance. When we watch the late Sir Abubakar at close range, we find that he was the embodiment of Nigeria's hopes and aspirations, guiding it towards the realisation of its cherished dreams. His greatness was reflected in his ability to symbolize the positive strivings of the people of Nigeria for freedom, peace and prosperity—the fundamental values of our contemporary society. Right to the very end his faith in Nigeria, in Africa and in humanity remained unshaken despite the obstacles thrown in his way which the manner and means of his death symbolised in the final stage.

Essentially a democrat, his approach to our problems was always humane and conciliatory. He was a just man as recognised even by those who saw nothing good in his actions and who despised him. He was free of intolerance and bigotry. As a man of peace who patiently looked to the future with courage and hope he compromised on many issues against his own judgement to accommodate the demands of others that were often excessive and inconsiderate. His untiring effort and sacrifice to guide our infant democracy, nurtured in his own hands, produced in him a too cautious approach in his dealing with those subverting the growth of our responsible government for their own dark designs. Such was the mark of his dedication to the rule of law and the ideal of democracy, a philosophy which brought martyrdom to many like Sir Abubakar, so that truth, untarnished, might always prevail. With the loss of men like him—men of patience and mending compromise— the unity of Nigeria, which they worked so hard to achieve, became gravely in danger.

He shouldered his heavy responsibilities in a way which revealed his greatness, and under his wise leadership Nigeria made stupendous progress in many fields. He was a respected leader, a much loved man, who abhorred injustice and lived simply. His reputation carried his name far beyond our borders and he easily occupied a prominent position among world leaders.

His single-mindedness, tenacity of purpose and patience in struggling with Nigeria's vast and intricate problems commanded universal respect. A man of great charm and humility whose many activities took him into a number of international fields where he made enduring contributions quietly and without fuss and earned the respect of his colleagues. A truly cultured man, he lived for his countrymen and died at the hands of an ungrateful section of murderers among them. As a great son of the North and one whose memory is cherished by the world, it is right that he should have a special place of remembrance in our hearts on this Day of Dedication.

But we did not just lose a leader, we lost leaders. In many ways, Sir Abubakar's close friend and colleague, the late Sir Ahmadu Bello was to Northern Nigeria what Ghandi was to India. The greatest symbol of Northern identity, Sir Ahmadu was first and last a Northerner and made no apology for being so. A great man by whatever yardstick we measure greatness, he worked and sacrificed his life for the North in order that Northerners too, proud of their past heritage, should have a place in modern Nigeria to contribute to her development on equal footing and in partnership with their compatriots from other regions. . . .

I must warn that the task which we have set ourselves to accomplish demands great resolution from us all. And it is not going to be easy. The North, more than ever before, needs men and women of dedication and action; men and women with intelligence, courage, foresight and ideas for solving the new problems of the time and, men and women who are capable of bringing about improvement in all aspects of our social and economic life. We are only beginning to see some of the difficulties that can be expected from murders such as occurred last year. It is within our means, Nigerians of whatever origin, to end the difficulties and to restore our country to the path of sanity and happiness. This is the test to prove our claim to maturity and some degree of civilisation. Although we in the North are behind in many fields, we are an adaptable people as has been very clearly demonstrated to us recently. In the past we relied on outsiders not only to perform nearly all the skilled jobs in various essential services of the economy but went so far as to appear to have surrendered even menial jobs which are not traditionally associated with us. We had been too slack in the past to allow the complete passing away of the control of our economy from our hands to those of outsiders. This and other shortcomings we must put right through hard work and by organising ourselves co-operatively. Since neither Government nor Native Authorities can come anywhere near meeting all our varied requirements, we must turn to ourselves to help ourselves. This is not a new phenomenon with us in the North, particularly at a time of national crisis. We tried in the 1950s when we embarked upon the Northern Self-Development Fund to fight a constitutional battle the issue of which was luckily resolved around the table before the funds were used. Those of you who remember that worthy cause would also remember the use to which the funds were put in training several Northerners from the primary school level to the university in the United Kingdom.

I am happy to say that the Treasurer of the Northern Self-Development Fund has recently informed me that there is still a few thousand pounds left in this fund and I have therefore decided to revive the Northern Self-Develop-

2 A

ment Fund by calling upon everyone throughout the Region to contribute generously to it. I hereby launch this Self-Development Fund. A steering committee has already met to consider the uses the Funds raised might be put to and their report is now under study. A co-ordinating Regional Committee consisting of Chiefs and prominent Northern Nigerians from all over the Region will be set up in due course in addition to Sub-Committees in every Native Authority area under the chairmanship of the local Chief. I ask you in the name of Northern Nigeria to assist these Committees when they come into being and thereby help towards a rapid development of the North. I hope very sincerely that you will answer this call and respond magnificently so that we can build a new North which will become an example to our part of the world. For its part the Military Government will do everything possible to create an ideal atmosphere under which these lofty objectives can be achieved. I call upon all those in authority in this Region to set an example and lead the way for the people to follow. . . .

Above all I must appeal to Native Authorities to think ahead and not to hesitate to introduce changes where desirable. I congratulate those Native Authorities who by the contribution of their people are planning education expansion on a large scale. I urge that others should follow this fine example of a march to progress. . . .

In conclusion I invite you, ladies and gentlemen, to join with me in praying for the souls of the late Alhaji Sir Abubakar Tafawa Balewa, Alhaji Sir Ahmadu Bello and our Army Officers who suffered death on the 15th of January, 1966. Let us also pray for the souls of all other Nigerians who suffered similar fate as a result of the events of the last twelve months throughout the Federation. May their souls rest in peace and may their sacrifices be an inspiration to us who live. Finally let us all together dedicate ourselves on this day to the service of our people, to the progress of Northern Nigeria and to peace and unity of all the peoples of Nigeria.

[1] *By courtesy of the Government Printer, Kaduna.*

85.
Gowon's Press Conference on the Aburi Meeting, 26 January 1967[1]

Our main concern at the Aburi meeting was how to keep the country together and restore normal conditions. We reviewed the situation in the Nigerian Army and we all agreed that there should be one Nigerian Army under a unified command as at present. We recognised that in the context of the events of 1966, the most practical way of achieving this aim is to organise the army into area commands. The preponderance of the army in each command will be drawn from the indigenes of that area. Each area command will be under an area commander who will take operational instructions from the military headquarters which will be directly under me as the Supreme Commander of the armed forces. Under the proposal, military governors can use the area commands for internal security purposes but this will normally be done with the express permission of the head of the federal military government. We definitely decided against regional armies. We also agreed that matters of policy in the armed forces and police should be vested in the Supreme Military Council. The Army, Air Force, and Police Councils, and the Navy Board will continue to function as at present.

Because of rumours of illegal recruitment and importation of arms, the Accra meeting agreed to establish a military committee to collect statistics of arms and the strength of the armed forces everywhere in the federation. All the regions are participating in this exercise.

There have been some speculations about the effect of our decisions on senior appointments and promotions in the Federal Public Service. It was agreed that top posts such as permanent secretaries and ambassadors will have to be approved by the Supreme Military Council. I would like to explain that the Federal Public Service Commission as well as the Police Service Commission will continue to function as at present.

We did not go to Aburi to write a new constitution for Nigeria. The constitution of Nigeria will be written in Nigeria by Nigerians on the authority of the people of Nigeria. We however agreed to return to the status quo as of January 17, 1966 and this is in keeping with my earlier public pronouncements that decrees or parts of decrees which tended towards over-centralisation should be repealed. We will continue to operate the existing Federal Constitution and the Federal System of Government until a new constitution is drawn up. A decree is now under preparation which will give effect to the decision to return to the constitutional position before 17th January, 1966 without prejudice to the sections of the constitution suspending parliament and related public offices.

There has been some confusion over the Aburi decision that the ad hoc committee on the constitution should resume sitting as soon as practicable. I did say in my broadcast of November 30, 1966[2] that if all delegates to the ad hoc committee can meet within Nigeria and agree to carry on from where they left off in October their final conclusion will assist the drafting committee in its work. The ad hoc committee will accordingly resume sitting to continue where they left off on September 30, 1966 as soon as the green light is given.

So far, I have not set up the Drafting Committee and the Constituent Assembly promised in my broadcast because it was the intention that normal conditions should be fully restored before they begin to function. We went to Aburi precisely to generate the necessary atmosphere and mutual confidence in which lasting constitution can be drawn up. We definitely agreed that the next meeting of military leaders should be held within Nigeria. I intend to arrange an early meeting of the Supreme Military Council accordingly.

In Aburi we made an excellent start in the bid for permanent peace but let us not deceive ourselves that it was possible to solve all Nigeria's problems in the two-day meeting of minds of Nigeria's military leaders.

I am still as anxious as when I first took office to associate reputable Nigerians drawn from all parts of the Federation with the work of the

Federal Executive Council and the Federal Military Government. We need to exercise some caution here because of our temporary difficulties and the emotions of the recent past. I am carrying on the necessary consultations with all sections of the Nigerian community and when eventually the names we are screening are announced, the general public will be satisfied.

On the economic front, I am fully aware that what the business community and the Nigerian masses want is the maintenance of peaceful conditions in which they can go about their daily business and improve their standards of living. The government will continue its efforts to repair the temporary set-backs in our economic life particularly in the field of transportation such as railways and road.

The major economic decision taken in Aburi was to continue to pay salaries of displaced persons to 31/3/1967 but each case is to be considered on its merit. In fairness to some of the public bodies that have to pay this money, the difficulties facing them have to be appreciated. . . . The insistence that all planes going to the East must first land in Enugu for military clearance has involved the Nigerian Airways in substantial additional running costs. The P and T is also losing substantial revenue as a result of the recent disturbances and the current situation in the country. All these made it very difficult for these statutory corporations to continue to pay their displaced employees.

The Federal Military Government will continue to encourage public officials who left Lagos to return to their posts. In this respect it is gratifying to note that traders and other civilians of eastern origin have of their own volition been returning to Lagos to carry on their legitimate trade.

It has been indicated that as a result of the Accra meeting the political programme of the Federal Military Government outlined in my broadcast to the nation on November 30, 1966 has been abandoned. I want to state categorically that this is not the case. The issues raised in that programmes have become more urgent than ever. In particular, the states issue will have to be given early consideration. The Federal Military Government will see to it that new states are created for those who want them in accordance with the criteria laid down in my broadcast. All those who sincerely believe in a permanent solution to our current constitutional crisis must face the nation's problems. I am sure that if this country were allowed to fall apart, it will disintegrate into more than the existing four regions. Without an effective central authority to hold the country together, the minorities in each region will definitely assert their right to self-determination.

I should like to take this opportunity to express once again my sincere gratitude to Lt.-Gen. Ankrah, Chairman of the National Liberation Council, his colleagues, the government and the people of Ghana for making it possible for Nigerian military leaders to meet.

I hope this brief resumé will give you an idea of what the Aburi spirit means to Nigeria. The press and the radio have a special responsibility in bringing this spirit of keeping Nigeria together to the people. I did say immediately after that conference that Nigeria will definitely remain united. Nigeria will remain one indivisible country by the will of the people of this country.

[1] *Held in Lagos. Federal Ministry of Information hand-out.*
[2] *See* DOC 75.

86.
Eastern Government's View of What was Agreed at Aburi[1]

i. All the military leaders solemnly declared that they renounced the use of force as a means of settling the problems confronting the country and they re-affirmed their faith in discussions and negotiations as the only way of resolving the Nigerian crisis.

ii. A Military Committee comprising representatives of the Regions should meet to exchange information on the quantity of arms and ammunitions held in each unit of the Army in all parts of the country. Unallocated stores of arms and ammunitions held in the country should be shared out equitably between the various commands in the Federation.

iii. The Army itself should be reorganised in order to restore discipline and confidence. Specifically, the Army should be governed by the Supreme Military Council under a Chairman to be known as Commander-in-Chief of the Armed Forces and Head of the Federal Military Government. Area Commands corresponding to existing Regions and under Area Commanders should be created. During the period of the Military Government, Military Governors should have control over Area Commands for internal security.

iv. There should be created a Lagos Garrison, including Ikeja Barracks. A Military Headquarters comprising equal representation from the Regions and headed by a Chief of Staff should also be established.

v. In accordance with the decision of 9 August, 1966, Army personnel of Northern Nigeria origin should return to the North from the West. In order to meet the security needs of the West, a crash programme of recruitment and training was necessary but the details should be examined after the Military Committee had finished its work.

vi. All matters of policy, including appointments and promotions to commissions or senior posts in the Armed Forces and the Police should be dealt with by the Supreme Military Council.

vii. The legislative and executive authority of the Federal Military Government should be vested in the Supreme Military Council to which any decision affecting the whole country should be referred for determination, provided that where it is not possible for a meeting to be held the matter requiring determination should be referred to the Military Governors for their comments and concurrence.

viii. Appointments to the Diplomatic and Consular service as well as to superscale posts in the Federal Public Service and equivalent positions in Statutory Corporations must be approved by the Supreme Military Council.

ix. All decrees or provisions of decrees passed since 15 January, 1966, which detracted from the previous powers and positions of Regional Governments should be repealed with a view to promoting mutual confidence. All the Law Officers of the Federation should meet in Benin on 14 January, 1967, and list all the Decrees or provisions of Decrees concerned, so that they may be repealed not later than 21 January, 1967, if possible.

x. A meeting of Permanent Secretaries of the Ministries of Finance should be convened within two weeks to consider ways and means of resolving the serious problems posed by displaced persons all over the country.

xi. Displaced civil servants and Corporation Staff (including daily-paid employees) should continue to be paid their full salaries until 31 March, 1967, provided they have not secured alternative employment. The Military Governors of the East, West and Mid-West should send representatives (Police Commissioners) to meet and discuss the problems of recovery of property left behind by displaced persons.

xii. The *Ad Hoc* Constitutional Committee should resume sitting as soon as practicable and the unanimous recommendations of that body made in September, 1966, should be considered at another meeting of the Supreme Military Council.

xiii. For at least the next six months there should be purely a Military Government having nothing whatever to do with politicians.

xiv. The late Military Leaders should be accorded full Military Honours due to them.

xv. All Government information media should be restrained from making inflammatory statements and causing embarrassment to various Governments in the Federation.

xvi. Lt.-Col. Ojukwu assured the Supreme Military Council that his order that non-Easterners should leave the Eastern Region would be kept under constant review with a view to its being lifted as soon as practicable.

[1] *Eastern Region Official Document no. 5 of 1967, pp. 6–8. See also its* The Meeting of the Supreme Military Council (*Feb. 1967*).

87.
Federal Government Attacks East's Lack of Loyalty over the Aburi Spirit[1]

I

It was expected that tact and restraint would be exercised by all concerned after the return of the military leaders in order to uphold the new spirit of Aburi.

Since his return however, the attitude of the Eastern Military Governor has raised genuine doubts as to the amount of faith which his Government reposes in the decisions of that conference.

In the first place, against agreement reached that Press or other controversy should be avoided in the interest of national unity and understanding, the Eastern Governor proceeded immediately on his return to convene a Press conference at which he made statements and remarks which gave a rather misleading impression of the decisions of that meeting.[2]

Such impression, for example, as the one that a confederation was decided upon or that the Regions of Nigeria should fall more and more apart instead of coming together to find lasting solutions to the country's problems.

Secondly, shortly after this Press conference, the Eastern Nigeria Government unilaterally decided and announced its withdrawal from the National Provident Fund, one of the economic institutions which exert a unifying influence on the country. This decision was clearly against the grain of the

Aburi meeting at which the military leaders re-affirmed their faith in the existing institutions of the Federation.

Thirdly, although the Eastern Military Governor gave an undertaking at Aburi that the ban against non-Easterners in his Region would be lifted, nothing has been done in this direction since the return of the military leaders to Nigeria. Of course, he was to do this 'as soon as practicable' but the discretion is his, in the light of prevailing circumstances.

Fourthly, it was a matter of positive regret that the Eastern Military Governor was credited with the statement that, even if the Northern Region were divided into 50 states, he would still not encourage Easterners to live in any such states.

The Federal Government regards this statement as most unfortunate since it amounts to inciting Easterners against any prospects of peace and friendship between peoples of the two Regions through freedom of association or movement. Coming after the Aburi meeting, when all efforts should be directed towards the restoration of mutual understanding and confidence amongst the various sections of Nigeria, this statement is a disservice to future national solidarity and good relations among Nigerians.

The Eastern Military Governor is also reported to have promised protection to those who may be attacked by unidentified agents from outside the Region. In the light of a general declaration by the Nigerian military leaders at Aburi renouncing force as a means of solving our national problems, this statement is also very unhelpful to the cause of unity.

The points raised in the foregoing paragraphs show that it is the Government of Eastern Nigeria, and certainly not the Federal Military Government, which seems to be losing faith in the new spirit of Aburi.

The Federal Military Government repeats its determination and commitment to the creation of a peaceful atmosphere for the rebuilding of mutual confidence amongst the various peoples of the Federation. But all impartial observers who have the interest of the Nigerian nation at heart will certainly be disappointed at the general tone and attitude adopted by the Eastern Military Governor since the Aburi meeting.

II

The Government appreciates and views with sympathy and understanding the anxiety being expressed of late by various media of public information over what seems a not-too-fast progress in the implementation of schemes and proposals arising from the Aburi meeting of Nigerian military leaders.

It should, however, be equally appreciated by all concerned that the speed with which these matters are handled must of necessity be dictated by administrative and other circumstances of the country, some of which were unforeseen at the time the decisions were taken.

In spite of these circumstances, the Government's efforts are progressing steadily. This is evident from the fact that since the Aburi meeting two conferences of Government functionaries have been held at Benin.

The first was the conference of the Solicitors-General of the Federal and Regional Governments at which the various decrees and edicts enacted since January 15, 1966, were examined with a view to recommending suitable amendments at the Federal and Regional levels.

It will be recalled that at his Press conference last week, the Head of the Federal Military Government and Supreme Commander of the Armed Forces did promise that a decree to give effect to this development would soon be published.[3]

It is pertinent to point out that the mechanics of doing this are intricate and the law officers need time to produce the sort of results that would forestall controversy and meet the requirements as decided and recommended by the Benin meeting.

Another conference has been taking place at Benin since last week, that of the Army officers drawn from the units stationed with four Regions as well as the Federal Territory of Lagos. Again the process of implementing the Aburi decisions on the Army can be delicate although the mere announcement of the decision sounded so simple and easy.

The undertaking to pay salaries of displaced workers until March 31 this year, still stands. As regards the case of the Railway workers, the Supreme Commander at his Press conference last week did explain that embarrassing circumstances in which the Nigerian Railway Corporation finds itself as a result of the disturbances of last year.

On the whole, the Federal Military Government reminds all concerned that these are difficult human circumstances whose handling cannot lend themselves to copy-book or precision-machine type of operation, even though this is a military Government.

[1] *Statements issued in Lagos on 30 and 31 January 1967. Full text in* New Nigerian, *1 and 2 February 1967.*

[2] *See* DOC *83.*   [3] *See* DOC *85.*

88.
The East Disputes the Federal Interpretation of Aburi[1]

The first draft decree sought to return Nigeria to the Constitutional position before 17 January, 1966, while in fact the decisions of the Supreme Military Council were on specific issues and were not limited by dates. In the draft decree the title of 'Supreme Commander' was still retained contrary to the decision at Aburi to alter it to 'Commander-in-Chief'. The draft decree also retained the word 'President' instead of 'Chairman of the Supreme Military Council' as was agreed at Aburi. Again it enlarged the membership of the Supreme Military Council to include 'Head of the Nigerian Army', the 'Chief of Staff of the Armed Forces' and the 'Chief of Staff of the Nigerian Army'. No such decisions were taken at Aburi. It was merely agreed that there should be one Chief of Staff at Headquarters. Contrary to the Aburi accord, the draft decree vested executive and legislative powers either in the Federal Military Government or in the Federal Executive Council. But the Aburi Meeting clearly decided that the legislative and executive authority of the Federal Military Government should vest in the Supreme Military Council to which any matter affecting the whole country should be referred for determination. The draft decree also completely ignored the decision at Aburi that appointments and promotions within the upper hierarchy of the Army, Police, the Public Service and Corporations must be approved by the Supreme Military Council. Lastly, the draft decree proceeded to restore sections 70, 71 and 86 of the old Constitution, which had been suspended; but without also restoring the safeguards provided in that Constitution. By this mischievous action Lt.-Col. Gowon, contrary to the spirit and letter of the Aburi agreements, arrogates to himself the power to declare a state of emergency anywhere in Nigeria.

The second draft decree was prepared by the Gowon Government after a meeting of Secretaries to the Military Governments and other officials, held at Benin on 17 and 18 February, 1967. But as has been said earlier, it fell short of the Aburi decisions. Whereas it was agreed at Aburi that on *all* matters affecting the Country as a whole, the concurrence of the Regional Military Governors must be obtained, the second draft decree limits the requirement for concurrence to a few enumerated subjects. Furthermore, the decree confers the power of appointment and removal of Judges of the Lagos High Court and of Justices of the Supreme Court of Nigeria on the Head of the Federal Military Government when in fact the power should vest in the Supreme Military Council. While sovereignty vests in the Supreme Military Council the Second Draft Decree transfers the prerogative of mercy to the Head of the Federal Military Government and thus deprives the Council of its legitimate right as the sovereign authority. Again the Second Draft Decree restores the suspended provisions of the Federal Constitution. What was decided at Aburi was that only Decrees or provisions of Decrees which detracted from the powers of the Regions should be identified and repealed. Consequently, those suspended provisions of the Federal Constitution which do not affect the powers of the Regions must remain suspended.

[1] *Official Document no. 5 of 1967, pp. 11–12.*

89.
'Unilateral Action'—A Personal Letter from Ojukwu to Gowon[1]

It is increasingly and ominously clear to me that we are not really serious to save the country in spite of our public protestations to that effect. For so long our country has been in continuous stalemate and it is now time to put an end to this state of affairs.

2. After the Aburi meeting, everybody rejoiced that it had been a success. From our mood in Ghana, I was convinced that this was the feeling of us all. Personally I returned to Enugu satisfied that we had faced our problems in earnest and realism. I, therefore, lost no time in re-assuring the people of the East, who had good reasons to doubt the usefulness of our meeting, that they had been wrong in their doubts and misgivings. It is a shame that subsequent developments tend, in fact, to prove them right and me wrong.

3. At Aburi, certain decisions were taken by the Supreme Military Council—

the highest authority of the land under the present Regime. For my part, I became dedicated to those decisions, only to discover soon that you and your Civil Service advisers, along with selfish and disgruntled politicians in Lagos, and perhaps elsewhere as well, did not feel the same. As a result you have seen to it that the decisions taken at Aburi are systematically vitiated or stalled.

4. Soon after our return from Aburi meeting you on your own volition got in touch with me to discuss the Federal publication *Nigeria '66*. You wondered if it would be advisable in the light of the spirit of Aburi to go ahead publishing the document. We discussed and agreed that since the publication had not already been put out to the public it might be wise to withhold it at least for some time. On the 15th of January the publication came out. I got in touch with you and you assured me that it was not a deliberate act but a leakage. This information turned out to be a deceit because evidence soon came through that the publication was, in fact, formally launched in Washington, London, Cotonou and other foreign capitals. What is more, its introduction shows that the draft was completed after the Aburi meeting, most likely even after our discussion.

5. Your Press conference to the world on the Aburi meeting[2] virtually amounted to a denunciation of the agreements reached at Aburi. At that Press conference you even brought in issues which were never discussed at Aburi, no doubt in order to embarrass me and cause dissatisfaction in the East. My reaction to that Press conference was clearly shown in my letter EMG/S.62/ of 30th January, addressed to Military Governors and copied to you.

6. Contrary to the decisions at Aburi, recruitment into the Army has continued with publicity in different parts of the country except the East; contrary to those agreements, you have proceeded to appoint Ambassadors without reference to the Supreme Military Council; contrary to the agreements, purchase and importation of arms have continued. The meeting of Military Officers to discuss the reorganisation of the Army as agreed at Aburi has been unilaterally postponed by you. The meeting of Finance Officials, with particular reference to the problem of rehabilitation, has not even been held because your Finance Permanent Secretary in Lagos does not think it will serve any useful purpose.

7. You failed to publish the Decree on 21st January, repealing all Decrees or aspects of Decrees which detracted from the previous powers and positions of the Regional Governments. After strong pressure from me and the Military Governor of the West, you have got a comprehensive Decree drafted which, for all intents and purposes, aim at strengthening the powers of the Federal Government at the expense of the Regions. You have denounced the decision (which incidentally was taken on your own personal initiative and proposal at Aburi) to pay employees who had been compelled to flee their places of work in other parts of the country until the 31st of March.

8. In support of these defaults on your part, you and your Federal advisers have looked for one reason or another. You have described the Press statement I gave soon after my return, as causing 'serious embarrassment to all', when, in fact, my honest motive was to assure the people of the East of the sincerity and determination of the Military Regime to face realities and save the country from ruin.

9. You have on another occasion accused me of distorting the decisions of Aburi, when in fact, I was very careful in my choice of words to conform with the actual ones we used. Another reason to support your efforts to abandon the Aburi agreements is the ridiculous one that I went to the meeting prepared while others were not. This is an information which has repeatedly filtered through to me and it surprises me that mature people should expose themselves to such ridicule. It was our first meeting since July 29 and it certainly could not be a picnic but business. The agenda was prepared beforehand in consultation with all concerned. If anybody went to that meeting unprepared, then one can only infer that he was not seriously concerned with the sad problems which had beset the country, let alone with how to solve those problems.

10. Following your denunciation of the agreement to pay fleeing employees up to the end of March, your officials have given the fact that railway wagons are now in the East as an excuse. When the decision was taken at Aburi, everybody knew that those wagons were here. One should have thought that the implementation of the Aburi agreement would be a pre-condition for the release of these wagons and not the other way round. Your Government has further complicated matters by denying the Coal Corporation the right to collect their just debts from the Nigerian Railway Corporation, and have refused to send the necessary funds for the payment of salaries for railway workers. These acts are nothing but a deliberate attempt to cause trouble and disaffection among the people of Eastern Nigeria, because you and your Federal officials know the large number of persons involved and the seriousness of their dissatisfaction following non-payment of their salaries at the beginning of a new year when they have to meet commitments for their children's school fees and other personal matters.

11. The authorities in Lagos have not stopped there. They are using all their power to impede the smooth operation of private industries in this Region. Not only are they doing everything to obstruct investors and industrialists coming to do business here, they are doing everything they can to kill even those industries which are operating in this Region.

12. On the political front, I have evidence that the Federal Government is encouraging acts of subversion and sabotage within this Region, all of which are unfriendly and unbecoming of a people who regard themselves as belonging to one corporate country.

13. I have in this letter tried in catalogue some of the actions of the Federal authorities which are nothing but breaches of faith and exhibition of hostility towards this Region. I do not want to go over what I have often repeated and of which you are well aware, of similar acts prior to the Aburi meeting and beginning from July 29.

14. Since your assumption of office you have constantly told me one thing and done another. You have never honoured any of our mutual agreements, let alone those reached by accredited representatives of our Governments at conferences. I had thought that the Aburi meeting would put an end to all these acts of hostility and deception.

15. As far as I am concerned, I have now on my hands one million eight hundred thousand refugees who must be catered for. In addition to these people thousands of people have left Secondary Schools and other training

institutions, and have entered the labour market looking for employment in the East. I accept with disfavour the attempts on the part of the Federal authorities to increase this problem by refusing to pay the railway employees up till 31st of March as agreed, following your own personal suggestion at Aburi, and of doing everything to see that the Coal Corporation folds up. I have separately addressed you on the subject of the Federal Government's refusal to pay to this Region its statutory share of revenue.

16. Now that I have been driven right to the wall, I have no alternative but to consider certain actions of which I have always hated to think. But I have a responsibility and as a soldier of honour, I will not run away from them. The people of this Region have a right to decent life, peace and harmony. As a people who once claimed the honour of being looked upon as the most matured in Africa, the leaders of this country must show that maturity by honouring agreements. Organised society, confidence, good faith and progress cannot exist if people who call themselves civilised cannot honour agreements voluntarily and maturely taken. The survival of this country, its normalcy and peace, hinge on the implementation of the Aburi agreements. I would be the last to say that those agreements were perfect. I have already on several occasions said that I took them as no more than interim arrangements for the smooth running of the Military Regime. Having admitted that they could not be perfect, I believe that they may have to be modified in the light of experience in their operation.

17. We are coming to the end of our fiscal year when estimates must be finalised and plans made for the coming year. These are not possible under the present stalemate and unsettlement. If, therefore, the Aburi agreements are not implemented by the 31st of March, I shall have no alternative but to feel free to take whatever measure is unilaterally possible to carry out the spirit of the Aburi agreements. I say this with the deepest sense of regret and fully conscious of the consequences of such unilateral action. But, I shall be able to tell the world when the time comes what part I have played at different stages and in different circumstances since the emergency which started in May last year, to avoid the situation. The responsibility will not be mine.

18. I still hope that good sense will prevail and that God will save us from such a bleak future. Let us at once implement the Aburi agreements, and preserve the country as one.

[1] *Sent from Enugu on 16 February 1967, with a copy to the other Regional Military Governors. This is another classified document leaked by the East. (Cf. DOC 68.)*
[2] *See DOC 85.*

90.
'On Aburi We Stand': Ojukwu's Dawn Broadcast, 25 February 1967[1]

Fellow Countrymen and Women,
    A little over a month ago, the whole country rejoiced at the prospect of a

fast return to normal conditions. This was after the historic meeting at Aburi
in Ghana where Nigerian Military Leaders held their first meeting since the
tragic events of July 29, 1966. We reached unanimous agreement on a wide
range of matters. On my return to Enugu I gave a Press Conference at which
I explained some of the decisions reached at that meeting.[2] I appealed to all
Eastern Nigerians to approach the problem facing the country in the same
spirit which marked the discussions at Aburi.

Today all the high hopes and confidence borne out of Aburi seem to be
waning. There is evidence that those in authority in Lagos are determined to
repudiate or evade the agreements reached unanimously. Unnecessary confusion has been infused into the whole issue both from within and from
without, and the country is once again drifting dangerously.

Eastern Nigeria has gone through terrible tragedies in recent months.
Apart from the wounds of the recent pogrom, we have on our hands one
million eight hundred thousand refugees who must be catered for. The people
of this Region have a right to decent life, peace and harmony. Conscious of the
gravity of the situation, I have spared no effort to inspire a sense of realism
and sanity in the approach to the crisis so that we might preserve the integrity of this country and enable our people to embark upon the enormous
task of reconstruction without fear of molestation. I tried hard for several
months to persuade my colleagues to hold a meeting outside Nigeria where
the security of all the participants would be assured. For long, this suggestion
was treated with levity by Lt. Col. Gowon, but eventually it was unanimously agreed that the meeting should hold in Ghana.

Why did I go to Aburi? I did so firstly, because after the events of July 29,
1966, there was no single authority in Nigeria which could command the
allegiance and obedience of the entire peoples of Nigeria, or, give protection
to their lives and property. It became imperative, therefore, to re-create the
Supreme Military Council in such a manner as to re-establish its authority
and ensure its impartiality in matters affecting Nigeria as a whole, thus
removing the possibility of the central authority being solely controlled either
by a Northerner, an Easterner, a Westerner or a Mid-Westerner. Secondly, in
order to preserve the integrity of the country, a solution must be found to the
question of national leadership and chain of command within the Armed
Forces. The Aburi meeting was intended to provide and did provide a working
basis for solving the problem. Thirdly, it was necessary to arrest the drift in
the country and to control the situation so as to enable constitutional arrangements to be made in an atmosphere devoid of fear, tension and suspicion. I
did not go to Aburi as an Easterner, I went there as a Nigerian seeking a
satisfactory solution to a Nigerian problem. I did not go to Aburi to seek
powers for myself nor did I go there for a picnic. I went there to work in
order to save this country from disintegration. The solutions proposed were
accepted without equivocation at Aburi. They were accepted because we all
saw in them the *only* formula that can keep Nigeria together. I am, therefore,
irrevocably committed to seeing that the Aburi decisions are fully implemented.

After deliberating for two days—4th and 5th of January, 1967, the Military
Leaders reached agreement on a wide range of matters including the following: re-organisation, administration and control of the Army; preparation of

statistics of present army strength; full implementation of the decisions of August 9, 1966, reached by the representatives of the Military Governors, including the return of Army personnel of Northern Nigeria origin to the North; suspension of recruitment and training of soldiers pending re-organisation of the army; announcement of the death of Major-General J.T.U. Aguiyi-Ironsi and Lt. Col. Adekunle Fajuyi; the relationship between the Central and Regional Governments; repeal of Decrees tending towards over-centralisation; re-creation of the Supreme Military Council; appointments to diplomatic and consular posts, superscale posts in the Federal Civil Service, senior ranks in the Armed Forces and the Police, and identical posts in the Federal Corporation service; rehabilitation of displaced persons and recovery of their properties.

My position regarding the implementation of the Aburi Agreements has been repeatedly made clear. Apart from my public statements on the subject, I have written a number of letters to my colleagues, all urging that the Aburi agreements be implemented without unnecessary delay.

Having regard, however, to the volume of letters, and other forms of enquiries, and the great uneasiness which appear to be pervading the Region, as a result of actions on the part of the Government in Lagos such as the non-payment of salaries to both its direct employees and those of its statutory corporations, I have no alternative but to make this statement for two reasons. First, to assure the people of this Region that I am bound in honour to the Aburi agreements, and secondly to call for continued calm and intensified vigilance.

I am fully conscious of the fact that people who are not in possession of the full facts about the feeling in the Region, and the circumstances of my present statement, will, as usual, read everything sinister into it. I shall soon be accused of trying to put difficulties in the way of implementing the Aburi agreements, or of attempting to embarrass certain quarters. But I would be failing the people of this Region if I did not explain to them what I consider the real causes of the present stalemate.

Soon after our return from Aburi, Lt. Col. Gowon got in touch with me and informed me that the Government in Lagos had prepared a publication called, *Nigeria '66*. He wanted my views as to whether the publication of that booklet would be contrary to the decision reached not to publish anything which would detract from the spirit of Aburi. I personally saw in this approach an encouraging sign for future co-operation and confidence. We discussed and agreed that since the publication had not been put out to the public it would be wise to withold it. On the 15th of January, 1967, that publication was released; its sole objective being to denigrate Eastern Nigerians, living and dead. I got in touch with Lt. Col. Gowon and he assured me that it was not a deliberate act but a leakage. This information turned out to be untrue because evidence soon came through that the publication was, in fact, formally launched in Washington, London, Cotonou and other foreign capitals. What is more, its introduction shows that the draft was completed after the Aburi meeting, most likely even after our discussion. It was the first act from Lagos after Aburi which shook my confidence in what we tried to do at Aburi.

Then came Lt. Col. Gowon's Press Conference to the world on the Aburi meeting which virtually amounted to a denunciation of the agreements reached at that meeting.[3]

Contrary to the decisions at Aburi, recruitment into the Army has continued in different parts of the country except the East; contrary to those agreements, important diplomatic and other public appointments have been made without reference to the Supreme Military Council as clearly agreed at Aburi; contrary to the agreements, purchase and importation of arms have continued. The meeting of Military Officers to discuss the re-organisation of the Army as agreed at Aburi has been unilaterally postponed by Lagos. The meeting of Finance Officials, with particular reference to the problem of rehabilitation, has not even been held because officials in Lagos do not think it will serve any useful purpose.

At a meeting of Representatives of the Military Governors held in Lagos on the 9th of August, 1966, it was agreed that all decrees or Provisions of decrees of the Regional Governments should be repealed. The Government in Lagos failed to implement that decision. At the Aburi meeting, all the Military Governors insisted that that decision of August 9 be fully implemented, and it was agreed that Solicitors-General should meet on the 14th of January to identify those decrees or provisions of decrees so that they could be repealed by the 21st of January. The Solicitors-General met and identified those decrees or provisions of decrees affected. Naturally they also discussed other aspects of the Aburi decisions and sought guidance on some of them.

Since they had pin-pointed the decrees or sections of decrees to be repealed, there should be no difficulty in repealing those decrees, while leaving the other questions asked by the Solicitors-General to the Supreme Military Council. After strong pressures from me and the Military Governor of the West, the Government in Lagos produced a draft decree which for all intents and purposes aimed at strengthening the powers of the Government at the expense of the Regions: the very opposite of what the Aburi decisions envisaged. The draft was, of course, not acceptable, and so that decree has not up till now been published.

At the Aburi meeting, the question came up of employees of Government and public Corporations who had found it necessary to flee their places of work because of the disturbances. On the suggestion and personal initiative of Lt. Col. Gowon himself, we decided that such employees should be paid their salaries until the 31st of March, 1967, unless they had in the meantime found alternative employment. This decision has not been implemented. Indeed, instructions have been received from Lagos that such people who are of Eastern Nigeria origin should not be paid their salaries.

In support of their defaults, the Lagos Government has looked for one reason or another. There have been suggestions that the Aburi agreements should be reviewed if not abandoned because some members did not understand their implications. Others have said that they went there unprepared. As it was our first meeting since July 29, 1966, we certainly could not have gone to Aburi unprepared. The agenda was prepared beforehand in consultation with all the Governments concerned. If anybody went to that meeting unprepared, then one can only infer that he was not seriously concerned with the said problems which had beset the country, let alone with how to solve them.

In support of the Lagos Government's refusal to honour the Aburi agreements as they affected the payment of fleeing employees up to the end of March, the fact that a number of railway wagons are now in the East has been proffered as an excuse. When the decision was taken at Aburi, everybody knew that those wagons were here. One should have thought that the implementation of the Aburi agreement would be a pre-condition for the release of these wagons and not the other way round. The Government in Lagos further complicated matters by denying the Coal Corporation the right to collect their just debts from the Nigerian Railway Corporation, and have refused to send the necessary funds for the payment of salaries for railway workers. These acts are nothing but a deliberate attempt to cause trouble and disaffection among the people of Eastern Nigeria, because they know the large number of persons involved and the seriousness of their dissatisfaction following non-payment of their salaries at the beginning of a new year when they have to meet commitments for their children's school fees and other personal matters.

The authorities in Lagos have not stopped there. They are using all their power to impede the smooth operation of private industries in this Region. Not only are they doing everything to obstruct investors and industrialists coming to do business here, they are doing everything they can to kill even those industries which are operating in this Region. I am aware also that plans to carry out a blockade of the East is being hatched.

On the political front, I have evidence that the Governments in Lagos and Kaduna are encouraging acts of subversion and sabotage within this Region. These Northern controlled Governments are prepared to sink their tribal and political differences in order to achieve an objective nearest to their hearts, namely, to dominate and rule the Southern Regions. It is this same policy that is now driving this country to the verge of disintegration. I, therefore, take this opportunity to call on the peoples of Southern Nigeria to open their eyes and see the hand-writing on the wall.

It has now become imperative that an end should be put to all this. As a people who once claimed the honour of being looked upon as the most mature in Africa, the leaders of this country must show that maturity by honouring agreements. The survival of this country, its normalcy and peace, hinge on the implementation of the Aburi agreements.

We are coming to the end of our fiscal year when estimates must be finalised and plans made for the coming year. These are not possible under the present unsettled state of affairs. For this reason I have recently informed my fellow Military Leaders that if the Aburi agreements are not fully implemented by the 31st of March, I shall have no alternative but to feel free to take whatever measures that are necessary to give effect in this Region to those agreements.

The Secretaries to the Military Governments and other officials have recently held a meeting in Benin to advise on the implementation of the Aburi agreements. I sincerely hope they will bring home to all concerned the pressing need to give immediate effect to the Aburi decisions. Friends of Nigeria in Africa and the rest of the world, and particularly in Ghana, are watching our actions with deep concern. Once the agreements are implemented, Nigerians will be assured of a faster and more peaceful march to the goal of normalcy.

Before concluding, I feel I must say something about the position of non-Easterners whom circumstances compelled me to ask to leave this Region some months ago. While at Aburi I gave assurance that this order will 'be kept under constant review with a view to its being lifted as soon as practicable.' It is not true, as has frequently been suggested in different quarters, that I had undertaken to ask them to return immediately we got back from Accra. I reserved my position in this respect because I felt that the implementation of the Aburi decisions would create the atmosphere conducive to their early return. I am anxious for this occasion to come and sincerely hope that conditions will soon materialise for this to be done.

Finally, I must warn all Easterners once again to remain vigilant. The East will never be intimidated nor will she acquiesce to any form of dictation. It is not the intention of the East to play the aggressor. Nonetheless it is not our intention to be slaughtered in our beds. We are ready to defend our homeland. We are prepared to crush any aggressors.

Fellow countrymen and women, on Aburi we stand. There will be no compromise. God grant peace in our time.

[1] *Eastern Ministry of Information Press Release No. 123/1967. (Cf. DOC 89.)*
[2] *See DOC 83.* [3] *See DOC 85.*

91.
Military Governor of the West Speaks on Aburi[1]

My fellow countrymen,

I have up till now refrained from making any public statement on the outcome of the conference of Nigerian military leaders which was held at Aburi in Ghana, early in January this year. As you know, that meeting came about as a result of the exertions and personal sacrifice of men of goodwill all over the country and through the generosity of Lieutenant-General Ankrah and his colleagues of the Ghana National Liberation Council.

Perhaps one of the greatest achievements of the conference was that it served to restore hope and to revive a constructive attitude towards finding a solution to the problem of rebuilding and working for a strong and united Nigeria.

We only have to look back on the path which we have trodden in these last fourteen months of strife and purposeless waste to realise fully all that we have lost. A broadcast to the people of Nigeria soon after the Aburi conference would have been most fitting and this might have been properly done on behalf of all of us at the Federal level by the Head of the Federal Military Government and Supreme Commander of the Armed Forces, Lieutenant-Colonel Yakubu Gowon. I know that he was not unmindful of his responsibilities in this direction; but he was ill immediately after his return from Aburi. He was also forestalled by the turn of events which followed.

Since then, a lot of water has passed under the bridge and today, it looks as if we are dangerously close to the pre-Aburi days which were notorious for their uncertainties and capriciousness. Practically all my colleagues on the

2 B

Supreme Military Council have made public statements of one kind or another on the Aburi Conference; but as I said earlier on, I have up till now maintained a studied silence and concentrated on working behind the scenes by offering advice and warning in the belief that I might, in this way, serve the people of this Region and the country better.

In view of a certain amount of restiveness which I observe, I consider it my duty to break that silence and to let the people of Western Nigeria know that my efforts in this direction have produced some encouraging results. There is still a tremendous lot to do, but all is not lost as some people fear.

First, let me tell you about Aburi. The communiqué issued by the Nigerian Military leaders at the conclusion of the conference showed clearly that the true interests of the nation had triumphed and that we derived immense benefit from our deliberations; indeed agreement was reached in broad terms on a variety of subjects, the most important items being the following:

i. All the military leaders solemnly declared that they renounced the use of force as a means of settling the problems confronting the country and they re-affirmed their faith in discussions and negotiations as the only way of resolving the Nigerian crisis.

ii. It was agreed to exchange information on the quantity of arms and ammunitions held in each unit of the Army in all parts of the country. Agreement was also reached to the effect that unallocated stores of arms and ammunitions held in the country should be shared out equitably between the various commands in the Federation.

iii. It was agreed that the Army itself should be re-organised in order to restore discipline and confidence. Specifically, it was agreed that the Army should be governed by the Supreme Military Council under the Chairman to be known as Commander-in-Chief of the Armed Forces and Head of the Federal Military Government. The creation of Area Commands corresponding to existing Regions was also agreed to. It was further agreed that all matters of policy including appointments and promotions to commissions or senior posts in the Armed Forces and the Police should be dealt with by the Supreme Military Council.

iv. The Military leaders agreed that the legislative and executive authority of the Federal Military Government should be vested in the Supreme Military Council to which any decision affecting the whole country should be referred for determination, provided that where it is not possible for a meeting to be held the matter requiring determination should be referred to the Military Governors for their comments and concurrence.

v. It was agreed that appointments to senior ranks in the Diplomatic and Consular service as well as to superscale posts in the Federal Public Service and equivalent positions in Statutory Corporations must be approved by the Supreme Military Council.

vi. It was agreed that all decrees or provisions of decrees passed since January 15, 1966, which detracted from the previous powers and positions of Regional Governments should be repealed with a view to promoting mutual confidence.

vii. It was agreed by the military leaders that a meeting of officials should be convened soon after the Aburi conference to consider ways and means of resolving the serious problems posed by displaced persons all over the country.

viii. It was agreed that the *Ad Hoc* Constitutional Committee should resume sitting as soon as practicable and that the unanimous recommendations of that body made in September, 1966, should be considered at another meeting of the Supreme Military Council.

There has been fierce criticism by the public during the past few weeks alleging tardiness in the implementation of those decisions. It would be futile to deny that difficulties of various kinds have not arisen since our return from Aburi. It is common knowledge that there have been moves and ill-considered pronouncements which have all tended to re-open old quarrels and age-old feuds. It must be admitted that there have been other difficulties as well, even though these have been largely administrative in character.

I should however like to emphasise that I have, for my part, done everything in my power to ensure that we stand by the undertakings freely entered into by all of us at Aburi. I am painfully aware that failure to implement these decisions would be seen at home and abroad as a dishonourable act, and that this would in turn wreck any chance of national reconciliation. I know that a majority of my colleagues on the Supreme Military Council feel the same way and that they have all been working in this spirit.

But you might well ask, where are we now? My answer is simply that although we have made considerable progress towards the implementation of these agreements, we still have a long way to go and I must ask you to endure and persevere a little longer. Let me remind you that while you are perfectly entitled to demand an end to uncertainties, you should not overlook the gravity and consequences of the disorder which took place in this country during 1966.

Upon careful reflection, you will appreciate that the task of reconciliation must necessarily take time. It would be unrealistic to suppose that a two-day meeting of military leaders will be sufficient for the purpose of finding a permanent and satisfactory solution to all our problems. It has always been my view that close and continuous consultation between all the military leaders is as urgent and essential today as it was prior to the Aburi conference. These conversations must go on until confidence and trust is firmly re-established among us.

I fully share the anxiety of members of the public that the country should be seen to move forward in a positive fashion; but I must insist that we have not been entirely idle in this regard. Since our return from Aburi, there has been a meeting of the Solicitors-General from all over the Federation for the purpose of drafting the necessary legal instrument for the implementation of the Agreements which I have mentioned earlier on in this broadcast.

When, some three weeks ago, the situation looked rather bleak, and it looked as though we were not getting anywhere, I urged that a meeting of Secretaries to the Military Governments should again be convened at Benin for the purpose of sorting out the confusion and misunderstanding which appeared to have arisen over the implementation of the Aburi Agreements.

I am glad to report that the Head of the Federal Military Government and Supreme Commander of the Armed Forces and other Regional Governors responded promptly and generously to this suggestion and a meeting of officials did take place at Benin. It is gratifying to note that the outcome of the meeting has assisted in no small way in bringing us closer together in our thoughts. I believe that I am in a position to say that we are today in a far better state to cope with the problems of the nation than we were at any time since our return from Aburi.

As you might have heard from recent press announcements, a meeting of the Supreme Military Council is planned to take place at Benin very soon. It is my earnest hope that we would, at that meeting, be able to promulgate the decree which will result in the implementation of, at least, the essential part of the Agreements reached by the military leaders at Aburi. Before long, a full report of the proceedings of the conference at Aburi will be placed in hands of the public and we should all be in a position to enter into considered judgement on the course of events.

In addition to the modest achievements recorded above, a representative body of Army Officers met in Benin during the month of January with a view to preparing detailed plans for the re-organisation of the Army as envisaged under the relevant clause of the Aburi Agreements.

Although we cannot claim to have made any significant progress in this direction, I would call the attention of the people of this Region to the fact that there has been some improvement in our position with regard to Army personnel. A sizable number of Yorubas have been recruited into the Army in recent months and the monthly in-take of recruits has been increased in fulfilment of the undertaking given to the people. While the common training facilities at Zaria will continue to be available for our use, a training depot is being constructed here in Western Nigeria and I expect that it will be possible within a matter of a few weeks for training to commence here in Western Nigeria.

In spite of the uneasiness and distrust which have unfortunately pervaded our affairs since the Aburi conference, I have considered it my duty to continue to confer with my colleagues all over the country. I have done this in the firm belief that the only way out of our present troubles is through consultation with a view to promoting and brightening the opportunities for tolerance and understanding and in order to rescue and rebuild this country.

I should like to make it absolutely clear that I do not desire any honours or preferments beyond the opportunity which has already been given to me to serve the people of Western Nigeria and through them, the nation. I do not lay claims to higher office of any kind, all I ask is the opportunity to discharge my responsibilities to the people of this Region and to the nation as a whole by lending such weight as I have in support of policies and measures which I genuinely believe to be in the true interest of us all.

People should therefore disabuse their minds about rumours going around that I am in conspiracy with some of my colleagues in order that I may take over the headship of the Federal Military Government.

As agreed by the Military leaders at Aburi, I would emphasise that I am unalterably opposed to the use of force in settling the problems of this nation. As I see it, we renounced the use of force not merely for reasons of charity and compassion, but because it would do us no good whatsoever. I know that I speak for the people of this Region when I say that we should leave no stone unturned in finding a peaceful solution to such disputes as plague this nation today.

I, for my part, have no doubt that a great deal can be achieved given tolerance, mutual understanding and above all genuineness of purpose. No one should harbour any illusions about the disastrous consequences of further acts of violence or the use of force in any form. We know for a fact that this can only do irreparable harm to the nation and deny us the achievement of the objectives which we seek.

It is my firm belief that a partisan spirit could only serve to aggravate our difficulties. When therefore I was confronted by representatives of the displaced persons in this Region a week ago, with the demand that we eject all persons from a particular Region from our midst, I had no doubts about my duty to the people of this Region and to the country at large.

I am sure you do not need me to remind you that we in Western Nigeria have passed through very trying times during the past five years. If we have not issued pamphlets to recount and commemorate these sad events, it is certainly not because we do not have a good story to tell. Our reticence has been governed by the belief that we should for once, endeavour to play a positive role in healing the wounds of the nation. I am convinced that we have a vital role to play in this connection, and I believe most passionately, that the stability of this Federation will be greatly endangered unless we in the West accept our fair share of responsibility for constructive leadership.

I am grateful to representatives of the displaced persons in Western Nigeria for their generous response to my appeal and for their recognition of the wider interests of the Region and the nation. I should like to take this opportunity to assure them that I will continue to use every available means at my disposal to ensure that their legitimate claims are met.

Already, agreement has been reached by the Commissioners of Police all over the country regarding practical steps for the recovery and safety of property left behind in various parts of the country. Beyond this, I trust that it may be possible before long to persuade my colleague, the Military Governor of the East, to co-operate with us by lifting the ban on the free movement of persons. I am sure, he is well aware that we cannot go on in this way indefinitely without provoking unpleasant reactions.

Before I end this broadcast, I should like to say a few words about a rather popular subject—the making of a Constitution. I entirely share the views of the Head of the Federal Military Government and Supreme Commander of the Armed Forces, to the effect that the task of preparing a Constitution is a matter for the people.

We in the armed Forces do not seek in any way to impose a Constitution of any sort on the people and I would urge most strongly that all talk of confederation and federalism should be put aside, until such a time as the *Ad Hoc* Committee resumes its work. I believe that all of us in the Supreme Council are agreed that we should not allow ourselves to be unnecessarily burdened or distracted by the controversy over the form of the country's Constitution under a civilian administration. Our priority task is to devise a suitable arrangement for keeping the country together and for running it in an effective manner under a military regime.

I would like to emphasise that I am personally committed to the sacred task of doing everything I can towards helping to keep this country together as a single unit and handing it back to civilian authorities better than we of the Armed Forces found it. I should like to be clearly understood that I would not subscribe to any arrangement or policy which might in any way conceivably lead to the break-up of this country, for we hold it in trust and we are in honour bound to maintain its integrity.

I wish I could end this broadcast by telling you tonight that our toils and troubles are over; but I must tell you in all honesty that there is still a lot to be done. I trust however that this broadcast will have persuaded you that we military Leaders have not been entirely idle and that considerable progress has been made. . . .

I should continue to need and depend on the efforts of mind and body of the people of this Region for the achievement of our common objective— the restoration of a united Nigeria, built, this time, on the principles of equality, fairness and trust.

[1] *Broadcast from Ibadan, 1 March 1967. Western Ministry of Information hand-out.*

92.
Gowon's Private Address to Heads of African Diplomatic Missions in Lagos, 1 March 1967[1]

Your Excellencies,

In October 1966, I addressed letters to our brother Heads of State and Government in Africa explaining the situation in Nigeria and the efforts we were making to come to an amicable settlement. I have been encouraged by the responses received and the sympathy shown by my colleagues.

When I addressed you a little under three months ago on the eve of this New Year, I expressed my hope that the New Year would bring its choicest blessings and good news to Nigeria. Since then we the military leaders of Nigeria have had the meeting at Aburi in Ghana and in spite of the various interpretations that have since been given to the broad conclusions, that meeting afforded the opportunity for all of us to meet for the first time since July 29, 1966.

I consider this meeting with you essential because as trusted envoys of your respective countries duly accredited to my Government, I expect you to send despatches to your Governments which will reflect as much as possible an objective analysis of the situation in Nigeria. It is my desire that my discussion with you should be in confidence and that is why I have not invited the press to be present. I equally expect that you will reciprocate by treating whatever we may discuss here with the same degree of confidence that I have assigned to it.

It is true that at Aburi we all signed an undertaking not to use force in an attempt to settle our present difficulties in the country, but I would like to make it abundantly clear that this undertaking is valid so long as there is no attempt anywhere on the part of anybody to disintegrate the country. In this connection I reiterate what I said in my broadcast of 30th November, 1966[2] that we shall be in honour bound to defend the integrity of the country even if we have to use force.

As I said earlier, we reached broad conclusions on a number of subjects at Aburi but the specific implementation of each item required detail examination by the administrative and professional experts in the various fields. In working out the details, major points of disagreement and interpretation have arisen between the Eastern Military Governor on the one hand, and the rest of us. These points require further clarification and decision by the Supreme Military Council before the relevant Aburi understandings can be given effect in concrete legislation.

It is pertinent here to recall the more important conclusions reached in Aburi. We agreed to return to the constitutional position before January 17, 1966. This means in effect that the Federal Government in Lagos and the Regional Governments will continue to carry on their respective functions as before. Thus any powers which were taken away from the Regions after January 17, were to be restored to them. In this context, we agreed that the Supreme Military Council should be given powers to deal with all matters of national importance affecting the whole country. I emphasise that it was never the intention that any Military Governor should have the power to veto decisions taken by the Supreme Military Council. This, as a matter of fact, is one of the major points of disagreement which has held up the Draft Decree on the constitution.

On the reorganisation of the Army, we agreed to continue to maintain one Nigerian Army under one command. It was agreed that there would be Area Commands to correspond with the existing regional boundaries, but we also agreed that the details should be worked out in view of the far reaching implications. This is another area where we have to clarify outstanding questions before the changes agreed in outline at Aburi can be fully implemented.

We also touched on problems of rehabilitation of displaced persons. Here things are moving in the right direction. We discussed the restoration of essential services such as the disruption of railway services in the East, where it affects a number of displaced persons. The Military Governor, East, assured us that he would look into this with the minimum delay. He was also to lift the ban on non-Easterners.

You must have heard a lot about senior Federal appointments in the Public Service at home and abroad becoming the responsibility of the Supreme Military Council. The interpretation given to this gesture of unity and good faith on my part by the Governor of the East, was that all current senior appointments in the Nigerian Foreign Service should be cancelled now and new appointments and postings made by the Supreme Military Council. An interpretation like this can only lead to administrative chaos and I assure you, Gentlemen, this was never my intention. The thinking here was in respect of appointments to posts such as Permanent Secretaries and Principal Representatives abroad.

You are aware from newspaper publications and radio broadcasts that the Military Governor of Eastern Nigeria has given an ultimatum which is due to expire on the 31st of March.[3] I do not intend to bandy ultimatums but I would like to re-emphasise my responsibilities as Head of the Federal Military Government towards the whole country both to Nigerian citizens and the foreigners amongst us.

Your Excellencies, Nigeria is passing through a very difficult time but history shows that many countries have passed through such difficult times and emerged in the end much stronger nations. There have been hints of unilateral action and desperate acts which could endanger the corporate existence of Nigeria. I take this opportunity to appeal to your Governments through you not to do anything which could in any way encourage such dangerous developments.

Africa desires unity; all our countries are struggling to achieve this goal. Each African nation must therefore maintain and consolidate its integrity to contribute effectively to this our common struggle. My country played its role in helping to contain the divisive efforts of certain elements in a sister Republic not long ago. In the event of any section of this country acting unilaterally to the extent of destroying the constitution, we will have to take necessary police action to contain the situation and maintain the integrity of the nation. I would like an assurance from your respective Governments through you individually that in such extremities your Governments will co-operate fully with us and will do nothing whatsoever tending to give any form of recognition or support to such dissident elements opposed to my Government.

Excellencies, all I am trying to do is to hold this country together. I am still trying my best to do so by peaceful means. We however live in a situation where we may be forced to take preventive measures to avoid disaster. You can all use your good offices to help.

[1] *This document was leaked by Enugu, according to a statement made by Lt.-Col. Gowon on 24 April 1967. See* DOC *103.*

[2] *See* DOC *75.*   [3] *See* DOC *90.*

93.
Eastern Government's Comments on Gowon's Address to Foreign Diplomats [1]

Yesterday, March 1st, Lt. Col. Yakubu Gowon summoned the Heads of the Diplomatic Missions in Nigeria to what was no less than a secret meeting. From the opening address delivered by him to the Heads of Diplomatic Missions,[2] it is clear that his intention was to use his position and access to the Heads of Diplomatic Missions in Lagos for blackmail. He made no secret of this intention because he excluded the Press, enjoined the Heads of Diplomatic Missions to regard everything he said as a matter of confidence and to send dispatches to their governments based on the distorted information he gave out to them.

He started his address by talking of 'various interpretations that have been given to the conclusions reached at Aburi'. The Aburi decisions as contained in the statements and communiqués issued at that meeting as well as in the

official minutes issued from the Cabinet Office in Lagos, were put in language
and phrases which for their simplicity allowed of no ambiguity.

Lt. Col. Yakubu Gowon made it 'abundantly clear'—and these are his very
words—that he had abandoned faith in the joint declaration to eschew the
use of force in the settlement of our problems. For this statement, he owes
Nigeria and the whole world personal responsibility for whatever may be
the consequences of any attempt to employ force in the settlement of our
current problems. As far as the East is concerned, it has been made repeatedly clear that we cannot be intimidated and that we are prepared to
match any force with force. He would be a fool who thought that the East
would be sleeping and therefore not apprehensive of intentions on the part
of Lagos and the North to destroy or enslave it by force.

Anybody who was present at the Aburi meeting or has read the minutes,
communiqués, statements and verbatim reports, would be surprised that a
person who calls himself a Head of State could so deliberately mislead accredited representatives of Foreign Governments by saying that the implementation of each item of the conclusions required prior detailed examination by the administrative and professional experts in the various fields.
The conclusions in Aburi were no proposals but decisions taken by the
highest authority in the land.

What happened in fact was that specific matters namely, the Decrees and
sections of Decrees to be repealed, the mechanics of Army reorganisation and
the question of rehabilitation of refugees, were referred to experts. The
meeting of the financial experts to consider the question of rehabilitation of
displaced persons has not been held because the Federal Permanent Secretary of the Ministry of Finance does not think that such a meeting would
serve any useful purpose. The Army experts met and started discussions but
the Federal representatives suddenly caused the meeting to be discontinued.
The legal experts met and reached agreements but these were rejected.

To talk of any of the decisions reached requiring further clarification and
further decisions by the Supreme Military Council before the relevant Aburi
'understandings' can be given effect in concrete legislation, is dishonest and
cannot therefore do any credit to Nigeria in the eyes of an inquisitive and
understanding world.

Lt. Col. Yakubu Gowon told the Heads of Missions that the agreement
about returning the Regions to their positions before January 17 also meant
in effect that the Federal Government in Lagos would continue to carry on
its functions as before. He failed to inform the world that by the decisions
taken at Aburi, the Federal Government meant no more than the Supreme
Military Council. No one of course who knows the sort of advice Lt. Col.
Gowon is receiving in Lagos would be surprised by this suppression and
distortion of truth.

It is difficult to understand the introduction of the word 'veto' into the
matter. The Aburi agreement was that any decision which affected the whole
country must receive the concurrence of all the Military Governors because
of their special responsibilities in their different areas of authority, and so to
the country as a corporate whole.

On the reorganisation of the Army, it is for Lt. Col. Gowon to explain to
the world what he means by the 'Army continuing to be under one com-

mand' when in the very next sentence of his statement he also speaks of an agreement to establish area commands corresponding with the existing Regional boundaries. This contradiction in itself tells the truth and one does not need to belabour the point.

It is clear that what was envisaged was a loosely-knit Army administered by a representative military headquarters under the charge of a Chief of Staff and commanded by the Supreme Military Council, not by Lt. Col. Gowon as he claimed in his recent Press Conference.[3]

Significantly, Lt. Col. Yakubu Gowon merely made a passing reference to the pervading question of rehabilitation of displaced persons and says that things are moving in the right direction. Judging from what is happening, one would agree that things are moving in the right direction as Gowon would like it in that the hated East is bearing the heaviest brunt to this misfortune. So long as this is so and the East is suffering under the heavy burden, Gowon and his accomplices can remain satisfied that things are moving in the right direction.

One does not need to mention his statement that the Aburi decisions discussed the restoration of essential services, such as the disruption of Railway services. In my recent broadcast, I touched on this point and told the country that the restoration of these services was to follow the general course of a return to normalcy following the implementation of the Aburi agreements.

Lt. Col. Yakubu Gowon informed the accredited Assembly of world representatives that the decision of the Aburi meeting that appointments to diplomatic and consular posts as well as to senior posts in the Federal Civil Service and public corporations was confined to the posts of Permanent Secretaries and Principal Representatives abroad. Nowhere in the decisions were the words 'Permanent Secretaries' or 'Principal Representatives abroad' mentioned. Such limitations never occurred in anybody's mind. The words used were 'appointments to diplomatic and consular posts' as well as to 'senior posts in the Federal Civil Service and public corporations'.

To confuse issues, Lt. Col. Gowon gave the impression that the main difference between him and me on this particular decision was that I insisted on cancelling the appointments of existing civil servants. I can think of nothing more slanderous. At my press conference on the 6th of January[4] explaining to the public what had happened at Aburi, I had [something] to say on this subject. . . . Nothing in that statement can be interpreted by any honest person to mean that my intention was that existing appointments should be concelled. The sum total of all this is to further confuse the situation in a deliberate attempt to hoodwink the diplomats. For this I apologise to them on behalf of all honest Nigerians.

Since it is now clear that Lt. Col. Yakubu Gowon and his aides in and outside Lagos now want to resort to blackmail and deceit, I am despatching to all Embassies in Nigeria all relevant and authentic documents available to me in connection with Aburi.

It is hoped that the Federal Government will not interfere with the movement of these documents and that those concerned will be able to base their despatches on the truth. As accredited representatives of their countries they must not lend themselves to blackmail, deceit or intimidation.

It is clear from Gowon's statement in question that he is prepared to distort the verbatim reports of the Aburi meeting. To keep the public informed, the Eastern Nigerian Broadcasting Service will be playing the tape records of the proceedings live at scheduled times as from today. Arrangements have been completed to transform those tape recordings to long playing gramophone records for those who may wish to have them and play at leisure. We are also going ahead to print and publish the documents and records of the Aburi meeting.

Finally, Gowon closing his statement, wanted reassurance from the respective governments through the Embassies that they will co-operate with him and do nothing whatsoever to give any form of recognition or support to dissident elements opposed to his government. The question that one would like to ask Gowon is 'Who are the dissident elements and which is his government?' At the Aburi meeting I made it perfectly clear that the East did not recognise Gowon as the Head of the Federal Military Government because he usurped that position. To talk, therefore, of 'his government' is presumptuous.

We in the East are anxious to see that our difficulties are resolved by peaceful means and that Nigeria is preserved as a unit but it is doubtful and the world must judge whether Lt. Col. Gowon's attitudes and other exhibitions of his insincerity are something which can lead to a return of normalcy and confidence in the country.

[1] *Statement issued from the Military Governor's Office, Enugu, 2 March 1967 (Ministry of Information hand-out).*
[2] *See* DOC *92.*   [3] *See* DOC *85.*   [4] *See* DOC *83.*

94.
'Nigeria's Last Hope': Press Statement by the Eastern Nigeria Union of Great Britain and Ireland[1]

Nigeria is on the brink of disintegration In Nigeria, no one military leader has commanded the allegiance of the whole country since July 29, 1966, when General Ironsi, the Military Head of State, was murdered by mutinous Northern Nigeria soldiers, and the chain of command was broken by Lt. Col. Gowon's 'assumption' of office. It was in recognition of this that the Supreme Military Council, made up of all Nigeria's military leaders, agreed, at a recent meeting in Ghana, that Government decisions affecting the entire country should be taken collectively by the Supreme Military Council and with the concurrence of the Regional Governors, the only people exercising effective authority in their respective territories. This agreement, so vital for the restoration of confidence and normalcy in Nigeria is now being vitiated by the Government in Lagos as a result of pressures from Northern Nigerian politicians and civil servants.

THE GHANA AGREEMENTS

In broad outline the agreements in Ghana were meant to reduce tension, break the impasse which had brought the country to a standstill and pave the way for the Regions of Nigeria to resume co-operation.

DECLARATION ON THE USE OF FORCE

In its declaration on the use of force, the members of the Supreme Military Council made up of Lt. Col. Gowon, the four Regional Military Governors, and the Head of the Nigerian Navy, solemnly and unequivocally renounced the use of force as a means of settling the crisis in the country and held themselves in honour bound by that declaration. The Council re-affirmed its faith in discussion and negotiation as the only way of resolving the Nigerian crisis and undertook to stop any further arms importation into the country.

Nevertheless, Northern Nigerians, in addition to stock-piling ammunition have continued with other war-like preparations. In particular, they have, on the 31st January, 1967, imported three jet fighters from Italy.

RE-ORGANISATION OF THE ARMY

The Nigerian Army, since the inter-tribal mutiny of July, 1966, has been under the effective command of the respective Regional Military Governors. In order to reintroduce some confidence and a measure of unity, the Supreme Military Council decided to exercise collective operational control over the entire army. Area commands corresponding to the various Regions were formally recognised and the military Governors given full control over their Army in matters of internal security. It was agreed to establish a Military Headquarters, to be headed by a Chief of Staff, in which the four Regions would be equally represented. It was agreed, therefore, that the Army would be governed by the Supreme Military Council whose Chairman would become the titular Commander-in-Chief and Head of the Federal Military Government.

Lt. Col. Gowon now insists that 'the Area Command will take operational instruction from the Military Headquarters which will be directly under me as the Supreme Commander of the Armed Forces.' By this action he has not only defied a decision freely reached with his colleagues, but has also re-introduced the fear of a one-man control of the Army which is unacceptable in the circumstances of Nigeria today.

OTHER AGREEMENTS

The Supreme Military Council, recognising the conditions which forced many Nigerians, mostly of Eastern origin, to return to their homes, agreed that the salaries and wages of all such displaced persons who have not found alternative employment should be paid by the Federal Government and its institutions up to the 31st of March, 1967. It was clear that fear of the activities of the Northern soldiers had been responsible for the exodus of workers and the consequent disruption of services. Now, Lt. Col. Gowon and Northern Nigerian leaders use this as an excuse for introducing a new clause in the agreement reached on this matter by saying that 'each case is to be considered on its merit.'

The Supreme Military Council reached other agreements, one of which was that all decrees passed since the first Military Government from January 15th 1966, which detracted from the autonomy of the Regions should be repealed by January 21st, 1967. January 21st has since passed without the agreement being honoured. Following on this, it was agreed that fiscal experts drawn equally from all the Regions should meet and devise a new formula of revenue allocation to take account of the changes in population disposition since May, 1966. This is significant for Eastern Nigeria because almost 2,000,000 people have now returned to the Region from other parts of Nigeria, especially the North. The basis of free population movement between all the Regions, on which the existing principle of revenue allocation was made is, therefore, altered.

The people of Eastern Nigeria, who have suffered extreme provocation from Northern Nigeria and have lost about 30,000 of their kith and kin in recent disturbances, are anxious that Nigerians should forget the past and look to the future. It is for this reason that they place such faith in the agreements recently reached by the military leaders in Ghana, the implementation of which would have created conditions for the restoration of confidence and stability. Eastern Nigeria, which is made up of the dynamic Efiks, Ibibios, Ibos and the Ijaws, is anxious that Nigeria should resume its onward march, and for its people to contribute their share to the country's progress by their talents, education and industry.

Eastern Nigerians believe in one country which should remain one economic unit. They also believe that every Nigerian in every part of the country should be free to realize his full potential. All the efforts and energies of the people were directed to creating a society on those lines. Seven years' experience of working a Federation with a strong centre, however, has demonstrated that:

(a) this belief is not generally shared; and
(b) the root-cause of crisis after crisis in Nigeria has been the struggle to control the Centre.

THE LAST CHANCE

Nigeria is on the brink of disintegration. Nigeria's last hope of remaining one country and solving her present problems lies in peaceful negotiation, not in the use of force, and in honouring agreements reached by such negotiation. Any attempt to impose a solution by force, or to introduce measures affecting Eastern Nigeria without the concurrence of her accredited representative at the highest organ of the land, the Supreme Military Council, will be regarded as a provocative act aimed at forcing the Eastern Region out of the Nigerian Association. The responsibility for this will, therefore, rest elsewhere, not in the East. Once this happens, Nigeria, as we know it, will be over the brink and cease to exist. Friends of Eastern Nigeria in the United Kingdom and the world will, no doubt, appreciate the determination of the people of Eastern Nigeria not to allow themselves to be subjected to the perpetual domination of the Northerners of Nigeria.

[1] *Published as a full page advertisement in* The Times *and the* Guardian, *2 March 1967, and in the* New York Times.

95.
Speech by the Chairman of the Eastern Region's Rehabilitation Committee[1]

It gives me great pleasure to be afforded this opportunity to address you at this first ever seminar which will study a new phenomenon never known to this part of the world until in recent months. . . .

The purpose of this seminar is not to examine the causes of the disaster either remote or immediate; indeed, the sponsors of this conference have urged everyone participating in it to eschew any matters or materials which would tend to lay emphasis or underscore unnecessarily the events that have transpired.

I am therefore making only a cursory and passing reference to the causes of the pogrom. One thing is however sure and that is that a great number of people mostly of Eastern Nigeria origin have been forced by circumstances beyond their control to leave or abandon some other parts of Nigeria where many of them had sojourned for many years. Suddenly and without warning they have been thrust out of these areas into this Region. Many of them in a state of helpless indigence and penury; others maimed permanently through injuries they received, quite a number naked and without clothing. Some have been left spiritually lonely and physically depraved.

So that in one short moment we have on our hands a complex situation which requires remedies that vary not only in nature but in degrees. Some of the refugees, and I insist on calling them refugees instead of displaced persons, need new homes, others need a complete psychological change, others want work, others want health.

It was in the maze of these events that His Excellency the Military Governor, Lt. Col. Chukwuemeka Odumegwu-Ojukwu inaugurated the Rehabilitation Commission, charging this new body with the responsibility of caring for those persons who have returned and providing £1m for this purpose. The Commission consists of your humble speaker as Chairman, three Commissioners and a Secretary. Added to these, are ten distinguished Eastern Nigerians of varying professions, skills and experiences on the Panel of Advisers. Naturally, on our inauguration, the Commission was faced with the immediate duty of arranging the reception of those who fled. They were arriving by train, by plane, by lorries, on foot, indeed by every conceivable means of transport. A refugee clutching his child and without any belongings became a regular feature for those four depressing weeks. Ever since, over 1·8 million people have come into this Region through many a highway and by-way. . . .

God in His infinite mercy worked on the side of the people of this Region. They arrived at a time when our harvest was at its peak and our barns were full with crops. Food therefore was not a pressing necessity. Secondly, this miracle has been performed as a result of our time honoured and respected extended family system. My Commission was saved the onerous duty of erecting transit camps with their natural unpleasant consequences and bitterness. These refugees returned and were absorbed in existing facilities of their homes. If anything, our villages without an additional housing became so elastic that they were able to absorb in this short period the great number that I have already indicated.

Ladies and Gentlemen, my Commission knew that very soon the honeymoon would be over; very soon the elasticity of the extended family system would become so distended that it would burst under its own inscrutable burden unless some drastic and quick action were taken. Our first task therefore was to anticipate that food in the next few months may become short. We quickly rallied round a group of knowledgeable skilled Eastern Nigerians. Thank goodness that this disaster has had a salutary effect of bringing together such a large concourse of experienced and seasoned skills whose services and knowledge had been denied to this Region. This group was asked to study and report on food production within two weeks. I am happy to report that the submissions made by them have formed the prop on which our food production programme has largely depended. . . .

My Commission likewise appreciated that during this period there was a necessity of adjustment and that there would be a strain on housing, employment and that indeed services themselves might be stretched to breaking point. In spite of the fact that Eastern Nigeria is backed with the magnanimous steadfastness of its peoples' warmth for their relations it was clear that this steadfastness could only be sustained by providing employment opportunities to those who had returned. We therefore decided that all public servants returning to the Region as well as those working for Public Corporations in other parts of Nigeria returning to the Region should be absorbed and that the burden of their salaries would be borne by my Commission up to the 31st of March 1967. This indeed worked miracles and as a result, in less than six months, over 28,000 persons had been given employment in the public sector and nearly 5,000 more had been absorbed in the private sector both through our personal persuasion and their own magnanimity.

Our next problem was that of the widows, and there are many of them as well as the orphans. My Commission decided to make an outright grant of £5 per widow and to pay 10/- per month per orphan for six consecutive months. I appreciate that these grants appear paltry but they were to be paid to a group of people who had lost all hopes and whose very existence was in jeopardy. These payments therefore were intended not to be a panacea of all their needs, wants or indeed problems but to act as temporary reliefs tiding them over the period of their darkest need. Furthermore, it was to make them less dependent on the members of their individual families. . . .

I cannot forget that my Commission also gave considerable thought to students, many of whom had lost their parents or guardians. We paid the school fees for the last quarter for those school children whose needs were ascertained and confirmed. £7,000 was made available to the University of Nigeria to set up a Revolving Loans Fund to enable needy undergraduates to continue with their studies without interruption. Another £10,000 was made available to enable the Law Students to carry on with their studies here in Eastern Nigeria. In recent weeks, my Commission has recognised the necessity of giving some form of assistance to the many thousands of elementary school children and the few hundreds of secondary school children whose education stands in danger of being halted as a result of last year's events. . . .

Ladies and gentlemen, the problem is here. So far the going has been smooth, uneventful and romantic. No one can forecast that it will remain like that all along. Already pressures are building up both in the civil service, the public sectors and the private sectors which admittedly have a limit they can absorb. As I speak to you now, nearly six thousand Railway men varying from administrators, accountants, engineers, other professions, engine drivers, coal men, clerks, station staff, etc. and about that number of daily paid workers have been unleashed on us. A couple of a thousand more are overflowing from the Posts and Telegraphs Department. The bulk of the Airways staff have neither planes to fly nor operations to maintain. They are there. They are our kinsmen. We must do something about them.

This is why my Commission lent its fullest support not only in principle but in more solid terms to gather all of you here, distinguished scholars, experienced administrators, chiefs and leaders of thought to consider this problem aggressively and assist my Commission in promulgating ideas and schemes that will combat the problem. I am not going to attempt whatsoever to anticipate those who are going to read papers. I would however wish to direct your thoughts to such questions as the priorities to consider in this problem. Should we go ahead with new industries and more capital works some of which will merely be infrastructures or should we continue to provide subsidies and grants or should our funds be made available only strictly on business terms? Will it be prudent to continue payment of school fees? Should we only concern ourselves with productive schemes? Should we let Government invest its funds for instance in the building of houses either directly or through its own agencies? What type of retraining schemes should be mounted? Amidst these unanswered questions, what should be the ultimate aim of whatever schemes we may have vis-à-vis the economy of the Region, and so on. These problems I leave in your able hands. . . .

Let me repeat what I said on our inauguration, that we shall give this assignment our time, our labour and our patience. We appreciate the task to be difficult but these difficulties are not insurmountable. In a few months, we have made some achievements. We have changed the faces and spirit of millions who have returned imbued with hate and rejected by others and we are now offering them life, new hope and new opportunities. We cannot, and I am sure you will agree with me here, perform miracles. It is abundantly true that the refugee problem has vindicated the tenacity, endurance and hard work of the Easterner. Some of those who have returned are making immense contributions to their own rehabilitation and the up-building of our

Region. In that spirit I wish to conclude in the words of the Pilgrim Fathers
who themselves were refugees from Europe and say:

> Give me your tired, your poor, your huddled masses
> yearning to breathe free air. . . .

[1] *Delivered by Mr. Iheanacho to a seminar on the problem of Eastern refugees held at the
University, Nsukka on 11 March 1967. Text by courtesy of a delegate to the seminar.*

96.
'Be Prepared and Avoid Panic': Public Poster displayed in Enugu, March 1967

See pp. 384-5.

[By courtesy of an Enugu resident.]

97.
Ojukwu's Press Conference, 13 March 1967[1]

. . . I have called you to this conference, this morning, for three reasons. First
to explain to you, in all sincerity and truth, our position in the tragic crisis
which has engulfed this country, embarrassed our friends and betrayed the
hopes of the world about Nigeria. Secondly, by explaining to you our position, to attempt to erase certain wrong and tendentious impressions which
have been created about this Region by people, who, because of their positions in Lagos and control of the country's oversea missions are more easily
accessible to you than we are in this Region. Thirdly to give you an idea of
the Region's expectations for the future.

As I have said our opponents, because of their position in Lagos, their easy
accessibility to representatives of and visitors from other parts of the world
and through our diplomatic channels, maintained and serviced with the
common funds of this country, have been issuing to the world information
and explanations about our present crisis in a way which has been far from
fair either to those who are expected to make use of such material or information or to Eastern Nigeria. Indeed the immediate cause of my asking you
to come is the impression which has recently been given to diplomats by Lt.
Col. Gowon about the position of Eastern Nigeria.[2] I did immediately put out
a rejoinder to the statement which Lt. Col. Gowon made to the foreign
diplomats.[3] In that rejoinder, I tried to expose the tendentious inaccuracies of
his statement. The main purpose of that approach to representatives of
foreign powers was to enlist their sympathy for the people in Lagos against
the people of this Region. Impressions have been inspired in many quarters

2 c

BE PREPARED AND AVOID PANIC

From the look of things, it would appear that the people of Eastern Nigeria would be forced by external violence to surrender their birthright. If this is attempted, there should be no panic. Eastern Nigeria is fully prepared for any action. Should any group of people make this attempt by attacking us, the public will be duly alarmed. When you hear any of the following alarms, know that the enemy is around:

    (i) Prolonged sounding of horns, trains, loco and fire Unit;
    (ii) Prolonged vehicle horns;
    (iii) Continuous toll of school and church bells;
    (iv) Market Masters and Town Criers bells or gongs;
    (v) Buggle alarm calls.

DO NOT PANIC BUT TAKE THE FOLLOWING PRECAUTIONS

A If you are in the open, immediately take cover and observe any enemy shooting. Thereafter hurry by the safest means to your home or to the nearest building or to the nearest trenches.

B If in the building, pregnant women and nursing mothers, children, old or otherwise disabled men and women should lie on the floor indoors, preferably at the corners.

C Shut all doors and windows leaving only small gaps for observation. If at night, put out lights.

D If you are in possession of shot-gun, take suitable firing position inside or outside the building and shoot to kill the enemy.

E If you have no gun, collect other implements of

J After destroying the enemy or after they shall have fled, you should resume normal life. Remove and bury all water and food that was left behind and made unfit for consumption. Also do not eat any food or drink any water left by the enemy. Do not touch any equipment or article left by the enemy.

K If you come across guerilla forces, you must get away from them quickly and report to your own people, otherwise they will arrest you.

L If an enemy catches you and interrogates you, on no account must you give him any information, his inhuman methods notwithstanding. Remember that after giving the enemy the information he requires, he must still kill you, and that any informa-

the class-rooms until they can be evacuated home in small groups. Teachers should organize themselves into fighting groups using any available implement under able leadership. There is an evacuation team in your zone. Call for its assistance.

G People in mountain areas will ensure that hills dominating approach routes are manned under cover by people who will hurl down stones and other implements on the aggressor to kill him or impede his move.

H If you are wounded, do not panic or despair. There are teams to give you medical care and evacuate you to a safe area. They will come round immediately.

I In the event of the enemy gaining control of your building or area, take as much food and water as you can carry and await your evacuation to a safe area. Before vacating your building or area for the enemy, destroy all food and pour away water that may be left behind, and alternatively render such food and water unsafe for the enemy to use.

N You must deny the enemy the use of essential supplies and services.

O Do not indulge in "loose talks" and do not let the enemy know your plans. Walls have ears and careless talks cost lives.

P Always move fast and out of the view of the enemy.

Q You should be able to identify your own troops from the enemy troops.

R From the very time an alarm is given indicating the approach of the enemy, you should not stampede and scramble out for your home towns and villages as this will create traffic problems and impede the quick movement of your combatant Forces.

S Whenever the alarm is given, all motorists should clear their vehicles out of the highway to allow free movement for the combatant forces.

BE PREPARED

If you have not a gun, get a cutlass, a bow and arrow or anything that can kill now and be ready. A few tins of canned food may be useful. **DO NOT PANIC. No enemy can overcome you.** We are proud to be Easterners and we must exist.

BE PREPARED. SAVE THE EAST

Issued by AUTHORITY OF CIVIL DEFENCE COMMITTEE, ENUGU

GPE 995/367/200,000

that we in the East have already completed plans to secede. With this as an excuse the authorities in Lagos thought they should solicit the sympathy and support of foreign powers for their plans to embark upon what they called 'Police' action against the 'rebellious' East. . . .

Nigeria is indeed in danger of disintegration. This danger is very real and can only be removed if we can restore in the country the vital elements of good faith and confidence—the two shattered essentials of mutual co-operation and trust. We shall do this only if we, the Military leaders now saddled with the responsibility for running this country, can approach our task and face our problems with a sense of realism, objectivity and a spirit freed from past prejudices and sectional ambitions.

In January last year, 1966, a group of officers and men of the Nigerian Army, with origins from different parts of the country mutinied and the old regime surrendered power to the Army. You all know what relief, enthusiasm and expectations that event brought, not only to the people of this country but also to all her friends beyond. . . . You all know that but for the advent of the military regime at the time it did, Nigeria would have disintegrated in the flames of sordid civil war.

On the assumption of power the military regime made it quite clear that it came to restore law and order, peace and confidence throughout the whole Country. They would also expose and punish as far as possible the malpractices of corruption and other abuses of the past regime. With the cleaning of our public life completed, they were to embark upon the final exercise of arranging for a realistic and lasting constitution for the country, such as would save the country from the sad and tragic experiences which it had passed through.

All the public declarations of policy and programmes made whether by the Supreme Commander and Head of the Federal Military Government at the time, Major-General J. T. U. Aguiyi-Ironsi, or by the Military Governors of the different Regions, received universal approbation and support. . . . All the military leaders appeared to share the passion for and faith in the unity of this country. It is a sad thing that events should now show that we did not have identical concepts as to the basis of that unity. I shall return to this point later.

It was in pursuance of that policy of unity that Decree No. 34 was passed after being considered, accepted and approved by the whole Supreme Military Council of which all the Regional Military Governors were members. It turned out that a section of the country, the North, had been nursing hate against the East and were eagerly looking for an opportunity to give violent expressions to that hate. The publication of the Decree provided a good pretext for them suddenly to unleash as from Sunday the 29th of May premeditated massacres of Easterners anywhere, and in whatever circumstances, such Easterners were found in the North.

Those gruesome massacres were alleged to have been carried as a protest against the passing of Decree No. 34. If in fact it was the passing of that decree which had provoked the violence, why was it that the violence was directed against the people of a particular Region, whereas the Supreme Military Council, which was collectively responsible for the decree, consisted of Military leaders representing all sections of the country? Subsequent events, to be mentioned later, will provoke direct and real answers from the mouths of the perpetrators of the hideous crimes.

That 'obnoxious' Decree has since been repealed. But in fairness to it and its authors, let us remind ourselves briefly of what it would have achieved. It could have achieved three things. First, it would have formalised the *de facto* administrative arrangement and organisation inherent in a Military Regime having a unified command. Secondly, it could have led to an imaginative deployment and distribution of the nation's talents and expertise, in the same way as material and financial resources were being deployed and distributed, for the common good of the country. Thirdly, by the deployment of the administrative, technical and other personnel from one section of the country to the other, mutual understanding would have been enhanced and a real sense and feeling of interdependence fostered among the different peoples of the land. It was mainly in furtherance of this last aim that the late Supreme Commander decided to rotate Military Governors.

However in spite of those massacres the people of the East in their faith in the country as a unit accepted those massacres as the last act of sacrifice for that faith. Meanwhile Easterners had been deserting their places of work and returning to the East in hundreds. Essential services in the North, and indeed the whole economy of that Region, faced imminent collapse. I had personally to appeal to the fleeing Easterners to go back to the North.[4] They obeyed me and went back.

Meanwhile the Emirs of the North met and announced that they had in their wisdom decided on how best the affairs of the country should be run and were despatching their decisions to the Supreme Military Council. It turned out that their solution was tantamount to a determined defiance of the Supreme Military Council. The Supreme Military Council met in Lagos and considered the Northern memorandum to which an appropriate reply was later sent. That meeting of the Supreme Military Council also decided to set up a high-powered Commission of Inquiry into the organised violence in the North with a view to apportioning blame and assessing compensation.

No sooner had this decision been announced than the Northern Leaders openly declared that the inquiry would be held over their dead bodies. The Supreme Military Council was not, of course, prepared to be so defied and showed a determination to go ahead with the implementation of Decree 34 but after assurances that the arrangements in that Decree were temporary and only meant for the Military administration. A permanent constitution for the country would be drawn up by the people. It also gave the North other assurances with regard to appointments in the Public Service and such matters which the world was told to be among those things which frightened the North most.

In search of peace and in order to reassure the people of this country and ascertain their wishes with a view to fostering harmony, the Supreme Commander, Major-General J. T. U. Aguiyi-Ironsi, planned a tour of the whole country. This tour took him to Ibadan towards the end of July. In the early hours of July 29th, while he was staying in the State House as the guest of the Military Governor of the West, Northern soldiers went there and kidnapped him. At the same time officers of Eastern Nigeria origin were taken out of their beds, shot and killed in cold blood in Ibadan, Abeokuta, Ikeja,

Kaduna and other military stations in the North. We in the East were saved by accident following an anonymous telephone message from Abeokuta warning me about what was happening in those parts.

It soon became clear that the aim of Northern soldiers, aided and abetted by civilian leaders of the North, was to exterminate military officers of Eastern Nigeria origin from the entire Nigerian army. During the few days beginning July 29th the Emirs and Chiefs of the North were holding a meeting in Kaduna. It was at that meeting that the Sultan of Sokoto openly invoked Allah to stand by and help their children now fighting for their freedom.

I did say early in this Address that subsequent events were to provoke from the Northern people the answer to the mystery of May 29 massacre. This statement of the spiritual leader of the North was the first indication of the true answer to that mystery. Later a group of so-called Northern intellectuals under the cloak of a nebulous organisation going by the name of 'Current Issues Society' had to boast, in a pamphlet, of the Northern conquest of the whole of Nigeria within two days from July 29th.

The Northern explanation of these atrocities of July was that it was a revenge of the event of January the 15th and that it was confined to the Army. Again the people who were responsible for the January 15th event were officers and men from all the tribes of Nigeria serving in the Army. If it was a revenge for what had happened on that occasion, why was it confined to members of a particular tribe or Region? Indeed one of the first acts of the July rebels was to travel to the prisons where Northern soldiers, detained along with others in connection with the event of January 15, 1966, were housed and released these Northern soldiers, killing in the process Eastern Nigeria soldiers who were kept in these prisons in protective custody.

It is well known that having thus achieved their purpose or felt to have achieved their purpose, the Northern soldiers wanted immediate secession from the rest of the country. Their desire would have been fulfilled but for the intervention of foreign friends who convinced them of the folly of such a move. Even after they had abandoned their threat for immediate secession, Lt. Col. Yakubu Gowon in his first broadcast on the assumption of office declared that 'The basis of unity in the country did not exist.' He made that statement on the 1st of August, 1966.[5] Making this statement he was merely echoing the general and consistent feeling of the North. How consistent the North has been in their belief that the basis of unity does not exist for Nigeria has been fully brought out in my Government publication entitled *The North and Constitutional Developments in Nigeria.*

I shall not bother you with detailed information about my conversations with Lt. Col. Gowon in those critical days and the various agreements we reached over the telephone which were, of course, never kept by Lt. Col. Gowon. . . . Troops have not all been posted to their respective regions of origin, the decrees which showed extreme centralisation—in other words, detracted from the previous powers of the Regions—have not been repealed. The enlarged body later known as Ad Hoc Constitutional Committee, which it was recommended should meet in a week from the 9th of August did not meet until after over five weeks, and then had to be suddenly dismissed because the trends developing there were seen by the North as not favouring them.

A point worth mentioning about this Ad Hoc Constitutional Committee is that in their original memorandum to that Committee, the North advocated what amounted to a Customs Union in the country, only to change their mind soon after the submission of that memorandum, and advocate for a Federal government with a strong centre, which they had never really before liked or fully accepted. The reason for this change was given unconsciously by Lt. Col. Gowon himself early in October following.

The Ad Hoc Constitutional Conference met for several weeks and began to reach agreements of a major and fundamental nature. The apparent success of this Ad Hoc Constitutional Conference began to cause a thaw in the ominous tension which had enveloped the country. But, alas, the understandings and the agreements reached at these meetings were seen in the North as not serving their purpose. To stop the work of that Ad Hoc Constitutional Committee they again resorted to an organised pogrom which started from the 29th of September. The nature and the intensity of this latest pogrom shocked the conscience of the whole world and led Lt. Col. Gowon to make a personal appeal to his people of the North to stop the killings. It was this speech which revealed exactly the reason for the massacres in the North and the sudden change of attitude of the Northern people from favouring a very loose political association in the country to that of a federal system with strong centre. In that speech Lt. Col. Gowon reminded the people of the North that another Northerner was in control of the affairs of the country, because God in His Wisdom had once again entrusted the control and destiny of Nigeria into the hands of the Northerners. This statement of Lt. Col. Gowon on that occasion finally explained the Northern intentions and in some way the inhuman atrocities against the people of the East. It revealed that the Northern idea of unity is that of horse and rider, the horse being the rest of the country and the rider being the North. It revealed that the Ironsi Regime was overthrown because it happened to be headed by a person who was not of Northern origin. Thirdly, it explained that the pogrom had been directed against Easterners because the North saw in them a source of obstacle to their eternal domination of the country. . . .

We went to Ghana in a genuine attempt to reach certain understandings, take decisions and reduce tension. Above all, we were to evolve arrangements whereby the Military Regime could re-organise itself in order to fulfil its responsibilities for the country. I went there not as an Easterner or Military Governor of the Eastern Nigeria, but as a Nigerian. . . . I want . . . to take this opportunity to explain to you the case of the East in the controversy which has raged the nation since our return.

The communiqués issued at the end of our meetings in Ghana clearly stated what decisions had been taken. The official minutes issued by the Cabinet Office and accepted by all after their circulation, also contain accurate records of the major decisions. In order to pave the way for regular meetings in Nigeria and reduce tension, certain actions were to be taken before the end of January. The Law Officers, representing all the Governments, were to meet in Benin on the 14th of January and pin-point those decrees or aspects of decrees which had detracted from the previous powers and positions of the Regional Governments. The repealing decree was to be published on the 21st of January. Financial experts of all the Governments were to meet within two weeks of the end of our meeting and consider the question of financial arrangements in the light of the present situation in the country. The case of those military officers and men who had been detained following the January incident and of those who had taken part in the rebellion of July 29 were to be considered by the 28th of January at a meeting of the Supreme Military Council which was to follow the passing of the decree on the 21st of January.

The Law Officers met on the 14th, reached agreements on what decrees and aspects of decrees should be repealed, while referring a number of questions affecting other aspects of Aburi Agreements to the Supreme Military Council for clarification. No decree was published on the 21st of January. After persistent pressures on Lagos, they eventually produced a draft decree which was totally contrary to the spirit and letter of Aburi Agreements in that instead of restoring the original powers to the Regions, it, in fact, actually gave more powers to the Federal Government. In other words, they went fairly a long way towards the provisions of the repealed Decree 34 which had been used by the North as an excuse for slaughtering innocent Easterners. Before the issue of that draft decree, Lt. Col. Gowon in his Press Conference on Aburi[6] openly expressed his intention not to abide by the decisions taken . . . advised by officials in Lagos to reject those agreements because they would detract from their powers and positions.

Every action, attitude and utterance of Lt. Col. Yakubu Gowon since our return from Aburi has portrayed his unwillingness to carry out those agreements or even to respect the spirit with which we appeared to have left Ghana. I shall now mention a few of such actions of bad faith:

1. Soon after our return from Aburi, Lt. Col. Gowon telephoned me and informed me that a Federal publication entitled *Nigeria 1966* had been prepared and he wanted my opinion as to whether it would be advisable to release that publication, having regard to the Aburi spirit. We discussed and agreed that since the publication had not already been put out to the public, it might be wise to withhold it, at least for some time. I saw this action of Lt. Col. Gowon in consulting me on this issue as the beginning of a period of good faith and confidence. You can imagine my disappointment when on the 15th of January the Lagos Press published extracts from this publication which was a blatant denigration of Easterners living and dead. I promptly got in touch with Lt. Col. Gowon and sought explanation. He regretted the publication which he described as a leak. His explanation turned out to be a deceit, because evidence soon came through that the publication was, in fact, and with the authority of Lagos, formally launched in all the capitals of foreign countries. Indeed, the introduction to that booklet was clearly written after our return from Aburi, most likely after Gowon's discussion with me.

2. Evidence abound in my possession that Lagos and the North are actively encouraging acts of subversion against this Region. They have been doing everything to sow seeds of discord and confusion among the peoples of this Region.

3. Contrary to the Agreements in Aburi, recruitment into the army continued with the authority or connivance of Lagos in other parts of the country except the East.

4. Contrary to the Aburi Agreements, appointments of ambassadors have

been made without reference to the Supreme Military Council and Easterners serving in foreign embassies have been forced into situations where they have to leave their posts and return home for absorption into the Eastern Nigeria Civil Service.

5. Contrary to the Agreements reached in Accra, purchase and importation of arms have continued.

6. The meeting of Military officers to discuss the reorganisation of the Army in order to enable the Supreme Military Council decide on how the Armed Forces Act should be amended, was unilaterally postponed by the Federal authorities after an encouraging start.

7. The meeting of Finance officials has not taken place because the Permanent Secretary, Federal Ministry of Finance does not think that such a meeting would serve any useful purpose.

8. I have already mentioned the failure to publish the decree on the 21st of January or take actions on those matters for which definite dates were set at Aburi.

9. Contrary to the Aburi Agreements, employees of Federal civil service and public corporations have not been paid their salaries up to the end of 31st of March.

10. The recent statement to diplomats[7] with its distortion of facts, threat of the use of force, was a negation of the Aburi spirit and agreement, particularly our agreement to eschew the use of force.

11. The employees of the Railway Corporation and of the Coal Corporation, both Federal institutions, have been without salaries and have had to be rescued with advances from the Eastern Nigeria Military Government.

12. The authorities in Lagos are doing everything in their power to impede the smooth operation of private industries in this Region. They not only mislead potential investors but are also doing everything they can to bring to a standstill industries already operating in Eastern Nigeria.

For the above lapses, the Federal Government and its officials in Lagos have tried to find one reason or another. Such reasons include the ridiculous one that they went to Aburi meeting unprepared and that some people did not understand the Agreements reached at that meeting. Because of this, they had to refer the decisions to civil service experts for final advice. For failing to honour the agreement to pay Federal employees who had been compelled to flee their places of work, the reason has been given that certain railway wagons are lying in the East and because of that the Federal Government has been unable to make money in order to fulfil its obligation in this regard. But the wagons were there when the decisions were taken at Aburi.

It was for the above reasons that I found myself compelled to issue the statement[8] in which I stated that unless the Aburi Agreements were implemented by an acceptable decree before the 31st of March, I shall consider myself free to take unilateral action to implement those Agreements.

Now, where do you go from here? My threat to take unilateral action to implement the Aburi agreements has been interpreted to mean a decision to secede. That interpretation appears to me far-fetched. There is no doubt that, if I find myself compelled to take such an action, the repercussions will be serious for the country, and where we go from there will depend on the attitude of other parts of the country particularly the North and Lagos. But that situation can be avoided if my friends decide to play fair.

You have all seen and read one of the latest outbursts of my colleagues, the Governor of the North, boasting of the North's ability to crush the East in a matter of hours. That such a statement should be uttered by such a responsible person in Nigeria is indicative of the thinking in certain quarters.

It has been announced that a decree implementing the Aburi agreements will be published in a few days' time. Having regard to the decision in Aburi that all matters affecting the whole country should be referred to all Military Governors for comments and concurrence, I regard that decision to publish a decree amending the country's constitution without my comments and concurrence irregular and *ultra vires*.

I have come across reports in certain foreign papers giving impression that the present struggle is tribal. Our struggle is by no means tribal. It is a struggle for freedom and equality among Nigerians. It will end whenever the North is able to accept the equality of all Nigerians to share in the control and running of the affairs of this country, and have by devious means tried to crush progressive forces in the South. The Eastern Government is today facing the same situation which the Action Group Government of the West faced some years ago. It was the struggle of that progressive party against the reactionary forces of the North which landed the country in its present state of impasse.

Finally, there is one question which many people have often asked. It is the question of my inability to accept Lt. Col. Gowon as the Supreme Commander. I fully explained my position regarding this during the Aburi meeting. I could not accept him—and I have told him so on many occasions—because he was heading a Government of rebels who had kidnapped their Supreme Commander. To accept him would be the acceptance of permanent indiscipline within the Army. All the same it is possible for us to reach an amicable *modus vivendi*, and the meeting at Aburi did agree on a formula acceptable to all. This is an added reason for implementing the Aburi agreements, so that necessary steps might be taken to save all concerned embarrassment. . . .

Appendix to Statement

New York Times: There have been some reports in the Lagos Press that you went to Benin yesterday and stayed for about three and half hours with Lt.-Col. Ejoor. Did you go to Benin?

O: Yes, I went to Benin for what was a private visit to an old friend of mine, Lt.-Col. David Ejoor. Of course, in a situation such as this we would amongst other things discuss the present crisis. We discussed generally their last meeting at Benin. We discussed again points arising from the Aburi meeting. I think we discussed too the possibility of opening the frontiers to Mid-Westerners, allowing them to come back to the East. . . .

New York Times: You used to say that you will not be willing to attend the Supreme Military Council Meeting at Benin as long as Northern troops were in the West. Does your trip yesterday to the Mid-West mean that you may consider attending the Supreme Military Council Meeting at Benin?

O: My visit to Lt.-Col. Ejoor cannot in any way be construed to mean a meeting of the Supreme Military Council. . . .

B.B.C.: There have been two rumours around. One is that ships of the Nigerian Navy are proceeding to the Eastern Region for action against the East. Do you believe that?

O: It is true that troops boarded four ships of the Nigerian Navy ostensibly for an exercise along the coast of the Eastern Region. . . . We were told that they would fire in the air and in the water. I immediately on hearing this warned Gowon as to the possible repercussions of this. . . . I was greatly worried until I spoke to my Army Commander who gave me assurance that he could quite conveniently line the bottom of the creeks with debris of the Nigerian Navy. I therefore sent instructions and told Gowon that it was my intention to sink the four ships should they menace any Eastern port. Later good sense prevailed. I now understand that the ships have been recalled. . . .

New York Times: You have persistently said that the East does not intend to secede unless pushed. How would you describe a push? Invasion by Lagos or what? I remember your telling me the other day that the line has been crossed. In short, what is the line that has been crossed? Could you define it?

O: I said a number of times that the East will not secede unless pushed. In the present situation, in very precise terms, the East would only secede if she were attacked and an attack can be in two ways. Physical Military Attack, or Economic Blockade. We all know that when you pick up a pistol and shoot somebody it is called murder, equally so when you strangle him.

Observer: The great difficulty most of us overseas have is to try and explain the reality of your thinking when you suggest that there is going to be an attack on the East, because what the Federal Government, the leaders and the diplomats say is that the rest of the country know that logistically it is not possible for what remains of the Nigerian Army to make any successful attack on the East. Then the question arises, do you really believe that an attack on the East is being planned now or in the near future, in the long future, or as some people would suggest, that you are merely keeping up the spirit of defiance, the warlike spirit in the East, in order to fall in with your diplomatic purposes in your struggle against the North? I shall be very grateful for your clarification on this.

O: There are two things there. Planning an attack on the East is one, being able to sustain that attack is another. Certainly I believe that the Northerners are planning and will continue to plan an attack on the East. I believe also that they will not be successful, but in the course of the last year till now, the East has taken so much that it might well be the last straw which might break the camel's back.

As to the Northern attitude to all this, one has to look through generally Northern approach to the Nigerian situation. You will see that even when we had a Federal Government which was functioning, the North quietly contrived to build in the Northern Region some forty-two airports and landing strips. The North throughout was over-sensitive about the siting of defence installations. Whilst we were talking unity and not bothering very much about this, all the key defence installations were sited in the North including the ammunition factory. Very soon after the departure of the Easterners, as a top priority the North obtained some eighteen technicians to get the ammunition factory again working and it is again now working.

The North started purchasing arms immediately after Aburi. They continued recruiting. As soon as it was possible after 29th July incident, they moved every bit of ordnance store to the North and then they were not satisfied with Kaduna, they had to go into the innermost North, they moved them from Kaduna to Zaria.

Then we have the fact that historically prior to the advent of the British, the North was already embarked on a war of conquest to the Sea. This was interrupted as Tafawa Balewa often reminded the entirety of this country by the advent of the British. Ahmadu Bello made it quite clear that his intention was to continue the unfinished work of his great-grand father Shehu Usman Dan Fodio. Finlly, we have Hassan Katsina threatening to crush the East within two hours.

All these are indicative of the state of mind in the North and I would be a complete idiot if I did not plan for the worst eventuality.

Observer: Could I follow that up with one question? You talk all the time about the North as if the North really ever existed or exists today. I wonder why it is that you don't differentiate between the different parts of the North. Do you really believe that the Middle Belt sections would participate in any plan of the North to attack the East?

O: I would like very much to be able to differentiate but the pogroms of May and particularly of September and again the activity of Middle Belt personnel within the Army during the 29th July attempt to exterminate Eastern soldiers from the Nigerian Army [combine] to give me no ground for optimism. The Middle Belt people did partake of all these atrocities, and really it will be wishful thinking on our part to think that with the feeling in the North today, I can well separate them from the main North. . . .

New York Times: Lagos Press carried a release that the January detainees in the East had been released. What is their future?

O: What reports from Lagos could be accurate? This is the first thing. Security reasons obviously preclude me from answering that question directly. But this I can say to you: they are still in the East and more comfortable.

New York Times: Can't you tell whether they are still in the army in the East?

O: I cannot tell you.

New York Times: I presume some of them have been discharged.

O: I presume so. There has been a note sent in from Lagos in which it was said some of them were no longer members of the army. I do not think that letter is worth more than the paper it is written on, the point being that it was the Supreme Military Council that put those people into protective custody. Lagos has not got the right to release or to do anything about them. It is a matter for the Supreme Military Council anyway.

New York Times: Is the release of these detainees in the spirit of Aburi?

O: What release are you talking about, the Lagos purported release or the one you said you saw in the newspapers about the East? Which one are you talking about? The one in the East is still ambiguous because all of them were detained in the East and not staying with you.

New York Times: Do I understand that you do not want to confirm that Majors Nzeogwu and Ifeajuna have been released?

O: I said that security reasons preclude me from answering that question directly. . . .

Newsweek: Have you made any suggestion to alter any plans for the meeting of your colleagues and yourself at the Supreme Military Council holding in the month?

O: No, I have not made any. I have continued to insist that the decisions at Aburi should be implemented as a first step before we have the meeting. This was, in fact, what we envisaged at the Aburi meeting itself. . . . We will not accept anything that deviates from the Aburi accord.

Reuters: Have they sent you the minutes?

O: They only sent me the papers to be discussed.

Voice of America: You said that you do not recognize Gowon. Do you recognize the Federal Military Government?

O: There is a Federal Government of which I am a member. At the moment there is a junta headed by Gowon which is assuming the functions of that Federal Government. It is this junta I do not recognize. . . .

Observer: I want to take you a little bit forward to March the 31st and the events thereafter, because unless one gets something to implement the Aburi decisions, it is likely that what you called the junta will pass a decree which will have no effect on the East. Would you implement Aburi in your own terms? If you would, the whole situation would become an open conflict as it was before Aburi. In that kind of situation, what happens in terms of negotiation? What is the general situation which you envisage after March?

O: This is really why I found it necessary to warn about what might happen after the 31st of March. I can envisage once I start implementing Aburi on my own terms—as I am bound to do if they will not play fair and honour agreements—I can see them in Lagos, in their foggy reasoning, taking this as an act of confrontation. I can see them probably accepting the first move, the second move, and then their misplaced pride being hurt by the third move. I can then see them—and this is the point of this open conflict— probably embarking on open hostility. Does that answer your question?

Observer: Rather disastrously, yes.

North American Newspaper Alliance; If the worst comes to the worst and the East secedes, do you believe that the East can be viable economically?

O: This is the point which I see a lot of emphasis has been placed on. You all are well travelled in the world. You know that in a question of independence and self-determination, viability is usually given a very, very low priority consideration. The point here and the crux of the whole matter in Nigeria today is that the North wants to dominate. The East believes that power in the Federal, in the centre, should be shared. As I said in my statement, the day they accept that power should be shared in the Federal Government, there would be no crisis. As a people we have a right at least to safeguard ourselves. We will not walk into servitude.

Washington Post: Do you feel that there is any chance of agreement between you and the Federal Government? Would you suggest to the Federal

Government to make some kind of gesture to avoid the kind of situation which you envisage?

O: I have often made suggestions. I have suggested to Gowon a possible line. As a first stage, he can commit himself now that there is so much suspicion to the Aburi Agreements, that he would implement those agreements in full. Indeed, he should go a stage further: he should state his stand on this impasse so that at least we may know where we are going, not this continual drift which has been the fate of Nigeria since he assumed office. There are many other things. Indeed I have suggested up to eight things which he could do.

Observer: When you say you suggested, do you believe that Gowon is able to do what you like him to do? In other words, who in fact has control over the direction of policies in Lagos?

O: You asked me this question last time. I think it is clear now. First, Gowon is not capable of doing anything. He is only a front man for the whole N.P.C./N.N.D.P. coalition, what was previously known as the N.N.A. in terms of Nigerian politics.

In fact the officers and men who took part in the 29th July massacre were being used as tools. If you remember, in the course of my first statement I said that the soldiers wanted secession. This is most significant. It is the soldiers not knowing what they were being used for who wanted secession. But the N.N.D.P./N.P.C. coalition which master-minded this pogrom definitely wanted to continue the old policy of the Sardauna, that is to dominate and to dictate. If you look back on our political history it will tell you that before the arrival of Independence there was only one effective power in the country which could challenge and did challenge the Northern idea about unity in this country, and that was the Action Group. The North then went out and most ruthlessly crushed the Action Group. In doing this they were to some extent aided by the N.C.N.C. of the East who were still talking in very idealistic terms about the problems of Nigeria. Once the Action Group was crushed and then a Pocket Government set up in the West, and you all know how this was done, the North turned its venom on the East. Indeed this was what I meant when I said that this was not a tribal conflict as such. It is in essence a power struggle. You will see that what the North objects to is a Government controlled perhaps by the Ibos or an effective Government. It is not the Ibos themselves that they are against. And all their efforts have been directed at removing them from positions of control, hence you will see that there are Mid-Western Ibos in Lagos today quite free. The Northern concept accepts this because the Mid-West Ibos do not control a Government which can be in opposition to them. What they are against is the Eastern Government, an opposition on the way to their complete domination of the Federation. In fact this gives you the only true explanation for 29th September. In July, they succeeded in removing an Easterner or Southerner from the position of headship of the Federation which to the North was an eyesore. They did it most ruthlessly. They got political power. The next stage was to remove Easterners from economic control and this really was why they went on for the September massacre, to get out every Easterner from any position of economic control in the whole country starting in the North. You notice of course that socially there has been an accepted apartheid between the North and the East, indeed, the North and the South. So that September actually was a culmination of all they had planned for their domination of Nigeria but for one thing which they miscalculated, and that was the stand which I maintained and also the success of that stand. They did not think that anybody or any power in Nigeria could, after what they had done in 1966, stand in their way.

Observer: How then would you explain the non-identification of the stand of Western Nigeria, in other words, the stand of the Action Group, Chief Awolowo and the Military Governor of the West?

O: I maintain, and I have every reason to believe that they see this the way I see it. It is true that I saw it earlier than most but, certainly, both the West and the Mid-West have come to see it that way. Indeed after Aburi, all letters by the Military Governor of the West about the interpretation of the Aburi Agreements have been absolutely identical in essence with mine. The Mid-West the same. But there are other things which prevent them from making as firm a stand as I do.

How would you feel being a Westerner, Governor of the West, with troops guarding your State House permanently being Northern soldiers? No matter what you feel intellectually, when it comes to the fact that your own life is in jeopardy you have to modify your public statements. The same thing goes for the Mid-West. You know that they never really got started, so they arrived at this crisis perhaps in the weakest position. It is for these people as much as it is for the East, that I am making my resistance. I refuse to accept the North permanently dictating to Nigeria just by virtue of their size. The day, I repeat it again, this people of the North accept that power at the Centre should be shared, the crisis in Nigeria would end.

A lot of talk has been given to unity, getting everybody together, everything together in Nigeria, but really have they paused to look at this in very practical terms? What form of Federation can we see arising out of a situation when a people, a group, the East cannot move about freely in two-thirds of the country? This is really what it means! How do we see this Federation in which the people of the East cannot deal with more than half the population of the country? Whoever talks of unity must think of these things. We do agree it would be nice to have, but the people of this country have shown over and over again that it is not unity that they want but association. This question of unity which keeps getting bandied around is a foreign concept. . . . What the people of Nigeria want is association and once you start on this premise, everything falls into line. You can understand it.

West Africa: Could you name some of these people you think are, in fact, organizing an attack on the East or who are behind the plan of the North to dominate?

O: If I start giving you the names of everybody, it will take about thirty minutes but in the North there are men like [here followed the names of certain N.P.C. politicians]; there are the Emirs, the 'dyed-in-the-wool' feudalists; there are some people in Lagos who aid and abet them, generally men without roots, men who cannot fit into their own regional societies or in the scheme of things in their various regions, people with vested interest in the continuance of a sort of dominance in Lagos; people like [here followed the names of senior bureaucrats in the Federal Civil Service] who [had] never felt happy in [their] own region ever; people like [X. Y. Z.], now absconded, serving overseas. There is the Majekodunmi group with all it entails. . . .

Indeed, if there are enemies of Nigeria today, these are the men. They are causing all the confusion purely for their own personal greed. Nothing else.

Voice of America: You said you will not attend any meeting of the Supreme Military Council until the Aburi agreements are implemented. Could such a meeting which you will attend take place within Nigeria? Is it possible, in other words?

O: Oh, yes! It is possible. You see, at Aburi, I just put the ball into their court. If they play it right, of course, yes. Indeed, when I came back from Aburi, I looked forward to a meeting at the end of the month. I was full of enthusiasm and hope, and again I am prepared to go anywhere, but first, they must implement these agreements, that's all.

Time Magazine: In view of everything you have said, if you and Gowon could reach some agreement, would you expect Gowon to be able to enforce it and get the North to accept?

O: I think actually the only person who can help Gowon out of his troubles is myself. No other person can. All Gowon has to do is to recognize this, and then come and we will discuss and find solutions. He cannot do it alone; I know that. He has tried but he has failed.

Reuters: Supposing Gowon wants to come to Enugu to discuss with you, do you guarantee him safety?

O: I have not stopped inviting him to Enugu since July. I have been constantly inviting him. It is up to him to accept. Indeed, I think he probably played his very worst card over the question of the death of the Supreme Commander. That gave him an opportunity of at least coming to the East and touring out a little bit. He failed there. And I did invite him.

Associated Press: Why is your Government opposed to the creation of more states in Nigeria when it is said that the troubles in Nigeria would be minimized when one region is not in a position to dominate the others?

O: My Government is not opposed to the creation of more states. What my Government is opposed to is the creation of more states at this time of tension and uncertainties. We have got to reduce tension first, generate confidence and then agree on the criteria for the creation of states and then set a date for the simultaneous implementation of those agreements. The North or Lagos is really not serious about the creation of states. . . . They mentioned it at the enlarged *Ad Hoc* Constitutional Committee when they found it very difficult to get the sort of Nigeria they wanted. We came back from Aburi, again they saw that the agreements had not given them a position of dominance; so they started again on the question of states. If they are really serious at a stage we will get round a table and discuss the criteria. This is what I said. But they even give impossible terms. They sit up in the North and then stay there in their usual way telling us what states should be created and where. They are not serious. I think everybody in and outside Nigeria knows about the struggle of the Middle Belt people for the creation of their state. Why does not the North do that as an act of faith and create the Middle Belt State? You have got to remember that there are certain emotions attached to this too. The East had a section of it cut out; the West had another section cut out. Up till today the North has been the only one keeping together and they have continued deceiving people with this talk of states. They are, in fact, not serious.

Observer: You have recently changed your ribbon to red. Has it any significance?

O: Dipped in the blood of our youth. . . .

B.B.C.: In the last twenty-four hours that I have been here, it seems to me you have all the facilities for setting up an alternative Government. Is that right?

O: Yes. I have every opportunity, that is true. It is just that I consider that if I did this, there would be the possibility of more deaths and I am only very anxious to avoid more deaths in this situation. We have lost enough. It has been such a waste. Even now, there is still the possibility but I am convinced that that sort of confrontation will be no answer to the situation. I do believe that once the North realizes that they cannot crush the East within two hours, they will perhaps come round a table and we continue our negotiations. It was for this that Aburi envisaged that the military will find a *modus vivendi* to continue whilst experts then get the constitutional issues thrashed out . . . .

[1] *Given at Enugu before foreign diplomats as well as press and radio representatives. Eastern Ministry of Information Press Release No. 140/1967.*
[2] *See* DOC *92.*   [3] *See* DOC *93.*
[4] *See* DOC *28.*   [5] *See* DOC *37.*
[6] *See* DOC *85.*   [7] *See* DOC *92.*
[8] *See* DOC *90.*

98.
'The Misguided Role of the Middle Northerners'[1]

No part of Nigeria has played a more misguided role in the present Nigerian crisis than our brother Nigerians who come from the southern North. Their role is misguided because for months now they have been fed the falsehood that they have only to exterminate their brother Easterners and their problems will for ever be solved. But the attempted extermination of Easterners has led only to starvation, poverty, terror and insecurity. In September 1966, the Tivs were told by the Fulani-Hausa emirs that it was the Easterners who prevented them from having their own state. The result of this Arabian Nights' tale was that as trains carrying Easterners arrived at Oturkpo, unholy bands of Middle Northerners attacked the trains, looting and killing. Some of the Tivs who understood tried to intervene but got no hearing.

The act of vandalism has not made the Middle Belters a better people nor has it given them a greater say in the affairs of Northern Nigeria. There are still today thousands of Middle Belters in the dungeons where they were flung by the Sardauna regime. They languish in jail and may perish there. The Middle Belters are misguided because all their bravado is based on their supposed reputation as press-button riflemen to be summoned by some

2 D

Fulani-Hausa emirs for self-protection and for the consummation of the Jihad. Does gun-carrying prevent a man from looking all around him and seeing the desolation? Is it enough to smoke Indian hemp and be under a fantastic delusion of being all-powerful temporarily? Of course, when the effect wears off, the great Middle Belt gunman is plunged into the depth of despair and frustration, and his next course of action is to take revenge on some innocent Fulani-Hausa soldiers. The outbreak at Ikeja in which 40 soldiers were killed; at Markurdi where soldiers and police had a gun battle; at Jebba where two officers, three privates and one civilian were recently killed and buried; at Sardauna Province where the Military Governor of the North had to fly in in person to try and restore some order; at Maiduguri where soldiers and police had to be quickly moved in: these outbreaks are no isolated cases but indicate remorse and frustration.

The question now being widely asked is: are the Mid-Northerners at last beginning to realise that the Fulani hierarchy and the Hausa officials are using them to further the Jihad? If the ordinary Middle Belter and the rifle-carrying soldiers are realising this, it is very doubtful whether the Middle Belt leadership is doing so. Otherwise these leaders who have no urgent problems to attend to would not waste their valuable time conferring with leaders of the Fulani-Hausa kingdom who have nothing for them but serfdom.

The Fulani and Hausa know exactly what they want out of Nigeria—domination in which their lieutenants would be planted everywhere. They know that they will fail in this ambition but they want to try. Wherever they stand they find that the real power is the hands of the non-Fulani, non-Hausa. Between them and the East lies the southern North. They want to march from Makurdi in the Middle Belt country. Between them and the East from Lagos are the West and the Mid-West.

It is therefore in their interest to promise the world to the Tivs whose home must be used as the firing ground when and if the clash begins. Under the guise of repatriating beggars from Lagos, the Fulani and Hausa have sent home all their men who are unable to carry arms. They do not mind if anyone else is killed provided it is not even a Fulani or Hausa beggar. But they want to kill more Westerners: they want to kill more Mid-Westerners: they want to kill more Tivs. Having done this, as Colonel Hassan fondly dreams, the East would be overrun in a few hours. This wishful thinking is a military matter which I cannot discuss.

The main point here is that the Middle Belters are having a raw deal, will always have a raw deal, and will perish under this raw deal, unless they make a stand and cease to be tools of emirs and their so-called leaders who have been given large sums of money in order to sell out the Middle North to the Northern North. Before the present crisis, all the cooks and stewards at the Hamdala Hotel in Kaduna were Tivs and Idomas. At the same time, all the Permanent Secretaries at Kaduna were Fulani-Hausa. In short, the Tiv has always been a third-class Northerner whose only value is to protect the emir and his Jihad whenever threatened as is the case now. His feet have always been too dirty to soil the emir's carpets. The Idoma, the Tiv, the Kanuri today cannot find markets for their products. The Idoma and the Tiv are good farmers. They deserve to sell their products in Eastern Nigeria but they dare not. There are no traders now in the Middle Belt, only rumours of imaginary planned attacks by Easterners. There is no substitute for the Easterner who was driven home. Where is the El Dorado promised by the northern Northerners? How many Tivs or Idomas are emirs in the far North? It is a well-known fact that 99·9 per cent of the emirs in the North are Hausa-Fulani. The mature students programme at the Ahmadu Bello University was designed to train Fulani-Hausas to continue their domination of other Northerners from the non-Hausa, non-Fulani-speaking areas, notably the Middle Belt. And now realising that one day the Tiv, the Idoma and Kanuri riflemen might turn against them, the emirs and their political accomplices have started a training camp at Funtua for their own army of suppression. There is not one Middle Belter on the role of recruits.

Is it not time for the Middle Belters, the non-Hausa and non-Fulani-speaking Northerners, to stop fooling themselves and try to think? What future lies ahead for them in the grand design by the Sardauna to dip the Koran in salt water? Nothing, absolutely nothing but penury and want. The mid-Northerners must understand that they are not fighting for their own war, but the war for the Fulanis and Hausas who will then turn round and continue to enslave them. Today, we hear Middle Belters moving their forces here and there along the border of Eastern Nigeria looking for imagined enemies and imaginary attacks. The East will never attack anyone. It is an entirely different matter if any misguided platoon or battalion becomes aggressive.

[1] *Talk on E.N.B.S., Enugu, 27 March 1967 (B.B.C. ME/2426/B/1).*

99.
Decree No. 8 of 1967[1]

The main feature of this Decree is the vesting in the Supreme Military Council of both the legislative and executive powers of the Government of the Federation. The Federal Executive Council which has hitherto exercised these powers has now been divested of them and it is henceforth to discharge those functions that are specifically delegated to it by the Supreme Military Council.

2. In the exercise of these legislative and executive powers, the concurrence of the Head of the Federal Military Government and of all the Military Governors is, for the first time, made essential in respect of certain matters which are set out in section 69 (6) of the Constitution. These are, to mention a few, matters affecting or relating to trade, commerce, industry, transport, the Armed Forces, the Nigeria Police, Higher Education, and the territorial integrity of a Region and the provisions of the sections listed in the proviso to section 4 (1) of the Constitution.

3. On the other hand, the legislative and executive powers of the Regions have been fully restored and vested in their respective Military Governors. But the provisions of section 86 of the Constitution of the Federation ensure that no Region shall exercise its executive authority so as to impede or pre-

judice the exercise of the executive authority of the Federation or to endanger the continuance of federal government in Nigeria.

4. The provisions of section 70 of the Constitution of the Federation give powers to the Supreme Military Council to take over the executive and legislative functions of a Regional Government during any period of emergency which might be declared in respect of that Region by the Supreme Military Council, while those of section 71 give the Supreme Military Council power to take appropriate measures against a Region which attempts to secede from the rest of the Federation, or where the executive authority of the Region is being exercised in contravention of section 86 of the Constitution.

5. On the question of amendment to a Regional Constitution, section 5 of the Constitution of the Federation has been suitably modified to the effect that in respect of certain matters mentioned in the section like, the appointment, tenure of office and terms of service of High Court judges, the functions of the Public Service Commission, the establishment of a Consolidated Revenue Fund, etc., any Edict made shall come into operation only with the concurrence of the Supreme Military Council.

6. The Advisory Judicial Committee established under Decree No. 1 of 1966 and which before now tendered advice to the Supreme Military Council regarding appointment of judges all over the Federation has been abolished. Each Military Governor now controls appointment of judges of the High Court of his Region. But the appointment of the judges of both the Supreme Court of Nigeria and the High Court of Lagos is made the sole responsibility of the Supreme Military Council.

7. All appointments to posts in the superscale Group 6 and above in the Public Service of the Federation and appointments to posts of Deputy Commissioner of Police and above in the Nigeria Police Force are now to be made by the Supreme Military Council. The functions formerly discharged under sections 110 and 146 of the Constitution of the Federation by the Federal Public Service Commission and the Police Service Commission respectively are now to that extent limited.

8. Appointments to the offices of Ambassador, High Commissioner and other principal representatives of the Republic in countries other than Nigeria are now, under the Decree, to be made by the Supreme Military Council.

[1] *This is the Explanatory Note attached to Decree No. 8 of 1967, Constitution (Suspension and Modification), Supplement to the Official Gazette of the Federation of Nigeria, vol. 54, A 91–2. The Decree was promulgated on 17 March 1967.*

100.
'Between One Ambitious Man and the Rest of the Country': Hassan Katsina's Statement to the Press on the Dispute with the East[1]

The Supreme Military Council and the Commander-in-Chief, Lt.-Col. Yakubu Gowon, have both publicly declared their determination to keep the

Federal Republic of Nigeria together. I want also to publicly declare my support to this solemn pledge.

For the sake of the country, it is important that we return at once to the path of sanity and normalcy. I have no desire to remain here and I am sure most of my colleagues are anxious to return to barracks as soon as we can do so.

We are dedicated to the use of peaceful means for restoring normality; for we all realise that the use of force cannot provide a permanent and successful settlement of our problems. Nevertheless, if it should become necessary in the interest of the country and should it become the only solution left, clearly it will then become our duty to use force, albeit, very reluctantly.

Many of you have met our friend, Lt.-Col. Ojukwu, and have read his many statements. You may draw your own conclusions. My own is that Lt.-Col. Ojukwu is determined to make any kind of settlement impossible. Every one of his actions, every utterance of his seems calculated to divide us, to increase bitterness and to provoke us.

For our part, we recognise our responsibility and have refrained from pursuing the same course and have cautioned our people against being provoked.

As a soldier, my duty is to be loyal to my country and to defend its integrity against both internal and external aggression. I, like every Nigerian soldier, am sworn to defend the Constitution. I said before that, if the Commander-in-Chief, who is a man of the highest integrity, every inch a soldier, and who is working hard for the survival of his country, were to give the order, it would take only hours to subdue Lt.-Col. Ojukwu and remove the cause of friction. I still stand by this statement.

Let me make it clear that this dispute is no longer between the East and the North. It is between one ambitious man and the rest of the country. In spite of his boast, Ojukwu knows that, if we had any aggressive intentions against the East, he cannot redeem his pledge to meet 'force with force'. The truth is that he cannot face us. But we have no desire to use force against our own countrymen.

The East Military Governor has told the world that, even if the North was split into 50 states, he would not allow Easterners to come and live in any of them. Note that he says he will not allow Easterners to come and live in any of them. The Easterners are not to have a free choice in the matter.

This is his attitude in spite of the fact that he is aware that many people of Eastern Nigeria origin still live and work here in the North and several now in the East write asking to come back to live with us. Perhaps Lt.-Col. Ojukwu regards these people as non-Easterners.

I understand that the people of Ogoja are prevented from crossing the provincial boundary by soldiers of Eastern Nigeria origin and the whole of the Eastern Region now is one big prison. Lt.-Col. Ojukwu himself is, I believe, not free; for he is surrounded by a clique of evil advisers. The other Military leaders are making sincere efforts to save the people of Eastern Nigeria from their tyranny.

When the Eastern Nigeria Military Governor talks about an economic blockade I wonder why no one asks him what he means. It is unnecessary to impose any blockade against the East. The place is very effectively barricaded and blockaded by Ojukwu himself. And this has been the state of affairs since August last year.

Rail and road transport are prevented from going to or coming from the East on his own orders. Since Northern produce cannot use Eastern ports, shipping through these ports has virtually come to a halt. His own partial blockade on aircraft going to the East also is in force. More recently he is understood to have interfered with the free navigation of the international waterway along the Niger.

Under these circumstances I cannot imagine why anyone should wish to impose another blockade. One is already in force.

Much has been said about the Aburi agreements. The only thing wrong about Aburi is that Lt.-Col. Ojukwu insists that only his understanding of it and his after-thoughts should be implemented. He has persistently refused to attend any meeting where these decisions could be ratified and where any differences in interpretation could be resolved. It is difficult to know how to meet his wishes.

As far as the North is concerned, you can see for yourself that life is normal. You can go anywhere, talk to anyone. We recognise that the events that have taken place have shaken the very existence of this country but we know from history that this is by no means an isolated case. Many a great nation has passed through worse times than ours but have overcome their difficulties.

We believe we have a special responsibility to keep Nigeria together and we are going to be faithful to our country. But, in this connection, it is alleged that we in this Region do not want anything other than federalism, and are sworn to keep the country together because we stand to lose most.

I must make it clear that our stand in this respect is not because we fear any system other than federalism but because, on the assumption of power by Lt.-Col. Yakubu Gowon, he declared that there would be no major constitutional changes without prior consultation with the people of Nigeria. If we must change the constitution from federation to confederation we must consult the people. In the present circumstances we cannot consult since Ojukwu would neither attend meetings, nor allow his delegations to attend.

Secondly, it must be clear that, if the East is to secede it can only do so by the consent of the rest of the country and by all sections of the East. We have evidence that the vocal group in favour of secession are the Ibos and even then not all the Ibos. What are we expected to do about the other sections of the East? Sit by and see them forced away and oppressed by Ojukwu's administration?

A new concept has also now been introduced to our crisis. For the first time Lt.-Col. Ojukwu has introduced the religious element. One can also blame the foreign press for this new element. We have observed very carefully that over the years but particularly in recent months, every foreign paper which has concerned itself with Nigeria's problems has always given a religious twist to these problems. Many of them know and certainly Emeka knows that religion has had nothing to do with any of Nigeria's crisis before or since after our independence.

We would like to inform them, if they do not already know, that there live in the North of Nigeria millions of Christians and that they too are part and parcel of our society. They enjoy the same rights and privileges, share the same hopes and anxieties, live in the same houses and are subject to the same laws. We cannot understand why the foreign press, but particularly sometime responsible church publications, should want to ignore them and regard them as Moslems.

Although this is a serious matter, it sometime amuses me to observe the length to which responsible newspapers go to hide the truth from their readers that there are Christians in Northern Nigeria. Take the example of our Head of State. At the end of July the foreign press could not believe that he is a Christian. When they could not escape this simple truth, they coined a new description of him, 'Yakubu Gowon from the Moslem North'.

But we have become accustomed now to many unflattering descriptions. We are feudal; we are desperately poor and we are very backward. We note these descriptions, but we like to say that in our own way we are introducing far-reaching reforms in Northern Nigeria. We intend to do so without the help of anyone and we intend to do so at our own pace. But when we do finish we would still give ourselves a sound structure of our own which will stand the test of time and win the confidence of the responsible sections of the world. . . .

[1] *Made in Kaduna on 20 March 1967*. New Nigerian, *21 March 1967*.

101.
Gowon's Broadcast to the Nation, 25 March 1967[1]

My dear countrymen: my every day feeling is for you. During the past few months, I and the other military leaders have met a few times to try to solve our problems, and while we have been meeting or thinking in our offices, the debate has been going on around us in the newspapers and on the radio, in the universities, and in your homes about issues of federation, confederation, secession, domination, and the possibility of military action. But what I want to do tonight is to bring this abstract issue down to earth. I want to consider with you what the problems we face mean to the lives of the ordinary people in this country. Our duty as leaders is not just to pursue ideologies or forms of government for their own sake. My main concern is the happiness of the ordinary Nigerian citizen. We must therefore look at matters concerning how we should run the government in the light of how they will affect people's lives. We must always assess how the political decisions that we reach will influence the way our peoples live, the things that they want for themselves and their families, and shape the future of us all. My words are not intended to convey any threat but to beg for a calm approach, for a serious consideration of all that we stand to lose if we continue to drift apart as some people urge. I am speaking to you, the common people of our country, and I want you to understand that my primary concern is about you and your lot.

Nigeria has been going through hard times in the last two or three years. Governments have fallen and often people have not known where to look for guidance and honest leadership. In the absence of true leadership, mistrust and suspicion have come to the surface, and as a result people have been killed, women have been left without husbands, and children without fathers.

Unfortunate people have been compelled to move from one part of the country to the other, trade has dropped. All through these days, people are worried about how long their jobs will last, how they will sell their crops, where they will find money for school fees, whether those they love are safe. People desperately want to know if the future will be better than the past has been. The whole country has been wounded and what it needs most now is peace and unity so that these wounds can heal. I want to say to you that I myself and the other men who share authority with me really and truly want to bring back peace to Nigeria. It would be unforgivable for anyone to try to prolong the agony of the nation and prevent the early return of genuine peace. Only when there is peace can all of us do those things that human persons most deeply want to do.

All men and women desire to live a happy, contented life, to have children and to bring them up well, to be respected as they grow older and to die full of years and honour. I myself, like many of you, would like to live the normal, happy life we all deserve, to have a family and to care for them. I want my children to grow up in peace. I should like to educate my children and I should like too to have them meet with other Nigerian children from different parts of the country. I want them to get to know people outside their own language group and to see these people as human beings. I want them to trust people and to be trusted. I should like to bequeath to them a future they can look forward to in a country that they will be proud of. It is for reasons of this kind that I want all of us to try for trust to grow between us all, and for us to realise that the true interest of all of us lies in the same direction. We must not allow ourselves to be misled.

But how do we proceed now in the search for a genuine peace? The recent past provides lessons for us all on the primary need to avoid selfishness and narrow self-interest in approaching national problems. They remind us of the need to create conditions of equality for all the groups in our diverse country and to pursue justice honestly and consistently. Although we must learn from the past, yet if we are to build peace in our present circumstances we must learn now to forget a little of our past quarrels and forgive a great deal. Let us resolve that those who have died in the service of the Federation have made the supreme sacrifice so that our country may live and prosper. Let us think of our children and their future very, very hard. Let us not through blind ambition or hate provoke still greater disaster than we have suffered so far: because if we remain divided and dwell forever on our losses, we shall only invite greater tragedy. I shall always do my best to prevent such a development.

Now, let us look at the economic consequences of the troubles since January 1966. The disturbances of the last year and a half have caused considerable damage to the economy of Nigeria. The railways in particular and road transport are not functioning properly. The loss of transport has hit the coal mines severely and tin mines as well. The miners are threatened with unemployment. Many factories cannot reach their customers and are losing money. They find it more difficult to obtain their raw materials. People in some areas are not able to sell food to people in other areas to whom they have traditionally sold it and farmers and traders are suffering. Unless we can remedy the situation quickly, many people will have lost their jobs. They will be short of money for food. They will be unable to find money to maintain their families properly, to keep their children in school, or to take part in traditional festivals. Believe me when I say from my heart that all these things are my primary concern and they underlie my conviction of the need to preserve the Federation as a going concern.

There are few things more demoralising than being unemployed and not being able to find work. I want people to keep their jobs. I want them to go on receiving their salaries. I want farmers to be able to sell their crops. I want traders to trade again with their customers. But I cannot ensure these things without your help and co-operation. Every honest leader must harken to your legitimate and normal needs. The sufferings of all the citizens should not be extended any longer. I and my colleagues in the Federal Military Government have exercised great patience. We have not rushed matters. We have made far-reaching political concessions to accommodate all the Regions. The railways in the East should now run again. If they do not run, they cannot earn money to pay their workers. Our goods should now be distributed as cheaply as possible. The whole country—North, East, West and Mid-West—will gain equally if normalcy is restored. The foreigners' confidence in us will be restored and there will be more work, more trade, and more money. You must all think of these things. I know that the desire of every citizen is that these important things should become normal without delay. I know I can rely on your support and understanding in my effort.

In time our country should become rich. We have good and varied crops—cocoa, palm produce, peanuts and cotton. We can also grow all the food we need, we have minerals—tin, coal, iron and petroleum. We have wealth in our educated people beyond what most developing countries have. Above all, our men and women can work with determination. We have only to think of how much has been accomplished in the last two or three decades. The future before our great generation can be much better. But wealth, prosperity and strength will come to our country only if we remain together and united. Despite all the misunderstanding and conflict that divide us, our people need one another. There are differences in every large and great country. We need one another still. We need the variety of crops that we produce and that saves our country from depending on one crop in the world market. We need to operate together a transport system that stretches throughout the whole country. We form the largest market in Africa. We are setting up and with time we shall set up more industries big enough for this market, industries that employ our people and turn the products of our soil into greater wealth.

My dear countrymen, I pray and I shall work for the early return of the conditions under which any Nigerian can live and work and enjoy himself everywhere in this country. We deeply regret the temporary difficulties preventing the free movement of people. But we must thank God that there is still free movement of the majority of Nigerians in most of the provinces of this large country. What we must do is to improve the situation, not to make it worse.

Despite our present difficulties, our currency remains strong and the Nigerian pound is used everywhere in this country and beyond. Goods produced anywhere in the country are freely sold everywhere in the country. We maintain one customs unit. These are very important things. They are what matter most. We must maintain our good money so that if you save your money, you can enjoy the fruit of your savings. These are positive things we should emphasise and it is wrong and dangerous to claim that the Federation of Nigeria should be torn apart because of the events of 1966. You must all help by ignoring such false propaganda. You are all familiar with village life. Within our small social groups, individuals share their hopes and ambitions, sorrows and joys. They feast together at the coming of a child; they harvest the crops co-operatively, they mourn the dead together. Now, disputes often break out within the village and may even involve loss of life and threaten the unity of the whole community. But when this stage is reached, the cry eventually goes up: Cease! Enough! We must settle our differences before the village is destroyed. I seem to hear this cry in our country at this stage.

This is why I have bent over backwards to accommodate the wishes of the Military Governor of the Eastern Region and ignored personal insults so far. But the true interest of every Nigerian, including the various people who inhabit the Eastern Region, demands that we who are now privileged to serve the country must resolve the crisis without further delay. We can move beyond our sorrow and ensure that the misunderstandings of one year do not destroy the community that has grown up in the last half century. We can work out a better political system than we had in the past. We can try to ensure that better political leaders emerge, and we can pray God to help us. I know that it will not be easy to solve our problems overnight. But I know too that we cannot solve them by separating from one another. People who suggest this not only give little thought to the economy, but to the history of the country from the time that the North and the South were amalgamated. Nor do they think of the hardship involved for the ordinary man.

It was when our politicians came on the scene that they thought they could solve our problems by weakening the bonds that tied us together. Such reasoning has been a good part of our history since 1960. If we go further now in the same direction we should destroy the links that hold us together as people of one country. We should thus invite the whole world to mock us, and interfere, and we would inevitably drift into war with one another—God forbid. We will take the first step towards solving our problems only if we resolve honestly to continue to work together and to hold the country together.

When we, the military leaders, went to Aburi we made a beginning at putting things together again. I know that since then disagreements have arisen over the decisions. Yet I think that the meeting was a beginning. I have every intention of maintaining the spirit that inspired the meeting at Aburi and I need help from my military colleagues to do so. But I cannot allow myself to be held to an interpretation that follows part of the wording and part of the agreements reached. I must implement the agreement with concern for justice and truth and the interest of the common people of the country who are the helpless victims of our crisis and who have no hope of earning their living if we damage the country and its economy.

Fellow citizens, we have now promulgated a Decree giving effect to the consensus at Aburi. It provides a framework to guide the discharge of government functions in the meantime. But we should now look ahead to the real problems facing the country and see how we can solve them. The first thing is to restore transport, other essential services, and trade. We should continue to plan and build more factories. I look forward to the co-operation of each and every one of my colleagues to see that progress is made without delay. You will be the judge of our efforts. I hope that the only sacrifice I shall require of you is hard work so as to enable all groups in the country to enjoy equality of status and opportunity in the Federation. We must also introduce reforms to ensure that the best politicians emerge to run the country in the future. We must now hope and resolve that the worst is over. We must resolve to act first now and avoid divisive talk. With your active co-operation, I hope these tasks can be accomplished in good time so that the army can resume its traditional role. Thank you and may God keep you all.

¹ *Broadcast live from Lagos, 25 March 1967. Full text in* New Nigerian, *27 March 1967.*

102.
Programme for Return to Civilian Rule: Communiqué issued by the Supreme Military Council, April 1967[1]

The Supreme Military Council adopted the political and administrative programme of action for preserving the Federation of Nigeria as one country. The main items in the approved programme include:

i. Creation of States as the basis of political stability in Nigeria.

ii. Preparation and introduction of a new Constitution.

iii. National economic reconstruction with particular reference to the early restoration of normal economic links such as the resumption of Nigeria Airways and Railway services to all parts of the Federation and the preparation and introduction of the Second National Development Plan.

iv. Purging of corrupt elements in our public life and the restitution of ill-gotten gains, and

v. Supervision of elections of new civilian governments.

The Council accepted the need to accelerate the implementation of the programme in order to return to civilian rule. As a first step, the Council decided that the adjourned Constitutional Conference should reconvene in Benin City not later than the 5th of May, 1967 to continue discussions where it left off on October 1, 1966 and complete its work on or before 2nd of June 1967. It was agreed that further efforts should be made for the representatives of Eastern Nigeria to attend.

Some of the important details of the approved programme are as follows:

Between April and December 1967

i. Definite action on Declaration of Assets Decree and the various Reports on Tribunals of Enquiry into the Federal Statutory Corporations.

ii. Revenue Allocation Commission.

iii. Appointment of Special Committee on States Question. Submission of Report by the Special Committee on States Question to the Supreme Military Council for decision on number and identity of new States.

iv. Supreme Military Council decision on methods of selection of Constituent Assembly.

v. Introduction of civilians as full members into Federal Executive Council and Regional Executive Committees.

vi. Appointment of Constitution Drafting Committee.

Between January and December 1968

i. Selection of Members of Constituent Assembly.

ii. Submission of Report of Drafting Committee to Supreme Military Council.

iii. Convening of Constituent Assembly to consider and approve Draft Constitution.

iv. Revision of Electoral Register.

v. Promulgation of New Constitution.

vi. Installation of Transitional Government.

vii. Resumption of Political Party Activities.

Early 1969

i. Preparation for Elections;

Elections to Federal and State Legislatures.

ii. Appointments of Heads of Governments for Federal and States Governments.

iii. Parliaments meet: New Governments approved.

iv. Formal hand-over to Civilian Governments.

The Supreme Military Council took the opportunity to review the latest actions of the Eastern Nigeria Military Governor, Lt.-Col. Odumegwu-Ojukwu and took a number of decisions to protect the revenue and other commercial interests of the Federation until such a time as the Military Governor East can have second thoughts on his actions. The Supreme Military Council authorised certain stern measures to be taken by the Federal Military Government should the Military Governor East continue his illegal actions.

[1] *Issued in Lagos on 22 April 1967. Text from* Blueprint for Nigerian Unity (*Lagos, 1967*).

103.
Gowon Addresses Heads of Diplomatic Missions in Lagos[1]

You will recall that on the 1st of March this year I had a meeting with you in this same venue.[2] On that occasion, I informed you of the steps which my Government was taking to resolve amicably the political problems facing the country. You will also recall that, on that occasion, I gave you the assurances of my colleagues and myself that we would spare no efforts provided nothing is done by anyone to impair the integrity and the corporate existence of the Federation of Nigeria.

In pursuance of our objectives to settle our problems peacefully, we have caused a series of meetings of the Supreme Military Council and officials of the

Federal and Regional Governments to be held to resolve the outstanding differences of interpretation of the Aburi conclusions. A meeting of the Supreme Military Council also followed at Benin with a view to enabling the Eastern Governor to attend. You are aware that he did not attend that meeting. Nevertheless, an opportunity was given to our colleague in the East to make his views available to the Council. Consequent upon this meeting and that of the Drafting Committee of Legal Officials from the whole Federation, Decree No. 8 of 17th March, 1967 was promulgated.[3]

The said Decree No. 8 in effect restored the powers of the Regional Governments to the constitutional position before January 17, 1966. In fact, the Decree went further than mere restoration and for the first time included Regional Governors as members of the Federal Executive. Thus, you will see that the position of Regional Governments has actually been considerably strengthened. This Decree also established Area Commands in an effort to re-establish confidence within the army and maintain discipline in order to ensure the continuation of the Nigerian Army under a unified command. It was in consonance with this spirit that the title of the High Office which I have the honour to hold was changed from Supreme Commander to Commander-in-Chief of the Armed Forces.

You must all have read the proposals by the Federal Military Government towards its handing over of the administration to the civilians hence I need not dwell on them. Copies of the Communiqué issued at the end of the meeting of the Supreme Military Council will be distributed to you.[4]

You must also have read from the newspapers, or received from your representatives in Enugu, the text of the statement made a few days ago by the Military Governor of Eastern Nigeria to the Foreign Representatives there. The statement was sent to me by telex (after it had been made) on Saturday the 22nd of April, 1967. You probably also have a copy of my memorandum referred to in that statement. This is a classified document and you all know as representatives of respective Governments how such documents should be handled. However, my colleague in Eastern Nigeria has long decided not to respect the basic and fundamental principle guarding classified documents for reasons best known to him. No doubt you all remember the issue of my statement to you on 1st March when I requested you to treat the information therein as confidential.[5] I sent a copy of the Statement to Lt.-Col. Ojukwu and he promptly released it to the Press. Therefore I shall make the text of this address available to the information media.

It seems quite obvious that Lt.-Col. Ojukwu, being aware that there are still some loyal civil servants of Eastern Nigeria origin in the Federal Public Service in Lagos, wants to make 'scapegoats' of them by pretending that classified documents 'leak' out from Lagos to him through such officials even when such documents are properly and officially circulated to him in his capacity as a member of the Supreme Military Council. What glaring distortion is made of such information is unfortunate, to say the least.

One clear example of this type of distortion is the decision that all Public Officers (including former Foreign Service Officers) who have now transferred to the service of Eastern Nigeria but who still retain Diplomatic passports although their present appointments do not entitle them to hold such passports should return them. The Military Governor of Eastern Nigeria has said that all Eastern Nigerians are being deprived of passports. This is not true.

I am aware of the havoc and mischief being done by some of these people illegally carrying Diplomatic Passports. They are being used among other things, to negotiate and buy arms not only illegally but falsely in the name of the Federal Government. I want to stop this.

Incidentally, Lt.-Col. Ojukwu accuses me of bad faith in preparing the memorandum to Council at the time we were making arrangements for a meeting of the Supreme Military Council. In fact, he promulgated an edict purporting to appropriate Federal Government properties in the Eastern Region at a time when we were seriously discussing arrangements for a meeting at which it was hoped he would be present. I telephoned my Eastern colleague to confirm whether the newspaper and radio reports were in fact correct. I indicated to him the difficulties he was creating for me by his action and that if the other Regional Governors took the same action, the consequences would be disastrous for the nation. It would also interest you to know that the initiative for telephone discussions between me and the East Military Governor has always come from me.

I must now draw your attention to the statement made by Lt.-Col. Ojukwu to the World Press in Enugu on the 13th of March.[6] You will recall that in answer to a question by the representative of the London *Observer*, who sought to know what general situation the Governor envisaged after March 31, 1967, he replied as follows:

I can envisage once I start implementing Aburi on my own terms—as I am bound to do if they will not play fair and honour agreements—I can see them in Lagos, in their foggy reasoning, taking this as an act of confrontation. I can see them probably accepting the first move, the second move, and then their misplaced pride being hurt by the third move. I can then see them—and this is the point of this open conflict—probably embarking on open hostility.

It appears that Lt.-Col. Ojukwu has begun to implement his threats. I have in mind the Edict which purported to appropriate revenue originating from the Eastern Region and the latest move, the take-over of Federal Government Corporations and other interests in the East, such as the Airways, Broadcasting, Railways, Shipping, Posts and Telecommunications, Electricity, Coal and Ports.

My Government is not unaware of its responsibility to this nation. There is no doubt that these so-called Edicts are contrary to the Laws and Constitution of Nigeria. Consequently, they have no legal validity. In spite of these illegal and treasonable acts, no drastic steps have yet been taken because of consideration for the common man, particularly in Eastern Nigeria and in the hope that our colleague in Enugu will see reason.

You are also aware of other acts of provocation and attempts by the Eastern Governor to disrupt the machinery of Government in the Federation. Examples of such acts have been the expulsion of all non-Easterners (with the exception of Mid-Western Ibos resident in Eastern Nigeria); his withdrawal of some civil servants of Eastern Nigeria origin from the services of the Federation; his recent instructions to members of the Police Force of Eastern Nigeria origin to return to that Region and strong indications of his interference with Naval personnel. In addition, there is the continued illegal importation by the Eastern Governor of arms and ammunition from various sources. These illegal acts have to and must be checked before they get out of hand. Since the Military Governor, Eastern Nigeria does not accept Decree No. 8 he has not even the faintest grounds of legality to justify his opposition to the creation of States.

I must emphasise my previous assurance that my colleagues and I will continue to seek a peaceful solution to the present problem as long as nothing is done to damage the national integrity and corporate existence of the country. You will agree with me that as the Head of the Federal Military Government, I am duty bound to protect the nation against any acts of rebellion, and any threats to our continued existence as a nation. We are approaching a Katanga situation.

Reference has been made to the proposal that the Military leaders should meet outside Nigeria in the presence of some African Heads of State. After due consideration, I am unable to agree to this proposal because of the following reasons:

a. the current situation in Nigeria is an internal affair:

b. the invitation, emanating from Lt.-Col. Ojukwu as it does, has the undertone of seeking de facto recognition by these African Heads of State. It also implies that there is a dispute between two sovereign and equal states;

c. to avoid possible division in the ranks of the O.A.U., and especially among those who would be genuinely interested in assisting Nigeria;

d. the fact that Lt.-Col. Ojukwu refuses to recognise the existence of the Federal Government and myself as the Head; and

e. the invitation to any Head of State must, as a matter of protocol, emanate from me as Head of the Federal Military Government. In reaching such a decision I would, of course, consult my colleagues on the Supreme Military Council.

We have given serious consideration to the series of provocations so far unwontingly launched against the rest of the country by the Eastern Governor. We shall be failing in our duty as soldiers and as the Federal Military Government if the interests of the State are not protected. Accordingly, appropriate measures are being taken to safeguard the sovereignty and territorial integrity of the Federation of Nigeria.

Your Excellencies, I would like to reiterate that my Government stands committed to protecting and respecting all international agreements as well as ensuring the safety of foreign investment and of all foreign nationals within the Federation. This duty includes the safeguarding of all the economic interests of the Federation wherever they may lie.

I have just heard, with dismay, of the hijacking of a Nigerian Airways Fokker Friendship aircraft on its way from Benin to Lagos on a scheduled flight. The aircraft is now known to be in Enugu and the list of passengers includes foreign nationals. It is my firm resolve that such shall not happen again and I am holding Lt.-Col. Ojukwu personally responsible for the safety of all the passengers on that aircraft and their return to their destination. Should any of you desire any special assistance with regard to your nationals, please contact the Ministry of External Affairs.

The situation is well within the capacity of my Government to resolve and all we ask for is your continued understanding and sympathy. You are familiar with similar events in history. We regard our present situation as an unfortunate but perhaps inevitable stage in our evolution towards national consciousness. Therefore any foreign intervention, direct or implied, unless requested by my Government, will be regarded as an unfriendly act. I trust that Lt.-Col. Ojukwu understands this. Your Excellencies, you are witnesses to the steps taken by my Government to ensure the peaceful settlement of the problems facing the country. Unfortunately these steps have failed to achieve the desired result. You will agree that the country cannot continue in its present state of uncertainty. My colleagues and I have decided to take measures which we consider necessary for keeping the country together. I am certain that in view of the known situation, I can continue to count on the support and co-operation of your Governments.

I want to make it abundantly clear that in the event of Lt.-Col. Ojukwu carrying out his threat to secede, this will be a clear signal in the first place to create a COR-State[7] for the protection of the minorities in Eastern Nigeria whom we know do not want to part from the rest of the country. This action of creating the COR-State will be backed by the use of force if need be.

Reference has been made by Lt.-Col. Ojukwu to the use of force and the agreement signed by us at Aburi. It appears, however, that his own interpretation is that force must not be used against him but that he can use it against anybody else. I receive scores of representations and petitions daily from people of Eastern Nigeria, especially from the Calabar, Ogoja and Rivers areas, of treatment meted out either on the directives or with the connivance of Lt.-Col. Ojukwu. For example wives and children are carried off to Enugu and locked up when husbands and fathers who may be wanted for political reasons cannot be found.

Finally, Your Excellencies, there is no change in my stand from what I said in my broadcast of November 30th 1966[8] and the stand I took at Aburi, namely that there will be no use of force provided nothing is done by anyone to impair the integrity and corporate existence of the Federation of Nigeria.

[1] *Speech made in Lagos on 24 April 1967. Ministry of Information hand-out.*
[2] *See* DOC *92.*   [3] *See* DOC *99.*
[4] *See* DOC *102.*   [5] *See* DOC *92.*
[6] *See* DOC *97.*
[7] *Calabar-Ogoja-Rivers State, the creation of which was a constant objective of minority groups in Eastern Nigeria during the 1950s.*
[8] *See* DOC *75.*

104.
Awolowo Promises West will secede if the East does[1]

The aim of a leader should be the welfare of the people whom he leads. I have used 'welfare' to denote the physical, mental and spiritual well-being of the people. With this aim fixed unflinchingly and unchangeably before my eyes I consider it my duty to Yoruba people in particular and to Nigerians in general, to place four imperatives before you this morning. Two of them are categorical and two are conditional.

Only a peaceful solution must be found to arrest the present worsening stalemate and restore normalcy.

The Eastern Region must be encouraged to remain part of the Federation.

If the Eastern Region is allowed by acts of omission or commission to secede from or opt out of Nigeria, then the Western Region and Lagos must also stay out of the Federation.

The people of Western Nigeria and Lagos should participate in the ad hoc committee or any similar body only on the basis of absolute equality with the other regions of the Federation.

I would like to comment briefly on these four imperatives. There has, of late, been a good deal of sabre rattling in some parts of the country. Those who advocate the use force for the settlement of our present problems should stop a little and reflect. I can see no vital and abiding principle involved in any war between the North and the East. If the East attacked the North, it would be for purpose of revenge pure and simple. Any claim to the contrary would be untenable. If it is claimed that such a war is being waged for the purpose of recovering the real and personal properties left behind in the North by Easterners two insuperable points are obvious. Firstly, the personal effects left behind by Easterners have been wholly looted or destroyed, and can no longer be physically recovered. Secondly, since the real properties are immovable in case of recovery of them can only be by means of forcible military occupation of those parts of the North in which these properties are situated. On the other hand, if the North attacked the East, it could only be for the purpose of further strengthening and entrenching its position of dominance in the country.

If it is claimed that an attack on the East is going to be launched by the Federal Government and not by the North as such and that it is designed to ensure the unity and integrity of the Federation, two other insuperable points also become obvious. First, if a war against the East becomes a necessity it must be agreed to unanimously by the remaining units of the Federation. In this connection, the West, Mid-West and Lagos have declared their implacable opposition to the use of force in solving the present problem. In the face of such declarations by three out of remaining four territories of Nigeria, a war against the East could only be a war favoured by the North alone. Second, if the true purpose of such a war is to preserve the unity and integrity of the Federation, then these ends can be achieved by the very simple devices of implementing the recommendation of the committee which met on August 9 1966, as reaffirmed by a decision of the military leaders at Aburi on January 5 1967 as well as by accepting such of the demands of the East, West, Mid-West and Lagos as are manifestly reasonable, and essential for assuring harmonious relationships and peaceful co-existence between them and their brothers and sisters in the North.

Some knowledgeable persons have likened an attack on the East to Lincoln's war against the southern states in America. Two vital factors distinguish Lincoln's campaign from the one now being contemplated in Nigeria. The first is that the American civil war was aimed at the abolition of slavery—that is the liberation of millions of Negroes who were then still being

2 E

used as chattels and worse than domestic animals. The second factor is that Lincoln and others in the northern states were English-speaking people waging a war of good conscience and humanity against their fellow nationals who were also English speaking. A war against the East in which Northern soldiers are predominant, will only unite the Easterners or the Ibos against their attackers, strengthen them in their belief that they are not wanted by the majority of their fellow-Nigerians, and finally push them out of the Federation.

We have been told that an act of secession on the part of the East would be a signal, in the first instance, for the creation of the COR state by decree, which would be backed, if need be, by the use of force.[2] With great respect, I have some dissenting observations to make on this declaration. There are 11 national or linguistic groups in the COR areas with a total population of 5·3 millions. These national groups are as distinct from one another as the Ibos are distinct from them or from the Yorubas or Hausas. Of the 11, the Efik/Ibibio/Annang national group are 3·2 million strong as against the Ijaws who are only about 700,000 strong. Ostensibly, the remaining nine national group number 1·4 millions. But when you have subtracted the Ibo inhabitants from among them, what is left ranges from the Ngennis who number only 8,000 to the Ogonis who are 220,000 strong. A decree creating a COR state without a plebiscite to ascertain the wishes of the peoples in the area, would only amount to subordinating the minority national groups in the state to the dominance of the Efik/Ibibio/Annang national group. It would be perfectly in order to create a Calabar state or a Rivers state by decree, and without a plebiscite. Each is a homogeneous national unit. But before you lump distinct and diverse national units together in one state, the consent of each of them is indispensable. Otherwise, the seed of social disquilibrium in the new state would have been sown.

On the other hand, if the COR State is created by decree after the Eastern Region shall have made its severance from Nigeria effective, we should then be waging an unjust war against a foreign state. It would be an unjust war, because the purpose of it would be to remove 10 minorities in the East from the dominance of the Ibos only to subordinate them to the dominance of the Efik/Ibibio/Annang national group. I think I have said enough to demonstrate that any war against the East, or vice versa, on any count whatsoever, would be an unholy crusade, for which it would be most unjustifiable to shed a drop of Nigerian blood. Therefore, only a peaceful solution must be found, and quickly too to arrest the present rapidly deteriorating stalemate and restore normalcy.

With regard to the second categorical imperative, it is my considered view that whilst some of the demands of the East are excessive within the context of a Nigerian union, most of such demands are not only wellfounded, but are designed for smooth and steady association amongst the various national units of Nigeria.

The dependence of the Federal Government on financial contributions from the regions—These and other such like demands I do not support. Demands such as these, if accepted, will lead surely to the complete disintegration of the Federation which is not in the interest of our people. But I wholeheartedly support the following demands among others, which we consider reasonable and most of which are already embodied in our memoranda to the Ad Hoc Committee. . . .

That revenue should be allocated strictly on the basis of derivation; that is to say after the Federal Government has deducted its own share for its own services the rest should be allocated to the regions to which they are attributable.

That the existing public debt of the Federation should become the responsibility of the regions on the basis of the location of the projects in respect of each debt whether internal or external.

That each region should have and control its own militia and police force.

That, with immediate effect, all military personnel should be posted to their regions of origin. . . .

If we are to live in harmony one with another as Nigerians it is imperative that these demands and others which are not related, should be met without further delay by those who have hitherto resisted them. To those who may argue that the acceptance of these demands will amount to transforming Nigeria into a federation with a weak central government, my comment is that any link however tenuous, which keeps the East in the Nigerian union, is better in my view than no link at all.

Before the Western delegates went to Lagos to attend the meetings of the ad hoc committee, they were given a clear mandate that if any region should opt out of the Federation of Nigeria, then the Federation should be considered to be at an end, and that the Western Region and Lagos should also opt out of it. It would then be up to Western Nigeria and Lagos as an independent sovereign state to enter into association with any of the Nigerian units of its own choosing, and on terms mutually acceptable to them. I see no reason for departing from this mandate. If any region in Nigeria considers itself strong enough to compel us to enter into association with it on its own terms, I would only wish such a region luck. But such luck, I must warn, will, in the long run be no better than that which has attended the doings of all colonial powers down the ages. This much I must say in addition, on this point. We have neither military might nor the overwhelming advantage of numbers here in Western Nigeria and Lagos. But we have justice of a noble and imperishable cause on our side, namely: the right of a people to unfettered self-determination. If this is so, then God is on our side, and if God is with us then we have nothing whatsoever in this world to fear.

The fourth imperative, and the second conditional one has been fully dealt with in my recent letter to the Military Governor of Western Nigeria, Col. Robert Adebayo, and in the representation which your deputation made last year to the head of the Federal Military Government, Lt. Col. Yakubu Gowon. As a matter of fact, as far back as November last year a smaller meeting of leaders of thought in this Region decided that unless certain things were done, we would no longer participate in the meeting of the ad hoc committee. But since then, not even one of our legitimate requests has been granted. I will, therefore, take no more of your time in making further comments on a point with which you are well familiar. As soon as our humble and earnest requests are met, I shall be ready to take my place on the ad hoc committee. But certainly—not before.

In closing, I have this piece of advice to give. In order to resolve this crisis amiably and in the best interests of all Nigerians certain attributes are required on the part of Nigerian leaders—military as well as non-military leaders alike—namely: vision, realism and unselfishness. But above all, what will keep Nigerian leaders in the North and East unwaveringly in the path of wisdom, realism and moderation is courage and steadfastness on the part of Yoruba people in the course of what they sincerely believe to be right, equitable and just. In the past five years we in the West and Lagos have shown that we possess these qualities in a large measure. If we demonstrate them again as we did in the past, calmly and heroically, we will save Nigeria from further bloodshed and imminent wreck and, at the same time, preserve our freedom and self-respect into the bargain.

May God rule and guide our deliberations here, and endow all the Nigerian leaders with the vision, realism, and unselfishness as well as courage and steadfastness in the course of truth, which the present circumstances demand.

[1] *Speech made to the Western leaders of thought, in Ibadan, 1 May 1967.* Daily Times, *2 May 1967. Cf.* DOC *200.*
[2] *See* DOC *103.*

105.
Hassan Katsina Addresses Northern Leaders of Thought[1]

I have found it necessary to invite you again to Kaduna in order to acquaint you with developments since the full Supreme Military Council meeting at Aburi early in the New Year and to seek your ever valuable guidance and advice on the measures so far introduced and on the new proposals recently announced by the Federal Military Government.[2]

Needless to emphasise, the Federal Military Government intends, with the co-operation of all well-meaning and responsible Nigerians, to implement faithfully those proposals within the period specified in the communiqué issued at the end of the recent meeting of the Supreme Military Council.

Since your last meeting in January, the Supreme Council and officials from all the Governments in the Federation have held a number of meetings in order to resolve the outstanding differences in the interpretation of the decisions and agreements reached at Aburi. A meeting of the Supreme Council was held at Benin as venue in order to enable our colleague from the East to attend.

You all know that he did not attend in spite of assurances and guarantees about his safety. Instead he made available his views in writing and through his officials. As a result of the Benin meeting Decree No. 8 was promulgated.

This Decree as you all know restored the powers of the Regional Governments to the constitutional position existing before January, 1966. More than this it strengthened the position of the Regional Governments by including, for the first time, Regional Governors as full members of the Federal Executive Council. Also in a bid to re-establish confidence within the Army as well as in order to maintain discipline and ensure the continuation of the

Nigerian Army under a unified command, it set up Area Commands in all the Regions and the Federal Territory of Lagos.

One other important thing introduced by this Decree was the change of the title of the Head of the Federal Military Government from the 'Supreme Commander' to the 'Commander-in-Chief' of the Nigerian Armed Forces.

These measures were adopted in the honest belief that they were conciliatory and would therefore be acceptable to all concerned, including the Eastern Regional Government. They had implemented the Aburi decisions which had provoked so much debate and controversy both within and outside Nigeria and the delay over the implementation of which had invited equally scathing criticisms from Lt.-Col. Ojukwu himself.

But this was not the case. Instead, the immediate reaction of the Eastern Military Governor was to repudiate the Decree and cast aspersion on all our efforts at conciliation. He argued with shameless untruth that the Decree did not in any way reflect the decisions reached at Aburi. As usual, he maintains that only his interpretation of the Aburi decisions is correct, that of all the other members of the Supreme Military Council is wrong. Like a spoilt child if he cannot have his way he will upset everything.

Like a man consumed by pride and ambition if he cannot rule all he will ruin all. He has, therefore, as everyone knows embarked on a callous and deliberate smear campaign against the Federal Military Government and the Commander-in-Chief in person and threatened that he would henceforth proceed with unilateral action to implement in his own Region what he considered were the decisions reached at Aburi.

Externally, he has launched a most vicious propaganda campaign in which the factors that disunite this country are emphasised rather than those that unite us.

Emissaries have been sent abroad to give prominence to the elements that make for the disintegration of this country rather than to the honest efforts being made by the Governments and the people and organisations all over the country to restore normalcy and goodwill and keep the country together.

Internally, the entire information media in the East has been geared to vilifying Northern Nigeria in particular. They have worked feverishly to spread discord between tribes in the North and to incite the feelings of our brothers in the West, Mid-West and Lagos against us. As soon as Nigeria sees a glimmer of hope for resolving our differences, the Eastern Governor deliberately takes provocative steps to dampen the spirits of men of goodwill all over Nigeria.

By the beginning of April this year it was clear that Lt.-Col. Ojukwu was bent upon carrying out his threats to pull the East, including the minority elements who are opposed to his plans, out of the Federation. First he promulgated an edict which empowered the Eastern Nigeria Military Government to appropriate all Federal revenues originating from the East, thus unilaterally altering the existing revenue allocation formula between the Federal Government and the Regions which is laid down by law.

Next he took over all the Federal Government institutions and corporations such as the Nigeria Airways, Broadcasting, Railways, Telecommunications, etc. in the East. These were followed by other illegal and unconstitutional acts such as the seizure and hi-jacking of aircraft belonging to the Nigeria

Airways: interference with the Nigerian Naval personnel and non-recognition of the authority of the Federal Supreme Court.

Other provocations included the recent call on the members of the Nigeria Police Force of Eastern Nigeria origin to return to the East, the persistent defiance of the powers of the Federal Military Government and the refusal to accept and acknowledge the authority of the Commander-in-Chief. In addition the whole world is aware that the Eastern Military Governor has continued to import arms and ammunitions illegally from various sources into his Region.

These are indeed grave and serious acts for which Lt.-Col. Ojukwu must be personally held responsible. The Supreme Military Council took the opportunity at its last meeting to review them and I assure you that the Federal Military Government is not merely sitting idle and allowing these illegal acts to go unchallenged. It is fully alive to its responsibility to the nation and intends to take appropriate and firm action to secure obedience to the Constitution of the Federal Republic by East [Military] Governor, to put a stop once and for all to any further acts of defiance from him and in this way maintain the unity and territorial integrity of the Federation of Nigeria.

The Commander-in-Chief has already warned the East Military Governor in unequivocal terms that should he carry out his threat to secede completely from the Federation, the consequences will be serious. The Federal Military Government has a duty to ensure that the minorities in Eastern Nigeria whose fervent desire is to remain Nigerians are not severed against their will from the rest of Nigeria. Whatever the cost they must be allowed to make their own voluntary choice.

I know it is the desire, the earnest prayer and sincere hope of all lovers of Nigeria that we may be able to find a peaceful and lasting settlement to our problems. Such also are the feelings of the Federal Military Government. The same cannot be said of the Government of the East.

It is clear from his recent acts and utterances that the East Military Governor has no interest in a peaceful settlement. Only an immediate change of heart and attitude by Lt.-Col. Ojukwu and his few advisers can accelerate a peaceful solution. As we all know where people differ there are two methods of reaching a settlement. They can adopt the well tried and civilised method of discussion and conciliation. They can also resolve to follow the path of war. This second method is barbarous and abhorred by all civilised communities. But by his acts of arrogance, defiance and ridicule the Eastern Military Governor shows himself clearly in favour of a settlement by force.

I want to warn that the use of force will only bring disaster and more misery to the people he claims to represent. The Federal Military Government acting in concert with the loyal Regions can end Lt.-Col. Ojukwu's outlawery, but only hesitates and continues to seek settlement by peaceful means purely in order to avoid suffering and hardship on those innocent people now forced against their wish to accept Lt.-Col. Ojukwu's dictatorship.

In an effort to find a permanent and peaceful settlement to our problems the Supreme Council met recently in Lagos and adopted a political and administrative programme of action to preserve the Federation as well as to facilitate a return to civilian rule by 1969. Copies of the communiqué issued at the end of this meeting in which the Federal Military Government's proposals in this regard are outlined more clearly will be distributed to you for study and I shall be only too pleased to transmit whatever additional advice or suggestions you will care to make to the Commander-in-Chief for the Supreme Council's consideration.

You will note that as a first step the Council has recommended the immediate reconvening of the adjourned constitutional conference on the future of Nigeria at Benin City not later than the 5th of May, 1967. Your advice and guidance to our delegates and advisers in the light of the new developments will be most useful. This need for your guidance and advice is in fact the main purpose of calling this meeting. My only hope is that out of today's deliberations will emerge constructive and useful suggestions for solving the problems of the country.

Gentlemen, in spite of pre-occupation with the national problems we have not altogether shut our eyes to our own local problems here in the North nor, for that matter, the need for introducing changes and reforms where these are desirable. Indeed we have spared no effort in our determination to find solutions to the peculiar problems of this Region.

Here I wish to refer to the recent judicial reforms and the decision to preclude Native Authority staff from taking active part in politics either directly or indirectly in the future. In my view these reforms are a step in the right direction and, having regard to the present circumstances, they are also timely.

I am sure every progressive man and woman in the North will welcome them. The judicial reforms have been introduced primarily in order to safeguard and protect the interest of the common man, and, secondly, to bring our judicial system in line with that obtaining in all progressive and civilized societies.

Similarly, the decision to prevent Native Authority staff from taking active part in politics has its advantages. Not only will it be possible for Native Authority staff to concentrate more on their work and in this way improve the efficiency of their Native Authorities but it will also enable this Region to produce, in numbers and quality, professional politicians who are independent both in outlook and thinking and better able to devote their entire time to political and parliamentary affairs.

This does not, of course, mean that Native Authority staff cannot contest elections, but it does mean that if they wish to take part in politics, they must cut their connection with their Native Authority. The same applies to their counterparts working under Government. Looked at from another angle one can see the logic and sense in the decision to prohibit Native Authority staff from engaging actively in politics.[3]

First as already explained, their counterparts in Government are so prohibited and secondly, just as it is important to separate the Judiciary from the Executive so also is it important to separate the Executive from the Legislature. When politics return this will relieve the Native Authorities of the charge of favouring one side or the other. Any Authority is established for a whole community and it cannot function effectively if one section feels that it is working against it.

This decision is therefore for the good of the North and for the good of Native Authorities and if we have more than one party in the North it will give each and every one of them a fairness. Fairness is always our aim in this Region. At any rate, the reforms which have just been introduced and those which are in the process of being worked out are inevitable if the North is to remain progressive in a rapidly and fast changing world.

The North is described as complacent and conservative. This is not true; change has been taking place and continues to take place among us, but certain of our actions and behaviour give to the outside world the impression that we are static. We must wipe away this impression and we can only do this by discarding outmoded practices and institutions. We must modernise according to our needs and conditions. We need to capture the imagination of the progressives and give no cause for the contempt with which the North is so often treated.

It is for these and other reasons that I commend to you wholeheartedly the reforms just introduced. I am confident that you will not read any sinister motives in them. The Military Government has nothing but the interest of the North and its people at heart and I shall do nothing which will frustrate or humiliate deliberately any class or group of people. I appeal to all of you again to co-operate fully with the Government in ensuring the success of these reforms. . . .

[1] *Speech made at Kaduna, 1 May 1967.* New Nigerian, *2 May 1967.*
[2] *See* DOC *102.*   [3] *Cf. speech of 19 April 1967.*

106.
Ojukwu's Terms to the National Conciliation Committee[1]

I
1. The East is willing, and indeed prepared, to participate in discussions designed to resolve the present Nigerian crisis.
2. With regard to the request made by the delegates of the Conciliation Committee that the Eastern Government should appoint representatives to the Committee, it would appear anomalous that whilst the other members of the Committee have been personally invited by the sponsors/conveners, the Eastern delegates should be appointed by their own Government.
3. Other members of the Committee, therefore, ought also to be appointed by their respective Governments. A Committee constituted in this way would be in a better position to achieve effective results.
4. Such a Committee should be set up in such a way that it is made up of people who have the authority and mandate of their Governments, with the Regions having equal representation and equality of status.
5. Necessary preparations should be made to ensure that there are:
a. agreed agenda, with emphasis on the terms of association between the Regions;
b. an acceptable venue, with due regard to conditions of safety and free discussion; and
c. a time limit set for the completion of the work of the Committee so that the discussions do not become unduly protracted.

6. If the delegates are to participate in the discussions in an atmosphere of freedom and equality, then

a. the economic strangulation of the East should be discontinued;

b. the occupation of West and Lagos by Northern troops should end.

II.
Mr Ojukwu said:

I started off this struggle in July with 120 rifles to defend the entirety of the East. I took my stand knowing fully well that doing so, whilst carving my name in history, I was signing also my death warrant. But I took it because I believe that this stand was vital to the survival of the South. I appealed for settlement quietly because I understood that this was a naked struggle for power and that the only time we can sit down and decide the future of Nigeria on basis of equality will always be equality of arms. Quietly I built. If you do not know it, I am proud, and my officers are proud that here in the East we possess the biggest army in black Africa. I am no longer speaking as an under-dog, I am speaking from a position of power. It is not my intention to unleash the destruction which my army can unleash. It is not my intention to fight unless I am attacked. If I am attacked I will take good care of the aggressor. That is why I really believe that our future must be for the South to halt a while and think, so whilst we are catching up something which is already written to the core, that is association with the North, we do not lose more the things that keep us in the South together.

In specific answer to a query by Chief Awolowo, the leader of the Peace Mission, regarding the attitude of the Eastern Leaders to the former Northern Region and secession, Mr Ojukwu replied: 'on the specific question of whether there is a possibility of contact with the North, the answer is at the battlefield.'

[1] *Ojukwu addressed the Delegation at State House, Enugu on 6 May 1967. The proposals were signed there on 7 May 1967. Texts taken from Ojukwu's subsequent address to the East's Consultative Assembly, 26 May 1967* (DOC 110), *and from Federal Government publication* The Collapse of a Rebellion (*Lagos, 1968*), *p. 7.*

107.
Lagos Clarifies Position on Presence of British Troops[1]

Attention has been drawn to radio and newspaper reports emanating from Eastern Nigeria Information media purporting that the Federal Military Government has asked for British Troops for the purpose of crushing the Eastern Nigeria Military Government. The truth is that in the continuing effort to search for a solution to the problems besetting this country, the need for creating a safe venue within Nigeria for a meeting of Nigeria's Military leaders has become most pressing. Since such a meeting within Nigeria is considered impracticable because of the objection in certain quarters to the disposition of army personnel, the question of a meeting in a British Aircraft Carrier or Frigate, which would serve as a safe neutral ground, was considered.

With the foregoing in view, the following message was sent to all the Military Governors on the 17th of May, 1967:

TO ALL MILITARY GOVERNORS (KADUNA, ENUGU, IBADAN & BENIN) FROM: HEAD OF THE FEDERAL MILITARY GOVERNMENT AND COMMANDER-IN-CHIEF OF THE ARMED FORCES.

TENTATIVE ARRANGEMENTS MADE FOR BRITISH ASSISTANCE MILITARY PERSONNEL ONE OR TWO COMPANIES STRICTLY TO CREATE NEUTRAL ZONE FOR US TO MEET. SUGGEST BENIN/NAIFOR IDEAL VENUE. ALTERNATIVE OFFER BRITISH AIRCRAFT CARRIER/FRIGATE. GRATEFUL CONFIRM YOU ARE AGREEABLE FIRM ARRANGEMENTS SHOULD BE CONCLUDED FOR MEETING ON OR ABOUT MAY TWENTYFOURTH. ALSO INDICATE ALTERNATIVE PREFERRED. LETTER WITH PROPOSED AGENDA FOLLOWS.

It is most uncharitable for any information media to begin to accuse anyone of requesting the assistance of British troops to crush Eastern Nigeria. It is up to each Military Governor, having been informed of the moves being made to make a meeting possible within Nigeria to communicate his objection, if any, to the Head of the Federal Military Government and not for any information media to go about casting aspersions on honest effort.

No official request has been made to the British Government in this context. Only tentative feelers were made.

[1] *Statement issued by the Cabinet Office on 18 May 1967: Federal Ministry of Information Press Release No. 1108/1967.*

108.
British High Commission Denies Dispatch of British Troops[1]

My attention has been drawn to allegations in the Eastern Region press and radio that Britain is planning to intervene militarily in Nigeria. I am well aware that attacks of this nature, which arise in times of stress do not in the long run alter the cordial and long established friendship between Britain and Nigeria. Nevertheless, in this case a reply is necessary.

It is ridiculous for anyone to suggest that Britain would even contemplate any form of military action against Nigeria. It is on a par with the stories about jet bombers being sent to Nigeria from an Asian State and warships from an African State. What Britain wants for Nigeria is just what the Nigerians want for themselves, to find a peaceful solution to their current political problems. Without taking sides, the British Government is convinced that such a solution can and must be found by Nigeria without any external interference from whatever source.

A suggestion has been raised that it would make it easier for all the Leaders of Nigeria to meet on Nigerian soil if the safety of their meeting place could be guaranteed by using a small body of troops lent by another friendly Power. No such request has in fact been made to the British Government. If all four Military Governors and the Federal Government wished for a meeting of this sort and a request was made to the British Government it would receive careful consideration; but it would only be given consideration if it was the unanimous wish of all Nigerians from all parts of the country.

[1] *By courtesy of the U.K. High Commission, Lagos.*

109.
Hassan Katsina's Interview on the Withdrawal of Northern Troops from the West[1]

H.K.: Our discussions concerned the honest desire of Col. Adebayo and myself to ensure that the relationship between the people of the West and Northern Nigeria continues to be as close and cordial as in the past. The bonds of history, culture, tradition, religion, outlook and economic interrelationship that have been forged over the years are very strong indeed. I have not the slightest doubt that it is the wish of the common man in the West and the common man in the North that these bonds should be further strengthened to the mutual benefit of the two peoples.

Q: Could Your Excellency elaborate on these bonds?

H.K.: Yes, I was coming to that. Take the question of the mutual acceptance of each other's way of life by the two peoples. In the North here, you have a greater proportion of Yorubas than any other Nigerian tribe actually living among Northerners within the city walls. Before Sabon Garis grew up for what some people call stranger elements, the Yorubas lived with Hausas, Fulanis, etcetera, within the same city walls. The leaders of the Yoruba communities in towns in the North have always been accorded recognition in the North as Sarkin Yorubawa. In the West the leaders of the Hausa communities in Yoruba towns have always been similarly recognised as Oba Hausa. In the economic field even before there were railways or motor roads, trade links had been developed between the West and the North. The advent of speedy means of transport and communications strengthened these trade links. . . . As the Governor of the West was telling me the day before yesterday, while we in the North sell large quantities of foodstuff to the West, the kolanuts purchased by the North from the West are on the order of £5,000,000 per annum. Take the question of culture and tradition. Our chieftaincy institutions are similar. Just as the Northerner holds his chief and emir in high esteem, so the Yorubaman holds his oba. In religion the West and the North are men following the Islamic and Christian faith. . . .

I will just mention one last and very important one. Here in the North we have a large number of Northerners who are Yorubas from Ilorin, and there is a large number of Northerners who regard the West as their only home. There are also Yorubas in Kabba; they form an inseparable link between the North and the West. In short, there are so many strong factors which unite the North and West that it would be a tragedy, not just for the two Regions, but for the entire nation, if the harmony between the two peoples is disturbed.

Q: I asked earlier on, Your Excellency, why should the discussions become so urgent?

H.K.: Yes, they became urgent following certain recent pronouncements that have made Yorubas resident in the North apprehensive, and also those Northerners in the West worried. A few weeks ago two Yorubas were alleged to have informed influential quarters in the West that there was tension in the North and that the Yorubas felt unsafe. This allegation was unfortunately made public, and of course it got people worried, especially as it was tied up with the statement involving major national issues at that time. As a matter of fact there was little to justify the allegation and the publicity it received. I immediately instructed action to be taken by chiefs, provincial secretaries, and divisional officers that all provincial headquarters, divisional headquarters, and district headquarters dispel the allegation and maintain the confidence that allegation could have eroded.

I am happy to say that the action taken by all was effective. It averted a serious situation. . . .

The second reason for my chief concern was the question of the withdrawal of troops of non-Western Nigeria origin from Ibadan and Abeokuta. An understanding had been reached by members of the Supreme Military Council that these troops would be withdrawn. This, as you know, is the reason for the present crash training programme to increase the Yoruba representation in the Nigerian Army. This was a military decision which, I believe, no one really wants to turn into a political issue.

The timing of the movement of the troops had to be agreed between all concerned, but suddenly, as you are probably aware, some newspapers reported pressure being exerted by civilian leaders in the West that these troops were to be removed. One of the reasons given was that the West would not feel on a par with the other Regions until the troops were removed. A great deal of suspicion was aroused here in the North by this demand and the persistence with which it was urged by civilians.

The fact that the demand had been first advocated largely by the East long before the civilians in the West took it up later aroused the suspicions of the people of the North. It was assumed that Southern solidarity against the North, which Ojukwu has been advocating, was being supported by the West. I did my best, of course, to disabuse the people on the subject and to educate them about the stand of the West.

When you add to all this the publicly-announced allegations that Yorubas in the North were unhappy, you can imagine the apprehension of the Northerner in the West as to what could happen to him if the troops were withdrawn. You can also imagine the apprehension of the Yorubaman in the North as to what would happen to him if the Northerners develop bitterness over utterances and demands made in the West. In a situation pregnant with possible grave misunderstanding of each other by both people, something had to be done and quickly too. . . .

Q: Why did you have to address the troops in Ibadan?

H.K.: You should realise that these men are human beings. The mere fact that they are in khaki does not mean that they have no feelings and no souls. Some of them have lived in the West for years. They have been under strain for almost 18 months now. They have been accused, often quite wrongly, of misbehaviour toward the civilian population. They have always been accused of acts they know nothing about. These men, I am told, voluntarily confined themselves to barracks. I have been very proud of the conduct of these men in this regard.

We must admit, of course, that in any Army you cannot but have a bad egg that could give the entire poultry a bad name. I decided to speak to the men in consultation with the Commander-in-Chief, therefore, to educate them as to the reason for their withdrawal. I wanted them to leave in the highest spirits without bitterness. I told them that I wanted their withdrawal to be accomplished without the slightest hitch.

Between the period of my visit to them and their departure, I instructed them to behave in exemplary way. I told them not to allow anyone to provoke them by irresponsible talk. There are always those who want to give a dog a bad name and hang him. These men are first-class soldiers and have their pride. The West Governor, as you know, paid them glowing tribute several weeks ago for their loyalty and excellent service during the many years they have been stationed in Ibadan and Abeokuta.

Q: How did the men receive Your Excellency's address?

H.K.: In a most gratifying way. It went on very well. You may or you may not know, of course, that my address to them was on the special instruction of the Commander-in-Chief. The Adviser to the West Military Governor was with me, and also Chief of Army Staff Lt.-Col. Akahan, and also the Commandant of the Battalion, Maj. Sotomi, together with officers from my office.

Q: How soon are these movements going to take place?

H.K.: Soon enough for the major part to be completed by 31st May. By the first few days of June it should have been completed.

Q: Where are the troops being deployed?

H.K.: This has been answered in the release issued by the Commander-in-Chief. They will move from Ibadan and Abeokuta, some to Lagos to strengthen the troops in Apapa and Ikeja, and some to Ilorin and Jebba to strengthen the garrisons in those places. . . .

[1] *Radio interview in Kaduna, 26 May 1967. Verbatim text from* New Nigerian, *27 May 1967.*

110.
Ojukwu's Address to the Eastern Consultative Assembly, 26 May 1967[1]

Highly respected Chiefs and Elders, Loyal Patriots of Eastern Nigeria, Distinguished Fellow Countrymen,

Once again it is my privilege to welcome you to this Assembly. I do this with all humility and a sense of duty. Although we have not met in this body for sometime, I have continuously and daily met people from all walks of life, visited various places and discussed with the people.

In tackling the day-to-day problems which have confronted us, my task has been made much lighter than it would otherwise have been by your absolute support and understanding in all we have tried to do. On all the occasions I have had the privilege of addressing you, either personally as I am now doing, or through other media of communication, I have made it clear that my paramount aim as the Military Governor of this Region has always been to preserve the integrity of this Region, to provide adequate security for its citizens, to assure peace and progress amongst us and to prevent any recurrence of ill-treatment and atrocity against this Region and its people; and also, in consultation with my military colleagues, to establish a framework within which all the component units of this country could work together in the future on a basis of absolute equality. These have been the joint objectives of everyone of us and our paths towards them have always been made very clear and unmistakable.

Your meeting today is very crucial. The East is at the cross-roads. Since our last meeting everything possible has been done by enemies of the East to escalate the crisis in an attempt to bring about the collapse of this Region. They have failed and will continue to fail. Nevertheless, I find it necessary to put all the facts before you, indicating the issues, the difficulties and the dangers, so that you can examine them fully and advise me on the path we are to follow from now on. As usual, I call upon you to be free, frank and objective.

For a better understanding and a proper appreciation of the problems facing the country today, and in particular of the attitude of Eastern Nigeria to them, we need to go back to the historic statements on Nigerian unity made by leaders of Northern Nigeria.

We all know that before the amalgamation in 1914 of Southern and Northern Nigeria, the North was administered as an entity quite distinct from the South. The amalgamation was, however, not intended to, and did not in fact, result in a fusion of either the peoples of both areas or of their institutions. When, for example, a Legislative Council was established in 1922, it could not, and did not, legislate for the North; rather the Governor-General in Lagos legislated for the North by means of Proclamations. This was so because the amalgamation was forced on Northerners who made no secret of their dislike for it. The late Sir Ahmadu Bello, in his book, *My Life*, at page 135, said:

> The Colonial master who ruled Nigeria introduced a system of unitary government not for the present or future unity or wellbeing of all the indigenes of the country but for his own administrative convenience. Lord Lugard and his amalgamation were far from popular amongst us at that time.

In 1953, the late Sir Abubakar Tafawa Balewa in a speech in the Legislative Council, said:

> Since the amalgamation of the Southern and Northern Provinces in 1914, Nigeria has existed as one country only on paper. It is still far from being united. The country is inhabited by peoples and tribes who speak different languages, who have different religions, different customs, and traditions and entirely different historical backgrounds in their way of life, and who have also attained different stages of development. . . . We do not want our southern neighbours to interfere in our development. . . . But I should like to make it clear to you that if the British quitted Nigeria now at this stage the Northern people would continue their interrupted conquest to the sea.

'Interrupted conquest'! That has always been the Northern intention Thank God that the East has now awakened to its responsibilities, and with that awakening, that ambitious dream will never be fulfilled in this country.

The Self-Government motion in the Central Legislature in March, 1953, evoked the following reply from late Sir Ahmadu Bello:

It is true that we politicians delight in talking loosely about unity of Nigeria. . . . What is now called Nigeria consisted of large and small communities all of which were different in their outlooks and beliefs. The advent of the British and of Western education has not materially altered the situation and these many and varied communities have not knit themselves into composite unit. . . . In 1914, the North and South were amalgamated though the administration of the two sections are distinctly different. Since then, no serious attempt has been made by the British or by the people themselves to come together and each section has looked upon the other with suspicion and misgiving.

In supporting him, Isa Kaita said. 'The mistake of 1914 has come to light and I should like to go no further.' During this period, secession was the talk of every Northern leader, and Sir Ahmadu again said during one of the Legislative Council Debates:

. . . There were agitations in favour of secession; we should set up on our own; we should cease to have anything more to do with the Southern people; we should take our own way.

. . . I must say it looked very tempting. We were certainly 'viable', to use the current phrase; we could run our own show; the Centre would have to hand over to us our share of Nigeria's accumulated sterling assets. We had the men and production and minerals and the will to act.

The Northern House of Assembly debated the issue of self-government for Nigeria later that year, and in the course of this, her leaders adopted the now famous 8-point proposal, the purport of which is that the political arrangement best suited to Nigeria was complete regional autonomy with common services maintained by a central agency which would have neither legislative nor executive powers.

This attitude of the North delayed Nigerian Independence for two years. History will record that leaders from Southern Nigeria, and from Eastern Nigeria in particular, preached and worked for twenty years to achieve the unity of this country. History will also bear witness to the fact that the North had for so long resisted the idea of unity, and had, on four occasions in the recent past, expressed this resentment through brutal killings.

In 1964 when the most farcical election in Nigeria took place, a Northerner, Mallam Bala Garuba, published the following statement in the December 30 issue of the *West African Pilot*:

The conquest to the sea is now in sight. When our godsent Ahmadu Bello said some years ago that our conquest will reach the sea shores of Nigeria, some idiots in the South were doubting its possibilities.

Today have we not reached the sea? Lagos is reached. It remains Port Harcourt. It must be conquered and taken after December 30, 1964.

I remember when the N.C.N.C. and the A.G. were boasting about their daydreams of snatching power from us. Today, their great brains are in our bag. Imagine such personalities as Akintola, Benson, Davies, Akinjide, Olowofoyeku. . . .

I still hope that it will not be long when Okpara, Adegbenro and Aminu Kano will come to beg. Osadebay and other Mid-West leaders are half way to us. As for Awo, he will spend the last day of his term of imprisonment there for his inordinate ambition. Some Southern fools must understand that to suggest secession after their defeat is suicide for them. Let them think about all these things and understand the implications in secession.

(a) Where is the Nigerian Military Academy? (b) Where is the Nigerian Air Force base built? All these are up here in our region.

After the election, we will call upon our leaders to make a Northerner the leader of the Nigerian Army. Those who propose Ironsi are day-dreaming.

After the next five years those southern so-called educated fools must realize where they are. Once we will be able to connect the Bornu Railway with those of our brothers in the neighbouring country and from there to Egypt, we can allow secession to take place.

Our exports could be sent out through that way. Thanks to Allah that the Kainji Dam will soon be completed. It is up to Tarka to come back now or face what will follow when we achieve our aim.

We must do anything possible to win the coming jihad. But we must keep our weather eyes open on those from the West as they could do anything at any time. Immediately we win, we can lose some members from the West at any time. We must not take things for granted.

With our 167 seats in the North we can go it alone. There is no need sharing the post of Prime Ministership and Presidentship with anyone. I have a genuine fear that we keep the posts and then concede some important ministries to some Yoruba members.

The time has come. We are going to show these intellectual fools that we are only in the morning of our leadership of this country.

We try N.N.D.P. in the next five years and see whether they will be too forward and ambitious as the ungrateful N.C.N.C. and A.G. If some still doubt that we haven't conquered our way to the sea, let them go through these facts.

(a) Who is the Prime Minister of the country?

(b) Who is the Minister of Lagos Affairs? Is Lagos not our capital?

Our only obstacle are the Ibos. They have played their card. They will sink.

This statement summarises the stand of the North in relation to the rest of the country. In August, 1966, just after the murder of Major-General Aguiyi-Ironsi Gowon stated publicly that there was no basis for Nigerian unity.

I have quoted those and other statements in order to remind us of the consistency of the North in their feeling of separateness except where they are in relation to other peoples of Nigeria as Master is to servant.

In May 1966, the ill-fated Decree No. 34 was promulgated after it had been discussed and approved by General Aguiyi-Ironsi's Supreme Military Council which was composed as follows:

North (Two members)	Lt.-Col. Hassan.
	Lt.-Col. Gowon.
East (Two members)	Lt.-Col. C. Odumegwu Ojukwu.
	Lt.-Col. G. T. Kurubo.
West and Lagos (Three members)	Lt.-Col. F. A. Fajuyi.
	Commodore J. Wey.
	Brigadier B. O. Ogundipe.
Mid-West (One member)	Lt.-Col. D. Ejoor.

At the same time, his Federal Executive Council consisted of:

North (Three members)	Lt.-Col. Hassan.
	Lt.-Col. Gowon.
	Alhaji Kam Selem—Deputy Inspector-General of Police.
East (Three members)	Lt.-Col. C. Odumegwu Ojukwu.
	Mr. L. E. Edet, Inspector-General of Police.
	Lt.-Col. G. T. Kurubo.
West and Lagos (Three members)	Lt.-Col. F. A. Fajuyi.
	Commodore J. Wey.
	Major M. Johnson.
Mid-West (One member)	Lt.-Col. D. Ejoor.

The Heads of the Federal Civil Service were distributed as follows: North 8, East 3, West and Lagos 5, Mid-West 7. The Heads of Federal Corporations and Institutions then were distributed thus: North 6, East 3, West 12, Mid-West 1.

I have given you these facts because after the promulgation of Decree No. 34, evil-minded persons in the North and elsewhere propagated the mischievous lie that Easterners were dominating the affairs of the country. At no time since independence did Easterners dominate the politics of the Federation.[2]

The reaction of the North to Decree No. 34 was to massacre Easterners in the North and to loot their property in May 1966.

Thereafter, the Supreme Military Council decided that a tribunal should be set up to enquire into the causes of that disturbance. Northern Emirs rejected it and demanded the secession of the North from the Federation. Nonetheless, the tribunal was scheduled to begin its sittings on August 2, 1966. On July 29, and for several days thereafter, Northern soldiers in conspiracy with Northern civilians unleashed against defenceless Easterners the bloodiest acts of brutality. Major-General Aguiyi-Ironsi was murdered. His host, Lt.-Col. Fajuyi, was also murdered. Dead they are but their memories will live from age to age as a shining example of heroism, courage and loyalty.

In the heat of these outrageous acts, Gowon, a fairly junior Colonel in the Army, and himself one of the rebels, hoisted himself on the seat of the Supreme Commander; his first act was to demand secession for the North as a condition for stopping the massacre. I was left with no other alternative than to agree. However, on the advice of certain foreign nationals, he abandoned the idea, telling his people of the North that Allah had once more put the Government of Nigeria into the hands of 'another Northerner'.

On August 8 and 9, 1966, representatives of all the Military Governors met in Lagos and recommended, among other measures, that:

a. Troops should be sent back to barracks in their region of origin.

b. All decrees which centralized affairs in Lagos should be abrogated.

c. Lagos should be garrisoned in a manner to be determined by the Military Governors.

d. A Constitutional Conference should be constituted to work out a constitution for Nigeria.

These recommendations were ignored by Gowon, and to this day Northern

2 F

troops have been stationed in Lagos and Western Nigeria. The proposed Constitutional Conference began its sitting on September 12, 1966. Gowon charged it to discover a form of association suitable for Nigeria no matter the name by which it may be called.

Memoranda were exchanged by the Delegates, and vital features of some of them are as follows:

NORTH

... In all, we have had two attempts at a Unitary system of Government. The first attempt proved unsatisfactory, and the second proved a disaster. We have also had two attempts at the Federal system. The two attempts ended in chaos, and we are again presented with an opportunity to look dispassionately at our future association.

In putting forward its suggestions, the Northern delegation has taken into account the mood of the people and the mood of the army which must be a matter for serious consideration if we are not to deceive ourselves. The delegation has also taken into account the very wise recommendations made recently by a meeting of the representatives of the Regional Governors that army personnel should be posted to barracks in their Regions of origin. It has also taken into account the areas of lasting mutual trust, in whatever pockets they may exist, which have so far not been completely destroyed by recent events. It has also taken into account the need to preserve the economy of the component parts of the country and avoid as far as possible its disruption.

The Northern delegation advocates a system of government which differs from anything that has been attempted in Nigeria in the past. As each Region has managed to preserve some measure of order and sense of unity within its confines, each region should be constituted into an autonomous state.

Subjects or groups of subjects which are of common interest to the component states should be delegated to a Common Services Commission to operate.

The North then proposed:

1. The new Nigeria shall comprise a number of autonomous States.
2. The autonomous States of Nigeria, that is to say, Northern Nigeria, Eastern Nigeria, Western Nigeria, Mid-Western Nigeria or by whatever name they may choose to be called later and such other States as may be formed subsequently should agree to enter into a Union which shall have a Central Executive Council, representation to which shall be on equal representation from all the States comprising the Association. The powers of the Central Executive Council shall be delegated by the component States except that powers connected with external or foreign affairs, immigration, can be unilaterally withdrawn by the State Government while all other functions or powers delegated to the Central Executive Council can only be withdrawn by the State Governments after a unanimous decision by their representatives in the Central Executive Council. The Chairmanship of the Council shall rotate. Each Chairman shall hold office for one year.
3. Any member State of the Union should reserve the right to secede completely and unilaterally from the Union and to make arrangements for co-operation with the other members of the Union in such a manner as they may severally or individually deem fit.
4. Each State must have its own Army, Air Force, Police, Civil Service and Judiciary. There shall be a Navy composed of personnel in proportion to the population of each State.

The Northern memorandum then went on to propose a detailed form of Common Services Organization within the existing Regions as sovereign states. The terms of this memorandum are in consonance with the eight-point proposal adopted by the North on the 23rd of May 1953.

WESTERN NIGERIA AND LAGOS

The alternative proposal of the Delegates of Western Nigeria and Lagos is as follows:

In the event of the other Regions feeling unable to accept the foregoing proposals for the establishment of true Federalism in Nigeria, then it is proposed that what is now the Federation of Nigeria should become the Commonwealth of Nigeria comprising the existing Regions and such other Regions as may be subsequently created, with Lagos forming part of the present Western Nigeria.

The Government of each State within the Commonwealth shall be completely sovereign in all matters excepting those with respect to which responsibility is delegated to the Council of States.

You can see that the position of the West then was very similar to the Northern proposal which suggested the loosest type of association for Nigeria. In the words of the late Sir Ahmadu Bello, this association would be:

A looser structure for Nigeria while preserving its general pattern—a structure which would give the Regions the greatest possible freedom of movement and action: a structure which would reduce the powers of the Centre to the absolute minimum.

The Gowon junta now preaches unity not because it believes in unity but because the dominating position of the North is threatened.

The Ad Hoc Constitutional Conference sat for about three weeks, and when it looked as if it was going to achieve a form of association unsuitable to Northerners, the pogrom of September and October was unleashed. The story of this pogrom is now being recorded by the Atrocities Commission in the interest of posterity.

The events of that period have made fundamental changes in the structure and pattern of Nigeria society and government. Some two million Eastern Nigerians have returned to the East. All the Northerners in the East have gone home. Relationship between peoples of the two Region have come to an end, and if ever revived, will be on an entirely different basis.

I refused to recognize Gowon for reasons which I gave at Aburi. To recognize him would mean to accept the authority of a rebel in the Army, and that would be bad for discipline. The stalemate which followed culminated in the Aburi Meeting.

The main decisions reached at Aburi were: [DOC 86 followed here].

It is to be noted that the meeting of the 4th and 5th of January at Aburi was held largely on my own initiative. Although I had strong forebodings about the outcome of the meeting, I went to it with a genuine desire to make it succeed. I decided that as soon as I set foot on the Ghana soil, I should be nothing but a Nigerian. It was my aim that the Military Leaders must come to an arrangement whereby the right climate could be created for all of us to carry out the duties and responsibilities to which we had dedicated ourselves.

I wanted an atmosphere created for a return of normalcy, peace and confidence in the country, an atmosphere in which all sources of fear and suspicion would be removed.

My genuine desire for all these was borne out by the fact that, before the start of the meeting, I pressed for a resolution eschewing the use of force in the settlement of our problems. I did so because of the widespread fear and suspicion in other parts of the country that the East was planning an attack. Nobody with knowledge or discernment could doubt our ability, even at that time, to take effective actions of revenge against the North, or even Lagos, if we had wanted. But our aim was and has remained that we should avoid further bloodshed, even though it has been the innocent blood of Easterners that has been most wantonly shed. Subsequent events seem to indicate that our opponents mistook my action in pressing for that resolution on the use of force as a sign of weakness.

On the question of political and administrative control of the country as a whole, executive and legislative powers were vested in the Supreme Military Council. In other words, all what used to be the legislative powers of the Nigerian Parliament, and what used to be the executive and policy-making powers of the Council of Ministers, under the civilian regime, were vested in the Supreme Military Council as a collective organ. To make sure that the Regions had effective voice in all decisions affecting the whole country, all such decisions must receive the concurrence of all Military Governors; and where any Military Governor was unable to attend a meeting of the Supreme Military Council, any decision reached in his absence must be referred to him for comments and concurrence.

This principle of concurrence by Military Governors was prompted by an appreciation of the special responsibilities which each Military Governor had over his area of authority. Having regard to the general welfare of the people under his charge, he should be in a position to delay any decision affecting the country as a whole until a consensus was reached.

As far as the Regions were concerned, it was decided that all the powers vested by the Nigerian Constitution in the Regions and which they exercised prior to 15th January, 1966, should be restored to the Regions. To this end, the Supreme Military Council decided that all decrees passed since the Military take-over, and which tended to detract from the previous powers of the Regions, should be repealed by 21st of January, after the Law Officers should have met on the 14th January to list out all such decrees.

None of these agreements has been carried out. The meeting of Military Officers was abandoned because Gowon withdrew the Federal representatives. The Law Officers met on the 14th of January as agreed and listed out the relevant decrees which had detracted from the previous powers and positions of the Regions, to enable the Supreme Military Council to promulgate the necessary decree by the 21st of January as decided at Aburi. The officers of the Ministry of Finance never met within the time stipulated at Aburi because the Permanent Secretary of the Federal Ministry of Finance did not consider that such a meeting would serve any useful purpose.

I have said that what the decisions at Aburi amounted to in terms of political and military control of the country was that the country should be governed as a Confederation. As soon as we came back from Aburi, I considered it my duty to explain to the Eastern Nigeria public, through the press, the decisions taken at Aburi, and as far as my sense of responsibility allowed me, the implications.[3] In Lagos, the Permanent Secretaries there studied the recommendations and, to their credit, brought out clearly and unmistakenly their meanings and implications. Having seen these, however, they unfortunately went beyond their rights and duty as civil servants to advise against the implementation of the Aburi agreements.[4] From here our difficulties started and have taken us to our present stalemate.

This leads me to the publication by Lagos of the controversial Decree No. 8. That is the Decree by which Gowon and his group claim to have implemented the Aburi agreements. I have mentioned that aspect of the Aburi decisions which stipulated that a Decree restoring the Regions to their position before the military take-over should be passed by 21st of January, 1967. The Law Officers met, as required, on the 14th of January but no signs of action appeared forthcoming from Lagos after that meeting. On or about the 19th of January, I despatched a telegram calling for the necessary draft decree to be circulated for concurrence.

Gowon's reply was the negative one of giving untenable reasons for his failure to carry out that aspect of the Aburi decisions. He, however, assured me that the decree was being drafted and asked for an urgent meeting of the Supreme Military Council. I promptly replied to his telegram as follows:

Glad learn Decree being drafted to repeal all decrees or aspects of decrees which detracted from position and powers of regional governments as they existed before January 15th 1966. Imperative that repealing decree be published immediately in order to confirm confidence and clear way of meeting Supreme Military Council. I agree that matters affecting constitution for which there were questions or reservations should be referred to Supreme Military Council which should follow soon after publication of decree repealing over-centralizing decrees or aspects of decrees. Surprised that my press statement embarrassed anyone. I know people with vested interests have tried through representations to you and others to capitalize viciously on that press conference. Honest acquaintance with and appreciation of feelings in East would show that it was in the interest of all that the conference was given. Silence would be misinterpreted here and difficulties created for smooth return to normalcy and of confidence. Every word spoken at Press Conference completely in accord with transcript of Aburi meeting.

You will see in that telegram my willingness to attend the Meeting of the Supreme Military Council provided the repealing Decree acceptable to all was published without delay. Such an action on the part of Gowon would have proved his sincerity to keep faith and honour agreements in the interest of public confidence. I should add here that the West Military Governor took the same stand with us on the need for an immediate publication of the repealing Decree.

Eventually a draft decree came forward from Lagos; but it was a document which was a complete departure from, indeed the very opposite of, what was intended at Aburi. It was even at variance with the agreements reached by the Solicitors-General at their Benin meeting of the 14th of January. Both the West and ourselves rejected the draft outright. Then followed a period of public controversy, confusion and uncertainty, until it was agreed that officials of the different Governments, led by their respective Secretaries to the

Military Governments, should meet at Benin to advise on how best the Aburi agreements should be implemented.

The officials of the five Governments of the Federation held meetings on the 17th and 18th of February and at the end made recommendations which have since been published and which I believe you all have seen. Another draft decree was prepared by Lagos. Although it must be admitted that this draft (which, incidentally, was, I am told, the 5th attempt!) was an improvement on the first one, yet it contained extraneous features which, at best, went contrary to the agreements of the officials and, at worst, were directed against the East. We promptly raised our objections to those features, but without any further comments from the Federal Government a meeting of the Supreme Military Council was arranged to be held in Benin on the 10th of March.

They expected me to attend that meeting even though they knew perfectly well that I could not do so for three obvious reasons. First, Northern troops were still present in the West and Lagos, and, secondly, all the confidence and marks of good faith generated at Aburi had been systematically undermined by Lagos. Thirdly, the passing of the right decree had been my precondition for attending such a meeting. However, they met on the 10th of March and, that very day, approved their Decree No. 8.

As if to underline their action of perfidy and double-dealing, a message was sent through, even after they had taken a final decision on the Decree, for Law Officers of the Regions to meet in Lagos to finalize a draft Decree. As a mark of my genuine desire for a peaceful settlement and return to normalcy, I sent my Law Officers to the meeting in Benin, where they were simply told that as the Decree had been passed by the Supreme Military Council, there was really nothing for them to do! All the same, our men reduced into writing and handed to their colleagues, this Region's objections. A few days later, on Friday the 19th of March, the Decree was formally published.

The Decree gave Gowon a veto power over the concurrence of all the Military Governors in matters affecting the exercise of legislative and executive powers of the Federation; it gave the Supreme Military Council power to declare a state of emergency in a Region against the wishes of the Governor. It is important that you should know that two days after the promulgation of the Decree, Gowon requested the other members of the Supreme Military Council to approve his proposal for a declaration of a state of emergency in the East. But for the wisdom of some members of the Council who refused to be so used, the story of the past two months would have been different.

For the foregoing reasons, I found Decree No. 8 unacceptable and rejected it. It was a Northern instrument for political power over the South. An important fact to bear in mind is that at Aburi it was agreed that all the members of the Supreme Military Council should meet to appoint the Commander-in-Chief and Head of the Federal Military Government. Up till now that decision has not been implemented.

I think I should here tell you my personal efforts since July to ensure a quick, realistic and peaceful settlement of our problems. Soon after the July 29th rebellion and the usurpation of office by Gowon, I told him that even though I was not prepared to accept him either as the Supreme Commander or the Head of the Federal Government, I would be prepared to co-operate with him in the task of keeping the country together, stopping further bloodshed and ensuring a quick return to normalcy.

It was for that reason that I sent representatives of this Region to Lagos on the 8th of August although I knew perfectly well the type of risks to which they were at that time exposed. It was for that reason that I did everything to make it possible for the meeting of the Ad Hoc Constitutional Conference to be held in Lagos with our representatives attending. All along Gowon and I were keeping in daily contact with each other on the telephone. Even after the pogrom which started on the 29th of September and which has, more than anything else, changed our previous conception of Nigeria as one country, I continued the daily dialogue with Gowon.

There was a meeting of Secretaries to the Military Governments immediately followed by that of Advisers to the Military Governors. The outcome of these efforts was the famous Aburi meeting of the 4th and 5th of January.

Although the attitude of Lagos to the Aburi agreements was nothing but a catalogue of bad faith, I still felt that all chances of a peaceful settlement, which would lead to the maintenance of this country as a unit, had not all been lost. Meanwhile the Federal Government was owing us heavy amounts of money due to us as our right under the Constitution. I pressed that this debt should be paid promptly in view of our pressing needs for funds to meet our refugee problems. Nothing was done; the drift continued; the stalemate persisted, and the clouds thickened.

On the 16th of February, I sent a lengthy letter to Gowon with copies to Commodore Wey and other Military leaders. Because of its interest a copy of that letter has been printed as an appendix to this speech for you to see.[5] I shall, therefore, not recount the details of that letter, but in it I brought out as forcefully as possible the dangers inherent in the continued stalemate. I pointed out to Gowon that, in spite of all his public protestations to that effect, he was not serious about saving the country. I repeated this Region's absolute stand on the Aburi decisions. I then gave him a catalogue of his acts of bad faith and perfidy following the Aburi meeting. Finally I gave the warning that if by the 31st of March the Aburi agreements were not implemented, I would have no alternative but to feel free to take whatever measure was possible to implement the decisions unilaterally. I ended my letter with these words:

I say this with the deepest sense of regret and fully conscious of the consequences of such unilateral action. But, I shall be able to tell the world when the time comes what part I have played at different stages and in different circumstances since the emergency which started in May last year, to avoid the situation. The responsibility will not be mine.

I still hope that good sense will prevail and that God will save us from such a bleak future. Let us at once implement the Aburi agreements, and preserve the country as one.

There was no reaction from Gowon to that letter. We continued to drift. On the 10th of March, a meeting of the Supreme Military Council was held in Benin, and on Friday the 19th of March, the so-called Decree No. 8 was promulgated. The financial year was coming to an end, as was fast approaching my dateline of 31st March.

My aim was still to avoid a point of no return. Thus, on Easter Sunday, the 26th of March, I paid a visit to Ghana for discussions with General Ankrah and his colleagues on the National Liberation Council. I explained to them the position of this Region and the dangerous consequences of Gowon's continued indifference. I undertook not to take unilateral action provided Lagos paid its debt to us before the 31st of March. General Ankrah and his colleagues for their part undertook to bring together in Ghana all the officials of the Nigerian Governments to discuss the settlement of Federal debts to this Region.

On Monday the 27th, I held a meeting at Onitsha with Colonel Adebayo, Military Governor of Western Nigeria, accompanied by Commodore Wey, Head of the Navy, and Mr. Omo-Bare, Deputy Inspector-General of Police. We held a lengthy, detailed and frank talk, in which I made the position of the East absolutely clear. The meeting ended on a high note of optimism. The delegation undertook to get Gowon to do two things: first, to make sure that the debt owed to the East was paid by 31st March; secondly, either to suspend Decree No. 8 or to repeal those sections which were obnoxious to the East. They also suggested that the North should express public apology to the East for their atrocities.

I should also have mentioned that I had previously paid a visit to my colleague and friend, Lt.-Col. David Ejoor with whom I held intimate discussions. I had made quite clear to him the course open to the East unless there was a change of attitude in Lagos.

True to their word, the Ghanaian authorities were able to bring together in Ghana representatives of the Governments of the Federation, comprising economists, financial experts and legal experts, for a meeting which was held on Wednesday the 29th of March. The painful result of that meeting was the knowledge that the Federal Government had no intention of paying to this Region debts owed to it.

Here, I must place on record my unqualified gratitude and tribute to General Ankrah and his colleagues for the untiring efforts in trying to help this country solve its problems. The sincerity in all their approaches has always been transparent. Apart from telephone contacts and letter correspondence, the Ghanaian Government has sent representatives to Nigeria on several occasions to hold personal discussions, all aimed at helping us resolve our difficulties. Even if it turns out that Nigeria cannot remain as one, the efforts of Ghana in trying to avoid that situation will never be forgotten. If in the end some other solution is achieved, Nigeria will have yet greater reason to be grateful to the Government and people of that sister country of Africa.

Eventually, the date-line of 31st March arrived, and I considered it my duty to take appropriate actions, effected through Edicts. Not surprisingly, the Federal Government and its associates immediately read everything vicious into my action. I think I should here explain again the reasons behind the various edicts passed since the 31st of March:

REVENUE COLLECTION EDICT
The purpose of this edict was to make sure that the Federal Government is no longer in a position to owe this Region its statutory revenues. It is

legitimate that we take what belongs to us; it did not attempt to change the formula for revenue allocation as provided in the Nigerian Constitution, nor to take away what rightly belonged to the Federal Government. The truth of this statement is borne out in our estimates for this year where the revenues expected from Federal sources have been shown strictly on the existing formula.

LEGAL EDUCATION EDICT

Following the disturbances of 1966, our students in the Lagos Law School were compelled to return to this Region. As a result of the stalemate, it became clear that they would never return to Lagos for their studies. We asked Lagos to open a law school at our expense but they refused even though under the Act it was possible. These students had a right to continue with their legal studies and also to practise their chosen profession. This Government would have failed in its duty to them if it did not take appropriate action to safeguard their interests. Our action was guided by the same principle that led us to establish a Medical School and a Teaching Hospital.

STATUTORY BODIES COUNCIL EDICT

As part of its acts of retaliation and repression the Federal Government stopped the payment of salaries and wages to the employees of the various Federal statutory bodies operating in this Region, stopped the supply of necessary equipment, material and spare parts for them, and suspended the services of some of them, while making every effort to stifle others. The aim of the edict was to enable this Region take over the control and administration of these bodies to ensure co-ordination and efficient management. I do not need to mention that the Federal Government had failed to honour the Aburi agreement to pay employees of Governments and Statutory Corporations up to the 31st of March. The result is that this Government had to take over responsibility for the payment not only of the salaries and wages of refugees, but even of other employees of those Corporations operating in this Region. As at the end of April, this Government had spent £600,000 on this account.

COURT OF APPEAL EDICT

This edict was enacted to ensure that our people have opportunities of prompt justice and redress. The Federal Supreme Court last held sessions in the East in February, 1965. As a result of the events which started in July 1966, our people, as lawyers or clients, could not pursue their appeals in Lagos. As the Federal Chief Justice was unwilling to arrange sittings of the Court in the East, the representative of Eastern Nigeria on the Supreme Court has since returned to the East, and the Bar Association of Eastern Nigeria has taken a resolute stand against its members going to Lagos for cases, we saw no alternative than to enact an edict establishing our own final Court of Appeal.

REGISTRATION OF COMPANIES EDICT

This edict requires companies to be registered in Eastern Nigeria; it does not deal with incorporation. It will enable us to collect and collate statistics of businesses operating in this Region for the purposes of planning.

No sooner had the Revenue Edict been passed than Lagos stopped all flights of Nigeria Airways, of which this Region is a joint-owner, to the East. Business and official travel has been disrupted and movement of mails has been disturbed. Talking of mails, I can illustrate the situation by mentioning that a letter signed in the Cabinet Office in Lagos on the 28th of April and addressed to my office was not received until the 19th of May.

In addition to this Lagos ordered that Federal employees serving in this Region, whether in Government or Corporations, should not be paid their salaries and abandoned all financial responsibility for Federal projects established in this Region.

As if all these were not enough, Gowon convened a meeting of his Military colleagues and presented to them a memorandum seeking authority for diplomatic, military and further economic sanctions against the East. You know the details of that iniquitous memorandum, which I promptly published as soon as it came into my hands.

You have heard about the withdrawal of diplomatic passports from citizens of this Region, the stoppage of postal order transactions between this Region and the rest of the country. There is, of course, the blockage of foreign exchange not only against this Government as such, but also against Statutory Corporations and institutions and even private industrial concerns in which this Government has a financial interest.

Importers from this Region have been denied import licences, and our industries the right to import essential raw materials for their operations. Further, Lagos has sent emissaries abroad to interfere with this Region's sale of its produce. Lagos has done everything within its power to strangle this Region economically.

I think that here I must mention the radio announcement by Gowon that his sanctions against the East have been lifted with effect from Tuesday the 23rd of this month. The unfortunate thing is that Gowon should tag on to his announcement the suggestion that the East should reciprocate by repealing the different Edicts which I have already mentioned and even the release of Railway rolling stock. If Gowon's action is to be taken as a sign of a change of heart, belated though it may be, let him go further and support it by paying to the East all moneys owed by Lagos, pay all Federal Corporation staff, reconstitute the Federal Supreme Court in a manner acceptable to all. No, we have had and known enough of Lagos not to be so foolish as to take Gowon's words on their face value. There must be concrete proof of genuine intentions and good faith.

Let me give you the background to Gowon's announcement about the lifting of his sanctions against this Region. I had repeatedly stated categorically that neither I nor my representatives would attend any further meeting to discuss the problems of Nigeria while the economic strangulation continued. I said it to the last delegation from Ghana; I said so to Mr. Justice Arthur Prest who came here as a representative of a body called the Nigerian Peace Committee; I said so to Chief Awolowo and others who came as the representatives of the so-called National Conciliation Committee.

Indeed I should say a little more on the visit of Chief Awolowo and his group. They had come, in the name of the so-called National Conciliation Committee, to plead with us to send delegates to attend a meeting of that

Committee. We could not understand the basis on which the Committee was constituted; it contained two self-exiled Eastern Nigerians resident in Lagos, in whom we have no confidence. The Committee has, however, invited two prominent men in this Region to serve as members, Sir Francis Ibiam, my Adviser, and Sir Louis Mbanefo, my respected Chief Justice. I informed the delegation that, as my Adviser, Sir Francis could not be expected to serve on a Committee to mediate between me and other military leaders; I told them that in this Region we regard the Judiciary as sacrosanct and would not want it involved in political matters of this nature.

However, we offered concrete proposals which were reduced into writings as follows [DOC 106 followed here].

We have heard that the Committee subsequently met, and submitted recommendations to Gowon, who has accepted them. Gowon is, of course, always prepared to accept recommendations from any body or any organization provided the Eastern viewpoint is not represented.

Last week, Gowon sent me a telegram informing me that he had arranged with the British Government to supply two companies of British troops to neutralize Benin or nearby so that the Military leaders might meet and that as an alternative to the supply of troops the British Government had agreed to make available an aircraft carrier or frigate on which we could hold a meeting.[6] I, of course, promptly rejected the proposals in a telegram which read as follows:

1. Meeting of Military Leaders without proper preparation and agreed agenda cannot achieve good results;
2. Request for British troops without prior consultation with East makes whole business suspicious in the extreme;
3. British agreement not in consonance with their policy of non-intervention nor your declared policy of non-internationalization of crisis;
4. Presence of British troops in Benin will be regarded inimical to East. In view of British attitude in present crisis other alternative not acceptable. East will resist British or Northern incursion into Mid-West with force.

If, however, you are now prepared to approach matter with realism and sincerity meeting of Military Leaders should be preceded by meeting of Government representatives on an agenda mutually agreed. Representatives would be fully briefed by respective Military Leaders so that they can reach agreement for ratification by Military Leaders or place proposals for them to decide upon. In any case, the East will not, repeat not, attend any meeting whilst subject to economic strangulation. See my letter of 16th May.

Two days before, I had addressed what I regarded as a final letter to him, part of which read as follows:

The purpose of this letter is to tell you that in the face of all these unfriendly and destructive acts, deliberate and well calculated against this Region, we have no alternative but to make plans for a separate existence in the interest of self-preservation. Contrary to what you have chosen to believe, and have taken great pains to get the world to believe, it has always been my genuine desire to keep this country in existence. But for this desire I could have taken all the measures now taken or proposed to be taken, six months ago, and there would have been no power to stop us. I believed that this country should exist as one in a realistic form of association. Since this wish cannot be fulfilled the responsibility is yours and history will know where to lay the blame.

Before I go on, I should like here to stress that while Gowon is only too anxious to ask Britain for troops, his attitude towards the efforts of African Heads of State and the OAU to mediate has been one of stout and consistent rebuff bordering on contempt.

Having said that, there are certain facts which we must bear in mind. In the context of Nigeria, the history of this Region has been one of retarded progress because we are too prone to compromise and sacrifice in the interest of national unity.

The year 1966 has been for us a year of great lessons, opening our eyes to realities and dispelling our illusions. We came to this position months ago, but unfortunately we were alone. We had seen the need that if this country was to be saved, its component parts were to move apart. For this we were misunderstood and even abused. But because we believed our stand to be right we stuck to it.

One thing that has come out of the evils of 1966 is that they have clearly identified for us areas of conflict and friction as well as what powers can be used or abused by one authority to the detriment of others.

I am happy that at last our brothers in the South have come to realize the wisdom and sanity of what we have been advocating these last months.[7] A great deal has, however, happened that our people are now demanding sovereignty.

Another good sign of the recent weeks is the acknowledgement by the people of the South that the stand of the East against the North has not been a mere struggle for itself; but a struggle against all forms of injustice, and for the natural rights of every citizen to have and enjoy life and property in an atmosphere and under environments free from fear and molestation. It has been a struggle of progress against reaction. If then, by hitherto standing alone, we have been able to convince others that we have been championing their cause as well as ours, we have every reason to feel proud of our stand, without regret for whatever sacrifices we have so far sustained.

Those of you who have been following the utterances in the North and Lagos during the past months would have heard threats of force against this Region. May I take this opportunity to assure you all that there is no power in this country, or in Black Africa, to subdue us by force. I make this statement not to intimidate anyone but to reassure you all, as well as to warn those who might be misguided.

As I pointed out in my letter of 16th May to Gowon, he seems to believe that time is on his side and against us. We know that the Federal Government has been importing arms, and preparing troops for purposes best known to them. We shall not launch an attack on anybody. But should anybody want to use force against this Region, he will find us neither unprepared nor inadequate. I think a word to the wise should be sufficient.

No Easterner would want to pass through the events of the past ten months again. Only a loose association, call it confederation or what you may, can ensure this. But Gowon and the North have categorically rejected confederation. The position of the East, and indeed the West and Mid-West on the one hand, and that of the North on the other, are at once irreconcilable. It is for you as the representatives of the 14 million people of Eastern Nigeria to choose from (a) accepting the terms of the North and Gowon and thereby submit to domination by the North, or (*b*) continuing the present stalemate and drift, or (*c*) ensuring the survival of our people by asserting our autonomy. If we have no alternative to the third choice, we shall leave the door open for association with any of the other Regions of the country that accepts the principle of association of autonomous units.

In such a situation the present units of the country would emerge as sovereign units each capable of maintaining its integrity at home and abroad but at the same time co-operating in the operation of common services in such fields as transport and communications, particularly shipping, harbours and ports, railways and airways. This form of association would envisage the movement of goods and services across the borders without customs restrictions. Appropriate machinery could be devised for co-ordination in currency management and monetary policy.

While I cannot here go into the details of this arrangement, the association could provide for dual citizenship so that nationals of the associating units need not carry passports from one territory to another.

It is my belief that such arrangements are the only practicable, and realistic ones in the present circumstance and hold greater promise for the future than complete disintegration. Given good faith on all sides we cannot rule out the possibility of closer ties in the near future.

I consider it my duty to warn that if we are compelled to take that decision we must be prepared for a period of real sacrifice, hardship, and inconvenience. To start with, we may be without friends for a period. We may have to face the hostilities of the North acting in desperation. For a time there would be financial and economic difficulties. There will be the problems of external communications, of immigration, including passports.

All these would prove uncomfortable but only for a while. But we are bound to pull through it all. We have already made contingency plans to mitigate as much of those difficulties as possible. I shall not pursue the point, except to warn that time is running out. The people of this Region are totally tired of the present stalemate and state of uncertainty. We do not have much longer to wait. If Lagos and the North are now prepared that we settle the matter peacefully, they must act quickly.

We have a way of life and proud heritage to defend and preserve. We want to preserve our democratic and free institutions as a progressive society unhampered in its progress and development by feudalistic and reactionary forces with which it has been our misfortune to contend all these years.

As I said at the beginning of this address, I shall need your advice and guidance on the path we are to follow from now. If, as is now customary, the Lagos and Kaduna authorities continue to spurn our genuine proposals for a form of association of sovereign units, merely because they wish to dominate the entire country, through a strong central government, I would expect the people of this Region to resist to the last man their aggressive designs on this Region. I am encouraged by the massive demonstrations throughout the Region supporting the Government's stand in this crisis. There have also been persistent requests and appeals to me for a formal break with some parts of the country. I now look to this august assembly for clear guidance on what to do should all our peaceful and constructive overtures fail.

Before concluding, I should like to refer to a few matters which are of particular interest to everyone in this Region at this moment. It has come to my notice that a number of expatriates have been worried about their future and personal safety. I want to assure them that Eastern Nigeria is safe for all friends; we need their services and their assistance and friendship. We guarantee them the safety and security not only of their persons but also of their property and business. I regret that in the past week or so circumstances have arisen where the people of this Region have had to react unfavourably towards a long-established expatriate business in this Region. I personally regret the incident and do sincerely hope that the type of circumstances borne out of the present crisis will not occur again.

This speech has been fairly long, and I must bring it to an end. Quite a number of you here might be wondering what this Government has been doing to give effect to the new Provincial Administration system. I want to assure you that everything is being done in this direction. There has been a lot of administrative and technical details to be completed before the system can come into full operation. What could be done has been done, such as the posting of administrative officers to the new Divisions and Provinces. What remains to be done will be done as expeditiously as possible.

I also appreciate the inconvenience which the absence of Customary Courts has caused to every man and woman of this Region as well as to the Local Government authorities, which have been handicapped in the collection of rates and in the maintenance of law and order. Here again things have been moving as fast as practicable and I hope, within a short time, to announce the constitution and members of the different Customary Courts.

Finally, it remains for me to thank you all for coming to this meeting. I do not need to extol the value of your understanding and co-operation which you have all along extended to me in the present crisis. The struggle has been the people's struggle, not the struggle of one individual. With God on our side we shall emerge from the dark clouds now overshadowing us into a glorious and happy future.

[1] *Delivered at Enugu, 26 May 1967. Biafran Ministry of Information hand-out.*

[2] *For the contrary Federal Statistics, see* Diversity in Unity (*Lagos, 1967*), *pp. 4-9.*

[3] *See* DOC *83.*   [4] *See* DOC *82.*   [5] *See* DOC *89.*

[6] *See* DOC *107.*   [7] *See* DOC *104.*

111.
Gowon's Broadcast to the Nation, dividing Nigeria into Twelve States[1]

Dear countrymen:

As you are all aware Nigeria has been immersed in an extremely grave crisis for almost eighteen months. We have now reached a most critical phase where what is at stake is the very survival of Nigeria as one political and economic unit. We must rise to the challenge and what we do in the next few days will be decisive.

The whole world is witness to the continued defiance of Federal Authority by the Government of Eastern Region, the disruption of the Railway, the Coal Corporation, the normal operations of the Nigerian Ports Authority, the interference with the flight schedules of the Nigeria Airways and other illegal acts by the Eastern Region Government culminating in the edicts promulgated last month by that Government purporting to seize all Federal Statutory Corporations and Federal revenues collected in the East.

The consequence of these illegal sets has been the increasing deterioration of the Nigerian economy. It has also produced uncertainty and insecurity generally and pushed the country with increasing tempo towards total disintegration and possible civil war and bloodshed on massive scale.

It has also led to increasing loss of foreign confidence in the ability of Nigerians to resolve the present problems. This has been reflected in the stoppage of the inflow of much badly needed additional foreign investment, it has put a brake on economic development so essential to the well-being of the common man and the ordinary citizen whose only desire is for peace and stability to carry on his daily work.

In the face of all these, I have shown great restraint, hoping that through peaceful negotiations a solution acceptable to all sections of the country can be found. Unfortunately, the hopes of myself and my other colleagues on the Supreme Military Council have been disappointed by the ever increasing campaign of hate by the Governor of the Eastern Region. Lt.-Col. Ojukwu has continuously increased his demands as soon as some are met in order to perpetuate the crisis and lead the Eastern Region out of Nigeria. We know very well the tragic consequences of such a misguided step. Not only will the regions themselves disintegrate further, but before then, pushed by foreign powers and mercenaries who will interfere, this dear country will be turned into a bloody stage for chaotic and wasteful civil war.

When the tragic events of 15th January, 1966 occurred, the country acquiesced in the installation of a Military Regime only because it desired that order and discipline should be restored in the conduct of the affairs of this country, that swift reforms will be introduced to produce just and honest Government, to usher in stability and ensure fair treatment of all citizens in every part of the country. The citizens of this country have not given the Military Regime any mandate to divide up the country into sovereign states and to plunge them into bloody disaster.

As I have warned before, my duty is clear—faced with this final choice between action to save Nigeria and acquiescence in secession and disintegration. I am therefore proclaiming a State of Emergency throughout Nigeria with immediate effect. I have assumed full powers as Commander-in-Chief of the Armed Forces and Head of the Federal Military Government for the short period necessary to carry through the measures which are now urgently required.

In this period of emergency, no political statements in the Press, on the Radio and Television and all publicity media or any other political activity, will be tolerated. The Military and Police are empowered to deal summarily with any offenders. Newspaper editors are particularly urged to co-operate with the authorities to ensure the success of these measures.

I have referred earlier to some illegal acts of the Eastern Region Government. You all know that about one-third of the entire rolling stock of the Nigerian Railways, including 115 oil-tankers, have been detained and that the services on the Eastern District of the Nigerian Railways have been completely disrupted for many months. You are also aware of the fact that they have disrupted the direct movement of oil products from the refinery near Port Harcourt to the Northern Region. They have hindered the transit of goods to neighbouring countries and have even seized goods belonging to foreign countries. These acts have flagrantly violated normal international practice and disturbed friendly relations with our neighbours. That refinery is owned jointly by the Federal Government and Regional Governments. Illegally, since last year, the Authorities at Enugu have interfered with the flight routes of the Nigeria Airways. Only recently they committed the barbaric crime of hi-jacking a plane bound for Lagos from Benin. They have placed a ban on the residence of non-Easterners in the Eastern Region—an action which is against the Constitution and the fundamental provisions of our laws. They have continuously on the Press and radio incited the people of Eastern Region to hatred of other Nigerian peoples and they have indulged in the crudest abuse of members of the Supreme Military Council, especially myself.

Despite all these, I have spared no effort to conciliate the East in recognition of their understandable grievances and fears since the tragic incidents of 1966. To this end I agreed with my other colleagues on the Supreme Military Council to the promulgation of Decree No. 8 which completely decentralized the Government of this country and even went further than the Republican Constitution as it existed before 15th January, 1966. But what has been the response of the Eastern Region Government? Complete rejection of Decree No. 8 and insistence on its separate existence as a sovereign unit.

Only recently, a group of distinguished citizens formed themselves into the National Conciliation Committee. They submitted recommendations aimed at reducing tension. These included the reciprocal abrogation of economic measures taken by the Federal Military Government and the seizure of Federal Statutory Corporations and Federal revenue by the Eastern Government. These reciprocal actions were to be taken within one week, that is by 25th May, 1967. It is on record that I accepted the recommendations and issued instructions effective from Tuesday, May 23. Indeed I now understand that certain vehicles of the Posts and Telegraphs Department which went to the East in resumption of services have been illegally detained in that Region. The response of the East has been completely negative and they have continued their propaganda and stage-managed demonstrations for 'independence'.

Fellow citizens, I recognize however that the problem of Nigeria extends beyond the present misguided actions of the Eastern Region Government. My duty is to all citizens. I propose to treat all sections of the country with equality. The main obstacle to future stability in this country is the present structural imbalance in the Nigerian Federation.

Even Decree No. 8 or Confederation or Loose Association will never survive if any one section of the country is in a position to hold the others to ransom.

This is why the item in the Political and Administrative Programme adopted by the Supreme Military Council last month[2] is the creation of states as a basis for stability. This must be done first so as to remove the fear of domination. Representatives drawn from the new states will be more able to work out the future constitution for this country which can contain provisions to protect the powers of the states to the fullest extent desired by the Nigerian people. As soon as these states are established, a new Revenue Allocation Commission consisting of international experts will be appointed to recommend an equitable formula for revenue allocation taking into account the desires of the states.

I propose to act faithfully within the Political and Administrative Programme adopted by the Supreme Military Council and published last month. The world will recognize in these proposals our desire for justice and fair play for all sections of this country and to accommodate all genuine aspirations of the diverse people of this great country.

I have ordered the reimposition of the economic measures designed to safeguard Federal interests until such a time as the Eastern Military Government abrogates its illegal edicts on revenue collection and the administration of the Federal Statutory Corporations based in the East.

The country has a long history of well articulated demands for states. The fears of minorities were explained in great detail and set out in the report of the Willink Commission appointed by the British in 1958. More recently there has been extensive discussions in Regional Consultative Committees and Leaders-of-Thought Conferences. Resolutions have been adopted demanding the creation of states in the North and in Lagos. Petitions from minority areas in the East which have been subjected to violent intimidation by the Eastern Military Government have been widely publicized. While the present circumstances regrettably do not allow for consultations through plebiscites, I am satisfied that the creation of new states as the only possible basis for stability and equality is the overwhelming desires of vast majority of Nigerians. To ensure justice, these states are being created simultaneously.

To this end, therefore, I am promulgating a Decree which will divide the Federal Republic into Twelve States. The twelve states will be six in the present Northern Region, three in the present Eastern Region, the Mid-West will remain as it is, the Colony Province of the Western Region and Lagos will form a new Lagos State and the Western Region will otherwise remain as it is.

I must emphasize at once that the Decree will provide for a States Delimitation Commission which will ensure that any divisions or towns not satisfied with the states in which they are initially grouped will obtain redress. But in this moment of serious National Emergency the co-operation of all concerned is absolutely essential in order to avoid any unpleasant consequences.

I wish also to emphasize that an Administrative Council will be established at the capitals of the existing regions which will be available to the new states to ensure the smoothest possible administrative transition in the establishment of the new states. The twelve new states, subject to marginal boundary adjustments, will therefore be as follows:

North-Western State comprising Sokoto and Niger Provinces.

North-Central State comprising Katsina and Zaria.

Kano State comprising the present Kano Province.

2 G

North-Eastern State comprising Bornu, Adamawa, Sardauna and Bauchi Provinces.

Benue/Plateau State comprising Benue and Plateau Provinces.

West-Central State comprising Ilorin and Kabba Provinces.

Lagos State comprising the Colony Province and the Federal Territory of Lagos.

Western State comprising the present Western Region but excluding the Colony Province.

Mid-Western State comprising the present Mid-Western State.

East-Central State comprising the present Eastern Region excluding Calabar, Ogoja and Rivers Provinces.

South-Eastern State comprising Calabar and Ogoja Provinces.

Rivers State comprising Ahoada, Brass, Degema, Ogoni and Port Harcourt Divisions.

The states will be free to adopt any particular names they choose in the future. The immediate administrative arrangements for the new states have been planned and the names of the Military Governors appointed to the new states will be gazetted shortly. The allocation of federally collected revenue to the new states on an interim basis for the first few months has also been planned. The successor states in each former region will share the revenue until a more permanent formula is recommended by the new Revenue Allocation Commission. Suitable arrangements have been made to minimize any disruption in the normal functioning of services in the areas of the new states.

It is my fervent hope that the existing Regional Authorities will co-operate fully to ensure the smoothest possible establishment of the new states. It is also my hope that the need to use force to support any new state will not arise. I am, however, ready to protect any citizens of this country who are subject to intimidation or violence in the course of establishment of these new states.

My dear countrymen, the struggle ahead is for the well-being of the present and future generations of Nigerians. If it were possible for us to avoid chaos and civil war merely by drifting apart as some people claim that easy choice may have been taken. But we know that to take such a course will quickly lead to the disintegration of the existing regions in condition of chaos and to disastrous foreign interference. We now have to adopt the courageous course of facing the fundamental problem that has plagued this country since the early 50s. There should be no recrimination. We must all resolve to work together. It is my hope that those who disagreed in the past with the Federal Military Government through genuine misunderstanding and mistrust will now be convinced of our purpose and be willing to come back and let us plan and work together for the realization of the Political and Administrative programme of the Supreme Military Council, and for the early restoration of full civilian rule in circumstances which would enhance just and honest and patriotic government. I appeal to the general public to continue to give their co-operation to the Federal Military Government; to go about their normal business peacefully; to maintain harmony with all communities wherever they live; to respect all the directives of the Government including directives restricting the movements of people while the emergency remains. Such directives are for their own protection and in their own interest.

Let us, therefore, march manfully together to alter the course of this nation once and for all and to place it on the path of progress, unity and equality. Let us so act that future generations of Nigerians will praise us for our resolution and courage in this critical stage of our country's history. Long live the Federal Republic of Nigeria.

[1] *Broadcast from Lagos on 27 May 1967. Federal Ministry of Information hand-out.*
[2] *See* DOC *102.*

112.
'The Republic of Biafra': Resolution by the Eastern Region Consultative Assembly[1]

We, the Chiefs, Elders and Representatives of Eastern Nigeria, gathered at this Joint Meeting of the Advisory Committee of Chiefs and Elders and the Consultative Assembly do solemnly declare as follows:

Whereas we have been in the vanguard of the national movement for the building of a strong, united and prosperous Nigeria where no man will be oppressed and have devoted our efforts, talents and resources to this end;

Whereas we cherish certain inalienable human rights and state obligations such as the right to life, liberty and pursuit of happiness; the right to acquire, possess and defend property; the provision of security; and the establishment of good and just government based on the consent of the governed;

Whereas in practical demonstration of these beliefs, our people settled in other parts of Nigeria, served their country in many capacities, and contributed immensely to the growth and development of Nigeria;

Whereas we are living witnesses of injustices and atrocities committed against Eastern Nigeria, among which are the premeditated murder of over 30,000 of our innocent men, women and children by Northern Nigerians, the calculated destruction of the property of our sons and daughters, the shameless conversion of two million Eastern Nigerians into refugees in their own country, all this without remorse;

Whereas in consequence of these and other acts of discrimination and injustice, we have painfully realized that the Federation of Nigeria has failed, and has given us no protection;

Whereas in spite of these facts, the Government and people of Eastern Nigeria have persisted in their efforts to find a practical and just solution that would preserve the continued existence of Nigeria as one corporate unit and restore peace and confidence as demonstrated by the initiative of our Military Governor in getting all the military leaders together at Aburi, Ghana;

Whereas the hopes which the Aburi Agreement engendered have proved to be misplaced and have been destroyed by a series of acts of bad faith and distortions and finally by a refusal on the part of the 'Lagos Government' to implement these and other Agreements notwithstanding the fact that they were freely and voluntarily entered into;

Whereas the Federation of Nigeria has forfeited any claim to our allegiance by these acts and by the economic, political and diplomatic sanctions imposed against us by the so-called Federal Government;

And whereas the object of government is the good of the governed and the will of the people its ultimate sanction;

Now, therefore, in consideration of these and other facts and injustices, we, the Chiefs, Elders and Representatives of all the Twenty Provinces of Eastern Nigeria, assembled in this Joint Meeting of the Advisory Committee of Chiefs and Elders and the Consultative Assembly, at Enugu this 27th day of May, 1967, we hereby solemnly:

a. Mandate His Excellency Lt.-Col. Chukwuemeka Odumegwu Ojukwu, Military Governor of Eastern Nigeria, to declare at the earliest practicable date Eastern Nigeria a free, sovereign and independent state by the name and title of the Republic of Biafra.

b. Resolve that the new Republic of Biafra shall have the full and absolute powers of a sovereign state, and shall establish commerce, levy war, conclude peace, enter into diplomatic relations, and carry out, as of right, other sovereign responsibilities.

c. Direct that the Republic of Biafra may enter into arrangement with any sovereign unit or units in what remains of Nigeria or in any part of Africa desirous of association with us for the purpose of running a common services organization and for the establishment of economic ties.

d. Recommend that the Republic of Biafra should become a member of the Commonwealth of Nations, the Organization of African Unity and the United Nations Organization.

e. Recommend the adoption of a Federal Constitution based on the new provincial units.

f. Re-affirm His Excellency's assurance of protection for the persons, properties and businesses of foreign nationals in our territory.

g. Declare our unqualified confidence in the Military Governor of Eastern Nigeria, Lt.-Col. Chukwuemeka Odumegwu Ojukwu, and assure him of our unreserved support for the way and manner he has handled the crisis in the country.

So help us God.

[1] *Adopted on 27 May 1967. Biafran Ministry of Information hand-out.*

113.
East's Reaction to the Creation of the States[1]

A stunned country and her friends have heard with amazement the ominous and disastrous announcement of Gowon proclaiming himself the Dictator of Nigeria, in what amounts to a one-man coup d'etat. By this act, Gowon has made the 27th May, 1967, the darkest date in the history of freedom and respect for human feelings in this country.

Gowon has unceremoniously dismissed the Supreme Military Council, contemptuously brushed aside the most senior military officer available in the country by proclaiming himself the Commander-in-Chief of the Armed

Forces and Head of a Federal Government that is now to consist of himself alone.

He has banished from the 56 million people of this country their natural right to personal liberty, freedom of expression and of movement even within their areas of abode. The personal lives of these 56 million people are now at the disposal of one man whose hands are already tarnished with the blood of thousands of innocent people of Eastern Nigeria.

Significantly, one of his very first acts as a dictator has been the farcical creation of states by the stroke of the pen. His vested interest in the creation of states has always been transparent, his denials on that score notwithstanding. His principal ambition and mission has always been the creation of the Middle Belt state. If he had had the courage to do this in the right way everyone in this country would have understood him. He purports to have created six States in the North when, in fact, he has left the North intact by creating more provinces still to be governed by Lt.-Col. Hassan Usman Katsina as Chairman of the so-called Council of States. He has left the Mid-West intact.

In the East he purports to have created three states. . . . It is manifestly clear that Gowon does not even know the political geography of Eastern Nigeria and therefore cannot expect any one to take him seriously. Besides, Gowon knows that he cannot enforce any of his decrees in the East. The whole exercise is therefore dishonest, cowardly and farcical because it serves as a cloak for a permanent subjugation of the West by the North; for it is clear that the declaration of the so-called state of emergency is directed principally against the occupied areas of the South, namely, Lagos and Western Nigeria.

We in the East know our stand. The people of the East cannot be intimidated, nor can they be deceived. Neither the so-called state of emergency that Gowon has declared nor the Decree purporting to create states can apply in this Region. We remain undisturbed but prepared to meet any challenge that may come from Gowon.

Gowon's statement and his proclamation of himself as a dictator may however be a signal for bloody conflict. For this the blame will not be ours. Gowon will bear the full responsibility while we, for our part, will do our duty.

[1] *Eastern Ministry of Information Press Release No. 1285/1967.*

114.
Ojukwu Secedes and Declares the 'Republic of Biafra'[1]

Fellow countrymen and women, you, the people of Eastern Nigeria:

Conscious of the supreme authority of Almighty God over all mankind, of your duty to yourselves and posterity;

Aware that you can no longer be protected in your lives and in your property by any Government based outside Eastern Nigeria;

Believing that you are born free and have certain inalienable rights which can best be preserved by yourselves;

Unwilling to be unfree partners in any association of a political or economic nature;

Rejecting the authority of any person or persons other than the Military Government of Eastern Nigeria to make any imposition of whatever kind or nature upon you;

Determined to dissolve all political and other ties between you and the former Federal Republic of Nigeria;

Prepared to enter into such association, treaty or alliance with any sovereign state within the former Federal Republic of Nigeria and elsewhere on such terms and conditions as best to subserve your common good;

Affirming your trust and confidence in me;

Having mandated me to proclaim on your behalf, and in your name, that Eastern Nigeria be a sovereign independent Republic, Now therefore I, Lieutenant-Colonel Chukwuemeka Odumegwu Ojukwu, Military Governor of Eastern Nigeria, by virtue of the authority, and pursuant to the principles, recited above, do hereby solemnly proclaim that the territory and region known as and called Eastern Nigeria together with her continental shelf and territorial waters shall henceforth be an independent sovereign state of the name and title of 'The Republic of Biafra'. And I do declare that—

i. all political ties between us and the Federal Republic of Nigeria are hereby totally dissolved;

ii. all subsisting contractual obligations entered into by the Government of the Federal Republic of Nigeria or by any person, authority, organization or government acting on its behalf, with any person, authority or organization operating, or relating to any matter or thing, within the Republic of Biafra, shall henceforth be deemed to be entered into with the Military Governor of the Republic of Biafra for and on behalf of the Government and people of the Republic of Biafra, and the covenants thereof shall, subject to this Declaration, be performed by the parties according to their tenor;

iii. all subsisting international treaties and obligations made on behalf of Eastern Nigeria by the Government of the Federal Republic of Nigeria, shall be honoured and respected;

iv. Eastern Nigeria's due share of all subsisting international debts and obligations entered into by the Government of the Federal Republic of Nigeria on behalf of the Federation of Nigeria shall be honoured and respected;

v. steps will be taken to open discussions on the question of Eastern Nigeria's due share of the assets of the Federation of Nigeria and personal properties of the citizens of Biafra throughout the Federation of Nigeria;

vi. the rights, privileges, pensions, etc., of all personnel of the Public Services, the Armed Forces and the Police now serving in any capacity within the Republic of Biafra, are hereby guaranteed;

vii. we shall keep the door open for association with, and would welcome, any sovereign unit or units in the former Federation of Nigeria or in any other parts of Africa desirous of association with us for the purposes of running a common services organization and for the establishment of economic ties;

viii. we shall protect the lives and property of all foreigners residing in Biafra; we shall extend the hand of friendship to those nations who respect our sovereignty, and shall repel any interference in our internal affairs;

ix. we shall faithfully adhere to the charter of the Organization of African Unity and of the United Nations Organization;

x. It is our intention to remain a member of the British Commonwealth of Nations in our right as a sovereign, independent nation.

Long live the Republic of Biafra!

And may God protect all who live in her!!

[1] *Declaration made at Enugu on 30 May 1967. Biafran Ministry of Information hand-out.*

115.
Gowon's Address to the First Civilian Members of the Federal Executive Council[1]

I have great pleasure in welcoming you to the first meeting of the enlarged Federal Executive Council. Before we proceed to the ceremonial side of the occasion, I would like to address you briefly on some of the basic questions which we have to face.

Your appointment to the Federal Executive Council marks a turning point in the history of the military regime. We are now embarking on the road back to full civilian rule. During this period of transition, however, we must continue with the work of national reconstruction in accordance with the political and administrative programme of the Supreme Military Council. My belief is that your wealth of experience will be of great assistance to the administration.

Left to me alone, I would have brought civilians into the Federal Executive Council in accordance with my promise to the nation long ago.[2] But the mention of civilian rule was one of the nightmares of Lt.-Col. Ojukwu. One of the many concessions I had to make to him was to keep civilians out of sight. He told me many times that we will be pushing him out of the Federation if I brought civilians into the Federal Executive Council. He always pleaded with me that he would find it very difficult to keep his own civilians and ex-politicians in the backroom if their counterparts elsewhere were to help me in running the Federal Government in Lagos. Any neutral observer who has recently been to Enugu knows that Ojukwu was bent on forcing the East out of the Federation to satisfy his personal political ambitions.

I had to assume full powers and declare a state of national emergency to deal with the situation when it became quite clear to me that no concession could stop Ojukwu from trying to secede; and Lt.-Col. Ojukwu declared his secession three days thereafter. Can any honest man say that it took the rebel regime in Enugu just those three days to compose an anthem and prepare Ojukwu's new flag displayed on public buildings on the 30th of May? The fact is that Ojukwu's preparations for taking Eastern Nigeria out of the Federation were complete long before the declaration of national emergency.

I have taken the irrevocable decision to crush Ojukwu's rebellion in order to re-unite Nigerians resident in the three Eastern States with their brothers and sisters in other parts of Nigeria as equal partners. In spite of the tragic experiences of 1966, I know that many Ibo officers and troops and the majority of the civilians in the former Eastern Nigeria are still prepared to live in peace with the rest of Nigeria. But Ojukwu will not let them. I have nothing against the Ibos as a people and I know also that in their hearts of hearts the majority of them have nothing against me but for Ojukwu's evil propaganda. Any form of reconciliation and peaceful settlement short of carving up Nigeria did not suit Ojukwu's political plans.

When the country has been re-united without Ojukwu, the Armed Forces will hand it over to civilians chosen by the electorate. The Ibos and other ethnic groups will be fully represented in such a civilian Government. No group or State will henceforth be in a position to dominate other groups since the twelve States established are equal in all respects and no one State is subordinate to any other State. This is the birth of a New Nigeria.

It will be for the people to choose their leaders. I have only invited you, gentlemen, on your individual merits and experience to help this administration in the critical days ahead. My choice has not been guided by any political bias. I will like to emphasise that your joining the administration is not a signal for the resumption of political activities and sectional controversies in the country.

I am not a politician. Honestly, I do not understand the politics of intrigue, but I do understand the politics of the heart and, like most other Nigerians, I know what is good for the people. The people of this country require honest administration and selfless service. People in a position of trust must discharge their responsibilities without fear or favour. Nigeria is a nation on trial. It is only men of honour and integrity who can save this great country, the hope of Africa. I firmly believe that all members of the Federal Executive Council can aspire to the highest ideals in all their actions.

I know from the public reactions to my first announcement to bring in civilians into the administration that many Nigerians are not anxious to see those who in recent years participated in government and politics back in Ministerial seats before the job of national reconstruction is completed. It will, to that extent, be misleading to the man-in-the-street if members of the Federal Executive Council were to be handed departmental responsibilities as Ministers. I have nevertheless decided to allocate you full responsibilities for Ministries and Departments but, for the time being, it will probably be better if civilian members of the Federal Executive Council are called Commissioners. This temporary nomenclature will not in any way detract from your departmental responsibilities.

I will, for the time being, retain responsibility for the Ministry of Defence and one or two other Ministries and I have also allocated some portfolios to senior members of the Armed Forces and the Police. This will no doubt help emphasise the Military character of the regime especially for the period of the national emergency. . . .

Since I assumed responsibility as Head of the Federal Military Government, I have been guided in all my actions by the overall interest of the whole country. Although civilian members of the Federal Executive Council are drawn from the twelve States, we must all recognise the national and objective approach to most of the problems which the Federal Executive

Council has to tackle. My hope is that you are here not spokesmen for the individual States but as elder statesmen and young reformers interested in assisting the Armed Forces to establish a New Nigeria.

I am most anxious to return to full civilian rule in accordance with the political and administrative programme of the Supreme Military Council. The smooth implementation of that programme with your rich experience and ability will ensure an early return to full civilian and democratic rule in which no group or state is in a position to dominate others. I must emphasise that flexibility is an essential part of the Supreme Military Council's programme and you are not therefore being invited to implement the law of the Medes and Persians.

I have invited you to come and serve the nation as full-time Commissioners. It is for you to set up the highest standards for future civilian governments to emulate. First, we will have to prepare a code of conduct which will ensure the good behaviour of all Commissioners and other public officers. As far as the Military administration is concerned, the so-called 'ten per cent' is dead for good. I will welcome any advice from you to the Supreme Military Council on the salaries and allowances which will be paid to the civilian members of the Federal and the State Executive Councils. From what some of you have already told me in private, your remuneration will be quite different from the fabulous salaries, allowances and privileges which, among other things, discredited the former civilian governments. I have some ideas which I will put to you in our private discussions. We have entered a new era in Nigeria where what is important is not what we get out of Nigeria but what services we can give to the nation in our life time. . . .

¹ *Made in Lagos on the occasion of the first meeting of the reconstituted Federal Executive Council, 12 June 1967. Federal Ministry of Information Press Release No. 1295/1967.*
² *See* DOC *75.*

116.
Operational Code of Conduct for the Nigerian Army¹

RESTRICTED

DIRECTIVE TO ALL OFFICERS AND MEN OF THE ARMED FORCES OF THE FEDERAL REPUBLIC OF NIGERIA ON CONDUCT OF MILITARY OPERATIONS

As your Commander-in-Chief of the Armed Forces of the Federal Republic of Nigeria, I demand from all officers and men the two most important qualities of a fighting soldier—*loyalty* and *discipline*. Nigerian Armed Forces, especially the Army, have established a very high international reputation for high discipline and fighting efficiency since their establishment until the events of

15th January, 1966 spoilt that reputation. Since then it has become most necessary to demand the highest sense of discipline and patriotism amongst all ranks of the Armed Forces. Success in battle depends to a large extent on this—discipline and loyalty of the officers and men and their sense of patriotism.

2. You are all aware of the rebellion of Lt.-Col. C. Odumegwu-Ojukwu of the East Central State and his clique against the Government of the Federal Republic of Nigeria. In view of this defiance of authority, it has become inescapable to use the force necessary to crush this rebellion. The hardcore of the rebels are Ibos. The officers and men of the minority areas (Calabar, Ogoja and Rivers and even some Ibos) do not support the rebellious acts of Lt.-Col. C. Odumegwu-Ojukwu. During the operations of Federal Government troops against the rebel troops many soldiers and civilians will surrender. You should treat them fairly and decently in accordance with these instructions.

3. You must all bear in mind at all times that other nations in Africa and the rest of the world are looking at us to see how well we can perform this task which the nation demands of us. You must also remember that you are not fighting a war with a foreign enemy. Nor are you fighting a religious war or Jihad. Your are only subduing the rebellion of Lt.-Col. Odumegwu-Ojukwu and his clique. You must not do anything that will endanger the future unity of the country. We are in honour bound to observe the rules of the Geneva Convention in whatever action you will be taking against the rebel Lt.-Col. Odumegwu-Ojukwu and his clique.

4. I direct all officers and men to observe strictly the following rules during operations. (These instructions must be read in conjunction with the Geneva Convention):

a. Under no circumstances should pregnant women be illtreated or killed.

b. Children must not be molested or killed. They will be protected and cared for.

c. Youths and school children must not be attacked unless they are engaged in open hostility against Federal Government Forces. They should be given all protection and care.

d. Hospitals, hospital staff and patients should not be tampered with or molested.

e. Soldiers who surrender will not be killed. They are to be disarmed and treated as prisoners of war. They are entitled in all circumstances to humane treatment and respect for their person and their honour.

f. No property, building, etc, will be destroyed maliciously.

g. Churches and Mosques must not be desecrated.

h. No looting of any kind. (A good soldier will never loot).

i. Women will be protected against any attack on their person, honour and in particular against rape or any form of indecent assault.

j. Male civilians who are hostile to the Federal Forces are to be dealt with firmly but fairly. They must be humanely treated.

l. All military and civilians wounded will be given necessary medical attention and care. They must be respected and protected in all circumstances.

m. Foreign nationals on legitimate business will not be molested, but mercenaries will not be spared: they are the worst of enemies.

5. To be successful in our tasks as soldiers these rules must be carefully observed. I will not be proud of any member of the Armed Forces under my command who fails to observe them. He does not deserve any sympathy or mercy and will be dealt with ruthlessly. You will fight a clean fight, an honourable fight in defence of the territorial integrity of your nation—Nigeria.

6. You must remember that some of the soldiers Lt.-Col. Ojukwu has now forced to oppose you were once your old comrade at arms and would like to remain so. You must therefore treat them with respect and dignity except any one who is hostile to you.

Good luck.

MAJOR-GENERAL YAKUBU GOWON,
Head of the Federal Military Government,
Commander-in-Chief of the Armed Forces
of the Federal Republic of Nigeria.

Note.—To be read and fully explained to every member of the Armed Forces. Sufficient copies will be made available to all members of the Armed Forces and Police. It will be carried by all troops at all times.

[1] *Not dated, but issued early in July 1967. Reproduced by courtesy of a Nigerian soldier. The English version promised a translation into Hausa, Ibo, Yoruba, Efik, and Ijaw. Tiv was not mentioned.*

117.
'Zero Hour': Ojukwu Warns that War is Imminent[1]

Fellow countrymen, people of Biafra, it is a month today since we took the irrevocable decision to assert our autonomy and sovereignty by becoming the Republic of Biafra. Gowon's immediate reaction to our decision was to vow to crush us. Since then he has consistently described his decision as irrevocable. I have conclusive evidence that he and his Northern bandits have now finalised their plans to attack us in our homes. They have taken all this time to prepare and accumulate arms. . . .

Yesterday, Gowon published and distributed a code of conduct for war. Yesterday, he and his gangster Cabinet decided that the time had come to launch the long-awaited attack on Biafra. Yesterday, Gowon began troop movements to complete his concentration menacing our borders. Furthermore, he has openly incited certain sections of this republic to insurrection and has tried to subvert the loyalty of the police of this republic. It is reliably learned that he has continued to negotiate for the passage of his troops through a neighbouring country.

I wish to take this opportunity to make it crystal clear that any territory through which Gowon's troops pass shall be considered enemy territory. Fellow countrymen and women, we have arrived at zero hour. Gowon is determined to come into our homes and to destroy us in order to carry away what belongs to us. His psychological warfare of lying propaganda calculated to create alarm, frighten our people and cause dissension among us has failed completely. Gowon feels that he must play the man and carry out his suicidal threats to launch a physical attack on us. I want you all to remain calm and determined as you have been. Our soldiers are ready. While they will be fighting in foreign lands, our civil defence organisations, men, women and children, must guard our homes.

If Gowon should make the mistake of crossing into our territory even by a few yards, we shall immediately go into an open, outright and total war against Nigeria. Our conduct of the war will not be confined to our territorial boundaries. We shall take the opportunity to ensure that they do not repeat their adventure ever again. This will be an opportunity for us to do honour to the memory of the thousands of our kith and kin savagely murdered last year, by avenging their death. If this is what the world wants in order to be convinced that we are determined to keep our sovereignty, we now eagerly await the opportunity of giving that proof. We shall not be blamed for the consequences of what is now imminent.

Fellow countrymen, proud and courageous Biafrans, this is your moment. When we go to war, it will be a war against Nigeria. For it is Nigeria that has vowed that we shall not exist. With God on our side we shall vanquish. Long live the Republic of Biafra.

[1] *Broadcast to the people of the East, in English and vernaculars, 30 June 1967* (*B.B.C. ME/2506/B/2*).

118.
The Count Down: Federal Government Proposes Six Conditions to avoid War[1]

1. Public announcement of the withdrawal of the declaration of independence of the so-called Biafra Republic and revocation of the Independence Edict and associated Edicts.
2. Public announcement of acceptance and recognition of Federal Government authority over Eastern Nigeria by the former Military Governor, East, Lt.-Col. Ojukwu or any other Eastern officer.
3. Public announcement of acceptance of the twelve States in Nigeria and the immediate installation of the new Military Administration in Rivers State and South-Eastern State subject to marginal boundary adjustments by the States Boundary Commission.
4. Acceptance of appointment of Civilians as Commissioners into the Federal Executive Council and State Executive Councils.
5. Agreement to revoke the Revenue (Collection) Edict and related measures.
6. Agreement that constitutional talks on the future of Nigeria will be held by the duly accredited and equal representatives of the twelve states.

[1] *Statement issued by the Federal Ministry of Information, 1 July 1967, and reprinted in its* Challenge to Unity (*Lagos, 1967*).

119.
General Gowon's First Wartime Press Conference[1]

The Head of the Federal Military Government, Major-General Yakubu Gowon, addressed a news conference on July 13th and gave details of the military situation in the 'police action' against the Eastern States. Major-General Gowon said that the university town of the East-Central State, Nsukka, would fall into the hands of the Federal Government troops 'any time from now'. Referring to rumours that the operation had been too slow, he commented: 'Those who say that we have been slow know nothing about warfare. It is not like motor-driving; you are bound to run into resistance on the way; you have to get off crooked roads; you have got to clear the bush and make sure you do not leave pockets of resistance on the way to attack you from the rear. But you can be sure we are moving extremely well. The morale of the Federal troops has been very high.'

Major-General Gowon said that so far one mercenary had been captured, and he was waiting for details about him. Several others had been encountered during the operations. About 500 rebel troops had been captured around the Ogoja area and a few around the area of Nsukka. There was no truth in the story that rebel troops had damaged the airport at Makurdi and no damage had been done to any DC-3 aircraft.

Major-General Gowon said that the present police action 'is not a total war against the Eastern States but against a rebellion'. 'It is not a personal struggle between Ojukwu and myself. Ojukwu has had this ambition since 1964.' He hoped to crush the rebellion as quickly as possible. Once Ojukwu was out of the way, the rest would come to terms with the rest of the country.

Referring to the possibility of reconciliation, the Commander-in-Chief said that Ojukwu wanted reconciliation 'only if we could sit as two separate sovereign nations.'

'Why,' Major-General Gowon asked, 'should we sit with him and discuss as two separate countries? Before we could start a reconciliation Ojukwu should publicly withdraw his unilateral declaration of independence, he should publicly withdraw edicts taking over certain government departments, he should recognise the Central Government, he should accept the recent creation of States, and should accept the introduction of civilians into the Federal Executive Council. If he is prepared to do these things, we could then get together and have some useful discussions.'

[1] Daily Times, *14 July 1967.*